Concepts of Athletic Training

Concepts of Athletic Training

Fifth Edition

RONALD P. PFEIFFER, EdD, ATC

Co-Director, Center for Orthopaedic and
Biomechanics Research (COBR)
Professor, Department of Kinesiology
Boise State University

BRENT C. MANGUS, EdD, ATC

Associate Professor
Department of Kinesiology
Director of Athletic Training Education
University of Nevada, Las Vegas

JONES AND BARTLETT PUBLISHERS

Sudbury, Massachusetts

BOSTON   TORONTO   LONDON   SINGAPORE

World Headquarters
Jones and Bartlett Publishers
40 Tall Pine Drive
Sudbury, MA 01776
978-443-5000
info@jbpub.com
www.jbpub.com

Jones and Bartlett Publishers Canada
6339 Ormindale Way
Mississauga, Ontario L5V 1J2
CANADA

Jones and Bartlett Publishers International
Barb House, Barb Mews
London W6 7PA
United Kingdom

Jones and Bartlett's books and products are available through most bookstores and online booksellers. To contact Jones and Bartlett Publishers directly, call 800-832-0034, fax 978-443-8000, or visit our website www.jbpub.com.

Substantial discounts on bulk quantities of Jones and Bartlett's publications are available to corporations, professional associations, and other qualified organizations. For details and specific discount information, contact the special sales department at Jones and Bartlett via the above contact information or send an email to specialsales@jbpub.com.

The authors, editor, and publisher have made every effort to provide accurate information. However, they are not responsible for errors, omissions, or for any outcomes related to the use of the contents of this book and take no responsibility for the use of the products and procedures described. Treatments and side effects described in this book may not be applicable to all people; likewise, some people may require a dose or experience a side effect that is not described herein. Drugs and medical devices are discussed that may have limited availability controlled by the Food and Drug Administration (FDA) for use only in a research study or clinical trial. Research, clinical practice, and government regulations often change the accepted standard in this field. When consideration is being given to use of any drug in the clinical setting, the health care provider or reader is responsible for determining FDA status of the drug, reading the package insert, and reviewing prescribing information for the most up-to-date recommendations on dose, precautions, and contraindications, and determining the appropriate usage for the product. This is especially important in the case of drugs that are new or seldom used.

Production Credits
Chief Executive Officer: Clayton Jones
Chief Operating Officer: Don W. Jones, Jr.
President, Higher Education and Professional Publishing: Robert W. Holland, Jr.
V.P., Design and Production: Anne Spencer
V.P., Manufacturing and Inventory Control: Therese Connell
V.P., Sales and Marketing: William J. Kane
Acquisitions Editor: Jacqueline Ann Geraci
Associate Editor: Patrice Andrews
Senior Production Editor: Julie Champagne Bolduc
Marketing Manager: Wendy Thayer
Marketing Associate: Meagan Norlund
Interactive Technology Manager: Dawn Mahon Priest
Composition: Graphic World, Inc.
Cover Design: Kristin E. Ohlin
Senior Photo Researcher and Photographer: Kimberly Potvin
Photo Researcher: Lee Michelsen
Cover Image: © David Madison/age fotostock
Printing and Binding: Malloy, Inc.
Cover Printing: Malloy, Inc.

Library of Congress Cataloging-in-Publication Data
Pfeiffer, Ronald P.
     Concepts of athletic training / Ronald P. Pfeiffer, Brent C. Mangus. — 5th ed.
        p. ; cm.
     Includes bibliographical references and index.
     ISBN-13: 978-0-7637-4949-1 (alk. paper)
     ISBN-10: 0-7637-4949-4
     1. Athletic trainers. 2. Sports injuries. 3. Sports medicine. I. Mangus, Brent C. II. Title.
     [DNLM: 1. Athletic Injuries--therapy. 2. Sports Medicine. QT 261 P528c 2007]
RC1210.P45 2007
617.1'027—dc22   2007010918
6048

Photo credits appear on page 409, which constitutes a continuation of the copyright page.

Printed in the United States of America
11 10 09 08 07   10 9 8 7 6 5 4 3 2 1

Brief Contents

Contents

Preface

The primary theme of this book continues to be the care and management of sport and activity–related injuries. Therefore, the target audience includes anyone planning a career in coaching, athletic training, or K–12 physical education. Coaching personnel, especially those in the public school system, continue to serve as "first responders" in the majority of sports-injury situations. This continues to be the case despite the fact that more Board of Certification, Inc. (BOC)–certified athletic trainers are presently employed in the nation's high schools than ever before. As such, the coach's initial decisions and subsequent actions are critical in determining the outcome of an injury. In order to make correct decisions, coaching personnel must be properly trained, not only in basic first aid, but in more advanced knowledge in order to properly manage injuries that are complicated by sports equipment such as helmets, face masks, mouth guards, and other equipment. Students majoring in athletic training will also find this new edition extremely relevant to their educational goals. The content will form a solid foundation for more advanced studies in this exciting and constantly evolving allied health field.

The majority of sport and activity–related injuries involve the musculoskeletal system. As such, much of the content of this text is devoted to the recognition, immediate care, and management of injuries such as sprains, strains, dislocations, and fractures in the extremities. Fortunately only a small percentage of sports and activity–related injuries are life threatening or result in permanent disability. However, deaths and permanent disability tragically continue to be an outcome in a small percentage of cases. Most of these injuries are related to trauma to the head and/or neck or are heat related. Detailed information on head and neck injuries as well as prevention of heat disorders is provided in Chapters 9 and 18.

This latest edition continues to feature a chapter devoted to the adolescent athlete. The rationale for this is simple: The vast majority of school-aged athletes (K–12) are, in fact, adolescents or pre-adolescents. As such, they represent an anatomically distinct population when compared to adult athletes. These differences must be recognized and considered by coaching personnel when making decisions regarding not only injury management, but also when designing and implementing injury prevention programs.

The general field of sports medicine continues to be a rapidly evolving field of study. The authors have made every effort to update critical material throughout the text in order to make the content as current as possible. Some of the major changes since the previous edition include:

- Chapter 1: Revised to reflect the most recent injury epidemiology data available at the time of publication.
- Chapters 1, 11, 12, 15–17: New figures have been added including X-ray, magnetic resonance imaging, and photos of acute injuries and dermatological conditions.
- Chapter 2: As education program requirements have changed recently, the current requirements for students completing entry-level athletic training education programs as well as components of the latest BOC Role Delineation Study have been included.
- Chapter 3: The list of states that now regulate the practice of athletic training has been updated.
- Chapter 4: The information describing the Preparticipation Physical Evaluation has been updated to reflect the latest guidelines from the American Academy of Pediatrics.
- Chapter 6: The "Supplements and Ergogenic Aids" section has been updated to include current information on ephedra, Andro, and creatine with ß-alanine.
- Chapter 7: Content describing first response to injuries has been updated to reflect the guidelines provided by the American College of Emergency Physicians.
- Chapter 8: Information on currently available NSAIDs has been included in Table 8.2.
- Chapter 9: New figures showing the correct use of spine boards in the care of head and neck injury have been provided.
- Chapters 13–15: The information on prevention of many different types of injuries has been expanded and includes additional and updated images of the latest types and style of injury prevention equipment.
- Chapter 19: New information on exercise-induced asthma has been included.
- Appendices 1 and 2 have been updated to reflect current guidelines for cardiopulmonary resuscitation, automated external defibrillator use, and management of bloodborne pathogens as recommended by the American College of Emergency Physicians.

Technology Integration

As with the fourth edition, information directing the reader to web sites providing additional information is given at the beginning of each chapter. The links found on **http://health.jbpub.com/book/concepts/5e** provide additional information to the chapter content and encourage students to become more proficient in using the web as a learning resource.

The updated and improved **Instructor's ToolKit** includes an instructor's manual, computerized TestBank, Image and Table Bank, and PowerPoint presentations with more than 500 slides. These slides make transitioning to the fifth edition easier, ensuring that you and your students get the most out of this text. They can be used in classroom presentations or printed directly onto overhead transparencies.

Features

- **What If?** features are "real life" scenarios that encourage students to work on critical decision-making skills. These sections provide the sort of information typically available to coaching personnel when confronted with an injury-related problem. These scenarios can have many applications, such as simple decision-making practice sessions alone or with another student or, ideally, as the script for role-play exercises in a sports-injury class laboratory practice session.
- **Time Out** boxes provide additional information related to the text, such as NATA Athletic Helmet Removal Guidelines, guidelines for working with an injured athlete, how to recognize the signs of a concussion, and first aid for epilepsy.
- **Athletic Trainers Speak Out** boxes feature a different athletic trainer in every chapter who discusses an element of athlete care and injury prevention.
- All relevant chapters begin with an **Anatomy Review** to introduce body parts to students unfamiliar with human anatomy and provide a refresher for students who have had human anatomy.

Conclusion

This book is an outstanding resource for students studying to become physical education teachers, coaches, and athletic trainers. Personnel charged with the responsibility of providing emergency care for athletes must be trained in the first aid procedures appropriate for sports injuries. The content of this text, the accompanying Instructor's ToolKit CD-ROM, and **http://health.jbpub.com/book/concepts/5e** will provide instructors and students with a wealth of information on topics related to the care and prevention of sports injuries. The goal, of course, is to give coaching and teaching personnel the necessary knowledge and critical-thinking skills to recognize and differentiate minor from more serious sports injuries. Once decisions are made regarding the nature of the injury, appropriate first aid care and/or medical referral can be instituted.

Acknowledgments

To Paul W. Pfeiffer, my father, mentor, and friend. You gave me many gifts, one of which was perseverance, and without perseverance, this book would never have been written.
Ron Pfeiffer

Thank you to my family for their support throughout this project.
Brent Mangus

The authors would also like to thank Ted Eaves, ATC, for all of his insight and help with creating the ancillaries for this edition.

This text would not have been completed had it not been for those colleagues who reviewed and contributed to the manuscript:

Scott Anderson
University of Oklahoma
Norman, OK

Ronnie P. Barnes
Head Athletic Trainer
New York Giants
East Rutherford, NJ

Kim Calvert
Alfred University
Alfred, NY

David L. Collins
East Texas Baptist University
Marshall, TX

Gary Craner
Assistant Athletic Director and Head Athletic Trainer
Boise State University
Boise, ID

Russell D. De Lap
Concordia University Wisconsin
Mequon, WI

Jamie Dolieslager
Bethel University
St. Paul, MN

Doris E. Flores
Program Director for the Athletic Training Curriculum
California State University, Sacramento
Sacramento, CA

Dr. Danny T. Foster
Associate Director of Athletic Training
University of Iowa
Iowa City, IA

Yasuo Fukuda
Head Athletic Trainer at Bishop Gorman High School
  and Las Vegas Gladiators Assistant Trainer
Las Vegas, NV

Jorge Garcia
Athletic Trainer
Kip Owen Orthopedics
McAllen, TX

Rick Griffin
Head Athletic Trainer
Seattle Mariners
Seattle, WA

Charles W. Hale IV
Bridgewater College
Bridgewater, VA

Ariko Iso
Assistant Athletic Trainer for the Pittsburgh Steelers
Pittsburgh, PA

Richard Leander
Head Athletic Trainer
Moscow School District
Moscow, ID

Sue Lerner
Assistant Athletic Trainer
University of Southern California
Los Angeles, CA

Dr. Larry J. Leverenz
Director of Athletic Training Education
  and Athletic Trainer
Purdue University
West Lafayette, IN

Karen Lew
Athletic Training Education Program Director
Southeastern Louisiana University
Hammond, LA

Malissa Martin
Director of Athletic Training Education
College of Mount St. Joseph
Cincinnati, OH

Dale Mildenberger
Head Athletic Trainer
Utah State University
Logan, UT

Robert E. Patton
Texas State University–San Marcos
San Marcos, TX

Dan Ruiz
High School Teacher and Athletic Trainer
Mark Morris High School
Longview, WA

Kenji Sasaki
Athletic Trainer
Morioka High School
Staff Athletic Trainer
Iwate Amateur Sports Association
Iwate, Japan

René Revis Shingles
Assistant Professor in the Athletic Training
  Education Program
Central Michigan University
Mount Pleasant, MI

Ellise Spaulding
Gloucester County College
Sewell, NJ

Barrie Steele
Director of Athletic Training Services
University of Idaho
Moscow, ID

Dr. Christine Stopka
Professor
Department of Health Education and Behavior
University of Florida
Gainesville, FL

Scott Sunderland
Knox College
Galesburg, IL

Eric Taylor
Head Athletic Trainer
Centennial High School
Boise, ID

Andrew Vanous
Fort Lewis College
Durango, CO

Katie Walsh
Director of the Sports Medicine/Athletic
  Training Program
East Carolina University
Greenville, NC

Susan P. Wehring
Loras College
Dubuque, IA

Sara Williamson
San Diego Mesa College
San Diego, CA

Michael Scott Zema
Slippery Rock University of Pennsylvania
Slippery Rock, PA

The Concept of Sports Injury

MAJOR CONCEPTS

After reading and studying this chapter, the reader will be familiar with the scope and breadth of the topic of sports injury. The chapter presents the most recent data available to provide a quantitative perspective on the number of participants injured while engaging in sport activities. It discusses the most popular definitions of sports injury currently in use, along with a variety of the most commonly used medical terms related to the type and severity of injury. These terms are used throughout the remainder of the book and can also prove useful to the coach when communicating with members of the medical community about sports injuries. The last section of the chapter introduces the concept of epidemiology as it applies to the study of sports injury.

http://health.jbpub.com/book/concepts/5e

The web site for this book offers many useful tools and is a great source for supplementary information for both students and instructors.

Visit the site at
http://health.jbpub.com/book/concepts/5e
to link to the following organizations and sites:

- National Collegiate Athletic Association
- Consumer Product Safety Commission
- National Center for Catastrophic Sport Injury Research

Organized competitive high school sports continue to be extremely popular among American children. Recent research indicates that approximately 6.7 million public school children are involved in these activities annually (NFSH, 2003). Along with modest growth in high school sports programs, there has been massive growth in the number of adolescent and pediatric-aged children playing sports. As a result of community-based programs, a total of approximately 30 million school-aged children are involved in sports in the United States (Adirim & Cheng, 2003). Although these sports often involve children as young as 6 to 8 years, the level of competition is often extremely high as attested by the fact that it is common for teams to travel hundreds and sometimes thousands of miles to compete in tournaments. Further, it is not uncommon for children in sports such as tennis and gymnastics to invest as much as 20 hours a week in their chosen activity (Maffulli & Caine, 2005).

With the implementation of the Title IX Education Assistance Act of 1972, growth in the participation of female athletes in the United States has been at 700% (Stanitski, 1989). Ironically, as a result of unfounded fears

FIGURE 1.2 Females are at no greater risk for injury when involved in sports than are their male counterparts.

in both the lay and coaching communities that girls were not tough enough to play sports, many young female athletes were historically discouraged from participation. Even more disturbing is the fact that such negative stereotypes still persist in some sports organizations. Fortunately, researchers have produced data demonstrating clearly that, with few exceptions, injuries to female participants are sport specific (Figure 1.1), not gender specific (Collins, 1987). These data support the premise that, overall, females are at no greater risk for **injury** when involved in organized activities than are their male counterparts (Figure 1.2).

In recent years, sports-injury researchers have determined that certain types of knee injuries, specifically, those involving the **anterior** cruciate ligament (ACL), occur more frequently in female high school athletes in two sports—basketball and soccer—than in males in the same sports (Powell & Barber-Foss, 1999). It is interesting to note that this same trend has been found at the collegiate level. Recent research conducted by the National Collegiate Athletic Association (NCAA) via the Injury Surveillance System found the following results: Female basketball players injured their ACLs seven times more often than males during practice and five times more often than their male counterparts in games (NCAA, 1999). The majority of these ACL injuries is classified as noncontact; that is, the injuries do not occur as a result of a collision with an opponent or inanimate object. Rather,

FIGURE 1.1 Data clearly indicate that injuries to female athletes are sport specific.

noncontact ACL injuries are related to sports that involve rapid directional changes or deceleration when running, or repeated jumping and landing. Research is ongoing in regard to understanding the precise causative factors, as well as how to prevent such injuries from occurring (Griffin et al., 2000, Hewett, Meyer, & Ford, 2006a, 2006b).

In spite of the best efforts of parents, coaches, and officials, injury continues to be an unavoidable reality for a significant number of participants. For example, Beachy and colleagues studied injuries in 32 sports over an 8-year span in one Honolulu school. They found that football yielded the highest injury rate for boys whereas soccer produced the highest rate for girls. When the football and wrestling results were removed from the analysis, the injury rates for boys and girls were not significantly different. (Beachy, Akau, Martinson, & Olden, 1997). To date, two other large-scale, comprehensive studies of injuries among high school–aged athletes have been completed, and their findings support the premise that injuries are a constant problem associated with sports participation (NATA, 1989; Powell & Barber-Foss, 1999).

Results from a National High School Injury Survey (1995–97) sponsored by the National Athletic Trainers' Association (NATA) found that national injury rates have remained close to those documented by Powell for the 3-year period from 1986 to 1988. For example, the more recent data compared to the 1986–88 data indicate that in sports such as football and basketball (boys and girls) the proportion of minor, moderate, and major injuries was similar (Powell, 1987). In a similar study of high school injuries in the state of Pennsylvania, Grollman and associates (1996) found overall 3069 reportable injuries from 10 sports (boys and girls) across 40 high schools for the 1994–95 school year. The sport with the highest percentage of injuries was tackle football (46.7%), followed by boys' basketball (10%) and wrestling (9.68%). The sport producing the highest percentage of injuries for girls was basketball (7.5%).

Research looking at a broader age distribution was conducted by Damore and colleagues (2003), who studied emergency department admissions of patients ranging in age from 5 to 21 years at four hospitals for two 1-month periods (October 1999 and April 2000). They recorded a total of 1421 injuries in a group of 1275 patients in the age range of their study. Of these injuries, 41% were attributed to sports participation. The average age for such patients in their study was 12.2 years, with sprains, contusions, and fractures being the most common injuries. Males sustained more injuries (62%) to the musculoskeletal system than did their female counterparts.

Radelet and colleagues (2002) studied injuries in a population of children (1659) involved in community sports programs over the course of 2 years. Specifically, they monitored the injuries in children ranging in age from 7 to 13 years who were involved in baseball, softball, soccer, and football. An injury was defined as "requiring on-field evaluation by coaching staff, or causing a player to stop participation for any period of time, or requiring first aid during an event." They further defined an "athlete exposure" as one athlete participating in one event (game or practice). Their results, expressed as the rate of injury per 100 athlete exposures, were that soccer had the highest rate at 2.1 injuries, followed by baseball at 1.7, football at 1.5, and softball at 1.0. In all sports, there were more injuries in games than in practices, with contusions being the most common injury overall. It is also interesting to note that in soccer, there were no gender differences in injury rates.

Definition of Sports Injury

Though logic would seem to argue that determining what constitutes a sports injury would be simple, just the opposite is the case. Despite the efforts of many in the sports medicine community, a single, universally acceptable definition of sports injury remains unavailable. Debates about precise definitions among academicians may seem petty to the injured athlete; however, from a clinical and scientific viewpoint, having a standard set of definitions would greatly improve the usefulness and impact of future injury studies.

Most current definitions of sports injury incorporate the length of time away from participation (time lost) as the major determinant (DeLee & Farney, 1992). Using this definition, an injury is said to have occurred when an athlete is forced to discontinue play and/or practice for a predetermined length of time—for example, 24 hours. In 1982, the NCAA established the Injury Surveillance System (ISS), which established a common set of injury and risk definitions for use in tracking collegiate sports injuries. To qualify as an injury under the ISS, that injury must meet the following criteria:

1. Occurs as a result of participation in an organized intercollegiate practice or game
2. Requires medical attention by a team athletic trainer or physician
3. Results in restriction of the student athlete's participation or performance for one or more days beyond the day of injury (Benson, 1995)

injury Act that damages or hurts.
anterior Before or in front of.

The NCAA monitors injuries at Division I, II, and III institutions across all regions of the country and produces an annual report of the findings.

The NATA has commissioned two national surveys of high school sports injuries, each spanning 3-year periods (i.e., 1986–88 and 1995–97). The injury definitions used in the NATA studies are similar to the ISS because they rely on estimates of time lost from play as the indicator of injury severity (Foster, 1996).

Even though time lost is a convenient method for identifying an injury, such a definition does not lend itself to an accurate reflection of the severity of the injury. Severity of injury determinations may be made by a variety of people, including the coach, physicians or other sports medicine personnel, parents, or perhaps even the athlete. A related problem is that no standard is currently in use by all organizations monitoring sports injuries for the amount of time—hours, days, weeks, or months—that must be lost to qualify as a specific level of injury severity.

From a scientific standpoint, using the amount of time lost as a definition of sports injury is subject to significant error as previously described, depending on the method of data collection and injury definitions employed. However, once an injury is identified, several qualifiers are available to enable sports medicine personnel to better describe the precise characteristics of the injury. These include the type of tissue(s) involved, injury location, and time frame of the injury, that is, either acute or chronic.

A commonly used medical classification system for injuries uses two major categories: acute and chronic. **Acute injuries** have been defined as those "characterized by a rapid onset, resulting from a traumatic event" (AAOS, 1991). Acute injuries are usually associated with a significant traumatic event (Figure 1.3), followed immediately by a pattern of signs and symptoms such as pain, swelling, and loss of function. In the case of an acute injury, **critical force** has been defined as the "magnitude of

a single force for which the anatomical structure of interest is damaged" (Nigg & Bobbert, 1990). The potential for critical force, and subsequent acute injury, is clearly seen in tackle football. Estimates demonstrate that the vertebral bodies in the human cervical spine have a critical force limit of 340–455 kilograms. Researchers, using devices to simulate a typical tackle, have estimated that compressive forces acting on the cervical spine can exceed these limits (Torg, 1982).

Chronic injuries have been defined as those "characterized by a slow, insidious onset, implying a gradual development of structural damage" (AAFP, 1992). Chronic sports injuries, in contrast to acute ones, are not associated with a single traumatic episode; rather, they develop progressively over time. In many cases, they occur in athletes who are involved in activities that require repeated, continuous movements, such as in running (Figure 1.4). Consequently, such injuries are sometimes called overuse injuries, implying the athlete has simply done too many repetitions of the given activity. Overuse injuries in tendons occur when the workload from exercise exceeds the ability of musculotendinous tissues to recover (Hess et al., 1989). Thus, activity serves to cause a progressive breakdown of the tissue, leading eventually to failure.

Common sites for overuse injuries are the Achilles tendon, the patellar tendon, and the rotator cuff tendon in the shoulder (Hess et al., 1989). The Achilles tendon is subjected to tremendous stress during running and

FIGURE 1.4 Chronic injuries are common in high-impact sports such as running.

FIGURE 1.3 Acute injury in an athlete.

FIGURE 1.5 Injuries to the Achilles tendon are common in track and field events.

FIGURE 1.7 Tennis places significant stress on the rotator cuff.

jumping (Figure 1.5). Research indicates that these forces may exceed the physiological limits of the tendon, thereby resulting in damage (Curwain & Stanish, 1984). Likewise, the patellar tendon must absorb repeated episodes of stress during sports. For instance, jumping and landing, as well as kicking a soccer ball (Figure 1.6), generate forces in this tendon that are many times greater than those produced during normal gait (Gainor et al., 1978). The rotator cuff tendon, specifically the supraspinatus, is also vulnerable to injury from overuse. Any activity requiring repeated overhead movements of the arm, such as overhead strokes in tennis (Figure 1.7), places significant stress on this tendon. This is especially true during the deceleration phase of a swing or throw, after the arm has reached peak velocity. It is during this period of movement that muscles are undergoing **eccentric contraction,** a type of contraction identified as a causative factor in tendon injury (Curwain & Stanish, 1984). Such stress can cause damage in the supraspinatus

FIGURE 1.6 Jumping and landing, as well as kicking a soccer ball, subject the patellar tendon to stress.

acute injury Characterized by rapid onset, resulting from a traumatic event.

critical force Magnitude of a single force by which an anatomical structure is damaged.

chronic injury One characterized by a slow, insidious onset, implying a gradual development of structural damage.

eccentric contraction The simultaneous processes of muscle contraction and stretching of the muscle–tendon unit by an extrinsic force.

tendon, resulting in a chronic injury. DiFiori categorizes factors contributing to overuse injuries as either intrinsic, such as immature (growth) cartilage, lack of flexibility, lack of proper conditioning, psychological factors; and extrinsic, including such factors as excessive training or lack of adequate recovery, incorrect technique, and playing on uneven surfaces or surfaces that are too hard (DiFiori, 1999).

Probably the most commonly used terms for differentiating tissues involved in a given injury are *soft* and *skeletal*. **Soft tissue,** as a category, includes muscles, **fascia,** tendons, **joint capsules,** ligaments, blood vessels, and nerves. Most soft-tissue injuries involve contusions (bruises), sprains (ligaments/capsules), and strains (muscles/tendons). Skeletal tissue includes any bony structure in the body. Therefore, under this system, a common ankle sprain would qualify as a soft-tissue injury; a fractured wrist would be deemed a skeletal injury. These injuries, and the forces that produce them, are discussed further in Chapter 8.

A notable exception to the general confusion in defining a sports injury has to do with injuries so severe that they are known as catastrophic. **Catastrophic injuries** involve damage to the brain and/or spinal cord and are potentially life threatening or permanent. In the context of high school and college sports, catastrophic injury has been defined as "sport injury that resulted in a brain or spinal cord injury or skull or spinal fracture" (Mueller & Cantu, 1999). Mueller and Cantu have defined direct catastrophic injuries as those that result directly from participation in the skills of a given sport. Indirect catastrophic injuries are defined as those caused by systemic failure resulting from exertion while participating in a sports activity, or by a complication that was secondary to a nonfatal injury (Mueller & Cantu, 1993). Given these definitions, a catastrophic injury can occur as either a direct result of participation (sustaining a neck fracture during a tackle in football) or an indirect result (suffering a systemic heat stroke during a cross-country run). Though catastrophic sports injuries account for a small portion of all sports-related injuries, their potential for serious complications has resulted in an increased awareness by members of the sports medicine community. The most recent data available, for the 2004 season, indicate that at the high school level football produced four direct fatalities and seven indirect fatalities. The majority of the direct fatalities resulted from brain injury, and the indirect fatalities resulted from heat stroke, one from lightning, and three from unknown causes. Other high school sports mentioned in the 22nd annual report of the National Center for Catastrophic Sport Injury Research (2005) as meriting special attention are wrestling, gymnastics, ice hockey, baseball, and track. Pole-vaulting is associated with the majority of track-related deaths.

Injury Classifications

Regardless of the specific force involved in producing an injury, it is critical that all personnel involved in supervision of sports and physical activities, particularly coaches, be familiar with and fluent in the use of the basic

Athletic Trainers SPEAK Out

Sports-injury prevention is the cornerstone of the athletic trainer. Sports-injury prevention begins with a comprehensive sport-specific physical examination given by a qualified medical professional and continues through the selection and proper fitting of equipment and developing the physical components for sports competition. I have always said that if an athletic trainer can take an injured body part and rehabilitate that body part and individual back into full participation, then why can't an athletic trainer take an uninjured body part and individual and provide a strength and conditioning experience that brings that athlete to a top level of participation for physical activity and competition? With the knowledge, skills, and experience certified athletic trainers have in the area of athletic injury prevention they can assist the coach and work with the athlete in flexibility, strength, plyometric, and aerobic fitness in the prevention of sports injury and in the enhancement of sports performance.

—*Malissa Martin, EdD, ATC, CSCS*

Dr. Martin is the Director of Athletic Training Education in the Department of Health Sciences at the College of Mount St. Joseph.

terminology of connective-tissue injury. It is essential that any injury be recognized and, whenever possible, be correctly identified as soon as possible after the injury occurs, and then clearly described when communicating with other members of the sports medicine team (e.g., the team physician or athletic trainer). It is also vital that a vocabulary of standardized terms universal to all members of the sports medicine team be mastered. In 1968, the Committee on the Medical Aspects of Sports, a branch of the American Medical Association (AMA), published *Standard Nomenclature of Athletic Injuries (SNAI)*. Though this text is no longer in print, it provided clearly defined, standardized terms that can and should be used by those providing care for sports injuries.

Because the vast majority of sports injuries involve damage to connective tissue, the terms that apply to these common conditions are listed hereafter. Obviously, a certain degree of variability is unavoidable in any clinical definition. However, these terms, when used properly, can greatly reduce the confusion that so often exists regarding specific injuries.

Sprains

Sprains are injuries to ligaments, which surround all synovial joints in the body. The severity of sprains is highly variable depending on the forces involved. *SNAI* describes three categories of sprains, based on the level of severity.

First-Degree Sprains

According to *SNAI,* first-degree sprains are the mildest form of sprain; only mild pain and disability occur. These sprains demonstrate little or no swelling and are associated with minor ligament damage.

Second-Degree Sprains

Second-degree sprains are more severe; they imply more actual damage to the ligament(s) involved, with an increase in the amount of pain and dysfunction. Swelling is more pronounced, and abnormal motion is present. Such injuries have a tendency to recur.

Third-Degree Sprains

Third-degree sprains are the most severe form of sprain and imply a complete tear of the ligament(s) involved. Given the extensive damage, pain, swelling, and **hemorrhage** will be significant and are associated with considerable loss of joint stability.

Strains

Strains are injuries to muscles, tendons, or the junction between the two, commonly known as the musculotendinous junction (MTJ). The most common location

of a strain is the MTJ; however, the exact reason for this is unknown. As is the case with sprains, there is tremendous variability with respect to the severity of strains seen in sports. *SNAI* presents three categories of strains.

First-Degree Strains

SNAI describes first-degree strains as the mildest form with little associated damage to muscle and tendon structures. Pain is most noticeable during use; there may be mild swelling and muscle spasm present.

Second-Degree Strains

Second-degree strains imply more extensive damage to the soft-tissue structures involved. Pain, swelling, and muscle spasm are more pronounced, and functional loss is moderate. These types of injuries are associated with excessive, forced stretching or a failure in the synergistic action in a muscle group.

Third-Degree Strains

Third-degree strains are the most severe form and imply a complete rupture of the soft-tissue structures involved. Damage may occur at a variety of locations, including the bony attachment of the tendon (**avulsion** fracture), the tissues between the tendon and muscle (MTJ), or in the muscle itself. A defect may be apparent through the skin and will be associated with significant swelling. Obviously, this type of injury involves significant loss of function.

---

soft tissue Includes muscles, fascia, tendons, joint capsules, ligaments, blood vessels, and nerves.

fascia Fibrous membrane that covers, supports, and separates muscles.

joint capsule Sac-like structure that encloses the ends of bones in a diarthrodial joint.

catastrophic injury One involving damage to the brain and/or spinal cord that presents a potentially life-threatening situation or the possibility of permanent disability.

sprain Injury to a joint and the surrounding structures, primarily ligaments and/or joint capsules.

hemorrhage Discharge of blood.

strain Injury involving muscles and tendons or the junction between the two, commonly known as the musculotendinous junction.

avulsion Forcible tearing away or separation.

Contusions

In all probability, common bruises or **contusions** are the most frequent sports injury, regardless of activity. Contusions result from direct blows to the body surface, which cause a compression of the underlying tissue(s) as well as the skin (O'Donoghue, 1984). They can occur in almost any activity; however, collision and contact sports such as tackle football, basketball, and baseball are more to blame in this regard. Curiously, many athletes and coaches view contusions as routine, minor injuries, but they can be serious, even life-threatening, injuries when the tissues involve vital organs such as the kidneys or the brain.

Contusions are typically characterized as being associated with pain, stiffness, swelling, **ecchymosis** (discoloration), and **hematoma** (pooling of blood). If not treated properly, such injuries to muscle tissue can result in a condition known as **myositis ossificans,** which involves the development of bonelike formations in the muscle tissue.

Fractures

Fractures and dislocations represent two categories of injuries involving either bones or joints of the body. Though such injuries can occur in any activity, they are more common in collision sports in which large forces come into play. **Fractures** have been defined by the National Safety Council (NSC, 1991) as "a break or crack in a bone." The NSC recognizes two types of fractures: closed (i.e., bone ends not breaking the skin) and open or compound (i.e., bone ends breaking through the skin surface). Compound fractures are potentially more serious because of the risk of infection related to the open wound. Furthermore, control of bleeding may be necessary depending on the severity and location of the wound.

Acute fractures are relatively uncommon sports injuries. When they occur, however, appropriate first aid is essential to prevent complications such as shock, excessive blood loss, or permanent damage. Fortunately, with modern diagnostic procedures, identifying traumatic fractures is relatively easy. The NSC provides the following descriptions of signs and symptoms:

- *Swelling.* Caused by bleeding; it occurs rapidly after a fracture.
- *Deformity.* This is not always obvious. Compare the injured with the uninjured opposite body part when checking for deformity.
- *Pain and tenderness.* Commonly found only at the injury site. The athlete will usually be able to point to the site of pain. A useful procedure for detecting fractures is to feel gently along the bones; complaints about pain or tenderness serve as a reliable sign of a fracture.
- *Loss of use.* Inability to use the injured part. Guarded motion occurs because movement produces pain, and the athlete will refuse to use the injured limb. However, sometimes the athlete is able to move the limb with little or no pain.
- *Grating sensation.* Do not move the injured limb in an attempt to see if a grating sensation called **crepitation** can be felt (and even sometimes heard) when broken bone ends rub together.
- *History of the injury.* Suspect a fracture whenever severe forces are involved, especially in high-risk sports such as tackle football, alpine skiing, and ice hockey. The athlete may have heard or felt the bone snap.

Fractures may also be described in terms of the specific nature of the break in the bone. The major types of traumatic fractures are shown in Figure 1.8.

Stress Fracture

A stress fracture is typically linked to sports because it develops over a relatively long time period, as opposed to other fractures caused by a single trauma. **Stress fractures** occur when a bone is subjected to repeated episodes of overloading (stress) that exceed its rate of recovery. In effect, the bone starts to break down and eventually begins to fail. Because stress fractures take time to develop, the signs and symptoms are easily confused with other, less-serious sports-related problems. This is especially true for stress fractures of the lower leg bones, which are often confused with shin splints. Although stress fractures can occur throughout the body, the majority occur in the lower extremities. Athletes at high risk for stress fractures are those who are in poor physical condition or overweight. However, even well-conditioned participants may develop such a fracture, particularly when they have made a recent and sudden increase in the intensity of their training program. Stress fractures may even be related to diet: A regimen low in calcium may predispose athletes, particularly females, to this problem (Nelson, 1989).

The symptoms of a stress fracture are nebulous at best; nevertheless, certain factors are usually present when one is developing:

- *Pain/tenderness.* Athlete complains of pain and/or tenderness. A constant ache is not relieved with rest.
- *Absence of trauma.* Suspect such a fracture when there is no history of traumatic event, yet the symptoms persist.

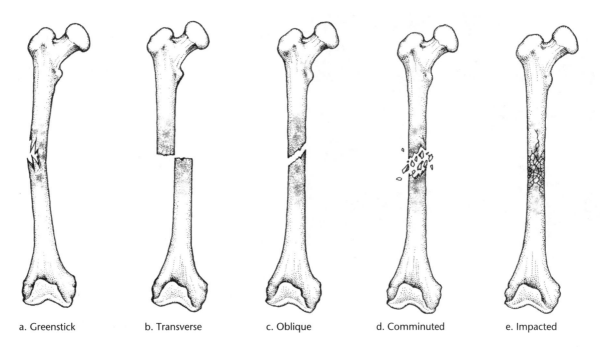

a. Greenstick   b. Transverse   c. Oblique   d. Comminuted   e. Impacted

FIGURE 1.8 Types of fractures.

- ***Repetitive activity.*** Athlete is involved in an activity that subjects the suspect area to repeated stressful episodes.
- **Duration.** Symptoms have slowly developed over a period of days, weeks, or even months.

Stress fractures often present the physician with a difficult diagnosis because, during the initial phases, X-ray examinations may not show the fracture. This is because stress fractures develop slowly and rarely result in large, visible cracks in the bones (O'Donoghue, 1984). Most stress fractures are not visible on standard X-rays until they actually begin to heal. It is this healing process, known technically as a callus, that signals that a fracture has occurred (see Figure 1.9.) As a result, the physician must base the diagnosis on the factors listed previously. The best approach is to treat athletes as if they have a stress fracture and repeat the X-ray evaluation on a weekly or biweekly basis until a callus is seen. In difficult cases, a bone scan or magnetic resonance imaging may be used to obtain a positive diagnosis.

Treatment of stress fractures involves rest and splinting or casting when necessary, followed by a slow, gradual return to participation. Athletes are often encouraged to maintain their fitness levels during recovery by cross training—that is, riding a stationary bike, jogging in shallow water, or swimming. All of these activities provide good stimulation of aerobic fitness while reducing stress on the skeletal system. Any program of recovery must be structured on an individual basis by the coach, athletic trainer, and physician.

Salter-Harris Fractures

A category of fractures unique to the adolescent athlete involves the epiphyseal growth plate and is known as Salter-Harris fractures. These fractures are classified based on the specific location of the fracture line(s) across the epiphyseal region of the bone. Five types (I, II, III, IV, V) have been identified (Figure 1.10).

Type I involves a complete separation of the **epiphysis** from the metaphysis.

contusion Bruise or injury to soft tissue that does not break the skin.

ecchymosis Black-and-blue discoloration of the skin caused by hemorrhage.

hematoma A localized collection of extravasated blood, usually clotted, that is confined within an organ, tissue, or space.

myositis ossificans Myositis marked by ossification within a muscle.

fracture A break or crack in a bone.

crepitation Crackling sound heard during the movement of a broken bone.

stress fracture Small crack or break in a bone related to excessive, repeated overloads; also known as overuse fracture or march fracture.

epiphysis Cartilaginous growth region of a bone.

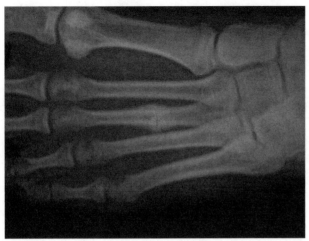

FIGURE 1.9 Stress fracture of the third metatarsal (approximately mid-shaft) in the left foot. Note callus formation around the site of the fracture.

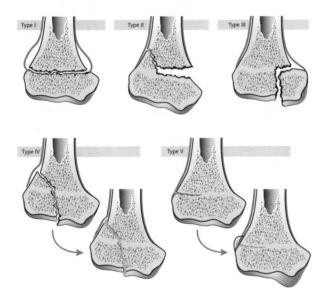

FIGURE 1.10 Salter-Harris epiphyseal fractures.

Type II involves a separation of the epiphysis from the metaphysis as well as a fracture through a small part of the metaphysis.

Type III involves a fracture of the epiphysis.

Type IV involves fracture of both the epiphysis and metaphysis.

Type V involves a crushing injury of the epiphysis without displacement.

Salter-Harris fractures can result in long-term complications for bone growth if not cared for properly. These complications include premature closure of the growth plate or abnormal joint alignment, which can result in the possibility of different leg lengths when growth ceases. These injuries must be evaluated by a physician, who will determine the best method of management. If there is a fracture associated with displacement of the fragments, reduction is required. This may be accomplished either with or without surgical intervention, depending on the specifics of the pathology as determined by the physician. Fixation may be accomplished via closed reduction in appropriate cases or through surgery and internal fixation (Stanitski & Sherman, 1997). Salter-Harris fractures are discussed further in Chapter 20.

Dislocations

Dislocations have been defined as "the displacement of contiguous surfaces of bones comprising a joint" (Booher & Thibodeau, 1989). Two types of dislocations can occur, based on the severity of the injury. A **subluxation** takes place when the bones of a joint are only partially displaced. A **luxation** happens when the bones of a joint are totally displaced. In a sense, any dislocation, whether it is a subluxation or luxation, should be viewed as a severe type of sprain. Recall that sprains involve damage to the tissues surrounding joints—that is, capsules and ligaments. As such, dislocations present many of the same signs and symptoms as those seen in sprains. First aid treatment for dislocations combines care given for both sprains and fractures.

Dislocations can occur in any articulation; however, specific joints seem to be more vulnerable. Two joints in the shoulder complex, the glenohumeral and the acromioclavicular, are injured frequently in sports such as tackle football and wrestling. The small joints in the fingers are commonly dislocated in baseball and softball. Fortunately, such dislocations are relatively easy to evaluate because their most definitive sign is deformity of the joint. Deformity is typically easily identified because the joint can be quickly compared to the same joint on the opposite side of the body or an adjacent joint such as in a finger or toe. Symptoms of dislocation include joint dysfunction, as well as the feeling of the joint having been forced out of normal position. Often the athlete reports having heard a snapping or popping sound as well. If treated properly, full recovery typically occurs. *It is important to note that at no time should the*

WHAT IF?

A student athlete asks you to explain the difference between a subluxation and a luxation of a joint.

coach attempt to reduce (put back in place) any disloca-tion, no matter how minor it may appear to be. All dislo-cations should be diagnosed and reduced by a physician after a complete medical evaluation.

Injury Recognition

From a practical standpoint, learning to recognize in-jury, regardless of the classification system used, is an essential skill to be mastered by the coach. To a great extent, the athlete's health and safety are determined by the decisions and subsequent actions of the coach be-cause the coach is most often the first to arrive at the scene of an injury. In addition, the dramatic increase in sports-injury litigation should serve as further incen-tive for coaching personnel to be prepared for emer-gencies. The premise that most injuries are best treated with the "run-it-out" approach is dangerous, to say the least. Today's coach should treat all possible injuries as such, until proven otherwise. It is imperative that coaching personnel develop the knowledge and skills to discriminate injuries requiring medical referral from those not necessitating such evaluation. Moreover, it should be noted that such decisions are best left to qualified health specialists, such as athletic trainers cer-tified by the Board of Certification, Inc. (BOC). Every effort should be made to have such a specialist em-ployed, either permanently or part-time, by the school or agency sponsoring the sports program.

Epidemiology of Sports Injury

Scientific sports-injury research is a relatively recent phenomenon. The majority of the early studies, some-times known as case-series studies, were based on in-formation collected by medical personnel at hospitals or clinics (Walter et al., 1985). Although these data have provided valuable information, significant problems are associated with this type of data collection. Typi-cally, only athletes with significant injuries seek medical attention at a hospital or clinic. Thus, a large number of athletes with injuries of minor to moderate severity may not be included in the study. Another problem with case-series research is the inability to accurately identify the cause or causes of a specific injury. For ex-ample, researchers at a particular clinic might conclude that less-experienced athletes are more susceptible to injuries. However, without knowing the general level of experience of all athletes—injured as well as unin-jured—it is impossible to determine what constitutes inexperience.

A better approach to sports-injury research involves the application of the principles of epidemiology. The science of **epidemiology** is the "study of the distribution of diseases, injuries, or other health states in human populations for the purpose of identifying and imple-menting measures to prevent their development and spread" (Caine, Caine, & Lindner, 1996). The sports epi-demiologist collects information in an effort to identify causative agents or **risk factors** that may have con-tributed to a particular injury. Hypotheses are then developed and tested to confirm a statistical relation-ship. Risk factors, such as collisions in tackle football or ice hockey, may be inherent in the sport. Equipment may increase the risk of injury—for example, a football helmet with a faulty design or a diving board set too close to the pool deck. The athlete may also possess risk factors—for example, muscle imbalances, obesity, or any of a variety of congenital conditions.

By determining statistical relationships between sus-pected risk factors and specific injuries, sports regula-tory organizations can implement strategies designed to reduce or eliminate the risk of sports injuries. The inci-dence of spine injury in tackle football was significantly reduced by a rule change implemented in 1976 that made the practice of **spearing** (tackling and/or blocking with the head as the initial point of contact) illegal (Torg, 1982). In this case, the available data indicated that the technique of spearing placed the cervical spine (neck) of athletes at risk.

Curiously, it was also hypothesized that improve-ments in helmet technology in the early 1970s may have contributed to the increase in cervical spine injury be-cause athletes were inclined to tackle with their heads down, essentially using their head as a weapon, in the belief they would not sustain a head injury. As men-tioned previously, this observation led to the rule change in 1976 that prohibited the practice of spearing.

dislocation The displacement of contiguous sur-faces of bones comprising a joint.

subluxation Partial or incomplete dislocation of an articulation.

luxation Complete dislocation of a joint.

epidemiology The study of the distribution of dis-ease or injury within a population and its envi-ronment.

risk factor Causative agent in a sports injury.

spearing A practice in tackle football whereby a player performs either a tackle or a block using the head as the initial point of contact.

Large-scale injury surveillance systems have been sponsored by several organizations in the United States since the early 1970s. The earliest to employ epidemiological methods was the National Athletic Injury/Illness Reporting System (NAIRS), which was instituted in 1974. More recently, the National Collegiate Athletic Association Injury Surveillance System (NCAA-ISS), the National High School Injury Registry, and the National Sports Injury Surveillance System (NSISS) have been implemented. Sports organizations such as the National Football League (NFL) and the National Hockey League (NHL) conduct ongoing injury surveillance annually as well.

The National Center for Catastrophic Sports Injury Research began operation during the early 1980s with a focus on the documentation of catastrophic injuries at the high school and college levels (Mueller & Cantu, 1993). This center monitors catastrophic injuries in the following sports:

Baseball	Ice hockey	Tennis
Basketball	Lacrosse	Track
Cross country	Skiing	Volleyball
Field hockey	Soccer	Water polo
Football	Softball	Wrestling
Gymnastics	Swimming	

The primary goal of all organizations involved in sports-injury research is to identify risk factors for injury and, whenever possible, to develop and implement strategies to reduce the risk(s). It is hoped that the information collected by these organizations will lead to continued reductions in both the frequency and severity of sports injuries.

Classification of Sports

Just as injuries can be defined and described using a variety of medical and scientific terms, sports can be classified based on their comparative risk of injury based on criteria such as the amount of physical contact between participants or on the relative intensity of the activities. The American Academy of Pediatrics (AAP) has classified many popular sports based on the likelihood of collisions between the participants (see Table 1.1). Some sports, such as tackle football and ice hockey, are by their very nature classified as contact/collision activities. In activities such as basketball and soccer, participants may make contact with each other; however, in the majority of instances, the magnitude of these collisions is less than in sports such as tackle football or ice hockey. As such, the potential for impact-related injuries is lower in limited contact and noncontact sports than in contact/collision sports. It

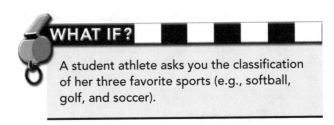

WHAT IF?

A student athlete asks you the classification of her three favorite sports (e.g., softball, golf, and soccer).

should be noted, however, that such classification systems do not imply that sports classified as something other than contact/collision are completely safe. To the contrary, not all injuries are related to the amount of physical contact between participants. For example, temperature-related injuries such as heat exhaustion or heat stroke can occur in virtually any sport when proper preventive measures are neglected. The reader will note that the AAP has stated that participation in boxing is not recommended (AAP, 1994).

Sports medicine personnel, coaches, administrators, and parents can use this information when athletes are found to have specific health-related problems during their preparticipation physical evaluations. For example, a child with a history of recent head injury would be ill-advised to participate in a contact/collision sport such as football. However, contrary to popular belief, noncontact sports can represent a risk to athletes as well. For example, a child with an identified, clinically significant congenital heart disorder might be advised to avoid aerobic activities such as track, swimming, or aerobic dance.

Extent of the Injury Problem: Some Examples

Despite rule changes, proper supervision, and improved coaching, experts report that from 3% to 11% of all children will suffer some type of sports injury every year (Goldberg, 1989). These data indicate that the type and severity of these injuries are sport specific. That is, every sport tends to generate specific types of injuries unique to that sport. This section presents current statistical information on injuries in six popular interscholastic sports, beginning with tackle football.

Tackle Football

Tackle football (Figure 1.11) continues to be popular, with approximately 1.5 million athletes participating, beginning as young as age 9 at the youth sport level, up through high school, collegiate, and professional levels (Stuart et al., 2002). Ramirez and colleagues conducted a 2-year duration study of high school football injuries

TABLE 1.1

CLASSIFICATION OF SPORTS BY CONTACT

Contact/Collision	Limited Contact	Noncontact
Basketball	Baseball	Archery
Boxing*	Bicycling	Badminton
Diving	Cheerleading	Body building
Field hockey	Canoeing/kayaking (white water)	Bowling
Football	Fencing	Canoeing/kayaking (flat water)
Tackle	Field events	Crew/rowing
Ice hockey	High jump	Curling
Lacrosse	Pole-vault	Dancing
Martial arts	Floor hockey	Ballet
Rodeo	Football	Modern
Rugby	Flag	Jazz
Ski jumping	Gymnastics	Field events
Soccer	Handball	Discus
Team handball	Horseback riding	Javelin
Water polo	Racquetball	Shot put
Wrestling	Skating	Golf
	Ice	Orienteering
	In-line	Power lifting
	Roller	Race walking
	Skiing	Riflery
	Cross-country	Rope jumping
	Downhill	Running
	Water	Sailing
	Skateboarding	Scuba diving
	Snowboarding	Swimming
	Softball	Table tennis
	Squash	Tennis
	Ultimate Frisbee	Track
	Volleyball	Weight lifting
	Wind surfing or surfing	

*Participation not recommended.

Source: Reproduced with permission from the American Academy of Pediatrics, Medical Conditions Affecting Sports Participation, Committee on Sports Medicine and Fitness, *Pediatrics.* 2001;107:1205.

that surveyed 87 schools in California. They reported an overall injury rate of 25.5 injuries for every 100 players with the highest rates occurring during games (Ramirez, Schaffer, Shen, Kashani, & Krauss, 2006). Earlier research conducted at the high school level found that 34% of the participants were injured, based on a study funded by the National Athletic Trainers' Association (Powell & Barber-Foss, 1999). The NATA survey suggests that the percentage of high school–level players injured annually has dropped slightly compared with the 3-year period of 1985–87. Many of these injuries are directly attributable to the fact that participants obviously collide with one another as part of the game. However, recent research has found that the incidence of injury is variable, based on the position played. For

example, offensive players sustain a higher percentage of injuries, 55%, than do defensive players, 35.8%. In addition, the data reveal that the most commonly injured body region was the hip/thigh/leg, followed by the ankle/foot and the knee. Of all the injuries, 2.4% required surgery, and of those, 59.4% involved the knee (Powell & Barber-Foss, 1999). In a study of high school football in Texas, a similar pattern of injury was noted (DeLee & Farney, 1992). For example, out of their sample of 4399 players, approximately 23% sustained sprains to the knee during the 1-year study period.

Recent research examining injuries in youth football has provided a wealth of information. For example, Stuart and colleagues (2002) examined the injury rates in 915 players aged 9 to 13 years distributed across

FIGURE 1.11 Up to 34% of participants in interscholastic tackle football can expect to be injured.

42 teams. Over the course of one season, these researchers recorded a total of 55 injuries during games. Of these, the majority were contusions (60%), with muscle strains, sprains, fractures, abrasions, and concussions accounting for 20%, 9%, 7%, 2%, and 2%, respectively. The majority of the injuries involved the lower extremity, including four fractures, all Salter-Harris type. It is interesting to note that their data also indicate a relationship between age and injury: Older players were found to be at a higher risk for injuries. In addition, the highest relative risk of injury by player position was found for running backs and quarterbacks, followed by defensive backs and then linebackers.

Malina and colleagues (2006) studied 678 players aged 9 to 14 years (PONY Football League) over two consecutive seasons. An injury was defined as "any injury that causes cessation of a player's customary participation on the day following the day of onset." BOC-certified athletic trainers were on-site to record all injuries, both at home games and practices, to ensure accuracy of the data. A total of 259 injuries were recorded over two seasons with 178 occurring in practice and the remaining 81 in games. Most injuries were minor (64%) with moderate and major injuries at

18% and 13%, respectively. Injury rates were similar for players in the 4th and 5th grades at 13.3 and 12.9 per 1000 exposures, respectively, with rates doubling for the 7th and 8th grades at 26.1 and 27.4 injuries per 1000 exposures, respectively. It is also interesting to note that, excluding the 6th-grade cohort, game injury rates were more than double the rates seen in practice for all other grade levels. Further, the game injury rates for the 7th and 8th grades were the same as the game rates for high school participants reported by Powel and Barber-Foss (1999). However, more striking is the finding that practice injury rates for the 7th and 8th graders were more than double that seen at the high school level. These findings reinforce the notion that coaching personnel at the youth football level must be trained in first aid and cardiopulmonary resuscitation (CPR), and whenever possible, a BOC-certified athletic trainer should be on hand for both practices and games (Powell & Barber-Foss, 1999).

A common area of concern in tackle football is the incidence of injuries involving the brain and spinal cord. The data compiled by Powell and Barber-Foss (1999) indicate an increase in the reported incidence of injuries to the head/neck/spine. Specifically, it was found that

10.3% of all the injuries reported during the 3-year period of 1995–97 were classified as neurotrauma (injuries to the nervous system such as mild brain injury). In this category, football exceeded a number of other sports such as wrestling, baseball, soccer, and basketball. It should be noted that the reported increase in the football-related incidence in neurotrauma may be the result of increased awareness and better reporting of the injury than in years past and is not necessarily because of an actual increase in this type of injury.

Basketball

Slightly fewer than 1 million high school students, boys and girls, participated in basketball programs in the United States during the 2004–05 school year (NFHS, 2006). Research continues to find that basketball places the lower extremities at risk. Ankle sprains are the most frequent injury in both sexes, followed by injuries to the hip/thigh/leg and knee (Powell & Barber-Foss, 1999). It should be noted that the incidence of knee injuries in basketball is consistently higher for girls than for boys (Figure 1.12). In addition, girls also demonstrate a higher percentage of knee injuries requiring surgery (Powell & Barber-Foss, 1999).

The most recent data (2005–06 season) available from the National Collegiate Athletic Association's Injury Surveillance System (NCAA-ISS) yield results similar to, but perhaps more striking than, the high school data reported by Powell and Barber-Foss. Women basketball players at the collegiate level were

FIGURE 1.12 Basketball places the lower extremities of female players at particular risk.

found to have injured their knees, specifically the anterior cruciate ligament (ACL), at a much higher rate than their male counterparts. Specifically, the women's injury rate during practice was approximately twice that seen in men's practice. The difference between women and men players' ACL injuries in games was even more striking in that the rate of ACL injury during games was three times higher for women than for men. As such, it appears that with respect to collegiate basketball, female athletes continue to exhibit a far greater risk for sustaining injuries to the ACL than do their male counterparts. Although a great deal of research has been and continues to be focused on explanations for these differences, no definitive cause has yet been identified. Research to date has attempted to identify risk factors in female athletes associated with a higher risk for noncontact ACL injuries (Arendt & Dick 1995; Griffin et al., 2000; Harmon & Ireland, 2000; Hewett et al., 2006a, 2006b; Kirkendall & Garrett, 2000). For a more detailed discussion of the issue of ACL injuries, see Chapter 15.

Baseball and Softball

Participation figures for the 2004–05 season show that 459,717 boys participated in baseball at the high school level (NFHS, 2003). The latest available injury data demonstrate that over a 3-year period (1995–97) slightly less than 12% sustained some type of injury, with the most common areas being the forearm/wrist/hand and the shoulder/arm. Of these, more than 50% were classified as either strains or sprains (Powell & Barber-Foss, 1999). Because of the advent of rules requiring safety equipment for catchers (full face mask and throat and chest protection) as well as helmets (double earflap design) for batters, the incidence of head injuries remains low, that is, less than 2% of all reported injuries at the high school level.

Approximately 4.8 million children between the ages of 5 and 14 years play baseball, softball, or tee-ball annually (AAP, 2001). According to the American Academy of Pediatrics, perhaps as many as 8% of these children are injured each year. Of these injuries, 26% are fractures and 37% are contusions/abrasions. It is worthy to note that the AAP has determined that children have an increased vulnerability to chest impacts from balls, perhaps because of the increased elasticity of the thorax in these young players (AAP, 2001). Between the years 1973 and 1995, 88 baseball-related deaths were reported in this age group. Forty-three percent resulted from direct ball impact with the chest. The AAP has made a number of recommendations designed to reduce the risk of such injuries, including the use of batting helmets and face protectors, both at bat and when on-base; outfitting catchers with a helmet, face mask, and chest and neck protector; eliminating the on-deck circle; and adding protective screening around dugouts and player benches. Eye injuries are a major concern in baseball, which is the most productive sport in this regard. One-third of these injuries result from being struck by a pitched ball.

A persistent area of concern is the possibility of chronic injuries to the elbow related to adolescent pitchers throwing excessive numbers of curve balls and/or breaking pitches. Specifically, the area of concern is the medial humeral epicondyle (see Chapter 12) and the muscles that attach at this location. In the adolescent elbow these attachments represent a growth plate; as such, they may be vulnerable to the repeated stresses that pitching can generate. Research by Adams (1965) raised serious concerns about elbow injuries among Little League pitchers. This condition, dubbed **Little League elbow,** created a considerable amount of worry among parents in the late 1960s. In response to these widespread concerns, sports medicine researchers began to investigate the problem. Two large-scale studies found no relationship between pitching and elbow damage (Gugenheim et al., 1976; Larson et al., 1976). In contrast to these studies, research conducted by Micheli and Fehlandt endeavored to identify what causes injuries to tendons and **apophyses** (bony attachments of tendons) in a population of 445 children aged 8 to 19 years. Their conclusion was that for boys, baseball was associated with the highest occurrence of injury. Further, softball was the fourth most commonly associated sport for injury in girls. Overall, they found that in their study group the most common injuries were to the elbow (Micheli & Fehlandt, 1992). It has also been reported that those pitching with a sidearm technique (Figure 1.13) are three times more likely to develop elbow problems than those who pitch using the more traditional overhand style (Stanitski, 1993).

Softball (fast pitch) provided a sport activity for 355,960 girls during the 2002 season (NFHS, 2003). The NATA data indicate that over the course of the 3 most recent years of their survey, 14.4% of softball participants sustained some type of participation-related injury during the season. As was noted for baseball, the most commonly injured body area was the forearm/wrist/hand, followed by the hip/thigh/leg and the shoulder/arm. As with baseball, more than 50% of all the softball-related injuries were categorized as either sprains or strains (Powell & Barber-Foss, 1999).

Wrestling

Wrestling at the high school level drew 243,009 participants during the 2004–05 season (NFHS, 2006). Its continued popularity is no doubt partly a result of the fact that participants are matched by body weight, thus allowing children of all body sizes to participate. However, given the nature of the sport, collisions/contact with opponents and mats do result in various injuries. In addition, joint injuries occur in takedown and escape maneuvers as well as in holds (Figure 1.14), which are essential parts of the sport.

According to the most recent data available, approximately 27% of participants sustained an injury during the competitive season. The most common body areas ivolved were the shoulder/arm, knee, and forearm/wrist/hand. More than 50% of these injuries were classified as either strains or sprains (Powell & Barber-Foss, 1999). Other injuries common to

FIGURE 1.13 The correct pitching technique can spare Little Leaguers possible elbow damage.

FIGURE 1.14 In wrestling, takedown and escape maneuvers can result in injuries.

wrestling are **friction** burns to the skin, skin infections, and irritation of the outer ear (sometimes referred to as cauliflower ear). Mandatory headgear that provides ear protection, improvements in mat surfaces, and vigilant cleaning and maintenance of facilities have significantly reduced the incidence of these problems. Because wrestling incorporates specific weight categories, the sport has historically been plagued with problems associated with rapid and excessive weight loss by participants. This issue is discussed further in Chapter 6 and Appendix 4.

Volleyball

The sport of volleyball continues to be extremely popular with high school girls. The latest participation figures show that for the 2004–05 season, 386,022 girls participated (NFSH, 2006). Volleyball involves jumping, diving, and overhand arm swinging (serves and spiking) and as such qualifies as a "limited contact" sport. Injury data from the 1995–97 NATA study (Powell & Barber-Foss, 1999) found that 14.9% of the volleyball participants sustained some type of participation-related injury. Of those, the majority were classified as sprains, 51.5%, which was the highest percentage of sprains for the 10 sports surveyed. Of these sprains, 41.8% involved the ankle/foot, exceeding girls' basketball in this regard for the same survey. Knee injuries in volleyball constituted 11.1% of the injuries reported in the survey. Data compiled by the NCAA-ISS found that for the 2002–03 season, women volleyball players sustained 0.21 ACL injuries for every 1000 game exposures at the collegiate level. This was a considerably higher rate than seen in practice for the same athletes; the practice rate was 0.03 ACL injuries per 1000 exposures (NCAA, 2003).

Soccer

Soccer (Figure 1.15) has grown in popularity throughout the United States with recent estimates of nearly 14 million participants younger than age 18. Soccer ranks as the fourth-highest participation sport in the United States, behind basketball, volleyball, and softball

(CPSC, 1995). According to the National Federation of State High School Associations, during the 2002 season, 339,101 boys and 295,265 girls participated in soccer programs at their respective high schools (NFHS, 2003).

Although soccer does not involve intentional collisions between players, incidental collisions frequently occur, and as such, it is classified by the AAP as a contact/collision sport (AAP, 1994). Protective equipment is limited, with most body areas exposed to external trauma. The most recent data available indicate that 20.2% of boys and 25.6% of girls were injured during their season in the 1995–97 academic years (Powell & Barber-Foss, 1999).

Not surprisingly, contusions are the most common type of injury; however, the majority are minor. Injuries involving the lower extremities, specifically the knee, ankle, and shin, are most common. The majority, however, are not severe. Data on injury types and rates in youth soccer show a similar pattern regarding injury location, that is, the majority of injuries are in the lower extremities, accounting for about 60% of the total with the knee and ankle joints representing the most commonly injured areas (Giza & Micheli, 2005). With respect to knee injuries, specifically the ACL, available data indicate that female youth participants sustain higher numbers of these

FIGURE 1.15 The most common injuries among soccer players involve the knee, shin, and ankle.

Little League elbow Condition related to excessive throwing that results in swelling of the medial epicondyle of the elbow, i.e., medial humeral epicondylitis.

apophysis Bony outgrowth to which muscles attach.

friction Heat producing.

injuries than their male counterparts do. Recently published research based on youth soccer insurance claims found that female participants dramatically increased the number of claims for ACL injuries at age 14, and compared with males, females demonstrated a higher ratio of knee injury compared to all injuries and a higher ratio of ACL injury compared to all injuries (Shea, Pfeiffer, Wang, Curtin, & Apel, 2004).

A unique aspect of the game involves the skill known as heading, in which a participant contacts a kicked ball with the head. Some medical experts have hypothesized that this practice may lead to possible head injury. Historically, little reliable research has been conducted attempting to confirm this hypothesis (Jordan et al., 1996; Smodlaka, 1984). However, research examining the incidence of head injury from all causes in soccer, as well as evidence of decreased neurocognitive function, has increased significantly in recent years. Boden and colleagues (1998) examined the rate of concussions in soc-

cer at the collegiate level and found that the majority of the concussions reported resulted from collisions with an opponent rather than from intentional heading of the ball.

In recent years, a number of deaths and severe injuries have been related to improperly constructed movable soccer goals. For the period from 1979 to 1994, at least 21 deaths were reported; an additional 120 nonfatal injuries occurred that were directly related to movable goals (CPSC, 1995). The majority of these injuries and fatalities occurred when the goals tipped over and struck the victims. As a result, numerous soccer organizations—such as the Federation Internationale de Football, the National Federation of State High School Associations, and the National Collegiate Athletic Association—have established strict criteria for the construction of soccer goals. In addition, the Consumer Product Safety Commission has published guidelines for the design and construction of movable soccer goals.

REVIEW QUESTIONS

1. Damore and colleagues (2003) recently conducted research on emergency department admissions in a population of patients ranging in age from 5 to 21 years. What percentage of these admissions was attributable to sports injuries?

2. What are the most commonly used criteria for defining a sports injury?

3. Describe briefly two major problems that arise regarding the most commonly used definitions of *sports injury.*

4. What are the three criteria necessary for an injury to be classified as such under the NCAA's Injury Surveillance System (ISS)?

5. Define and differentiate between acute and chronic forms of injury.

6. What constitutes a catastrophic sports injury?

7. What specific tissue types are involved in sprains and strains? How is the severity of these injuries defined?

8. What makes a stress fracture unique when compared with other types of fractures?

9. Define and differentiate between subluxation and luxation.

10. What is the science of epidemiology?

11. According to the most recent NATA high school sports injury study, what has been the most recent trend with respect to injuries to the head/neck/spine?

12. *True or false:* Offensive football players sustain fewer injuries when compared to those who play in defensive positions, according to the most recent NATA data.

13. What is the most frequent injury in basketball?

14. What were the conclusions of Micheli and Fehlandt regarding the relationship between elbow injuries and participation in baseball?

15. What piece of equipment related to soccer has been found to play a direct role in the majority of deaths related to this sport?

REFERENCES

Adams JE. (1965). Injury to the throwing arm: A study of traumatic changes in the elbow joint of boy baseball players. *California Med.* 102:127–132.

Adirim TA, Cheng TL. (2003). Overview of injuries in the young athlete. *Sports Med.* 33(1):75–81.

American Academy of Family Physicians (AAFP). (1992). *Preparticipation Physical Evaluation* (1st ed.). Chicago: American Academy of Family Physicians.

American Academy of Orthopaedic Surgeons (AAOS). (1991). *Athletic Training and Sports Medicine* (2d ed.). Park Ridge, Ill.: American Academy of Orthopaedic Surgeons.

American Academy of Pediatrics (AAP). (1994). Committee on Sports Medicine and Fitness. Medical conditions affecting sports participation. *Pediatrics.* 94(5):757–760.

American Academy of Pediatrics (AAP). (2001). Risk of injury from baseball and softball in children. *Pediatrics.* 107(4):782–784.

American Medical Association (AMA). (1968). *Standard Nomenclature of Athletic Injuries* (1st ed.). Chicago: American Medical Association.

Arendt E, Dick R. (1995). Knee injury patterns among men and women in collegiate basketball and soccer: NCAA data and review of literature. *Am J Sports Med.* 23(6):694–701.

Beachy G, Akau CK, Martinson M, Olden TF. (1997). High school sports injuries: A longitudinal study at Punahou School, 1988–1996. *Am J Sports Med.* 25:657–681.

Benson M. (1995). *1995–96 NCAA Sports Medicine Handbook* (8th ed.). Indianapolis, Ind.: National Collegiate Athletic Association.

Boden BP, Kirkendall DT, Garrett, Jr. WE. (1998). Concussion incidence in elite college soccer players. *Am J Sports Med.* 26:238–241.

Booher JM, Thibodeau GA. (1989). *Athletic Injury Assessment.* St. Louis: Times Mirror/Mosby.

Caine DJ, Caine CG, Lindner KJ (eds.). (1996). *Epidemiology of Sports Injuries.* Champaign, Ill.: Human Kinetics.

Collins RK. (1987). Injury patterns in women's intramural flag football. *Am J Sports Med.* 15(3):238–242.

Consumer Product Safety Commission (CPSC). (1995). Guidelines for movable soccer goal safety. CPSC Document #4326.

Curwain S, Stanish WD. (1984). *Tendinitis: Its Etiology and Treatment.* Lexington, Mass.: D. C. Heath and Company.

Damore DT, et al. (2003). Patterns in childhood sports injury. *Pediatr Emerg Care.* 19(2):65–67.

DeLee JC, Farney WC. (1992). Incidence of injury in Texas high-school football. *Am J Sports Med.* 20:575–580.

DiFiori JP. (1999). Overuse injuries in children and adolescents. *Phys Sportsmed.* 27(1):75–89.

Foster T. (1996, April). NATA releases results from high school injury study. *NATA News.*

Gainor BJ, et al. (1978). The kick: Biomechanics and collision injury. *Am J Sports Med.* 6:185–193.

Giza E, Micheli LJ. (2005). Soccer injuries. *Med Sport Sci.* 49:140–169.

Goldberg B. (1989). Injury patterns in youth sports. *Phys Sportsmed.* 17:175–186.

Griffin LY, et al. (2000). Noncontact anterior cruciate ligament injuries: Risk factors and prevention strategies. *J Am Acad Orthop Surg.* 8(3):141–150.

Grollman LJ, Irrgang JJ, Dearwater SD. (1996). Statewide surveillance of interscholastic sports injury: PATS, Inc. injury reporting system (PIRS). Poster presentation at the annual meeting of the National Athletic Trainers' Association, Orlando, Fla.

Gugenheim JJ, et al. (1976). Little-League survey: The Houston study. *Am J Sports Med.* 4:189–199.

Harmon KG, Ireland ML. (2000). Gender differences in noncontact anterior cruciate ligament injuries. *Clin Sports Med.* 19(2):287–302.

Hess GP, et al. (1989). Prevention and treatment of overuse tendon injuries. *Sports Med.* 8:371–384.

Hewett TE, Myer GD, Ford KR. (2006a). Anterior cruciate ligament injuries in female athletes: Part 1, Mechanisms and risk factors. *Am J Sports Med.* 34:299–311.

Hewett TE, Ford KR, Myer GD. (2006b). Anterior cruciate ligament injuries in female athletes: Part 2, A metanalysis of neuromuscular interventions aimed at injury prevention. *Am J Sports Med.* 34:490–498.

Jordan SE, et al. (1996). Acute and chronic brain injury in United States national team soccer players. *Med Sci Sports Exerc.* 24:205–210.

Kirkendall DT, Garrett WE Jr. (2000). The anterior cruciate ligament enigma. Injury mechanisms and prevention. *Clin Orthop.* 372:64–68.

Larson RL, et al. (1976). Little-League survey: The Eugene study. *Am J Sports Med.* 4:201–209.

Maffulli N, Caine DJ (eds.) (2005). Epidemiology of pediatric sports injuries. Individual sports. *Med Sports Sci.* 48:1–7.

Malina RM, et al. (2006). Incidence and player risk factors for injury in youth football. *Clin J Sport Med.* 16(3): 214–222.

Micheli LJ, Fehlandt AF. (1992). Overuse injuries to tendons and apophyses in children and adolescents. *Clin Sports Med.* 11:713–726.

Mueller FO, Cantu RC. (1993). *National Center for Catastrophic Sport Injury Research—tenth annual report—fall 1982–spring 1992.* Unpublished manuscript. Chapel Hill: University of North Carolina, Department of Physical Education.

Mueller FO, Cantu RC. (1999). Glossary of injury terms. Available at www.unc.edu/depts/nccsi/InjuryTerms.htm.

National Athletic Trainers' Association (NATA). (1989). 3-year study finds "major injuries" up 20% in high-school football. *Athletic Training.* 24:60–69.

National Center for Catastrophic Sport Injury Research. (2005). *Twenty-First Annual Report, Fall 1982–spring 2004.* Chapel Hill: University of North Carolina.

National Collegiate Athletic Association (NCAA).(1999). ACL injuries in women's basketball far exceed the rate in men's game. *NCAA News.* Indianapolis, Ind.

National Collegiate Athletic Association (NCAA). (2003). Sports specific injury data (2003). Available at: www1.ncaa.org/membership/ed_outreach/health-safety/iss/Reports2002-03. Accessed 12/1/03.

National Federation of State High School Associates (NFSH). (1999). *1999 High School Athletics Participation Survey.* Kansas City: National Federation of State High School Associations.

National Federation of State High School Associations (NFSH). (2006). Participation in high school sports increases again; confirms NFHS commitment to stronger leadership. Available at: http://www.nfhs.org/web/2006/09/participation_in_high_school_sports_increases_again_confirms_nf.aspx. Accessed 3/26/07.

National Federation of State High School Associates (NFSH). (2003). Surveys and Resources. Available at: www.nfhs.org/nf_survey_resources.asp. Accessed 12/1/03.

National Safety Council (NSC). (1991). *First Aid and CPR* (1st ed.). Sudbury, Mass.: Jones and Bartlett.

Nelson RA. (1989). Nutrition for the athlete. In Ryan AJ, Allman FL (eds.). *Sports Medicine* (pp. 165–182). San Diego: Academic Press.

Nigg BM, Bobbert M. (1990). On the potential of various approaches in load analysis to reduce the frequency of sports injuries. *J Biomech.* 23(Suppl. 1):3–12.

O'Donoghue DH. (1984). *Treatment of Injuries to Athletes.* Philadelphia: W. B. Saunders.

Powell JW. (1987). 630,000 injuries annually in high school football. *Athl Train JNATA.* 22:19–22.

Powell JW, Barber-Foss KD. (1999). Injury patterns in selected high school sports: A review of the 1995–97 seasons. *J Athl Train.* 34:277–284.

Radelet MA, et al. (2002). Survey of the injury rate for children in community sports. *Pediatrics.* 110:e28.

Ramirez M, Schaffer KB, Shen H, Kashani S, Kraus JF. (2006). Injuries to high school football athletes in California. *Am J Sports Med.* 34:1147–1158.

Shea KG, Pfeiffer R, Wang JH, Curtin M, Apel PJ. (2004). Anterior cruciate ligament injury in pediatric and adolescent soccer players: An analysis of insurance data. *J Pediatr Orthop.* 24:623–628.

Smodlaka V. (1984). Medical aspects of heading the ball in soccer. *Phys Sportsmed.* 12:127–131.

Stanitski CL. (1989). Common injuries in preadolescent and adolescent athletes—recommendations for prevention. *Sports Med.* 7:32–41.

Stanitski CL. (1993). Combating overuse injuries—a focus on children and adolescents. *Phys Sportsmed.* 21:87–106.

Stanitski CL, Sherman C. (1997). How I manage physeal fractures about the knee. *Phys Sportsmed.* 25(4):108–121.

Stuart MJ, et al. (2002). Injuries in youth football: A prospective observational cohort analysis among players aged 9 to 13 years. *Mayo Clin Proc.* 77(4):317–322.

Torg JS. (1982). *Athletic Injuries to the Head, Neck and Face.* Philadelphia: Lea & Febiger.

Walter SD, et al. (1985). The aetiology of sport injuries—a review of methodologies. *Sports Med.* 2:47–58.

The Athletic Health Care Team

MAJOR CONCEPTS

The cornerstone of providing optimal care to those suffering from sports injuries is the athletic health care team, which is made up of a variety of highly trained medical and allied medical personnel, as well as nonmedical personnel such as coaches, parents, and administrators. This chapter provides an overview of the principal members of the team and reviews the evolution of the field of sports medicine. In addition, it describes specific services provided by the athletic health care team, giving special attention to the team physician and the BOC-certified athletic trainer. It also outlines educational requirements for BOC certification and employment options for certified athletic trainers.

http://health.jbpub.com/book/concepts/5e

The web site for this book offers many useful tools and is a great source for supplementary information for both students and instructors.

Visit the site at
http://health.jbpub.com/
book/concepts/5e
to link to the following organizations and sites:

- Board of Certification, Inc.
- The American College of Sports Medicine

Effective delivery of health care to participants in sports and other physical activities is best achieved through a team approach that includes, at the least, the coach, a team physician, and a Board of Certification, Inc. (BOC)–certified athletic trainer. Known as the athletic health care team, these personnel must coordinate their activities to provide essential health care to young athletes. For example, in the vast majority of cases it is not practical for a physician to be on campus daily in the high school setting to provide medical services to the athletes. As such, an allied health practitioner such as a BOC-certified athletic trainer presents a cost-effective solution to the problem. An athletic trainer can be on campus on a daily basis and is in position to observe injuries as soon as they occur. In such cases, the athletic trainer can make decisions regarding injury severity, medical referral, and return to play. In cases where an athletic trainer is not present, coaches trained in first aid and cardiopulmonary resuscitation (CPR) can, and should, offer basic first aid and life-support services to the athletes in their charge.

The physician, athletic trainer, and coaching staff should coordinate their efforts regarding injury prevention through constant dialogue regarding conditioning programs; equipment inspection, purchases, and repair; and environmental conditions. The sports medicine team should provide services such as preparticipation health screening, development and implementation of an emergency plan, medical supervision of practice and games/ contests, injury recognition and treatment (including rehabilitation), implementation of injury prevention strategies, adequate record keeping, and education programs for coaches, athletes, and where appropriate, parents. It is also critical that the athletic health care team communicate with the local emergency care providers, such as paramedics or emergency medical technicians (EMTs) to plan ahead of time regarding matters such as access to game and practice facilities, practice and game schedules, and specific procedures such as helmet removal in tackle football. This is discussed further in Chapter 7, "Emergency Plan and Initial Injury Evaluation."

Sports Medicine

Sports medicine has been defined as "a field that uses a holistic, comprehensive, and multidisciplinary approach to health care for those engaged in a sporting or recreational activity" (Dirckx, 1997). Historically, those most often associated with the practice of sports medicine have included physicians who work directly with athletes, typically orthopedic surgeons and athletic trainers. As the field of sports medicine has evolved over the past several decades, a number of related professionals have been added to the list of potential practitioners in the field of sports medicine. These include primary care physicians (family practice, internal medicine, OB-GYN, pediatrics), osteopathic physicians, chiropractic physicians, sports physical therapists, sport-massage practitioners, dentists, sports psychologists, sports nutritionists, exercise physiologists, strength and conditioning coaches, and, in school settings, school nurses.

At the professional level, today's athletes may have access to a wide variety of sports medicine services. These often include comprehensive preseason physical examinations; proper instruction on sports skills; supervision of conditioning programs; psychological assessments; nutrition education and dietary counseling; help with preventive taping, strapping, and bracing; acute injury care with medical referral; and injury rehabilitation. Sports medicine services at the interscholastic level are typically much more limited, but at the very least they include some type of required preseason physical examination. Additionally, an increasing number of high schools employ a certified athletic trainer, certified by the Board of Certification, Inc. (BOC). In some instances, however, in the absence of an athletic trainer, athletic events may be supervised by a medical doctor or other health professional or left up to the discretion of the coaching staff. The National Athletic Trainers' Association (NATA) has published a document entitled "Appropriate Medical Care for Secondary School Aged Athletes—Consensus Statement" that outlines the essential components and members of the athletic health care team. This document can be obtained by visiting the NATA web site at www.nata.org/publicinformation/position/htm.

With few exceptions, the health care of professional and college athletes was traditionally the domain of the **orthopedic surgeon.** This was logical because many of the serious injuries involved bones and joints. However, with the increased popularity of sports across all age groups and a subsequent rise in demand for services, many different medical specialists are now providing sports medicine services.

It is generally acknowledged that more sports medicine services in the future will be offered to the athletic community by primary care physicians. Because medical schools typically don't provide specialized training in the care of sport- and activity-related injury, a wide array of specialized fellowships are available today in the area of sports medicine. Sports medicine fellowships lasting 1 to 2 years are now available that can lead to an additional credential, the Certificate of Added Qualifications in Sports Medicine (CAQ). The CAQ is available to any primary care practitioner and is awarded on successful completion of an examination as well as completion of either a sports medicine fellowship or 5 years of practice, 20% of which must have involved sports medicine (Rich, 1993).

Key Members of the Team

Although each member of the athletic health care team is important, three are essential: the coach, the team physician, and the BOC-certified athletic trainer. Although typically not recognized as experts in sports injury, coaches are critical in the process of injury prevention and, in many cases, also function as a "first responder" when an athlete is injured. Regardless of their academic backgrounds, coaches in the public schools should receive training in basic conditioning procedures, maintenance and fitting of protective equipment, first aid and CPR, operation of an automatic external defibrillator (AED), and recognition and management of common sports injuries. In addition, coaches should teach correct technique of sports skills to their athletes.

Although it would be ideal if all public schools sports programs had a team physician and a BOC-certified athletic trainer, the reality is that in the majority of cases, the coach must provide basic sports medicine services to his or her athletes. Even when a school does employ an athletic trainer, it is impossible for one athletic trainer to be physically present at all practices and games at the same time. As such, when an injury occurs, the coach is often the first person on the scene of the injury and, further, must make the initial decisions regarding the status of the athlete and administer appropriate first aid procedures. Coaches must be good communicators and be willing to follow the recommendations of the athletic trainer and team physician when making decisions about an injured athlete's recovery plan and return-to-play schedule. At the same time, the athletic trainer and team physician need to include the coach in matters such as development of the conditioning programs and the emergency plan.

Team physicians are medical doctors (allopathic or osteopathic) who agree to provide (either voluntarily or for pay) at least limited medical care to a particular sports program or institution. These services range in scope from a pediatrician who volunteers to be present for home football games at the local high school to the team orthopedic surgeon who is under contract with a professional football program.

The team physician must be willing to commit the necessary time and effort to provide care to the athlete and team. In addition, the team physician must develop and maintain a current, appropriate knowledge base of the sport(s) for which he or she is accepting responsibility. The duties for which the team physician has ultimate responsibility include the following (ACSM, 2001):

Medical management of the athlete

- Coordinate preparticipation screening, examination, and evaluation
- Manage injuries on the field
- Provide for medical management of injury and illness
- Coordinate rehabilitation and return to participation
- Provide for proper preparation for safe return to participation after an illness or injury
- Integrate medical expertise with other health care providers, including medical specialists, athletic trainers, and allied health professionals
- Provide for appropriate education and counseling regarding nutrition, strength and conditioning, ergogenic aids, substance abuse, and other medical problems that could affect the athlete
- Provide for proper documentation and medical record keeping

Administrative and logistical duties

- Establish and define the relationships of all involved parties
- Educate athletes, parents, administrators, coaches, and other necessary parties regarding concerns pertaining to the athletes
- Develop a chain of command
- Plan and train for emergencies during competition and practice
- Address equipment and supply issues
- Provide for proper event coverage
- Assess environmental concerns and playing conditions

A qualified team physician has an understanding of sports injuries that most other doctors simply do not possess. Furthermore, a team physician generally knows the common risk factors regarding sports injuries, is familiar with the athletes, and should have a genuine interest in the welfare of each participant. These attributes

---

sports medicine Branch of medicine concerned with the medical aspects of sports participation.

orthopedic surgeon Physician who corrects deformities of the musculoskeletal system.

team physician A medical doctor who agrees to provide at least limited medical coverage to a particular sports program or institution.

are a great advantage to both coaches and athletes. Acquiring the services of a team physician may not be an easy task, especially in rural communities and in situations where little or no money is available. However, team physicians report that the major reason they become involved with sports is because of a strong personal interest (Rogers, 1985). Thus, it may be possibleto obtain a team physician on a volunteer basis, at least for the purposes of providing medical care at athletic events. To expect more will, in all likelihood, require that some sort of contractual payment plan be arranged. Contacting your state medical association may provide information on how to locate interested physicians. Also, if a college or university is nearby, its team physician may be willing to provide services to your program as well. If not, he or she may know of other physicians in the area who would be willing to do so.

A variety of continuing education programs are currently available to team physicians through workshops, seminars, and postgraduate courses offered by hospitals, medical schools, and professional groups. In addition, numerous medical organizations exist that promote the study of sports medicine through membership. Some of these include the American Medical Society for Sports Medicine, the American Orthopedic Society for Sports Medicine, the American College of Sports Medicine, the American Osteopathic Academy of Sports Medicine, and the Canadian Academy of Sports Medicine (Rich, 1993).

The best way to provide comprehensive medical care for student athletes (during both practice and games) is to hire a BOC-certified athletic trainer who works in conjunction with the team physician. Athletic trainers are recognized allied health care professionals who complete a bachelor's or master's degree with extensive academic and clinical training in the broad area of the care

and prevention of sports injuries. The BOC (2006) defines certified athletic trainers as "medical professionals who are experts in injury prevention, assessment, treatment and rehabilitation, particularly in the orthopedic and musculoskeletal disciplines." Including a BOC-certified athletic trainer on the high school staff can greatly enhance the overall quality of sports medicine services (Figure 2.1).

The latest BOC role delineation study, 5th edition, determined that BOC-certified trainers provide the following services in a wide array of professional settings (BOC, 2006):

- Prevention
- Clinical evaluation and diagnosis
- Immediate care
- Treatment, rehabilitation, and reconditioning
- Organization and administration
- Professional responsibility

The NATA is the national governing body for the profession of athletic training in the United States. Becoming a BOC-certified athletic trainer requires qualifying to sit for, and then passing, the BOC certification examination, which, beginning in the spring of 2007, will be offered via a national network of computerized testing centers. To qualify to sit for the examination, you must have completed an educational program accredited as an entry-level program by the Commission on Accreditation of Athletic Training Education (CAATE). Applicants must have an endorsement on the examination application from their CAATE program director. In addition, applicants must have proof of current certification in emergency cardiac care. A document titled *BOC Exam Candidate Handbook* is available for review and download at the BOC web site (www.bocatc.org/becomeatc/CANDIDATE/).

Guidelines for the development and implementation of entry-level education programs in athletic training have been developed and are published by CAATE in the document titled *Standards and Guidelines for an Accredited Educational Program for the Athletic Trainer*. Educational programs in athletic training must be intensively reviewed for initial accreditation and continued accreditation by both on-site visits and annual reports. The program review process is conducted by the Commission on Accreditation of Athletic Training Education (CAATE).

The CAATE-accredited curriculum offers specific courses designed to prepare students in essential cognitive, affective, and psychomotor domains. More than 500 specific skills have been identified and must be included in the educational program by way of classroom instruction as well as clinical education. Clinical

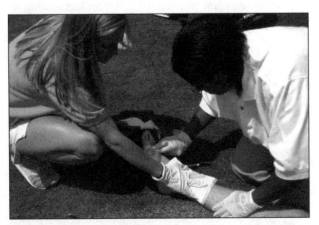

FIGURE 2.1 An athletic trainer evaluates an athlete with an acute injury.

education involves students acquiring skills under the direct supervision of clinical instructors in settings that are typical in the athletic training facilities located on the campus of the institution sponsoring the educational program. In addition, through formal affiliations, students may gain clinical experience off campus in settings such as high schools, other colleges and universities, or professional sports organizations that are located in the immediate geographic vicinity of the institution sponsoring the educational program. Entry-level athletic training education programs must incorporate competency-based classroom and clinical education experiences. Accredited programs must include formal instruction in the following subject matter areas:

Foundational Courses

- Human anatomy
- Human physiology
- Exercise physiology
- Kinesiology/biomechanics
- Nutrition
- Statistics and research design
- Strength training and reconditioning
- Acute care of injury and illness

Professional Courses

- Risk management and injury/illness prevention
- Pathology of injury/illness
- Assessment of injury/illness
- General medical conditions and disabilities
- Therapeutic modalities
- Therapeutic exercise and rehabilitation
- Health care administration
- Weight management and body composition
- Psychosocial intervention and referral
- Medical ethics and legal issues
- Pharmacology
- Professional development and responsibilities

In addition to the formal instruction, students must also complete Clinical Education over the course of a minimum of 2 years and must include a component of working with patients with general medical conditions. Students are evaluated by either approved clinical instructors or physicians across the following settings (NATA, 2005):

- Colleges/universities
- Secondary schools
- Professional sports
- Clinic
- Industrial settings
- Hospitals
- Olympic sports

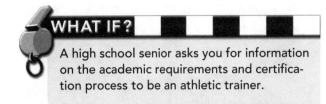

WHAT IF?

A high school senior asks you for information on the academic requirements and certification process to be an athletic trainer.

CAATE recommends additional classes in other subjects, including chemistry, physics, pharmacology, statistics, and research design.

To remain certified, an athletic trainer is required to earn continuing education units (CEUs) and report these activities to the BOC every 3 years by participating in activities such as attending or participating in professional meetings, writing articles for journals, making presentations, and enrolling in college classes that pertain to sports medicine. In addition, CPR certification must be maintained during each 3-year CEU cycle. For more information regarding the BOC certification examination as well as continuing education requirements, contact the BOC at www.bocatc.org.

Professional Settings for the Practice of Athletic Training

Historically the practice of athletic training was confined to the collegiate sports setting, with an emphasis on caring for injuries in tackle football. It was not until the 1970s that this situation changed significantly, as the services of athletic trainers began to be recognized as extremely valuable in the high school sports setting. The high school setting is discussed later in this chapter.

The major expansion in professional settings for athletic trainers has occurred since 1980 with the growth in the field of sports medicine and sports medicine clinics. Since 1980, there has been a 300% increase in the number of registered sports medicine clinics in the United States (Figure 2.2). A broad range of services is provided by these centers, including fitness evaluation and exercise prescription, lifestyle counseling, evaluation and treatment of injuries, and even sports medicine research (Weidner, 1988). This exponential growth in sports medicine clinics has not gone unnoticed by the nation's hospitals. As such, there has been recent growth in hospital-based sports medicine outpatient services. Because BOC-certified athletic trainers possess expertise in the care of those injured in sports and recreational activities, they have found employment opportunities in these new settings. A major source of employment for newly certified athletic trainers continues to be the sports medicine clinic and hospital-based outpatient sports medicine services.

FIGURE 2.2 Since 1980 there has been a 300% increase in the number of sports medicine centers in the United States.

Another relatively recent addition to the professional settings available to athletic trainers is the corporate setting. Major corporations have found it beneficial and profitable to employ athletic trainers to provide direct services to their employees involved in on-site health and fitness programs or in the area of ergonomics. In the most recent NATA salary survey, the average annual salary of athletic trainers employed in the corporate setting, providing health/wellness/fitness services, was $49,012 (NATA, 2005). Although the corporate setting still represents a small percentage of all employment of athletic trainers, it is anticipated that placement in this venue will increase in the future.

To practice in the professional sports setting is often considered to be the dream job for many entering the profession of athletic training. Although the thrill of working with highly paid, marquee athletes may be attractive to some, there are some less-attractive aspects to working in this setting. These include the tremendous pressure to win that is placed on the coaching staff that can, and often does, affect the sports medicine staff and the lack of job security associated with changes in coaching staffs that occur frequently at the professional level. It is not anticipated that there will be any significant growth in employment in this setting in the near future.

The Secondary School Setting

"Why doesn't your school employ an athletic trainer?" When asked this question, most administrators respond that they cannot afford to hire such a person. This argument is no longer as valid as it once may have been. Today, schools have a variety of options available to them if they want to hire a BOC-certified athletic trainer. The most

cost-effective approach appears to be employing one individual as both teacher and athletic trainer. This person is typically hired as a teacher and in addition provides athletic training after school. Ideally, classroom loads can be adjusted to give the teacher/athletic trainer time in the afternoons or mornings to see athletes before practice. This allows an opportunity for rehabilitation, evaluation of injury recovery, counseling, and any other tasks that cannot be effectively completed otherwise. Administrators find this option to be very affordable because the teacher/athletic trainer can be given a standard teaching contract and can provide educational services to the general student population. Additional monetary stipends, often similar to those given a head coach in the same school or district, are sometimes negotiated to pay for the athletic training services provided. A recent study found that the national average annual salary for high school athletic trainers was $43,884 (NATA, 2005).

A less-affordable but more effective option is for the school to hire a full-time athletic trainer. This individual has no formal teaching responsibilities at the school, but is responsible for implementing a comprehensive sports medicine program. This can include follow-up care and rehabilitation of injured athletes during the morning hours prior to practice (during study hall, for example). In addition, the full-time athletic trainer may be able to arrange a schedule so that it more closely approximates the normal number of hours per week provided by other personnel at the school. Though this option often results in the best health care for student athletes, school districts are generally reluctant to commit to the initial financial outlay necessary to develop such a position. Given the financial realities of many school districts around the country, this option may not see significant growth in the foreseeable future.

Other options are available to schools; however, they all offer fewer services to both the school and the athletes. Some alternatives include hiring a part-time athletic trainer or a graduate student/athletic trainer if a university is located nearby, contracting to provide in-service training on various aspects of services with a local sports medicine clinic, or using a substitute teacher/athletic trainer. Though all of these options may save the school money in the short term, they obviously short-change the student athletes with respect to the availability of sports medicine services.

Having a BOC-certified athletic trainer on staff provides many indirect benefits to the school. From a legal standpoint, the school is less vulnerable to tort claims related to sports injuries. This is because such claims are often based on the premise that the school failed to provide adequate medical care to athletes. By hiring a BOC-certified athletic trainer, the school had demonstrated a

Athletic Trainers SPEAK Out

As student athletic trainers, not many of us had one specific goal or vision of the athletic training setting in which we would want to work. Getting broad experiences by working with high school athletes, world-class athletes, male and female athletes, diverse ethnic populations, different age groups, and by exposing yourself to various geographical areas will truly help in your professional growth.

Work ethics and professionalism play a big part in our success. One often forgets to maintain a professional attitude toward what we do and the people we encounter each day. All the small things, such as treating patients and co-workers with respect, maintaining cleanliness at the work site, using respectful language and attire, continuing to educate ourselves, and keeping our skills and knowledge updated, demonstrate our professionalism. The true keys to success are to enjoy what you are doing and being passionate for your profession.

—*Ariko Iso, MA, ATC*

Ariko Iso is Assistant Athletic Trainer for the Pittsburgh Steelers.

commitment to providing the best possible care for student athletes (Stopka & Kaiser, 1988). A qualified athletic trainer also offers many unique educational opportunities for the school. For example, such a professional can teach classes in basic sports injury care, first aid and CPR, nutrition, and physical conditioning. The athletic trainer can also implement a student athletic trainer program at the school to provide educational opportunities for high school students interested in a career in sports medicine. High school student athletic trainers wishing to continue their education at the university level may qualify for scholarships or other types of financial aid. Such funds are typically made available through the sports medicine program at the sponsoring institutions. Finally, the athletic trainer can provide in-service training on various aspects of sports-injury management for the coaching staff. Obviously, the school can realize many returns on its investment when it hires a BOC-certified athletic trainer (see Time Out 2.1).

BOC-certified athletic trainers signify a marked improvement in the health care services provided to athletes, regardless of level of competition. This is partly because of the fact that even under the best of circumstances team physicians are typically available to athletes only on a part-time basis. The BOC-certified athletic trainer can provide a direct link between the injured athlete and the appropriate medical services. In this way, the coach is relieved of much of the responsibility of providing care for the injured participants.

Sports Medicine Delivery

Once the decision is made to hire a certified athletic trainer, potential applicants can be located by listing the position with the NATA's placement service. This can be accomplished by visiting the NATA web site (www.nata.org) and following the links to the placement service. Another option is to contact universities that offer CAATE-approved curriculums in athletic training for a listing of their recent graduates. A listing of all universities with NATA-approved curriculums is available at the NATA web site or by contacting the NATA national office at 214-637-6282.

TIME OUT 2.1

Major support for the placement of BOC-certified athletic trainers in secondary schools was provided by the AMA's House of Delegates in June of 1998. The AMA House of Delegates adopted the following statements as policy:

1. The AMA believes that (a) the Board of Education and the Department of Health of the individual states should encourage that an adequate Athletic Medicine Unit be established in every school that mounts a sports program; (b) the Athletic Medicine Unit should be composed of an allopathic or osteopathic physician director with unlimited license to practice medicine, an athletic health coordinator (preferably a BOC-certified athletic trainer), and other necessary personnel; (c) the duties of the Athletic Medicine Unit should be prevention of injury, the provision of medical care with the cooperation of the family's physician and others of the health care team of the community, and the rehabilitation of the injured; (d) except in extreme emergencies, the selection of the treating physician is the choice of the parent or guardian and any directed referral therefore requires their consent; (e) Athletic Medicine Units should be required to submit complete reports of all injuries to a designated authority; and (f) medical schools, colleges, and universities should be urged to cooperate in establishing education programs for athletic health coordinators (BOC-certified athletic trainers) as well as continuing medical education and graduate programs in Sports Medicine.

2. The AMA urges high school administrators, athletic directors, and coaches to work with local physicians, medical societies, and medical specialty societies, as well as government officials and community groups, to undertake appropriate measures to ensure funding to provide the services of a certified athletic trainer to all high school athletes.

3. Recognizing that not all high schools have the resources to procure the services of a certified athletic trainer and further recognizing that athletic trainers cannot be present at all practices and competitions, the AMA encourages high school administrators and athletic directors to ensure that all coaches are appropriately trained in emergency first aid and basic life support.

Source: Lyznicki JM, Riggs JA, Champion HC. (1999). Certified athletic trainers in secondary schools: Report of the Council on Scientific Affairs, American Medical Association. *Journal of Athletic Training.* 34(3):272–276. Reprinted with permission.

1. Define the term *sports medicine*.

2. What is the CAQ and how does it relate to the team physician?

3. List the specific services that should be provided to the athlete by the team physician.

4. What are the six areas that comprise the role of the BOC-certified athletic trainer?

5. List several professional medical organizations that promote the study of sports medicine.

6. What has been the largest employment market for athletic trainers in recent years?

7. Briefly describe six different employment options for a BOC-certified athletic trainer in the school setting. Elaborate on the advantages and disadvantages of each option.

8. *True or false:* It is generally acknowledged that sports medicine services in the future will be provided by medical specialists rather than primary care physicians.

9. List the 20 specific subject matter areas that are required by the CAATE for accredited curriculums in athletic training.

REFERENCES

American College of Sports Medicine (ACSM). (2001). Team physician consensus statement. Available at www.acsm.org/pdf/teamphys.pdf. Reprinted with permission.

Board of Certification, Inc. (BOC). (2006). Defining athletic training. Available at: http://www.bocatc.org/athtrainer/DEFINE/. Accessed 6/1/06.

Dirckx JH (ed.). (1997). *Stedman's Concise Medical Dictionary for the Health Professions.* Baltimore: Williams & Wilkins.

National Athletic Trainers' Association (NATA). (2005). Athletic training overview. Available at: http://www.nata.org/brochures/general/1015_Athletic%20Training%20Education%20Overview.pdf. Accessed 3/26/07.

National Athletic Trainers' Association Board of Certification (NATABOC) (1999). *Role Delineation Study* (4th ed.). Omaha: National Athletic Trainers' Assocation Board of Certification, Inc.

Rich BSE. (1993). "All physicians are not created equal": Understanding the educational background of the sports-medicine physician. *J Athletic Training.* 28(2): 177–179.

Rogers CC. (1985). Does sports medicine fit in the new health-care market? *Phys Sports Med.* 13(1):116–127.

Stopka C, Kaiser D. (1988). Certified athletic trainers in our secondary schools: The need and solution. *Athletic Training.* 23(4):322–324.

Weidner TG. (1988). Sports-medicine centers: Aspects of their operation and approaches to sports-medicine care. *Athletic Training.* 23(1):22–26.

3

The Law of Sports Injury

As with medicine in general, the field of sports medicine has witnessed a dramatic increase in the amount of litigation over the last decade. This chapter introduces the reader to legal terminology and outlines what constitutes the coach's duty when working with athletes. It provides a listing of the major forms of coaching liability along with information on how to reduce the risk of litigation. It also presents appropriate steps to take in the event of a lawsuit and concludes with a discussion on the ethics of sports-injury care.

http://health.jbpub.com/book/concepts/5e

The web site for this book offers many useful tools and is a great source for supplementary information for both students and instructors.

Visit the site at
http://health.jbpub.com/book/concepts/5e
to link to the following organizations and sites:

- Cornell Law School—The Legal Information Institute

FIGURE 3.1 A coach evaluates an injured athlete.

The coach is often the first on the scene when a sports injury occurs. The coach's decisions and actions at the time of the injury are critical to the welfare of the athlete (Figure 3.1). Moreover, inappropriate decisions and actions may jeopardize the injured participant and lead to legal action by the athlete and/or parents or legal guardians (in the case of minors). A 1996 study of 104 high school athletic coaches found a significant percentage lacked adequate first aid knowledge in accordance with nationally recognized guidelines. Perhaps even more alarming was the finding that when a close game was at stake, a significant percentage of the coaches reported a conflict of interest when a starting player was injured (Dunn & Ransone, 1996). Perhaps at no other time in the history of sports has the potential for legal action against coaching personnel been as great as it is today.

There are several reasons for this increase in the number of lawsuits. They include an increase in the number of participants, greater visibility of sports through the media, rising expectations regarding legal negligence, improved accessibility of legal services, more acceptance by the courts of comparative negligence settlements, and greater consumer awareness about sports services and products (Baley & Matthews, 1988).

The Concept of Tort

A **tort** is harm, other than a breach of contract, done to another for which the law holds the wrongdoer responsible (Ray, 1994; Schubert, Smith, & Trentadue, 1986). In the context of sports, an injured athlete may argue that an injury resulted from someone else's behavior—that of an opponent, an official, or a coach. Tort cases involving sports-related injuries generally seek to recover money to compensate the athlete for damages resulting from someone's alleged negligence.

Essential to proving a tort is establishing that someone, other than the athlete, acted in a negligent manner, which resulted in an injury. **Negligence** is a type of tort and is defined as the failure to do what a reasonably careful and prudent person would have done under the same or like circumstances or, conversely, as doing something that a reasonably careful and prudent person would not have done under the same or like circumstances (Baley & Matthews, 1988; Ray, 1994). Negligence involves either an act of **commission** (acting in an improper way) or an act of **omission** (failure to act). An example of negligence by an act of commission is the high school football player (plaintiff) who claims that permanent **quadriplegia** resulted from improper first aid rendered by the coach (defendant) at the time he sustained a neck injury during a game. In such a case, the athlete might claim the coach's actions caused additional spinal damage that would not have occurred if proper first aid had been rendered. In this case, the athlete would argue that the coach's actions constituted negligence. A coach presented with the same situation could be found negligent by an act of omission if he or she failed to act to protect the injured player from being moved by concerned teammates or other nonmedical personnel on the scene. The defendant would then be judged, in part, on the basis of what a similarly trained person would have done in the same situation. Coaching staff are held to a predetermined standard of care for all those under their supervision. The question that will be asked is, "Should the coach have anticipated the risk to the injured participant?" This is known as the "foreseeability" of the injury and, in essence, determines if the coach provided the appropriate standard of care to the injured athlete. If not, then the coach may be found to have been negligent.

In school sports cases, tort claims often name as many defendants as possible. For example, in the scenario given, the list of defendants might include the coach, an official or officials, the athletic director, the school district, and perhaps even the state high school athletic association. Tort claims generally ask for monetary rewards; therefore, it is only logical that defendants would be selected, in part, based on their ability to pay such awards. This is commonly referred to as "going for the deepest pocket."

Appenzeller (1978) identifies four elements that must be present in order to prove negligence. They are listed in Time Out 3.1.

According to Appenzeller, proving the absence of one or more of the four elements in Time Out 3.1 is the best method of defense in a negligence suit. Other ways of defeating a negligence suit involve showing proof of one of the following legal doctrines:

TIME OUT 3.1

Four Elements of Negligence

1. **Duty:** An obligation recognized by the law requiring a person to conform to a certain standard of conduct for the protection of others against unreasonable risks
2. **Breach of duty:** A failure to conform to the standard required
3. **Proximate or legal cause:** A reasonably close causal connection between the conduct and the resulting injury
4. **Damage:** Actual loss resulting to the interests of another

Contributory negligence. The plaintiff is found to be in part or totally responsible for the injury.

Comparative negligence. This allows for the plaintiff to receive partial compensation on a prorated basis, dependent upon a judgment regarding the extent of **contributory negligence**. In other words, if a monetary reward is given, it will be based only on the percentage of negligence assigned to the defendant.

Assumption of risk. This means that the plaintiff assumes responsibility for injury. In other words, the plaintiff agrees to participate in the sport knowing that there is a chance of suffering an injury. For this defense to work it is essential that the athlete (plaintiff) be fully informed of the potential dangers related to participation. Failure to warn the athlete of such dangers has been found to constitute negligence (Graham, 1985).

Act of God (act of nature). This concedes that the injury occurred as a result of factors beyond the control of the defendant. Being injured or killed by an earthquake that occurs during a cross-country running event would, in all probability, be considered an act of God.

What Is Your Liability?

Anyone serving in a coaching capacity, whether voluntarily or paid, bears considerable responsibility for the health and safety of athletes. Historically, a coach employed by government institutions such as school districts or universities has enjoyed a certain degree of immunity from tort litigation under the doctrine of sovereign immunity. This in essence protects government institutions and their personnel from liability claims. However, some states have

determined through legislative action that tort litigation against such agencies may be possible, depending on the specific circumstances. Consequently, more injury liability cases are now being contested successfully against coaching personnel. Therefore, it appears that protection under the doctrine of sovereign immunity is no longer guaranteed (Berry, 1986).

The coach must always use reasonable care to avoid creating a foreseeable risk of harm to others (Schubert, Smith, & Trentadue, 1986). Whether on staff or volunteer, a coach should have some sort of written contract outlining specific duties (Graham, 1985). Such a document provides a level of protection from litigation as long as the coach functions within the context of the contract. Schubert, Smith, and Trentadue (1986) outline seven potential actions for which a coach may be found negligent. These are explained in Time Out 3.2.

Are You Protected?

The best protection a coach can have against the risk of litigation is to avoid the problems listed in Time Out 3.2. Today's coach must be constantly aware of potential risks to athletes and must take appropriate action to reduce or eliminate those risks. This ongoing process of being ever vigilant for potential risks to athletes helps reduce the chances of successful litigation because it indicates the coaching staff has met the standard of care by eliminating all foreseeable risks for injury.

Good Samaritan Law

Most states have Good Samaritan laws in place, which serve to protect citizens who voluntarily provide first aid to an injured person. Such laws were developed, in

tort Harm, other than a breach of contract, done to another for which the law holds the wrongdoer responsible.

negligence The failure to do what a reasonably careful and prudent person would have done under the same or like circumstances, or doing something that a reasonably careful and prudent person would not have done under the same or like circumstances.

commission A legal liability arising when a person commits an act that is not legally his to perform.

quadriplegia Paralysis affecting all four limbs.

contributory negligence Negligence arising when an injured party is at least partly responsible for an act that causes his own injury.

TIME OUT 3.2

Potentially Negligent Actions by Coaches

- **Failure to provide competent personnel.** When a head coach hires an assistant, he or she assumes some responsibility for the competence, or lack thereof, of that assistant. If the assistant coach fails to give proper instruction to the athlete, the head coach could be found to be negligent.

- **Failure to provide instruction.** This involves providing proper instruction on the fundamental and advanced skills required for participation, as well as those for injury prevention. The coach must make sure that the participants receive adequate conditioning exercises and use the appropriate protective equipment. The coach must also instruct athletes on the rules and regulations regarding participation.

- **Failure to provide proper equipment.** Because the coach may be responsible for the selection and purchase of protective equipment, he or she must make sure that any such equipment does not place an athlete in jeopardy. The coach may also be held responsible for failure to maintain and/or replace damaged equipment.

- **Failure to warn.** The coach has the obligation to warn participants of any dangers that may not be obvious. It may be advisable, in light of recent cases, to warn athletes *in writing*, even of dangers that appear obvious (Graham, 1985). When dealing with minors, any written warning should be given to the parent(s) or guardian.

- **Failure to supervise.** The coach is required to supervise activities to an extent that is determined, in part, by the age, skill, and experience of the participants. Thus, inexperienced children involved in a high-risk sport such as football require a higher level of supervision than do senior varsity athletes in the same sport. Anytime children are involved, regardless of the activity, the coach is responsible for providing supervision.

- **Moving or improperly treating an injured athlete.** The coach is required to provide medical care to an injured athlete. Given this mandate, the prudent coach should have basic training in proper first aid procedures for common athletic injuries. Coaches have been found liable for failing to provide appropriate first aid as well as for having applied inappropriate procedures. It is also critical that a coach remove a child from participation if there is any question about immediate health status.

- **Selecting participants.** The coach is responsible for ensuring that an athlete is ready to play—that is, the athlete possesses an adequate level of physical fitness, or if recently injured, is ready to resume participation. In most cases, examination by a medical doctor should be required before an athlete is allowed to resume participation after an injury.

Source: Schubert GW, Smith RK, Trentadue JC. (1986). *Sports Law*. St. Paul: West Publishing Company. Reprinted with permission of Thomson West.

---

part, to encourage the average citizen to render first aid in an emergency, even though such individuals do *not* have a duty to provide such care. In contrast, coaches and other school personnel do have a duty to provide appropriate emergency care and, as a result, do not enjoy immunity from tort claims under the tenets of Good Samaritan laws.

Because most tort claims seek monetary rewards, it is obvious that a coach's personal assets may be in jeopardy in the event of an unfavorable court decision. Therefore, it is imperative that the coach be protected by some form of liability insurance. A coach in an interscholastic or intercollegiate setting is generally covered by insurance provided by the employer. However, it is wise to ascertain the specific type of coverage provided. Don't assume you are protected. A volunteer coach may not have any liability coverage, in which case the purchase of personal liability insurance is advisable.

A good rule of thumb is never to assume that you are covered. Before beginning the playing season, contact your employer, sponsoring organization, or an insurance company representative to determine what type of coverage you have and whether it offers the best protection.

How to Reduce Your Chances of Going to Court

The following is a list of nine important preventive steps a coach can implement to reduce the chances of being sued:

1. **Written contract.** This document should state in detail the expectations and limitations of your service as a coach. (It is advisable to have an attorney examine any contract to determine what liabilities may be included.)

Athletic Trainers SPEAK Out

In most secondary school settings, the sport coach is still the primary provider of health care services to the student-athlete. Because of this charge, it is imperative that they stay abreast of current information and skills regarding athletic-training techniques, ideas, regimes, and injury prevention. This will not only allow the coaches to provide appropriate and efficient care, but it may also help reduce the possibility of putting themselves in a potentially litigious situation.

—*Barrie Steele, MS, LAT, ATC*

Barrie Steele is the Director of Athletic Training Services at the University of Idaho and is District 10 Representative, NATA Board of Directors.

2. **Certification in basic or advanced first aid and CPR.** Make sure your certification is current and that you periodically practice your skills. Such training is available through the National Safety Council.

3. **Emergency plan.** It is essential that a formal emergency plan be developed for both home and out-of-town contests. These plans should be in written form; all parties involved with their implementation should have copies. Furthermore, any emergency scheme should be periodically rehearsed to ensure that it will function effectively during a real crisis. It is advised that the plan be examined by an attorney to ensure that it meets all legal requirements (Baley & Matthews, 1988). Details for the development of an emergency plan are presented in Chapter 7.

4. **Parental consent form** (for athletes under 18 years of age). These forms provide an excellent opportunity to inform both the athlete and parents/guardians regarding the potential for injury that is inherent in participation.

5. **Comprehensive preparticipation physical examination (PPE).** Such an examination must be a requirement of all participants. This exam should be administered by a medical doctor (MD, DO), and all pertinent information should be recorded on an appropriate form. Athletes should not be allowed to participate in sports activities until they have undergone the physical. Most school districts, colleges, and universities have standard forms for these physical exams. Information collected should be on file with the athletic administrator and handled confidentially. Whenever possible, the PPE should include some sort of neuropsychological or postural stability testing to establish a baseline for comparative purposes later if the athlete sustains a head injury at some point in the future (Osborne, 2001).

Comprehensive guidelines for the PPE have been published by a consortium of medical groups, including the American Academy of Family Physicians, the American Academy of Pediatrics, the American Medical Society for Sports Medicine, the American Orthopaedic Society for Sports Medicine, and the American Osteopathic Academy of Sports Medicine. A complete document, *Preparticipation Physical Evaluation,* can be purchased by contacting the American Academy of Family Physicians (www.aafp.org; 800-944-0000). Physicians who administer PPEs should consider following these guidelines; doing so is likely to be interpreted by the courts as exercising reasonable care toward athletes under their care. A detailed description of a PPE is given in Chapter 4.

6. **Document all injuries.** Regardless of severity, a detailed description of the initial care and treatment—as well as the cause(s)—of all injuries must be recorded on a standard form. The coach should make sure that all pertinent information regarding an injury is collected and placed on file with the athletic administrator. It is advisable that a history of injuries be maintained on all athletes. In this way, coaching and medical personnel will be aware of all recent injuries a given athlete may have sustained.

Recently introduced federal regulations known as the Health Insurance Portability and Accountability Act (HIPAA) have had a dramatic impact on the entire health care industry, including the sports medicine field. Although a comprehensive discussion of HIPAA is beyond the scope of this text, coaches and other members of the athletic health care team should be familiar with those aspects of the new regulations that can affect their professional practice. For example, these new regulations place strict limitations on the release of personal health information to third parties, such as the media. Because sports are of great interest to the general public and because sports injuries are often somewhat public by their very nature, members of the athletic health care team must carefully monitor how information regarding an athlete's injury is distributed to the media, if at all.

7. **Attendance at in-service seminars and/or postgraduate classes.** Owing in large part to the increased concern regarding sports-injury litigation, most school districts conduct periodic in-service training on the topic of the care and prevention of athletic injuries. Many times such seminars are offered by the school district, local hospitals, or a regional university. In addition, coaches are often encouraged by school administrators to enroll in postgraduate classes pertaining to the care and prevention of sports injuries. Attendance at such seminars demonstrates a willingness on the part of coaching personnel to remain informed regarding current standards of care and prevention of sports injury.

WHAT IF?

You are asked to take a part-time position coaching girls' volleyball at a local junior high school. What specific steps can you take to protect yourself from a potential lawsuit if an injury occurs to one of your athletes?

8. **Periodic inspections of facilities and/or equipment.** Such inspections must be conducted to ensure that any potential hazards are corrected. In addition, it is advisable to notify the athletic administrator, in writing, of any hazards that remain uncorrected.

9. **Develop and maintain effective lines of communication.** Communication with athletes, parents, athletic administrators, and medical personnel is essential to providing safe activity for sports participants.

What to Do If You Get Sued

If you are about to be sued in a tort case, it is critical that you take the appropriate steps to protect yourself. It is recommended that you first call your insurance company and contact your lawyer (Appenzeller & Appenzeller, 1980). In this way, you will be given proper advice on how to protect yourself. Furthermore, all pertinent facts related to the case can be recorded while events are still recent.

It is important to write a detailed description of all events leading up to and immediately following the injury. This should include signed statements by eyewitnesses if possible. It is also advised that you not make statements to the media or to other parties without the advice of your attorney (Appenzeller & Appenzeller, 1980). In this way you will avoid compromising your position during a subsequent trial or appeal.

Ethics of Sports-Injury Care

The athlete's health and safety should be the ultimate priority for all those involved in organized sports. However, society's values have changed significantly since the days of the Olympian games held in ancient Greece. More and more, sports are now seen as a business, with an increasing emphasis on winning and earning monetary rewards. Very often, a coach's livelihood and career depend on a win-loss record. In addition, athletes (and often parents) bring pressure to ensure an opportunity to play.

More than ever before, the coach must resist the temptation to circumvent the recommendations of medical personnel when returning an injured athlete to participation. Under no circumstance should an athlete be allowed to resume sports without the consent of a medical doctor. Remember: Unethical behavior by a coach will in all probability be considered as negligence by a court of law.

State Regulation of Athletic Training

Medical and allied health professions are regulated at the state level, with the intent being to protect the public from incompetent practitioners. Because the profession of athletic training has continued to evolve, more and more states now regulate the practice of athletic training. Several different types of regulation of athletic trainers are presently in place in 44 of the 50 states. Licensure is considered the "gold standard" for professional regulation of ethlects trainers; to date, 33 states require athletic trainers to be licensed to practice. Other forms of state regulation include registration, certification, and exemption. In general, regulation defines the scope and practice of athletic training in a particular state. Anyone with Board of Certification, Inc. (BOC) certification who plans to practice as an athletic trainer in a state that regulates the practice of athletic training must contact the state regulatory body to determine his or her eligibility to practice in that state. Most often an application process is required and strictly enforced. A current listing of states that regulate athletic training is shown in Time Out 3.3.

TIME OUT 3.3

Governmental Affairs Committee List of Regulated States

The following states (33) have licensure:
Alabama
Arizona
Arkansas
Connecticut
Delaware
Florida
Georgia
Idaho
Illinois
Indiana
Iowa
Kansas
Maine
Massachusetts
Michigan
Mississippi
Missouri
Nebraska
Nevada
New Hampshire
New Jersey
New Mexico
North Carolina
North Dakota
Ohio
Oklahoma
Rhode Island
South Dakota
Tennessee
Texas
Utah
Virginia
Wisconsin

The following states (6) have certification:
Kentucky
Louisiana
New York
Pennsylvania
South Carolina
Vermont

The following states (2) have registration:
Minnesota
Oregon

The following states (3) have exemption:
Colorado
Hawaii
Wyoming

The following states (6) have none of the above:
Alaska
California
Maryland
Montana
Washington
West Virginia

Source: National Athletic Trainers' Association. Reprinted with permission.

REVIEW QUESTIONS

1. Define the terms *tort* and *negligence* as discussed in the text.

2. Briefly describe the two types of negligence—commission and omission—mentioned in the chapter.

3. What are the four elements that must be present to prove negligence?

4. Describe briefly the five ways that a negligence suit may be defeated.

5. Does liability differ for a paid coach versus a volunteer?

6. Do Good Samaritan laws protect school personnel, such as coaches, from litigation?

7. List and describe the reasons a coach may be found negligent.

8. Outline the nine steps that can reduce a coach's chances of being sued.

9. What are the first two things a coach should do when notified of an impending lawsuit?

10. Elaborate on the sociologic pressures exerted on today's coach that may challenge one's sense of professional ethics.

11. *True or false:* The courts have found that a coach is responsible for giving instruction to athletes regarding the rules and regulations of participation in sports.

12. *True or false:* The first thing to do if you are sued is to phone your insurance company and your lawyer.

13. What does the acronym HIPPA stand for?

14. What is the purpose of state regulation of athletic trainers, and how many states presently regulate the profession?

REFERENCES

Appenzeller H. (1978). *Physical Education and the Law.* Charlottesville: The Michie Company.

Appenzeller H, Appenzeller T. (1980). *Sports and the Courts.* Charlottesville: The Michie Company.

Baley JA, Matthews DL. (1988). *Law and Liability in Athletics, Physical Education, and Recreation.* Dubuque, Ia.: William C. Brown.

Berry RC. (1986). *Law and Business of the Sports Industries. Vol. II: Common Issues in Amateur and Professional Sports.* Dover, Mass.: Auburn House.

Dunn LR, Ransone JW. (1996). Assessment of first aid knowledge and decision-making of high school coaches. Poster presentation at the annual meeting of the National Athletic Trainers' Association, Orlando, Fla.

Graham LS. (1985). Ten ways to dodge the malpractice bullet. *Athletic Training.* 20(2):117–119.

Osborne B. (2001). Principles of liability for athletic trainers: Managing sport-related concussion. *J Athl Train.* 36(3): 316–321.

Ray R. (1994). *Management Strategies in Athletic Training.* Champaign, Ill.: Human Kinetics.

Schubert GW, Smith RK, Trentadue JC. (1986). *Sports Law.* St. Paul: West Publishing Company.

4

Sports-Injury Prevention

MAJOR CONCEPTS

Prevention of sports injuries must be a priority for everyone involved in athletics, particularly coaches, officials, administrators, and sports medicine personnel. This chapter describes the critical steps that must be taken to reduce the likelihood of injury. First, it differentiates between two major categories of injury risk factors—intrinsic (age, gender, skill) and extrinsic (equipment, environment, sport). It then distinguishes between two essential prevention strategies: preparticipation physical evaluation (PPE) and physical conditioning with an emphasis on periodization of the training year. Finally, it concludes with a description of the major factors to be considered to modify the common extrinsic risk factors related to sports injuries.

http://health.jbpub.com/book/concepts/5e

The web site for this book offers many useful tools and is a great source for supplementary information for both students and instructors.

Visit the site at
http://health.jbpub.com/ book/concepts/5e
to link to the following organizations and sites:

- The American Academy of Pediatrics
- The National Strength and Conditioning Association
- The Riddell Corporation

FIGURE 4.1 In some sports, the cause of an injury might seem obvious, but other factors may also contribute.

Previous chapters have discussed the scope of the sports-injury problem, sports medicine personnel involved in treating injuries, and the legal implications of injuries. Obviously, it would be in everyone's best interest to reduce the number of injuries through a well-planned, co-ordinated program of injury prevention. However, before such an endeavor can be effective, causative factors must be identified that contribute to injuries. In this way, all parties involved—coaches, officials, and athletes—can take steps to eliminate or at least reduce the risk of injury. At first, this may seem to be a simple process with regard to common sports injuries. For example, when a football running back collides with a linebacker and sustains a sprained knee ligament, the cause of the injury would seem to be the force of the collision (Figure 4.1). However, other factors may have played a role in creating the injury. The player's skill, age, hamstring/quadriceps strength ratio, shoe type, playing surface (natural turf or artificial), fatigue, and previous injuries may all have contributed.

Causative Factors in Injury

Sports scientists have collected considerable information regarding injuries, and some have conducted research to identify causative factors. Two general categories have been proposed: extrinsic factors and intrinsic factors. Extrinsic factors include equipment, environment, type of activity, and conditioning errors. Intrinsic factors include age, gender, body size, history of injury, fitness, muscle strength (especially imbalances), ligamentous laxity, skill, psychological status, and perhaps even overall intelligence (Taimela, Kujala, & Osterman, 1990). Moskwa and Nicholas (1989) identified a number of risk factors by body area, for example, in the upper extremity ligamentous laxity, tight shoulder muscles, and shoulder girdle weakness all increase the risk for injury. In the lower extremity such factors as tight, weak hamstrings, weak lower extremity muscles, joint malalignments, and poor stretching and muscle conditioning were all identified as risk factors.

It is clear that not all of these factors can be eliminated or changed. However, it is certainly possible to reduce or eliminate problems such as poor or faulty equipment, inadequate muscle strength, poor skills, and training errors.

Intervention Strategies

It is the responsibility of all members of the sports medicine team to remain vigilant in an effort to identify causative factors before an injury occurs. Many of the extrinsic factors are quite easily recognized. For example, regular inspections of protective equipment and athletic facilities can alert personnel to potential problems. Athletes in high-risk sports must be informed of the potential hazards and prevention strategies. For example, in tackle football athletes should be taught proper blocking and tackling techniques in an effort to avoid using the helmeted head as a weapon. It has been found that the incidence of serious head and neck injuries can be greatly reduced in this way.

Both the National Collegiate Athletic Association (NCAA) and the National Federation of State High School Associations (NFHS) have developed and implemented guidelines regarding medical evaluations of student athletes. The NCAA Guideline 1B (Medical Evaluations, Immunizations, and Records) requires that all student athletes receive a preparticipation medical evaluation at the initial entrance into the institution's athletic program. Thereafter, only an updated medical history is required unless an additional medical examination is warranted based on the updated history (Benson, 1995). The National Federation of State High School Associations continues to recommend a medical evaluation prior to participation in interscholastic sports. The NFHS policy, entitled "Recommended Eligibility Standards for Athletics," states, "Prior to the first year of participation in interscholastic athletics, a student shall undergo a medical examination and be approved for interscholastic athletic competition by the examining medical authority. Prior to each subsequent year of participation, a student shall furnish a statement, signed by a medical authority, which provides clearance for continued athletic participation."

Two factors have contributed to the development of these comprehensive guidelines regarding preparticipation physical evaluation (PPE). First, since the late 1970s there has been explosive growth in the number of sports participants. It has become ever more difficult for school officials to monitor the health of all of their incoming student athletes on an annual basis. Second, our society has become more litigious in recent years and, as a result, coaches, educational institutions, and sports associations have a greater fear of being sued if and when a student is injured as a result of inadequate health screening. Therefore, the PPE is an important tool for all concerned. The primary purposes of the PPE should be to identify preexisting risk factors for injury as well as to ascertain any injuries or diseases that may create problems for the student athlete later on.

Typically the PPE will be administered by a licensed physician (MD or DO), although it has been reported that not all states require a physician to conduct the PPE (Feinstein, Soileau, & Daniel, 1988). A well-administered PPE can provide a great deal of information about the athlete's readiness for participation. Commonly identified conditions include congenital disorders such as spina bifida occulta (incomplete closure of the vertebral neural arch), absence of one of a paired set of organs (eye, kidney, testicle), postural problems such as abnormal spinal curvatures or abnormalities of the extremities, muscle imbalances, obesity, high blood pressure, cardiac defects or disorders of cardiac rhythm, respiratory conditions such as asthma, drug allergies, skin infections, and vision problems.

Historically, PPEs all too often have consisted of a simple quick check of the major physiological systems. With the increased numbers of sports participants over the past two decades, the demand on the medical community for these services has increased as well. Obviously, as the costs

of health care in general have escalated, so have the costs of undergoing a PPE. As a result, many young athletes simply cannot afford to visit a personal physician (assuming they have one) each year for such an evaluation. It was reported that the PPE is often the *only* time healthy children come into contact with a physician during the year (Koester, 1995). In an effort to improve the overall quality of PPEs nationally, a consortium of professional medical organizations developed and published a comprehensive set of guidelines for PPEs in 1992; the guidelines have since been updated twice, with the most recent version published in 2005. In addition, in 1996 the American Heart Association developed guidelines for detection of preexisting cardiovascular conditions during the PPE.

Two basic PPE formats are currently recommended. One option is for the athlete's personal physician to perform the PPE in the physician's office; this is considered the ideal option. The other option accommodates groups of athletes in one session and is called the "coordinated medical team" approach (American Academy of Family Physicians, 2005).

Both formats can be highly effective tools for the delivery of the PPE. The advantages of the individual PPE performed by the athlete's personal physician include familiarity of the physician with the athlete's medical history and, immediate access to medical records that include such information as immunization history. In addition, the athlete's personal physician in all likelihood has established a relationship of trust with the athlete that will allow for some discussion regarding health risk behaviors such as drug use and sexual behavior. In some situations, however, the office visit with a personal physician may not be possible. For example, when a group of athletes such as a basketball or volleyball team all need PPEs, the team physician may prefer to arrange for the team to be evaluated by a team of clinicians that include primary care physicians as well as athletic trainers, physical therapists, exercise physiologists, and nutritionists. According to the American Academy of Family Physicians, this approach to the administration of the PPE does have some advantages over the office visit format. These include possible cost savings to the athletes as well as provision of PPEs to athletes who do not have a personal physician. To expedite the PPE process, it is recommended that the athlete complete a PPE medical history in advance of the actual evaluation. Whenever possible the medical history should be done with the athlete and parent(s) or guardian(s) together.

Regardless of which type of PPE is employed, the procedure can provide valuable information relative to an athlete's readiness for participation. Coaches as well as sports medicine personnel must be aware of any preexisting conditions that may make the athlete vulnerable to specific medical problems. A thorough medical history, including previous injuries, represents information essential to the welfare of the athlete.

Athletes with medical conditions such as diabetes, epilepsy, and drug allergies should be identified in case of subsequent injury or other problems related to their condition. Special populations need to be evaluated on the basis of injury risk factors that may not be present in the general population. Athletes with special physical and mental problems must be assessed by physicians who are familiar with the medical implications of each specific disorder. Obviously, all information obtained during a physical examination should be handled confidentially.

Concern has been raised in the sports medicine community regarding athletes who are missing one of a paired set of organs—for example, those who have only one eye, kidney, or testicle. The consensus is that when loss of the remaining organ can be life threatening, as in the case of a single kidney, the athlete should not be involved in a collision sport (Dorsen, 1986).

Considerable debate exists about the appropriate frequency of the preparticipation physical evaluation. Many school districts require a PPE on an annual basis. However, as costs for such procedures increase, there is pressure to amend this requirement to a format that would require an updated physical evaluation whenever an athlete reaches a new level of competition—for example, when going from junior high to high school (McKeag, 1985). It is also advised that whenever an athlete has sustained a more serious injury, such as head or spinal trauma, he or she should receive a complete physical evaluation by a physician prior to being allowed to return to participation. The American Academy of Pediatrics

(AAP), along with five other consensus groups, has recommended that younger secondary-school-level athletes receive a comprehensive PPE biannually and at 2- to 3-year intervals for older athletes. In addition, it is recommended that a comprehensive PPE be administered for athletes entering either middle or high school or those transferring to a new school. Further, all athletes should receive annual updates that consist of a comprehensive history, along with assessment of height, weight, and blood pressure. Follow-up examination for any problem(s) detected in the history is also recommended (American Academy of Family Physicians, 2005).

Injury Prevention and Preseason Conditioning

Many of the intrinsic risk factors, such as fitness level and skill, can be significantly modified as a result of effective conditioning programs and coaching. An essential aspect of any injury prevention program is the optimal development of physical fitness in the athlete. The old saying "You don't play sports to get fit, you get fit to play sports" is certainly valid today. A significant body of evidence exists supporting the premise that a fit athlete is less likely to suffer an injury (Taimela, Kujala, & Osterman, 1990).

The components of fitness include cardiorespiratory (aerobic) fitness, muscular strength and endurance, flexibility, nutrition, and body composition (Fox, Dirby, & Roberts, 1987). Athletes in any sport would be well advised to develop a total conditioning program that addresses all of these components. By so doing, the athlete will benefit in two ways—improved performance

Athletic Trainers SPEAK Out

The athletic trainer and the strength and conditioning specialist can work as a team in order to prepare the athlete for the rigors of athletic competition. By exchanging ideas, they can formulate a plan that will maximize the athlete's program. The more successful the off-season conditioning program, the less likely that the athlete will experience a significant injury.

An off-season program that involves strength training, cardiovascular conditioning, and proper rehabilitation programs will work to the advantage of the athlete. An athletic trainer can make a significant difference as long as he or she works collaboratively to help athletes reach their full potential.

—*Dan Ruiz, ATC*

Dan Ruiz is a high school teacher and athletic trainer at Mark Morris High School in Longview, Washington.

and reduction in injuries. It is important to remember that a conditioning program consists of two primary components, general conditioning and sport-specific conditioning. The general conditioning program focuses on the major fitness components as listed earlier, whereas the sport-specific conditioning focuses on any aspect of a particular sport or activity that is unique to it. For example, the shoulder girdle and glenohumeral joint muscles in a tennis player need to receive special attention to avoid overuse injuries related to repetitive overhand strokes, which are inherent to the sport. To be effective, the conditioning program should allow for general conditioning on a year-round basis. This is best accomplished by incorporating the concept of periodization in the total conditioning program.

Aerobic Fitness

Aerobic fitness, also commonly termed aerobic power, is defined as the amount of work that can be accomplished using the oxidative system of converting nutrients into energy. Aerobic power can be tested in the laboratory and is normally expressed in an equation that states the volume of oxygen consumed per unit of body weight per unit of time. The most common expression is in milliliters of oxygen per kilogram of body weight per minute (ml/kg/min^{-1}). Continuous activities with a duration in excess of a minute or longer rely on aerobic power for muscle energy. However, athletes involved in anaerobic (energy production in the absence of oxygen) activities can benefit indirectly from having a high level of aerobic fitness. It has been shown that aerobic fitness can assist in avoiding injuries related to general fatigue. This is true even in sports that do not, in themselves, require high levels of aerobic fitness for athletes to be successful (Taimela, Kujala, & Osterman, 1990). Fatigue can have a detrimental effect on muscle strength, reaction time, agility, and neuromuscular coordination (Wilmore & Costill, 1988).

In short, regardless of the sport, athletes who enter the season with a high level of aerobic fitness are less prone to injury. Aerobic fitness can be enhanced by regular participation in activities such as running, bicycling, swimming, cross-country skiing, in-line skating, stair-stepping, and aerobic dance. As a general rule, athletes who are not participating in an aerobic sport should include some sort of aerobic training at least 3 days per week.

Muscle Strength, Power, and Endurance

Muscle strength is defined as the maximum amount of force that can be produced in one repetition, often referred to as a repetition maximum (1 RM). Muscle power can be defined as "the time rate of performing work" and can be expressed in the equation "Power = Force × Velocity" (Knuttgen, 1995). In essence, for most athletic applications, muscle power is much more important to performance than pure strength because performance is most often time dependent. That is, to be effective, athletes need to be quicker and more explosive in their performance. Muscle endurance, in contrast to strength, is defined as the ability to sustain a muscle activity. Muscle strength, power, and endurance are typically improved with some form of strength training, most often involving "free weight" exercises. Each requires distinctly different types of training, which is achieved by manipulation of the training volume, training intensity, training frequency, and placement of rest periods.

Training volume is defined as the total amount of weight lifted in a given workout session. This can be calculated by multiplying the total number of sets and repetitions by the amount of weight lifted in each set. For example, 10 repetitions of 175 pounds in the first set, 185 pounds in the second set, and 195 in the third set would be calculated as follows: 175 × 10 = 1750; 185 × 10 = 1850; 195 × 10 = 1950, for a total training volume of 1750 + 1850 + 1950 = 5550 pounds. As a general rule, the higher the training volume in a given workout, the lower the amount of weight lifted in any given set of repetitions.

Training intensity is most often defined as the amount of weight lifted per repetition; as such, lifting 50 pounds for 10 repetitions would be a 50% lower intensity when compared to lifting 100 pounds for 10 repetitions in the same exercise. Another way to define intensity is in terms of velocity of movement; that is, the faster the repetition is performed, the higher the intensity (Wathen, 1994a). As such, without changing the actual amount of weight lifted, the intensity of the lift can be increased by simply increasing the velocity of the movement. In some types of weight training the velocity of the repetition is maximal or near maximal and is known as explosive power training. Explosive power training should only be performed under the guidance of someone with expertise in training program design because inappropriate forms of explosive power training can result in injury.

Training frequency is the number of training sessions completed in a given period of time (Wathen, 1994c). The most common way to express frequency is by recording the number of workouts per week, or in some cases, number of workouts per day. A number of factors must be considered when determining the training frequency. These include the current fitness status of the athlete, the training volume and intensity, and the specific type(s) of exercises planned (Wathen, 1994c). As a general rule, most strength-training programs incorporate between three to five workouts per week. As programs become more sophisticated and complex, frequency can be increased; however, such programs usually divide the training into segments such as legs, trunk, or arms, and as such, each area is developed in separate workouts throughout the week. It is critical to remember that physiologically there are limits as to how quickly muscle tissue can adapt to a given workout. In general, moderate- to high-intensity training requires 24 to 48 hours for full recovery to occur. Failure to consider these physiologic adaptations may result in overuse injuries related to the training program.

Rest periods can be specific to the amount of time allowed between sets in a given training session, or in a broader sense, the amount of time allowed for the body to recover between training sessions. The rest period allowed between sets of lifts in a given training session can, to a great extent, determine the specific effects of that session. For example, when the goal of the training session is absolute strength or muscle power, the training intensity will be high; therefore, the recovery period between sets should be relatively long, for example, 3 to 5 minutes (Wathen, 1994b). Conversely, when training for muscle endurance, the rest periods between sets can be shorter, sometimes as short as 15 to 30 seconds, and may be extended up to 60 seconds. The question of "inserting" rest periods between training sessions has more to do with ensuring adequate tissue recovery between training sessions. The process of arranging training around specific goals and objectives with predetermined amounts of time spent training and resting is known as **periodization.** The purpose of periodization is to tailor the training program to meet the specific needs of the individual athlete to maximize performance at the time of competition(s), but at the same time avoiding training-related injury. The process of periodization is discussed later in this chapter.

Improved muscle strength has also been found to be helpful in reducing the chances of injury. Several physiologic and morphologic changes have been attributed to strength training (Fleck & Falkel, 1986). Taken individually or as a group, these adaptations will have the effect of making the body more resistant to injury. Specifically, research has found that connective tissues (fascia, tendons, ligaments) all become stronger as a result of strength training. Furthermore, bone density increases and bone becomes less susceptible to both trauma and fractures related to overuse. Improving the strength of muscles that surround a joint will help the athlete protect it from injury. Improving the strength ratio between opposing muscle groups, such as hamstrings and quadriceps, continues to be a generally well-accepted technique for preventing injury. Muscular endurance has been found to increase after appropriate strength-training programs. This is particularly true of programs that incorporate a greater number of repetitions in each set of exercises.

Flexibility

Improved flexibility has been determined to reduce the incidence of musculoskeletal injuries (Shellock & Prentice, 1985). Muscles that cross two or more joints have been found to be those most commonly injured. This increase probably results, in part, because of the greater levels of stretching during activity within these muscles (Safran, Seaber, & Garrett, 1989). **Flexibility** has been defined by Jensen and Fisher (1972) as "the range of motion (ROM) in a given joint or combination of joints." They report that several factors determine the **ROM** of a given joint. These include bone structure; tissue mass surrounding the joint; and extensibility of tendons, ligaments, muscles, and skin surrounding the joint. Temperature of the tissue, which is mediated by local blood flow and external (ambient) temperature, can significantly affect tissue extensibility. Warm-up exercises have been found to be effective in increasing tissue temperatures temporarily. Both chronological age and gender have also been found to affect flexibility (Wilmore & Costill, 1988). In general, flexibility decreases with age, although maintaining an active lifestyle may greatly reduce such changes. In addition, females have been found to be more flexible than their male counterparts. This is most likely related to differences in gonadotropic hormone levels between the sexes.

Two types of flexibility have been identified: static and dynamic (Safran, Seaber, & Garrett, 1989). Static flexibility involves the ROM achieved through passive manipulation of a given joint by another person while the muscles are relaxed. Dynamic flexibility is the ROM achieved by contracting the muscles around the joint, such as the ROM of knee flexion when contracting that joint's flexor muscles. Stretching exercises have been found to be effective in improving the extensibility of muscle tissue and can serve as a preventive factor with respect to muscle strains (Safran, Seaber, & Garrett, 1989).

Stretching exercises can be grouped into four different categories, based on the method employed. **Ballistic stretching** involves powerful contractions of muscles to force a joint to a greater ROM. **Static stretching,** as the name implies, involves moving a joint to a position of stretch that is then sustained (held) for a period ranging from 3 seconds up to a minute or longer (Shellock & Prentice, 1985). **Proprioceptive neuromuscular facilitation (PNF)** involves a technique originally developed for use with patients suffering from paralysis. Essentially,

PNF uses the body's proprioceptive system to stimulate muscles to relax. A variety of manual techniques have been developed, all using PNF principles. To use PNF techniques effectively, specialized training is required. Finally, passive stretching involves having someone other than the athlete move a joint through an ROM. This is commonly seen in sports such as swimming or gymnastics, in which an athlete will work with a partner to stretch the shoulders and arms behind the body.

Some research indicates that, when comparing these techniques, static stretching is probably the most effective, with effects lasting up to 90 minutes (Safran, Seaber, & Garrett, 1989). Evidence suggests that the best time to use static stretching is at the end of a workout when the tissues are warmer as a result of increased blood flow (Weaver, Moore, & Howe, 1996). Ballistic stretching is considered the least effective method and may even result in injury. The medical evidence is overwhelming in discouraging the use of ballistic forms of stretching.

Nutrition and Body Composition

The dietary habits of any athlete, regardless of the sport, have a profound influence on overall performance and on recovery from injury. Obviously, the body will respond to a conditioning program in a more positive manner when adequate amounts of essential nutrients are consumed in the daily diet. An overemphasis on leanness—by society, parents, coaches, and athletes themselves—has resulted in abnormally high ratios of lean body weight to fat body weight among many young athletes. Specific nutritional considerations for athletes are presented in Chapter 6.

Periodization

As mentioned earlier in this section, a conditioning program should be designed to develop all fitness components to an optimal level, while at the same time allowing adequate intervals for rest and recovery. The periodization model includes several components that represent increasingly smaller units of training time. The largest unit is known as a macrocycle and typically encompasses one calendar year. The macrocycle can then be divided into smaller units known as mesocycles, which last from several weeks to a month or more, depending on the number of competitive seasons in the macrocycle. The smallest component is called a microcycle and consists of 2 to 4 weeks of training with fluctuations in intensity, duration, and frequency (Kontor, 1986). A mesocycle consists of several successive microcycles leading to a specific conditioning goal—for example, **hypertrophy** of leg muscles. A transition phase is a period of 2 to 4 weeks that occurs between training seasons or between successive mesocycles. During a transition phase, training is adjusted gradually, either to bring an athlete to peak fitness or to allow the athlete to rest and recover after the competitive season. In short, the function of the transition phase is to give the body time to recover from the previous cycle to be ready for the next segment of the training season.

The components of a macrocycle are determined by the number of competitive seasons contained in a given calendar year. For an athlete who competes in one sport per year with one competitive season, the macrocycle will typically include postseason, off-season, preseason, and in-season components. Conversely, for an athlete with more than one competition season in the same calendar year, there may be two or more groups of training cycles composed of an off-season, preseason, and in-season. This would be a model for the college-level football player who has two seasons each year, "spring ball" and the "regular season."

Periodized programs that include a goal of the development of muscle power include the preparatory period, normally placed in the off-season portion of the training year, which progresses the athlete through

periodization The organization of training into a cyclical structure in order to attain the optimal development of an athlete's performance capacities.

flexibility The range of motion (ROM) in a given joint or combination of joints.

ROM Range of motion.

ballistic stretching Stretching technique that uses repetitive bouncing motions.

static stretching Passively stretching an antagonistic muscle by placing it in a maximal stretch and holding it there.

proprioceptive neuromuscular facilitation (PNF) Stretching techniques that involve combinations of alternating contractions and stretches.

hypertrophy Enlargement of a part caused by an increase in the size of its cells.

three distinct phases. They are hypertrophy/endurance, strength, and, finally, power. The rationale for this progression is based on sound science of muscle physiology. The purpose of the hypertrophy/endurance phase is to strengthen the connective tissue surrounding the muscle fibers and the tendons attaching the muscles to bones. This development of connective tissue enables the athlete to safely progress to more high-intensity training that follows without risking training-related injury. The intensity levels in the hypertrophy/endurance phase are generally low with higher volumes, which equates to more repetitions completed per session with a smaller percentage of the 1-RM weight for each exercise. The strength phase is next and represents a significant change in both the objectives and the protocol. The objective of this phase is obviously to increase the strength of the involved muscle groups. The exercise intensity levels are increased progressively to as high as 80% of 1 RM for each exercise. Conversely, volume is decreased to several sets of 5-RM to 8-RM levels (five to eight repetitions per set) (Wathen & Roll, 1994). The final phase, known as the power phase, focuses on the development of higher-velocity movements. By definition, the intensity during the power phase is very high—often as high as 90% of 1 RM for each exercise with lower training volumes.

A typical application of periodization for a two-season-per-year athlete can be illustrated with a collegiate-level football lineman preparing for the spring football season. During the preseason phase, he may spend the first 3 weeks working on muscle strength and hypertrophy (microcycle), followed by 3 weeks of high-intensity, low-volume strength training to develop muscle power (microcycle). These two microcycles would constitute a mesocycle with the goal of improving lower-extremity power. A transition phase would then be inserted just prior to the onset of the competitive season. During the spring season, the player would reduce his weekly frequency of weight training to maintain the gains achieved during the preseason

phase. This player would have a similar program established for his preparation for the regular season as well, and it would build on the gains made in the program just described.

Modification of Extrinsic Factors

Extrinsic risk factors for sports injuries include the practice/competition environments, facilities, protective equipment, and officiating and coaching. It is critical that coaching personnel, athletic program administrators, and, if on staff, BOC–certified athletic trainers monitor all of these factors in an effort to identify and eliminate any potential risks to the athletes.

Practice/Competition Environment

Whether outdoors or indoors, the environment must be assessed to determine if it represents a potential health risk. This is particularly true when athletes exercise in conditions of high relative heat and humidity. Specific guidelines for preventing heat-related problems are presented in Chapter 18. It is important to remember that indoor activity can pose a significant risk of thermal injury, particularly if the participant is not properly hydrated or if the indoor temperature and humidity are high.

Facilities

All sports facilities must be designed, maintained, and frequently inspected for the safety of the participants. Budgets and local building codes must be considered; however, these factors should never be allowed to supersede safety. Shared facilities are common; for example, football fields are often surrounded by an outdoor running track with field event equipment (landing pits for high jump and pole-vault, shot-put ring, etc.) either on the playing field or on the ends of the field. Baseball fields may be located next to a soccer field or perhaps even share some of the same ground. Regardless of the specific situation, it is critical that care be taken that all facilities meet the minimum requirements for safe participation. These include such things as integrity of safety fences, batting cages, location of dugouts in baseball and softball, type of bases used (breakaway or fixed), soccer goals that are correctly constructed and anchored, location of water and sanitation facilities, and emergency medical services (EMS) access routes.

With respect to indoor facilities, primary concerns center on lighting, playing surfaces, and room dimensions. Poor lighting may contribute to accidents resulting from poor visibility. A floor that is not cleaned regularly or improperly finished may become slippery and thus contribute to collisions. Budgetary constraints may mean that some gymnasiums are built that do not provide adequate space between the basketball baskets and the adjacent wall. This is especially common at the junior high and elementary school levels. In such situations it is critical that protective padding be placed on the walls behind the basketball backboards to reduce players' collisions with the wall. Locker rooms and shower facilities should be designed to enable participants to move around safely, with adequate ventilation, lighting, and nonskid floors. It is imperative that medical equipment such as whirlpool baths and other therapeutic modalities such as ultrasound or diathermy machines *not* be available for use in the locker room. Such equipment represents a significant safety risk and greatly increases the legal liability of the school.

Protective Equipment

Protective equipment plays a vital role in the prevention of injuries. This is especially true in sports such as tackle football, ice hockey, baseball, and softball. However, virtually all sports can benefit from the use of some form of safety equipment, be it something as simple as shin guards in soccer or mouth guards in basketball or wrestling. A variety of the major forms of protective equipment are discussed in Appendix 7.

REVIEW QUESTIONS

1. Differentiate between intrinsic and extrinsic types of causative factors leading to sports injury. Provide several examples of both types.

2. List four types of intrinsic factors related to sports injury that a medical doctor might identify during a preparticipation physical evaluation.

3. What are two disadvantages to using an individual format for a preparticipation physical evaluation?

4. List the seven components of fitness as described in the chapter.

5. Briefly describe the relationship between volume, intensity, and frequency of training as they relate to periodization.

6. Define the terms *macrocycle, mesocycle,* and *microcycle* as they relate to a sports training program.

7. *True or false:* According to the chapter, athletes, regardless of sport, can benefit from possessing a relatively high level of aerobic fitness.

8. What is the meaning of the acronym *ROM?*

9. Discuss the advantages and disadvantages of the four categories of stretching exercises.

REFERENCES

American Academy of Family Physicians (2005). *Preparticipation Physical Evaluation*. Minneapolis, Minn. McGraw Hill/Physician and Sportsmedicine.

Benson M (ed.). (1995). *1995–96 NCAA Sports Medicine Handbook* (8th ed.). Overland Park, Kans.: The National Collegiate Athletic Association.

Dorsen PJ. (1986). Should athletes with one eye, kidney, or testicle play contact sports? *Phys Sportsmed*. 14(7):130–138.

Feinstein RA, Soileau EJ, Daniel WA. (1988). A national survey of preparticipation physical-examination requirements. *Phys Sportsmed*. 16(5):51–59.

Fleck SJ, Falkel JE. (1986). Value of resistance training for the reduction of sports injuries. *Sports Med*. 3:61–68.

Fox EL, Dirby TE, Roberts AF. (1987). *Bases of Fitness*. New York: Macmillan.

Grace T. (1985). Muscle imbalance and extremity injury: Perplexing relationship. *Sports Med*. 2:77–82.

Jensen CR, Fisher AG. (1972). *Scientific Basis of Athletic Conditioning*. Philadelphia: Lea & Febiger.

Knuttgen HG. (1995). Force, work, power in athletic training. *Sports Science Exchange*. 8(4).

Koester MC. (1995). Refocusing the adolescent preparticipation physical evaluation toward preventative health care. *J Athl Train*. 4:352–360.

Kontor K (ed.). (1986). Periodization: Roundtable. *NSCA Journal*. 8(5):24.

McKeag DB. (1985). Preseason physical examination for the prevention of sports injuries. *Sports Med*. 2:413–431.

Moskwa CA, Nicholas JA. (1989). Musculoskeletal risk factors in the young athlete. *Phys Sportsmed*. 17(11):49–59.

Safran MR, Seaber AV, Garrett WE. (1989). Warm-up and muscular injury prevention: An update. *Sports Med*. 8(4):239–249.

Shellock FG, Prentice WE. (1985). Warm-up and stretching for improved physical performance and prevention of sports-related injuries. *Sports Med*. 2:267–278.

Taimela S, Kujala UM, Osterman K. (1990). Intrinsic risk factors and athletic injuries. *Sports Med*. 9(4):205–215.

Wathen D. (1994a). Load assignment. In Baechle TR (ed.). *Essentials of Strength Training and Conditioning* (pp. 435–446). Champaign, Ill.: Human Kinetics.

Wathen D. (1994b). Rest periods. In Baechle TR (ed.). *Essentials of Strength Training and Conditioning* (pp. 451–454). Champaign, Ill.: Human Kinetics.

Wathen D. (1994c). Training frequency. In Baechle TR (ed.). *Essentials of Strength Training and Conditioning* (pp. 455–458). Champaign, Ill.: Human Kinetics.

Wathen D, Roll F. (1994). Training methods and modes. In Baechle TR (ed.). *Essentials of Strength Training and Conditioning* (pp. 403–415). Champaign, Ill.: Human Kinetics.

Weaver J, Moore CK, Howe WB. (1996). Injury prevention. In Caine DJ, Caine CG, Lindner KJ (eds.). *Epidemiology of Sports Injuries* (Chapter 26). Champaign, Ill.: Human Kinetics.

Wilmore JH, Costill DL. (1988). *Training for Sport and Activity: The Physiological Basis of the Conditioning Process* (3d ed.). Dubuque, Ia.: William C. Brown.

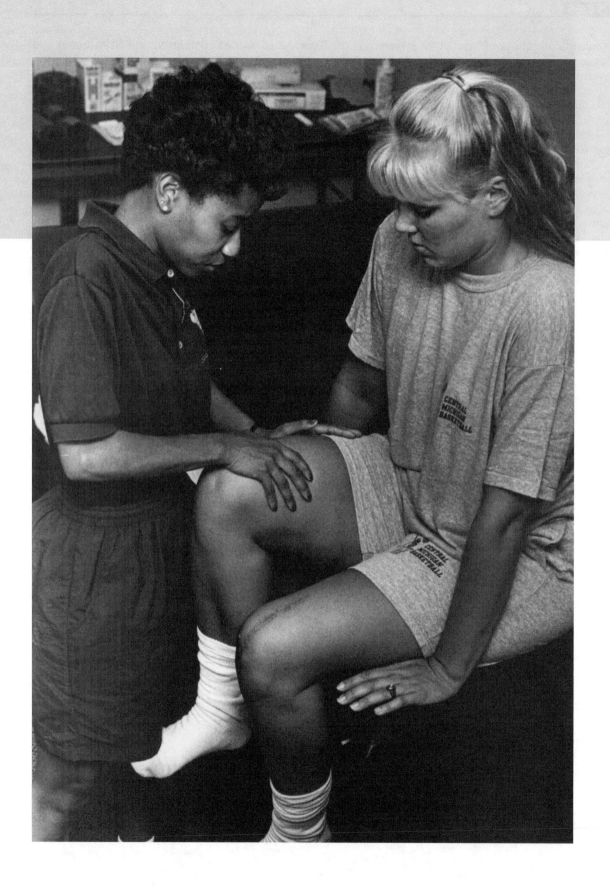

5

The Psychology of Injury

MAJOR CONCEPTS

Sports injuries involve more than damaged ligaments, tendons, and muscles; the athlete's perception of and reaction to an injury will also play a major role in the recovery process. This chapter introduces the reader to seminal research on the psychology of sports injuries. It begins with an examination of primary personality variables: trait anxiety, general personality, and locus of control. The relationship between athletes and social environment is examined, with a focus on how their social environment can induce significant stress, predisposing them to injury. Research into the disorder known as seasonal affective disorder (SAD) is presented, along with its implications for the athletic community. The chapter also gives special attention to the effects of competitive stress on the adolescent athlete. In addition, it presents the results of recent research into the psychological effects of injury. The chapter concludes with an in-depth discussion of eating disorders as they affect today's athletes. It discusses both anorexia nervosa and bulimia nervosa in terms of early warning signs and recommended treatments.

http://health.jbpub.com/book/concepts/5e

The web site for this book offers many useful tools and is a great source for supplementary information for both students and instructors.

Visit the site at
http://health.jbpub.com/book/concepts/5e
to link to the following organizations and sites:

- The Association for the Advancement of Applied Sports Psychology

The concept of risk factors for sports injuries was introduced and discussed in Chapters 1 and 4. Phenomena such as environmental conditions, type of playing surface, quality of protective equipment, player skill, years of experience, relative muscle strength, and type of sport were all identified as being possible contributors to an injury. Implementation of strategies designed to reduce or eliminate the impact of these risk factors represents a major responsibility of all those involved in the administration of organized sports programs. However, despite significant improvements in coaching and physical-conditioning techniques, rule changes, better officiating, advances in protective-equipment technology, and enhanced facilities, injuries still occur. Although this phenomenon may be partly a result of increased numbers of participants as well as improved systems for reporting injuries, both acute and chronic injuries continue to be a significant threat to a large percentage of young athletes.

In an effort to explain these trends, sports scientists have recently begun searching for additional risk factors. Increased attention has been given to the possible relationship between psychological variables and sports injuries (Figure 5.1). This would seem to be a logical avenue of research because it has long been hypothesized that a wide variety of psychological factors may affect both the mental and physical health of an individual. For example, early research investigating the relationship between psychological stress and disease in the general population indicated that individuals experiencing high levels of stress were more prone to illness (Holmes & Rahe, 1967). There is evidence that high levels of stress in athletes can result in physical fatigue as well as reduced peripheral vision, either of which could conceivably increase the chances of an injury (Hanson, McCullugh, & Tonymon, 1992; Perna & McDowell, 1995). As sports psychologists continued to investigate the relationship between the mind and sports injuries, the psychological attributes of athletes were divided into two general categories—personality variables and psychosocial variables.

Personality Variables

According to Kerr and Fowler (1988), personality characteristics refer to the "stable, enduring qualities of the individual." Characteristics such as general personality makeup, trait anxiety, locus of control, and self-concept have all been examined relative to their possible relationship to sports injuries. General personality makeup can be classified in a variety of ways, for example, aggressive or passive, introverted or extroverted. **Trait anxiety** has

FIGURE 5.1 Competition can create a great deal of psychological stress.

been defined as "a general disposition or tendency to perceive certain situations as threatening and to react with an anxiety response" (Kerr & Fowler, 1988). **Locus of control** has to do with people's belief, or lack thereof, that they are in control of events occurring in their lives. Two general types of individuals have been identified—those with an external locus of control and those with an internal locus of control. The former feel they have very little control over events in their lives. These people believe factors such as destiny, luck, or fate determine life events. Individuals with an internal locus of control feel they are responsible for what happens to them—they are in charge. Research to date that has attempted to link incidence and/or severity of injury to locus of control has yielded inconclusive results. There is evidence that such connections, if they do exist, may be sport specific—that is, locus of control may play a role in injury in certain types of sports. For example, in a study of intercollegiate football players, Petrie (1993a) found a relationship between trait anxiety and days missed because of injury. Conversely, research conducted on collegiate athletes participating in track and field events failed to find statistically significant evidence of a relationship between

Personality Variables **57**

injury and locus of control or trait anxiety (Hanson, McCullugh, & Tonymon, 1992).

Self-concept may also be a risk factor with regard to injury. Athletes with low self-concept have been found to demonstrate a statistically significant relationship with sports injuries (Kerr & Fowler, 1988; Lamb, 1986). Lamb established a strong negative correlation (−0.917) between self-concept and frequency of injury among a group of female collegiate field hockey players. Lamb reported similar results by Irvin in an earlier study that examined self-concept and injury rates in a group of collegiate football players. These findings support the theory that low self-concept functions as a significant risk factor for athletic injury. Apparently, athletes with a low self-concept are less able to deal effectively with the stress of competition. This inability may even result in behavior that leads to injury. In extreme cases, being injured may become an attractive alternative to participation because it gives the athlete a legitimate excuse to avoid playing. Ironically, such injured athletes often get more attention from coaches and peers than they would otherwise have received. The prudent coach should consider the administration of a screening test such as the Tennessee Self-Concept Scale (TSCS) to identify athletes with low self-concept. Coaches lacking experience in the administration of these tests should seek the services of a trained professional, such as a sports psychologist, school psychologist, or guidance counselor. Athletes identified as having a low self-concept may be aided by a variety of intervention strategies. There is evidence that self-concept can be raised through a program of individualized counseling and exercise. Obviously, a coach should attempt any sort of counseling with extreme caution so as not to make a bad situation worse. Once identified, athletes with low self-concept should be advised to consult a professional sports psychologist, guidance counselor, or even a clinical psychiatrist for help. The coach must exercise good judgment and tact to avoid labeling an athlete in a negative manner.

WHAT IF?

You are coaching wrestling in a northern Michigan high school. It is early December, and one of your athletes comes to you complaining of chronic fatigue, a craving for sweets, and a loss of interest in the sport. Could these complaints be symptoms of a psychological disorder and, if so, what would you do to help this athlete?

Seasonal Affective Disorder

Seasonal affective disorder (SAD) is a psychiatric disorder that affects the general population, including athletes, primarily in the fall and winter seasons. SAD has been linked to a wide array of symptoms, including a loss of physical capacity and energy, increased appetite (carbohydrate craving), decreased libido, hypersomnia (excessive sleep or drowsiness), anhedonia (lack of interest in normally pleasurable activities), and impaired social activity (Rosen et al., 1996).

Rosen and colleagues studied 68 NCAA Division I ice hockey players to ascertain the frequency of SAD (Rosen et al., 1996). Specifically, these players were all located in northern latitudes, with decreased daylight in the fall and winter months. The players were studied for one complete season, during which time they were given a set of questionnaires designed to identify those players exhibiting either symptomatic or subsyndromal SAD (a mildly dysfunctional state, which is insufficient in intensity to meet criteria for a major depressive disorder) (Kasper et al., 1989). The findings of this research were alarming: 22 of the 68 players in the study were found to be suffering from either symptomatic SAD ($N = 6$ [9%]) (Newcomer & Perna, 2003) or subsyndromal SAD ($N = 16$ [25%]).

Considering the fact that many of the symptoms of this disorder may negatively affect performance or, worse, predispose some to injury, it seems prudent for parents, coaches, and sports medicine personnel to become familiar with the signs and symptoms of SAD. Although subsyndromal SAD represents a less severe form of the affliction, the potential for serious problems is high given that athletes thus affected may fail to seek medical attention. Accurate diagnostic tests are available for SAD, and anyone exhibiting such symptoms as described herein should be referred to a specialist for evaluation. Regarding treatment, Rosen and colleagues have reported promising results using light therapy (Rosen et al., 1996).

Psychosocial Variables

Although overall correlations between general personality traits and injuries have been weak, more convincing findings have been produced from research examining

trait anxiety A general disposition or tendency to perceive certain situations as threatening and to react with an anxiety response.
locus of control People's belief, or lack thereof, of being in control of events occurring in their lives.

the relationship between psychosocial factors and injury rates. Psychosocial variables develop through the interaction between the individual and a changing social environment (Kerr & Fowler, 1988). Specifically, attention has been given to studying the effects of stressful life events on athletes. Stressful life events has been defined as positive or negative episodes that usually evoke some adaptive or coping behavior or significant change in the ongoing life pattern of the individual (Holmes & Rahe, 1967). This theory holds that life events can be very stressful—even those most people would consider positive, such as getting married, taking a vacation, or even winning the lottery. Researchers have endeavored to study the effects of life events on different populations, including athletes. A variety of questionnaires has been developed, including the Social Readjustment Rating Scale (SRRS), the Social and Athletic Readjustment Rating Scale (SARRS), the Life Event Scale for Adolescents (LESA), the Life Event Questionnaire (LEQ), the Life Event Survey for Collegiate Athletes (LESCA), and the Athletic Life Experience Survey (ALES).

A number of studies have revealed a strong relationship between stressful life events and sports injuries (Andersen & Williams, 1988; Hanson, McCullugh, & Tonymon, 1992; Kelley, 1990; Lamb, 1986; Lysens, Auweele, & Ostyn, 1986; Petrie, 1993a; Williams & Andersen, 1998). Evidence suggests that when an athlete is experiencing significant personal changes, especially those seen as negative, the chances of injury increase. As was the case with determination of self-concept status, the coaching staff may find it helpful to assess the life-stress status of athletes prior to the beginning of the season as well as on a follow-up basis. In this way, athletes who are at high risk—that is, those with high life-stress scores—can be identified and referred to a counselor in an effort to improve coping skills. There is evidence that athletes with a higher degree of such skills were less likely to be injured (Hanson, McCullugh, & Tonymon, 1992). The administration and interpretation of psychometric tests are most effectively conducted by sports psychologists and other trained professionals. Coaching personnel should avoid the temptation to play amateur

Athletic Trainers SPEAK Out

At football practice, a wide receiver goes up for the ball. A safety, heading for the receiver, makes contact as his helmet strikes the receiver's ribs. The resulting injuries are severe: the wide receiver suffers a pneumothorax; the safety has seven broken vertebrae and a fractured first rib. The wide receiver will miss four weeks of the season and very likely could lose his starting position. The safety will never be able to play tackle football again. Both players will struggle emotionally and psychologically.* Being sensitive to the psychological side effects of physical injury is part of the job of an athletic trainer, who must try to return the player to productivity, not only in their sport, but also in their life in general. Although it is not the job of an athletic trainer to provide psychotherapy, it is the athletic trainer's job to develop a relationship of trust with young athletes through caring communication. Physical injury is not the only agent that stimulates psychologically related difficulties. Athletic trainers are often the first to notice symptoms arising from a variety of problems, such as external pressures to participate in sports, eating disorders, chemical imbalance, attention deficit disorder (ADD), etc. In working with athletes, athletic trainers should be concerned with the total well-being of each person. We need to be able to recognize symptoms of emotional and psychological problems. We need to know when to listen, when to talk, when to act, and when to refer an athlete for outside help.

—Gary E. Craner, MEd, ATC/R

Gary Craner is Assistant Athletic Director and Head Athletic Trainer at Boise State University and is a member of the NATA Hall of Fame.

*True incident. Both players continued their education. The safety switched sports and now competes in judo. The wide receiver came back to compete and received all-conference honors.

psychologist with athletes because they may only make a bad situation worse.

Competitive Stress and the Adolescent

With the number of adolescents participating in sports increasing annually, serious concerns have been raised by professionals regarding the psychological impact of competition on youngsters (Nash, 1987). It is probable that the majority of children, even today, get involved in sports for recreational and social reasons. However, it is also true that the intensity of competition is being increased drastically in some sports at exceedingly early ages. Sports such as women's gymnastics, tennis, figure skating, bicycle motocross (BMX) cycling, and professional skateboarding routinely produce regional and national champions under the age of 16. The pressure to win can come from parents, coaches, peers, sponsors, and even the media. Although the immediate effects of such pressure on children may be difficult to gauge, it is safe to assume that youngsters do not possess the psychological coping skills of adults. Consequently, the stress of competition may result in significant problems for some kids. Young athletes may be more prone to injury, psychosomatic illnesses, emotional burnout, and other stress-related afflictions. Parents and coaches must take care not to force children beyond their ability to cope with the activity. It is a sad commentary on the values of today's society to think that some children may be driven from a sport that they love simply because they were pushed too hard, too early.

Psychology of the Injured Athlete

An injury represents a potent form of psychological stress for the athlete. For most, the possibility of being sidelined by a traumatic episode is an ever-present fear (Figure 5.2). What little research is available on this topic seems to support the premise that, for most athletes, an injury produces a predictable psychological response. Groundbreaking research by Weiss and Troxel (1986) reported that an injury will cause a psychophysiological reaction in the athlete that follows the classic stress-response model originally formulated by Selye (Figure 5.3).

As can be observed, in phase 1 the injury serves as a potent **stressor** and requires the athlete to adapt to a restriction of normal activity. Phase 2 involves an appraisal of the significance of the injury, both in a short- and long-term sense. Weiss and Troxel (1986) reported that this phase is when an athlete may engage in negative self-doubt ("What if I can't recover by the next game?").

FIGURE 5.2 The potential for injury is an ever-present fear for most athletes.

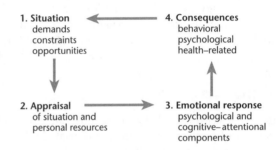

FIGURE 5.3 The stress process.

Phase 3 of the stress model involves an emotional response that can precipitate a host of physical and psychological reactions, ranging from severe anxiety, depression, and anger to increased muscle tension, blood pressure, and heart rate. Ermler and Thomas (1990) as well as Pedersen (1986) have developed models of injury response that fit well into this phase of the stress-response model. Ermler and Thomas theorized that an injury causes an athlete to experience feelings of alienation. Pedersen compared the effects of an injury with the grief response experienced following the death of a loved one. The fourth stage involves the long-term consequences of the emotional response in phase 3. If an athlete fails to respond to an injury in a positive manner, he or she may suffer from a wide variety of problems, including sleep disorders, loss of appetite, and perhaps decreased motivation (Weiss & Troxel, 1986).

stressor Anything that affects the body's physiological or psychological condition and upsets the homeostatic balance.

Recent research examining the effects of severe sports injuries on adolescents has yielded some disturbing results. Boys and girls (average age 16.7 years) who played football, girl's soccer, basketball, and volleyball were studied to determine if an injury classified as severe by the NCAA-ISS rating system (see Chapter 1) resulted in post-traumatic distress. The study found significant effects, resulting in both avoidance behaviors and intrusive thoughts in the study group. The researchers also noted that these effects "may persist even after physical recovery has occurred" (Newcomer & Perna, 2003). Although more research is needed in this area, these results do indicate that sports injuries may well be responsible for lingering psychological effects in young athletes.

Recommendations

As a result of the development of these injury-response models, recommendations have been made regarding how to best assist the injured athlete in coping with an injury. Weiss and Troxel (1986) developed a list of guidelines for personnel to follow when working with an injured athlete. These are enumerated in Time Out 5.1.

Eating Disorders

With few exceptions, all sports impose an extremely narrow set of parameters for the appropriate body type required for success. It is difficult to imagine, for example, a world-class gymnast who is 6 feet tall and weighs 240 pounds or a successful long-distance runner or figure skater who is obese.

Reality dictates that specific sports require specific body types in order for athletes to be competitive. Some sports, such as those mentioned, demand leanness for at least two reasons. First, the **biomechanics** of the sport may require a lean and muscular body in order to perform highly complex skills effectively. Second, the sports community and society as a whole have come to expect

TIME OUT 5.1

Guidelines for Working with an Injured Athlete

1. Treat the person, not just the injury.
2. Treat the athlete as an individual.
3. Keep in mind that communication skills are critical to an open coach–athlete relationship.
4. Remember the relationship between physical and psychological skills.
5. Seek the help of a sports psychologist for further ideas and strategies.

Source: Weiss MR, Troxel RK. (1986). Psychology of the injured athlete. *Athletic Training*. 21(2): 109–10. Reprinted with permission.

that successful athletes look lean and muscular. In recent years, media exposure of many top athletes has focused as much on physical appearance as on performance. This has created the need for many aspiring athletes to conform to a certain, very narrowly defined body type (Figure 5.4). This is especially true for female athletes.

WHAT IF?

You are coaching high school girls' volleyball and one of your players keeps excusing herself from practice to go to the bathroom. Other members of the team tell you that she is vomiting each time she goes. What could such behavior imply? What would be your best course of action?

FIGURE 5.4 Many athletes feel compelled to conform to a certain body type.

Psychologists are beginning to discover that this emphasis on the ideal body has resulted in serious negative effects on the athletic community. An increasing number of athletes are demonstrating abnormal, even pathogenic, eating behaviors that may have deeper psychological origins. Bulimia nervosa and anorexia nervosa are on the increase within the athletic community, with the former being more prevalent. The majority of athletes with eating disorders are female; likewise, the majority of people within the general U.S. population who have eating disorders are female.

Anorexia Nervosa and Bulimia Nervosa

Anorexia nervosa is characterized by a pattern of self-starvation motivated by an obsession with being thin and an overwhelming fear of being fat. Anorexic individuals typically have a grossly distorted body image; they think of themselves as being fat when they are, in fact, abnormally lean. **Bulimia nervosa** is characterized by repeated bouts of binge eating followed by some form of purging—for example, vomiting, taking laxatives, fasting, or undertaking vigorous, excessive exercise. Both anorexia and bulimia are considered to be serious psychological problems that are most common among adolescent and young-adult females (Johnson & Tobin, 1991).

Research

Research indicates that a significant percentage of female collegiate athletes may practice dietary habits considered to be **pathogenic,** that is, unhealthy (Grandjean, 1991). Such behavior, at the very least, may be a precursor of more serious eating disorders. When questioned, athletes report they engage in abnormal eating behaviors in an effort to improve either performance or appearance, or both. Perhaps more alarming, one study found that 70% of those reporting pathogenic eating behaviors felt such practices were harmless (Rosen et al., 1986).

Rosen and colleagues (1986) surveyed the eating habits of 182 female collegiate athletes and determined that 32% regularly practiced pathogenic eating—whether binges followed by self-induced vomiting that occurred more than twice weekly or the regular use of laxatives, diet pills, and/or diuretics. Another survey of both male and female collegiate competitors yielded similar results. Of 695 athletes questioned, 39.2% of the females and 14.3% of the males were classified as bulimic, and 4.2% of the females and 1.6% of the males were found to be anorexic (Burkes-Miller & Black, 1988). Johnson and colleagues (1999) surveyed 1445 athletes from 11 NCAA Division I institutions regarding the prevalence of disordered eating. Their results seem to indicate an improvement in eating behaviors in collegiate-level athletes when compared with earlier studies. For example, their results indicated that 10.85% (females) and 13.02% (males) reported binge-eating behaviors on a weekly, or greater, basis. In a similar study, Gutgesell and associates (2003) surveyed both female athletes and nonathletes regarding their eating habits and behaviors. Of interest is that the nonathlete control subjects reported more problematic eating behaviors than did the female athletes.

Little is known about pathogenic eating behaviors among male athletes. Historically, the sport of wrestling has received the most attention with regard to this problem. It is common knowledge that many wrestlers routinely practice a variety of strange eating and training behaviors, especially just prior to competition. These include fasting, restriction of fluids, the use of laxatives, vomiting, and sweating off weight by wearing a rubber suit in the sauna. Obviously, all of these practices are to be discouraged. At best they will result in a short-term water loss; at worst they can cause severe illness and even death. Specific recommendations regarding minimal competitive weight are discussed in Chapter 6 as well as in Appendix 4.

Recent research indicates that although males comprise around 10% of the diagnosed cases of eating disorders, male athletes report relatively higher indices of eating disorders when compared to male nonathletes than when the same comparison is done with females (Hausenblas & Carron, 1999). Also, as noted earlier, NCAA research found that 13.02% of males reported binge eating on a weekly basis, versus 10.85% of females (Johnson et al., 1999). More research is needed to determine if male athletes are vulnerable to the same pressures as their female counterparts when it comes to maintaining body build and leanness. Additionally, it needs to be determined if the reported low incidence of eating disorders in male athletes is an accurate reflection of the true incidence in this population.

biomechanics Branch of study that applies the laws of mechanics, internal or external, to the living body.

anorexia nervosa Characterized by a pattern of self-starvation with a concomitant obsession with being thin and an overwhelming fear of being fat.

bulimia nervosa Characterized by repeated bouts of binge eating followed by some form of purging, e.g., vomiting, use of laxatives, fasting, or vigorous and excessive exercise.

pathogenic Causing disease.

Sport Specificity and Eating Disorders

It has been well documented that certain sports carry a high risk that participants will develop eating disorders. These include women's gymnastics, ballet, diving, and figure skating. All of these activities place a heavy emphasis on lean, muscular body builds. Petrie (1993b) recently surveyed 215 female gymnasts in college and determined that over 60% reported a variety of disordered eating behaviors. A meta-analysis of 92 published studies on eating disorders concluded that female athletes involved in sports that place a premium on physical appearance (aesthetic sports) demonstrated a significantly higher prevalence of eating disorder symptoms than female nonathletes (Hausenblas & Carron, 1999). Not surprisingly, there is growing evidence that eating disorders may be gaining a foothold in sports historically immune to such problems. Rosen and colleagues (1986) found that significant percentages of female athletes participating in field hockey, softball, volleyball, track, and tennis reported pathogenic eating behaviors. In a survey of young (9 to 18 years old) competitive swimmers, Dummer and colleagues (1987) found that of 289 postmenarcheal females, 24.8% reported practicing some form of pathogenic eating behavior.

A variety of physical and psychological problems are associated with both anorexia and bulimia. Thornton (1990) reports that anorexic and bulimic athletes run the risk of esophageal inflammation, erosion of tooth enamel, hormone imbalances that can lead to osteoporosis and **amenorrhea,** and kidney and heart problems related to electrolyte imbalances. In addition, a variety of psychological problems, including depression and anxiety disorders, is also common.

Prevention

Prevention of eating disorders, including bulimia and anorexia nervosa, must be the goal of all those involved with organized sports. Coaches need to place less emphasis on body weight and fat when working with

---

TABLE 5.1

SAMPLE DISORDERED EATING QUESTIONNAIRE

Part 1: How often do eating behaviors interfere with your:

	Never	Rarely	Sometimes	Often	Always
Daily interactions with peers & coaches	1	2	3	4	5
Daily thoughts or feelings about yourself	1	2	3	4	5
Daily participation in athletics	1	2	3	4	5

Part 2: How often do you weigh or measure your body size?

____ > 5 times a day	____ once a week	____ once every 2 mos.
____ 3–5 times a day	____ 3 times/week	____ once every 3 mos.
____ 1–3 times daily	____ once every 2 weeks	____ once a year
____ once a day	____ once a month	____ never

Part 3: Please respond to the following using the scale below in regard to your sport.

	Never	Rarely	Sometimes	Often	Always
Weight loss is required for increased performance	1	2	3	4	5
Weight loss was required to meet a lower weight category	1	2	3	4	5
Weight loss was required to reach an aesthetic ideal	1	2	3	4	5
Coaching staff makes remarks concerning my weight	1	2	3	4	5
I am weighed in front of my teammates	1	2	3	4	5
Team members' weights are made public	1	2	3	4	5
Mandated decrease in body fat percentage	1	2	3	4	5
Fear of losing a position on team if weight is not controlled	1	2	3	4	5

*Source: Koszewski W, Chopak JS, Buxton BP. (1997). Risk factors for disordered eating in athletes. *Athletic Therapy Today.* 2 (2): 7-11. Reprinted with permission from Human Kinetics (Champaign, IL).

athletes. Referring to weight in a negative manner, requiring mandatory weigh-ins, or publicly ostracizing an athlete for being overweight are all practices to be condemned.

Coaches and parents need to be alert to the early warning signs of eating disorders. Screening for athletes who may be at risk for an eating disorder can commence at the time of the preparticipation physical evaluation (PPE). A simple questionnaire (Table 5.1) can be completed by the athlete during the PPE. If an athlete achieves a score indicative of someone who may be at risk, he or she can be referred for psychological counseling (Koszewski, Chopak, & Buxton, 1997).

Treatment

Treatment of eating disorders ranges from simple counseling and education (when diagnosed in early stages) to hospitalization in severe cases. It must be remembered that in many cases an eating disorder may be a symptom of a psychological problem such as depression or anxiety. Despite improved treatment programs, experts report that at least one-third of these cases will not respond to therapy. It is hoped that continued research will improve the prognosis for these individuals.

amenorrhea Absence or suppression of menstruation.

REVIEW QUESTIONS

1. Briefly define several of the personality variables described in the chapter.

2. Discuss the relationship between an athlete's self-concept and the risk of sports injury.

3. Describe briefly the relationship between psychosocial variables and the risk of sports injury.

4. List several sports in which adolescent athletes routinely achieve national-championship status. Discuss the possible relationship between this high level of competitive stress and the psychology of the adolescent athlete.

5. Discuss the psychological impact of a sports injury on an athlete in terms of the stress model shown in the chapter.

6. List the recommended guidelines for dealing with an injured athlete.

7. Define both anorexia nervosa and bulimia nervosa.

8. *True or false:* Recent research found that 70% of those reporting pathogenic eating behaviors felt such practices were harmless.

9. List several common forms of pathogenic eating behaviors found to be practiced by athletes.

10. List five common signs or behaviors that may indicate the development of an eating disorder.

11. Define the acronym SAD and discuss its implications for competitive athletes.

REFERENCES

Andersen MB, Williams JM. (1988). A model of stress and athletic injury: Prediction and prevention. *J Sport Exercise Psychol.* 10: 294–306.

Burkes-Miller ME, Black DR. (1988). Male and female college athletes: Prevalence of anorexia nervosa and bulimia nervosa. *Athletic Training.* 23(2):137–140.

Dummer GM, et al. (1987). Pathogenic weight-control behaviors in young competitive swimmers. *Phys Sportsmed.* 15(5):75–84.

Ermler KL, Thomas CE. (1990). Interventions for the alienating effect of injury. *Athletic Training.* 25(3):269–271.

Grandjean AC. (1991). Eating disorders: The role of the athletic trainer. *J Athletic Training.* 26(2):105–112.

Gutgesell ME, et al. (2003). Weight concerns, problem eating behaviors, and problem drinking behaviors in female collegiate athletes. *J Athletic Training.* 38(1):62–66.

Hanson SJ, McCullugh P, Tonymon P. (1992). The relationship of personality characteristics, life stress, and coping resources to athletic injury. *J Sport Exercise Psychol.* 14:262–272.

Hausenblas HA, Carron AV. (1999). Eating disorder indices and athletes: An integration. *J Sport Exercise Psychol.* 21:230–258.

Holmes H, Rahe RH. (1967). The Social Readjustment Rating Scale. *J Psychol Res.* 11:213–218.

Johnson C, Tobin DL. (1991). The diagnosis and treatment of anorexia nervosa and bulimia among athletes. *J Athletic Training.* 26(2):119–128.

Johnson C, et al. (1999). Athletes and eating disorders: The National Collegiate Athletic Association Study. *Int J Eat Disord.* 26(2):179–188.

Kasper S, et al. (1989). Epidemiological findings of seasonal changes in mood and behavior. *Arch Gen Psychiatry.* 40:823–833.

Kelley MJ. (1990). Psychological risk factors and sports injuries. *J Sportsmed Phys Fit.* 30:202–221.

Kerr G, Fowler B. (1988). The relationship between psychological factors and sports injuries. *Sports Med.* 6:127–134.

Koszewski W, Chopak JS, Buxton BP. (1997). Risk factors for disordered eating in athletes. *Athletic Therapy Today.* 2(2):7–11.

Lamb M. (1986). Self-concept and injury frequency among female college field-hockey players. *Athletic Training.* 21(3):220–224.

Lysens R, Auweele YV, Ostyn M. (1986). The relationship between psychological factors and sports injuries. *J Sportsmed.* 26:77–84.

Nash HL. (1987). Elite child-athletes: How much does victory cost? *Phys Sportsmed.* 15(8):129–133.

Newcomer RR, Perna FM. (2003). Features of posttraumatic distress among adolescent athletes. *J Athletic Training.* 38(2):163–166.

Pedersen P. (1986). The grief response and injury: A special challenge for athletes and athletic trainers. *Athletic Training.* 21(4):312–314.

Perna FM, McDowell SL. (1995). Role of psychological stress in cortisol recovery from exhaustive exercise among elite athletes. *Int J Behav Med* 2(1):13–26.

Petrie TA. (1993a). Coping skills, competitive trait anxiety, and playing status: Moderating effects on the life stress-injury relationship. *J Sports Exercise Psychol.* 15:261–274.

Petrie TA. (1993b). Disordered eating in female collegiate gymnasts: Prevalence and personality/attitudinal correlates. *J Sports Exercise Psychol.* 15: 424–436.

Rosen LW, et al. (1986). Pathogenic weight-control behavior in female athletes. *Phys Sportsmed.* 14(1):79–86.

Rosen LW, et al. (1996). Seasonal mood disturbances in collegiate hockey players. *J Athletic Training.* 31(3):225–228.

Thornton JS. (1990). Feast or famine: Eating disorders in athletes. *Athletic Training.* 18(4):116–122.

Weiss MR, Troxel RK. (1986). Psychology of the injured athlete. *Athletic Training.* 21(2):104–105.

Williams JM, Andersen MB. (1998). Psychological antecedents of sport injury: Review and critique of the stress and injury model. *J Appl Sport Psychol.* 10: 5-25.

6

Nutritional Considerations

MAJOR CONCEPTS

Research has shown that, regardless of the sport, an athlete's diet plays a critical, if not essential, role in performance. Yet, misinformation and misconceptions persist among coaches and athletes regarding what constitutes an adequate diet. This chapter first examines available evidence concerning the dietary knowledge and practices of coaches and athletes. It next identifies specific problems and outlines dietary recommendations pertaining to protein intake. Special attention is given to the sport of wrestling, which has been plagued with the problem of athletes attempting to lose body weight rapidly by dehydration, and a simple method is provided to assess an athlete's ability to rehydrate adequately. This chapter concludes with brief discussions of the relationship between nutrition and recovery from injury and of the use of supplements to enhance performance.

http://health.jbpub.com/book/concepts/5e

The web site for this book offers many useful tools and is a great source for supplementary information for both students and instructors.

Visit the site at
http://health.jbpub.com/book/concepts/5e
to link to the following organizations and sites:

- Healthtouch Online
- The Gatorade Sports Science Institute
- The U.S. Department of Agriculture

An athlete's diet has a direct impact on performance, recovery from training and competition, resistance to environmental extremes, recovery from injury, and, to some extent, likelihood of injury. In essence, diet influences virtually all aspects of sports participation. Yet, research demonstrates that both coaches and athletes often lack adequate knowledge on the subject or incorporate unfounded nutritional practices into training programs. Published studies consistently indicate that coaching personnel lack adequate knowledge in the general area of nutrition. For example, Parr, Porter, and Hodgson (1984) surveyed 348 coaches, 179 Board of Certification, Inc. (BOC)–certified athletic trainers, and 2977 athletes at the high school and college levels about their nutritional knowledge and practices. The majority of coaches (61%) reported they had no formal training in nutrition, and 78% reported they lacked adequate knowledge about it. However, the majority of athletes (68%) were familiar with the four food groups, and 71% reported incorporating them into their diets. Not surprisingly, certified athletic trainers were found to be the most knowledgeable regarding nutrition, with 73% reporting having had at least one college course on the subject. Perhaps what was most significant about this survey was that athletes reported that parents were their leading sources of information about nutrition—followed by TV commercials and magazines. Although the knowledge of most parents concerning nutrition cannot be measured, it is probably safe to assume that both parents and the media represent, at best, marginal sources of current information. Sossin et al. (1997) surveyed high school wrestling coaches with respect to their knowledge on specific nutrition concepts, including training diets, dehydration, and body composition. Test scores were below 60% correct on these topics, which tends to support the premise these coaches are ill prepared to provide good counsel to their athletes on these critical topics. This conclusion is reinforced by the fact that the same study found that fewer that 40% of these same coaches reported having attended nutrition workshops.

Nutrients: An Overview

The following section provides an overview of the fundamental concepts of nutrition and is presented as a basis for the chapter content that follows. Although a comprehensive investigation of both macro- (required in large amounts) and micronutrients (required in small, or trace, amounts) is beyond the scope of this text, a brief review of the six classes of nutrients is presented. These are carbohydrates, fats, and proteins, which comprise the macronutrients; vitamins and minerals, which comprise the micronutrients; and finally water.

Carbohydrates

Carbohydrates (CHO) are molecules that, by way of their metabolic breakdown, provide energy for high-intensity exercise. The specific forms of CHO used within the body are blood glucose, as well as glycogen (the storage form of glucose) found in the liver and skeletal muscle. Carbohydrates fall into three general categories, based on the complexity of the molecule. They consist of carbon, hydrogen, and oxygen atoms, with the number of carbon atoms ranging from three to seven. The simplest forms of CHO are the monosaccharides (a single molecule), which include sugars such as fructose, glucose (blood sugar), and galactose. The next group are the disaccharides (two monosaccharide molecules combined), which include commonly known sugars such as lactose (milk sugar), sucrose (the most common form of sugar in the diet), and maltose. The complex carbohydrates are known as polysaccharides (10 to thousands of monosaccharides linked together) and include compounds such as glycogen, starch, and cellulose.

The majority of dietary CHO is derived from plant sources, primarily grains, seeds, fruits, and, to a lesser extent, vegetables. In a practical context the most common forms of dietary CHO intake are from simple sugars, primarily foods high in sucrose such as soft drinks, candies, and cereals that are high in sugar. Although high in caloric content, these foods provide little in the way of other nutrients and therefore are often referred to as "empty calorie" foods. A superior form of dietary CHO is derived from eating whole-grain cereals, whole-grain breads, and fruits. The CHO in these foods is in the form of starch found in the cereals and breads, commonly known as the complex carbohydrates. An added benefit of consuming complex CHO is that they typically contain dietary fiber (indigestible CHO), which may lower cholesterol absorption and is also beneficial to the digestive tract. Another excellent source of CHO is fruits, which can provide a significant amount of CHO in the form of fructose. Fructose, a monosaccharide, is much sweeter than sucrose; however, the benefit of fructose is that it "does not stimulate pancreatic insulin secretion" and, as a result, "helps to stabilize blood-glucose and insulin levels" (McArdle, Katch, & Katch, 1999). An added benefit of these foods is they typically contain a wide variety of other nutrients and, as such, help to provide a balanced diet.

The recommended percentage proportion of CHO in the diet should range between 60% and 70% of the total calories consumed daily, depending on the exercise intensity (McArdle, Katch, & Katch, 1999). Regardless of the type of CHO consumed, they all provide approximately 4 kcals/gram. (A kilocalorie, or kcal, sometimes called a nutritional calorie, is the energy equivalent required to raise the temperature of 1 kilogram of water 1°C). The average person stores approximately 1500 to 2000 kcals, the majority of which is in the form of muscle and liver glycogen, with a small portion available as blood glucose (McArdle, Katch, & Katch, 1999).

Carbohydrate (Glycogen) Loading

As stated earlier, the majority of CHO in the body is stored in the skeletal muscles and liver in the form of glycogen. Physiologically, it is to the athlete's advantage if the total amount of stored glycogen can be increased prior to a competition. Athletes involved in aerobic sports, especially those with a duration in excess of 60 minutes, benefit the most from an increased level of stored glycogen.

Essentially, the process of CHO loading involves the systematic decrease of dietary CHO intake in conjunction with a significant increase in exercise intensity. Early procedures for CHO loading were particularly Spartan in nature, requiring multiple days of intense exercise (depletion phase) combined with dietary restriction of CHO intake. Ironically, although such protocols often did result in an increase in stored glycogen, the negative impacts often outweighed the benefits to performance. These included severe physical fatigue associated with the depletion phase, along with negative emotional changes such as hyperirritability. In addition, another problem related to CHO loading is that for every gram of CHO stored, an additional 2.7 g of water is also stored. As such, the process of CHO loading results in an overall increase in body weight that, in sports such as distance running, may represent a performance detriment.

Modified, less draconian, versions of CHO loading have been developed and have been found to be highly effective in elevating stored glycogen levels well above what can be achieved by consuming a high-CHO diet. Research has verified that a properly executed regimen of CHO loading can boost the level of stored glycogen from the normal of 1.7 g of glycogen/100 g of muscle tissue to 4 to 5 g of glycogen/100 g of muscle tissue. A typical regime begins approximately one week prior to the competition and includes high-intensity exercise combined with a low-CHO, high-protein diet for four days followed immediately on days 5–7 with a diet high in CHO along with a normal protein intake. A high-CHO meal is then consumed on the day of the competition (McArdle, Katch, & Katch, 1999).

Fats (Lipids)

Fats serve a variety of functions in the body, including providing energy for muscle contraction; insulation, primarily in the form of subcutaneous fat; and protection of vital organs such as the kidneys and heart. Dietary fats are either simple or complex, depending on their specific molecular structure. Fats, like CHO, consist of carbon, hydrogen, and oxygen atoms; however, the ratio of hydrogen to oxygen is far greater in fats. Depending on their molecular structure, fats can exist either in liquid (oils) or solid form. Simple fats consist of two components, glycerol and a fatty acid, and can be either saturated or unsaturated. The term *saturated* describes the fact that in this form of fat all of the available bonding sites on the fatty acid molecule are occupied by a hydrogen atom. Most dietary sources of saturated fats are derived from animal sources (i.e., beef, pork, poultry, and dairy products) and are generally solid at room temperature. Unsaturated fats, as the term implies, are structured in such a way as to prevent all of the available bonding sites from being occupied by a hydrogen atom. The majority of unsaturated fats exist as liquids at room temperature. Unsaturated fats exist in two forms, monounsaturated and polyunsaturated. Monounsaturated fat molecules include a single site on the carbon chain where a double bond exists, thus preventing hydrogen atoms from bonding at that site. Polyunsaturated fats have two or more double bonds and, as such, have at least two sites that cannot be occupied by hydrogen atoms.

Dietary sources of fats, as stated earlier, are animal products such as beef, poultry, and pork. Other sources include dairy products, such as milk, butter, and cheese. In addition, plant sources of fats include nuts and plant oils such as corn, olive oil, and soybean oil. The recommended percentage proportion of fats in the diet should be 30% or less of the total calories consumed daily (McArdle, Katch, & Katch, 1999). It is recommended that the majority of fats consumed be unsaturated to avoid the problems attributed to excessive consumption of saturated fats related to cardiovascular disease. Regardless of the type of fat consumed, all forms provide approximately 9 kilocalories (kcals)/gram. The available amount of energy in the form of stored body fat is significantly greater than what is available from CHO. For example, the available energy in a 70-kg person who has 18% body fat is calculated to be around 113,400 kcals (70 kg × 0.18 = 12.6 kg of fat; 12.6 × 1000 = 12,600 g of fat; 12,600 × 9 kcal = 113,400 kcals).

Proteins

As with both carbohydrates and fats, proteins also contain carbon, hydrogen, and oxygen atoms in their molecules. However, proteins also include nitrogen and, as

Athletic Trainers SPEAK Out

In today's society when fad and crash diets are targeted at those looking for a quick fix, individuals looking for overall nutrition must be careful. As an athlete begins to design a comprehensive training program, it is necessary to consider the importance of diet and nutrition. Each individual must create a proper diet that will be best for him or her. The athlete should consider including a variety of carbohydrates, proteins, fats, vitamins, and minerals as well as the required amount of water. The athlete should consult the certified athletic trainer and team dietitian or nutritionist in planning the appropriate diet. An athlete has different caloric needs as a result of greater energy expenditure as compared to the sedentary or less-active person. We as athletic trainers must be knowledgeable to give the athletes correct advice. The athlete's diet is what fuels performance.

—Karen M. Lew, MEd, ATC, LAT

Karen Lew is the Athletic Training Education Program Director at Southeastern Louisiana University.

such, they are unique molecules compared to the other nutrients. Protein molecules are assembled by combining amino acids using peptide bonds to form large, complex molecules. There are 20 specific amino acids required in the body to produce the thousands of proteins necessary for life. The majority of the body's protein is found in muscle and connective tissues. Proteins are also found in the body fluids and in the blood from thousands of different enzymes and structures related to blood clotting such as fibrin and fibrinogen. In addition, muscle protein is used as an energy source during prolonged exercise, producing as much as 10% to 15% of the energy requirements for activity. Research suggests that a regimen of regular aerobic exercise enhances the body's ability to generate energy from the metabolism of proteins (Sumida & Donovan, 1995).

The body builds proteins from the amino acids that are available from the protein that is consumed in the diet. Of the 20 amino acids required to construct the body's proteins, 8 cannot be synthesized by the body and must, therefore, be ingested in the diet. These eight amino acids are known as "essential," implying that they must be present in the diet. They are isoleucine, leucine, lysine, methionine, phenylalanine, threonine, tryptophan, and valine. The best dietary sources of the essential amino acids are eggs, meats, and dairy products, all known as complete proteins. Incomplete proteins are those that lack one or more or contain insufficient amounts of one or more of the essential amino acids. They include foods found in the legume and grain categories. Athletes who are on vegetarian diets must take care

to eat foods in the correct combination to provide all of the essential amino acids. A solution to the problem is for such athletes to include either eggs (ovolactovegetarian), milk products (lactovegetarian), or both to ensure adequate supplies of essential amino acids.

Protein Supplementation

Because dietary protein is associated with building muscle mass, many athletes are curious about the benefits of extra protein consumption beyond that found in their regular diets. At least two problems are associated with the practice of consuming additional protein. The first is that many sources of dietary protein also contain a large amount of saturated fat, such as beef and pork products. The second problem is that in certain cases the body may be unable to efficiently eliminate the by-products of excess protein breakdown, and, as such, organs such as the liver and kidney are stressed.

Today there is a huge commercial market for what are commonly known as protein supplements, often sold at health food stores, grocery chains, and sporting good stores and through mail order and the Internet. Most of these products consist of meat by-products that are processed into a powder form that is then mixed with water or some other liquid and consumed orally. Unfortunately, because these products are marketed as food supplements, their purity is not monitored by the Food and Drug Administration. In addition, many of them are extremely expensive on a per-pound basis, often exceeding the cost of more common sources of protein such as meat and dairy products.

Unfortunately, there is virtually no scientific research that supports the premise of protein supplementation enhancing muscle development. At present, available research indicates athletes involved in intense training, particularly strength training, need to consume between 1.2 and 1.8 g of protein for each kg of body weight (McArdle, Katch, & Katch, 1999). To put this into a practical context, the calculated protein requirement for a 60-kg athlete would range from a low of 72 g up to 108 g per day. Eight ounces of broiled salmon provides approximately 62 g of protein, 8 ounces of lean sirloin steak provides approximately 65 g of protein, and an 8-ounce skinless chicken breast yields a little over 70 g of protein. It can be seen that adequate protein to meet the daily requirements of an athlete in heavy training can easily be achieved through meals without the need of additional supplements.

Vitamins

Vitamins are chemicals that are needed by the body in relatively small amounts and, therefore, are classified as micronutrients. This should not be interpreted, however, to mean that vitamins have little importance nutritionally. To the contrary, adequate amounts of vitamins are essential to health and human performance. Vitamins serve a multitude of functions in the body, essentially helping to regulate biochemical reactions such as energy metabolism and cell and tissue generation, as well as serving as antioxidants (antioxidants protect structures such as cell membranes from the damaging effects of free radicals that are released during vigorous exercise). Vitamins contain no caloric value and, as such, do not directly provide energy for muscle contraction.

So far, 13 specific vitamins have been identified and are divided into two groups, water soluble and fat soluble. The water-soluble group includes vitamins C (ascorbic acid) and the B vitamins (B_1, B_2, B_6, B_{12}, niacin, folic acid, biotin, and pantothenic acid). Water-soluble vitamins, with the exception of B_{12}, are not stored in the body, and excess amounts are excreted via the kidneys and urine. Fat-soluble vitamins are vitamins A, D, E, and K, and because of their solubility, they are stored in the fat tissues of the body. In fact, excess consumption of fat-soluble vitamins beyond what is recommended (RDA) can result in buildup of and eventual toxic reaction to the stored vitamin.

There is no evidence that taking any vitamin in an amount greater than the recommended level provides any sort of performance enhancement. Athletes who consume balanced diets most likely are getting adequate amounts of vitamins through their food and beverage consumption. For athletes who are eating less than an ideal diet, a daily multivitamin supplement that meets the Recommended Dietary Allowances (RDAs) for all necessary vitamins is advised. There is no evidence that vitamins marketed as organic or natural provide any benefit over those that are manufactured synthetically and often sold at a lower cost. To be effective, vitamins should be taken after meals to optimize absorption because they work best in the presence of other nutrients (Clark, 1997).

Minerals

Minerals are elements that must be consumed regularly to ensure normal body functions. A typical over-the-counter daily vitamin and mineral supplement will usually include all of the minerals listed in Table 6.1.

The best-known mineral is calcium, which is metabolically associated with normal bone and dental health. It is the most prevalent mineral in the body and is easily obtained in the diet by consuming dairy products or other foods/beverages that have been artificially fortified with calcium. As is the case with vitamins, there is no scientific evidence that consuming minerals in excess of the RDA provides any advantage in performance. In addition, a well-balanced diet will provide all

---

TABLE 6.1

MAJOR MINERALS AND TRACE MINERALS

Major Minerals (100 mg daily minimum)

Calcium
Chloride
Magnesium
Phosphorus
Potassium
Sodium
Sulfur

Trace Minerals (less than 15 mg daily)

Boron
Chromium
Copper
Fluorine
Iodine
Iron
Manganese
Molybdenum
Nickel
Tin
Selenium
Silicon
Vanadium
Zinc

the necessary dietary minerals. However, evidence suggests that some athletes do not eat well-balanced diets and, therefore, should be advised to include a daily vitamin and mineral supplement in their diet. It must be emphasized that this supplement should be of the type that provides only the RDA of each nutrient and not a product that contains megadoses of the nutrients.

Scientific evidence suggests that some groups of athletes may be at an increased risk of calcium deficiency (Deuster et al., 1986; Moffatt, 1984). Female athletes involved in aerobic running sports, as well as gymnasts, have been found to be consuming too little calcium. This places these people at risk for inadequate bone development and can contribute to osteoporosis in later life. In these high-risk groups, calcium supplementation is most certainly warranted. Again, it is important to note that a supplement that provides the RDA is appropriate because consuming calcium in excess of this level may lead to other problems. The recommended daily dosage for adolescent females is 1500 mg.

Water

There is virtually no debate in the sports medicine community regarding the importance of water, not only to human performance but to survival as well! Water serves a myriad of functions in the body because the molecule is necessary for cellular function, heat regulation, and elimination of waste products. Water is housed in the body in two general locations. They are extracellular fluids (those fluids outside of the cells, commonly called "interstitial fluid") and intracellular fluids (those fluids contained in the cell). Water is constantly being lost through normal body functions such as breathing, elimination of wastes, and sweating.

At rest the adult requirement for water is approximately 2.5 L of water daily. Under conditions of heavy exercise, especially in conditions of high ambient temperature, water requirements can escalate to 5 to 10 L daily (McArdle, Katch, & Katch, 1999). During exercise, a significant amount of body water is lost to eliminate metabolic heat. The circulatory system transports this excess heat by way of the blood to the skin, where, in

harmony with the body's sweat glands, heat is carried from the surface by way of evaporation. The process of sweat evaporation from the skin surface can easily result in an hourly water loss from the body of 2 L or more for each hour of exercise. This fluid must be replaced or serious, even life-threatening, consequences can result. The process of controlling the body's core temperature during exercise is known as thermoregulation and is discussed in detail in Chapter 18.

Dietary Habits of Athletes: What the Research Shows

The limited amount of information available indicates that many athletes, in a variety of sports, fail to incorporate sound principles of nutrition into their training diets. Eck and colleagues (1988) surveyed 43 university football players and found that the distribution of dietary nutrients for carbohydrates, protein, and fat was not in accord with current recommendations. The averages for that team were 34.7% carbohydrates, 17% protein, and 48.2% fat. These percentages conflict with recommendations by experts who advise a distribution of 45% to 70% carbohydrates, 12% to 15% protein, and 20% fat (Coyle, 1988; Nelson, 1989). It is interesting to note that in a survey of coaches involved primarily with football, the majority (51%) advocated a diet consisting of 45% carbohydrates, 45% protein, and 10% fat (Bentivegna, Kelley, & Lalenak, 1979). The findings of these studies indicate that football players as well as coaches persist in the myth that excessive dietary protein is a prerequisite to success. The elevated levels of fat consumed by players in the study by Eck and colleagues (1988) may indicate that they were consuming a high percentage of red meats and other protein sources high in fat. Such dietary practices may create several cardiovascular problems, including arteriosclerosis and heart disease. It may be more than a curious coincidence that the life expectancy of an NFL football player is 52 to 55 years (Nelson, 1989).

As more women become involved in organized sports, concerns have been raised regarding special nutritional considerations for female athletes, especially those involved in sports associated with eating disorders, such as gymnastics. Moffatt (1984) surveyed the dietary habits of 13 female high school gymnasts who competed at advanced levels. The average body fat of these athletes was found to be 13.1%, yet 9 of the 13 girls were found to consume fewer calories than recommended. Because gymnastics is a sport that places great emphasis on being lean, it is not surprising that the majority of these girls demonstrated a deficient caloric intake. The gymnasts

WHAT IF?

A female high school gymnast asks you for recommendations for her training diet. What would you suggest she consume on a daily basis to remain competitive?

were also found to have diets low (below the RDA) in vitamin B_6, folic acid, iron, calcium, zinc, and magnesium. Loosli and Benson found very similar results in their survey of 76 adolescent female gymnasts. Their results indicated these young athletes were consuming less than the RDA in a number of vitamins and minerals and, in addition, were consuming too few total calories, especially in the form of carbohydrates (Loosli & Benson, 1990).

The nutritional habits of male and female high school cross-country runners were examined; the results were similar to those of related studies (Upgrove & Achterberg, 1990). Ironically, in a sport in which a diet high in carbohydrates is a prerequisite to success, these young runners were found to be poorly versed in the role of this essential nutrient. In addition, they reported that coaches were their preferred source of information on nutrition. This is particularly alarming considering that many coaches are ill prepared to give sound advice on nutrition. Deuster and colleagues (1986) examined the dietary habits of a group of 51 top-level female distance runners. Their reported intake of protein, fat, and carbohydrates was 13%, 32%, and 55%, respectively. These percentages indicate a diet somewhat high in fat and low in carbohydrates. Even with the high-fat content, their diets were still too low in caloric content. In effect, these women were training and racing while adhering to diets that failed to provide adequate calories for such activity. Further analysis revealed that although many of the runners reported taking some sort of iron supplement, 43% were found to be consuming less than the adult RDA for iron, which is 18 milligrams. Current thought among sports scientists is that iron deficiency is common in athletes involved in endurance sports (Pattini & Schena, 1990). It is speculated that iron may be lost through sweating, gastrointestinal bleeding, and excessive red blood cell destruction (**hemolysis**) in the blood vessels. Females are at particular risk because menstruation increases the loss of blood on a regular basis. During menstruation, athletes may lose as much as 2 milligrams of iron daily. This loss may be offset by a dietary adjustment of iron-rich foods, such as organ meats or enriched whole-grain products. A convenient method of supplementation is a daily multivitamin and mineral tablet. Numerous products are available over the counter that provide the adult RDA of iron.

Perron and Endres (1985) investigated the nutritional habits of 31 female high school volleyball players. Seventy percent of them did not meet the RDAs for energy (total calories), calcium, and iron. It is not surprising that 81% of these athletes reported a concern about body weight; perhaps their low caloric intake was part of an attempt to lose weight.

Conclusions

Based on the results of research pertaining to the nutritional behavior of athletes, it appears that some important conclusions can be made regarding the dietary practices of athletes:

1. Many athletes do not consume the proper proportions of protein, carbohydrates, and fat. There is growing support in the sports science community that adolescent athletes may require as much as 1.5 to 2 grams of protein per kilogram of body weight per day. For example, to compute the recommended one-day protein intake for an 85-pound female gymnast, make the following calculations:

   Body weight in kilograms = 38.63
   (85 pounds/2.2 pounds per kilogram)
   38.63 kilograms × 1.5 grams of protein
   = 57.94 grams daily protein requirement
   A chicken breast weighing 8 ounces will provide this amount of protein.

2. Many athletes involved in tackle football follow diets that are too high in fat and protein content (Figure 6.1).

3. Athletes participating in sports that stress lean builds and low body fat tend to follow diets too low in total calories.

4. Athletes tend to consume too many calories in the form of junk food (Figure 6.2).

5. Most athletes' diets are deficient in at least some important minerals, such as calcium, iron, and zinc.

FIGURE 6.1 Some red meats contain excessive amounts of fat.

FIGURE 6.2 Fast foods contain many nutrients but are typically high in fat content.

Wrestling: Special Considerations

Despite improved efforts by sanctioning bodies, officials, parents, and even many athletes, the sport of wrestling continues to be plagued with the problem of athletes practicing rapid, often unhealthy weight-loss procedures. Wrestling is one of only a few sports that matches participants on the basis of weight. Yet, in an effort to gain an advantage, many wrestlers attempt to shed pounds rapidly to compete in a lighter weight category. Unfortunately, the only form of rapid weight loss, short of surgical removal of tissue, is through **dehydration.** Water weighs approximately 7 pounds per gallon; therefore, an athlete can significantly reduce weight by reducing the body's water content. Wrestlers have been known to use a variety of methods to rapidly lose weight, including fluid restriction, the use of laxatives and diuretics, artificially induced sweating, and even starvation. There is no definitive proof that such tactics actually present an advantage, and there are plenty of reasons not to engage in such behavior. The short-term effects of repeated bouts of extreme, rapid weight loss include strength depletion, increased blood viscosity (blood thickening), blood clots, kidney and liver problems, swelling of the pancreas (which produces insulin), and ulcers (Nelson, 1989; Williams, 1992). The long-term effects are not known at this time; however, there is speculation in the scientific community that these techniques may interfere with normal growth and development in the adolescent athlete.

In an effort to reduce the likelihood of unhealthy weight-loss practices ("weight cutting") in high school wrestlers, the state of Wisconsin instituted the Wrestling Minimum Weight Project (WMWP) in 1989 (Oppliger et al., 1995). This project involved the establishment of minimum weight-loss and body-composition criteria that limited all participants to a body fat minimum of

7% and a maximum of 3 pounds of weight loss per week. A trained network of volunteers tested the athletes and provided an extensive offering of nutrition education for coaches around the state. Feedback regarding the program has been positive from 95% of the coaches, and wrestling participation has increased in Wisconsin as well. As a result of the WMWP, starting with the 1996–97 season, the National Federation of State High School Associations (NFHS) has modified wrestling rule 1-3-1 to include the following statement: "An ideal program would be one where a medical professional would assist in establishing a minimum weight through the use of checking body fat and hydration. The recommended minimum body fat should not be lower than 7%" (NFHS, 1996). In addition, the American College of Sports Medicine (ACSM, 1996) has published a position statement regarding weight loss in competitive wrestling (see Appendix 4).

Educating Athletes: What Can the Coach Do?

Research indicates that many athletes consider the coach to be responsible for providing guidelines on proper diet (Upgrove & Achterberg, 1990). Unfortunately, most coaches lack any sort of formal training on basic nutrition. Therefore, those planning to enter the coaching profession should incorporate at least one course on the subject into their academic programs. Coaches earning either a major or minor in physical education or a related field will probably be required to take at least one class in nutrition. The same is often true for those earning a coaching endorsement or minor. Another option for coaches is attendance at in-service meetings, professional conferences, and community education programs on nutrition-related topics. Subscribing to a professional journal in the field of coaching or sports science may also provide an excellent source of current information. Furthermore, many excellent books on sports nutrition are now on the market. In addition, hospitals often employ registered dietitians who are highly trained and may be more than happy to provide information on nutrition for your athletes. For assistance in locating an expert in your area, contact the American Dietetic Association, 208 S. LaSalle, Chicago, IL 60604–1003.

Another option for coaches who live near a university is to contact a member of the institution's sports medicine staff. Typically, this is a BOC-certified athletic trainer. In addition, universities often employ faculty with graduate degrees in nutrition science, and they may be willing to serve as a resource as well.

Coaches should encourage, perhaps even require, that athletes keep a daily record of what they eat and drink. This information can be combined with a training diary. Coaches should periodically review what athletes are eating and make recommendations based on sound nutritional principles. Such a record need not be a complex, detailed document. Athletes need only record the content and approximate amount of foods and beverages consumed during each meal. Most food packages provide information regarding the nutritional content of the product. With practice, it is relatively simple to determine if an athlete is consuming the correct amount of nutrients.

When working with children, coaches should discuss the nutritional needs of athletes with parents. A significant amount of nutritional information is available online at the United States Department of Agriculture's (USDA) Nutrient Data Laboratory web site. This site provides an extensive, searchable listing of the nutrient contents of hundreds of different foods. This information can be useful when making decisions about food choices. Another useful site is maintained by the USDA Center for Nutrition Policy and Promotion and allows for an online dietary analysis. After registering and entering all necessary dietary information, a detailed nutritional assessment is generated. Because this analysis is completed online, athletes should be encouraged to complete it at home, hopefully with parental involvement as well. It does little good to provide information to an athlete if an uninformed parent controls his or her diet.

General Dietary Guidelines for Athletes

Daily Diet (Nutritional Maintenance)

Although each sport and each athlete have specific nutritional requirements and preferences, some general recommendations can be made based on current knowledge. It should be noted, however, that (like a conditioning program) the athlete's diet should be tailored to meet individual needs. A gymnast may need to control her body composition within a very narrow set of parameters; a football lineman may wish to gain additional lean body mass. Thus, the nutrition program must be based on the physical characteristics of the athlete and the individual demands of the sport.

According to Brotherhood (1984), all sports nutrition programs should have three goals:

1. Nutritional maintenance and development during training to ensure adequate recovery between training sessions
2. Precompetition preparation
3. Nutrition during competition

Athletes need to be educated about proper food selections to maintain the correct proportions of carbohydrates, fat, and protein. Sport scientists recommend that 10% to 15% of dietary calories be supplied by protein, 30% by fat, and the remainder in the form of carbohydrates. It may be best to keep dietary recommendations as simple as possible because most foods contain significant amounts of carbohydrates. It is important that athletes understand that many protein sources contain significant amounts of fat; therefore, these foods should be consumed less frequently than carbohydrates. Most experts agree that even highly active athletes need only 1.5 to 2 grams of protein per day for each kilogram of body weight. This means that a football player who weighs 195 pounds (88.6 kilograms) needs to consume a maximum of 177 grams of protein per day. This amount would be supplied by consuming:

4 cups of milk	32 grams
9 ounces of lean beef	72 grams
4 cups of macaroni and cheese	72 grams
Total =	176 grams

Research shows that many football players routinely consume amounts of protein far in excess of the recommended levels (Slavin, Lanners, & Engstrom, 1988). Not only are such diets expensive, but they may be unhealthy as well. As described earlier in this chapter, excess protein produces metabolic waste products, especially nitrogen, that can put stress on both the kidneys and liver. Dehydration may also occur as the kidneys increase urine output.

Assuming athletes are sticking to a balanced diet, there is no need to be concerned about them getting enough vitamins and minerals. These compounds are needed in small amounts, and there is little evidence that athletes need to consume extra vitamins and minerals to perform. As discussed previously, one mineral that may prove an exception is iron. Dietary iron supplementation may be warranted in cases of identified iron deficiency. Athletes at risk of iron deficiency who complain of chronic fatigue, loss of fitness, and inability to perform—despite adequate diet and rest—should be referred to a physician for evaluation. A simple blood test can determine if a true iron deficiency is the problem. Researchers recommend that high-risk groups be tested periodically for iron deficiency, with subsequent supplementation of iron when deemed appropriate by a physician (Magazanik et al., 1988).

Coaches should be conservative when making dietary recommendations, especially to younger athletes. Offering a few well-proven, simple guidelines probably represents the most effective approach. An excellent resource is the interactive web site MyPyramid.gov that is made available to the public by the U.S. Department of Agriculture (Figure 6.3). This site enables the user to develop a personalized dietary plan based on factors such as age, gender, and physical activity level. This site has replaced the Food Guide Pyramid and can be found at www.MyPyramid.gov. Athletes interested in developing a more sophisticated dietary regimen should consider performing a dietary analysis using a computerized analysis system as described earlier in this chapter. Such an analysis will enable the athlete, coach, and parents to compare the actual diet with what is recommended.

Precompetition Diets

Precompetition diets should be determined based on the sport or activity. As a general rule, it is advised that athletes, regardless of sport, not consume a meal immediately

FIGURE 6.3 MyPyramid. (Source: U.S. Department of Agriculture, www.MyPyramid.gov)

prior to an event. The process of digestion takes 2 to 3 hours or longer; thus, foods eaten just before a contest will contribute virtually nothing to performance. Experts recommend that the typical pregame diet should consist of low-fat, easily digestible foods eaten no later than 3 to 4 hours prior to the contest (Brotherhood, 1984). If acceptable to the athlete, liquid diets offer some distinct advantages over the more traditional precompetition meal. Commercially manufactured liquid meals typically contain a high percentage of CHO in a form that facilitates rapid digestion and absorption. In addition, they contain water, which helps the athlete with respect to achieving adequate precompetition hydration. It is recommended that the precompetition diet contain between 150 g and 300 g of CHO (3–5 g/kg body weight) (McArdle, Katch, & Katch, 1999). These guidelines are especially important for athletes participating in endurance sports. However, athletes involved in power sports such as football would also benefit from such a regimen. The traditional meal of steak and potatoes just prior to the game provides only a psychological effect; it may cause bloating and a feeling of heaviness in some athletes.

Nutrition During Competition

Research has shown that consumption of CHO during activity, both aerobic and anaerobic, can be beneficial. Considerable attention has recently been given to the effects of carbohydrate ingestion during long-duration exercise. It is known that the body has a limited capacity for storing glycogen and that athletes may deplete glycogen supplies in the muscles and liver before completing an event. This is commonly referred to as "hitting the wall." Research supports the premise that consuming carbohydrates during long-duration exercise (1 to 3 hours at 70% to 80% maximum aerobic capacity) will allow active muscle tissue to rely on blood glucose for energy (Coyle, 1988). The recommended dosage of carbohydrate feeding during exercise is 8 ounces of solution containing a 5% carbohydrate mixture taken every 15 minutes. Many commercially made carbohydrate products are now available. Coaches and athletes can also prepare their own preferred beverages.

Weight vs. Fat Management

Athletes wishing to gain or lose weight must be educated about the various ways that body weight can be changed. Body weight can be categorized as three basic forms: water, fat tissue, and lean tissue. Water makes up a substantial portion of nearly all the tissues in the body.

Skeletal muscles make up the majority of lean tissue in the body. The majority of body fat is found just under the skin and is known as subcutaneous fat. The human body has devised a highly efficient method of storing excess dietary calories. When an athlete consumes more calories each day than the body requires for a given activity level, the excess calories are converted to fat. Conversely, if an athlete fails to consume enough calories to meet the daily requirement, stored fat will be metabolized to form energy. Curiously, when an athlete severely restricts caloric intake, such as in fasting, the body will consume muscle tissue to generate energy (Williams, 1992). Therefore, an athlete will reduce lean-tissue mass, which in most cases will result in loss of performance.

It is important to note that a given volume of muscle tissue will weigh more than the same volume of fat. The ratio of fat to lean body weight is commonly referred to as body composition. From a practical standpoint, skeletal muscles make up the majority of lean-tissue weight. Determining body weight by standing on a scale is of limited value. For the vast majority of athletes, it is really a moot issue because activity and diet allow them to maintain a desirable body weight. That is the case when an athlete's caloric intake equals caloric expenditure—that is, basic metabolic needs and exercise demands. Athletes should weigh themselves weekly, at about the same time of day, after going to the bathroom. Their body weight should not fluctuate from week to week. It is important to remember that female athletes may experience weight gains immediately preceding their menstrual period.

There are athletes who, for a variety of reasons, desire to change their body weight. Those involved in sports that require a specific body weight, such as wrestling, may attempt to lose pounds rapidly to compete in a lighter weight category. These competitors need to understand that rapid weight fluctuations involve dehydration and that significant water loss can cause a number of undesirable consequences resulting in loss of performance. Wrestlers should determine their healthy body weight during the off-season, and then concentrate on preparing for that weight category in the upcoming season.

Minimal Competitive Weight

For male athletes, it has been recommended that not less than 5% of total body composition be in the form of fat. The minimal competitive weight can then be calculated by dividing the athlete's lean body weight by 0.95 (Wilmore & Costill, 1988). To use this formula, the body weight and percentage of fat of the athlete must be determined. Although there are many ways of estimat-

ing body fat, the most practical method employs skinfold measurements. However, the technique is only as good as the person administering the test. Hence, testing of body composition should be conducted by a person who has been properly trained, such as an exercise physiologist or BOC-certified athletic trainer. After the percentage of fat has been determined, lean body weight (**LBW**) can be calculated with the following formula:

LBW = total body weight − fat weight

If an athlete weighs 135 pounds and has 14% body fat, fat weight can be determined by multiplying percentage of fat times body weight: 0.14 × 135 = 18.9 pounds. Thus, fat weight is approximately 20 pounds. Determining this athlete's LBW is calculated by subtracting fat weight from total body weight: 135 − 18.9 = 116.10 pounds. To determine the minimal competitive weight for this athlete, make the following calculation:

Minimal competitive weight = 116.10/0.95 = 122.21 pounds

Thus, this athlete should not compete if weight drops below 122.21 pounds. Although no formal guidelines currently exist for female athletes, experts recommend that their levels of body fat not drop below 8% to 10% (Wilmore & Costill, 1988). Using the same equation, a 115-pound female athlete who has 12% body fat should not be allowed to compete if her weight drops below 106.53 pounds:

115 × 0.12 (% body fat) = 13.8 pounds of fat

115 − 13.8 pounds of fat = 101.20 pounds LBW

Minimal competitive weight = 101.20/0.92

= 110.0 pounds

Athletes involved in sports such as gymnastics or diving, which tend to emphasize an ideal body type, may be faced with a dilemma when attempting to alter their appearance. First, these activities are considered to be anaerobic, deriving the required energy from glycogen supplies in working muscles. If a gymnast wishes to reduce her level of body fat, she will be required to engage in some form of aerobic exercise in addition to gymnastics training. In this way she will be able to eliminate excess body fat while at the same time sparing muscle tissue, which is needed for gymnastics.

Any athlete who demonstrates abnormal eating behaviors or exhibits unusual or unwarranted concerns

LBW Lean body weight.

about excess body fat should be referred to an expert for evaluation and dietary counseling.

Nutrition and Injury Recovery

Obviously, proper nutrition is vital to tissue healing and recovery. Although there is no evidence that supplementing vitamins and minerals will shorten recovery time, it is essential that their consumption be adequate (Wilmore & Costill, 1988).

A major concern for many injured athletes is weight gain during periods of forced inactivity. Some athletes find it difficult to adjust eating habits to reduce caloric intake when they are not exercising. It is important that the coach advise an injured athlete about dietary changes during recovery. It may be possible for some injured athletes to continue exercising with some form of alternate activity. Runners can often ride a stationary bicycle or run in a swimming pool, thereby maintaining aerobic fitness and burning off excess calories. Players who are suffering from infectious illnesses may be unable to exercise and should take care to reduce total caloric intake until they are healthy.

Supplements and Ergogenic Aids

Sport nutritional supplements have become very popular with athletes of all calibers. The use of supplements, once basically confined to professional or Olympic athletes, has now become a popular technique for gaining an edge for athletes of all ages and categories. Many coaches tell their athletes that by using nutritional supplements they can become bigger, stronger, and faster. This is exactly what the athlete wants to hear, and he or she will often spend significant amounts of money buying a variety of supplements to help reach the goal of becoming the best athlete. For many high school athletes, being a top-tier athlete can mean a college scholarship. The collegiate athlete may want to become better so he or she can obtain a professional contract and possibly make millions of dollars. These are just two of the many reasons athletes will take nutritional supplements and demonstrate their desire to become better athletes. It should be pointed out early in this discussion that not all supplements make the athlete bigger, stronger, and faster. Many supplements are marketed to make athletes think that by taking a pill or powder or drinking an ergogenic beverage they will improve their performance.

Supplements can also be called **ergogenic aids.** For something to be ergogenic, it must have the potential to increase the work output of the person using it. When work output is increased, the person is able to work longer and thus is capable of putting greater stresses on the body, thereby increasing his or her potential (size, speed, etc.) through the overload principle commonly used by most athletes in their normal training programs.

Ergogenic aids (Table 6.2) can be divided into two groups: legal and illegal. Legal ergogenic aids are those that can be legally purchased (via retail outlets, catalogs, magazines, and the Internet) and are frequently marketed as natural substances that the body needs and uses every day. The manufacturers claim that these substances are either needed by athletes in greater amounts than the body can acquire through normal dietary habits or are not available through the athlete's regular diet and are necessary for improved performance. There are thousands of products in the legal category, from amino acids (very popular) to zinc tablets.

Until the end of 2003, the most popular legal supplements for ergogenic purposes were a combination of caffeine and ephedra. In early 2004, the Food and Drug Administration (FDA) banned the use of ephedra as a supplement; ephedra will, however, continue to be available in foreign countries and thus can be purchased over the Internet or by other illegal means. Ephedra is very controversial as an ergogenic aid. The FDA ban in 2004 was challenged in court and the substance was again allowed to be sold over the counter (OTC) in 2005, but OTC sale of products containing ephedra was again challenged as an OTC preparation by the government in 2006. Caffeine continues to be touted as a safe and helpful aid in providing a boost of energy for the athlete. Caffeine and ephedra both affect the way the brain recognizes exhaustion during exercise. These supplements, in separate ways, override the brain's recognition of exhaustion during exercise and permit the athlete to continue training when the brain is telling the body to stop. The use of these supplements can be dangerous and even deadly when environmental factors such as excessive heat and humidity or excessive training efforts are coupled with the athlete's unwillingness to stop exercising at the appropriate time.

Other caffeine and ephedra combination supplements may be sold under various names. It is important for the coach or athletic trainer to discourage the use of these supplements during exercise situations. The use of these mixtures is most prevalent during two-a-day practices to boost energy levels and has been suspected in the deaths of some major league athletes.

Other commonly known supplements the athlete may be tempted to use are testosterone precursors. Androstenedione (andro) was made famous by professional baseball player Mark McGwire. Andro is a testosterone

TABLE 6.2

EXAMPLES OF VARIOUS ERGOGENIC SUBSTANCES USED BY ATHLETES

Generic and Brand Names	Perceived Benefits	Potential Adverse Effects
Androstenedione	Development of muscle mass	Reduction of testosterone production
		Banned by the United States government (2005), International Olympic Committee (IOC), and National Football League (NFL)
		This substance is available by prescription in the United States.
Dehydroepiandrosterone (DHEA complex)	Development of muscle mass Reduction of body fat and "antiaging"	Banned by the IOC and National Collegiate Athletic Association (NCAA)
β-hydroxy-β-methylbutyrate (HMB)	Muscle repair	Undetermined
Amino Acids (Pro Complex) (Max Pro) (Primo Max) (BCAA Stack) (Supreme Pure Whey) (Max Glutamine) (Glutamine Powder) (Glutacine GH—chewable)	Development of muscle mass	Undetermined
Creatine (Juiced Creatine) (Creatine Monohydrate) (Cell-Tech) (Phosphagen XT) (Swole—Jungle Juice)	Production of energy at the muscle cell by converting ADP to ATP	Kidney damage, fluid retention, muscle cramps, upset stomach, and diarrhea
Estrogen Inhibitors (6–OXO) (Biotest M)	Inhibits estrogen activity to enhance muscle development (typically used in conjuction with androstenedione)	Reduction of estrogen activity in males and females
Gammahydroxybutyrate (GHB)	Promotes deep sleep —argued to enhance GH release Also known as the "date rape drug"	ILLEGAL SUBSTANCE Can result in death This substance is available by prescription in the United States.

precursor taken by the athlete with the intent to build muscle tissue. Over-the-counter sales of andro were banned by the United States government in January 2005; however, an athlete may be able to purchase this drug over the Internet, and it is also available by prescription— thus an athlete may be able to obtain it illegally. Another testosterone precursor currently popular

ergogenic aids Food or beverages that have the potential to increase the work output of the person using them.

with athletes is dehydroepiandrosterone (DHEA), a hormone found in the blood that is converted to androstenedione, which is then converted to testosterone (Brown et al., 1999; Wallace et al., 1999). Both of these supplements break down into testosterone, which then is used by the body to generate increased muscle bulk. The adverse effect of using testosterone precursors is the reduction in testosterone production by the body. Additionally, andro is banned by the International Olympic Committee (IOC) and the NFL, and DHEA is banned by the IOC and the NCAA. Many of the athletes using testosterone precursors also use an estrogen inhibitor, which increases the effectiveness of the andro. Using an estrogen inhibitor reduces the estrogen in the body. In female athletes, this reduction of estrogen combined with the increase in overall testosterone over a long period of time leads to an increase in male characteristics.

Creatine is the ergogenic aid that most coaches and athletes are familiar with; it is typically used to produce an increase in energy, allowing the athlete to train for longer periods of time. Creatine is a component in the cell that converts ADP to ATP and thus produces energy for the cell. By putting more creatine in the system, the cell can produce more energy and the athlete can train longer. Thus, the athlete can overload the body and produce greater muscle mass. The scientific evidence regarding the effectiveness of creatine in generating muscle mass is equivocal. There are many published studies on creatine that report conflicting results. Therefore, many athletes follow the advice of fellow athletes when it comes to deciding if they will use creatine. It has been demonstrated that creatine is more helpful to the athlete who uses short bursts of energy (sprinters, weight lifters, etc.) than to endurance athletes (soccer players, swimmers, etc.). (Bemben & Lamont, 2005). Now it appears that for strength training by supplementing the diet using creatine with β-alanine, the athlete will experience a higher-quality workout, resulting in greater strength gains. The addition of β-alanine as a supplement appears to have a positive effect on lean-tissue accruement and body fat composition (Hoffman et al., 2006). The adverse effects associated with creatine are kidney damage, fluid retention, muscle cramps, upset stomach, and diarrhea. Creatine is available in many different forms, but most athletes use the powdered form combined with some type of fruit juice. It is an expensive supplement and can be purchased without a physician's prescription, that is, over the counter (OTC). Athletes considering the use of creatine should be encouraged to carefully weigh the purpose of using this or any supplement before they begin its use.

Amino acids (including whey protein) along with β-hydroxy-β-methylbutyrate (HMB) are marketed for muscle building and repair. Amino acids used for the purpose of muscle building have not been shown to be effective for this purpose in rigorous research studies. Amino acids are water soluble, and when excess amounts are taken they will be eliminated through the urine if not used by the body. A well-balanced diet provides the essential amino acids for most people. Athletes needing extra amino acids are encouraged to eat increased amounts of food during training and conditioning periods to obtain them.

Herbal supplements can also be readily purchased by the athlete and taken as ergogenic aids. Some of the herbs produce a stimulatory effect (ginseng, yohimbe, kava, etc.), and others produce relaxation (chamomile, St. John's wort, etc.) to reduce stress in the athlete. Some athletes don't understand that using herbs in combination with OTC or prescription drugs can result in either reducing the effectiveness of both the drug and the herb or increasing the action of both the herb and the drug in the body.

In contrast to the legal supplements are the illegal substances, which are usually legal substances when prescribed by a medical professional for the proper reasons. The most notable supplements in this category are anabolic steroids, erythropoietin, and stimulants. These products cannot be purchased in a retail store, but are typically purchased through an underground source. Athletes will go to extreme measures to obtain and use these supplements. They will also go to extreme lengths to hide the use of these illegal supplements.

Anabolic steroids are legal products, used by many medical doctors and veterinarians in therapeutic dosages to help heal muscle damage, but used illegally by athletes in much higher dosages to build large muscles. Athletes can use oral or injectable steroids, and many times they use both types in a "stacking" routine. Because the athlete is obtaining these supplements through an illegal source, the dosages used are sometimes as high as 100 times or more of the therapeutic dose. Steroids injected directly into the muscle are more effective than those taken by mouth because a higher percentage is delivered directly to the muscle after injection. Many times the athlete injecting steroids does not have the proper equipment for injections and must share needles and syringes, which is very dangerous. Oral intake subjects the drug to metabolism in the internal organs; much of the steroid is degraded in the digestive and organ metabolism period. By using anabolic steroids in large amounts, athletes can damage many internal organs and cause changes to their body composition that may not help them in their preferred sport.

Erythropoietin (EPO) is a natural substance produced by the kidneys that stimulates red blood cell proliferation.

EPO can now be synthesized in the laboratory and is used for cancer patients on chemotherapy and other individuals with chronic illnesses who need to augment their red blood cell levels. Athletes who compete in endurance activities can benefit from an increase in the number of circulating red blood cells. The red blood cells carry oxygen; the more oxygen the blood stream can carry to the cells, the longer the cells can function. The longer the cells function, the longer the athlete can compete at a higher level. Endurance athletes such as swimmers, marathon runners, cyclists, and others have been known to use this drug. The adverse effect of using EPO is that the athlete may take too much and get too many red blood cells circulating. This situation increases the viscosity of the blood and makes the heart work much harder to pump this thick blood through the body. If the heart has to work too hard for too long, the athlete can experience heart failure and die.

Stimulants can also be obtained by athletes and used to give them some energy when they are tired. Caffeine and ephedra are considered stimulants and, as mentioned previously, are easily obtained legally. There are also prescription stimulants athletes can obtain illegally. In general, stimulants provide an energy boost and are commonly used during two-a-day practices or prior to competition. The prescription stimulants affect the brain and body much the same way as the OTC stimulants do because they block the fatigue messages to the brain. The athlete then exercises beyond the capability of the body and can experience heat or cardiac problems.

Gammahydroxybutyrate (GHB) is an illegal substance (it is also known as the "date rape drug"), but can be obtained by some athletes. Those who sell GHB to athletes claim it helps the athlete get into the deepest phase of sleep and stay in that sleep phase longer. Deep sleep is suggested to be the cycle during which human growth hormone is released, making longer deep sleep potentially valuable for increased muscle growth (Van Cauter et al., 1997). The use of GHB can be lethal to the athlete. It is an illegal substance, and all athletes should be discouraged from its use.

REVIEW QUESTIONS

1. Describe the similarities and the differences between the basic molecular structure of carbohydrates, fats, and proteins.

2. Describe the major problems associated with excessive consumption of dietary protein.

3. According to the chapter, a survey of coaches, athletes, and BOC-certified athletic trainers revealed that athletes depended on what sources for their information about nutrition?

4. What is the recommended level of dietary protein for adolescent athletes?

5. What is the approximate weight of a gallon of water?

6. Discuss briefly the short-term effects of repeated episodes of extreme, rapid weight loss.

7. What should be the three goals of any sports nutrition program?

8. What are the recommended percentages of protein, fat, and carbohydrates in an ideal training diet?

9. Using the equation provided in the chapter, compute the protein requirement (in grams) for a football player who weighs 94 kilograms.

10. Briefly restate the five guidelines regarding a precompetition diet.

11. *True or false:* During times of heavy exertion, it is not possible to lose more than 0.5 to 1 liter of water for each hour of exercise.

12. Compute the fluid deficiency of an athlete who weighs 5.5 pounds less after practice than he did prior to practice.

13. Briefly review the effects of dietary fasting on muscle tissue.

14. *True or false:* Sports scientists recommend a training diet in which 30% to 40% of daily calories consumed are in the form of protein.

15. What is often the major nutritional concern of an injured athlete who is recovering from an injury?

REFERENCES

American College of Sports Medicine (ACSM). (1996). Position statement on weight loss in wrestlers. *Med Sci Sports.* 28(6):ix–xii.

Bemben MG, Lamont HS. (2005). Creatine supplementation and exercise performance: Recent findings. *Sports Medicine.* 35(2):107–125.

Bentivegna A, Kelley EJ, Lalenak A. (1979). Diet, fitness, and athletic performance. *Phys Sportsmed.* 7(10):99–105.

Brotherhood JR. (1984). Nutrition and sports performance. *Sports Med.* 1:350–389.

Brown GA, et al. (1999). Effect of oral DHEA on serum testosterone and adaptations to resistance training in young men. *J Appl Physiol.* 87(6):2274–2283.

Clark N. (1997). Eating for vitamins: Do you need supplements? *Phys Sportsmed.* 25(7):103.

Coyle EF. (1988). Carbohydrates and athletic performance. *Sports Science Exchange.* 1(7).

Deuster PA, et al. (1986). Nutritional survey of highly trained women runners. *Am J Clin Nutr.* 44:954–962.

Eck LH, et al. (1988). Composition of training-table selections in a group of male university athletes. *Athletic Training.* 23(2):141–144.

Hoffman J, et al. (2006). Effect of creatine and β-alanine supplementation on performance and endocrine response in strength/power athletes. *Int J Sport Nutrition Exercise Metabolism.* 16:430–446.

Loosli AR, Benson J. (1990). Nutritional intakes in adolescent athletes. *Pediatr Clin North Am.* 37(5):1143–1152.

Magazanik A, et al. (1988). Iron deficiency caused by 7 weeks of intensive physical exercise. *Eur J App Phys.* 57:198–202.

McArdle WD, Katch FI, Katch VL. (1999). *Sports & Exercise Nutrition.* Philadelphia: Lippincott Williams & Wilkins.

Moffatt RJ. (1984). Dietary status of elite female high-school gymnasts: Inadequacy of vitamin and mineral intake. *J Am Diet Assoc.* 84(11):1361–1363.

National Federation of State High School Associations (NFHS). (1996). *Wrestling Rules Book.* Kansas City: National Federation of State High School Associations.

Nelson RA. (1989). Nutrition for the athlete. In Ryan AJ, Allman FL (eds.). *Sports Medicine* (pp. 165–181). San Diego: Academic Press.

Oppliger RA, et al. (1995). The Wisconsin Wrestling Minimum Weight Project: A model for weight control among high school wrestlers. *Med Sci Sports.* 27(8):1220–1224.

Parr RB, Porter MA, Hodgson SC. (1984). Nutrition knowledge and practice of coaches, trainers, and athletes. *Phys Sportsmed.* 12(3):127–138.

Pattini A, Schena F. (1990). Effects of training and iron supplementation on iron status of cross-country skiers. *J Sportsmed Phys Fit.* 30:347–353.

Perron M, Endres J. (1985). Knowledge, attitudes, and dietary practices of female athletes. *J Am Diet Assoc.* 85(5):573–576.

Slavin JL, Lanners G, Engstrom MA. (1988). Amino-acid supplements: Beneficial or risky? *Phys Sportsmed.* 16(3):221–224.

Sossin K, Gizis F, Marquart LF, Sobal J. (1997). Nutrition beliefs, attitudes, and resources use of high school wrestling coaches. *Int J Sport Nutr.* 7(3):219–228.

Sumida KD, Donovan CM. (1995). Enhanced hepatic gluconeogenic capacity for selected precursors after endurance training. *J Appl Physiol.* 79:1883–1888.

Upgrove NA, Achterberg CL. (1990). The conceptual relationship between training and eating in high-school distance runners. *J Nutr Educ.* 23(1):18–24.

Van Cauter E, et al. (1997). Simultaneous stimulation of slow-wave sleep and growth hormone secretion by gamma-hydroxybutyrate in normal young men. *J Clin Invest.* 100:745–749.

Wallace MB, et al. (1999). Effects of dehydroepiandrosterone vs. androstenedione supplementation in men. *Med Sci Sports Exerc.* 31(12):1788–1792.

Williams MH. (1992). *Nutrition for Fitness and Sport.* Dubuque, Ia.: William C. Brown.

Wilmore JH, Costill DL. (1988). *Training for Sport and Activity: The Physiological Basis of the Conditioning Process.* Dubuque, Ia.: William C. Brown.

7

Emergency Plan and Initial Injury Evaluation

MAJOR CONCEPTS

Coaching personnel have a legal duty to develop and implement an emergency action plan to be followed if an athlete is injured while participating in sports. To be effective, the emergency plan must be carefully planned by all the principle parties involved, including all members of the athletic health care team in conjunction with emergency medical services (EMS) providers. In the public school setting, the appropriate institutional representatives, such as the athletic director and school principal, should be involved as well. The plan must be flexible to allow for changes in personnel or in facilities and venues. In addition, it must incorporate an education component that includes periodic rehearsal to ensure that it will work effectively if and when an emergency arises. Skills of available personnel must be recognized, and roles and responsibilities should be carefully documented. Details such as emergency equipment inventory, communications, and transportation must all be carefully considered. In addition, the emergency plan must extend beyond the traditional game day and practice paradigm to include off-season components such as summer conditioning camps and, if it is a separate facility, the strength and conditioning room. The plan must also address the potential issue of an injured or ill fan, sideline participant, or official. This chapter provides a step-by-step outline of the vital components in the development of an effective emergency plan. It discusses the process of injury evaluation in the unique situations presented in the sports environment.

http://health.jbpub.com/book/concepts/5e

The web site for this book offers many useful tools and is a great source for supplementary information for both students and instructors.

Visit the site at
http://health.jbpub.com/book/concepts/5e
to link to the following organizations and sites:

- Occupational Safety and Health Administration

As has been discussed in previous chapters, sports injuries are an inevitable outcome of participation for tens of thousands of athletes each year. Proper planning is essential to ensure appropriate initial first aid management of an injury. There are two good reasons for developing a formal emergency plan for sports injuries. First, anything that can be done ahead of time to improve the health care of injured athletes should be a priority. Second, from a legal standpoint, failure to have an emergency plan in place has been found to constitute negligence in litigation resulting from a sports injury (Shea, 1995). According to Ball (1989), "failing to identify and properly deal with injuries in order to avoid unnecessary aggravation or complication" is a major source of liability for coaches.

According to Andersen and colleagues (2002), the emergency plan should be a written document that accounts for the following components:

1. An emergency plan for athletics identifies the personnel involved in carrying out the emergency plan and outlines the qualifications of those executing the plan. Sports medicine professionals, officials, and coaches should be trained in automatic external defibrillation, cardiopulmonary resuscitation, first aid, and prevention of disease transmission.

2. The emergency plan should specify the equipment needed to carry out the tasks required in the event of an emergency. In addition, the emergency plan should outline the location of the emergency equipment. Further, the equipment available should be appropriate to the level of training of the personnel involved.

3. Establishment of a clear mechanism for communication to appropriate emergency care service providers and identification of the mode of transportation for the injured participant are critical elements of an emergency plan.

4. The emergency plan should be specific to the activity venue. That is, each activity site should have a defined emergency plan that is derived from the overall institutional or organizational policies on emergency planning.

5. Emergency plans should incorporate the emergency care facilities to which the injured individual will be taken. Emergency receiving facilities should be notified in advance of scheduled events and contests. Personnel from the emergency receiving facilities should be included in the development of the emergency plan for the institution or organization.

6. The emergency plan specifies the necessary documentation supporting the implementation and evaluation of the emergency plan. This documentation should identify responsibility for documenting actions taken during the emergency, evaluation of the emergency response, and institutional personnel training.

7. The emergency plan should be reviewed and rehearsed annually, although more frequent review and rehearsal may be necessary. The results of these reviews and rehearsals should be documented and should indicate whether the emergency plan was modified, with further documentation reflecting how the plan was changed.

8. The emergency plan should be reviewed by the administration and legal counsel of the sponsoring organization or institution.

In the high school setting, it is recommended that all personnel directly involved with the interscholastic sports program take part in the development and implementation of the emergency plan. This should include coaches, administrators, the team physician and athletic trainer (if available), local emergency medical services (EMS) personnel, student athletic trainers (if present), and other staff members involved with the program. These personnel make up what is known as the emergency team, and they provide four functions with respect to the emergency plan: (1) immediate care of the athlete, (2) equipment retrieval (emergency equipment), (3) activation of EMS (when situation is deemed of sufficient magnitude), and (4) directing EMS to the scene of the injury. Courson (1999) recommends that the most qualified person on the emergency team be the one to administer the initial care to the injured athlete. Further, he recommends that the individual responsible for activation of EMS be someone who not only is "calm under pressure" but is also a good communicator (Courson, 1999). The plan must be comprehensive, specifically outlining procedures for both home and out-of-town contests and practices. In addition, the emergency plan should provide for the possibility of sudden illness or injury involving a fan or sideline participant (Andersen et al., 2002). Furthermore, it must be written so that new staff members will be able to implement the plan when necessary (Ball, 1989). The written plan must include locations of telephones, emergency phone numbers, directions to the contest site, access points to the facility, and other critical information.

Regardless of the sport, location, and personnel available, certain questions must be answered well in advance. With respect to emergency medical services, it is important that arrangements be made to have EMS personnel present at any athletic event whenever possible

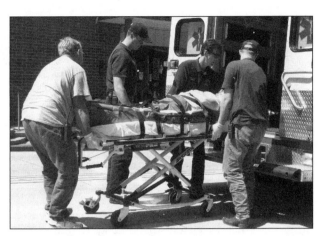

FIGURE 7.1 It is important that arrangements be made to have EMS personnel present at athletic events whenever possible.

(Figure 7.1). Moreover, coaches and staff should know where the EMS vehicle is parked, the access route to the playing area, and the location of keys to gates and doors that may present barriers to emergency personnel. If EMS personnel are not present at the event, all staff members should know the EMS phone number and the location of the nearest telephone. Given the available technology, it seems prudent that all key members of the coaching staff should carry a cellular telephone (make sure batteries are charged and tested regularly), with EMS phone numbers programmed in memory, at all times during both practice and contest situations. In this way, valuable time will not be wasted finding the nearest telephone in the event of an emergency that requires EMS. A decision should be made ahead of time as to who will summon emergency personnel and who will remain with the injured athlete. On a playing field, coaches should stipulate ahead of time what type of signal will be used to alert EMS personnel to come onto the field and render care (Harris, 1988).

Important Questions and Considerations

Nowlan and colleagues (1996) recommend the following major elements of an emergency plan:

1. Phones
   ____ Location/access at all times
   ____ Emergency numbers
   ____ Who makes the call?
2. Gates/Passageways
   ____ Which one is to be used?
   ____ Who has the keys?

____ Will emergency vehicles have easy access?
____ Who will guide emergency vehicles to the site?

3. Emergency Supplies
   ____ Location
   ____ Responsible party
   ____ Procedure for use

4. Emergency Evaluation/Care
   ____ Role of each individual

The emergency plan should be rehearsed periodically to ensure that it will work smoothly and effectively. Changes in staff, facilities, playing schedules, EMS, and playing seasons can all affect the effectiveness of any plan. It is the responsibility of all those involved with organized sports programs to provide proper emergency care in the event that it is needed.

First Aid Training

It should be obvious that all personnel involved with organized sports programs must be trained in basic first aid and cardiopulmonary resuscitation (CPR). Recent developments in automated external defibrillators (AEDs) have made it possible for these devices to be made available to institutions such as schools. As such, members of the athletic health care team should be trained in the use of AEDs. First aid, CPR, and AED training is available through several different agencies nationwide, including the National Safety Council, the American Heart Association and the Emergency Care and Safety Institute. It is strongly recommended that all personnel upgrade their training every 3 years, or more frequently, to keep first aid skills current. Periodic mock emergency drills should be practiced to verify the effectiveness of the emergency plan. CPR skills deteriorate quickly and should be reviewed regularly (Figure 7.2).

Injury-Evaluation Procedures
The Coach's Responsibility

Immediate management of an acute sports injury presents the coach with a challenge unlike any other related to the profession. Immediate care is critical in determining the location and severity of the injury. It is important to remember that sports injuries generally occur amid the confusion of a contest or practice. Therefore, it is imperative that the coach maintain a clear head and remain objective in the initial assessment of any injury. Every situation is unique, and the coach must make it clear to everyone in the immediate vicinity of the injured athlete that he or she is in charge. By law, the

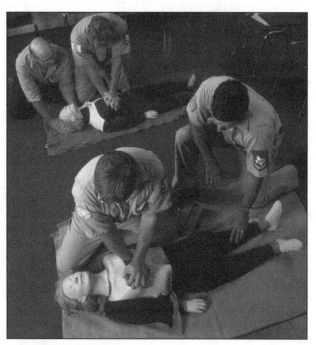

FIGURE 7.2 CPR training.

coach is the person most often held accountable for proper injury management when no athletic trainer or physician is present.

It is critical to note that coaches will typically be seen as "first responders" to an injured athlete and should focus on providing emergency care to the extent of their training and expertise. Coaches should be trained in emergency first aid, CPR, and in the operation of an automated external defibrillator (AED); however, coaches must avoid going beyond their level of training when evaluating an injured athlete. For example, performing clinical tests for the integrity of the ligaments of a joint goes beyond the training of most coaches and should be performed only by those personnel who have advanced training such as physicians and Board of Certification, Inc. (BOC)–certified athletic trainers.

As stated earlier, coaching personnel should be properly trained in first aid procedures, including CPR and operation of an AED. The primary objective of coaching personnel trained in emergency care is so that when confronted with an injured athlete, they can provide appropriate initial care, including sustaining the injured athlete's life until EMS personnel arrive at the scene. Knowing how to care for life-threatening conditions such as airway obstructions and respiratory and cardiac arrest is critical. If left unattended, any of these conditions can result in death within minutes. Thus, the primary skills developed during emergency care instruction focus on dealing effectively with respiratory and cardiac

problems—that is, airway assessment, techniques for opening the airway, rescue breathing, CPR, and the use of an AED. All of these techniques are learned skills that require periodic practice. It is important that coaches maintain their emergency care skills through regular review sessions as well as in annual recertification from agencies offering such instruction.

As stated earlier, each injury presents the coach with a unique set of circumstances; however, the coach's responsibilities remain the same. Coaches must have a basic knowledge of sports injuries and, more important, *the ability to differentiate minor from major injuries.* A central theme in the remainder of this book is the development of initial assessment skills necessary to determine which injuries should be referred to medical personnel and which can be treated with simple first aid. Such determinations represent a major dilemma for many in the coaching profession. This is especially true when no athletic trainer or physician is immediately available, which more often than not is the case. Critical to the process of immediate injury management is current certification in at least basic first aid and CPR. Furthermore, the coach must be familiar with the preexisting emergency plan and be able to function effectively as a primary player on the athletic health care team.

The Evaluation Process

To be effective in the initial process of injury management, the person rendering first aid must have a prepared protocol to follow. The emergency treatment protocol must be generic enough to be effective regardless of the type of injury. By following a preplanned format, the coach is assured of first evaluating all vital life functions and following up with a step-by-step examination to determine any and all injuries that the athlete may have sustained. In this way, tragedy can be avoided—for example, treating an unconscious athlete's head wound without first checking to see if he or she has an open airway and is breathing.

Assessment of the Injured Athlete

The assessment of the injured athlete consists of two phases known as the initial check and the physical exam. The purpose of the **initial check** is to determine if the athlete's life is in immediate jeopardy. According to the American Academy of Orthopaedic Surgeons, the initial check must include assessments of the following (in order of importance) (AAOS, 2006):

- Responsiveness
- Airway
- Breathing
- Severe bleeding

Generally, it is best not to move an athlete unless you have a good reason. Therefore, during the initial check make every effort to perform the assessment without moving the athlete. In some cases, this may not be possible; for example, it may be necessary to roll an athlete onto his or her side to determine if he or she has an open airway. It is important to follow appropriate first aid procedures whenever moving an athlete. Refer to Appendix 1 for details on the initial assessment and treatment of airway and cardiac emergencies.

Responsive Athlete?

Before making any decisions about rendering care to an injured athlete, it is essential that his or her level of responsiveness be determined. Assessment of the neurologic status of an injured person can be a daunting task, even for the experienced medical professional. The complexity of the central nervous system (CNS) cannot be disputed; however, from an assessment standpoint, dividing the CNS into the brain and spinal cord is helpful. As recommended by the National Safety Council (NSC, 2001), this can be accomplished quickly and consistently by using the AVPU scale. That is, A = Alert and Aware, V = responds to Verbal stimulus, P = responds to Painful stimulus, U = Unresponsive to any stimulus.

When assessing "alertness," note if the athlete's eyes are open and, further, if he or she can accurately state the date, time, and/or location, as well as his or her name. If the athlete can successfully accomplish these simple tasks, he or she is said to be *alert*. If the athlete does not appear to be alert, then attempt to verify his or her ability to respond to verbal stimulus. If verbal communication can be established, regardless of the accuracy of the communication, the athlete is said to be *"responsive to verbal stimulus."* In the event the athlete does not appear to be able to communicate verbally at any level, attempt to verify a response to painful stimuli by pinching the skin overlying a bone such as the clavicle, or skin on the inside of the upper arm or thigh. If you observe a response to these stimuli, either verbally, through facial gestures, or by attempts to move a limb to avoid being pinched, the athlete is said to be *"responsive only to painful stimuli."* If the athlete fails to show any form of response, that is, opening of the eyes, verbal communication, or response to painful stimuli, the athlete is said to be *"unresponsive to any stimulus."* If spinal or head injury is suspected, steps must be taken immediately to immobilize the head and neck to prevent aggravation of the injury. This process is described in detail in Chapter 9.

Respiratory System

Assessment of the respiratory system is the first priority when rendering first aid to an injured athlete. This portion of the initial check should require only a few seconds and can be initiated en route to the injured athlete if he or she is within visual proximity. If the athlete is obviously responsive, then it can be assumed that the airway is open and respiration is occurring. When level of responsiveness is in question or the athlete is unresponsive, then other means of airway and respiration assessment may be necessary.

Airway Assessment

Initial assessment can be facilitated by asking the athlete a simple question. If the athlete responds, the airway is open, and the level of responsiveness is high, which indicates that circulation is adequate (Hargarten, 1993). If the victim is unresponsive, assess for breathing first at the victim's head in the position he or she was found, if at all possible. If the victim is not breathing, either use the jaw-thrust technique (if serious head or spinal injury is suspected) or the head-tilt/chin-lift method (if there appear to be no indications of serious head or spinal injury).

If there is no possibility of serious head or spinal injury, use the head-tilt/chin-lift technique (Figure 7.3). Place one hand on the athlete's forehead while gently lifting the chin with the other hand. In the case of a helmeted athlete, such as a football player, *do not remove the helmet or face mask* to open the airway. Opening an airway and checking for breathing can be accomplished with the helmet in place. Attempts to remove the helmet can easily aggravate an existing spinal injury. (A detailed description of proper care of the injured helmeted player is presented in Chapter 9.)

When there is reason to believe a spinal injury may have occurred, the preferred method of opening the airway is the jaw-thrust technique (Figure 7.4). While at the athlete's side, place fingers below the ear lobes and gently push the jaw upward while not moving the head; this

FIGURE 7.3 Head-tilt/chin-lift method.

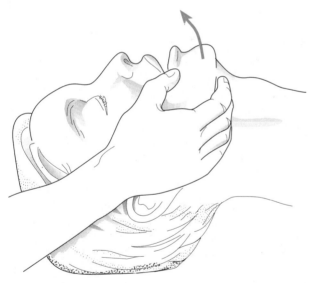

FIGURE 7.4 Jaw-thrust maneuver.

should open the airway. Remember to check for a foreign object in the airway, such as gum, a mouthpiece, chewing tobacco, a dental appliance, or other material. Remove such objects using the finger-sweep method (Figure 7.5).

Breathing Assessment

The responsive athlete is obviously breathing; however, continue to observe for difficulty in breathing and listen for sounds that may indicate a problem. The unrespon-

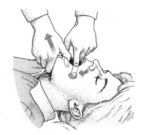

Finger-sweep method
- With index finger of your hand, slide finger down along the inside of one cheek deeply into mouth and use a hooking action across to other cheek to dislodge foreign object.
- If foreign body comes within reach, grab and remove it. Do not force object deeper.

FIGURE 7.5 Finger-sweep method.

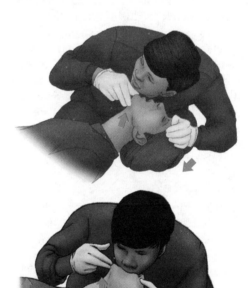

FIGURE 7.6 Check for breathing.

sive athlete can be assessed quickly once the airway is established. Remember three words: look, listen, feel. Look for the chest to rise and fall, listen for the flow of air exiting the athlete's nose and mouth, and feel for the air flow (Figure 7.6).

Circulatory System

Determination of the status of the circulatory system is a critical component of the initial survey and is intended to verify the integrity of the heart and blood vessels. The two major concerns are the presence or

FIGURE 7.7 After initial breaths check for breathing, coughing, and movement.

absence of the signs of circulation (breathing, coughing, movement), and presence or absence of loss of blood (hemorrhage), either internally or externally. Circulation assessment, as described in the following, should be executed quickly, whereas identification of hemorrhage may present the coach with a greater challenge, especially in the case where bleeding is internal. External signs of internal bleeding can be noted by changes on the skin surface and are associated with shock related to blood loss.

Circulation Assessment

A responsive athlete who is breathing will have the signs of circulation—breathing, coughing, and movement. Determine if the signs of circulation are present in an unresponsive victim after initial breaths by looking for breathing, coughing, and movement in response to the breaths (Figure 7.7). If you see no signs of circulation, begin CPR. In such a situation, the coach's primary responsibility is to keep the athlete alive and to ensure that help is summoned. There is no reason to move the athlete from the playing field or practice area. The possibility of delaying a game or practice does not justify moving someone in this situation.

Hemorrhage Assessment

Extensive external bleeding is extremely rare in athletics. Most external bleeding will be obvious and can be controlled by the appropriate first aid procedures—use of direct pressure, elevation, pressure points, and/or a pressure bandage. Any time blood or other bodily fluids are exposed, the coach should, whenever possible, take precautions: Wear eye protection and medical exam gloves to help prevent the possibility of bloodborne pathogen transmission (see Appendix 2).

Internal hemorrhaging is difficult if not impossible to detect during the initial survey. One of the earliest signs of severe internal bleeding will be **hypovolemic shock,** which is caused by too little blood in the vascular system. Two important signs of this condition are rapid, weak pulse and rapid, shallow breathing. Changes in the condition of the skin surface may also provide clues to this condition. Moist, clammy-feeling skin, associated with blue color inside the lips and under the nail beds, indicates shock. Such cases represent true medical emergencies, and the primary objective must be to treat for shock and arrange for transport to a medical facility.

The Initial Check: Summary

Remember that the purpose of the initial check is to determine whether there is a life-threatening injury. If an airway exists, breathing and pulse appear normal, and no bleeding is detected, the next step in the evaluation process is the physical exam. The purpose of the physical exam is to give the injured athlete a complete evaluation for any other injuries not found during the initial check. To be effective, the physical exam must be conducted in a preplanned, sequential fashion. In cases in which injuries are obvious, it may be possible to skip certain portions of the physical exam to render appropriate first aid sooner. However, even after attending to the obvious injury, the remaining portions of the survey should be completed. A good example would be a basketball player who falls to the floor immediately after having attempted to get a rebound. If you saw the incident—and noticed that she grabbed her ankle and was in obvious pain—you would be correct in performing a quick initial check followed by the application of ice and compression as well as elevation of the injured ankle. This entire process should take no more than a few minutes, after which you should perform a more thorough physical exam.

Physical Exam

The **physical exam** should include specific components that enable the coach to collect as much information about the injury as possible under the circumstances.

> **hypovolemic shock** Inability of the cardiovascular system to maintain adequate circulation to all parts of the body.
>
> **physical exam** Checking a victim of an emergency for signs and symptoms associated with injury and/or illness.

The essential parts of the survey are as follows:

History—having a discussion with either the athlete and/or onlookers

Observation—observing for obvious signs and/or symptoms related to the injury

Palpation—feeling the injured area to collect more information

It is important that while administering the physical exam the coach continually monitors the injured athlete's signs of breathing and circulation. Although the purpose of the initial check is to verify both circulation and respiration, both of these vital functions may change quickly related to the body's response to the injury. For example, an athlete who has sustained a significant head injury may initially have normal circulation and respiration that rather quickly decline as bleeding in the skull continues. As such, the coach must remain ever vigilant during the physical exam for changes in the condition of the athlete that may be life threatening. The coach must also be observant for signs and symptoms of shock, which can also escalate into a life-threatening phenomenon. Note signs and symptoms related to the injury. Critical to this is a basic understanding that a **sign** involves objective findings such as bleeding, swelling, discoloration, and deformity. **Symptoms** are subjective in nature and may not be as reliable in determining the nature of the injury. Symptoms include findings such as nausea, pain, and **point tenderness.**

Begin observing for signs and symptoms related to the athlete even before you are near enough to render any aid. As you approach the injured athlete, note the body position and look for signs of possible significance such as odd behavior or actions. If you saw the injury occur, you will have a good idea of the mechanism of injury. This is important because you will have an idea of the forces involved and the possible type(s) of injury.

With a responsive athlete, ask him or her to point out the site(s) of injury. Look and feel for the signs of injury, including deformity, open wounds, tenderness, and swelling. Whenever possible, compare the injured side with the uninjured area on the opposite side of the body. In cases of possible significant injury, in which much of the body is covered with equipment and clothing, it is best to remove garments from the suspected area of injury by cutting away clothing with scissors rather than removing it in a normal fashion. In this way, unnecessary movement of the athlete can be avoided. Obviously, care must be taken not to cause embarrassment to the athlete. However, in the case of a potential life-or-death situation, saving the athlete's life must always take priority over modesty.

Essentially, the physical exam should be thought of as a head-to-toe assessment of the athlete. The goal is to identify all injuries, regardless of severity, treat them appropriately, and refer the athlete for medical care if it is deemed necessary. Look and feel for deformity, open wounds, tenderness, and swelling by starting at the head and progressing through the neck, chest, abdomen, pelvis, and extremities.

Shock

Shock is an acute, life-threatening condition that involves the body's failure to maintain adequate circulation to the vital organs. As previously described, shock may result from severe hemorrhage; however, shock can be caused by a number of other conditions, including cardiogenic (heart failure), neurogenic (dilated vessels), and simple psychogenic conditions (fainting). The signs and symptoms of shock can include any combination of the following: profuse sweating; cool, clammy-feeling skin; dilated pupils; elevated pulse and respiration; irritable behavior; complaints of extreme thirst; and nausea and/or vomiting. Treatment for shock includes having the athlete in a supine position with the legs elevated approximately 8 to 12 inches. To avoid further loss of body heat, cover the athlete with a blanket. In the case of a suspected spinal injury, do not move the athlete from the position he or she is in. Rather, monitor vital signs and cover with a blanket if environmental conditions are such that loss of body heat is possible.

Medical History

Whether the athlete is responsive or unresponsive, collecting a history is considered the third part of victim assessment. Obviously, if the athlete is unresponsive, you will need to collect information from bystanders, typically teammates. Regardless of the circumstances, when rendering care to an unresponsive athlete always assume that there are serious head and spinal injuries that require the stabilization of the athlete's head and neck. Your priorities must be basic life support—airway, cardiac function, and breathing—followed by contacting EMS. In the case of the conscious athlete, the history process begins as soon as you arrive on the scene (Figure 7.8). Its purpose is to collect information critical to identifying the body areas involved as well as the severity and mechanism(s) of injury (Booher & Thibodeau, 1989). Traumatic injuries usually present a more obvious set of complaints and possible causes than chronic, long-term ones do.

Although each injury is unique, your questions to the athlete should be phrased in simple, easy-to-understand terms that will elicit the desired information without leading the athlete into giving a preferred answer. Avoid using terminology too advanced for the athlete, and always take care not to increase the anxiety level by losing

FIGURE 7.8 A coach obtains a history of injury from an injured athlete.

your composure. Questions should require only brief responses—preferably a yes or a no. Initially attempt to gain the confidence of the athlete by letting him or her know what you are doing and that you are there to ensure the athlete's welfare. Ask the athlete to explain what happened and to describe perceptions of the injury. Inquire if there is pain—and if so, where. Also ask whether the athlete heard any strange sounds during the injury or feels anything abnormal. The answers will provide essential information to assist you in your evaluation of both the location and magnitude of the injury. Do not forget to inquire about the injury history (both long and short term) of the involved area. A good example of how such information could be useful is the case of a suspected shoulder subluxation (partial dislocation). Such an injury may be very difficult to evaluate. However, if during your history taking the athlete informs you that the shoulder has been dislocated several times in the past year, you may then focus your efforts on determining the integrity of that specific joint. Information regarding the injury history of the athlete should always be passed on to medical personnel who will evaluate the athlete later.

In some cases, the medical emergency may be difficult to ascertain, as is the case with certain conditions such as diabetes, **exercise-induced asthma,** or a head injury. Clues to the problem may be given during the history process, if done correctly. In the case of metabolic emergencies, the questions are obvious. ("Do you have diabetes—and if so, did you take your insulin today?" "Do you have epilepsy—and if so, are you on any sort of medication?") In the case of the conscious athlete with a possible head injury, behavior may be incongruent with the circumstances. Your questions should assist in determining the level of consciousness, as well as the integrity of higher thought processes. The protocols for the initial treatment of athletes with head injuries are presented in Chapter 9.

Palpation

The palpation phase of the evaluation can usually be included in both the initial check and physical examination. The National Safety Council (2001) defines **palpation** as "the act of feeling with the hands for the purpose of determining the consistency of the part beneath." For example, in the unconscious athlete, initial evaluation should include careful palpation of the head and neck areas to determine if any noticeable irregularities are present that could indicate fractures, dislocations, or other types of damage. With practice, palpation skills can be refined to the point where identification of injury-related problems such as swelling, muscle spasm, localized fever, abdominal rigidity (sign of internal bleeding in abdominal cavity), deformity, crepitus (grating feeling beneath the skin surface), and skin tension can be easily detected.

Palpation is a learned skill and does involve some amount of contact with the injured athlete (Figure 7.9). Consequently, it is important that great care is taken to avoid aggravation of existing injuries. Also, when evaluating a conscious athlete, an explanation of the purposes of the evaluation can be helpful in relieving anxiety. It is recommended that whenever possible the palpation process

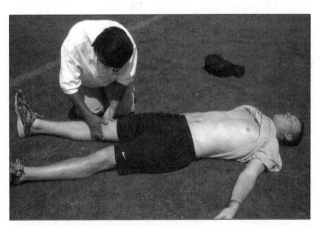

FIGURE 7.9 Palpation of a knee injury.

sign Objective evidence of an abnormal situation within the body.

symptom Subjective evidence of an abnormal situation within the body.

point tenderness Pain produced when an injury site is palpated.

exercise-induced asthma (EIA) Acute, reversible, self-limiting bronchospasm occurring during or after exercise.

palpation The act of feeling with the hands for the purpose of determining the consistency of the part beneath.

should begin in a body area away from where there are obvious injuries (Booher & Thibodeau, 1989). This allows the athlete to develop confidence in the coach's palpation skill prior to actual evaluation of the injury(ies). In the case of injury to an extremity, evaluation of the uninjured limb first is recommended as well. This provides an immediate basis for comparison when the actual injury is evaluated.

Removal from Field/Court

It is important that during all phases of the athlete examination process, significant findings are noted and recalled for later use. Normally the entire evaluation process should be completed in a matter of minutes, after which the appropriate first aid treatment should be initiated. If further evaluation is deemed necessary, the decision must be made to move the athlete from the playing field or practice area. Athletes who are conscious, responsive, and have no obvious lower-extremity injuries that preclude walking may be able to leave the area under their own power (with assistance). If a lower-extremity injury exists, it is best to use some form of transport device, such as a stretcher, spine board, or even a two-person carry, to remove the athlete from the site of injury. In the case of an unconscious athlete, or one who may have sustained a head or neck injury, the best policy is to stay with the athlete, monitor vital signs, treat for shock, and summon EMS personnel. Unless the athlete is in immediate danger of being injured further, there is *no justification* for movement prior to the arrival of EMS personnel.

Return to Play?

In the absence of a trained medical professional such as a physician or BOC-certified athletic trainer, the coach must answer the question, "Should this athlete be allowed to return to play?" In some cases, this decision will be quite easy, as in the case of a suspected head or neck injury. Any athlete who must leave a practice or game because of a neurologic injury should *not* be allowed to return until evaluated by a trained medical professional. This is true even in a case of what is commonly known as "getting one's bell rung."

Such an episode can lead to serious, even life-threatening complications if the athlete is allowed to return to participation without medical evaluation. Likewise, an athlete who appears to be suffering from heat-related problems, as discussed in Chapter 18, should be removed from participation and cleared for return only by a medical professional.

Without question, the most difficult decisions will involve injuries to the musculoskeletal system such as joint injuries, muscle strains, and contusions. In general, if the injury results in any degree of functional loss, the athlete should not be allowed to return to participation. Functional loss in the lower extremity can be verified by asking the athlete to perform simple drills such as hopping up and down on one leg or running a figure eight. In the case of upper-extremity injury, for example, in the shoulder region, asking the athlete to place his hand on the center of his upper back as if to scratch his back will verify normal range of motion. To test muscle strength and joint integrity, ask the athlete to perform a push-up. Failure to execute any simple functional test should result in removal from participation that day and medical referral. Such an athlete should be allowed to return to participation only after receiving medical clearance from a physician.

It is important to always remember that signs such as swelling, discoloration, limping, and facial expressions related to pain, and symptoms such as pain, popping, clicking in a joint, or uncontrolled muscle spasm all indicate a potentially more serious injury. When in doubt, always err on the conservative side and remove the athlete from participation until a more complete evaluation can be performed by a medical professional.

The Coach's Limitations

In the absence of a BOC-certified athletic trainer, medical doctor, or other designated health care provider, the coach will be responsible for the initial management of injuries sustained by an athlete. Yet coaches must take special care not to overstep the bounds of their training, experience, and expertise. In short, coaches should avoid the urge to assume a doctor's role. All of the procedures

Athletic Trainers SPEAK Out

Emergency medical services (EMS) operates similarly in the United States and Japan. By simply dialing 9-1-1, one is able to request emergency medical assistance. The primary difference between emergency sport medicine procedures in Japan and the United States is the availability of on-site first aid. This is particularly apparent in high school and higher education settings. Although it is common for an athletic trainer to provide on-site first aid, such as CPR, in the United States, the inverse is true in Japan. Although there are more athletic trainers in educational settings than in the past, full-time medical professionals are still uncommon for financial reasons. Because the Japanese sports industry is not as well developed as in the United States, especially at the university or collegiate level, there is minimal to no funding available for sports medicine initiatives. Because the settings and circumstances in Japan are culturally and socially different from those in the United States, the U.S. system of athletic training is not always applicable. High-risk sports such as American football and hockey are not as popular in Japan as soccer and baseball are. The resultant low percentage of catastrophic injuries minimizes the necessity of providing on-site first aid. Finally, athletic training is still a new profession in Japan, meaning public and school officials are less aware of its availability than their American counterparts are. Athletic training in Japan is rapidly growing and seeking the best way to fit the needs of its own society.

—Yasuo Fukuda, ATC, CSCS, and Kenji Sasaki, ATC

Yasuo Fukuda is the Head Athletic Trainer at Bishop Gorman High School and the Las Vegas Gladiators Assistant Trainer; **Kenji Sasaki** is the Athletic Trainer for the Morioka High School in Morioka, Iwate, Japan, and is a Staff Athletic Trainer for the Iwate Amateur Sports Association.

---

described so far can be classified as appropriate first aid care that should be rendered by coaching personnel at the time of an injury. *The critical point to remember, however, is that the coach should not perform procedures that are clearly in the domain of medical doctors or allied health personnel such as a BOC-certified athletic trainer.* *For example, performing special tests on joints to determine injury to ligaments, attempting to reduce (put back into place) a dislocated joint, or removing stitches, a splint, or cast are clearly procedures that fall in the domain of trained medical professionals and not coaching staff members.*

REVIEW QUESTIONS

1. List the questions that must be addressed when coaches are given the charge of providing emergency care without the services of a BOC-certified athletic trainer.

2. Briefly describe both the initial check and physical exam as they relate to the initial assessment of an injured athlete.

3. When performing an initial check of an injured athlete, what is the recommended procedure for opening an airway when a neck injury is suspected?

4. *True or false:* It is imperative that the helmet be removed from an injured, unresponsive football player as soon as possible to establish an open airway.

5. What is one of the earliest clues that internal bleeding may be occurring?

6. List the essential components of the physical exam.

7. What things should the coach do prior to reaching the athlete?

8. Differentiate between a sign and a symptom.

9. *True or false:* When collecting a history from an injured athlete, questions should be kept brief and use minimal complicated terminology.

REFERENCES

American Academy of Orthopaedic Surgeons (AAOS). (2007). *First Aid, CPR, and AED* (5th ed.). Sudbury, Mass.: Jones and Bartlett Publishers.

American Academy of Orthopaedic Surgeons (AAOS). (1991). *Athletic Training and Sports Medicine* (2d ed.). Park Ridge, Ill.: American Academy of Orthopaedic Surgeons.

Andersen J, et al. (2002). National Athletic Trainers' Association position statement: Emergency planning in athletics. *J Athletic Training.* 37(1):99–104. Adapted with permission.

Ball RT. (1989). Legal responsibilities and problems. In Ryan AJ, Allman FL (eds.). *Sports Medicine* (pp. 447–489). San Diego: Academic Press.

Booher JM, Thibodeau GA. (1989). *Athletic Injury Assessment.* St. Louis: Times Mirror/Mosby.

Courson R. (1999). Example template—sports medicine emergency plan. *Sports Science. NCAA.* Available: http://www.ncaa.org/sports_sciences/emergency_plan.html.

Hargarten KM. (1993). Rapid injury assessment. *Phys Sportsmed.* 21(2):33–40.

Harris AJ. (1988). Disaster plan—a part of the game plan? *Athletic Training.* 23(1):59.

National Safety Council (NSC). (2001). *First Aid and CPR* (4th ed.). Boston: Jones and Bartlett Publishers.

Nowlan WP, Davis GA, McDonald B. (1996). Preparing for sudden emergencies. *Athletic Therapy Today.* 1(1):45–47.

Shea J. (1995). Duties of care owed to university athletes in light of Kleinecht. *J Coll Univ Law.* 21:591–614.

8

The Injury Process

MAJOR CONCEPTS

This chapter examines the complex topic of the inflammatory reaction of tissues to trauma. It begins with an overview of the types of tissues involved in sports injuries, followed by a detailed, phase-by-phase description of the process of inflammation, which includes the acute, resolution, and regeneration/repair phases. It is critical that coaching personnel grasp the basic physiology of this process to better understand the recommended procedures for treating inflammation. Treatment can include ice application, compression, and elevation as well as the administration of therapeutic heat (hot packs, ultrasound) and pharmacologic agents (anti-inflammatories) if recommended by the attending physician. This chapter concludes with a discussion of the role of exercise in the rehabilitation process.

http://health.jbpub.com/book/concepts/5e

The web site for this book offers many useful tools and is a great source for supplementary information for both students and instructors.

Visit the site at
http://health.jbpub.com/book/concepts/5e
to link to the following organizations and sites:

- The PharmInfoNet
- The MCW Healthlink

The Physics of Sports Injury

The human body consists of many different types of tissue, each serving a specific purpose. Some are highly specialized; for example, the retina of the eye contains tissue that is sensitive to light and that is not found anywhere else in the body. Other types of tissue are distributed throughout the body. **Connective tissue,** for example, is the most common type in the body (Cailliet, 1977). Included in this category are ligaments, retinaculum, joint capsules, bone, cartilage, fascia, and tendons. Cailliet (1977) classified other general categories of tissue as epithelial (for protection, secretion, and absorption), muscular (for contraction), and nervous (for touch and conductivity). Because both connective and musculoskeletal tissue comprise a significant portion of all tissues in the body, it is no surprise that they are commonly involved in sports injuries. Existing research substantiates this: Nearly 50% of all injuries in some sports are acute in nature and involve either muscle or tendon tissue (Safran, Seaber, & Garrett, 1989).

Muscles and fascia are thought to be injured when excess tension is applied while contraction is occurring. Furthermore, it is commonly held that more injuries to muscles and fascia occur during eccentric contractions, which have been described as "the simultaneous processes of muscle contraction and stretch of the muscle-tendon unit by an extrinsic force" (Safran, Seaber, & Garrett, 1989). Tendons are extremely strong structures able to withstand stresses ranging from 8,700 to 18,000 pounds per square inch. Yet, activities such as running and jumping may generate forces in excess of these physiologic limits (Curwin & Stanish, 1984). Research has demonstrated that, with respect to strains, the distal musculotendinous junction (MTJ) is usually the site of failure (Safran, Seaber, & Garrett, 1989). As of yet, no scientific explanation has surfaced explaining why the majority of strains occur at this region. More research into the specific causes of such injuries is warranted because it has been well documented that, of all soft-tissue injuries related to sports, musculotendinous strains are the most common (Taylor et al., 1993).

The Mechanical Forces of Injury

Three types of forces can affect connective tissues such as tendons. They are tensile, compressive, and shear (Figure 8.1). Tendons are designed to resist tensile forces. They are less effective when subjected to shear forces and are poorly designed to deal with compressive forces. Conversely, bone tissue is designed to absorb compressive forces, but it is less effective against tensile

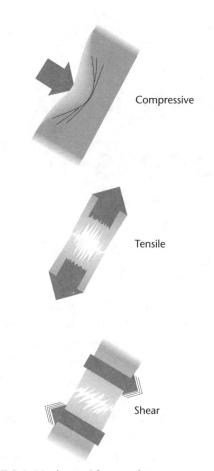

FIGURE 8.1 Mechanical forces of injury.

and shear forces (Curwin & Stanish, 1984). Ligament tissue, like that of tendons, is best suited to resist tensile forces while being more vulnerable to shear and compressive mechanisms.

Regardless of tissue type, each has a limit to how much force it can withstand. This limit has been referred to as the critical force (Nigg & Bobbert, 1990). The critical force value varies for each type of tissue in the body. Even within the same type of tissue, the critical force value may vary owing to changes in the tissue itself. For example, it has been reported that factors such as age, temperature, skeletal maturity, gender, and body weight can affect the mechanical properties of ligaments (Akeson, Amiel, & Woo, 1986).

The Physiology of Sports Injury
The Inflammatory Process

Whenever tissues are damaged as a result of an injury, the body reacts quickly with a predictable sequence of physiologic actions designed to repair the involved tissues. Regardless of what tissue has been injured, the body's initial response to **trauma** is inflammation, commonly referred to as swelling. This process begins during the first few minutes following the injury. The normal signs and symptoms of inflammation include swelling, pain, reddening of the skin (known as **erythema**), and an increase in the temperature of the area involved (AAOS, 1991).

The inflammatory process has been described as consisting of several specific stages. It begins with the acute phase, is followed by the resolution phase, and ends with the regeneration and repair phase (Lachmann, 1988). Each serves a specific purpose, and all are essential to proper repair of the structures involved.

Acute Inflammatory Phase

When tissues such as ligaments, tendons, or bones are damaged as a result of trauma, millions of cells are destroyed. Initially, the blood flow into the area is reduced (**vasoconstriction**); however, after only a few minutes this is followed by an increased blood flow (**vasodilation**). The mechanical force of the injury usually results in damage to a variety of soft tissues, including the blood vessels. As a result, the sudden increase in blood flow into the interstitial ("between the cells") spaces results in the formation of a hematoma. *Dorland's Pocket Medical Dictionary* (1977) defines hematoma as a "localized collection of extravasated blood"; it represents an important step in the inflammatory process. A hematoma can develop quickly because during the acute phase of an injury, blood flow may increase 10 times over normal (Lachmann, 1988). The clotting and cessation of blood flow distal to the site of injury result in a diminished blood flow to the tissues surrounding the primary area of injury. This reduction or, in some cases, cessation of blood flow to otherwise healthy tissue results in cell death and membrane disruption resulting from lack of adequate oxygen supply, known as "secondary hypoxic injury" (Knight, 1976). Secondary hypoxic injury involves additional cellular breakdown and subsequent release of chemicals from within an intracellular structure known as the lysosome. Lysosomes contain powerful enzymes that, when released, hasten the breakdown of cellular structure (degradation effect). In addition, other chemicals are released that affect neighboring cells, causing changes in nearby capillaries (vasodilation and vascular permeability effect) or signaling the need for scavenger cells to migrate to the injured area (chemotactic effect).

Three specific groups of chemicals have been identified as being active during the acute phase of the inflammatory response. They are degenerative enzymes (cellular breakdown), vasoactive substances (vasodila-

tors), and chemotactic factors (attracting other types of cells) (Fick & Johnson, 1993).

Histamine, a powerful inflammatory chemical, is released from a number of different types of cells, resulting in short-term vasodilation and increased vascular permeability. An enzyme known as Hageman factor (XIIa) is carried in the blood, and under the conditions of tissue damage it becomes active. The Hageman factor induces a number of localized changes in the region of damage. The complement system is then activated; this includes a variety of chemically similar structures that play major roles in the inflammatory reaction as well as assist in attracting other cellular structures into the area. This process of attracting cells such as **leukocytes** (white blood cells) is known as chemotaxis and is essential to the process of inflammation. The Hageman factor is also responsible for the manufacture of another powerful inflammatory chemical, **bradykinin.** Bradykinin affects the vasculature by increasing vascular permeability. In addition, bradykinin triggers the release of **prostaglandins,** which are among the most powerful chemicals in the human body (Wilkerson, 1985). Prostaglandins have a number of effects in the damaged area, including vasodilation, increased vascular permeability, and pain, as well as some related to the clotting mechanism (Lachmann, 1988).

---

connective tissue The most common tissue in the body; includes ligaments, bones, retinaculum, joint capsules, cartilage, fascia, and tendons.

trauma Wound or injury.

erythema Swelling and red discoloration of the skin.

vasoconstriction Decrease in the diameter of a blood vessel resulting in a decreased blood flow.

vasodilation Increase in the diameter of a blood vessel resulting in an increased blood flow.

histamine Powerful inflammatory chemical that causes an increase in vascular permeability as well as vasodilation.

leukocytes White blood cells.

bradykinin Inflammatory chemical released when tissues are damaged; it results in increased pain in the area and may play a role in the production of other inflammatory chemicals such as prostaglandins.

prostaglandins Perhaps some of the most powerful chemicals produced within the body. Related to the inflammatory process, they cause a variety of effects including vasodilation, increased vascular permeability, pain, fever, and clotting.

Physiologically, several chemicals conspire to cause an increase in vascular permeability. This allows large structures—plasma proteins, platelets, and leukocytes (primarily neutrophils)—to pass out of capillaries and into the damaged tissue (Wilkerson, 1985). By way of **phagocytosis** (cell eating), leukocytes dispose of damaged cells and tissue debris. The number of neutrophils in the damaged area can increase greatly in the first few hours of acute inflammation—to as high as four to five times the normal levels (Guyton, 1986). Neutrophils arrive quickly to the site of injury; however, they live for only a short time period (approximately 7 hours) and have no means of reproduction. When neutrophils expire, they release chemicals that attract a second type of leukocyte known as a macrophage. Macrophages also consume cellular debris via the process of phagocytosis. However, unlike neutrophils, macrophages can live for months and do have the ability to reproduce (Knight, 1995).

Another important chemical mediator of the acute inflammatory process is **arachidonic acid,** which is the product of the interaction between enzymes supplied by leukocytes and phospholipids derived from the membranes of destroyed cells (AAOS, 1991). Arachidonic acid serves as the catalyst for a series of reactions that yield a variety of substances, including leukotrienes, which play a role in the inflammatory phase by attracting leukocytes to the damaged area.

In essence, the entire acute inflammatory phase results in a walling off of the damaged area from the rest of the body—along with the formation of a mass of cellular debris, enzymes, and chemicals that serves to clean up the destroyed structures while also providing the necessary components for tissue repair. The acute inflammatory phase of injury lasts up to 3 to 4 days (Arnheim, 1989), unless aggravated by additional trauma, as happens when an athlete returns to participation too soon after injury.

Resolution (Healing) Phase

As previously stated, in the absence of further irritation or trauma, the acute inflammatory phase usually ends in 3 to 4 days after the initial injury. At this time, the earliest steps in tissue repair begin to occur, with the migration into the area of specialized cells, including polymorphs and monocytes (both specialized forms of leukocytes) as well as histocytes (a type of macrophage). These cells begin the process of breaking down the cellular debris, setting the stage for generation of new tissue. The stage is then set for the final phase of the inflammatory process—regeneration and repair.

Regeneration and Repair

With the exception of bones, connective tissues of the body heal themselves by forming scar tissue, which begins to form as early as 3 to 4 days after the injury. This process begins with the migration into the area of fibroblasts. According to *Dorland's Pocket Medical Dictionary* (1977), **fibroblasts** are immature, fiber-producing cells of connective tissue that can mature into one of several different cell types. Fibroblasts become active at this time, producing collagen fibers as well as proteoglycans (protein macromolecules), which help retain water in the tissues.

This is particularly important in tissues such as articular cartilage, which act much like a sponge when exposed to fluids in joints.

The circulatory system, specifically the damaged capillaries, begins to repair itself in just a few days after the initial injury. This process, known technically as **angiogenesis**, involves the actual formation of new capillaries, which interconnect to form new vessels.

With the formation of a new vascular supply, the new tissue is able to continue maturing, a process that may last up to 4 months. Scar tissue, under ideal conditions, can be 95% as strong as original tissue; it may, however, achieve considerably less strength, perhaps as much as 30% less (AAOS, 1991). A certain amount of stress is helpful to the new tissue in that it encourages the new collagen fibers to form in parallel lines, a much stronger configuration. Appropriate rehabilitative exercises are critical to this process. Figure 8.2 is a diagrammatic representation of the sequence of steps in the inflammatory process.

Bone injuries heal in a similar fashion to soft tissues; however, specialized cells known as osteoclasts migrate to the region of injury and remove destroyed cells as well as other debris. Specialized fibroblasts known as osteoblasts migrate to the injured area from adjacent periosteum and bone. In addition, new osteoblasts are manufactured on a large scale in the same region (Guyton, 1986). The function of the osteoblasts is to develop a zone of collagen and cartilage that is vascularized; this is known as a callus. A callus fills the space between the fractured bone ends and can be seen quite clearly on a standard X-ray photograph (Figure 8.3). The callus is not of sufficient strength to substitute for the original bone; however, through a process of maturation it becomes fully functional bone. With the majority of fractures, some type of immobilization will be required, usually in the form of a splint or a plaster or synthetic cast. In severe fractures, surgical placement of appliances such as plates and screws may be necessary.

Pain and Acute Injury

Although inflammation is often the most visible aspect of an acute injury, from the athlete's perspective, pain is often the biggest immediate problem. It is important to remember that although everyone has experienced pain associated with injury, everyone copes with pain differently, and further, pain is as much psychological (emotional) as it is physiological (tissue damage) (Thomas, 1997). As a physiological phenomenon, pain is essentially the result of sensory input received through the nervous system that indicates the location of the damage.

When damage occurs to tissues, the result is an alteration of the normal homeostasis of the structures involved. It is the process of altered homeostasis that triggers the pain response, resulting in sensory nerve receptors (afferents) transmitting impulses to the central nervous system (CNS). When pain is the result of external forces, impulses travel on relatively slow nerve fibers known as nociceptive C fibers. These fibers are labeled as slow because their conducting velocity is comparably slower than other afferent nerve fibers, such as those for the sense of touch and temperature. The nociceptive fibers are slower because of two primary factors: First, they are smaller in diameter than other afferent nerves, thus limiting the volume of information they can carry at any given time. Second, unlike most nerve cells, they have little or no fat in their bodies. It is the fat, known as myelination, that is responsible for substantially increasing conduction velocities of the impulses traveling from the periphery to the CNS. Myelination acts as an insulator that tends to help maintain high velocities of resultant stimuli.

The speed of nerve conduction is important and plays a primary role in the effective treatment of pain. As afferent messages are sent to the CNS they are "ranked" based on the number of impulses received per unit of time. As such, messages with the highest velocities receive priority status by the CNS. For example, if a pain message (relatively slow) and a touch message (relatively fast) reach the CNS simultaneously, the touch message is given higher priority. As a result, the CNS first recognizes the touch message, with the pain message being given a lower priority. This can be demonstrated by noting that more often than not, when a person suffers a blow, such as hitting one's head on something, the first reaction is to rub the area. The process of rubbing the injured area stimulates the fast velocity touch receptors, thus blocking the pain signals. This explanation of pain is based on the gate control theory of pain, which was first developed in the 1960s and published in the journal *Science* (Melzack & Wall, 1965). The gate control theory of pain is only one possible explanation of the pain process, and it should be noted that research continues regarding our understanding of pain.

phagocytosis Destruction of injurious cells or particles by phagocytes (white blood cells).

arachidonic acid Chemical released when cells are damaged that serves as a precursor to the formation of other inflammatory chemicals including leukotrienes and prostaglandins.

fibroblast Immature, fiber-producing cells of connective tissue that can mature into one of several different cell types.

angiogenesis Formation of capillaries, which interconnect, resulting in the formation of new vessels.

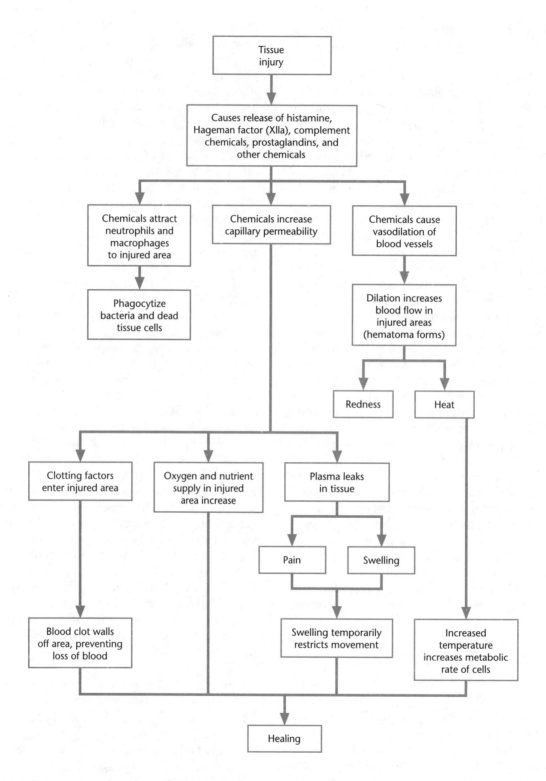

FIGURE 8.2 The inflammatory process. (Source: Adapted from Chiras DD. 1999. *Human Biology: Health, Homeostasis, and the Environment*, 3d ed. Sudbury, Mass.: Jones and Bartlett Publishers.)

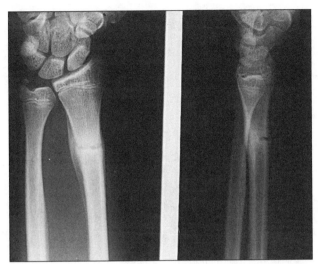

FIGURE 8.3 Callus forming around a fracture of the distal radius.

Sports medicine personnel can use a variety of **modalities** to treat pain associated with injury. Shown in Table 8.1 are the commonly used modalities that take advantage of the gate control theory to control pain.

Perhaps as important as understanding the precise mechanisms of pain is understanding how each athlete responds to pain. Pain has been defined as "the perception of an uncomfortable stimulus or the presentation or response to that stimulus by the individual" (Thomas, 1997). As such, it must be remembered that each individual responds to pain differently. It is essential to the process of the initial evaluation of an injury to be familiar with the athlete's typical response to pain. An athlete with an extremely high pain tolerance may underestimate the severity of an injury; conversely, an athlete with low pain tolerance may grossly exaggerate the severity of an injury. In essence, pain may not be a useful indicator of the severity of an injury. When a coach must make a decision about the significance of an

injury, it is best to err on the conservative side and, when in doubt, refer the athlete to medical personnel. Pain may also be thought of as the athlete's friend, in that it serves as a mechanism to reduce the athlete's activity level until adequate tissue healing has occurred. It is critical to remember that the treatment of pain should be the domain of sports medicine personnel. Coaches, athletes, and parents should not treat the pain associated with an injury to enable an athlete to return to participation.

Intervention Procedures

Although it is clear that the acute inflammatory process is a necessary component of healing, athletes, coaches, and even many sports medicine personnel typically think of inflammation as something to be avoided at all cost. This sentiment is so common in the sports community that the variety of suggested first aid treatments for acute injuries is overwhelming. Curiously, even today, no clear, concise set of criteria has been universally accepted in the sports medicine community regarding first aid treatment of acute soft-tissue injury. Suggested treatments of inflammation include the application of **cryotherapy** (therapeutic use of cold), such as crushed-ice packs, ice cups applied via massage, ice-water baths, commercially available chemical cold packs, and aerosol coolants (ethyl chloride). After the acute inflammatory phase has passed, usually 48 to 120 hours following injury, **thermotherapy** (therapeutic use of heat)—including commercially available hydrocollator packs, warm and moist towels, and ultrasound diathermy—may be appropriate. It should be noted, however, that use of modalities such as ultrasound should always be done under the direct supervision of trained allied health personnel such as a Board of Certification, Inc. (BOC)–certified athletic trainer, physical therapist, or physician.

In addition to cold and heat therapy, pharmacologic agents—drugs designed to prevent swelling (**anti-inflammatories**) or drugs designed to prevent pain (**analgesics**)—are often used to treat the inflammatory

TABLE 8.1	
COMMON MODALITIES USED TO TREAT PAIN	
Modality	**Afferent Nerve Stimulated**
Ice	Temperature receptors
Heat	Temperature receptors
Electrical stimulation	Touch receptors
Massage	Touch receptors
Prophylactic wrapping	Touch and proprioceptive receptors

modalities Physical agents that help create an optimal healing environment.

cryotherapy Therapeutic use of cold.

thermotherapy Therapeutic use of heat.

anti-inflammatories Drugs designed to prevent swelling. Two basic categories are currently in use: steroidal and nonsteroidal.

analgesic Agent that relieves pain without causing a complete loss of sensation.

response. The majority of these drugs must be prescribed by a medical doctor and represent treatment beyond the training of coaching personnel. However, there are anti-inflammatory drugs, such as aspirin, that are available over the counter (OTC) and are often effective for minor acute injuries. Caution should be exercised, however, particularly when the coach is dealing with athletes under the age of 18; he or she should consult with parents prior to recommending any sort of pharmacologic agent.

Experts agree that some sort of treatment, beyond simple rest, be applied during both the acute inflammatory phase as well as in the later stages of healing. Available research supports the use of modalities such as ice, compression, and elevation as well as pharmacologic agents such as anti-inflammatory drugs during the acute phase of the injury process. Likewise, clinical evidence strongly supports the use of modalities such as ice massage, ice immersion, therapeutic heat (moist hot packs, whirlpool, paraffin) as well as more sophisticated approaches such as ultrasound, diathermy (radio-frequency energy), and electrotherapies, transcutaneous electrical nerve stimulation (TENS), neuromuscular electrical stimulation (NMES), interferential stimulation (IFS), and galvanic stimulation. Application of any of these modalities may be regulated by medical practice acts in each state and therefore should only beapplied by qualified allied health personnel under the direct supervision of a physician and in the parameters stipulated by the practice act.

Cryotherapy and Thermotherapy

It has been found that changing the temperature of injured tissues can have dramatic effects on the physiologic activities of inflammation and healing. During the first few minutes of the acute inflammatory phase, direct application of cold (generally in the form of crushed ice) may reduce vasodilation, thereby reducing the amount of initial swelling. Additionally, in the case of an injury to an extremity, rest, ice, compression, and elevation (RICE) are all extremely helpful and effective. The application of RICE is a standard first aid procedure for injuries such as sprains, strains, dislocations, contusions, and fractures.

Though many variations on application exist, experts recommend that the most effective way of applying cold to the body is a plastic bag filled with crushed ice (Figure 8.4). Nothing exotic need be used—just a simple sandwich bag with some type of closure is most effective. Crushed ice is made relatively inexpensively by ice machines, which are a good investment for a school athletic department. Crushed ice can even be purchased prior to a game or practice session and be stored in a cooler for later use. Commercially available chemical

FIGURE 8.4 Bags filled with crushed ice are the most convenient way of applying cold to an injury.

cold packs and aerosol sprays (ethyl chloride) are less effective than crushed ice is and can even be dangerous in some situations. Research has shown that the risk of **frostbite** during the application of a bag of crushed ice is minimal. Human tissues freeze at around 25°F; a bag of crushed ice reaches a low temperature of only 32°F. It is recommended that the ice bag be left in place for 30-minutes, then be removed. If medical help is delayed for more than 30 minutes, allow the injury to rewarm for a period of 2 hours; then, follow up with another 30-minute application of cold if needed (Knight, 1985).

Compression is best achieved by using a commercially available elastic wrap (Figure 8.5). They come in a variety of sizes, ranging in widths that will accommodate almost any anatomic site and body size. It is best to place the ice bag directly against the skin with the elastic wrap secured over the bag. Wrap in a closed spiral fashion, starting distally and finishing proximally. Care must be taken not to make the wrap excessively tight because this could compromise circulation. Always check the pulse distal to the wrap after it is in place. You should be able to easily slip two fingers under the elastic after it is secured. Leave the wrap in place until the injury is seen by medical personnel.

Elevation of the injury is self-explanatory; however, some precautions are necessary. When elevating an injury to the lower extremity, make sure adjacent joints are supported with padding. Elevation during sleep can be accomplished simply by raising the foot end of the bed a few inches off the floor.

Generally there is some sort of delay in transporting the participant from the playing field to the sideline or perhaps to a treatment area a considerable distance

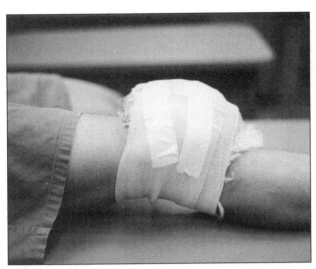

FIGURE 8.5 Elastic wrap provides a convenient method of compression.

from the site of injury. The period immediately after the injury has occurred is generally considered to be the best time to evaluate the extent of injury. Coaching personnel should avoid the temptation, however, to perform medical tests, such as ligament laxity assessments. As described in Chapter 7, such testing should be performed only by properly trained medical personnel such as a physician, BOC-certified athletic trainer, or sports physical therapist. When such tests are performed improperly, the injury may be aggravated.

Knight (1985) has reported that the application of ice to an injury during the acute inflammatory phase helps decrease the recovery time. This occurs because tissue cooling reduces the metabolic activity of the cells in the injured area, thereby reducing their need for oxygen. Consequently, the cells are better able to survive the initial period of inflammation when oxygen is in short supply. This sparing of cells contributes to a smaller collection of debris in the region of the injury, thereby promoting an earlier repair phase. In essence, the immediate application of ice helps reduce the severity of the secondary hypoxic injury, as described earlier in this chapter. Finally, application of cold provides an analgesic effect and reduces muscle spasm. These two effects allow the athlete to engage in therapeutic activities more effectively.

Thermotherapeutic agents such as moist heat packs or ultrasound may also have a beneficial effect on soft-tissue injury. However, available research is unanimous that such treatments should never be applied during the acute inflammatory phase. By heating the tissue during the early phases of the injury, the metabolic activity of the inflammatory agents will be increased, thereby resulting in an increase in inflammation (Wilkerson, 1985).

Thermotherapies may be useful during the final phases of injury repair by increasing available oxygen and stimulating vasodilation in the region of the injured tissues. In addition, heat increases local metabolic activities, including those resulting in regeneration of tissues.

Pharmacologic Agents

A wide variety of pharmacologic agents is currently available for the treatment of inflammation. Based on fundamental chemical configuration, they can be classified into two groups: steroidal and nonsteroidal anti-inflammatory drugs (NSAIDs). Both groups seem to interfere with some aspect of the inflammatory process, thereby reducing either the amount of swelling (anti-inflammatory) or pain (analgesic).

Steroidal Anti-inflammatory Drugs

Steroidal drugs are manufactured in such a way as to resemble a group of naturally occurring chemicals in the body known collectively as glucocorticoids, which are active in the body relative to the metabolism of carbohydrates, fats, and proteins. Curiously, the exact mechanism of action of steroidal drugs on the inflammatory process is not clearly understood. There is evidence that steroids lower the amount of chemicals released from intracellular lysosomes, decrease the permeability of capillaries, diminish the ability of white blood cells to phagocytize tissues, and reduce local fever (Guyton, 1986). Probably the best known of the steroidal preparations is cortisone; however, others commonly used include hydrocortisone, prednisone, prednisolone, triamcinolone, and dexamethasone.

Steroidal preparations are generally either orally ingested or injected. They may even be introduced through the skin via **phonophoresis** (using ultrasound

WHAT IF?

A parent asks you for advice on what over-the-counter drug would be best to give his daughter to help her recover from a second-degree ankle sprain. What would you suggest?

phonophoresis Introduction of ions of soluble salt into the body through ultrasound.

energy) or **iontophoresis** (using electrical current) (Fick & Johnson, 1993). Problems with steroidal chemicals involve the negative effects they have on the process of collagen formation. In essence, steroids can decrease the overall strength of the connective tissue structures in an injured region. Great care must be taken when using these powerful drugs. Discuss both the risks and benefits with the athlete prior to treatment.

Nonsteroidal Anti-inflammatory Drugs

Nonsteroidal anti-inflammatory drugs (**NSAIDs**) block specific reactions in the inflammatory process; however, they do not negatively affect collagen formation. These drugs have become extremely popular in the medical community: A reported 1.3 million prescriptions were written in 1991 (Fick & Johnson, 1993). The commonly used NSAIDs are listed in Table 8.2.

As a group, these drugs appear to block the breakdown of arachidonic acid to prostaglandin, which in turn decreases the inflammatory response to injury (AAOS, 1991). Aspirin, known chemically as acetylsalicylic acid, produces several effects—anti-inflammatory, analgesic, and **antipyretic** (reducing fever).

Though the physiologic effects of NSAIDs on inflammation are quite clear, what remains to be clarified is their effect, if any, on the healing process. Does using a particular drug in any way enhance the healing process by decreasing the healing time or by increasing the strength of the new tissue? Research to date is inconclusive; however, two studies have shed some light on both questions. Dupont, Beliveau, and Theriault (1987) reported the effects of a commonly used NSAID on the treatment of acute ankle sprains. They compared the effects of the NSAID with treatment that used ice, elevation, and taping only. The duration of the study was 28 days, and effects were evaluated on the basis of a variety of subjective criteria, including pain and the number of painful ligaments on palpation. The results indicated that a positive trend occurred in favor of the NSAID group; however, none of the trends was found to be statistically significant.

TABLE 8.2

SAMPLE NONSTEROIDAL ANTI-INFLAMMATORY DRUGS

Generic Name	Brand Name(s)	Manufacturer
Diclofenac, misoprostol	Arthrotec	GD Searle LLC, Chicago, IL
Celecoxib	Celebrex	GD Searle LLC
Diclofenac	Voltaren	Novartis Pharmaceuticals Corp, East Hanover, NJ
Diclofenac	Cataflam	Novartis Pharmaceuticals Corp
Diflunisal	Dolobid	Merck & Co, Inc, West Point, PA
Etodolac	Lodine	Wyeth-Ayerst International Inc, Madison, NJ
Flurbiprofen	Ansaid	Pharmacia & Upjohn Co, Kalamazoo, MI
Ibuprofen	Motrin	McNeil-PPC, Fort Washington, PA
	Advil	Wyeth, Madison, NJ
Indomethacin	Indocin	Merck & Co, Inc
Ketoprofen	Orudis	Rhône-Poulenc Rorer New Zealand Ltd, Auckland, New Zealand
Ketorolac	Toradol	Roche Pharmaceuticals, Nutley, NJ
Nabumetone	Relafen	GlaxoSmithKline, Research Triangle Park, NC
Naproxen	Naprosyn	Roche Pharmaceuticals
	Aleve	Bayer, Morristown, NJ
Oxaprozin	Daypro	GD Searle LLC
Piroxicam	Feldene	Pfizer Inc, New York, NY
Rofecoxib	Vioxx	Merck & Co, Inc
Salsalate	Disalcid	3M Pharmaceuticals, Northridge, CA
Sulindac	Clinoril	Merck & Co, Inc

Source: Miller MG, Weiler JM, Baker R, Collins J D'Alonzo G. (2005). National Athletic Trainers' Association position statement: Management of asthma in athletes. *Athletic Training.* 40(3):224–245. Reprinted with permission.

Dahners and colleagues (1988) aspired to determine if a commonly used NSAID would in any way affect the healing process of damaged ligaments. They studied damaged medial collateral ligaments in rats and compared the drug-treated group with a nondrug group. Their conclusion was that the drug did not increase the strength of the ligament after the normal time for complete healing, which was 21 days. Curiously, it was found that the drug did seem to decrease the time required for the healing ligaments to get stronger when compared with subjects not receiving the drug. This finding could have significant implications for athletes, particularly those who feel the need to decrease injury recovery time. However, it is important to remember that this study involved nonhuman subjects; consequently, implications for athletes must be evaluated in that context.

Until more conclusive research is available, it would appear that the best approach to treating the majority of soft-tissue injuries involves the application of RICE during the acute inflammatory phase, followed by a combination of RICE, prescribed pharmacologic agent(s), and prescribed and properly supervised rehabilitative exercises. From a legal and ethical standpoint, the coach or physical educator should provide only initial first aid to any soft-tissue injury and then refer the athlete to the appropriate medical authority. Nonmedical personnel should avoid prescribing any type of medication, even an OTC drug such as aspirin. It is always best to have any injury seen by medical personnel before further treatment (in any form) is given.

The Role of Exercise Rehabilitation

It may seem paradoxical, but the most effective treatment for many sports injuries, especially those involving soft tissues, is physical activity. Obviously, asking an athlete to run on a sprained ankle is incorrect, but a properly constructed and supervised exercise regime can have a dramatic impact on the healing process (Figure 8.6). Research indicates that rehabilitative exercise can exert a variety of positive effects on collagen formation (AAOS, 1991). Because **collagen** is a major constituent of tendon and ligament tissues, exercise is a logical form of treatment. According to Knight, exercise is essential during the healing process for two reasons. First, exercise results in increased circulation with a concomitant increase in oxygen supply to the healing tissue. Second, exercise stresses the healing tissue and in essence "guides" the proper structuring of collagen (Knight, 1995). It is important to remember, however, that although exercise is essential to proper tissue healing, the old saying "too much too soon" is worth remembering during the rehabilitation process.

At the very least, the process of collagen formation and tissue regeneration will require 2 to 3 weeks (Page, 1995). Further, after the final phase of healing the athlete should, when appropriate, have the area properly protected with adhesive taping, wrapping, or bracing. Decisions concerning any return to participation should be made by a medical professional with experience in sports injuries. Coaches should avoid returning an athlete to participation too early just because he or she may be critical to the team's success.

Any injury severe enough to warrant a medical diagnosis should be treated with a comprehensive program of exercise rehabilitation. Such a program must consist of essential components and must be planned by professionals with the appropriate training—either a BOC-certified athletic trainer or a physical therapist who has sports medicine training. Responsibility for implementation and supervision of the exercise program usually falls on the coach or physical educator. Thus, communication between the athlete, coach, and medical personnel is essential for any program to be effective.

Rehabilitative exercise, often called therapeutic exercise, is a four-phase process consisting of categories of exercise based on a continuum of severity and recovery. If the athlete's injury is severe, the initial exercise protocol may make the athlete a passive participant; a therapist actually moves the injured extremity through a series of passive exercises. The benefits are the reestablishment of a normal range of motion (ROM) as well as reduction of

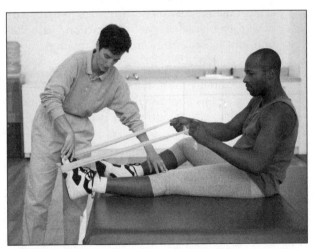

FIGURE 8.6 Exercise can be the most effective treatment for many athletes who have sustained sports injuries.

iontophoresis Using an electrical current to drive a chemical directly through the skin.

NSAID Nonsteroidal anti-inflammatory drugs.

antipyretic Agent that relieves or reduces fever.

collagen The major protein of connective tissue.

swelling and muscle spasm. As the injury improves, the next phase of exercise becomes active assisted. During this phase, the athlete becomes a working partner in the exercise process, making a voluntary effort to move the injured joint while being assisted by a therapist. The benefits of this phase are improved ROM and increased muscle strength. The next phase in the rehabilitation process is active exercise. At this point the athlete continues moving the joint through a full ROM, using gravity as resistance to stimulate development of muscle strength. The important aspect of this phase is that the therapist merely supervises the activity; no physical assistance is given to the athlete. The final phase of the recovery program is known as resistive: External resistance is applied to the joint movements. This can be done via manual resistance provided by the therapist, through the use of resistive exercise machines, or even with free weights. The primary objective of this phase is to improve the strength of the muscles surrounding the injured area to protect the injured area from future injury.

Injury rehabilitation should be considered an ongoing process: Injury-specific exercise should be a permanent component in the total training and conditioning program of the athlete. Without such an approach the likelihood of reinjury is high in many cases. The coach must communicate with the appropriate members of the athletic health care team—athletic trainer, physical therapist, and/or physician— to plan and implement an effective program of therapeutic exercise. (For more information see Appendix 6.)

REVIEW QUESTIONS

1. During what type of muscular contraction do the majority of muscle and/or fascia injuries occur?

2. *True or false:* The proximal musculotendinous junction has been found to be the most common site for injuries.

3. List the three types of mechanical forces that can cause soft-tissue injury.

4. Define *critical force*.

5. Describe the major steps that occur during the acute inflammatory phase of an injury—with particular emphasis on vasoconstriction, vasodilation, and subsequent hematoma formation.

6. Define *chemotaxis*.

7. Describe briefly the group of chemicals known as prostaglandins and discuss some of their known physiologic effects during the acute phase of an injury.

8. Briefly describe the overall purpose of the acute inflammatory phase of an injury.

9. What is the typical duration in hours of the acute inflammatory phase?

10. List the types of cells that migrate into the injured area during the early part of the resolution phase.

11. What type of tissue does not heal itself with scar tissue?

12. What are fibroblasts?

13. What is angiogenesis?

14. What is the relationship between a bony formation known as a callus and the healing of a fracture?

15. Describe the mechanism for the secondary hypoxic effect as described by Knight.

16. What is the effect of ice application on the secondary hypoxic effect?

17. *True or false:* Nerve messages sent to the CNS are ranked based on the number of impulses received per unit of time.

18. Explain how rubbing an injured area reduces the pain perception.

19. Explain the gate control theory of pain.

20. Explain briefly the physiologic effects of the application of ice, compression, and elevation on acute inflammation.

21. What is an easy and effective way of applying cold and compression simultaneously to an injury?

22. What is the recommended duration of ice application for the treatment of acute inflammation?

23. At what temperature do human tissues freeze?

24. At what point during the process of injury repair can thermotherapies be useful?

25. Differentiate between steroidal and nonsteroidal anti-inflammatory pharmacologic agents.

26. What is the mode of action of NSAIDs with respect to the acute inflammatory phase of an injury?

27. Give a definition of the acronym *OTC*.

28. Give a brief explanation of the four types of therapeutic exercise outlined in the chapter—passive, active assisted, active, and resistive.

REFERENCES

Akeson WH, Amiel D, Woo SL-Y. (1986). Cartilage and ligament: Physiology and repair processes. In Nicholas JA, Hershman EB (eds.). *The Lower Extremity and Spine in Sports Medicine* (pp. 3–41). St. Louis: Mosby.

American Academy of Orthopaedic Surgeons (AAOS). (1991). *Athletic Training and Sports Medicine* (2d ed.). Park Ridge, Ill.: American Academy of Orthopaedic Surgeons.

Arnheim DD. (1989). *Modern Principles of Athletic Training* (7th ed.). St. Louis: Times Mirror/Mosby, pp. 198–231.

Cailliet R. (1977). *Soft-Tissue Pain and Disability.* Philadelphia: F. A. Davis.

Curwin S, Stanish WD. (1984). *Tendinitis: Its Etiology and Treatment.* Lexington, Mass.: D. C. Heath and Company.

Dahners LE, et al. (1988). The effect of a nonsteroidal anti-inflammatory drug on healing of ligaments. *Am J Sports Med.* 16:641–646.

Dorland's Pocket Medical Dictionary. (1977). Philadelphia: W. B. Saunders.

Dupont M, Beliveau P, Theriault G. (1987). The efficacy of anti-inflammatory medication in the treatment of the acutely sprained ankle. *Am J Sports Med.* 15:41–45.

Fick DS, Johnson JS. (1993). Resolving inflammation in active patients. *Phys Sportsmed.* 21:55–63.

Guyton AC. (1986). *Textbook of Medical Physiology.* Philadelphia: W. B. Saunders.

Knight KL. (1976). Effects of hypothermia on inflammation and swelling. *Athletic Training.* 11:7–10.

Knight KL. (1985). *Cryotherapy: Theory, Technique, and Physiology.* Chattanooga, Tenn.: Chattanooga Corp.

Knight KL. (1995). *Cryotherapy in Sport Injury Management.* Champaign, Ill.: Human Kinetics.

Lachmann S. (1988). *Soft-Tissue Injuries in Sport.* Oxford, England: Blackwell Scientific Publications.

Melzack R, Wall PD. (1965). Pain mechanisms, a new theory. *Science.* 150: 971–979.

Nigg BM, Bobbert M. (1990). On the potential of various approaches in load analysis to reduce the frequency of sports injuries. *J Biomech.* 23:3–12.

Page P. (1995). Pathophysiology of acute exercise-induced muscular injury: Clinical implications. *J Athletic Training.* 30:29–34.

Safran MR, Seaber AV, Garrett WE. (1989). Warm-up and muscular injury prevention—an update. *Sports Med.* 8:239–249.

Taylor DC, et al. (1993). Experimental muscle-strain injury—early functional deficits and the increased risk of reinjury. *Am J Sports Med.* 21:190–193.

Thomas CL (ed.). (1997). *Taber's Cyclopedic Medical Dictionary* (18th ed.). Philadelphia: F. A. Davis.

Wilkerson GB. (1985). Inflammation in connective tissue: Etiology and management. *Athletic Training.* 20:298–301.

9

Injuries to the Head, Neck, and Face

MAJOR CONCEPTS

Injuries to the head, neck, and face present some of the most perplexing problems associated with sports injury. This chapter begins with a review of the gross anatomy of the head, neck, and face. It goes on to describe the central nervous system, giving special attention to the structures often involved in head and neck injuries, along with data on the incidence and severity of such injuries in a variety of sports. It provides a classification system for cerebral concussion that lists clear, concise signs and symptoms for each category and also discusses more severe forms of head injury, including intracranial injuries. Information on second impact syndrome is presented, along with recommendations on how best to avoid this potentially lethal problem. In addition, this chapter contains a special section on the helmeted football player that includes guidelines on the initial treatment of suspected head injuries.

Next, the chapter outlines major mechanisms of cervical spine injuries, followed by a discussion of the various types of injuries that can occur, including simple sprains and strains, as well as more severe forms such as disk herniations and vertebral fractures. In addition, it presents information regarding the mechanisms and signs and symptoms of brachial plexus injuries. As with head injuries, it features guidelines for the initial treatment of suspected injuries to the cervical spine in an easy-to-use format.

The remainder of the chapter deals with recognition and care of injuries to the face, teeth, eyes, nose, and ears.

http://health.jbpub.com/book/concepts/5e

The web site for this book offers many useful tools and is a great source for supplementary information for both students and instructors.

Visit the site at
http://health.jbpub.com/book/concepts/5e
to link to the following organizations and sites:

- University of Central Florida—Psychology Electronic Teaching Source
- University of Geneva School of Dentistry—The Dentaltrauma Server
- The American Academy of Opthalmology
- The University of Washington—Department of Otolaryngology/Head and Neck Surgery

In a practical sense, the head may be considered as a single structure with a variety of functions. These include housing the brain; providing sockets for the eyes and openings for the ears, nose, and mouth; and providing a site of attachment for the vertebral column. The neck serves as the mechanism for attachment of the head to the body. Though this arrangement works well for the day-to-day functions of our species, in the context of sports such an anatomic arrangement provides significant potential for a multitude of injuries. The brain, consisting of neural tissues that are easily damaged, must be protected, especially when one considers the potential forces involved in many different sports and activities.

Skull

The skull, which consists of 8 cranial bones and 14 facial bones, is a complex structure. The brain (encephalon) is housed in the cranium and is afforded considerable protection via an ingenious system of bony and soft-tissue structures.

The bones of the cranium (Figure 9.1) form a rigid housing for the brain and are held together by specialized articulations known as suture joints.

Curiously, the suture joints of the cranium are not rigid at birth; in fact, they do not complete their ossification process until human beings are between 20 and 30 years old (Gray, 1985). However, the anatomic arrangement of the cranial bones and their respective joints provides a protective outer structure for the brain.

The soft-tissue structures that serve a protective function include the five layers of tissues of the scalp. These are illustrated in Figure 9.2; they include the skin, a layer of dense connective tissue, the galea aponeurotica (essentially a broad, flat tendon), loose connective tissue, and the periosteum of the cranial bone.

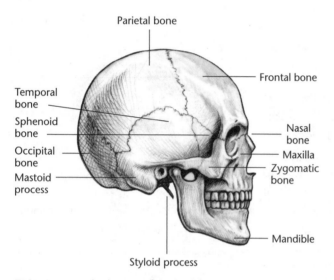

FIGURE 9.1 The bones of the human cranium.

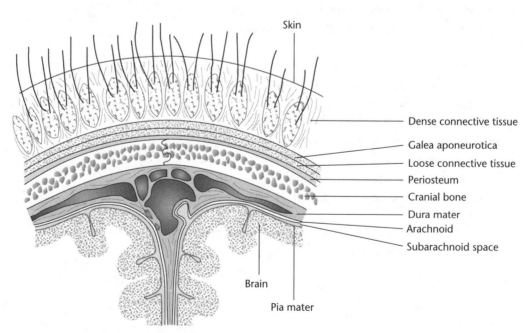

FIGURE 9.2 The human scalp: a cross section.

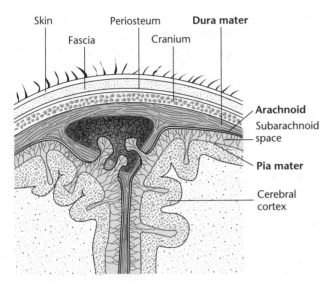

Skin Periosteum **Dura mater**

Fascia Cranium

Arachnoid
Subarachnoid
space

Pia mater

Cerebral
cortex

FIGURE 9.3 The cerebral meninges.

The Meninges

Below the cranial bones another group of soft-tissue structures can be found that protect the brain as well. These are collectively referred to as the cerebral meninges (Figure 9.3). They consist of three distinct layers of tissues located between the underside of the cranium and the surface of the brain. The outermost layer is known as the *dura mater.* It consists of tough, fibrous connective tissue that functions as periosteum to the inside surfaces of the cranial bones as well as a protective membrane to the brain (Gray, 1985). The dura mater is highly vascular, containing both arteries and veins that transport blood to and from the cranial bones. The middle meningeal layer is the *arachnoid;* compared with the dura mater, it has significantly less strength and contains no blood supply. The arachnoid is separated from the dura mater by a small amount of fluid. Below the arachnoid is the subarachnoid space containing cerebrospinal fluid (**CSF**). The purpose of CSF is to cushion the brain and spinal cord from external forces such as those encountered in collision and contact sports. The innermost meningeal layer is the *pia mater,* which is physically attached to the brain tissue and serves to provide a framework for an extensive vasculature that supplies the brain. The pia mater is a very thin, delicate membrane; like the arachnoid, it is more susceptible to trauma than the dura mater is.

The Central Nervous System

The brain (encephalon) along with the spinal cord compose the central nervous system (**CNS**). Both the brain and spinal cord are protected by the meninges as well as the bony structure of the cranium and vertebrae. The CNS tissue consists of both gray and white matter that represent two distinct types of neural tissues. The brain of an adult weighs 3 to 3.5 pounds and contains approximately 100 billion neurons (Van De Graaff, 1998). The brain consists of three basic parts: cerebrum, cerebellum, and brain stem. The cerebrum is the largest of the three and is involved in complex functions such as cognition, reasoning, and intellectual functioning. The cerebellum, located in the lower posterior portion of the cranial area, performs functions related to complex motor skills. The brain stem is located at the base of the brain and serves to connect the brain to the spinal cord.

Neural impulses travel to and from the CNS via the cranial nerves (directly from the brain) or by way of the spinal nerves exiting the spinal cord. There are 12 pairs of cranial nerves that are directly attached to the base of the brain and exit the CNS through openings (foramina) in the base of the skull. The spinal nerves are attached to either side of the spinal cord and exit the CNS at precise intervals through the intervertebral foramina of the spinal column. There are 31 pairs of spinal nerves: 8 cervical, 12 thoracic, 5 lumbar, 5 sacral, and 1 coccygeal. The cranial, spinal, and autonomic nerves compose that portion of the nervous system known as the peripheral nervous system.

The CNS receives an extensive blood supply that must remain constant for it to function. Even brief interruptions of blood flow lasting only seconds may result in loss of consciousness. Neural tissue may be destroyed when deprived of blood for only a few minutes.

The Face

The human face is composed of an outer layer of skin placed loosely over underlying bones. There are some subcutaneous muscles, cartilage, and fat deposits offering minimal protection from trauma. The facial bones consist of the maxilla (upper jaw), the right and left palatine, the right and left zygomatic, the right and left lacrimal, the right and left nasal, the right and left inferior nasal concha, the vomer, the mandible (lower jaw), and the hyoid.

Several areas around the face are especially prominent and thus prone to injury. The orbits for the eyes, particularly the supraorbital regions, are vulnerable to

CSF Cerebrospinal fluid.
CNS Central nervous system.

contusions. The nasal bones are located centrally on the face and can also receive direct blows, often resulting in fractures. The lower jaw (mandible) is subject to excessive external forces as well.

The Neck (Cervical Spine)

The bones of the neck are the seven cervical vertebrae (Figure 9.4) that provide support for the head as well as protection for the upper portion of the spinal cord. The first cervical (C-1) vertebra (atlas) articulates directly with the occipital bone to form the right and left atlanto-occipital joints. The skull and C-1 articulate as a unit with the second cervical (C-2) vertebra (axis) to form the atlantoaxial joint, which allows for rotation of the head on the neck. The remaining five cervical vertebrae become progressively larger as they approach the thoracic spine.

Head Injuries in Sports
Background Information

Although the majority of contusions to most parts of the body result in injuries that are self-correcting and without serious consequence, even relatively minor trauma to the head can result in severe, sometimes life-threatening injury. Because of the inability of brain tissue to repair itself, any loss of tissue results in some level of permanent disability. If the injury is severe enough, death can result. The possible mechanisms, types, and

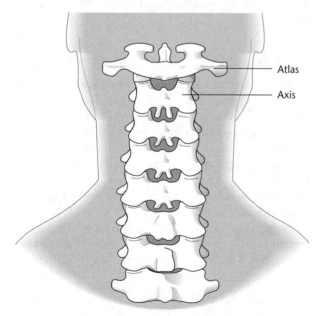

FIGURE 9.4 The cervical spine (posterior view).

severity of head injuries in sports are nearly infinite. However, significant advances in our understanding regarding head injuries in sports have been made in recent years. As a result, with appropriate education coaches can learn to recognize head injuries and render effective first aid when necessary. Although head injuries can occur in almost any sport or activity, scientific surveys have provided additional insight into which sports appear to carry a higher risk. Epidemiologic research on the incidence of head, brain, and neck injuries is ongoing, with accurate data available from relatively recent playing seasons. Guskiewicz and colleagues (2000) conducted a 3-year study of head/brain injuries in the United States among high school and collegiate football players. Overall, they estimated that there are approximately 300,000 traumatic head or brain injuries annually. In addition, they found that players sustaining a concussion had a threefold increased risk of sustaining an additional concussion when compared with their nonconcussed teammates.

When examining high school female sports/activities separately, cheerleading leads the list of those activities resulting in directly related catastrophic injuries. These deaths and injuries have been attributed to the escalation in the degree of difficulty in cheerleading routines as it has become a competitive sport. These include front and back flips, complex partner/spotter-dependent routines such as pyramids, and the use of minitrampolines (Cantu & Mueller, 1999).

In spite of these alarmingly high numbers of potentially catastrophic injuries, the most recent research available from the National Center for Catastrophic Sport Injury Research indicates that a relatively small percentage results in irreversible damage. For the 2004 football season, there were 19 direct catastrophic injuries, 4 of which resulted in deaths (Mueller & Cantu, 2006). Although this number is extremely encouraging, it must always be remembered that even one permanent neurologic injury related to head trauma is too many.

There is a multitude of descriptive classifications for head injuries. However, all can be placed into three general categories: mild head injury or concussion, intercranial hemorrhage, and skull fracture (Shultz, Houglum, & Perrin, 2000).

Mechanism of Injury

The vast majority of head injuries associated with sports involve either direct or indirect injury mechanisms. Direct mechanisms involve a blow to the head resulting in brain injury at the site of impact, known as a *coup* type of injury, as well as injury on the opposite side of the skull from the site of impact, known as a *contrecoup* type of injury. The contrecoup associated injury occurs when the head is moving and stops abruptly, for example, when a tackle is made in football, while the brain keeps moving in the skull, subsequently being compressed on the side opposite from the initial impact. Indirect mechanisms of injury involve damaging forces traveling from other areas of the body, such as blows to the face or jaw. Rapid and violent movement of the cervical spine, such as seen in whiplash injuries related to automobile accidents, may also result in indirect injuries to the brain. An understanding of these mechanisms of injury highlights the validity of the often-used cliché in sports medicine circles, "Treat every head injury as if there is a neck injury, and every neck injury as if there is also a head injury."

Concussion (Mild Head Injury)

Concussion, sometimes called *mild head injury* (MHI), has been defined by Jordan (1989) as "a clinical syndrome characterized by immediate and transient impairment of neurologic function secondary to mechanical forces." The clinical manifestations of concussion can include unconsciousness or other neurologic signs such as those listed in Time Out 9.1. In essence, any sort of external blow of sufficient magnitude can cause temporary disruption of normal neurologic function. Recent evidence suggests that in some concussions there is some level of structural damage. In addition, brain cells not destroyed remain

TIME OUT 9.1

Signs of Concussion (Mild Head Injury)

- Headache from the impact
- Dizziness
- Confusion
- Inability to quickly answer questions about orientation
- Irritability
- Poor concentration
- Pupils react to light
- Poor ability to track with the eyes
- Poor depth perception
- Ringing in the ears
- Vomiting
- Nausea
- Actions uncharacteristic of the individual

Source: Hunt V. (2000, August). Second impact heightens need for concussion management. *NATA News.* Reprinted with permission.

TABLE 9.1

EVIDENCE-BASED CANTU GRADING SYSTEM FOR CONCUSSION

Grade 1 (mild)	No loss of consciousness; post-traumatic amnesia* or postconcussion signs or symptoms lasting less than 30 minutes
Grade 2 (moderate)	Loss of consciousness lasting less than 1 minute; post-traumatic amnesia* or postconcussion signs or symptoms lasting longer than 30 minutes but less than 24 hours
Grade 3 (severe)	Loss of consciousness lasting more than 1 minute or post-traumatic amnesia* lasting longer than 24 hours; postconcussion signs or symptoms lasting longer than 7 days

*Retrograde and anterograde.
Source: Cantu, RC. (2001). Posttraumatic retrograde and anterograde amnesia. *J Athletic Training.* 36(3):244–248. Reprinted with permission.

extremely vulnerable to subsequent trauma, resulting in phenomena such as minor changes in blood flow, intracranial pressure, or anoxia (Cantu, 2001).

A variety of classification systems for cerebral concussion are currently in use; the majority base the level of severity on duration of unconsciousness as well as the presence or absence of post-traumatic amnesia (PTA). Any such system can be problematic when used in a crisis situation because it is often extremely difficult to gauge the length of time a person is unconscious. In an effort to simplify this process, Cantu (2001) has developed what he terms an "evidence-based" system for grading concussion (Table 9.1). The intent of this system is to simplify the decision-making process by members of the athletic health care team when evaluating the status of an athlete suspected of having sustained a head injury. Given the potential implications of a bad decision in such situations, these guidelines can help the coaching staff avoid errors in judgment.

Grade 1 concussions are by far the most common of those seen in sports; ironically, they are the most difficult to identify. The major distinction between grades 1 and 2 using the Cantu system is loss of consciousness and/or PTA lasting longer than 30 minutes in the latter grade. Grade 3 concussions are distinct because they involve either loss of consciousness lasting more than 1 minute or PTA of greater than 24 hours. According to Cantu, research indicates that the majority of sports-related concussions involve periods of unconsciousness lasting 1 minute or less. In addition, PTA lasts longer than 24 hours (Cantu, 2001). As such, Cantu's evidence-based grading system indicates that the majority of concussions in sports are of the grade 3 (most severe) level.

Two types of PTA resulting from head injury have been identified: anterograde and retrograde. Anterograde amnesia involves an inability to recall events that have transpired since the time of the injury. **Retrograde amnesia** is present when the athlete is unable to recall events that occurred just prior to the injury. It is generally thought that retrograde amnesia is indicative of more severe forms of head injury. When evaluating an athlete, the coach should ask several specific questions designed to elicit the presence of such forms of amnesia. (See Initial Treatment of a Suspected Head Injury: Guidelines.)

Grades 2 and 3 concussions differ from grade 1 in that they involve a loss of consciousness. Level of consciousness is a qualitative phenomenon to be determined as soon as possible after a head injury is suspected. This is generally accomplished by first determining if the athlete is alert and will respond to simple questions. Though almost any sort of questioning will yield some useful information, the best approach is to keep questions simple to evaluate the athlete's perspective of time and place: Cantu recommends questions such as the game score, name of the opponent, and so forth to determine the presence of retrograde amnesia and tasks such as reciting four words or numbers immediately and again 2 minutes later to detect the presence of anterograde amnesia (Cantu, 2001). Unconsciousness is usually identified when the athlete fails to respond to verbal stimuli or is obviously knocked out. Generally, consciousness is considered a positive sign; however, consciousness does not guarantee the absence of a potentially serious head injury.

Second Impact Syndrome

Recent research related to the phenomenon known as second impact syndrome (SIS) has raised concern in the sports medicine community that there needs to be a more cautious approach to the care and management of athletes who sustain minor concussions. SIS, according to medical experts, "occurs when an athlete who has sustained an initial head injury, most often a concussion, then sustains a second head injury before symptoms associated with the first have fully cleared" (Cantu & Voy, 1995). Essentially SIS involves the rapid development of catastrophic swelling of the brain, specifically a region known as the uncus of the temporal lobes, which puts pressure directly against the brain stem (Figure 9.5a, b).

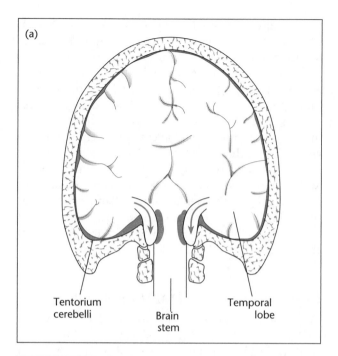

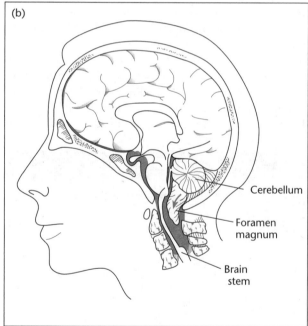

FIGURE 9.5 In second impact syndrome, vascular engorgement in the cranium increases intracranial pressure, leading to herniation of the uncus of the temporal lobes (arrows) below the tentorium in this frontal section (a), or to herniation of the cerebellar tonsils (arrows) through the foramen magnum in this midsagittal section (b). These changes compromise the brain stem, and coma and respiratory failure rapidly develop. The shaded areas of the brain stem represent the areas of compression. (Source: Robert Cantu, MD, FACSM, Neurological Surgery, Inc., Concord, Mass. Reprinted with permission.)

A typical scenario involves an athlete receiving a minor concussion with associated symptoms that include headache, nausea, and tinnitus (ringing in the ears). Several days later the same athlete, while engaging in the same activity, receives a relatively minor blow to the head. Shortly thereafter the athlete collapses, becomes unresponsive, and is taken to a health care facility. While there, the athlete dies in a deep coma. On autopsy, the cause of death is confirmed as massive cerebral edema resulting from uncontrolled vascular engorgement of brain tissue (or SIS). It is crucial to realize that any athlete who sustains what appears to be even a minor concussion should be examined carefully by a physician before being allowed to return to participation. This concern is especially acute in the case of an athlete with a recent history of concussion. It is important to remember that symptoms related to a concussion may take days or even weeks to be resolved. As such, it seems prudent that medical personnel, athletes, coaches, and parents apply extreme caution when making decisions regarding return to play for an athlete with a history of head injury.

Intracranial Injury

Intracranial injury in sports represents a potentially life-threatening situation. These injuries can be the result of a variety of mechanisms, including direct blows, rapid deceleration, and even rapid rotational motions of the head. By far, the majority of intracranial injuries result from blunt trauma to the head. The injury is characterized by disruption of blood vessels, either veins or arteries, resulting in the development of a hematoma or swelling in the confines of the cranium. Such a condition places the brain tissues in jeopardy because these structures are extremely sensitive to pressure.

Jordan (1989) has identified the major forms of **intracranial injury** as **epidural hematoma** (bleeding between the dura and the cranial bones), **subdural hematoma** (bleeding below the dura mater), **intracerebral hematoma** (bleeding within the brain tissues), and **cerebral contusion** (bruising of the brain tissue). It is important to note that an epidural hematoma involves arterial bleeding; therefore, the signs and symptoms of injury will usually develop rather quickly. Because of the vascular anatomy of the dura mater, a subdural hematoma can involve rapid arterial bleeding with symptoms developing in minutes, or bleeding may be venous, with pooling and clotting developing over many hours. In some cases, symptoms don't appear for hours or even days after the initial injury. Any of these conditions can result in some degree of permanent neurologic damage and even death.

Cranial Injury

Cranial injuries involve injuries to the bones of the skull. In the majority of cases, the force injuring the bones is of sufficient magnitude to also cause damage to the tissues of the scalp. Thus, along with cranial injury there may also be some bleeding and soft-tissue damage. Skull fractures can be simple, linear fractures with no damage to underlying tissue. In many cases these injuries produce few neurologic problems. The more severe forms of cranial injuries involve what are known as depressed skull fractures. These are potentially much more serious because bone fragments have been pushed into the cranial region. Obviously, this type of injury is more likely to produce serious, perhaps life-threatening, neurologic damage. A variety of signs and symptoms of cranial injuries may be present. These are discussed in some detail later in this chapter.

retrograde amnesia Inability to recall events that occurred just prior to an injury.

intracranial injury Head injury characterized by disruption of blood vessels, either veins or arteries, resulting in the development of a hematoma or swelling within the confines of the cranium.

epidural hematoma Bleeding between the dura and the cranial bones.

subdural hematoma Bleeding below the dura mater.

intracerebral hematoma Bleeding within the brain tissues.

cerebral contusion Bruising of brain tissue.

Initial Treatment of a Suspected Head Injury: Guidelines

Though the numbers of head injuries in all sports, including tackle football, are low *when compared to the total number of participants,* those that do occur are significant when one considers the potential seriousness of this type of injury. As mentioned previously, as a general rule, any athlete who sustains an apparent head injury should be treated as if a neck injury is also present; conversely, any athlete sustaining a neck injury should be treated as if there is also a head injury. The mechanism of injury for both is similar; consequently, it is possible that both could occur simultaneously.

The following guidelines for the emergency care of an athlete suspected of having sustained a head injury are divided into procedures while the athlete is at the site of injury, followed by guidelines for the injured athlete after he or she has been removed to a secondary site (sideline, courtside, etc.). It is critical to understand that if any signs and/or symptoms of head or neck injury are present when evaluating the athlete at the site of initial injury, he or she should not be moved until emergency medical services (EMS) personnel have arrived on the scene. It should be remembered that history has shown that at least 50% of all cases of permanent neurologic consequences from head or neck trauma are the result of inappropriate first aid care, *not the actual injury!*

Initial Check

After the coach reaches the athlete, the first step in the management of an athlete with a suspected head injury is based on basic first aid procedures: Determine if the athlete is in either respiratory or cardiac arrest. This is accomplished by executing the initial check. Any problems, such as an obstructed airway or cardiac arrest, must be attended to before continuing with any further evaluation of injuries. The first few seconds of the initial

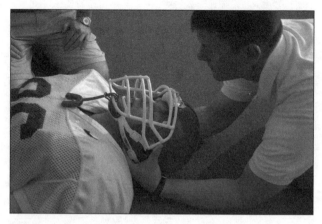

FIGURE 9.6 Stabilizing an athlete's head and neck.

check should provide important information about the injured player. On reaching the athlete note body position, movement or lack thereof, unusual limb positions, and (if present) the position of helmet, face mask, and mouth guard. If the athlete appears to be unconscious, attempt to arouse him or her by placing your hands on the shoulders, chest, or upper back and speaking loudly directly toward the athlete's head. If the athlete is conscious, the airway in all probability is open. If the athlete appears to be unconscious, make a mental note of the time; this will be of great value when the athlete arrives later at an emergency health care facility. It is critical that the coaching staff be trained and well rehearsed in dealing with such situations because immobilization of the head and neck should also take place at this time. This is accomplished quickly by having a person stationed at the athlete's head to stabilize it with both hands (Figure 9.6).

In the case of a helmeted football player, it is not necessary to remove the helmet to determine if the athlete is breathing. (Refer to the guidelines later in this section regarding removal of a face mask from a football player with a head and/or neck injury.) Breathing can usually be detected by placing your ear near the athlete's face and listening for the typical sounds of respiration. By doing this you may also detect sounds indicating airway obstruction, such as gagging, wheezing, or choking. You may also note movements of the thorax or abdomen, both of which can confirm normal respiration.

Circulation Assessment

A responsive athlete who is breathing will have the signs of circulation—breathing, coughing, and movement. Determine if the signs of circulation are present in an unresponsive victim after initial breaths by looking for breathing, coughing, and movement in response to the breaths. If you see no signs of circulation, begin

---

WHAT IF?

You are confronted with a situation during a tackle football game in which a player is apparently knocked unconscious during a play. When you arrive at the scene, the player is lying facedown and is not moving. What would you do to ascertain the athlete's level of injury? What would you NOT do, and why?

cardiopulmonary resuscitation (CPR). In such a situation, the coach's primary responsibility is to keep the athlete alive and to ensure that help is summoned. There is no reason to move the athlete from the playing field or practice area. The possibility of delaying a game or practice does not justify moving someone in this situation. After the decision is made to initiate CPR, EMS must be summoned. Carefully logroll the athlete to a supine position following accepted first aid guidelines that include vital steps such as stabilizing the head and maintaining an airway while performing the logroll.

Physical Exam

Obviously, an athlete who is conscious and alert represents a less complicated case than does a player who appears to be unconscious and not breathing. Once the initial check has been completed, *which can be accomplished with practice in around 30 seconds,* and the athlete's vital signs have been ascertained, proceed to the physical exam, in which the coach collects as much information about the suspected head injury as possible. The physical exam must include assessments of the following:

C—Conscious or unconscious

E—Extremity strength (if conscious) (Test without moving neck.)

M—Mental function (if conscious)

E—Eye signs and movements

P—Pain specific to the neck

S—Spasm of neck musculature

It is important for the coaching staff to remember the following statements when evaluating an athlete with a suspected head injury:

Don't remove the helmet of a football player.

Don't move the athlete.

Don't use ammonia capsules.

Don't rush through the physical exam.

Determining whether an athlete is conscious is not always an easy process. Obviously, an athlete who cannot be aroused by loud talking and is not moving presents an easy assessment of unconsciousness. However, head injuries result in many variations of signs and symptoms. If the athlete appears to be conscious, attempt to communicate by asking simple questions requiring the use of short-term memory. For example, ask the name of the opposing team, what day it is, the location of the contest, or the score of last week's game. Loss of short-term memory is indicative of a concussion and possibly a serious head or neck injury.

Do not attempt to revive an unconscious athlete by using a commercially made inhalant such as ammonia capsules. An athlete may attempt to jerk his head away from the inhalant, resulting in aggravation of an existing neck injury.

If the athlete is conscious, a series of quick, simple tests can be conducted to determine if any significant neurologic damage has occurred. Place two of your fingers in one of the athlete's hands and ask him or her to squeeze as hard as possible. Then perform the test on the opposite hand and compare grip strength. You can also place your hands on the tops of the athlete's feet and ask the player to dorsiflex (move the toes/top of foot toward the leg) to compare bilateral strength. Check sensation on both sides of the body by pinching the skin on the insides of the arms, thorax, and legs.

To determine possible brain injury, monitor the athlete's eyes by noting the size of the pupils. Place your

Athletic Trainers SPEAK Out

I recently had a player hit in the face with a line drive that knocked him face down on the mound. The player remained conscious but was incoherent. He gathered his senses and after having passed a neurological review was allowed by the attending physician to sit up. At this time there was immediate bloody drainage from both nostrils. He was once again placed lying down, a stretcher was asked for, and the player was taken by ambulance to the hospital, where a CAT scan revealed a bilateral fractured sinus.

—Rick Griffin

Rick Griffin is the Head Athletic Trainer for the Seattle Mariners.

hand over one eye and remove it quickly to determine if the pupil reacts to light. Perform the same test on the other eye. Pupils are generally the same size; however, in rare cases, some people normally have pupils of unequal size, known technically as **anisocoria.** Hold a finger or pen directly in front of the athlete's face and move it from side to side slowly. Ask the player to tell you when it is no longer visible. Note any difference in peripheral vision, comparing right and left, and also any jerking movements of the eyeballs, especially when the athlete is looking to the side. Loss of peripheral vision or jerking of the eyes is indicative of possible brain injury.

Gently palpate the athlete's neck, beginning at the base of the skull and working slowly down to the bottom of the neck. Note any deformity, such as cervical protrusions or muscle spasms. Ask the athlete if pain occurs at any specific area during your evaluation.

Based on the results of this portion of the injury evaluation, you should be able to determine what level of concussion, if any, the athlete may have sustained. If the athlete was rendered unconscious, even if only for a few seconds, by default he or she has sustained a grade 2 or 3 concussion. If the athlete never lost consciousness, but demonstrates some form of amnesia, either retrograde and/or anterograde, by definition, he or she has sustained a concussion. Any level of concussion represents a potentially serious medical emergency. The coach should follow the emergency plan for such situations. In all probability, an athlete who suffers a grade 1 concussion will be able, with assistance, to walk to the sideline or courtside. At that point he or she should be monitored and a decision should be made as to how best to obtain a complete medical evaluation by a physician. This process should be predetermined by way of the emergency plan. An athlete who suffers a grade 2 or 3 concussion should not be moved from the site of initial injury. Rather, the coach should continue to monitor the vital signs of the athlete and summon EMS. Prior to the arrival of EMS, no attempt to move the athlete away from the site of initial injury is warranted because to do so may aggravate the injury.

If, after your initial check and physical exam, the athlete appears not to have sustained a grade 1 concussion and vital signs appear to be normal, he or she can be safely moved away from the site of initial injury. This process should, however, be done with great care and without haste. Assuming the athlete is in a laying-down position, the first step in moving the athlete is to raise her to a sitting position. With assistance on both sides of the athlete by two members of the emergency team, assist her to a sitting position by applying some force under her armpits while giving her support in the event

she loses her balance. After the athlete is in a sitting position, monitor her vital signs and overall behavior for 1 to 2 minutes. If they appear to be normal, the next step is to assist the athlete to a standing position, again with support on both the right and left sides by members of the emergency team. After the athlete is in a standing position, again monitor her vital signs and sense of balance for 1 to 2 minutes. If they appear to be normal, ask her to begin walking slowly toward the area where she can be examined more carefully away from the site of the initial injury. Again, it is critical that members of the emergency team provide continual physical support on each side of the athlete as she walks in the event that she loses balance and begins to fall. After she arrives at the site for further evaluation, assist the athlete to a seated position and begin the next phase of the examination.

Sideline Assessment

Once the athlete is seated away from the playing area and can be assessed without interference from fellow athletes, a more detailed assessment of his or her condition must be conducted. The objective of this phase of the evaluation is to determine the presence of any signs or symptoms of head injury that may have developed since the time of the initial injury. This information is of vital importance when confronted with making decisions regarding medical referral, as well as clearance for return to participation. The concussion classification systems described earlier in this chapter provide guidelines for recognizing signs and symptoms of the most common forms of cerebral concussion. It has been said that "the single most important indicator of the severity of brain injury is the level of consciousness" (Jordan, 1989). However, in the majority of sports-related head injuries, the athlete never loses consciousness. The Cantu (2001) guidelines make it quite easy to differentiate between the three categories of concussion based on the nature of the PTA and/or unconsciousness. Even in the case of a grade 1 concussion, typically the athlete will appear dazed, confused, and may demonstrate dizziness along with an unstable gait. These signs may be accompanied by complaints of **tinnitus** (ringing in the ears) as well as some loss of memory, either anterograde or retrograde. Based on the guidelines, an athlete who sustains a grade 1 concussion must be pulled from participation and should not return until he or she is asymptomatic for 1 week. By default, any athlete who, based on the initial evaluation, has sustained any level of concussion should be removed from play and examined by a physician.

To assist in ascertaining the condition of the athlete who may have sustained a grade 1 concussion, it is helpful to administer one or more field tests for neurologic integrity prior to allowing an athlete to return to play. The finger-to-nose test (Figure 9.7) is administered by asking the athlete to stand with feet together, arms extended away from both sides of the body with elbows straight, and eyes closed. The athlete is then asked to touch the nose with an index finger—first with one arm, then the other. If the athlete is unable to touch the nose easily with either finger, return to play should not be allowed. The Romberg's test (Figure 9.8) involves asking the athlete to stand with feet together, arms at sides, and eyes closed. If the athlete is unable to maintain an erect posture and begins to sway, losing balance, the test is positive for a serious head injury. When administering such a test, be sure to position yourself to catch the athlete in case he or she loses balance and begins to fall. After administering these tests, have the athlete rest for 5 to 10 minutes and repeat the tests. If he or she is able to successfully complete the tests and does

FIGURE 9.7 The finger-to-nose test.

FIGURE 9.8 The Romberg's test.

not demonstrate any signs of PTA, he or she may be cleared to return to participation.

Cervical Spine Injuries
Background Information

Injuries involving the cervical spine occur in a variety of sports, but most often in football, rugby, ice hockey, soccer, diving, and gymnastics. Although any injury to this region of the body is potentially extremely serious, it is interesting to note that those that meet the criteria for the catastrophic category are quite rare: 2 in 100,000 of all neck injuries reported (Wiesenfarth & Briner, 1996). The annual incidence of cervical spine injuries among high school tackle football players has been consistently lower than prior to the early 1970s. This is no doubt a result, in part, of rules changes banning spearing as well as improved player fitness and skill level. In 1990, for example, no catastrophic injuries were reported for high school football, and the incidence has been less than 1 such injury for every 100,000 players for a number of years (Mueller & Cantu, 2006).

With the possible exception of a severe head injury, neck injuries are considered to be potentially the most serious category of sports injury. Many in the sports medicine community refer to the more severe forms of these injuries as catastrophic, which seems to be an appropriate term considering the potential outcome of trauma to this area. Neck (cervical) injuries occur in almost any sport and can involve a variety of tissues in the region, including bones, ligaments, intervertebral disks, spinal cord, spinal nerve roots, and/or the spinal nerves themselves (Torg, 1989).

The extent and severity of neurologic damage that occur in a neck injury depend on the magnitude of the mechanism of injury, the resulting movement of the neck, and the extent of tissue damage. In the case of simple neck strains, neurologic involvement is extremely rare.

Cervical injuries are expressly more serious when displacement of an intact vertebra occurs, when fragments of a vertebral fracture are displaced, or when an intervertebral disk ruptures, placing pressure directly on the spinal cord or nerve roots. In these situations, the potential for permanent neurologic damage is high.

anisocoria Rare, but naturally occurring condition where the pupils are of unequal size, not related to any acute condition such as head injury.

tinnitus Ringing in the ears.

Curiously, significant neurologic symptoms may be totally absent even when significant damage has occurred to tissues surrounding the spinal cord. Therefore, it is critical that the coach be objective and complete during the initial assessment process to avoid converting a treatable injury into a permanent one. Although it is not expected that the coach conduct a complete neurologic evaluation that would be expected of an athletic trainer or a physician, a few simple field tests, as described earlier in this chapter, will often yield sufficient information to make an informed decision regarding initial management of the athlete.

Mechanisms of Injury

Historically, the mechanism of injury considered to be potentially the most common and serious was excessive forced flexion (hyperflexion) of the cervical spine. However, extensive film analysis and objective research have disputed this long-held belief. Most experts now agree that the mechanism known technically as axial load produces the majority of serious cervical spine injuries. This is especially true in tackle football; prior to the mid-1970s tackling with the crown of the helmet (spearing) was a common practice. Axial loading of the cervical spine occurs when the head is lowered (flexed slightly) just prior to impact—the net effect being a straightening of the normal vertebral curve (extension) (Burstein, Otis, & Torg, 1982). In this position, forces applied to the top of the head are absorbed directly by the bones of the vertebral column without the protective assistance of surrounding ligaments and muscles. In 1976 the National Collegiate Athletic Association (NCAA) enacted a rule change that prohibited spearing

TABLE 9.2

ANNUAL SURVEY OF CATASTROPHIC CERVICAL CORD FOOTBALL INJURIES 1977–2005*

Year	Sandlot	Pro and Semi-Pro	High School	College	Total
1977	0	0	10	2	12
1978	0	1	13	0	14
1979	0	0	8	3	11
1980	0	0	11	2	13
1981	1	0	6	2	9
1982	1	1	7	2	11
1983	0	0	11	1	12
1984	1	0	6	0	7
1985	0	0	6	3	9
1986	0	0	4	0	4
1987	0	0	9	0	9
1988	0	0	10	1	11
1989	0	1	12	2	15
1990	0	0	11	2	13
1991	0	1	1	0	2
1992	0	1	6	0	7
1993	0	1	8	0	9
1994	0	0	1	1	2
1995	0	0	8	1	9
1996	0	0	6	3	9
1997	0	1	7	1	9
1998	0	0	4	0	4
1999	1	0	7	1	9
2000	0	0	6	2	8
2001	0	0	8	0	8
2002	0	0	5	1	6
2003	0	1	7	1	9
2004	1	1	10	0	12
2005	0	0	3	0	3
Total	**5**	**9**	**211**	**31**	**256**

*Figures are updated annually due to new cases investigated after publication.
Source: National Center for Catastrophic Sport Injury Research. (2006). Annual survey of catastrophic football injuries, 1977–2005. Available: http://www.unc.edu/depts/nccsi/CataFootballInjuries.htm. Reprinted with permission.

or leading with the head for contact. The results were impressive; there was a significant drop in the number of cervical cord injuries the following year. The National Center for Catastrophic Sport Injury Research has been tracking catastrophic injuries in high school and collegiate-level football since 1977. Data presented in their 2003 annual report are shown in Table 9.2. These data represent the annual incidence of cervical spine injuries that resulted in incomplete recovery.

Although the data in Table 9.2 show graphically an obvious decrease in the incidence of permanent cervical cord injuries resulting from high school and collegiate football, a study calls into question the effectiveness of the mentioned rule change. Heck (1996) examined game films from a New Jersey high school for two seasons, 1975 and 1990, to determine if the incidence of spearing, by position, had been reduced. Curiously, the overall rate of spearing differed very little; that is, the incidence was 1 in 2.5 plays in 1975 compared with 1 in 2.4 plays in 1990. Spearing by running backs actually increased in 1990 when compared with 1975, and it was noted that tacklers were more likely to spear if the running back was spearing. The only decrease in spearing was noted among defensive linemen and independent tacklers. Heck determined that the majority of spearing involved defensive backs and linebackers.

Assuming Heck's research is representative of high school football participants nationally, compliance or, rather, noncompliance with the no-spearing rule makes it seem that more emphasis needs to be given to teaching these young athletes not to practice this extremely dangerous maneuver. Coaches, officials, parents, and sports medicine personnel all share some responsibility in monitoring these young athletes during both games and practice. In 2005, the NCAA updated their tackle football rules in an effort to discourage athletes from contacting an opponent with the top or crown of the helmet, as well as the face mask, and also stated that spearing is not allowed. The National Athletic Trainers' Association (NATA), National Football League (NFL), and NCAA are actively working to educate football participants regarding the dangers of these high-risk maneuvers. A Microsoft Office PowerPoint slide presentation on this topic is available for viewing to NATA members at the following web site: www.nata.org/members1/committees/cuatc/spearing/highschool_spearing.ppt.

Although spearing has been identified as a continuing problem and an extremely hazardous practice among football players, it is also true that any forced movement of the cervical spine can result in injury. These mechanisms can be grouped into the following categories:

Hyperflexion

Hyperextension

Rotation

Lateral flexion

Axial loading

The types and severity of injury to the cervical spine are extensive; however, they can be classified according to the tissues involved and the extent of the damage. In order of severity, these range from simple compressions of the brachial plexus, which are self-correcting within minutes of the injury, to more severe problems involving ruptures of the intervertebral disks and fractures of the vertebrae.

Brachial Plexus Injuries

Known commonly as "burners" or "stingers," brachial plexus injuries are a frequent occurrence in sports such as football where the athlete's body may be forced in one direction while an arm may be pulled in the opposite direction. An injury to the brachial plexus typically results in significant but transient symptoms ranging from an intense burning sensation in the shoulder, arm, and hand to loss of sensation in the same areas. As can be seen in Figure 9.9, injury to the brachial plexus involves an abnormal traction or compression of one or more of the large nerves that comprise the entire plexus (Sallis, Jones, & Knopp, 1992).

Signs and symptoms of brachial plexus injury include the following:

1. Immediate neurologic symptoms radiate into the affected arm, often described as an intense burning or stinging sensation.

2. There is significant decrease in voluntary use of the arm (often the arm appears limp).

3. Symptoms should be self-correcting and the involved extremity should return to normal sensation in a few minutes.

4. In repeat cases, symptoms as described may persist for days or even weeks. Muscle atrophy, especially of the deltoid muscle, may be apparent. In such cases, medical evaluation is essential before the athlete is allowed to return to participation.

First aid care:

1. Because of the nature of brachial plexus injuries, little can be done with respect to first aid other than to remove the athlete from participation until the symptoms subside.

2. Once on the sideline, continue to monitor the athlete's recovery and do not allow him or her to return to participation until the symptoms have abated and grip strength in the affected extremity is normal compared to the opposite arm.

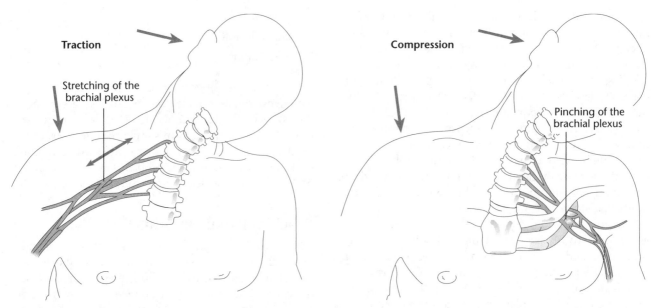

FIGURE 9.9 Common mechanisms of injury to the brachial plexus.

3. If symptoms as described do not abate after 10 minutes, refer the athlete for a medical evaluation and require medical clearance prior to return to participation.

Sprains

Sprains of the cervical spine are common in some sports and generally involve portions of the major ligaments that serve to stabilize the vertebrae. The common mechanism for these injuries are hyperflexion, hyperextension, lateral flexion, and rotation. These injuries generally involve a significant amount of force, as is seen in contact/collision sports such as football, ice hockey, and wrestling. Such injuries are usually self-correcting and resolve themselves over a period of days. Occasionally, however, the mechanism of a sprain is severe enough to result in an actual displacement of vertebrae, which can result in more serious neurologic problems.

Signs and symptoms of sprains include the following:

1. Localized pain in the region of the C-spine
2. Point tenderness over the site of the injury
3. Limited range of motion in neck movements
4. No obvious neurologic deficits (as verified by the neurologic test described under physical examination)

First aid care:

1. Remove the athlete from practice/competition that day.

2. Apply ice (best accomplished with a plastic bag filled with crushed ice).
3. If available, place a properly sized commercial cervical collar on the athlete.
4. Refer the athlete for a medical evaluation prior to being allowed to return to participation.

Strains

Strains involve the muscles and tendons of the neck region and are normally more painful than serious. Exceptions to this are injuries such as a whiplash, which consists of a combination of joint sprain and musculotendinous strain to the region. In addition, in severe whiplash injuries, indirect head injury is also possible. The mechanism of injury for strains is virtually the same as described previously for sprains.

Signs and symptoms of strains include the following:

1. Localized pain in the region of the C-spine
2. Muscle spasm
3. Limited range of motion in neck movements
4. No obvious neurologic deficits (as verified by the neurologic test described under physical examination)

First aid care:

1. Remove the athlete from practice/competition that day.
2. Apply ice (best accomplished with a plastic bag filled with crushed ice).

3. If available, place a properly sized commercial cervical collar on the athlete.

4. Refer the athlete for a medical evaluation prior to being allowed to return to participation.

Fractures and Dislocations

The most extreme forms of cervical injury occur when the damage involves fractures or dislocations resulting in pressure being placed directly on the spinal cord. The spinal cord is extremely sensitive to such trauma, and permanent neurologic damage and even death can occur depending on the specific location of the injury. The spinal cord may also suffer damage secondary to the initial trauma as a result of circulatory problems related to blood supply. When the spinal cord is bruised, bleeding and swelling may ensue, resulting in neurologic problems (Bailes, 1990). Any of the mechanisms described earlier can result in either a fracture or dislocation; however, axial loading is associated with many of the more severe forms of injury. It is critical to remember that these injuries represent true medical emergencies and therefore require the best care possible.

Signs and symptoms are as follows (in the case of an unconscious athlete, the primary objectives are to provide basic life support, stabilize the head and neck, and summon EMS):

1. Athlete reports having felt or heard something pop or snap in his or her neck at the time of injury
2. Severe pain localized in the region of the cervical spine associated with muscle spasm
3. Difficulty in swallowing
4. Deformity in the vertebrae, as detected by palpation
5. Burning, numbness, or tingling sensations in the extremities and/or trunk
6. Weakness in grip strength and/or dorsiflexion, either bilaterally or unilaterally
7. Complete absence of sensation in the extremities and/or trunk
8. Complete absence of motor function in the extremities and/or trunk
9. Loss of bowel/bladder control

First aid care:

1. Complete the initial check and ascertain status of vital signs.

2. After initial check is complete, proceed to the physical examination. If any of the previously listed signs/symptoms are present, proceed to the following steps.

3. Stabilize the head and neck immediately. The emergency plan should designate a team leader who will immediately apply manual spinal stabilization (Figure 9.6)—in the case of a helmeted football player, do *not* remove the helmet; rather, use the helmet to assist in stabilization of the head and neck (see Figure 9.18).

4. If CPR is necessary, the front of the shoulder pads can be opened to allow access for CPR. This is recommended prior to the decision to remove any equipment (Kleiner, 1998). If the decision is made to remove the shoulder pads, the helmet should be removed as well to maintain proper spinal alignment.

5. Summon EMS.

6. Do *not* attempt to move the athlete—rather, when EMS personnel arrive, assist them in placing the athlete onto the spine board or other spinal immobilization device.

7. Continue to monitor vital signs until arrival of EMS.

Initial Treatment of a Suspected Neck Injury: Guidelines

When considering specific actions in treating an athlete with a suspected neck injury, an immediate distinction must be made. Is the athlete conscious or unconscious? The answer to this question determines the initial treatment approach. With the unconscious athlete, it must be assumed that both head and neck injuries are present. The primary objective is to determine if the athlete's life is in immediate jeopardy. Does the athlete have an open airway? Is the athlete breathing? Does the athlete have a pulse? These questions are answered during the initial check discussed earlier. If the answer to any of these questions is no, then basic life support must be initiated and continued until the arrival of airway, breathing, and circulation (EMS).

The coaching staff should have a preplanned emergency protocol for handling athletes with head and neck injuries. One staff member must be designated as the emergency team leader, whose primary responsibility is the supervision of the entire management process. In addition, the team leader must monitor the position of the athlete's head and neck, making sure that the injured player is not moved unnecessarily. Although sports medicine literature is replete with explanations of how to effectively and safely transport athletes with head and neck injuries, there does not seem to be much practice of these measures when actual cases are examined in retrospect. In the vast majority of school sports situations, which are normally located in population centers, emergency medical services (EMS) should be readily available. Even in rural settings, EMS are typically only minutes away. Although it is important that coaching personnel be trained in proper transportation techniques, it should be remembered that training does not mandate implementation. This is especially true when considering the potential for catastrophic injury if a head or neck injury is improperly handled. As was discussed earlier in this section, special consideration must be given to the care and handling of the helmeted football player.

In general, when dealing with an unconscious athlete the most important criterion should be prevention of further injury (Vegso, Bryant, & Torg, 1982). The team leader or designate should immediately stabilize the head and neck manually and continue doing so throughout the evaluation. The next step involves checking airway, breathing, and pulse. If the athlete is breathing and has a pulse, the next step is to summon EMS while maintaining support to the athlete's head and neck as well as continuously monitoring the airway, breathing, and circulation (ABCs).

If any delay of EMS is anticipated in excess of 30 minutes, it is prudent to place the athlete on a spine board to ensure adequate immobilization. This procedure requires a properly constructed spine board (Figure 9.10) and a trained staff of a minimum of five people, including the team leader. The team leader is charged with maintaining the head and neck in a neutral position as well as in directing the actions of the other team members. As shown in Figures 9.11

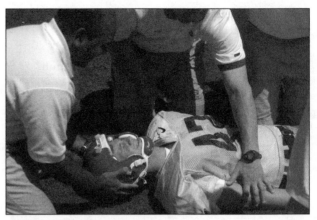

FIGURE 9.11 Members of the rescue team are stationed at the legs, hips, and shoulders, with the team leader providing stabilization to the head and neck.

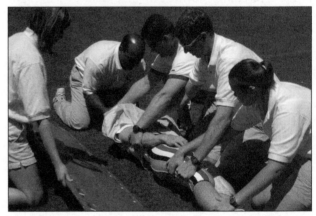

FIGURE 9.12 At the command of the team leader, the team rotates the athlete, as a unit, to enable movement of the spine board.

through 9.14, team members should be positioned at the athlete's shoulders, hips, and legs to properly roll the athlete onto the spine board. A fifth team member is required to slide the spine board under the athlete after he or she has been rolled onto the side by the other team members. The athlete should then be secured to the board and the head and neck supported by sandbags or towels, with straps properly placed to immobilize not only the head and neck, but also the entire body. Adhesive tape works well to provide additional immobilization to the head; place a strip across the athlete's forehead and chin. It is important to remember that placing an injured athlete on a spine board should be done only if absolutely necessary and, further, that the procedures for placing an athlete on this device be rehearsed frequently according to the recommendations of the emergency plan.

With the conscious athlete, the initial treatment procedures differ from those employed with the unconscious athlete. With the conscious athlete, the coach can

FIGURE 9.10 Examples of spine boards used to immobilize injured athletes.

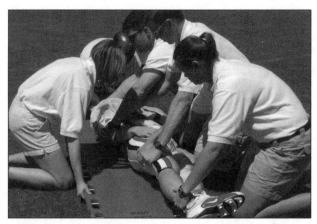

FIGURE 9.13 A fifth team member slides the spine board under the athlete. Note how the straps are placed to facilitate ease of securing the athlete to the board.

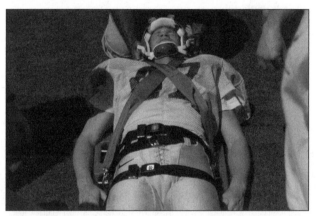

FIGURE 9.14 The athlete is firmly secured to the board with straps holding the ankles/feet, thigh/pelvis/arms, shoulders, and head and neck.

obtain immediate feedback regarding the player's condition. The athlete should be questioned regarding numbness of extremities, **dysesthesia** (impairment of the sense of touch), weakness, or neck pain (Bailes, 1990). In addition, if the athlete reports a loss of ability to move a limb or limbs or significant strength deficit (involving grip strength, or plantar or dorsiflexion), arrangements must be made to stabilize the head and neck, and EMS must be summoned.

Emergency Procedures for the Treatment of Head and Neck Injuries in Football

Though head and neck injuries carry the potential of catastrophic results regardless of the sport, football players who sustain such injuries present special problems because of their equipment. The standard equipment

protecting the player's head and neck is a helmet with an attached face mask, chin strap, and some type of mouth guard. This apparatus can make dealing with airway problems very difficult. Management procedures for the helmeted athlete have become a major issue in the sports medicine community—with strong opinions on how best to handle such an athlete (Feld, 1993; Putman, 1992; Ray et al., 2002; Segan, Cassidy, & Bentkowski, 1993). The National Athletic Trainers' Association (NATA) convened an interagency task force in 1998 to develop standardized medical guidelines for the proper care of the spine-injured athlete. The intent was to eliminate the confusion that existed at that time between different medical providers as to what constituted the proper care for athletes suspected of this type of injury. The task force published a position statement titled "Pre-hospital Care of the Spine-Injured Athlete," and the entire document is available on the NATA web site. Specific guidelines are presented in the document for the management of a helmeted athlete suspected of a cervical spine injury, and these are presented in Time Out 9.2. Coaching personnel are advised to exercise extreme caution when making decisions on immediate care of a helmeted athlete with possible head and/or neck injury. Removal of the helmet, unless executed by a physician or other emergency care provider such as an athletic trainer or paramedic, should be avoided unless absolutely necessary.

In situations in which an airway must be established, careful and properly executed removal of the face mask is the most prudent approach. Depending on the age and design of the helmet, removal of the face mask can be accomplished in a variety of ways. Although intense research on the most effective method of face mask removal is ongoing, the best technique to date appears to be cutting all the plastic clips (typically four: two upper and two lower) that hold the face mask to the helmet. It is critical to remember that the *head and neck must be stabilized at all times,* including during removal of the face mask. The majority of current designs secure the face mask to the helmet with small plastic clips attached to the helmet with screws (Figure 9.15). Cutting the plastic straps on each side of the face mask—using devices such as a Trainer's Angel (Figure 9.16), anvil pruner, wire cutters, or tin snips—while the head and neck are stabilized will allow the mask to be rotated up and away from the face (Figure 9.17). It is imperative that coaching personnel be aware of the specific types of equipment their athletes are wearing in the event that such an emergency arises.

dysesthesia Impairment of the sense of touch.

TIME OUT 9.2

GUIDELINES FOR APPROPRIATE CARE OF THE SPINE-INJURED ATHLETE

General Guidelines

- Any athlete suspected of having a spinal injury should not be moved and should be managed as though a spinal injury exists.
- The athlete's airway, breathing, circulation, neurological status and level of consciousness should be assessed.
- The athlete should not be moved unless absolutely essential to maintain airway, breathing and circulation.
- If the athlete must be moved to maintain airway, breathing and circulation, the athlete should be placed in a supine position while maintaining spinal immobilization.
- When moving a suspected spine-injured athlete, the head and trunk should be moved as a unit. One accepted technique is to manually splint the head to the trunk.
- The Emergency Medical Services system should be activated.

Face Mask Removal

- The face mask should be removed prior to transportation, regardless of current respiratory status.
- Those involved in the prehospital care of injured football players should have the tools for face mask removal readily available.

Football Helmet Removal

The athletic helmet and chin strap should only be removed:

- if the helmet and chin strap do not hold the head securely, such that immobilization of the helmet does not also immobilize the head;
- if the design of the helmet and chin strap is such that, even after removal of the face mask, the airway cannot be controlled nor ventilation provided;

- if the face mask cannot be removed after a reasonable period of time;
- if the helmet prevents immobilization for transportation in an appropriate position.

Helmet Removal

Spinal immobilization must be maintained while removing the helmet.

- Helmet removal should be frequently practiced under proper supervision.
- Specific guidelines for helmet removal need to be developed.
- In most circumstances, it may be helpful to remove cheek padding and/or deflate air padding prior to helmet removal.

Equipment

Appropriate spinal alignment must be maintained.

- There needs to be a realization that the helmet and shoulder pads elevate an athlete's trunk when in the supine position.
- Should either the helmet or shoulder pads be removed—or if only one of these is present—appropriate spinal alignment must be maintained.
- The front of the shoulder pads can be opened to allow access for CPR and defibrillation.

Additional Guidelines

- This task force encourages the development of a local emergency care plan regarding the pre hospital care of an athlete with a suspected spinal injury. This plan should include communication with the institution's administration and those directly involved with the assessment and transportation of the injured athlete.
- All providers of prehospital care should practice and be competent in all of the skills identified in these guidelines before they are needed in an emergency situation.

Source: Kleiner DM Almquist JL, Bailes J, et al. (2001). Prehospital care of the spine-injured athlete: A document from the Inter-Association Task Force for Appropriate Care of the Spine-Injured Athlete. Reprinted with permission from the National Athletic Trainers' Association (NATA).

Do not attempt to move the player until the physical exam is completed and your evaluation determines that he or she is not injured. An athlete who appears to have recovered fully during the initial check or physical examination should be escorted from the playing field, taken to the bench, and observed for a few minutes to determine if he or she is developing any signs or symptoms of head injury. Any player who was unconscious qualifies as having a grade 3 concussion and should be taken to a medical facility for evaluation.

If, on the other hand, your evaluation yields some suspicious signs and symptoms or the player is unconscious, stabilize the head and neck, summon EMS personnel, and monitor the athlete's vital signs. As can be

FIGURE 9.15 Plastic straps and screws secure the face mask to most football helmets.

WHAT IF?

You are asked to provide first aid care to a high school basketball player who just received a blow to his mouth from an opponent's elbow. On examination, you note that two teeth appear to be completely knocked out of their sockets. The teeth are still in the athlete's mouth. What would you do for this athlete?

FIGURE 9.16 In the event of an injury, qualified personnel can use cutting tools such as the FM Extractor (FME) or Trainer's Angel (right) to cut the straps on each side of the player's face mask.

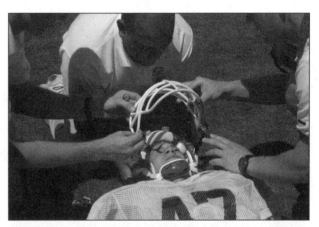

FIGURE 9.17 Once the straps are cut, the face mask can be rotated up and away from the player's face or, as recently recommended, completely removed.

seen in Figure 9.18, the helmet provides an excellent adjunct to cervical immobilization in the case of possible neck injury (Fourre, 1991). In most instances, there is no reason to move an injured player from the field before EMS personnel arrive. No game or practice is so important that it cannot be delayed to ensure proper first aid for an injured player.

In the vast majority of head injuries related to football, the best course of action is typically unclear; in many cases the injury may be difficult to identify. It is not uncommon for athletes with varying degrees of concussion to appear normal, at least for brief periods of time following the initial trauma. Therefore, the football coach, officials, and fellow players may be totally unaware that anything is wrong with the athlete. *In general, when in doubt regarding the athlete's head injury, it is best to err on the conservative side; pull the player out of the game until he or she has been properly evaluated.*

FIGURE 9.18 In the event of a neck injury, the helmet provides an excellent means of cervical immobilization.

Injuries to the Maxillofacial Region

A variety of injuries can occur to the maxillofacial region of the body, which includes the jaw and teeth, eyes, ears, nose, throat, facial bones, and facial skin. Fortunately, with the advent of modern technology, protective equipment has been developed for use in high-risk sports (Matthews, 1990). These devices have significantly reduced the overall numbers of injuries to this region.

Dental Injuries

There are 32 teeth in the adult human jaws, the majority of which are located just inside the front and sides of the mouth, where they are vulnerable to external blows common in both collision and contact sports. Teeth are firmly secured into either the maxilla (upper jaw) or mandible (lower jaw) by way of the root, which is cemented into the sockets of the jaws with a specialized form of bone known as cementum. In addition, the sockets are lined with periosteum that aids in securing the teeth to the jaw.

Specific Injuries

The majority of dental injuries in sports are from direct blows resulting in tooth displacement, a fracture or avulsion, and, in extreme cases, fracture of the jaw or other facial bones. Signs and symptoms of dental injury are listed in Time Out 9.3 along with the most likely injury.

Initial Check and Treatment: Guidelines

Whenever rendering first aid to someone suffering a dental injury, it is important to avoid exposure to any injury-related blood. As such, bloodborne pathogen prevention steps should be taken, which include protective gloves (latex) and, if possible, eye protection, such as goggles. (See Appendix 2.) Collect the history of the accident; this is an important component of the physical exam. Check to see if the athlete can open and close the mouth without pain or difficulty. Assess the general symmetry of the teeth; that is, look for irregularities visible in adjacent teeth. Examine the upper and lower teeth separately and carefully note any bleeding around the gum line or teeth or obvious chips or fractures.

Treatment for dental injuries includes direct finger pressure with a sterile gauze over the area of bleeding, if any. For loose teeth, gently push them back into their normal position. In the case of avulsions, make every effort to locate the tooth and protect it by placing it into either a commercially prepared solution or sterile saline (Matthews, 1990). Send the athlete to a dentist or physician immediately to have the tooth put back in place.

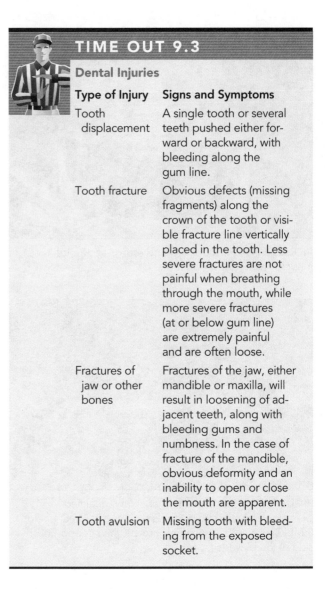

TIME OUT 9.3

Dental Injuries

Type of Injury	Signs and Symptoms
Tooth displacement	A single tooth or several teeth pushed either forward or backward, with bleeding along the gum line.
Tooth fracture	Obvious defects (missing fragments) along the crown of the tooth or visible fracture line vertically placed in the tooth. Less severe fractures are not painful when breathing through the mouth, while more severe fractures (at or below gum line) are extremely painful and are often loose.
Fractures of jaw or other bones	Fractures of the jaw, either mandible or maxilla, will result in loosening of adjacent teeth, along with bleeding gums and numbness. In the case of fracture of the mandible, obvious deformity and an inability to open or close the mouth are apparent.
Tooth avulsion	Missing tooth with bleeding from the exposed socket.

Time is of the essence in these situations, and the prognosis for the tooth is poor if more than 2 hours elapse between the time of the injury and time of replantation (Godwin, 1996).

Protection Against Injury

The most common method of dental protection in sports is the mouth guard, and many varieties are currently available. Properly fitted, a mouth guard can significantly reduce or even prevent many dental injuries. In addition, evidence suggests that mouth guards can also reduce the likelihood of concussions and dislocations of the temporomandibular joint, as well as jaw fractures. All mouth guards fall into one of three groups: stock, mouth-formed, and custom (Godwin, 1996). Stock versions are the least expensive; however, they are generally thought to be the least effective as well. The most commonly used are the mouth-formed type and, short of visiting the dentist to get a custom fit, they are probably the most cost effective for junior and senior high school athletes. The custom mouth guard provides the best possible fit and protection; however, the costs can be prohibitive for many athletes.

Obviously, in high-risk sports such as tackle football, a well-fitted mouth guard should be utilized to protect the athlete from such injuries. In the United States the use of mouth guards has been required in high school football since 1966. In 1974 the NCAA mandated their use in tackle football as well. Since then, ice hockey, field hockey, and men's and women's lacrosse have been added to the list of sports that require a mouth guard at both the high school and collegiate levels. The use of either stock or custom-made mouth guards is strongly recommended—by both the American Association of Oral and Maxillofacial Surgeons and the U.S. Olympic Committee—for protection in a variety of sports, including ice hockey, field hockey, rugby, wrestling, boxing, basketball, lacrosse, skiing, weight lifting, shot-putting, discus throwing, and even horseback riding (Kerr, 1986).

Eye Injuries

The human eye is an incredibly complex structure located in the orbit of the skull (Figure 9.19). The front of the eye consists of clear tissue known as the cornea, behind which the iris (pupil) and lens are situated. Located in the eyeball is the vitreous body, consisting of transparent, semigelatinous material that essentially fills the globe of the eye. The posterior surface of the inside of the eye is covered by the retina, which contains the specialized neural cells of vision known as rods and cones. With the exception of the clear tissue on the anterior surface of the eye, the majority of the eyeball is encased in a tough tissue known as the sclera.

It has been reported that approximately 40,000 sports-related eye injuries occur annually in the United States. The sports with the highest associated risks are basketball, baseball, and racket sports. Water sports are also responsible for a number of eye injuries. Perhaps most distressing is the conclusion by medical experts that the majority of these injuries (90%) are preventable (Rodriguez et al., 2003). With their increasing popularity, sports such as racquetball, squash, and badminton have produced an increase in eye trauma as well. Problems related to these sports include the small size of the striking objects (balls and shuttlecocks) as well as their velocity (Table 9.3) and the confined areas in which the games are played. Together, these factors greatly increase the probability of injury.

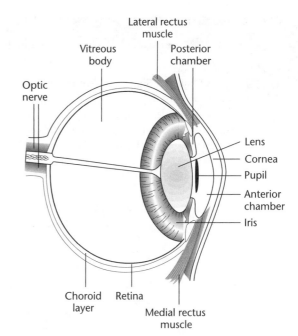

FIGURE 9.19 Anatomy of the eye.

TABLE 9.3	
POTENTIAL SPEED* OF OBJECTS IN RACKET SPORTS	
Squash ball	62 [140]
Badminton shuttlecock	57 [130]
Racquetball	48 [110]
Tennis ball	48 [110]

*Velocity is measured first in meters per second, then in miles per hour.
Source: Jones NP. (1989). Eye injury in sport. *Sports Med.* 7(3):168. Reprinted with permission.

Specific Injuries

Jones (1989) groups eye injuries into two different categories: contusional and penetrating. A contusional injury is the result of a blow from a blunt object such as a squash or tennis ball. Contusional injuries vary greatly in severity, ranging from simple corneal abrasions to major distortions of the eyeball resulting in rupture of the eye, fracture of the inner orbit, or a combination of the two. Additionally, the retina may be torn away from the inside of the eye, resulting in an injury commonly known as a detached retina. Penetrating injuries of the eye are less common, but can occur in shooting

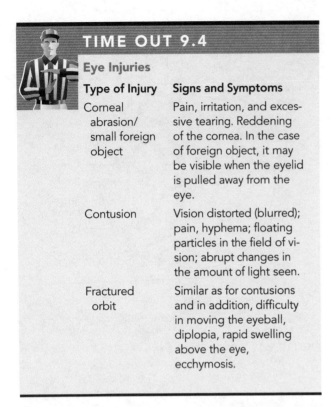

TIME OUT 9.4

Eye Injuries

Type of Injury	Signs and Symptoms
Corneal abrasion/ small foreign object	Pain, irritation, and excessive tearing. Reddening of the cornea. In the case of foreign object, it may be visible when the eyelid is pulled away from the eye.
Contusion	Vision distorted (blurred); pain, hyphema; floating particles in the field of vision; abrupt changes in the amount of light seen.
Fractured orbit	Similar as for contusions and in addition, difficulty in moving the eyeball, diplopia, rapid swelling above the eye, ecchymosis.

sports or even as the result of protective eye equipment that is defective. Signs and symptoms of eye injury are listed in Time Out 9.4.

Initial Check and Treatment: Guidelines

The majority of sports-related eye problems will involve either simple corneal abrasions or a small foreign object in the eye. The symptoms for each are often nearly identical: pain, irritation, and excessive tearing. A quick examination of the eye can be conducted by gently holding the upper eyelid up and away from the eye while checking the anterior of the eyeball for any problems (Figure 9.20). Small foreign bodies are usually washed away from the center of the eye by tears. Therefore, the particle may be located below the lower eyelid or on the side of the eyeball at a site known as the medial canthus.

If the foreign object can be seen, it can usually be carefully removed with a moist cotton swab. If the object appears to be imbedded in the eye tissue, cover *both* eyes carefully with clean gauze and immediately arrange for transport of the athlete to a medical facility. It is important to cover the uninjured eye to avoid movement of the damaged eye because the eyes normally move together to produce a visual image. This is known as "sympathetic eye movement."

If no object can be seen in the eye, the injury is most likely a corneal abrasion. Do not allow the athlete to

continue participation until the symptoms abate. If they persist or vision is severely disturbed, the athlete should be referred to the appropriate medical specialist for further evaluation.

When the eye receives a significant blow or contusion—from being hit by an elbow in a game of basketball or by a racquetball, for example—vision is usually at least temporarily disturbed. In most cases this causes a black eye resulting from hemorrhaging of tissue surrounding the eye. The immediate care of this injury is periodic application of cold for 24 hours after the injury. In the case of severe contusions, bleeding into the anterior portion of the eye (**hyphema**) may occur quickly. This is a potentially serious sign because it may indicate vascular damage in the eyeball. In addition, the eyeball itself may have been ruptured, or the socket (orbit) may be fractured, an injury known as orbital blowout. Symptoms of such an injury include pain (especially when attempting to move the eye), double vision (**diplopia**), and obvious hemorrhaging in the eye. An athlete with any of these signs or symptoms should be immediately referred for further medical evaluation.

Injuries resulting in a detached retina can be caused by the mechanisms previously described; however, the symptoms may not be immediately apparent. An insidious aspect of this injury is that the retina may slowly fall away from the posterior section of the eye over a period of days, weeks, or even months in some cases. Early symptoms include seeing particles floating inside the eye, distorted vision, and abrupt changes in the amount

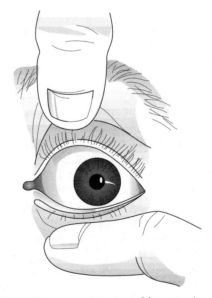

FIGURE 9.20 Proper positioning of fingers when initially examining the eye.

of light seen. Any athlete with a history of blunt trauma to the eye who later complains of any of these symptoms should be referred to a medical specialist.

Contact Lens Problems

Many athletes are fitted with contact lenses (both hard and soft). Few difficulties occur with these appliances; however, as a rule, more problems arise with hard lenses. Most result from the lens slipping out of place or dust that gets trapped between the lens and the eye. Soft lenses cover the entire anterior portion of the eye and are less able to migrate around on the eye surface. The coach should have the necessary materials handy in the first aid kit—including commercially prepared wetting solution, a small mirror, and perhaps even a contact-lens case—to deal with problems involving contact lenses.

Protection Against Injury

Although presently not required by the NCAA or high school sports regulatory bodies, protective eyewear is strongly recommended and is growing in popularity. It is interesting to note that experts report wearing eye protection can prevent 90% of eye injuries (Hamou & Zagelbaum, 1999). The primary forms of protective eyewear are goggles, used in sports such as basketball and racket sports, and face shields (usually attached to a safety helmet), used in sports such as football, ice hockey, and baseball/softball. Although many of these products are made of plastic, the best material is polycarbonate, which is extremely strong and protects well against impacts. It is recommended when purchasing protective eye devices that the device be approved by the American Society for Testing and Materials (ASTM) or the Canadian Standards Association (CSA). Refer to Appendix 7 for examples of protective eyewear.

Nose Injuries

The human nose is, by nature of its location, often subjected to trauma in sports. The classic nosebleed **(epistaxis)** may well be one of the most common facial injuries in sports. Anatomically, the nose consists of a combination bone-cartilage framework over which the skin is attached. The nose consists mostly of soft tissue (cartilage and skin) and can absorb significant amounts of force. The bones of the nose include the right and left nasal bones and the frontal processes of the maxilla (Gray, 1985). The superior portions of the nasal bones meet with the frontal bone between the orbits. The nose has two openings, commonly called nostrils (nares), which are separated in the middle by the cartilaginous septum. The areas immediately inside the nares contain hairs that trap large particles during respiration. Further up, the nares tissue is covered with mucous membrane.

Initial Check and Treatment: Guidelines

When an athlete receives a blow to the nose that results in bleeding, the nose should immediately be examined for the possibility of fracture. The signs of such a fracture include an obvious deformity of the bridge of the nose, which usually swells quickly. Fractures of the nasal bones constitute the most frequent fractures of the facial region (Booher & Thibodeau, 1989). If one is suspected, first control the nosebleed and then immediately refer the athlete for medical evaluation. Generally, uncomplicated nasal fractures are easily corrected by a physician.

Care of a simple nosebleed should include application of finger pressure directly against the nostril that is bleeding. The person rendering first aid should wear a latex glove for protection against exposure to blood. If the bleeding persists, application of a cold compress against the nasal region is usually effective in causing immediate vasoconstriction of the affected vessels. In addition, the athlete should be instructed to lie on one side (the same side as the bleeding nostril). If the athlete needs to continue participation, the nose can be packed with gauze, which should be allowed to protrude slightly from the nose to aid with extraction later.

Septal injuries present unique problems and the possibility of later complications. As a result of external blows, the septum can be bruised; bleeding can occur between the septum and the mucous membrane covering it. This injury is referred to as a septal hematoma and can lead to serious septal erosion if not corrected. The signs of a septal hematoma are swelling that is usually visible both inside and outside the nose. In addition, the nose may appear red and infected externally, and the athlete will complain of pain, especially when the nose is gently palpated. This injury should be referred to the appropriate medical specialist for diagnosis and correction. The coach or athlete should not attempt to drain a septal hematoma, as the likelihood of infection and permanent damage is high.

Ear Injuries

Anatomically, the human ear shares some common characteristics with the nose. Externally it appears as a

hyphema Bleeding into the anterior portion of the eye.

diplopia Double vision.

epistaxis Nosebleed.

cartilaginous framework covered with a layer of skin, but it has an extensive internal structure as well. Specifically, the ear can be divided into several anatomical components. The external ear consists of the large expanded portion, called the auricula, and the opening into the ear canal, known as the external acoustic meatus. The middle ear, which is a small space within the temporal bone, contains a small group of bones that transmit vibrations to the tympanic membrane (eardrum). The inner ear comprises the complex structure known as the labyrinth or specialized bones (vestibule, semicircular canals, and cochlea) that are directly attached with the vestibulo-cochlear nerve (Gray, 1985). The structures of the inner ear also play a major role in the maintenance of equilibrium (Van De Graaff, 1998). Thus, injuries to this area often affect not only hearing but balance as well.

With the exception of aquatic sports, the majority of sports-related medical problems with the ear affect its external parts. Sports such as wrestling, which involves a great deal of body contact between opponents and the playing surface, result in a large number of abrasions and contusions to the auricula. Although the use of protective equipment has reduced the overall numbers of such injuries, they do still occur. Because the tissues of the auricula have some degree of vascularity, trauma can lead to the development of a hematoma between the skin and underlying cartilage, known technically as an auricular hematoma (Matthews, 1990). If this condition is not treated properly or is repeatedly irritated prior to treatment, a serious cosmetic problem known as cauliflower ear can occur. In extreme cases the cartilage of the auricula may even begin to break down, thereby complicating the problem. Signs and symptoms of auricular hematoma include skin redness, local increase in tissue temperature, pain, and/or a burning sensation. This condition should be treated immediately with a cold pack. If swelling in the auricula occurs, the athlete should be referred to a physician so the fluid can be removed via aspiration. The ear will then be packed with a special material to prevent swelling from returning. Athletes with a history of this injury or those involved in high-risk sports such as wrestling should be required to wear properly fitted protection.

Any time an athlete receives a blow to the ear region that is immediately followed by a sudden reduction in hearing and/or dizziness, immediate referral to a physician is required. Blows to the outer ear can produce dramatic increases in pressure in the ear, resulting in ruptures of either the eardrum or a specialized structure known as the round window. When such an injury occurs, the immediate effects are significant reduction in hearing as well as transient loss of equilibrium. Other signs and symptoms may include bleeding from the ear as well as persistent and intense ringing in the ear. Damage to the round window may require surgical intervention to correct the problem (Matthews, 1990). Athletes with ear infections should be advised not to participate in aquatic sports until the problem has resolved itself. This is particularly true in diving because infection and subsequent inflammation in the ear may make it impossible for the athlete to clear the ears while underwater, often resulting in injury to the eardrum.

Fractures of the Face (Nonnasal)

Though fractures can occur almost anywhere on the face, certain sites are more often involved in sports-related injuries. A relatively common form of facial fracture involves the mandible (lower jaw) and occurs in boxing and other collision sports. The signs and symptoms of such an injury include obvious pain and swelling at the site of the fracture, observable deformity, and malocclusion (misalignment of the maxillary and mandibular teeth). Treatment entails gentle application of a cold pack and immediate referral to a physician. If a fracture has occurred, the jaw will be treated by wiring the mouth closed; in severe cases, surgical fixation may be required until the fracture is healed (Matthews, 1990).

A related injury is dislocation of the jaw, which can result from the same type of mechanism. Here the joint involved is the temporomandibular joint (**TMJ**), which is classified as ellipsoid and is formed by the union of the mandibular condyle and the mandibular fossa of the temporal bone (Figure 9.21). The TMJ is held together by numerous ligaments and joint capsules. Because of its

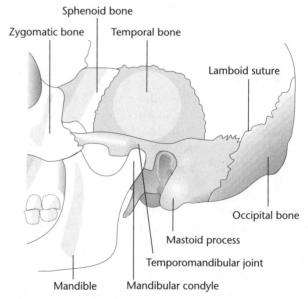

FIGURE 9.21 The temporomandibular joint.

bony configuration, this joint tends to dislocate relatively easily. The signs and symptoms of this injury include extreme pain and deformity in the region of the TMJ and inability to move the lower jaw; in some cases the mouth may be locked in an open position. Treatment for this injury is essentially the same as for a fracture. It is important that on-site reductions (putting the joint back in place) not be attempted.

Other bones of the face may be fractured, including the zygomatic bone. Generally, the signs and symptoms will include pain and swelling at the site of injury. In the case of the zygomatic bone, swelling and discoloration may spread to the orbit of the eye as well. Any athlete with a history of a blow to the face who has some or all of the previous signs and symptoms should be referred immediately to a physician for diagnosis and treatment.

Wounds of the Facial Region

Wounds to the face may take many forms; in general, their treatment should be based on basic first aid guidelines. Carefully clean the wound with mild soap and warm water; apply a sterile, commercially prepared dressing (not loose cotton); and refer the athlete to a physician. Facial wounds take on greater significance than injuries to other parts of the body primarily because of cosmetic reasons. Thus, any wound to the face, whether it is a simple **abrasion** (scraped skin), a more serious incision (smooth edged, bleeds freely), or laceration (skin cut with jagged, irregular edges), should be evaluated relative to the potential long-term cosmetic effects. As a general rule, any incision or laceration resulting in an observable space between the margins of the skin should be seen by a physician for suturing (Matthews, 1990). Usually, athletes can return to participation after the wound has been treated and (when necessary) sutured. The decision to release such an athlete to return to activity is best determined by the attending physician, especially in the case of a minor (Crow, 1993).

TMJ Temporomandibular joint.
abrasion Rubbing or scraping off of skin.

REVIEW QUESTIONS

1. List the names of the cranial bones and give a description of their anatomic relationship.

2. What are the correct names of specialized tissues known collectively as the cerebral meninges?

3. What is located in the subarachnoid space?

4. What is the approximate weight in pounds of an adult human's brain?

5. What are the three basic components of the human brain?

6. List the correct number of cervical, thoracic, lumbar, sacral, and coccygeal nerves.

7. According to the chapter, what is a cerebral concussion?

8. What is the major difference between a grade 2 and a grade 3 concussion as described in the chapter?

9. Describe the condition known as anisocoria.

10. What is anterograde amnesia as it relates to a head injury?

11. Define *subdural, epidural,* and *intracerebral hematomas;* also define *cerebral contusion.*

12. When rendering first aid to an athlete with a suspected head injury, what are the top three objectives?

13. *True or false:* The single most important indicator of the severity of head injury is the level of consciousness.

14. Describe the administration of the finger-to-nose test and the Romberg's test.

15. What is the most likely mechanism of a sports-related injury to the cervical spine?

16. What conditions must be assumed present whenever treating an unconscious athlete?

17. What types of information should be obtained when treating a conscious athlete with a suspected head and/or neck injury?

18. *True or false:* Experts agree that 90% of eye injuries could be prevented if athletes wore adequate eye protection.

19. What is the cause of the majority of dental injuries?

20. What is a simple, practical form of dental protection in sports?

21. *True or false:* The majority of sports-related eye injuries occur in basketball.

22. What is the recommended method of removing a small, nonimbedded object from an athlete's eye?

23. What is an orbital blowout?

24. What materials should the coach have available in a first aid kit for treating problems related to athletes wearing contact lenses?

25. Define the term *epistaxis.*

26. Describe the appropriate method for controlling a nosebleed.

27. *True or false:* With the exception of aquatic sports, the majority of sports-related medical problems with the ear involve the auricula.

28. Briefly describe the process leading to the condition known as cauliflower ear.

29. Why are facial wounds of greater significance than wounds on other areas of the body?

REFERENCES

Bailes JE. (1990). Management of cervical spine sports injuries. *Athletic Training.* 25:156–159.

Booher JM, Thibodeau GA. (1989). *Athletic Injury Assessment.* St. Louis: Times Mirror/Mosby.

Burstein AH, Otis JC, Torg JS. (1982). Mechanisms and pathomechanics of athletic injuries to the cervical spine. In Torg JS (ed.). *Athletic Injuries to the Head, Neck, and Face* (pp. 139–145). Philadelphia: Lea & Febiger.

Cantu RC. (2001). Posttraumatic retrograde and anterograde amnesia: Pathophysiology and implications in grading and safe return to play. *J Athletic Training.* 36(3):244–248.

Cantu RC, Mueller FO. (1999). Fatalities and catastrophic injuries in high school and college sports, 1982–1997. *Phys Sportsmed.* 27(8):35.

Cantu RC, Voy R. (1995). Second impact syndrome—a risk in any contact sport. *Phys Sportsmed.* 23(6):27–34.

Crow RW. (1993). Sports-related lacerations—promoting healing and limiting scarring. *Phys Sportsmed.* 21:143–147.

Feld F. (1993). Management of the critically injured football player. *J Athletic Training.* 28(3):206–212.

Fourre M. (1991). On-site management of cervical spine injuries. *Phys Sportsmed.* 19(4):53–56.

Godwin WC. (1996). A tale of two teeth. *Training Conditioning.* IV(3):39–42.

Gray H. (1985). *Anatomy of the Human Body.* Philadelphia: Lea & Febiger.

Guskiewicz KM, et al. (2000). Epidemiology of concussion in collegiate and high school football players. *Am J Sports Med.* 28(5):643–650.

Hamou DC, Zagelbaum BM. (1999). Incidence of sports related eye injuries. *Athletic Therapy Today.* 4(5):27–31.

Heck JF. (1996). The incidence of spearing during a high school's 1975 and 1990 football seasons. *J Athletic Training.* 31:31–37.

Jones NP. (1989). Eye injury in sport. *Sports Med.* 7(3):163–181.

Jordan BD. (1989). Head injury in sports. In Jordan BD, Tsairis P, Warren RR (eds.). *Sports Neurology* (pp. 75–83). New York: Aspen Publishers.

Kerr IL. (1986). Mouth guards for the prevention of injuries in contact sports. *Sports Med.* 3:415–427.

Kleiner DM. (1998). New guidelines for the appropriate care of a suspected spine injury. *Athletic Therapy Today.* 3(5):50–51.

Matthews B. (1990). Maxillofacial trauma from athletic endeavors. *Athletic Training.* 25:132–137.

Mueller FO, Cantu RC. (2006). Twenty-third Annual Report—Fall 1982–Spring 2005. National Center for Catastrophic Sport Injury Research. Chapel Hill: University of North Carolina (Available: http:/www.unc.edu/depts/nccsi/AllSport.htm.

Putman LA. (1992). Alternative methods for football helmet face-mask removal. *J Athletic Training.* 27(2):170–172.

Ray R, et al. (2002). Cervical spine motion in football players during three airway-exposure techniques. *J Athletic Training.* 37(2):172–177.

Rodriguez JO, Lavina AM, et al. (2003). Prevention and treatment of common eye injuries in sports. *Am Fam Physician.* 67(7):1481–1488.

Sallis RE, Jones K, Knopp W. (1992). Burners—offensive strategy for an underreported injury. *Phys Sportsmed.* 20:47–55.

Segan R, Cassidy D, Bentkowski J. (1993). A discussion of the issue of football helmet removal in suspected cervical spine injuries. *J Athletic Training.* 28(4):294–305.

Shultz SJ, Houglum PA, Perrin DH. (2000). *Assessment of Athletic Injuries.* Champaign, Ill.: Human Kinetics.

Torg JS. (1989). Athletic injuries to the cervical spine. In Jordan BD, Tsairis P, Warren RR (eds.). *Sports Neurology* (pp. 133–158). New York: Aspen Publishers.

Van De Graaff KM. (1998). *Human Anatomy* (5th ed.). Dubuque, Ia.: William. C. Brown.

Vegso JJ, Bryant MH, Torg JS. (1982). Field evaluation of head and neck injuries. In Torg JS (ed.). *Athletic Injuries to the Head, Neck, and Face* (pp. 39–52). Philadelphia: Lea & Febiger.

Wiesenfarth J, Briner W. (1996). Neck injuries—urgent decisions and actions. *Phys Sportsmed.* 24:35–41.

10

Injuries to the Thoracic Through Coccygeal Spine

MAJOR CONCEPTS

This chapter presents a brief review of the gross anatomy of the thoracic spine and thoracic cage along with a discussion of possible injuries to the region. Although relatively uncommon in sports, injuries to the thoracic spine do occasionally occur. These injuries are usually sprains; much less frequently they involve fractures. The chapter covers typical mechanisms of injury as well as common signs and symptoms and recommended initial treatment for both sprains and fractures. Injuries to the lumbar spine in sports are quite common: The vast majority are related to an anatomic defect known as spondylolysis. This chapter provides descriptions of the common problems associated with this part of the spinal column along with information regarding the signs and symptoms of related lumbar spinal disorders. It also discusses traumatic sprains, strains, and intervertebral disk injuries, with a focus on recognition and initial management.

http://health.jbpub.com/book/concepts/5e

The web site for this book offers many useful tools and is a great source for supplementary information for both students and instructors.

Visit the site at
http://health.jbpub.com/book/concepts/5e
to link to the following organizations and sites:

- The Southern California Orthopedic Institute

ANATOMY REVIEW OF THE THORACIC SPINE

The portion of the human vertebral column known as the thoracic spine consists of 12 vertebrae that articulate at the top with the cervical spine and with the lumbar spine at the bottom. Viewed from the side, the human vertebral column includes several curvatures that correspond with specific regions of the spine. Both the cervical and lumbar portions of the spine represent concave curves, whereas the thoracic portion of the vertebral column is convex, curving in the opposite direction to both the cervical and lumbar components. The curves of the spine, along with the ligaments and intervertebral discs, are important to the overall strength of the spinal column (Figure 10.1). The thoracic vertebrae are commonly numbered 1 through 12, beginning with the uppermost vertebra and ending with the 12th at the junction with the lumbar spine. An intervertebral disk is located between each thoracic vertebra. A unique aspect of the thoracic vertebrae is their relationship with the 12 pairs of ribs in the human skeleton. The

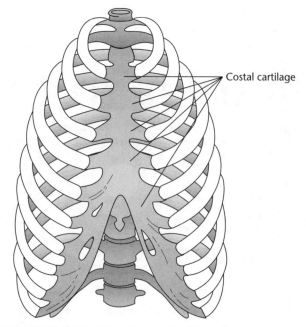

FIGURE 10.2 The thoracic cage (anterior view).

thoracic vertebrae, their corresponding ribs, and the sternum form a strong **thoracic cage** (Figure 10.2), which among other things serves to protect the internal organs of the region, including the heart and lungs (Gray, 1985).

Because of the bony union of the ribs and adjacent vertebrae, the thoracic spine is much less mobile than either the cervical or lumbar sections of the spine. The majority of movements in the thoracic region of the spine result from the process of respiration (Rasch, 1989). The limited movements of the thoracic vertebrae help to make injuries to this part of the body uncommon.

Common Sports Injuries

As stated, sports injuries to the thoracic spine are rare. Those sports-related injuries that do occur can be divided into two groups: skeletal and soft tissue (ligaments, muscles and tendons, and intervertebral disks). Available data demonstrate that bone-related injuries in this region are more common than those involving soft tissues (AAOS, 1991).

Skeletal Injuries

The most common injury to the thoracic spine involves a compression type of fracture to the vertebral body (O'Leary & Boiardo, 1986). This injury occurs near the junction of the thoracic and lumbar spines and is usually related to violent, ballistic movements that are unique to sports involving high velocities. An athlete

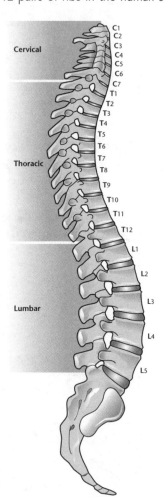

FIGURE 10.1 Lateral view, human vertebral column.

with a history of recent trauma to the thoracic spine who complains of severe pain in the region or perhaps even neurologic signs (pain or numbness of the extremities) should be referred to a medical doctor immediately for evaluation.

Another problem related to the vertebrae of the thoracic spine is Scheuermann's disease, which is sometimes seen in adolescents and is characterized by **kyphosis** (an abnormal amount of convexity of the spine). Children involved in activities that subject the spine to severe bending, such as gymnastics, may develop this condition. A child who complains of recurrent pain in the region of the thoracic spine that is associated with activity should be evaluated. A quick visual examination may confirm an abnormal amount of spinal curvature, which is made worse when the child bends forward as if to touch the toes. In some cases, related spinal problems such as **scoliosis** (lateral curvature) and lumbar **lordosis** (swayback) may also be present. Children with either of these disorders need to be referred to a doctor for extensive evaluation. If a diagnosis of Scheuermann's disease is made, treatment will involve both prescribed exercises and spinal bracing.

Vertebral Fractures

Fractures involving the thoracic spine are extremely rare; however, they can result from either a direct blow to the posterior thorax or extreme flexion of the thoracic spine, resulting in a compression of the vertebral body. In spite of the fact that neurologic complications related to vertebral fractures in this region are rare, significant soft-tissue damage can occur to the skin and underlying muscles. The mechanism of injury described earlier can occur in a tackle in football, a collision in soccer, or while landing on the opponent's knee during a takedown move in wrestling.

Signs and symptoms include the following:

1. Pain in the area of the injury.
2. Although the athlete may be able to stand and even move about, any motion specific to the trunk such as extension, flexion, or rotation will be extremely painful.
3. Swelling and discoloration in the area of injury may be apparent.
4. Muscle spasm over the injured area.

First aid care:

1. Immediately apply RICE.
2. Remove the athlete from participation for 24 hours, with a follow-up evaluation.

3. If symptoms persist, referral to a physician is warranted.
4. If neurologic symptoms are present during the initial evaluation, refer immediately to a physician.

Rib Fractures

Another type of fracture that may occur in this region involves the ribs and is known as a posterior rib fracture (AAOS, 1991). The mechanism for this injury is typically a direct blow to the lateral or posterior thorax. Fractures may occur anywhere along the rib; however, most commonly they occur near an angle of the rib, which is anatomically the weakest point (Booher & Thibodeau, 1989).

Signs and symptoms include the following:

1. Painful respiration.
2. Deformity in the region of the injury, including a protruding rib or a depression where the normal contour of the rib should be.
3. Swelling and discoloration.
4. Pain when the rib cage is compressed gently by the examiner.
5. In severe cases, lung damage may result in symptoms associated with pneumothorax (see Chapter 13).

First aid care:

1. Immediately apply RICE (generally best accomplished with a 6- or 8-inch-wide elastic wrap and a bag of crushed ice).
2. Treat for shock.
3. Refer for medical evaluation by a physician.

Complications of these injuries are rare; however, when they do occur they can be quite dangerous. Displaced rib fractures may damage internal thoracic structures, particularly the lungs, resulting in either a traumatic **pneumothorax** (Figure 10.3) or **hemothorax** (blood and air in the thorax). Such injuries will result in

---

thoracic cage Thoracic vertebrae, their corresponding ribs, and the sternum.

kyphosis Exaggeration of the normal curve of the thoracic spine.

scoliosis Lateral and/or rotary curvature of the spine.

lordosis Abnormal curvature of the lumbar vertebrae.

pneumothorax Collapse of a lung as a result of air in the pleural cavity.

hemothorax Bloody fluid in the pleural cavity.

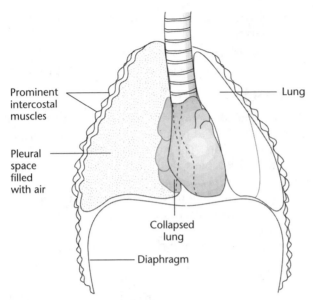

Prominent intercostal muscles

Pleural space filled with air

Collapsed lung

Diaphragm

FIGURE 10.3 Pneumothorax.

Lung

significant changes in breathing and may also induce shock. For more detailed information on the care and management of these injuries, refer to Chapter 13.

Sprains

Sprains occur whenever a joint is forced through an abnormal range of motion (ROM) that results in damage to supporting structures such as ligaments and joint capsules. Because the thoracic spine is well supported, limited movement is allowed, thereby reducing the incidence of sprains. Evaluation of a sprain to the thoracic spine is difficult and must be based on a detailed history of the injury. An athlete with such an injury will usually report having sustained an unusual movement of the

thoracic spine that is associated with localized pain, a feeling of popping or snapping, and in some cases swelling. A consistent symptom of injury to the thoracic area is painful respiration, which is associated with many different injuries to the region, including rib fractures and contusions. First aid for sprains to the thoracic spine includes the application of RICE. If significant symptoms such as **dyspnea** (difficulty breathing) persist for more than 24 hours, the athlete should be referred to a medical doctor.

Strains

Strains involve primarily contractile tissues and their support structures—muscles, fascia, and tendons. The muscles of the thoracic spine region include the erector spinae and the intercostals. Strains may occur related to maximum exertion in sports requiring large amounts of force, such as tackle football, wrestling, or ice hockey. Signs and symptoms of strains may be very difficult to differentiate from sprains. Often the injury mechanism will be identical to that of a sprain. Muscle spasms of erector spinae in the region may be noticeable. These muscles may also be sensitive to touch (palpation) and should be inspected for this symptom. First aid for suspected strains of this region is the same as for sprains: application of RICE.

Intervertebral Disk Injuries

Although extremely rare in the thoracic region of the spine, injuries can occur to the intervertebral disks located between each of the vertebrae. Disk problems may

dyspnea Difficult or painful breathing.

Athletic Trainers SPEAK Out

To be in this field [one] definitely has to be a people person. Good communication skills are a necessity for [being effective] because you deal with so many individuals and groups as part of your responsibilities. Organizing the care of the athlete, from prevention to total rehabilitation, involves a number of people with [you] at the core.

—Doris E. Flores, ATC

Doris Flores is the Coordinator for the Athletic Training Program and she is the Director of the Athletic Training Laboratory at California State University at Sacramento.

be secondary to a compression fracture of thoracic vertebrae. Any athlete who complains of persistent neurologic symptoms, such as numbness or pain radiating around the thoracic region or into one or more of the extremities, should be referred immediately to a medical doctor for a more detailed evaluation.

ANATOMY REVIEW OF THE LUMBAR SPINE DISTALLY TO THE COCCYX

The lumbar spine consists of five vertebrae that articulate superiorly with the thoracic vertebral column and inferiorly with the sacrum. The lumbar vertebrae are the largest vertebrae of all those that move—that is, cervical, thoracic, and lumbar (Gray, 1985). The lumbar vertebrae are numbered L-1 to L-5, from proximal to distal. As is the case with the thoracic and cervical sections of the spine, intervertebral disks are located between each of the lumbar vertebrae, as well as between T-12 and L-1 and between L-5 and S-1 (the first sacral vertebra). Additionally, large, strong ligaments assist in stabilization of the lumbar vertebrae (Figure 10.4), along with the thoracic spine and the sacrum. The anterior and posterior longitudinal ligaments are located on the anterior and posterior surfaces of the vertebral bodies (within the spinal cord canal), respectively. Both of these important ligaments span the vertebral column from the level of C-2 (axis) distal to the sacrum.

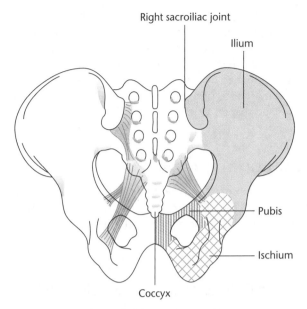

FIGURE 10.5 The pelvis (posterior view).

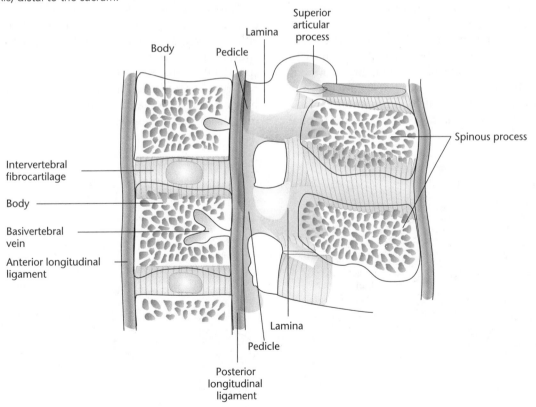

FIGURE 10.4 The lumbar vertebrae (sagittal view).

The sacrum, consisting of five fused vertebrae, is located between the two pelvic bones posteriorly. In essence, the sacrum serves to connect the spinal column to the pelvis (Figure 10.5). Two articulations, the right and left sacroiliac joints, are formed by the union of the sacrum and the pelvis.

The most distal portion of the vertebral column is a small, arrowhead-shaped structure called the coccyx.

Common Sports Injuries

Injuries are more common to the lumbar spine than to the thoracic. Of all the injuries that can affect the bony portion of the lumbar spine, the most common is spondylolysis.

Spondylolysis and Spondylolisthesis

Spondylolysis (Figure 10.6) is a defect in the part of a vertebra that forms the bony ring around the spinal cord known as the neural arch (Figure 10.7). Spondylolysis involves the portion of the neural arch known as the pars interarticularis (there are two on each vertebra, one on the right side and one on the left). The significance of bony defects in this region relates to superior articulations with adjacent vertebrae. Thus, any defect of the neural arch in this area can compromise the integrity of the articulation between any two vertebrae.

In cases in which both the right and left neural arches are affected, the involved vertebra has the potential to slide forward, thus producing a condition known as **spondylolisthesis.** As can be seen in Figure 10.8, the most common site for this condition is between L-5 and the sacrum (O'Leary & Boiardo, 1986). Given the normal

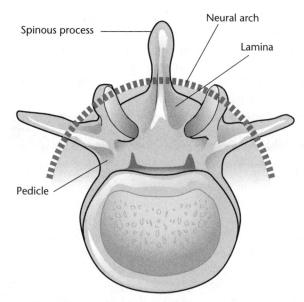

FIGURE 10.7 Overhead view of the neural arch of a typical lumbar vertebra.

slope of the sacrum, bony instability of the last lumbar vertebra makes anterior displacement possible, especially when the lumbar region is subjected to abnormal amounts of stress, such as occurs in gymnastics, tackle football, or competitive weight lifting.

The exact **etiology** of spondylolysis is not clear; however, evidence suggests that the bony defects may be either congenital (present at birth) or related to excessive stress to the bones during childhood. The symptoms of spondylolysis include lower back pain, which becomes particularly acute when the lumbar spine is placed into **hyperextension.** When the defect is unilateral (one side only), standing on one leg in conjunction with lumbar

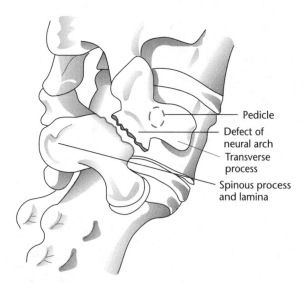

FIGURE 10.6 Defect of the neural arch that causes spondylolysis.

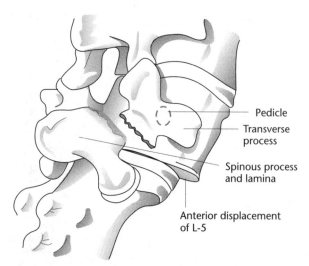

FIGURE 10.8 Anterior displacement of the L-5 vertebra that induces spondylolisthesis.

hyperextension will elicit pain only on the side of the defect (Halpern & Smith, 1991). If spondylolysis progresses to spondylolisthesis, symptoms may become more severe. Pain in the lumbar region may increase during activity, and in some cases radiating pain may occur in the buttocks and upper thighs (Booher & Thibodeau, 1989).

Any athlete complaining of symptoms of this type, particularly those involved in high-risk sports for lumbar injuries (gymnastics, tackle football, and weight lifting), should be referred to a medical doctor for further evaluation. Treatment for spondylolysis and spondylolisthesis may include rest, drug therapy, lumbar bracing, exclusion from certain sports, and in severe cases surgical spinal fusion.

Traumatic Fractures

Traumatic fractures of the lumbar vertebrae are infrequent in sports. Such injuries will normally be associated with a history of a severe blow to the lumbar region. Depending on the specific location and type of fracture, neurologic symptoms, such as radiating pain into the buttocks or legs, may be present. Such injuries need to be treated initially with great care via immobilization on a spine board and transport to a medical facility, where complete evaluation by a physician can take place. It must be remembered that an external blow to the lumbar region may also cause injury to internal organs, specifically the kidneys. Thus, it is important that the athlete be evaluated for such an injury. Special attention should be given to the signs and symptoms of internal injury, such as deep abdominal pain, **hematuria,** or shock.

Injuries to the sacrum or coccyx are generally limited to those caused by direct blows. Such injuries are normally self-limited and require only protection from future trauma. One notable exception is a severe blow to the coccyx, which may result in a fracture or severe bruise. Such an injury can occur when an athlete falls backward, landing hard on the buttocks and impacting the coccygeal region. The signs and symptoms of this injury involve an observable bruise in the coccygeal region, severe point tenderness, and swelling. This injury needs to be evaluated by a medical doctor because a fracture may be present.

Sprains and Strains

By far the most common soft-tissue injuries to the lumbar region are strains and sprains (O'Leary & Boiardo, 1986). Strains involve the contractile tissues of the region, or the erector spinae muscles (Figure 10.9).

Sprains involve the many ligaments and joint capsules of the region. As previously mentioned, there are large

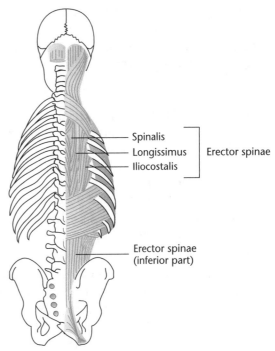

FIGURE 10.9 The erector spinae muscles of the upper and lower back.

ligaments (the anterior and posterior longitudinal ligaments) that bind the vertebral bodies together. In addition, there are ligaments and capsules binding the joints between adjacent neural arches (facet joints). Major joints in the region include the lumbosacral, sacroiliac, and the sacrococcygeal. Generally, injuries to the joints are rare in this region. However, muscle strains occur frequently, particularly in sports that place significant stress on the lumbar spine. Activities such as gymnastics, tackle football, and weight lifting can place the athlete in situations in which abnormal loads are exerted on the lumbar region of the spine.

Signs and symptoms include the following:

1. Localized muscle spasm.
2. Pain that is increased with trunk movements.
3. Postural abnormality of the trunk, which often involves a lateral tilting of the trunk away from the affected side.

spondylolysis A defect in the neural arch (pars interarticularis) of the vertebrae.

spondylolisthesis Forward slippage of vertebra, usually between the fifth lumbar and the sacrum.

etiology Science dealing with causes of disease.

hyperextension Extreme stretching of a body part.

hematuria Blood in the urine.

4. The athlete can link a specific incident with the onset of symptoms.

5. In simple strains or sprains, pain will *not* radiate into the buttock or lower extremities.

First aid care:

1. Remove the athlete from participation with assistance, as any voluntary attempts to move will usually increase the pain.

2. Place the athlete in a position of lying supine, with the legs parallel and both knees drawn up so the knees and hips are flexed (Figure 10.10).

3. Place a rolled towel or some other soft material into the lumbar region for support.

4. Place a bag of crushed ice into the lumbar region.

5. Athlete should be instructed to sleep in this position and to continue ice application over the next 24 hours.

6. If symptoms are not significantly reduced during the first 24 hours after the injury, medical referral is warranted.

It is important to remember that an injury mechanism of sufficient magnitude to cause a strain may have also caused more severe injury. It is always best to refer such athletes for further evaluation by a medical doctor (Shankman, 1991). This is especially important in cases in which the athlete complains of pain radiating into one or both legs. Such symptoms can indicate a significant injury, such as a herniated disk (O'Leary & Boiardo, 1986).

Lumbar Disk Injuries

A more serious form of soft-tissue injury to the lumbar region involves damage within an intervertebral disk, commonly known as a **herniated disk**. Though such injuries can occur to any of the disks of the spine, those most commonly injured in the lumbar region are L-4 and L-5 (Anderson, Hall, & Martin, 2000). Most often these injuries occur when an athlete is subjected to a great deal of force while in an awkward position. The anatomy of a typical intervertebral disk consists of an outer ring called the annulus fibrosus and a softer, inner portion known as the nucleus pulposus (Gray, 1985). In the case of a herniation, a weakness develops in the annulus, which then allows the nucleus pulposus to cause a protrusion through the wall of the annulus. Depending on the exact location of the herniation, pressure may be placed directly on the large spinal nerves passing through the region (Figure 10.11).

Signs and symptoms include the following:

1. Intense local pain that is aggravated with any attempts to sit up, walk, or stand.

2. Pain radiating into the buttock and lower extremity—radiating pain follows the distribution of the sciatic nerve.

3. Sensory loss or tingling/burning sensation radiating into the lower extremity.

4. Pain will be greatly increased by attempting maneuvers such as a straight-leg raise or a sit-up.

5. Muscle spasm and postural abnormalities.

6. In severe cases, disk herniation may interfere with normal bladder and/or bowel function.

FIGURE 10.10 Recommended position for an athlete with acute lower back pain.

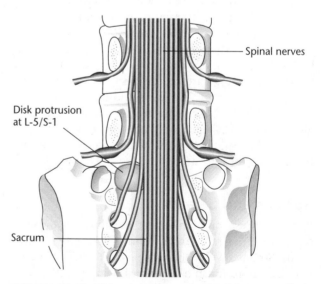

FIGURE 10.11 Disk protrusion at level L-5/S-1 may affect sacral nerves.

WHAT IF?

You are coaching gymnastics. One of your athletes just overrotated on a "double-back" on floor. As soon as she hit the mat, she collapsed to the floor, complaining of severe pain in her lumbar region. In addition, she complains of a burning sensation in the back of her thigh and lower leg. What type of injury might she have? What type of first aid care would you provide?

First aid care:

1. Remove the athlete from participation with assistance because any voluntary attempts to move will usually increase the pain.
2. Place the athlete in a position of lying supine, with the legs parallel and both knees drawn up so the knees and hips are flexed (Figure 10.10); if this position is uncomfortable, allow the athlete to assume a position that is the least painful.
3. Place a rolled towel or some other soft material into the lumbar region for support.
4. Place a bag of crushed ice into the lumbar region.
5. Arrange for transport to a medical facility for evaluation.
6. Although little can be done in the field for such injuries, much can be done to alleviate long-term symptoms with a combination of physical therapy and drug therapy. The major goal of such a strategy is to return the athlete to participation and avoid the need for surgery.

herniated disk Rupture or protrusion of the nucleus pulposus through the annulus fibrosus of an intervertebral disk.

REVIEW QUESTIONS

1. *True or false:* Because of the bony relationship between the ribs and adjacent vertebrae, the thoracic spine is much less mobile than either the cervical or lumbar region of the spine is.
2. *True or false:* Available data indicate that soft-tissue injuries of the thoracic spine are more frequent than bone-related injuries are.
3. Describe briefly the condition known as Scheuermann's disease along with its signs and symptoms.
4. Define scoliosis, kyphosis, and lordosis.
5. What is a posterior rib fracture, and what are its common signs and symptoms?
6. What is a consistent symptom related to sprains in the thoracic spine?
7. *True or false:* Intervertebral disk injuries are extremely common to the thoracic spine.
8. Anatomically, the sacrum consists of how many fused vertebrae?
9. Describe the condition known as spondylolysis.
10. Describe briefly the condition known as spondylolisthesis, including both the signs and symptoms as well as recommended treatment.
11. What is the recommended immediate treatment for a suspected strain or sprain of the lumbar spine?
12. Describe briefly the normal anatomy of a typical lumbar intervertebral disk as well as the process of disk herniation.
13. What are the signs and symptoms of lumbar disk herniation?

REFERENCES

American Academy of Orthopaedic Surgeons (AAOS). (1991). *Athletic Training and Sports Medicine* (2d ed.). Park Ridge, Ill.: American Academy of Orthopaedic Surgeons.

Anderson MK, Hall SJ, Martin M. (2000). *Sports Injury Management* (2d ed.). Philadelphia: Lippincott Williams & Wilkins.

Booher JM, Thibodeau GA. (1989). *Athletic Injury Assessment.* St. Louis: Times Mirror/Mosby.

Gray H. (1985). *Anatomy of the Human Body.* Philadelphia: Lea & Febiger.

Halpern BC, Smith AD. (1991). Catching the cause of low-back pain. *Phys Sportsmed.* 19:71–79.

O'Leary P, Boiardo R. (1986). The diagnosis and treatment of injuries of the spine in athletes. In Nicholas JA, Hershman EB (eds.). *The Lower Extremity and Spine in Sports Medicine* (pp. 1171–1229). St. Louis: Mosby.

Rasch PJ. (1989). *Kinesiology and Applied Anatomy.* Philadelphia: Lea & Febiger.

Shankman G. (1991). *Athletic Injury Care and Sports Conditioning.* Woodstock, Ga.: Sports Health Education.

11

Injuries to the Shoulder Region

MAJOR CONCEPTS

The initial sections of this chapter review the gross anatomy and arthrology of the articulations of the shoulder, followed by a brief discussion of acute and chronic injuries common to the shoulder region. This chapter describes clavicular fractures with respect to the common mechanisms of injury, signs and symptoms, and recommended first aid care. It also covers injuries to the acromioclavicular, sternoclavicular, and glenohumeral joints, outlining the common mechanisms of injury, signs and symptoms, and recommended first aid care.

Next the chapter reviews musculotendinous injuries of the shoulder region related to common mechanisms of injury such as throwing and swinging; it summarizes the basic kinesiology with identification of the various types of muscle contractions during each phase of movement. This is followed by specific information regarding strains to the rotator cuff, with special attention given to the signs and symptoms of this debilitating injury. It then discusses a related injury known as impingement syndrome with respect to its anatomy, signs and symptoms, and recommended treatment.

The concluding portions of the chapter contain information regarding two groups of injuries—problems with biceps tendons and contusions of the shoulder region. They present practical information about the signs and symptoms of these injuries along with the suggested first aid.

The web site for this book offers many useful tools and is a great source for supplementary information for both students and instructors.

Visit the site at
http://health.jbpub.com/
book/concepts/5e
to link to the following organizations and sites:

- The Southern California Orthopedic Institute

ANATOMY REVIEW

The shoulder allows for a great deal of movement while at the same time providing a point of attachment for the arm to the thorax. The skeleton of the shoulder (Figure 11.1) consists of the bones of the shoulder girdle and the upper arm bone (humerus). The *clavicle* and the *scapula* make up the shoulder girdle, so named because these two bones surround (girdle) the upper thorax. The head of the *humerus* combines with the shallow glenoid fossa of the scapula to form the highly mobile **glenohumeral (GH) joint,** commonly known as the shoulder joint (Figure 11.2). The GH joint is given additional stability by a fibrocartilaginous cuplike structure known as the glenoid labrum, which is directly attached to the glenoid fossa (Gray, 1985). The shoulder region also includes the **acromioclavicular (AC) joint,** located between the distal end of the clavicle and the acromion of the scapula (Figure 11.2), and the **sternoclavicular (SC) joint,** located between the proximal end of the clavicle and the manubrium of the sternum (Figure 11.3). Each of these joints is held together with ligaments and joint capsules that provide stability while also allowing for necessary movement, which is quite limited.

Many muscles move both the shoulder girdle and the GH joint in a multitude of directions. In nearly all motions the shoulder girdle and the GH joint work together to move the arm. Consequently, any limitation from injury to the shoulder girdle will indirectly affect the GH joint. The muscles in the region of the shoulder can be divided into two groups—those that act on the shoulder girdle and those that act on the GH joint (Figures 11.4 and 11.5). The muscles of the shoulder girdle are the levator scapulae, trapezius, rhom-

boids, subclavius, pectoralis minor, and serratus anterior. These muscles collectively contribute to the movements of the shoulder girdle, which include scapular retraction and protraction, upward and downward scapular rotation, elevation, and depression. The muscles are listed with their specific actions and innervations in Time Out 11.1.

The muscles that act on the GH joint include the pectoralis major, latissimus dorsi, deltoid, teres major, rotator cuff muscles (supraspinatus, infraspinatus, teres minor, subscapularis), and coracobrachialis. The GH joint enjoys an astounding amount of movement, virtually in any direction; however, the following are the movements normally attributed to the joint:

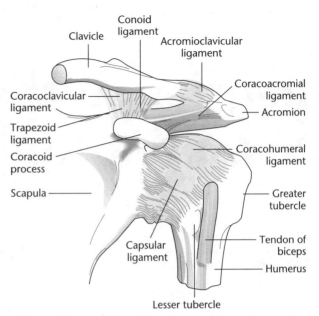

FIGURE 11.2 Ligaments of the acromioclavicular and glenohumeral joints.

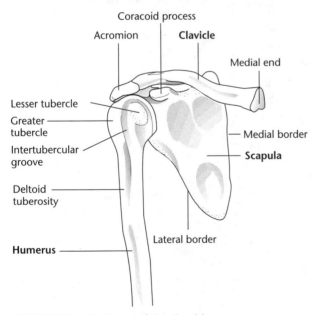

FIGURE 11.1 Skeleton of the shoulder region.

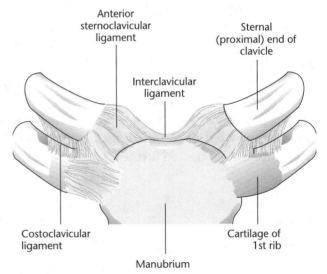

FIGURE 11.3 Ligaments of the sternoclavicular joint.

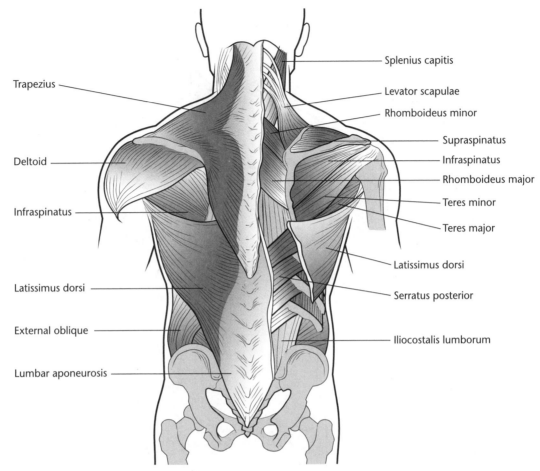

FIGURE 11.4 Muscles of the posterior trunk region.

flexion, extension, horizontal flexion and extension, internal and external rotation, abduction, and adduction. The muscles are listed with their specific actions and innervations in Time Out 11.2.

In athletes a large amount of soft tissue covers both the shoulder girdle and the GH joint; as a result, they are somewhat protected from external blows. However, even in extremely muscular athletes both the AC and SC joints lie just under the skin and are therefore more exposed to injury. The blood supply to the entire upper extremity, including the shoulder, originates from branches of the subclavian artery. As this artery passes into the axillary region it becomes the axillary artery; it continues into the upper arm, becoming the brachial artery, and splits just distal to the elbow into the radial and ulnar arteries that extend into the forearm and hand (Figure 11.6).

The major nerves of the shoulder and upper extremity originate from that group known collectively as the brachial plexus (Figure 11.7). The brachial plexus originates from the ventral primary divisions of the fifth through the eighth cervical nerves and the first thoracic nerve (Gray, 1985). Through a complex series of divisions the brachial plexus provides all the major nerves to the entire upper extremity.

Common Sports Injuries

Injuries to the shoulder region are common in many sports and in some cases are highly sport specific. For example, injuries to both the GH and AC joints are quite common in wrestling. Sports that emphasize a throwing

glenohumeral (GH) joint Articulation (spheroid) formed by the head of the humerus and the glenoid fossa of the scapula.

acromioclavicular (AC) joint Articulation (arthrodial) formed by the distal end of the clavicle and the acromion process.

sternoclavicular (SC) joint Articulation (arthrodial) formed by the union of the proximal clavicle and the manubrium of the sternum.

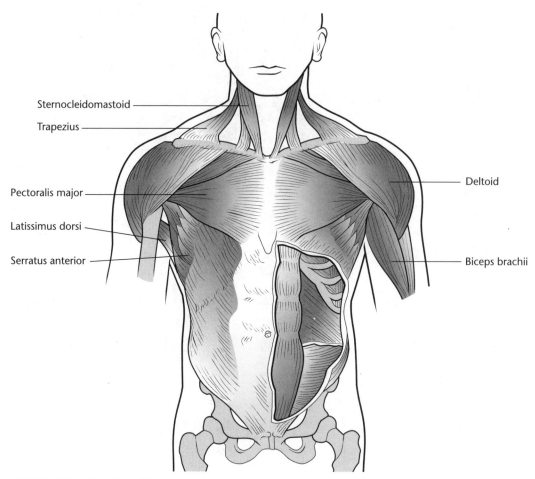

FIGURE 11.5 Muscles of the pectoral region.

TIME OUT 11.1

Muscles, Actions, and Innervations of the Shoulder Girdle

Muscle	Action(s)	Innervation
Levator scapulae	Scapular elevation	Dorsal scapular
Rhomboids	Scapular retraction Downward rotation	Dorsal scapular
Trapezius	Elevation Retraction Upward rotation Depression	Spinal accessory
Pectoralis minor	Depression	Medial pectoral
Serratus anterior	Protraction Upward rotation	Long thoracic
Subclavius	Depression Stabilization of the SC joint	Nerve to the subclavius

TIME OUT 11.2

Muscles, Actions, and Innervations of the Glenohumeral Joint

Muscle	Action(s)	Innervation
Pectoralis major	Adduction Internal rotation Flexion Extension	Med. & lat. pectoral
Latissimus dorsi	Extension Adduction Internal rotation	Thoracodorsal
Deltoid	Abduction Internal rotation Extension & lateral rotation Flexion & internal rotation	Axillary
Teres major	Adduction Internal rotation	Lower subscapular
Coracobrachialis	Flexion Adduction	Musculocutaneous
Rotator Cuff		
Supraspinatus	Abduction	Suprascapular
Infraspinatus	External rotation	Suprascapular
Teres minor	External rotation	Axillary
Subscapularis	Internal rotation Adduction	Upp. & lower subscapular

or swinging action often produce injuries caused by overuse to the muscles of the rotator cuff (infraspinatus, supraspinatus, teres minor, subscapularis), which act on the GH joint. The rotator cuff muscles are extremely important to the stability of the GH joint because this large ball-and-socket structure lacks inherent strength. Sports such as cycling and skating produce a large number of fractures of the clavicle brought about by falls. Injuries of the shoulder region can be classified as either acute (of sudden onset) or chronic (resulting from overuse). Sports involving heavy contact or collisions yield more acute injuries; those necessitating repeated movements tend to produce more chronic injuries.

Skeletal Injuries

Fractured Clavicle

The most common fracture of the shoulder region is a fracture of the clavicle. Such fractures can result from direct blows to the bone; however, the majority occur as a result of falls that transmit the force to the clavicle either through the arm or shoulder. The majority of clavicular fractures occur about midshaft (Figure 11.8);

the remainder involve either the proximal or distal end of the bone (AAOS, 1991). In the adolescent athlete another type of clavicular fracture, commonly known as a greenstick fracture, can occur. This fracture occurs in immature bone and involves a cracking, splintering type of injury. Although a fractured clavicle is potentially dangerous given the close proximity of the bone to major blood vessels and nerves, the vast majority of these injuries cause few complications. It is critical that appropriate first aid be applied to prevent unnecessary movement of the fracture that can result in additional soft-tissue damage.

Signs and symptoms of a fractured clavicle include the following:

1. Swelling and/or deformity of the clavicle
2. Discoloration at the site of the fracture
3. Possible broken bone end projecting through the skin
4. Athlete reporting that a snap or pop was felt or heard
5. Athlete holding the arm on the affected side to relieve pressure on the shoulder girdle

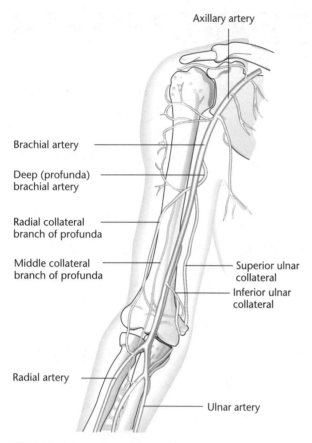

FIGURE 11.6 Major arteries of the arm.

Axillary artery

Brachial artery

Deep (profunda) brachial artery

Radial collateral branch of profunda

Middle collateral branch of profunda

Superior ulnar collateral

Inferior ulnar collateral

Radial artery

Ulnar artery

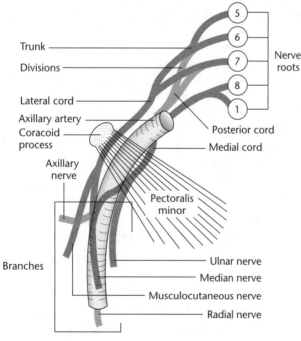

FIGURE 11.7 The nerves of the brachial plexus.

Trunk

Divisions

Lateral cord

Axillary artery

Coracoid process

Axillary nerve

Branches

Nerve roots

Posterior cord

Medial cord

Pectoralis minor

Ulnar nerve

Median nerve

Musculocutaneous nerve

Radial nerve

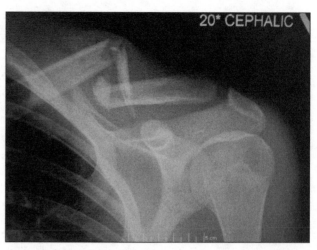

20° CEPHALIC

FIGURE 11.8 Fracture of the left clavicle (left shoulder).

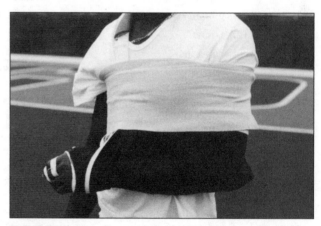

FIGURE 11.9 A sling-and-swathe bandage is effective for a variety of injuries to the upper extremity.

First aid care:

1. Treat for possible shock.
2. Carefully apply a sling-and-swathe bandage as shown in Figure 11.9 (National Safety Council, 1991).
3. Apply sterile dressings to any related wounds.
4. Arrange for transport to a medical facility.

Fractured Scapula

A much less common type of fracture in the shoulder region involves the scapula. A unique group of scapular fractures among professional football players was described by Cain and Hamilton (1992) in the *American Journal of Sports Medicine*. In all cases these fractures resulted from direct blows to the shoulder region. The symptoms of this type of fracture are less clear than those related to fractures of the clavicle. An athlete with a history of a severe blow to the shoulder region, followed immediately by considerable pain and loss of function, should be referred to a physician for further evaluation. This injury can be identified only by X-ray analysis. Treatment is determined by the specific location and extent of the fracture(s). Typically the athlete's arm will be placed in a sling, and the player will be removed from sports participation for a period of 6 weeks.

Soft-Tissue Injuries

A variety of sprains and strains involving any number of specific ligaments and tendons occurs in this region of the body. Although any joint can sustain a sprain, the GH and AC joints are the most commonly injured in the shoulder region.

Acromioclavicular Joint Injuries

Located just under the skin on the lateral superior surface of the shoulder is the AC joint. This synoviated articulation is supported by the superior and inferior AC ligaments and contains an intra-articular cartilaginous disk as well (Dias & Gregg, 1991). Additional support to the AC joint is provided by the coracoclavicular (CC) ligament (see Figure 11.2), which comprises the trapezoid and conoid ligaments. The CC ligament is attached between the superior coracoid process and the inferior lateral surface of the clavicle.

The typical mechanism of injury for the AC joint is a downward blow to the outer end of the clavicle, which results in the acromion process being driven inferiorly while the distal clavicle remains in place. Another possible mechanism is a fall forward on an outstretched arm, which then transmits the force up the extremity and results in the humeral head driving the acromion superiorly and posteriorly while the clavicle remains in place (O'Donoghue, 1976). Either of these two mechanisms can result in varying degrees of ligament damage. According to O'Donoghue (1976), the severity of the injury is graded based on the amount of damage to specific ligaments; however, any injury can be placed into one of the three following categories:

1. **First degree:** No significant damage, all ligaments intact.
2. **Second degree:** Relatively severe damage (tearing) of the ligaments. There will be no abnormal movement, and the clavicle will be in the normal position.
3. **Third degree**
   a. Complete rupture of the AC ligament with an intact CC ligament (Figure 11.10).
   b. Complete rupture of the AC and CC ligaments (Figure 11.11).

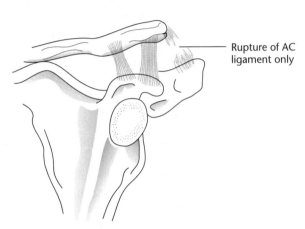

FIGURE 11.10 Complete rupture of the acromioclavicular ligament with an intact coracoclavicular ligament.

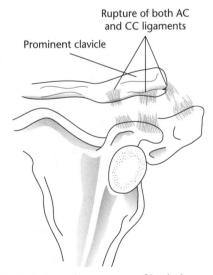

FIGURE 11.11 Complete rupture of both the acromioclavicular and coracoclavicular ligaments.

Signs and symptoms of AC joint sprains include the following:

1. With first- and second-degree sprains there will be mild swelling with point tenderness and discoloration around the AC joint.

2. Any movement of the shoulder region will elicit pain.

3. With a third-degree sprain there will be significant deformity in the region of the AC ligament. In the case of ruptures of both the AC and CC ligaments, there will be total displacement of the clavicle.

4. The athlete may report having felt a snap or heard a pop.

First aid care:

1. Immediately apply ice and compression. This is best accomplished by placing a bag of crushed ice over the AC joint and securing it with an elastic wrap tied in a figure-eight configuration.

2. Once the ice and compression are in place, apply a standard sling-and-swathe bandage as described by the National Safety Council (1991).

3. Immediately refer the athlete to a medical facility for further evaluation. In the event of severe injury, arrange for transport and treat for shock.

Long-term treatment for AC separations is dependent on the level of severity of the injury. In the case of first-degree and relatively minor second-degree sprains, rest and immobilization are normally effective. Considerable debate exists regarding the appropriate care for severe second- and third-degree AC injuries. Several surgical procedures have been employed; however, research indicates that more conservative, nonsurgical approaches may be just as effective (Bach, VanFleet, & Novak, 1992; Dias & Gregg, 1991).

WHAT IF?

You are at a high school wrestling tournament examining an athlete who just sustained a shoulder injury. You notice a large mass in the armpit area as well as a definite sloping of the shoulder's contour. The athlete is holding his arm in slight abduction and states that he felt his shoulder "pop out." What would you conclude based upon all of this information? How would you manage this injury?

Glenohumeral Joint Injuries

This articulation consists of the relatively large humeral head opposing the rather shallow glenoid fossa of the scapula. This bony arrangement is effective in giving the joint a great deal of mobility. The GH joint is classified as a spheroidal articulation that moves within all three planes of motion: frontal, sagittal, and transverse. However, this mobility makes the GH joint very unstable (Grabiner, 1989). The major soft-tissue structures of the GH joint (Figure 11.2) include the capsular ligament and the coracohumeral ligament (Gray, 1985).

The typical mechanism of injury for the GH joint involves having the arm abducted and externally rotated. In this position the anterior portion of the joint capsule, specifically the GH ligament, can be stressed beyond its capacity. If the ligament fails, the head of the humerus can move forward and out of place, resulting in the most common type of GH joint dislocation, an anterior dislocation (Figure 11.12). Depending on the severity, this injury may be either a subluxation or a complete dislocation.

Signs and symptoms of an anterior GH dislocation include the following:

1. Deformity of the shoulder joint: The normal contour of the shoulder is lost, and it appears to slope down abnormally.

2. The arm of the affected side will appear longer than normal.

3. The head of the humerus will be palpable with the axilla.

4. The athlete will be supporting the arm on the affected side with the opposite arm; the affected arm will be slightly abducted at the shoulder and flexed at the elbow.

5. The athlete will resist all efforts passively or actively to move the GH joint.

6. *Special Note:* In cases of subluxations of the GH, the shoulder may appear normal. However, it will be extremely painful for the athlete to attempt any movement. In addition, the joint may be point tender.

First aid care:

1. Immediately apply ice and compression. Put a rolled towel in the axilla. Place a bag of crushed ice on the front and back of the shoulder joint and secure with an elastic wrap tied in a figure-eight configuration.

2. After the ice and compression are in place, apply a standard sling-and-swathe bandage as described by the National Safety Council (1991).

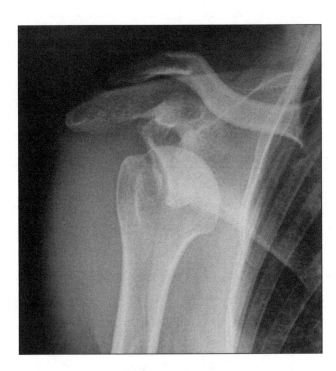

FIGURE 11.12 Anterior (inferior dislocation of the glenohumeral joint (right shoulder). Note the position of the humeral head relative to the glenoid fossa.

3. Immediately refer the athlete to a medical facility for further evaluation.

4. Because soft-tissue injury may be extensive, treat for shock.

A common complication of GH joint sprains is chronic GH joint subluxation. It has been reported that, once sustained, up to 85% to 90% of all traumatic anterior GH joint dislocations recur (Arnheim, 1987). The joint capsule, ligaments, and supporting musculature are often stretched; therefore, as the athlete continues to participate in stressful activity the joint becomes progressively less stable. The athlete typically will report that during certain movements, often those placing the GH joint in abduction and external rotation, the joint will pop out and then return to its normal position.

Such cases are usually treated conservatively with rest and exercises that specifically focus on the muscles surrounding the joint, including those of the rotator cuff. In severe cases surgical reconstructive procedures may be prescribed.

Sternoclavicular Joint Injuries

The SC joint is formed by the union of the proximal end of the clavicle and the manubrium of the sternum. This synoviated articulation is strengthened by several ligaments (Figure 11.3). These include the joint capsule, the anterior and posterior SC ligaments, the interclavicular and costoclavicular ligaments, and an articular disk located within the joint (Gray, 1985).

Although there are fewer injuries to the SC joint than to either the AC or GH joints, the coach should be prepared to recognize and treat them correctly. The mechanism of injury for the SC joint involves an external blow to the shoulder region that results in a dislocation of the proximal clavicle, most commonly with the bone moving anteriorly and superiorly. A sprain to the SC joint can range in severity from minor stretching, with no actual tearing of tissues, to a complete rupture of ligaments and extensive soft-tissue damage. Fortunately, anterior/superior dislocations cause few additional problems and are easily treated. Occurring much less frequently, but potentially more dangerous, is a posterior SC dislocation. In this instance the proximal end of the clavicle is displaced posteriorly, with the possibility of placing direct pressure on soft-tissue structures in the region, such as blood vessels or even the esophagus and trachea (AAOS, 1991).

Signs and symptoms of SC joint injuries include the following:

1. In most cases (second- and third-degree sprains) there will be gross deformity present at the SC joint.

2. In all but the least severe cases, swelling will be immediate.

3. Movement of the entire shoulder girdle will be limited owing to pain within the SC joint.

4. The athlete will typically report having heard a snapping sound or may have experienced a tearing sensation at the SC joint.

5. Note the body position of the athlete, because in this injury the arm may be held close to the body and the head/neck may be tilted/flexed toward the injured shoulder (Wroble, 1995).

WHAT IF?

You are examining a baseball player (center fielder) who is complaining of chronic pain in the back of his shoulder. He notices the pain especially after he throws a ball, and he is point tender in the region of the posterior scapula. What structure could be involved in this case?

First aid care:

1. Apply ice and compression, which is best accomplished using a plastic bag filled with crushed ice that is secured with an elastic wrap tied in a figure-eight configuration. Take care not to put pressure over the airway when wrapping the shoulder for compression of the SC joint.

2. Place the arm of the affected shoulder in a standard sling-and-swathe bandage as described by the National Safety Council (1991).

3. In cases of severe soft-tissue damage, treat the athlete for shock.

Medical treatment for the majority of SC joint sprains is conservative, that is, reduction of the dislocation if present followed by 2 to 3 weeks of support with a sling-and-swathe bandage. It is very rare that any sort of surgical correction is attempted, especially in the case of anterior dislocations. Obviously a sound program of rehabilitation exercises prescribed by a competent sports medicine professional will be helpful in getting the athlete back into action.

Strains of the Shoulder Region

A large number of muscles attach to the bones of the shoulder girdle, any one of which can suffer a strain. As was mentioned earlier, certain sports produce very specific injuries to the shoulder. Perhaps the most common strain involves the muscles of the rotator cuff.

Rotator Cuff

The muscles of the **rotator cuff** (Figures 11.13 and 11.14) serve a variety of purposes, including stabilization of the humeral head in the glenoid fossa as well as abduction and internal and external rotation of the GH joint.

To better understand the mechanism of injuries involving the rotator cuff, it is necessary to review the kinesiology of the overhand throw and/or swing. Throwing has been described as a five-phase process involving windup, cocking, acceleration, release, and follow-through (AAOS, 1991). Essentially, the windup phase requires putting the entire body into the best position to generate throwing forces. The cocking stage involves pulling the throwing arm into an abducted and externally rotated position at the GH joint; this incorporates a **concentric contraction** of several of the rotator cuff muscles, as well as other muscles of the shoulder region. The acceleration phase involves a sudden reversal of cocking: The arm is moved rapidly into internal rotation, horizontal flexion, and adduction of the GH joint via concentric contractions of muscles such as the pectoralis major, anterior deltoid, teres major, latissimus dorsi, and triceps. Depending on

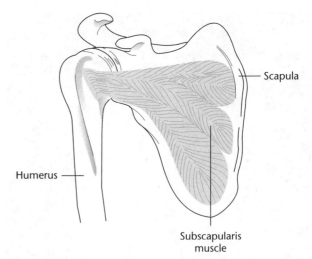

FIGURE 11.13 The rotator cuff (anterior view).

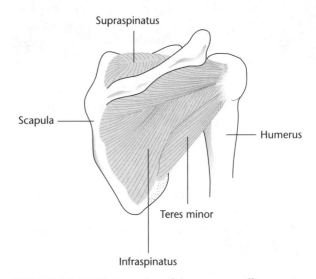

FIGURE 11.14 The muscles of the rotator cuff (posterior view).

the skill and strength of the athlete, the forces generated during the acceleration phase can be substantial and must be dealt with effectively during follow-through. The release phase is the shortest in the throwing cycle and involves timing the release at the point of maximum velocity. The follow-through phase requires that the entire upper extremity be decelerated immediately after the release. It is critical to note that several muscles of the rotator cuff are actively contracting eccentrically in an effort to slow the arm down.

The vast majority of strains to the rotator cuff occur during the follow-through phase, specifically during the eccentric phase of the contraction. This problem is made worse when the muscles of the rotator cuff are significantly weaker than those muscles involved in the acceleration phase. This problem can best be addressed with a properly designed conditioning program aimed at strengthening the muscles of the rotator cuff.

Strains to the rotator cuff are normally the result of overuse: They develop slowly over many weeks or months. Athletes who are involved in sports that require throwing and swinging are at risk for this type of injury, especially athletes with weak rotator cuffs or those who are older. Proper warm-up of the throwing and/or swinging arm can help reduce the stress on the musculature of the shoulder girdle. Often errors in execution of the throw or swing can contribute to overuse injury. Therefore, it is critical that athletes learn correct techniques to reduce the chances of developing an injury.

Signs and symptoms of rotator cuff injuries include the following:

1. Pain within the shoulder, especially during the follow-through phase of a throw or swing.

2. Difficulty in bringing the arm up and back during the cocking phase of a throw or swing.

3. Pain and stiffness within the shoulder region 12 to 24 hours after a practice or competition that involved throwing or swinging.

4. Point tenderness around the region of the humeral head that appears to be deep within the deltoid muscle. (It should be noted that rotator cuff injuries can mimic many others common to the shoulder region, including **bursitis** and **tendinitis**.)

First aid care of rotator cuff strains must take the following into consideration:

1. Overuse injuries are difficult to treat effectively without a thorough medical evaluation. When symptoms occur, the application of ice and compression may prove helpful in reducing the pain and loss of function associated with the injury.

2. In the majority of cases, the athlete will report repeated episodes of symptoms spanning many weeks or even months. Therefore, medical referral for a complete evaluation is essential.

Glenohumeral Joint–Related Impingement Syndrome

To *impinge* means to be forced "upon or against something" (Guralnik & Friend, 1966). A **syndrome** is defined as "a number of symptoms occurring together and characterizing a specific disease" (Guralnik & Friend, 1966). Hence, an impingement syndrome of the shoulder occurs when a soft-tissue structure such as a bursa or tendon is squeezed between moving joint structures,

resulting in irritation and pain. In the case of the GH joint, the most common impingement occurs to the tendon of the supraspinatus muscle as it passes across the top of the joint en route to its insertion (Lo, Hsu, & Chan, 1990). The normal anatomy of the GH joint is a tight fit relative to the amount of available space for structures above the joint capsule. This region, located directly beneath the acromion process, is known as the subacromial space. The floor of the subacromial space is the GH joint capsule. The ceiling comprises the acromion process and the coracoacromial ligament, which form an arch across the top of the GH joint known as the coracoacromial arch (Figure 11.15).

Any condition, whether related to sports or congenital, that decreases the size of the subacromial space may result in the development of an impingement syndrome. Various experts in the sports medicine community have reported that the most common causes of GH joint–related impingement syndromes are "anatomic variations in the coracoacromial arch" that cause damage to the structures found in the subacromial space (Burns & Turba, 1992).

Athletes who participate in sports placing an emphasis on arm movements above the shoulder level demonstrate a higher rate of impingement problems when compared with athletes who take part in sports not emphasizing such movements. A survey of athletes in sports requiring repetitive arm motions found the high-risk sports to include volleyball, badminton, basketball, gymnastics, squash, swimming, table tennis, tennis, and track and field events (Lo, Hsu, & Chan, 1990).

Signs and symptoms of impingement syndromes include the following:

1. Pain when the GH joint is abducted and externally rotated in conjunction with loss of strength

2. Pain whenever the arm is abducted beyond 80 to 90 degrees

3. Nocturnal pain (AAOS, 1991)

4. Pain felt deep within the shoulder (AAOS, 1991)

---

rotator cuff Group of four muscles of the glenohumeral joint: subscapularis, supraspinatus, infraspinatus, and teres minor.

concentric contraction Occurs when a muscle shortens and there is movement at the joint accompanied by contraction against resistance.

bursitis Inflammation of a bursa.

tendinitis Inflammation of a tendon.

syndrome Group of typical symptoms or conditions that characterize a deficiency or disease.

First aid care of impingement syndromes involving the GH joint is not required because they tend to develop over many days, weeks, or even months. Rather, any athlete complaining of the signs and symptoms listed should be referred for a complete medical evaluation. Treatment will consist of rest, anti-inflammatory drugs, and physical therapy. If these fail, surgery to correct the problem may be prescribed. In many cases this can be done via arthroscopy; typically it involves procedures such as removal of bone spurs from beneath the acromion process, release of the coracoacromial ligament, or a resectioning of a portion of the undersurface of the acromion process (partial acromionectomy) (AAOS, 1991).

Biceps Tendon Problems

The anatomy of the GH joint (Figure 11.16) includes the tendon of the long head of the biceps brachii muscle. The tendon passes into the joint capsule and is surrounded by a specialized portion of the synovium of the joint. As the tendon continues through the joint, it runs across the superior surface of the humeral head; in this position the tendon helps to stabilize the humeral head when the joint is abducted. The tendon of the long head of the biceps brachii originates from the supraglenoid tubercle (Gray, 1985). The short head of the biceps brachii derives from the nearby coracoid process. This tendon, however, remains anatomically separate from the GH joint.

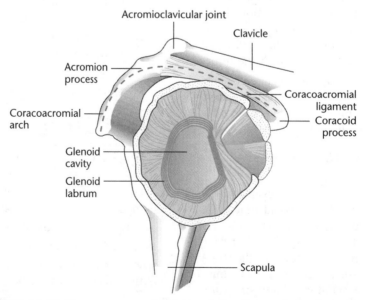

FIGURE 11.15 The coracoacromial arch and glenohumeral joint (lateral view).

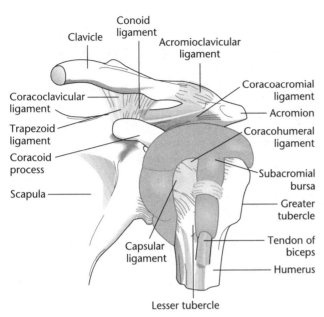

FIGURE 11.16 The glenohumeral joint (anterior view).

The tendon of the long head of the biceps brachii is located directly beneath the acromion process; therefore, it can suffer a type of impingement similar to that seen in the supraspinatus tendon. As the joint is abducted the tendon may be compressed within the subacromial space. Consequently, symptoms similar to those of impingement of the supraspinatus will develop. Athletes at risk for this injury include those involved in sports that place an emphasis on repetitive overhead movements with the arms.

Another problem related to the long head tendon of the biceps brachii is tendinitis, which may lead to a subluxation of the tendon from the bicipital groove. In most cases, tendinitis will develop slowly over a period of weeks or months. As the tendon enlarges as a result of the inflammation, it becomes less stable in the groove, where it is held by way of the transverse humeral ligament.

In chronic cases, a sudden violent force such as is commonly generated in throwing may cause the tendon to subluxate out of the groove, thereby stretching and tearing the ligament. The athlete will notice significant symptoms if the tendon should subluxate from the bicipital groove.

Signs and symptoms of biceps tendon problems include the following:

1. Painful abduction of the shoulder joint similar to that seen in impingement problems.

2. Pain in the shoulder joint when the athlete supinates the forearm against any resistance.

3. When actively flexing and supinating the forearm against resistance, the athlete may note a popping or snapping sensation as the tendon of the long head of the biceps brachii subluxates.

First aid care of biceps tendon problems is not a practical concern because they generally develop over time and fall into the category of a chronic injury. However, if the athlete should subluxate the biceps tendon from the bicipital groove, the initial episode of this injury can require first aid. In such cases, the immediate application of ice and compression is recommended. Long-term care for this injury includes rest, anti-inflammatories, and gradually progressive exercise rehabilitation. If symptoms persist and the tendon continues to subluxate from the bicipital groove, then surgery may be required to stabilize the tendon.

Contusions of the Shoulder Region

External blows around the shoulder region are a common occurrence in a variety of sports. The GH joint is well protected by muscles crossing over the joint, such as the deltoid. The nearby AC joint, however, is exposed and quite vulnerable to external blows. If the athlete should sustain a contusion to this joint, the result can be an extremely painful condition known as a **shoulder pointer.**

Signs and symptoms of shoulder contusions include the following:

1. History of a recent blow to the shoulder, with resulting pain and decreased range of motion

2. Spasm if muscle tissue is involved

3. Discoloration and swelling, especially over bony regions such as the AC joint

First aid care:

1. Immediately apply ice and compression directly over the area(s) involved. This is best accomplished with a bag of crushed ice and an elastic wrap.

2. In cases of severe pain apply an arm sling to relieve stress on the shoulder region.

3. If significant swelling persists for more than 72 hours in the region of the AC joint, refer the athlete to a physician. In some cases the AC ligament may have sustained a sprain.

shoulder pointer Contusion and subsequent hematoma in the region of the acromioclavicular joint.

1. Which two bones make up the shoulder girdle?

2. To what structure is the glenoid labrum attached?

3. Which one of the following arteries provides the blood supply to the shoulder region and upper extremity?
   a. Common iliac
   b. Ulnar
   c. Internal carotid
   d. Subclavian
   e. Axillary

4. Which one of the following is the correct derivation of the brachial plexus?
   a. C-5/T-2
   b. C-3/T-1
   c. C-1/T-5
   d. C-1/T-1
   e. C-5/T-1

5. List the four muscles of the rotator cuff group and identify one action common to each muscle.

6. List four signs and/or symptoms of a fractured clavicle.

7. Describe and/or demonstrate the appropriate first aid procedures for a fractured clavicle.

8. Describe the major ligaments that form the AC joint.

9. Describe briefly the two mechanisms of injury for the AC joint as discussed in the chapter.

10. Describe the common signs and symptoms of AC joint injuries.

11. Explain and/or demonstrate the appropriate first aid care for AC joint injuries.

12. List the major ligaments of the GH joint.

13. *True or false:* The most common type of GH joint dislocation is posterior.

14. Describe the common signs and symptoms of a GH joint dislocation.

15. Explain and/or demonstrate the appropriate first aid treatment of an athlete with a suspected GH joint dislocation.

16. Define the condition known as chronic GH subluxation.

17. Describe the primary ligaments of the SC joint.

18. Describe the common signs and symptoms of injury to this articulation.

19. Explain and/or demonstrate the appropriate first aid treatment of an athlete with a suspected SC joint injury.

20. Explain the five phases of an overhand throw and/or swing and give a brief description of the types of muscle contractions involved in each.

21. *True or false:* The vast majority of strains of the rotator cuff occur during the windup and cocking phases of the throw and/or swing.

22. List several of the signs and symptoms of rotator cuff strain as described in the chapter.

23. What anatomic structure forms a ceiling for the subacromial space?

24. *True or false:* Athletes involved in sports placing a heavy emphasis on arm movements below the shoulder level demonstrate a higher incidence of impingement syndromes.

25. List four signs and/or symptoms of impingement syndrome of the GH joint.

26. Which one of the following structures (ligaments) holds the biceps (long head) tendon in the bicipital groove?
   a. Annular ligament
   b. Medial collateral ligament
   c. Capsular ligament
   d. Transverse humeral ligament

REFERENCES

American Academy of Orthopaedic Surgeons (AAOS). (1991). *Athletic Training and Sports Medicine* (2d ed.). Park Ridge, Ill.: American Academy of Orthopaedic Surgeons.

Arnheim DD. (1987). *Essentials of Athletic Training* (1st ed.). St. Louis: Times Mirror/Mosby.

Bach BR, VanFleet TA, Novak PJ. (1992). Acromioclavicular injuries—controversies in treatment. *Phys Sportsmed.* 20:87–101.

Burns TP, Turba JE. (1992). Arthroscopic treatment of shoulder impingement in athletes. *Am J Sports Med.* 20:13–16.

Cain TE, Hamilton WP. (1992). Scapular fractures in professional football players. *Am J Sports Med.* 20:363–365.

Dias JJ, Gregg PJ. (1991). Acromioclavicular joint injuries in sport—recommendations for treatment. *Sports Med.* 11:125–132.

Grabiner MD. (1989). The shoulder complex. In Rasch PJ (ed.). *Kinesiology and Applied Anatomy.* Philadelphia: Lea & Febiger.

Gray H. (1985). *Anatomy of the Human Body.* Philadelphia: Lea & Febiger.

Guralnik DB, Friend JH (eds.). (1966). *Webster's New World Dictionary of the American Language.* Cleveland: The World Publishing Company.

Lo YPC, Hsu YCS, Chan KM. (1990). Epidemiology of shoulder impingement in upper-arm sports events. *Br J Sports Med.* 24:173–177.

National Safety Council. (1991). *First Aid and CPR.* Boston: Jones and Bartlett.

O'Donoghue DH. (1976). *Treatment of Injuries to Athletes.* Philadelphia: W. B. Saunders.

Wroble RR. (1995). Sternoclavicular injuries—managing damage to an overlooked joint. *Phys Sportsmed.* 23:19–26.

12

Injuries to the Arm, Wrist, and Hand

MAJOR CONCEPTS

This chapter begins with a brief review of the gross anatomy of the region with special emphasis on arthrology. It goes on to discuss upper-arm (brachial region) injuries, focusing especially on contusions and fractures. Given the potentially serious consequences of fractures of the humerus, the chapter provides detailed instructions for proper first aid care of these injuries. Next, the chapter reviews elbow injuries, outlining current information regarding the typical mechanisms, signs and symptoms, and critical first aid procedures. Again, because there are potential catastrophic consequences of a mismanaged elbow injury, this section provides specific first aid instructions. It also discusses problems related to the muscle attachments surrounding the elbow, clinically known as epicondylitis, along with special attention paid to the possible causes, signs and symptoms, and care.

Although quite rare, forearm injuries do occasionally occur, and the chapter reviews the more frequent varieties, along with guidelines on signs and symptoms as well as first aid care. Next it discusses injuries to the wrist, emphasizing relatively common injuries such as fractures of the scaphoid bone and dislocations of the lunate bone. Nerve injuries of the wrist region are common; carpal tunnel syndrome is perhaps the most well known. Therefore, the chapter outlines specific signs and symptoms for nerve problems involving the median and ulnar nerves.

Finally, the chapter discusses hand and finger injuries, which are both extremely common in sports.

http://health.jbpub.com/book/concepts/5e

The web site for this book offers many useful tools and is a great source for supplementary information for both students and instructors.

Visit the site at
http://health.jbpub.com/book/concepts/5e
to link to the following organizations and sites:

- The Southern California Orthopedic Institute
- Human Anatomy Online

The bones of the arm are the humerus (upper arm), the radius, and the ulna (forearm). The proximal end of the humerus (head) articulates with the glenoid fossa of the scapula to form the shoulder (glenohumeral) joint. The distal end of the humerus articulates with both of the forearm bones to form the elbow joint, which actually comprises three specific articulations—the **humeroulnar, humeroradial,** and proximal **radioulnar** joints. The distal end of the forearm articulates with the wrist (carpal) bones, forming the **radiocarpal** (wrist) and distal radioulnar joints. The joints of the arm allow for a great variety of motions, including flexion/extension and pronation/supination at the elbow as well as flexion/extension and radial and ulnar deviation at the wrist. The elbow (Figure 12.1) and wrist joints are held together with several ligaments that may be subject to trauma related to sports participation. Certainly one of the more distinctive ligament structures in the human body is the annular ligament of the elbow (Figure 12.2). This ligament holds the head of the radius in the proximal radioulnar joint; in so doing it allows that articulation to pronate and supinate while simultaneously allowing the radial head to articulate with the capitulum of the humerus.

As can be seen in Figure 12.3, the musculature of the arm is extensive. It is dominated by the elbow extensor and flexors that include the biceps brachii, brachialis, triceps brachii, and the anconeus. The muscles of the arm collectively contribute to several of the movements of the elbow; they are extension, flexion, and supination. The muscles are listed along with their specific actions and innervations in Time Out 12.1.

The forearm includes a large number of muscles for the movements of the forearm, wrist, hand, and fingers. The majority of the forearm muscles originate from the regions of the humeral epicondyles, either lateral or medial, that are located immediately proximal to the elbow joint. The muscles

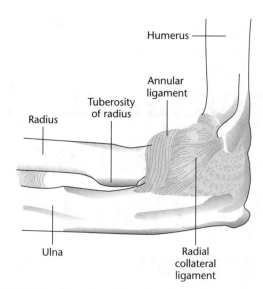

FIGURE 12.2 The elbow joint (lateral view).

of the forearm can be divided into the extensor/supinator and flexor/pronator groups (Figures 12.4 and 12.5). These muscles collectively contribute to the pronation and supination of the elbow, flexion and extension of the wrist and fingers, flexion and extension of the thumb, and radial and ulnar deviation of the wrist. The muscles are listed with their specific actions and innervations in Time Out 12.2.

The vasculature of the arm has been described in the previous chapter, as has the neural distribution.

Soft-Tissue Injuries to the Upper Arm

The majority of injuries to the upper arm are either contusions or fractures. Though strains do occur to this region, they are exceedingly uncommon. Because of the nature of contact sports, blows to the arm region are a common occurrence. A typical scenario involves a football lineman blocking with arms flexed at the elbows and receiving blows to the lateral surfaces of the upper arms. The underlying muscle tissue is compressed between the overlying skin and the bone of the humerus. Depending on the magnitude of the blow(s), damage to the muscle tissue may be significant. If such episodes are repeated, the athlete may develop a condition known as myositis ossificans traumatica.

Myositis Ossificans Traumatica

Myositis ossificans traumatica involves chronic inflammation of muscle, leading to the development of bonelike tissue in the muscle. It is quite common in football—so much so that the condition has become known as **tackler's exostosis** (AAOS, 1991). An **exostosis** is defined

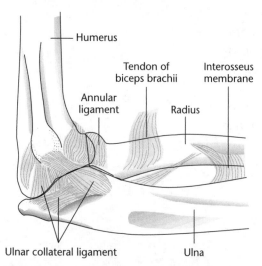

FIGURE 12.1 The elbow joint (medial view).

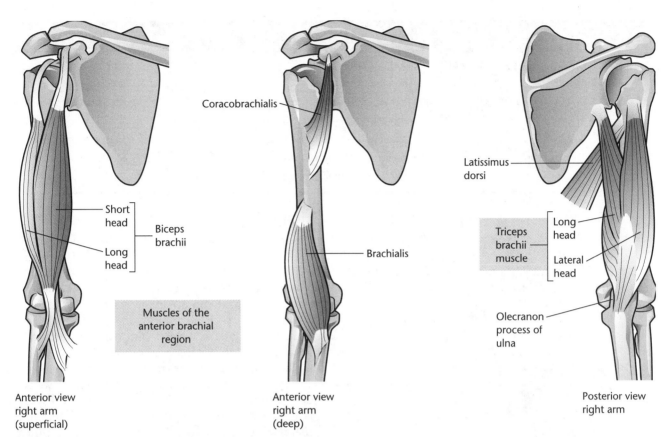

Coracobrachialis

Short head
Biceps brachii
Long head

Muscles of the anterior brachial region

Brachialis

Latissimus dorsi

Triceps brachii muscle
Long head
Lateral head

Olecranon process of ulna

Anterior view right arm (superficial)

Anterior view right arm (deep)

Posterior view right arm

FIGURE 12.3 Muscles of the arm, anterior and posterior.

as "a benign growth projecting from a bone surface characteristically capped by cartilage" (Friel, 1977). Myositis ossificans traumatica develops over a period of weeks or even months and therefore tends to be ignored in early stages of development, when it is typically dismissed as a simple bruise. It is important that the coach recognize that such an injury can develop into a more serious one and evaluate it accordingly.

Signs and symptoms of upper-arm contusions include the following:

1. Recent history of contusion to the region
2. Pain, discoloration, and swelling in the region of the injury
3. Muscle spasm and subsequent loss of strength in the affected muscle
4. Possible neurologic symptoms, including loss of sensation or muscle function distal to the site of injury

First aid care:

1. Immediately apply ice and compression. This is best accomplished by using a bag of crushed ice that is secured with a wide elastic wrap tied around the arm.

humeroulnar joint Articulation (ginglymus) formed by the proximal end of the ulna, specifically the trochlear notch, with the distal end of the humerus, specifically the trochlea.

humeroradial joint Articulation (arthrodial) formed by the proximal end of the radius and the distal end of the humerus, specifically the capitulum.

radioulnar joints Two articulations (pivot) formed by the proximal and distal radius and ulna, known commonly as the proximal and distal radioulnar joints.

radiocarpal joint Articulation (ellipsoidal) formed by the distal end of the radius and three bones of the wrist: navicular, lunate, and triquetral.

myositis Inflammation of muscle.

tackler's exostosis Formation of a benign growth projecting from the humerus that is caused by repeated blows to the upper arm region; common in tackle football.

exostosis Bony outgrowths that protrude from the surface of a bone where there is not a typical bony formation.

TIME OUT 12.1

Muscles, Actions, and Nerves of the Arm

Muscle	Action(s)	Innervation
Biceps brachii	Flexion of the forearm at the elbow	Musculocutaneous
	Supination of the forearm	
Brachialis	Flexion of the forearm at the elbow	Musculocutaneous
Triceps brachii	Extension of the forearm at the elbow	Radial
Anconeus	Extension of the forearm at the elbow	Radial

2. Place the arm in a sling to immobilize the limb for a period of 24 hours.

3. In cases of severe acute pain or symptoms that persist beyond 72 hours, refer the athlete for a complete medical evaluation.

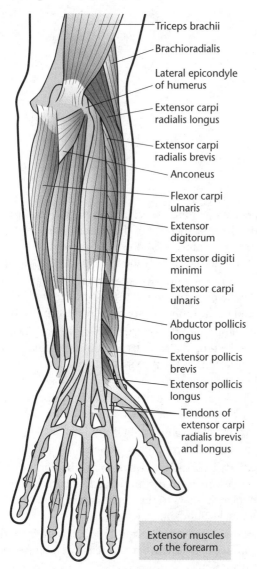

Triceps brachii

Brachioradialis

Lateral epicondyle of humerus

Extensor carpi radialis longus

Extensor carpi radialis brevis

Anconeus

Flexor carpi ulnaris

Extensor digitorum

Extensor digiti minimi

Extensor carpi ulnaris

Abductor pollicis longus

Extensor pollicis brevis

Extensor pollicis longus

Tendons of extensor carpi radialis brevis and longus

Extensor muscles of the forearm

FIGURE 12.4 Extensor muscles of the forearm.

Triceps Injuries

A less common group of injuries to the upper arm involves the triceps muscle. The mechanism of injury may be either a direct blow to the posterior elbow or a fall on an outstretched hand. Either mechanism can result in a partial or complete rupture in the muscle or its tendon. Although rare, such an injury can be extremely disabling and may be associated with either a fracture of the radial head or the olecranon process. A recent report on these injuries found that they occurred among a wide range of athletes, including a competitive weight lifter, a body builder, an alpine skier, and a volleyball player. By definition, all these injuries fall into the general category of muscle strains; depending on their relative severity and precise location, they may require immediate medical attention. In severe cases of partial or complete ruptures of the triceps or its tendon, surgical intervention may be necessary. Even in less severe cases involving only partial tears, the injury requires an extensive period of immobilization (1 month) in a splint with the elbow positioned at 30 degrees of flexion (Holleb & Bach, 1990).

Signs and symptoms of injuries to the triceps muscle include the following:

1. The athlete may report having experienced a sudden popping in the region of the posterior humerus or elbow.

2. Significant pain in the elbow region or just proximal in the area of the triceps tendon.

3. Visible defect in the triceps muscle or in the tendon near the olecranon process.

4. Discoloration and possible swelling, although both may be delayed for a period of hours after the injury.

First aid care:

1. Immediately apply ice and compression. This is best accomplished with a bag of crushed ice that is secured with a wide elastic wrap tied around the arm.

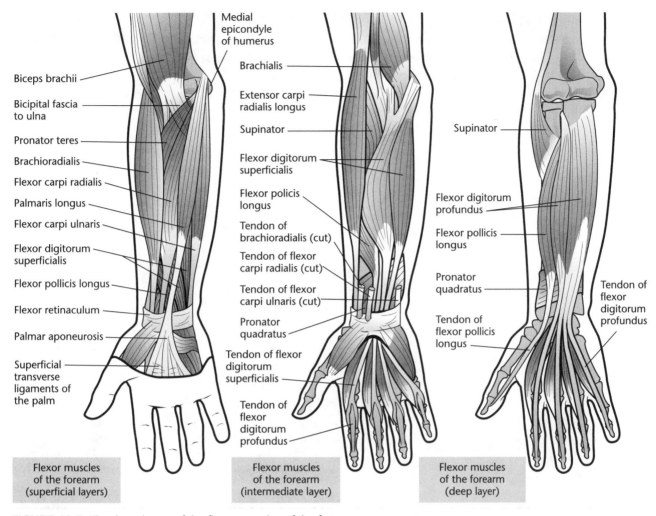

Biceps brachii

Bicipital fascia to ulna

Pronator teres

Brachioradialis

Flexor carpi radialis

Palmaris longus

Flexor carpi ulnaris

Flexor digitorum superficialis

Flexor pollicis longus

Flexor retinaculum

Palmar aponeurosis

Superficial transverse ligaments of the palm

Medial epicondyle of humerus

Brachialis

Extensor carpi radialis longus

Supinator

Flexor digitorum superficialis

Flexor policis longus

Tendon of brachioradialis (cut)

Tendon of flexor carpi radialis (cut)

Tendon of flexor carpi ulnaris (cut)

Pronator quadratus

Tendon of flexor digitorum superficialis

Tendon of flexor digitorum profundus

Supinator

Flexor digitorum profundus

Flexor pollicis longus

Pronator quadratus

Tendon of flexor pollicis longus

Tendon of flexor digitorum profundus

Flexor muscles of the forearm (superficial layers)

Flexor muscles of the forearm (intermediate layer)

Flexor muscles of the forearm (deep layer)

FIGURE 12.5 The three layers of the flexor muscles of the forearm.

2. Place the arm in a sling with the elbow positioned at approximately 90 degrees of flexion if pain can be tolerated.

3. If pain is severe or there is a visible defect in the triceps muscle or its tendon, immediate medical referral is necessary.

Fractures of the Upper Arm

Little information is available about the frequency of humeral fractures related to sports. It would seem that activities involving collisions between participants, such as tackle football and ice hockey, or sports with a potential for high-speed falls, such as cycling or inline skating, would carry a higher risk for such injuries (Figure 12.6). Although considered to be quite rare, humeral stress fractures have been reported related to high-intensity weight training (Bartsokas, Palin, & Collier, 1992).

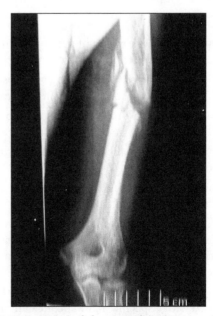

FIGURE 12.6 Mid-shaft fracture of the humerus (left arm).

TIME OUT 12.2

Muscles, Actions, and Innervations of the Muscles of the Forearm

Muscle	Action(s)	Innervation
Flexor digitorum profundus	Flexion of the distal interphalangeal joints of the fingers, as well as PIP and MP joints	Median & ulnar
Flexor digitorum superficialis	Flexion of the proximal interphalangeal joints of the fingers, as well as MP joints	Median
Flexor pollicis longus	Flexion of the thumb	Median
Pronator quadratus	Pronation of the forearm	Median
Brachioradialis	Flexion of the forearm at the elbow	Radial
	Supination of the forearm	
Extensor carpi radialis longus	Extension of the hand at the wrist	Radial
	Radial deviation of the hand at the wrist	
Extensor carpi radialis brevis	Extension of the hand at the wrist	Radial
	Radial deviation of the hand at the wrist	
Extensor digitorum	Extension of the fingers	Radial
	Extension of the hand at the wrist	
Extensor digiti minimi	Extension of the little finger	Radial
Extensor indicis	Extension of the index finger	Radial
Extensor carpi ulnaris	Extension of the hand at the wrist	Radial
	Ulnar deviation of the hand at the wrist	
Supinator	Supination of the forearm	Radial
Abductor pollicis longus	Abduction of the thumb	Radial
Extensor pollicis longus	Extension of the thumb	Radial
Extensor pollicis brevis	Extension of the thumb	Radial

Signs and symptoms of humeral fractures include the following:

1. Severe pain in the region of the upper arm with a recent history of trauma to the area.
2. Deformity may be present and visible, especially when compared with the opposite extremity.
3. Loss of function or an unwillingness to use the extremity.
4. Muscle spasm in the musculature surrounding the extremity.
5. The athlete may report having felt a snap or heard a pop at the time of injury.
6. If the radial nerve is involved there may be loss of sensation into the dorsum of the forearm and wrist. This may also result in loss of strength in the wrist extensors (AAOS, 1991).
7. In cases of stress fracture, pain may not be associated with a specific traumatic incident. Instead, the athlete may report a change in a training program—for example, a sudden increase in the intensity or volume of a strength-training program.

First aid care:

1. Immediately apply ice and compression in conjunction with a properly constructed splint. Many commercial splints are available and will work well when used according to the manufacturer's specifications. The application of ice and compression is best accomplished with a bag of crushed ice that is secured with a wide elastic wrap tied around the arm. Discontinue ice application if radial nerve involvement or circulatory deficiency is observed.
2. Apply a standard sling-and-swathe bandage as described by the National Safety Council (1991).
3. As with any injury requiring the application of a splint, periodic evaluation of circulation distal to the site of the splint is essential to guarantee that blood flow has not been impaired. This can be

Athletic Trainers SPEAK Out

Wrist problems are a common occurrence in sports. Sometimes they can develop into a serious situation and may sideline an athlete for an indefinite period of time. A diver, who was a former gymnast, developed bilateral de Quervain's disease. The condition in her left wrist was more severe than in her right. It was difficult for her to go through a workout, especially the portion that included diving from the 10-meter tower. After weeks of ice, rest, and modalities with no improvement, she received a steroid injection in her left wrist and was immobilized in a thumb spica cast intermittently during a 6-week period. This also failed, and it was decided the only way of correcting this injury was to perform surgery.

The young woman successfully recovered from her surgery and is now diving competitively, pain free.

—*Sue Lerner, MS, ATC*

Sue Lerner is Assistant Athletic Trainer at the University of Southern California.

WHAT IF?

You are asked to examine the elbow of a young softball pitcher. She has been suffering from elbow pain and reports that her elbow "locks" occasionally. When this happens she experiences sharp pain and swelling. What might be the cause of the problem and what would you recommend?

accomplished simply by squeezing the nail bed of a finger and observing the return of blood to the fingertip.

4. Humeral fractures are serious injuries often associated with significant soft-tissue damage. In such instances, the athlete should be treated for shock and immediately transported to a health care facility.

Elbow Injuries

Elbow injuries are common in sports and range from simple abrasions or contusions to complete dislocations or fractures. In sports involving repeated throwing or swinging actions, the elbow may develop an overuse injury related to muscular attachments on the humeral epicondyles, sometimes resulting in a condition known as **epicondylitis.** The joint can also sustain sprains;

the most common involve hyperextensions in which the joint is forced beyond its normal locked position in extension. Dislocations and fractures are probably the most severe types of injuries to this complex joint; if not cared for properly, either can lead to permanent complications.

Sprains and Dislocations

The three articulations of the elbow are bound together by several ligaments that combine to give support to the joint throughout its wide range of motion. The joint capsule of the elbow is extensive and is reinforced both medially and laterally by the ulnar and radial collateral ligaments, respectively. These two ligaments serve to protect the elbow from **valgus** and **varus** forces acting across the joint. In addition, the radial head is held in position by the annular ligament described previously.

The elbow may be sprained through a variety of mechanisms, including falls, particularly when an athlete falls backward with the elbow locked in extension. This mechanism results in a stretching and/or tearing of the anterior joint capsule as well as other soft-tissue structures in the anterior portion of the joint. Two other mechanisms for elbow sprains are valgus and varus forces that can occur suddenly in situations in which the

epicondylitis Inflammatory response at the epicondyle.

valgus Position of a body part that is bent outward.

varus Position of a body part that is bent inward.

arm is trapped in a vulnerable position, such as can happen in tackle football or wrestling.

Dislocations of the elbow are sprains in the extreme sense and involve damage to significant soft-tissue structures around the joint. The mechanism of injury is typically a fall in which the elbow is in either an extended or flexed position. The force of the impact causes the forearm bones to be driven posteriorly out of their normal position, with the olecranon process of the ulna coming to rest well behind the distal end of the humerus. The deformity is obvious, which makes the initial evaluation relatively straightforward. This injury may be associated with a fracture of either the radius or the ulna, or both.

Signs and symptoms of elbow sprains and dislocations include the following:

1. In cases of minor sprains, mild swelling and localized pain.
2. Difficulty in gripping objects or in making a fist.
3. In cases of dislocations, gross deformity of the elbow with abnormal positioning of the forearm bones behind the distal end of the humerus (Figure 12.7).
4. Severe pain and total dysfunction of the elbow joint.
5. Possible neurologic symptoms distal to the elbow characterized by numbness along the

distribution of major nerves. The ulnar nerve appears to be the most vulnerable to this specific injury (AAOS, 1991).

First aid care:

1. In cases of minor sprains the immediate application of ice and compression, using a bag of crushed ice held in place with an elastic wrap, is effective.
2. Once ice and compression are properly situated, the arm should be placed in a sling-and-swathe bandage as recommended by the National Safety Council (1991).
3. In cases of obvious dislocations, the primary concern is to prevent complications, which can be extremely serious and include compression on the neurovascular structures in the elbow region. Immediately apply ice and compression in combination with a properly applied splint.
4. Splinting of this injury requires special attention to avoid moving the displaced forearm bones. It is recommended by the National Safety Council (1991) that the splint be applied on either or both sides of the elbow as illustrated in Figure 12.8.
5. Elbow dislocations are serious injuries. The athlete should be treated for shock, and arrangements must be made for transportation to a medical facility.

Fractures

Elbow fractures generally involve the distal humerus, just above the epicondyles, or the proximal ulna or radius. Because of the complexity of the joint, any fracture represents potential problems for the athlete. As is the case with dislocations, neurovascular structures are in jeopardy when fractures result in displacement of bones. This is especially true if broken bones are moved inadvertently by the athlete or by someone else attempting to render first aid. A simple elbow fracture can easily be converted into an irreversible injury in such a situation. If the radial artery is compressed by broken bone ends, circulation to the forearm can be significantly reduced or stopped, resulting in a condition known as **Volkmann's contracture** (Figure 12.9). This condition involves the reaction of the forearm musculature to a lack of blood supply. If left uncorrected, it becomes a permanent deformity; therefore, it is imperative that elbow fractures be handled very carefully during the application of first aid procedures. Furthermore, it is important that the blood supply distal to the elbow be

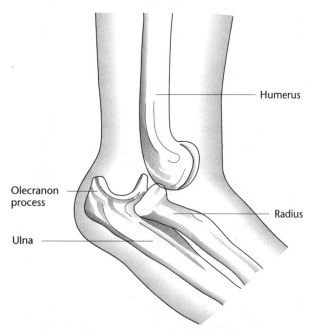

FIGURE 12.7 Posterior dislocation of the elbow.

Humerus

Radius

Olecranon process

Ulna

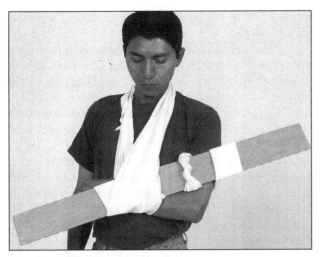

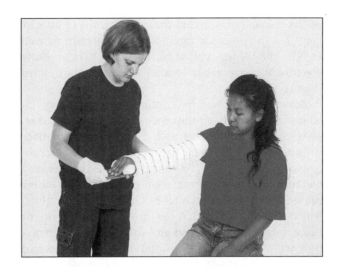

FIGURE 12.8 Splinting of an elbow injury.

monitored until the athlete is transported to a medical facility.

The mechanisms of injury are similar to those of sprains and dislocations. Fractures of the olecranon process of the ulna are often associated with falls in which the elbow is in a flexed position and the impact occurs on the tip of the joint. When elbow fractures occur in adolescents, they require special attention to ensure that the injury will not adversely affect the growth centers of the bones involved.

Signs and symptoms of elbow fractures include the following:

1. Recent history of significant trauma to the elbow in association with significant pain and dysfunction.

2. Immediate swelling in the region of the injury.

3. In the case of displaced fractures an obvious deformity will be noted.

4. In cases of problems with the blood supply, a lack of proper blood flow will be noted in the forearm and hand, both of which will feel cold and clammy. In addition, the victim will report pain or numbness in the hand.

First aid care:

1. Immediately apply ice; however, it is critical to avoid compression around the joint owing to the increased risk for vascular compromise with this particular injury.

2. Place a bag of crushed ice over the region of injury and hold it in place with a nonelastic cloth bandage such as a commercially prepared triangular one.

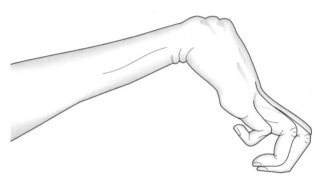

FIGURE 12.9 Volkmann's ischemic contracture.

3. The National Safety Council (1991) recommends applying some type of splint, taking great care to avoid moving the bones of the elbow, as shown in Figure 12.8.

4. Treat the athlete for shock and arrange for transport to a medical facility.

Epicondylitis of the Elbow

The epicondyles of the humerus are located immediately proximal to the distal articular surfaces of that bone—the capitulum and the trochlea. The more prominent medial epicondyle serves as the common site of attachment for flexor muscles of the forearm as well as for the ulnar collateral ligament. The smaller

Volkmann's contracture Contracture of muscles of the forearm related to a loss of blood supply caused by a fracture and/or dislocation of either of the bones in the forearm or the humerus.

lateral epicondyle serves as the common site of attachment for the extensor muscles of the forearm as well as for the radial collateral ligament. These bony prominences are easily located near the elbow joint (Figure 12.10).

Activities that require continuous gripping of an object along with simultaneous wrist actions, such as is common in racket and throwing sports, place considerable stress on the tissues of the epicondylar regions. During the 1970s considerable debate existed regarding the possible negative effects on the elbow caused by excessive pitching in Little League baseball. A major concern was that the throwing motion might cause degenerative changes and subsequent inflammation within the medial epicondyle of the elbows of young players, resulting in medial epicondylitis. This condition results in significant pain around the epicondyle and can severely limit the athlete's ability to flex or pronate the wrist and hand. In the adolescent, extreme cases can lead to actual fracturing of the epicondyle away from the humerus. Concerned parents and physicians coined the phrase Little League elbow to describe the injury among these young players. Subsequent studies did produce convincing evidence of a strong relationship between the throwing mechanism and medial epicondylitis (Larson et al., 1976). As a result, rules that limited the maximum number of innings young pitchers could throw during a season were instituted.

Another sport identified as a cause of medial epicondylitis in some athletes is golf. The condition, known as **golfer's elbow,** has been linked to players who have problems with their swing (Hutson, 1990). Available data support the premise that epicondylitis is less common on the medial side of the elbow when compared with the lateral side. Tennis has also been identified as a cause of epicondylitis. Tennis elbow involves the lateral humeral epicondyle and the tendon of the extensor carpi radialis brevis tendon (Hannafin & Schelkun, 1996). It has been reported that from 10% to 50% of all tennis players may suffer from this condition at some point in their career (Jobe & Ciccotti, 1994). Hutson (1990) reports that the problem is related to a variety of sports-related factors, including the following:

1. Overload related to the sheer frequency of shots played
2. Incorrect technique, particularly on the backhand
3. Too small a racket handle
4. Recent change of racket—for instance, from wood to graphite
5. Too tight a grip between shots
6. Muscle imbalance and/or loss of flexibility

Regardless of the type of epicondylitis, the first step in treating the problem is to identify the cause(s), including skill- and/or equipment-related problems. If the athlete treats only the symptoms without identifying the underlying problems, epicondylitis will most likely recur. After the cause(s) is identified, a program of aggressive treatment of symptoms with ice application (before and after practice) as well as strengthening exercises, including wrist curls and extensions as well as pronation and supination against mild resistance, may prove helpful. During the early phase of treatment, exercises without weight may be advised, such as squeezing a tennis ball (finger flexors) and finger extension against the resistance of the opposite hand. Any rehabilitation program should be developed and supervised by a competent sports medicine practitioner such as an athletic trainer or a sports physical therapist.

Signs and symptoms of epicondylitis include the following:

1. Pain in the region of either the medial or lateral epicondyle. Symptoms become worse during or immediately after participation.
2. Pain radiating distally into either the flexor/ pronator or extensor/supinator muscles, depending on which epicondyle is involved.

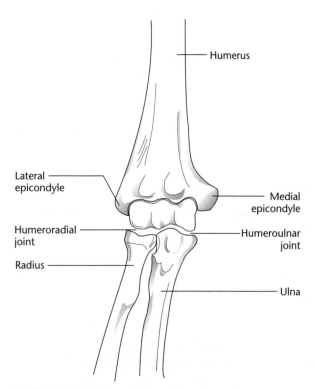

FIGURE 12.10 Epicondyles of the elbow joint.

3. Pain may be elicited in the region of the epicondyles during resisted wrist flexion or extension, depending on which epicondyle is involved.

4. Swelling in the region of the painful epicondyle.

5. In severe and chronic cases, crepitus (feeling hardened fragments through the skin) may be noted over the region of the affected epicondyle.

First aid care:

1. Both medial and lateral epicondylitis tend to be chronic injuries resulting from overuse; therefore, first aid is not a practical solution. When symptoms worsen, however, the application of ice and compression can be helpful; this is best accomplished with a bag of crushed ice that is secured with an elastic wrap.

2. If symptoms persist, medical referral is necessary.

3. Long-term treatment includes rest, reduced participation in the activity, and possible use of anti-inflammatory drugs.

Osteochondritis Dissecans of the Elbow

The mechanism of throwing can lead to a type of impingement syndrome in the elbow joint occurring between the radial head and the capitellum of the humerus. The action of high-velocity extension can cause the elbow to develop a valgus overload resulting in abnormal compression of the elbow on the lateral side of the joint (Hutson, 1990). Over time and with continued throwing, the cartilage on the proximal end of the radius can become inflamed and even begin to fracture, resulting in a condition known as **osteochondritis dissecans.**

Another possible mechanism for this type of elbow injury is axial loading of the forearm. Such a mechanism is common in falls or in sports that place the forearms in a weight-bearing position, which typically occurs in gymnastics. In either case, the impact force is transmitted up the forearm and causes the head of the radius to be jammed against the humerus. Over time osteochondritis dissecans can result from such repeated insults to the joint.

Signs and symptoms of osteochondritis dissecans include the following:

1. During the initial phases of development the athlete will experience pain during participation.

2. Joint inflammation and stiffness may be noted, particularly 12 to 24 hours after participation.

3. In well-established cases, cartilage fragments (loose bodies) may form in the joint; these are commonly known as joint mice.

4. The athlete may experience a locking of the elbow, which occurs when a loose body is caught between the moving bone ends in the joint.

5. In advanced cases the elbow may develop osteoarthritis.

First aid care:

1. An athlete with a history of trauma to the elbow joint associated with the symptoms just described should be referred to the appropriate physician for a thorough diagnostic evaluation.

2. Immediate symptoms are best treated with a bag of crushed ice held in place with an elastic wrap.

3. If fragments are identified in the joint, the physician may recommend arthroscopic surgery to remove the loose bodies.

4. The conservative (nonsurgical) treatment for this condition involves rest followed by an extensive period of rehabilitative exercise designed to strengthen both the muscles surrounding the elbow and the ligaments of the joint.

Contusions of the Elbow

External blows to the elbow region are common in sports. Little protective equipment is available for the joint, and its large range of motion and irregular shape make taping and wrapping impractical. Fortunately, the vast majority of contusions result in only temporary discomfort that normally improves in a few days. An exception, however, is the olecranon bursa, which is a large sac located between the skin and the olecranon process of the ulna. Falling on a flexed elbow or sustaining repeated blows to the olecranon area can irritate this **bursa** and cause acute bursitis. Although bursitis does not directly affect the

---

golfer's elbow Medial humeral epicondylitis related to incorrect golf technique.

osteochondritis dissecans Condition in which a fragment of cartilage and underlying bone is detached from the articular surface.

bursa Small synovial sac typically located over bony prominences that assists in cushioning and reducing friction.

integrity of the elbow joint, persistent swelling, stiffness, and pain associated with this problem can reduce the quality of athletic performance.

Signs and symptoms of olecranon bursitis include the following:

1. The most obvious sign of this injury is swelling located around the olecranon process of the ulna.
2. Pain and stiffness, especially when the elbow is flexed.
3. Skin temperature over the olecranon may be elevated.
4. Skin over the olecranon process may appear taut, and the joint may show signs of internal hemorrhage.

First aid care:

1. Immediate care of elbow contusions includes the application of a bag of crushed ice held in place with an elastic wrap.
2. If the signs and symptoms of olecranon bursitis appear, refer the athlete to the appropriate physician.

Wrist and Forearm Injuries

The anatomy of the human wrist is highly complex. Within this compact joint exist a large number of tendons (for the wrist, fingers, and thumb) that are tightly bound together underneath bands of connective tissue known as retinaculum (transverse carpal ligaments). Also passing through this region are the major nerves and blood vessels of the hand and fingers (Figure 12.11).

Aside from simple contusions, injuries to the forearm in sports are relatively uncommon. Usually contusions can be easily treated with ice, compression, and elevation; this can be followed later with the application of protective padding. Probably the most serious forearm injuries involve fractures distal in the forearm, just proximal to the wrist joint. The most well known of these is a **Colles' fracture,** which involves a transverse fracture of the distal radius (Figure 12.12). Variations of this fracture include simultaneous fractures of both the radius and ulna as well as compound fractures of either bone; such injuries are serious and must be properly cared for to avoid complications. The mechanism of injury is highly variable; whatever the mechanism, a great deal of force will be required and many soft-tissue structures may be damaged in conjunction with the fracture.

Signs and symptoms of distal forearm fractures include the following:

1. The athlete will have a recent history of significant trauma to the wrist region associated with having heard a popping sound and/or felt a snapping of the bones.
2. A deformity, known as the silver fork deformity, between the arm and wrist is typical; in the case of a Colles' fracture the hand is driven backward and outward (radial deviation) (Figure 12.13).

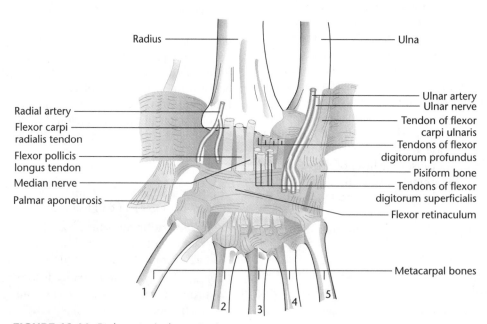

FIGURE 12.11 Right wrist (palmar view).

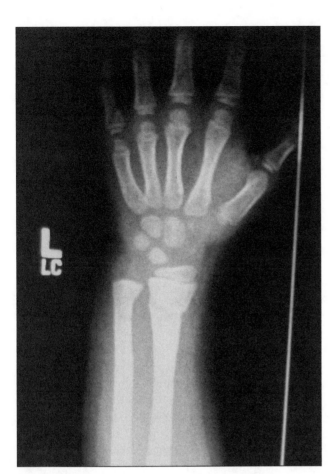

FIGURE 12.12 Distal forearm fracture (Colles').

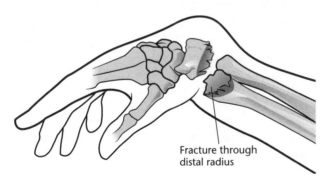

Fracture through
distal radius

FIGURE 12.13 A Colles' fracture demonstrating the "silver fork" deformity.

3. Swelling, often severe, develops quickly and may affect the hand and fingers.

4. Pain is generally severe, and motion of the wrist, hand, or fingers will be significantly curtailed.

5. In cases in which a broken bone(s) puts pressure on nerves, loss of sensation may be noted in either the hand or fingers or both.

First aid care:

1. Immediately apply ice, compression, and elevation (**ICE**). This is best accomplished with a bag of crushed ice that is held in place with an elastic wrap. Do not apply ice if you suspect either vascular or nerve supply is compromised. In addition, some type of splint must be applied to protect the area from further injury (see Figure 12.23).

2. Make sure that the fingertips are exposed to monitor the blood supply to the hand. This is easily accomplished by squeezing a nail bed and noting the return (or lack thereof) of normal reddish color to the tissue.

3. Once in place, the ice, compression, and splint should be elevated carefully using a standard sling-and-swathe bandage as recommended by the National Safety Council (1991).

4. Because of the pain and damage associated with this type of injury, it is imperative that the athlete be treated for shock and transported to a medical facility immediately.

Wrist Fractures

Fractures of the carpal bones do occur in sports. According to Booher and Thibodeau (2000), the most common involve the scaphoid bone (Figure 12.14). This bone can receive considerable force when the wrist is placed into extension in sports such as tackle football

Colles' fracture Transverse fracture of the distal radius.
ICE Ice, compression, and elevation.

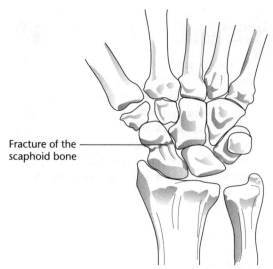

Fracture of the scaphoid bone

FIGURE 12.14 Fracture of the scaphoid bone is common in sports.

(blocking) and gymnastics (vaulting and floor exercise). Simple falls can also cause fractures to this critical bone of the wrist. The fracture generally occurs in a specific site on the scaphoid bone known as the waist, which is the narrowest section of the bone.

Other bones of the wrist may be fractured as well: fractures of the lunate, pisiform, and hamate have been reported. Regardless of which specific bone is fractured, the signs and symptoms will be similar. Because the carpal bones are small, gross deformity is typically not present, and evaluation of these injuries is difficult. When doubt exists about the extent or nature of the injury, the best policy is to refer the athlete to a physician for a more complete diagnostic evaluation.

Signs and symptoms of wrist fractures include the following:

1. A recent history of trauma to the wrist, specifically forced extension associated with a snapping or popping sensation in the wrist.

2. Pain in the wrist that is aggravated by movement. A simple test for the integrity of the scaphoid bone involves pressing lightly into the region at the base of the thumb known as the anatomical snuff-box (Figure 12.15), which is bordered by several tendons that attach within the thumb. The radial surface of the scaphoid bone is located within the anatomical snuff-box. Consequently, external pressure in this region may elicit a painful response from the athlete, which is a positive sign of a fracture of that bone.

3. The athlete may be unable or unwilling to move the wrist, and doing so may result in considerable pain.

4. The athlete may state that the wrist feels locked in a certain position; this can be an indication of a displaced fracture.

First aid care:

1. Immediately apply ice, compression, and elevation in conjunction with some type of splint that immobilizes the wrist (see Figure 12.23).

2. Once in place, the ice, compression, and splint should be elevated carefully by way of a standard sling-and-swathe bandage as described by the National Safety Council (1991).

3. Leave the fingertips exposed to facilitate monitoring blood flow to the hand beyond the level of the splint.

Wrist Sprains and Dislocations

The mechanism producing a fracture of the wrist may also produce a sprain or dislocation in that region when of lesser severity. Essentially, the wrist (radiocarpal) joint is bound together by a network of large, strong ligaments known as the palmar and dorsal radiocarpal ligaments (Figures 12.16 and 12.17). In addition, several smaller ligaments bind the remaining bones of the wrist to form a well-supported series of joints known collectively as the intercarpal joints.

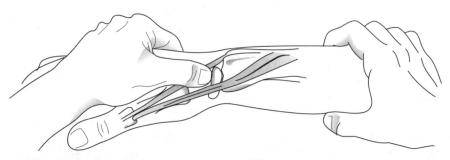

FIGURE 12.15 Palpation in the anatomical snuff-box.

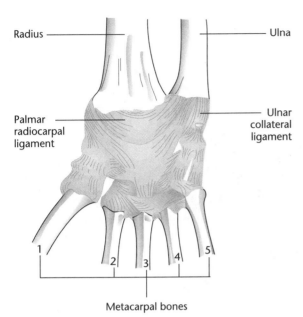

FIGURE 12.16 Palmar radiocarpal ligament.

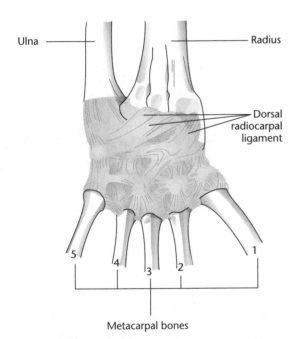

FIGURE 12.17 Dorsal radiocarpal ligament.

The most common sprain of the wrist is caused by forced hyperextension, which results in a stretching and possible tearing of the palmar radiocarpal ligament. Such an injury can, if severe enough, result in a dislocation of one or more of the carpal bones. In the case of a simple sprain, the carpal bones will remain in their normal position.

The most common dislocation of the wrist involves the lunate bone, which is located between the distal end of the radius and the capitate bone (Booher & Thibodeau, 2000). The mechanism of injury is forceful hyperextension; this causes the bone to shift out of its normal position and slide toward the palmar side of the wrist. In severe cases, the lunate will put pressure on the tendons and nerves of a region of the wrist known as the carpal tunnel, resulting in significant symptoms in the hand and fingers.

Signs and symptoms of wrist sprains and dislocations include the following:

1. The athlete will report having sustained a forced hyperextension of the wrist in conjunction with a snapping or popping sensation in the bones of the joint.

2. Movement, or attempted movements, of the wrist will be painful and meet with little success.

3. In cases of dislocations, the wrist may be locked so that the athlete will be unable to voluntarily move the wrist.

4. Numbness and/or pain may radiate from the wrist into the hand and fingers. In the case of lunate dislocations, these symptoms may involve the distribution of the median nerve, producing the symptoms known commonly as carpal tunnel syndrome.

5. Swelling of the wrist may be limited owing to the nature of the ligaments of the region.

First aid care:

1. Immediately apply ice, compression, elevation, and some type of splinting device designed to immobilize the wrist joint. A bag of crushed ice held in place by an elastic wrap is effective in most cases. Do not apply ice if you suspect either vascular or nerve supply is compromised. The splint may even be secured with the wrap as well.

2. Elevation is best achieved using a standard sling-and-swathe bandage.

3. In cases of significant pain or a possible dislocation, it is important to refer the athlete to a health care facility for further evaluation and treatment.

Nerve Injuries to the Wrist

Three major nerves cross the wrist from the forearm into the hand to supply both sensation and motor function to the hand and fingers. These nerves are the radial, the median, and the ulnar. Though any of these nerves may be damaged in a sports-related injury, the most commonly injured nerve is the median. This nerve

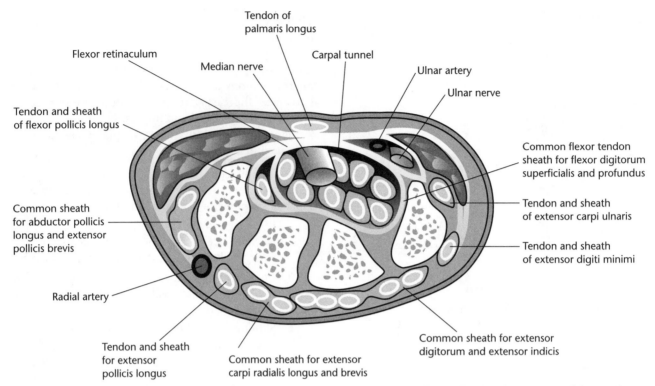

FIGURE 12.18 Cross-section view of the forearm at the wrist showing the carpal tunnel. Note the position of the median nerve.

passes through a region of the wrist known as the **carpal tunnel** (Figure 12.18), which also houses eight flexor tendons that pass into the hand. The tunnel is surrounded by dense, strong ligaments as well as bone.

The exact cause of **carpal tunnel syndrome** is unknown, but it probably involves swelling within the tunnel caused by tendinitis or sprains of the region. In any event, the pressure of the swelling has a negative effect on the median nerve. Although carpal tunnel syndrome can be caused by a single traumatic episode, such as a dislocated lunate bone, the majority of cases involving athletes tend to be the result of chronic overuse injuries. Sports with a high incidence include racket sports and those requiring the participant to grip an object tightly for extended periods of time. Unless treated properly, carpal tunnel syndrome can be extremely disabling and can often preclude an athlete from returning to the sport.

Another nerve-related injury in the wrist involves the ulnar nerve as it passes through the region on the ulnar side of the forearm. Specifically, the ulnar nerve is located in the vicinity of the pisiform bone and the hook of the hamate bone within the **tunnel of Guyon** (Hoppenfield, 1976). A blow to the wrist or tendinitis in the tendon of

flexor carpi ulnaris can result in irritation to the nerve and a variety of symptoms. These include loss of sensation to a portion of the hand and fingers as well as loss of muscle strength in the fingers affected by the ulnar nerve. The region of the hand that receives sensory impulses from the ulnar nerve is the medial portion of the palm, including the region known as the hypothenar eminence, as well as the medial half of the ring finger and the entire little finger.

Signs and symptoms of nerve injuries to the wrist include the following:

1. Loss of sensation to a portion of the hand and/or fingers that follows the distribution of a major nerve in the region. In some cases pain may radiate into the hand as well.

2. Pain and tenderness around the region of the wrist on the palm side.

3. Associated tendinitis of the wrist or recent history of trauma to the area, such as a contusion or sprain.

4. Symptoms may become worse when the wrist is fully flexed or extended or an object is gripped tightly in the hand.

First aid care:

1. This type of injury tends to develop slowly over time. The exception is when a nerve of the wrist is aggravated by an acute injury such as a severe contusion or sprain.

2. When associated with an acute trauma, the best approach is the immediate application of ice, compression, and elevation. Do not apply ice if you suspect either vascular or nerve supply is compromised. Splinting may be necessary depending on the specific injury.

3. Any athlete with a history of recurrent pain and stiffness in the wrist associated with the neurologic symptoms just described should be referred to a health care facility for a complete evaluation by a medical doctor.

4. If the medical diagnosis confirms a nerve-related problem, the initial care will generally involve rest, anti-inflammatory drugs, and in some cases a splint. In severe cases surgical decompression of the nerve may be required.

Unique Tendon Problems of the Wrist

By definition, **tenosynovitis** is an "inflammation between tendon and surrounding tissues with consequent loss of smooth gliding motion" (AMA, 1968). Perhaps the most common form of tenosynovitis in the wrist involves the tendons of the thumb (Figure 12.19) and is known as **de Quervain's disease.** In reality this is not a disease in the classic sense but rather a type of overuse injury specific to the wrist. de Quervain's disease most commonly involves the tendons of the extensor pollicis brevis and the abductor pollicis longus muscles as they pass across the radial styloid process. There is a third

tendon in the region, the extensor pollicis longus; however, it is rarely involved in this condition.

The mechanism of injury for de Quervain's disease is vague, but it probably involves overuse of the wrist and/or thumb. Initially, the tendons and the synovial sheath around the tendons become inflamed, resulting in pain, swelling, and stiffness. As the injury progresses the tendons begin catching within the anatomic tunnel, at times with such force that the athlete will feel them as they break free. Using the thumb, particularly in flexion and extension, will be extremely painful, and even wrist movements will be impeded. Conservative treatment includes rest, heat and drug therapy, and splinting of the wrist to reduce movements of the thumb. In many cases this problem tends to recur and eventually may require surgical treatment to release (decompress) the tendons as they pass near the radial styloid process.

Signs and symptoms of de Quervain's disease include the following:

1. Pain and tenderness within the region of the radial styloid process, specifically involving the tendons of the abductor pollicis longus and the extensor pollicis brevis.

2. Swelling in the area of the radial styloid process and, in advanced cases, the development of a nodule on one or more of the tendons.

3. The athlete may report that the tendons are catching within the wrist during activity.

4. Thumb flexion in conjunction with ulnar deviation of the wrist will cause a significant increase in pain and related symptoms.

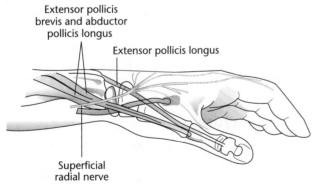

Extensor pollicis brevis and abductor pollicis longus

Extensor pollicis longus

Superficial radial nerve

FIGURE 12.19 Tendons of the thumb.

---

carpal tunnel Anatomic region of the wrist where the median nerve and the majority of the tendons of the forearm pass into the hand.

carpal tunnel syndrome A complex of symptoms resulting from pressure on the median nerve as it passes through the carpal tunnel of the wrist, causing soreness and numbness.

tunnel of Guyon Anatomic region formed by the hook of the hamate bone and the pisiform bone, whereby the ulnar nerve passes into the hand.

tenosynovitis Inflammation of the sheath of a tendon.

de Quervain's disease Inflammation of sheaths surrounding the extensor tendons of the thumb.

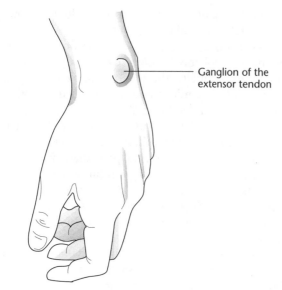

FIGURE 12.20 Ganglion of the wrist.

1. The most obvious symptom is a visible swelling through the skin of the wrist in the region of the extensor or flexor tendons.
2. In more advanced cases a painful, hardened nodule may be present directly over a tendon (see Figure 12.20).

Care of a ganglion:

1. In some cases ganglions regress on their own spontaneously.
2. In cases in which the ganglion does not interfere with performance, most physicians recommend leaving it alone.
3. In cases in which the ganglion does interfere with performance or is cosmetically unattractive, surgical removal in conjunction with repair of the synovial hernia is an option. It should be noted, however, that even after surgery ganglions may recur.

Hand Injuries

The hand, fingers, and thumb are often injured in many sports, with some of the highest frequencies occurring in sports such as baseball, softball, basketball, and football. The variety of injuries seen is nearly infinite; however, those described in this section represent the most common injuries seen.

The hand contains 19 bones: the 5 metacarpals and the 14 separate **phalanges** of the fingers (Figure 12.21). The joints of the hand include the carpometacarpal joints at the base of the hand, the metacarpophalangeal joints (knuckles), and the interphalangeal joints of the fingers and thumb. All of these joints are freely movable and are supported by many ligaments and capsular tissues. Movements at each of these joints are affected by the many muscles originating from the forearm that pass tendons into the hand and fingers. Also within the hand there are small, intrinsic (originating within the hand) muscles that precisely move the thumb and fingers. The nerves and vessels of the hand are continuations of the major structures that cross the wrist: the radial, median, and ulnar nerves as well as the radial and ulnar arteries.

Hand Fractures

Fractures can occur to any of the 19 bones of the hand; however, certain types of fractures are seen more commonly in sports. An injury unique to the thumb is **Bennett's fracture** (Figure 12.22). This injury often results from a blow to the hand while it is in a clenched-

Care of de Quervain's disease:

1. If diagnosed early, the condition is treated with rest, immobilization with some type of splint, and drug therapy.
2. In advanced or recurring cases, surgical treatment has been found to be highly effective with this condition. The basic surgical objective is to create more room within the tunnel for the tendons.

Another unique tendon-related wrist problem is known as a ganglion. Technically, a **ganglion** is a herniation of the synovium surrounding the tendons at the wrist. When this occurs the herniated tissue will gradually begin to fill with synovial fluid, producing a protrusion often visible as a bump on the surface of the wrist (Figure 12.20). The most common site for wrist ganglions is on the extensor tendon (dorsal) side of the wrist, although cases have been reported on the flexor tendon side of the wrist as well. Considerable debate continues concerning the specific cause of ganglions; however, it appears that they are related to the chronic strain of wrist tendons (O'Donoghue, 1976). Ganglions are highly variable in appearance. Some appear as a soft, apparently fluid-filled mass just under the skin; others materialize as a hard, painful mass over a tendon. Depending on their specific location, ganglions may interfere with an athlete's performance, but in most cases the problem is seen as primarily cosmetic.

Signs and symptoms of a ganglion include the following:

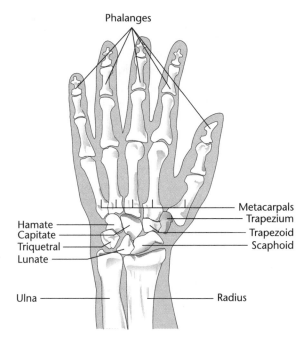

FIGURE 12.21 Bones of the hand and wrist.

Phalanges

Hamate
Capitate
Triquetral
Lunate

Ulna

Metacarpals
Trapezium
Trapezoid
Scaphoid

Radius

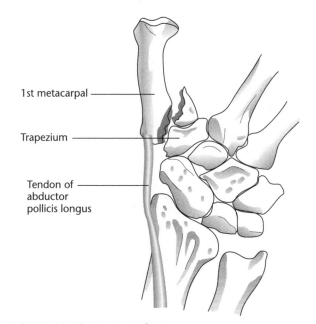

FIGURE 12.22 Bennett's fracture.

1st metacarpal

Trapezium

Tendon of
abductor
pollicis longus

fist position; the force of the mechanism causes the proximal end of the first metacarpal bone to be driven into the wrist. The result is a **fracture-dislocation** of the first metacarpal bone away from the greater multangular (trapezium) bone of the wrist. An obvious deformity appears with this injury, characterized by the thumb being shorter in appearance when compared with that of the opposite hand. Significant swelling will also be present near the base of the thumb over the carpometacarpal joint.

Fractures of the metacarpal bones of the fingers can also occur via a mechanism similar to that described for Bennett's fracture, that is, a blow with a clenched fist. The most common injury involves the fourth and/or fifth metacarpal bone(s) near the proximal end(s) (base) and is known as **boxer's fracture.** Because of the ligamentous structure of this area, displaced fractures are rare; consequently, deformity is usually not a common sign of injury. Another mechanism of injury for metacarpal fractures is a crushing force, such as having the hand stepped on by another athlete, which is common in sports such as tackle football.

Fractures of the phalanges also occur frequently in sports, particularly fractures of the proximal phalanges (O'Donoghue, 1976). Most of these fractures remain undisplaced and are easily treated with splinting; few if any long-term complications ensue. In cases in which the phalangeal fracture resists fixation and remains unstable, surgically implanted fixation is effective. This is critical because a serious complication of a finger fracture is rotational deformity, which results when the broken bone ends fail to unite in the correct position (Hutson, 1990).

Signs and symptoms of hand fractures include the following:

1. Recent history of significant trauma to the hand followed immediately by specific pain and dysfunction of the hand and/or finger(s).

2. In cases of displaced fractures, deformity may be observable, either as a bump or protrusion in the hand or as an oddly shaped finger.

3. In cases of compound fractures the skin will be broken over the region of the fracture.

4. There will be significant inflammation associated with any fracture in the hand or finger.

---

ganglion Herniation of the synovium surrounding a tendon and subsequent filling of the area with synovial fluid, resulting in a visible bump seen through the skin.

phalanges Anatomical name for the bones of both the fingers and/or toes.

Bennett's fracture Fracture and/or dislocation of the first metacarpal bone away from the greater multangular bone of the wrist.

fracture-dislocation An injury resulting in both the fracture of a bone and dislocation at the joint.

boxer's fracture Fracture of the proximal fourth and/or fifth metacarpal bones.

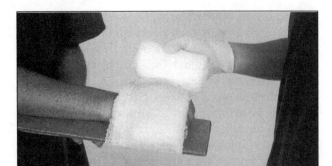

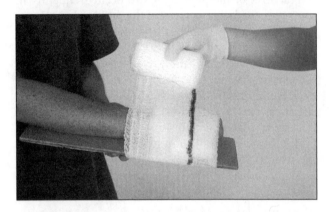

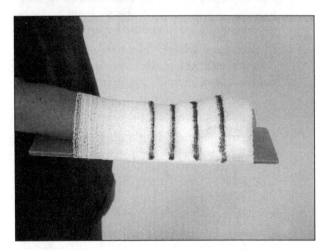

FIGURE 12.23 A splint provides immobilization for fractures of the forearm, wrist, and hand.

First aid care:

1. Immediately apply ice, compression, elevation, and some type of splinting device. This is best accomplished using a small bag of crushed ice held in place with a narrow elastic wrap; take care to leave the fingernails exposed.

2. Elevation can be easily achieved by placing the arm in a standard sling-and-swathe bandage.

3. Depending on the specific site of the fracture, a variety of splinting techniques can be used. For example, for an isolated phalangeal fracture a procedure known as buddy taping can be used, which simply involves taping the fractured finger to an adjacent one. Fractures of the metacarpal bones are best treated by immobilzation of the entire hand (Figure 12.23).

4. The athlete should be transported to the appropriate health care facility for further medical evaluation and treatment. *It is critical that fractures of the hand be treated as serious injuries.*

Sprains and Dislocations of the Hand

Any of the many joints in the hand can be subject to sufficient trauma to cause a sprain of the supporting ligaments. If the force is severe enough a dislocation of the joint may occur as well. Although virtually any of the joints of the hand may be injured, available information regarding sports-related injuries indicates that certain types are quite common. These include gamekeeper's thumb, mallet (baseball) finger, and boutonnière deformity.

Gamekeeper's Thumb

The metacarpophalangeal (MP) joint of the thumb is a large, condyloid joint allowing a considerable range of

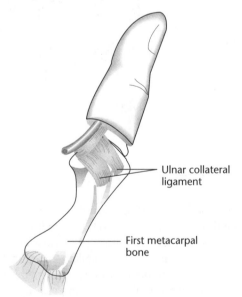

FIGURE 12.24 Damage to the ulnar collateral ligament of the metacarpophalangeal joint can result in gamekeeper's thumb.

Ulnar collateral ligament

First metacarpal bone

motion in flexion and extension as well as a slight amount of abduction and adduction. The joint is supported by both capsular and collateral ligaments. The latter are named according to their location relative to the radius and ulna: the collateral ligament on the lateral side of the joint is the radial collateral ligament, and the one on the medial side is the ulnar collateral ligament (Figure 12.24).

The term **gamekeeper's thumb** originated in the 1950s to describe an injury unique to gamekeepers, whose profession required them to break the necks of rabbits. Apparently this procedure resulted in considerable damage to the ulnar collateral ligament of the thumb, causing chronic instability of the MP joint (Hutson, 1990). Although there are few gamekeepers today, the injury occurs with surprising frequency in sports such as alpine skiing. The mechanism of injury involves a valgus (force applied to the medial side of the joint) stress across the MP joint of the thumb; this results in stretching, partial tearing, or even complete rupture of the ulnar collateral ligament. (In skiing, certain types of pole grips place considerable stress on the MP joint of the thumb when planting a pole.)

Injury to the ulnar collateral ligament can produce a grossly unstable thumb, particularly when an athlete attempts to grasp or hold an object. Recent evidence suggests that in 30% of the cases ligament injuries occur in conjunction with an avulsion fracture of a bone fragment from the base of the proximal phalanx (Isani, 1990). Regardless of the specific type of injury, any significant sprain of the ulnar collateral ligament within the MP joint of the thumb must be carefully evaluated by a physician to determine the extent of joint laxity as well as bony integrity. It is important to note that if left uncorrected this injury can lead to a chronically unstable joint that can negatively affect use of the hand.

Signs and symptoms of gamekeeper's thumb include the following:

1. Significant point tenderness over the region of the ulnar collateral ligament.

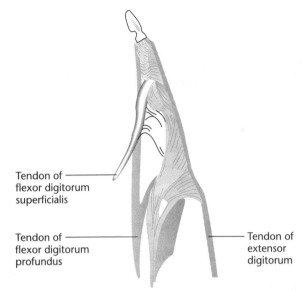

FIGURE 12.25 Tendons of the finger.

2. The athlete may report having felt a snap during the initial injury.
3. Significant swelling over the MP joint of the thumb.
4. Inability and/or unwillingness by the athlete to move the thumb.

First aid care:

1. Immediately apply ice, compression, and elevation. This is best accomplished by placing a small bag of crushed ice around the injured joint and securing it with an elastic wrap.
2. The easiest method of achieving elevation is to place the arm in a simple sling.
3. Refer the athlete to a health care facility for further evaluation and treatment of the injury.

Mallet (Baseball) Finger

Mallet finger involves the distal phalanx of a finger, oftentimes the index or middle finger. The injury is so named because the resulting deformity gives the distal segment of the finger the appearance of a mallet. The

gamekeeper's thumb Sprain of the ulnar collateral ligament of the metacarpophalangeal joint of the thumb.

mallet finger Deformity of the distal interphalangeal joint of the finger caused by an avulsion of the tendon of the extensor digitorum muscle from the distal phalanx.

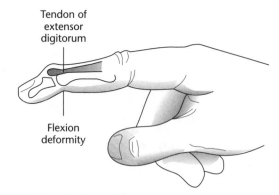

FIGURE 12.26 Mallet finger.

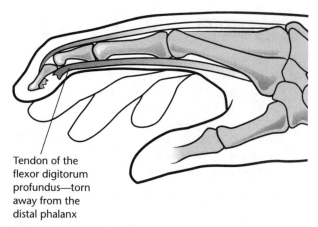

FIGURE 12.27 Jersey finger.

term *baseball finger* arose because the injury is so common in that sport: getting hit on the fingertip by a ball is a frequent occurrence.

The anatomy of the distal finger includes the **distal interphalangeal (DIP) joint,** which functions as a hinge. The muscles acting at this joint are the flexor digitorum profundus and the extensor digitorum. These two muscles are located in the forearm; however, their tendons pass through the hand, inserting into the bases of the distal phalanges of each of the four fingers (Figure 12.25). The mechanism of injury for mallet finger is quite precise: The tip of the finger must receive a blow at the time the finger is extending from a flexed position. The result is that the distal phalanx is suddenly and forcefully taken into flexion against the action of the extensor digitorum muscle. This can lead to an avulsion of the extensor tendon, with or without a small fragment of bone, from the insertion at the base of the distal phalanx. After this injury occurs the athlete is unable to extend the affected finger; it remains in a flexed position at the DIP joint (Figure 12.26).

Signs and symptoms of mallet finger include the following:

1. The single most important sign is the deformity itself, which is associated with a recent history of trauma to the fingertip.
2. Point tenderness on the dorsal surface of the base of the distal phalanx, directly over the site of insertion of the extensor digitorum tendon.

First aid care:

1. Immediately apply ice, compression, and elevation. This is best accomplished by placing a small bag of crushed ice around the involved finger and holding it in place with a small elastic wrap.
2. Immediately splint the finger with the DIP joint extended. Do not let the distal phalanx fall back into the flexed position.

3. The easiest method of achieving elevation is to place the arm in a simple sling.
4. Refer the athlete to a health care facility for further evaluation and treatment of the injury.

Jersey Finger

Jersey finger, much like mallet finger, involves a tearing away of a finger tendon from its attachment. In this case, however, the mechanism of injury involves catching a finger in an opponent's clothing, for example, a football jersey. In the attempt to grip the clothing, as the opponent pulls away, the tendon of the flexor digitorum profundus (FDP) is torn away from its attachment on the distal phalanx (Figure 12.27). Because the FDP is the only muscle that flexes the distal phalanx at the distal interphalangeal joint, this injury results in an inability to flex the DIP joint.

Signs and symptoms of jersey finger include the following:

1. Inability to flex the DIP joint of the affected finger.
2. Athlete reports having felt something snap, or tear away, at the area of the fingertip.
3. Point tenderness on the volar surface of the distal phalanx of the finger.

First aid care:

1. Immediately apply ice, compression, and elevation. This is best accomplished by placing a small bag of crushed ice around the involved finger and holding it in place with a small elastic wrap.
2. Splint the finger in a position of extension at the DIP and proximal interphalangeal joints.

3. The easiest method of achieving elevation is to place the arm in a simple sling.

4. Refer the athlete to a health care facility for further evaluation and treatment of the injury.

Boutonnière Deformity

Boutonnière deformity (French for *buttonhole*) involves the **proximal interphalangeal (PIP) joint** of the fingers (Hutson, 1990). The structure of the extensor digitorum tendon is unique as it crosses the dorsal surface of the PIP joint. The tendon is divided into three distinct bands: one central and two lateral bands (Figure 12.28). This arrangement allows for full flexion of the PIP joint without interference from the extensor digitorum muscle.

The mechanism for this injury is characterized by severe forced finger flexion, such as having the hand contact a playing surface during a fall with the fingers in a flexed position while an attempt is made simultaneously to extend the fingers. This results in tearing the central portion of the extensor tendon. Initial symptoms are limited; the athlete will be able to extend the injured PIP joint, but with limited strength. If left uncorrected, the PIP joint will eventually pop through the opening in the central portion of the tendon like a button popping up through a buttonhole. This results in a deformity that places the finger in a position of flexion at the PIP joint in conjunction with hyperextension at both the MP and DIP joints (Figure 12.29). Treatment for the injury consists of splinting the finger in a position of extension of the PIP joint to allow the central portion of the extensor tendon to heal. Surgical correction is not recommended (Hutson, 1990).

Signs and symptoms of boutonnière deformity include the following:

1. The athlete will report a violent flexion to the finger, perhaps associated with the sensation of tearing or popping over the PIP joint.

2. The injury will be followed immediately by significant weakness in extending the injured finger at the PIP joint.

3. The PIP joint will become painful and swollen, then stiff.

4. If left unattended, the injury may progress to the classic deformity, which is characterized by hyperextension of the MP and DIP joints, with flexion of the PIP joint.

First aid care:

1. Initially, this injury should be treated as any soft-tissue and/or skeletal injury of the hand or finger: Apply ice, compression, and elevation. This is best accomplished by using a small bag of crushed ice that is held in place with a small elastic wrap.

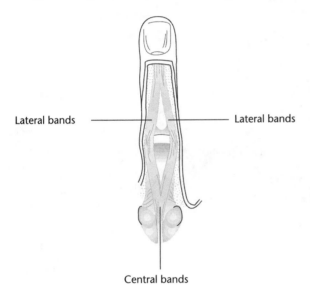

FIGURE 12.28 Bands of the extensor tendons.

Lateral bands — Lateral bands

Central bands

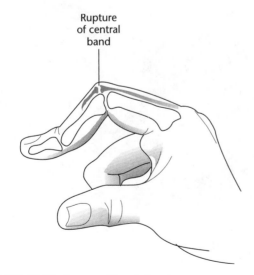

Rupture of central band

FIGURE 12.29 Boutonnière deformity.

distal interphalangeal (DIP) joint The joint formed by the articulation between the intermediate and distal phalanges of the digits (hinge type of joint).

boutonnière deformity Buttonhole deformity whereby the proximal interphalangeal joint of the finger is forced through the central band of the tendon of the extensor digitorum muscle.

proximal interphalangeal (PIP) joint The joint formed by the articulation between the proximal and intermediate phalanges of the digits (hinge type of joint).

2. Elevation can be easily achieved using a simple sling.

3. If any of the above signs and/or symptoms are present, the athlete should immediately be referred to a health care facility for medical evaluation.

4. In cases in which the initial injury has not been treated and has progressed to actual deformity, medical referral is mandatory.

Wrist and Thumb Taping

One of the taping procedures that can help prevent injuries in athletes involved in contact and collision sports is wrist and thumb taping. Taping the wrist and thumb before activity can help reduce excessive movement from contact, thus reducing the number of sprains to the area. It should be recognized that taping is both a science and an art that requires learning and practice. Once the coach or certified athletic trainer learns the basic concepts of a taping procedure, he or she needs to practice the application of the procedure. There are books available that demonstrate different taping procedures for many different joints. These books depict how the tape should be applied, but to really understand the reasons behind the procedures and to become a proficient applicator of the tape, an educational background is most helpful. The wrist and thumb taping pictures presented in Figures 12.30 through 12.39 provide an overview of a preventive procedure that can be applied.

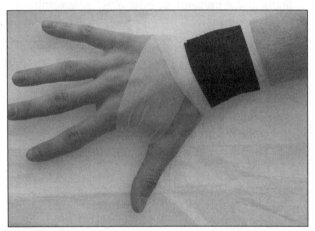

FIGURE 12.30 Start by applying pre-wrap as shown, followed by anchor strips around the wrist.

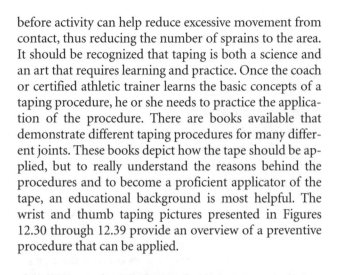

FIGURE 12.31 Apply figure-eight strips to stabilize wrist flexion and extension. A helpful hint in this step is to "pinch" the tape between the thumb and first finger to make the tape narrower and easier to follow the contours of the hand.

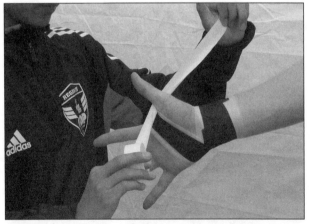

FIGURE 12.32 Apply thumb spica strips in an alternating pattern, moving from the base of the thumb to the nail.

FIGURE 12.33 Use the technique shown to minimize any compromised blood flow.

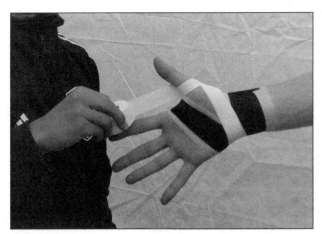

FIGURE 12.34 Thumb spica strips should be applied in opposite directions as they are placed in an alternating fashion.

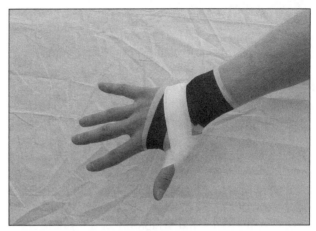

FIGURE 12.35 Wrist stabilization with thumb spicas applied.

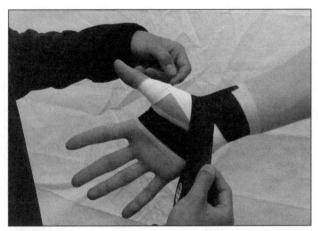

FIGURE 12.36 Apply stabilizing strips to reduce thumb movement (extension).

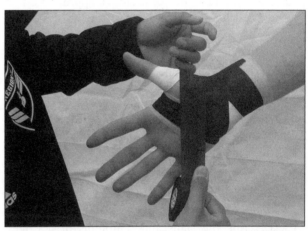

FIGURE 12.37 Alternate stabilizing strips from base of thumb, moving toward the nail.

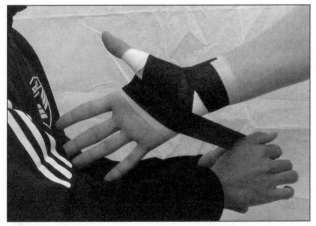

FIGURE 12.38 Apply finishing figure-eight strips to cover the thumb stabilizing strips.

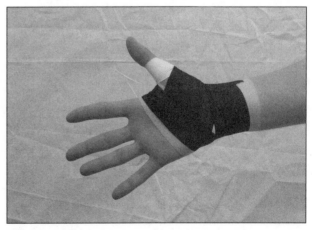

FIGURE 12.39 Complete wrist and thumb taping procedure. Check the thumbnail for compromised blood flow. A blue thumbnail indicates that the tape is too tight.

REVIEW QUESTIONS

1. List the three articulations of the elbow.
2. Explain the term *myositis ossificans traumatica* as it relates to a condition of the upper arm known as tackler's exostosis.
3. List the signs and symptoms of a humeral fracture.
4. Explain and/or demonstrate the first aid procedures for an athlete with a suspected fracture of the humerus.
5. Describe briefly the mechanism of injury for a posterior dislocation of the elbow.
6. List the signs and symptoms of a dislocation of the elbow.
7. *True or false:* The ulnar nerve is the most commonly damaged nerve in a dislocation of the elbow.
8. Explain and/or demonstrate the appropriate first aid care for an athlete with a suspected dislocation of the elbow.
9. Define the term *Volkmann's contracture.*
10. Review the signs and symptoms of either medial or lateral epicondylitis of the elbow.
11. Define osteochondritis dissecans.
12. What are the signs and symptoms of osteochondritis dissecans of the elbow?
13. What is the location of the olecranon bursa of the elbow?
14. *True or false:* A Colles' fracture involves the carpal bones of the wrist.
15. Describe the signs and symptoms of a Colles' fracture.
16. Explain and/or demonstrate the appropriate first aid procedures for an athlete with a suspected Colles' fracture.
17. Which one of the following carpal bones can be located within a region at the base of the thumb known as the anatomical snuff-box?
    a. Lunate
    b. Hamate
    c. Capitate
    d. Pisiform
    e. Scaphoid
18. *True or false:* The most common form of wrist sprain is the result of forced hyperextension.
19. What anatomic structures in the wrist form the tunnel of Guyon?
20. Which major nerve passes through this tunnel?
21. What musculotendinous unit is most often involved in the condition known as de Quervain's disease?
22. Define the condition known as a ganglion.
23. Explain and demonstrate the appropriate first aid care for a suspected phalangeal fracture of the hand.
24. Which specific ligamentous structure is damaged in the condition known as gamekeeper's thumb?
25. Describe the signs and symptoms of gamekeeper's thumb; explain and demonstrate the appropriate first aid for an athlete suspected of having sustained such an injury.
26. Explain the mechanism of injury and the structures involved in the condition known as mallet finger.
27. Explain the mechanism of injury and the structures involved in the condition known as boutonnière deformity.
28. Explain the mechanism of injury and the structures involved in the condition known as jersey finger.

REFERENCES

American Academy of Orthopaedic Surgeons (AAOS). (1991). *Athletic Training and Sports Medicine* (2d ed.). Park Ridge, Ill.: American Academy of Orthopaedic Surgeons.

American Medical Association (AMA). (1968). *Standard Nomenclature of Athletic Injuries* (1st ed.). Chicago: American Medical Association.

Bartsokas TW, Palin DW, Collier DB. (1992). An unusual stress fracture site: Midhumerus. *Phys Sportsmed.* 20: 119–122.

Booher JM, Thibodeau GA. (2000). *Athletic Injury Assessment.* Boston: McGraw-Hill.

Friel JP (ed.). (1977). *Dorland's Pocket Medical Dictionary.* Philadelphia: W. B. Saunders.

Hannafin JA, Schelkun PH. (1996). How I manage tennis and golfer's elbow. *Phys Sportsmed.* 24:63–68.

Holleb PD, Bach BR. (1990). Triceps brachii injuries. *Sports Med.* 10:273–276.

Hoppenfield S. (1976). *Physical Examination of the Spine and Extremities.* New York: Appleton-Century-Crofts.

Hutson MA. (1990). *Sports Injuries—Recognition and Management.* New York: Oxford University Press.

Isani A. (1990). Prevention and treatment of ligamentous sports injuries to the hand. *Sports Med.* 9:48–61.

Jobe FW, Ciccotti MG. (1994). Lateral and medial epicondylitis of the elbow. *J Am Acad Orthoped Surg.* 2:1–8.

Larson RL, et al. (1976). Little-league survey: The Eugene study. *Am J Sports Med.* 4:201–209.

National Safety Council. (1991). *First Aid and CPR.* Boston: Jones and Bartlett.

O'Donoghue DH. (1976). *Treatment of Injuries to Athletes.* Philadelphia: W. B. Saunders.

13

Injuries to the Thorax and Abdomen

MAJOR CONCEPTS

This chapter begins with an overview of the gross anatomy of the thorax and abdomen. Additionally, it discusses the internal organs associated with the thorax and abdomen that can be injured through sports participation. The internal organs and structures covered include the heart and lungs, liver, kidneys, spleen, stomach, and diaphragm.

The chapter also discusses external injuries such as fractures to the ribs, various joint-related problems, and breast injuries and contusions. It gives signs and symptoms of internal injuries to the heart, lungs, liver, kidneys, spleen, and bladder. At times, coaches overlook serious injuries to the internal organs; however, many injuries can have debilitating and even life-threatening effects if proper care is not applied.

http://health.jbpub.com/book/concepts/5e

The web site for this book offers many useful tools and is a great source for supplementary information for both students and instructors.

Visit the site at
http://health.jbpub.com/book/concepts/5e
to link to the following organizations and sites:

- Uniformed Services University of the Health Sciences
- The Loyola University Medical Education Network

ANATOMY REVIEW

The thorax and abdominal cavities contain the majority of the vital organs of the body. This area is enclosed by the spinal column, the rib cage, and the clavicle, which provide bony protection for the area. The vertebrae in this area include the 12 thoracic vertebrae and the 5 lumbar vertebrae located posterior to the abdomen. There are 12 pairs of ribs in both males and females. The first 7 (sometimes 8) pairs of ribs are connected to the spinal column posteriorly and the sternum anteriorly; therefore, they are known as true ribs. The anterior connection of the true ribs is made via a costal cartilage for each rib (Moore & Dalley, 1999). The remaining ribs, specifically ribs 8 through 10, connect via a common costal cartilage. Ribs 11 and 12 do not connect to the sternum anteriorly; thus, they are called floating ribs. The 8th to 12th pairs are sometimes referred to as false ribs. All of the joints between the ribs and the spinal column are reinforced with strong ligamentous support. This area is further strengthened by the anterior longitudinal ligament, which runs on the anterior surface of the spinal column from the occipital bone of the skull to the pelvic surface of the sacrum.

The main joints of the thorax include the intervertebral joints, the vertebral and rib joints, the sternocostal and costochondral joints, and the sternoclavicular joints. The intervertebral joints are those between each of the vertebral bodies. These joints are stabilized by ligaments and the intervertebral disks located between each vertebral body. The intervertebral disks are mostly fibrocartilaginous and play an important role in the weight-bearing ability of the spine. The ribs articulate with the vertebrae in an interesting manner. Each rib articulates with two adjacent vertebrae and the intervertebral disk. These joints are strengthened by ligaments that allow the gliding movements of the ribs at the vertebral column. Anteriorly, the first through the seventh ribs articulate with the sternum directly from their costal cartilage. Ribs 8 through 10 articulate with the sternum through a common cartilage. These joints are known as the sternocostal joints. The point at which the rib attaches to the costal cartilage is known as the costochondral joint. Typically, there is no movement at this joint (Gray, 1974).

One of the main joints of the thorax is the sternoclavicular joint. This is an articulation between the clavicle and the sternum; it is discussed in Chapter 11. This is the only bony articulation between the thorax and the arm, and it is supported by strong ligaments. There is movement at this joint even though it is not viewed as a major site of movement, as are other joints within the region. Several muscles surround the thorax and abdomen. The main thoracic muscles include the intercostal muscles, both internal and external, which function primarily to lift the rib cage and assist with breathing. More superficially, the pectoralis major and minor are located in the upper chest area and mainly control arm movement. In the posterior thorax several muscles run the length of the spinal column that are responsible for a variety of movements as well as stabilization of the spine. Most of the deep muscles running the length of the back, including the spinalis, longissimus, iliocostalis, and others, are responsible for keeping the spine erect. More superficially, muscles such as the latissimus dorsi, rhomboids, trapezius, and deltoid are mainly responsible for movements of the upper extremity. See Time Out 13.1 for specifics of muscle activity and innervation.

In the abdominal region there are also several important muscles. The main muscles of the anterior abdominal region are the external and internal obliques and the rectus

TIME OUT 13.1

Main Muscles, Actions, and Innervations of the Thorax and Abdomen

Muscles	Action(s)	Innervation
Latissimus dorsi	Adducts, extends, & medially rotates the arm	Thoracodorsal
Rhomboids	Scapular adduction	Dorsal scapular
Trapezius	Elevates, rotates, & retracts scapula	Accessory & C3–4
Pectoralis major	Adduction & medial rotation of arm	Lateral & medial pectoral
Pectoralis minor	Draws shoulder anterior and inferior	Lateral & medial pectoral
External oblique	Tenses abdominal wall & flexes and rotates vertebral column	T6–12
Internal oblique	Tenses abdominal wall & rotates the vertebral column	T6–12 & T1
Rectus abdominis	Tenses abdominal wall & flexes vertebral column	T7–12
Diaphram	Inspiration	Phrenic
Transverse abdominis	Tenses abdominal wall	T6–12 & L1

abdominis. The oblique muscles help to flex and rotate the trunk; they also assist with support of the abdominal viscera. The rectus abdominis is the main muscle of the anterior abdominal wall. In the abdomen the rectus abdominis acts to support the abdominal viscera and to flex the trunk. This muscle also assists in the lower extremity by helping to fixate the pelvis during movement, which allows the muscles of the lower extremity to function more effectively.

Internal Organs

The two main organs in the thorax (Figure 13.1) are the lungs and the heart. Each lung is encased in a separate and closed space called the pleural sac, which assists the lungs by helping to make respiration a smooth process. The lungs oxygenate blood as it circulates; they

WHAT IF?

You are coaching a tackle football game at the high school level. On the last play your quarterback was sacked and in the process received a severe blow to his abdomen. On further examination, he complains of extreme abdominal pain, has a rigid abdomen, and also reports pain radiating into his left shoulder and upper arm. Based on these signs and symptoms, could this athlete have a serious injury, and, if so, what?

are normally light, soft, spongy, and pinkish in a healthy person. The right lung has three lobes, and the left lung has two, which makes the right one a little larger and heavier than the left. Located directly between the two lungs is the heart. The heart is situated in an area called the mediastinum, which also houses major blood vessels and parts of the respiratory and digestive systems (trachea and esophagus) along with nerve and lymphatic tissues. Inferior to the pleural cavities and the mediastinum is a muscle called the diaphragm. Essentially the diaphragm separates the thoracic and abdominal cavities; it is considered the main muscle of respiration. The diaphragm is basically a circular muscle with a tendon in the middle that allows the muscle to contract and assist with breathing. There are several openings for blood vessels, nerves, and digestive structures to pass through the diaphragm.

For descriptive purposes the abdominal region (Figure 13.2) is typically divided into four quadrants: the right upper and lower quadrants and the left upper and lower quadrants, with the umbilicus serving as the

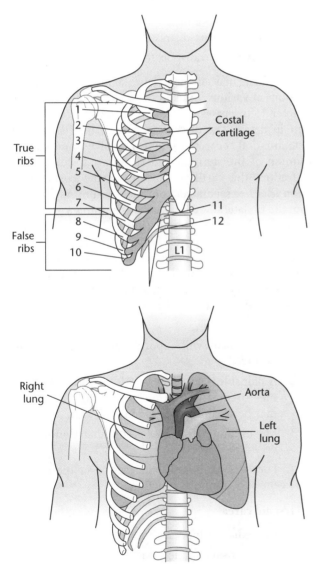

FIGURE 13.1 The internal organs of the thorax.

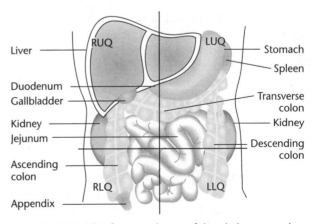

FIGURE 13.2 The four quadrants of the abdomen and the organs they house.

center point. The organs located within the right upper quadrant are the liver, gall bladder, and right kidney. In the right lower quadrant are the ascending colon and the appendix. In the left upper quadrant are the stomach, spleen, pancreas, and left kidney. In the left lower quadrant is the descending colon.

Common Sports Injuries

Sports injuries to the thorax and abdomen are relatively uncommon in children and adolescents. However, there are some injuries to the region that require immediate attention to prevent long-term disability and possibly even death. The discussion first focuses on external injuries involving the skeletal, muscular, and other external components of the region. The discussion then reviews injuries to the internal organs of the thorax and abdomen.

External Injuries

Fractures

Fractures to the bones of the skeleton can occur as a result of direct trauma. An athlete may fracture a rib, the sternum, the clavicle, or possibly some part of a vertebra. Fractures to any of these structures should be cared for immediately. Without proper care, complications can occur; the athlete may develop a pneumothorax or hemothorax, both of which are life-threatening conditions. A pneumothorax is the presence of air in the pleural cavity; a hemothorax is the presence of blood in the pleural cavity (Weissberg & Refaely, 2000).

In the case of a sternal fracture, which is infrequent in sports, two complications may arise. First, if the manubrium is dislocated and moves posteriorly, the possibility of an airway obstruction exists (Booher & Thibodeau, 2000). Second, if the sternum and ribs are separated completely, there is a likelihood of flail chest (loss of stability to the thoracic cage); the possible complications of this condition include a pneumothorax or hemothorax (Simoneauz, Murphy, & Tehranzadeh, 1990; Widner, 1988).

The other type of fracture to this region, which is more common in sports, is a rib fracture. Most often ribs are fractured in contact sports when two players collide and the rib cage is violently compressed. The fifth through the ninth pairs of ribs are most susceptible to fracture (Widner, 1988). However, almost any one of the ribs can be fractured under specific circumstances. As with other bones in the body, the ribs can be broken in varying degrees of severity, from greenstick

to displaced fractures. If a rib fracture is suspected, the athlete must be referred to the appropriate physician as soon as possible.

Signs and symptoms of a sternum or rib fracture include the following:

1. Extreme localized pain at the site of injury that is typically aggravated by sneezing, coughing, forced inhalation, or sometimes movement.
2. The athlete may grasp the chest wall at the point of injury.
3. Mild swelling may occur at the site, and there may be bony deformity.
4. The athlete may complain of breathing difficulties and take rapid, shallow breaths.

First aid care:

1. Monitor the athlete's vital signs and watch for any respiratory distress.
2. Arrange for transport to a health care facility.

The athlete may also experience subluxations and dislocations at various joints in the skeleton of the thorax. Chapter 11 discusses dislocation of the sternoclavicular joint in detail. The discussion here mainly deals with costochondral separations, which involve some type of disunion of the sternum and ribs. In a costochondral separation, the cartilage portion of the costosternal union is either separated from the sternum medially or from the rib laterally. Obviously this requires a great deal of force, and this type of injury is usually associated with contact or collision sports. Typically, the athlete with a costochondral separation will experience a great deal of pain at the time of the injury and in many cases will complain of pain for weeks after the injury.

Signs and symptoms of a costochondral separation include the following:

1. The athlete will report that a pop or snap occurred.
2. A palpable defect may be felt because deformity may or may not be present; in addition, there may be swelling in the immediate area.
3. Maximum or near-maximum inhalation may be very difficult.
4. Localized pain and tenderness over the area of the costochondral junction.

First aid care:

1. Immediately apply ice and light compression.
2. Treat for shock if necessary.
3. Arrange for transport to a medical facility.

Athletic Trainers SPEAK Out

During a routine high school varsity football practice on a Thursday afternoon, our players were running through the pass patterns when one of the receivers caught the ball and then tripped and fell on his stomach on the ball. Initially he appeared to have had the wind knocked out of him but nothing more. I helped him from the field and sat him on a bench to let him recover. After getting his breath he still complained of pain in the upper abdominal region. It was different than the pain one might expect with a bruise. Although the possibility of an abdominal injury was considered, I felt that the mechanism did not seem to be violent enough to cause any serious injury. I decided, though, that since the athlete was not improving it might be wise to get him to the training room and contact our team physician. I escorted him to the locker room; at this time he was complaining of pain moving to the shoulder. By the time the physician saw the athlete all the signs and symptoms were present to indicate a spleen injury. Within one hour the athlete was in the operating room. Given the nonviolent nature of the drill and the lack of immediate signs, [the coaches admitted] they probably would have sent the athlete home to rest. This action would have delayed the treatment and certainly led to more serious consequences.

—Larry J. Leverenz, PhD, ATC

Larry Leverenz is the Director of Athletic Training Education and Athletic Trainer at Purdue University.

Breast Injuries

The breast is subject to injury depending on the type of sport and the gender of the athlete. Women do incur breast contusions as a result of contact in some sports. Sports bras typically do not provide protection from direct contact, but they do help to support the breast during activity. Women will have various preferences regarding the type and size of sports bra that will provide the required support. Conversely, some women will elect not to wear a bra during sports participation. This decision should be left up to the athlete, based on comfort and performance. However, if the athlete elects not to wear a sports bra, she should be aware of the possible long-term effects of not supplying proper breast support during activity. Most often the major long-term effect is that the breast tissue stretches, resulting in loss of stability and natural breast contour.

Both men and women will at times experience nipple irritation. This problem is easily remedied by either changing tops or (if that is not possible) by placing a bandage over the nipple during competition so that irritation is reduced or eliminated.

Internal Injuries

Many organs and structures can be injured from direct trauma in collision and contact sports. It is not always easy to determine if an internal injury has occurred; therefore, the coach or athletic trainer must be educated and knowledgeable about the signs and symptoms of possible injury to an internal organ. The discussion here begins with the heart and lungs and continues with the internal viscera.

Heart Injuries

It has been noted that sudden death among athletes is more often a result of insult to the heart than any other factor (Aubrey & Cantu, 1989). This is not a common occurrence, yet even youth league baseball players and hockey players have experienced heart contusions (Karofsky, 1990). Any time the heart is compressed between the sternum and the spinal column by a violent external force, such as might be caused by being hit by a baseball or hockey puck, a cardiac contusion or chest pain can result (Karofsky, 1990; Steine, 1992; Widner, 1988). When an athlete is hit in the chest and the impact

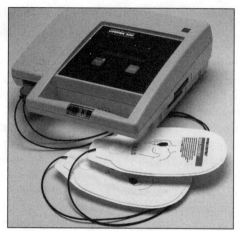

FIGURE 13.3 Example of a commercially available AED for use by a trained individual.

FIGURE 13.4 Softball chest protector.

is timed exactly with the repolarization phase of the contracting heart, it is possible for the athlete to experience ventricular fibrillation leading to death. This injury is known as commotio cordis and is most common in male youth in their early teen years playing baseball (Maron et al., 2002; Vincent & McPeak, 2000). Because of the increased incidence of this injury in youth baseball, the development and study of a softer baseball is ongoing (Link et al., 2002). The use of softer baseballs in youth games may be helpful in reducing the incidence of commotio cordis but may not be practical in games involving teenage athletes. Early intervention by trained professionals using an automated external defibrillator (AED) (Figure 13.3) appears to be the most practical approach to saving lives threatened by commotio cordis (Vincent & McPeak, 2000).

A blunt trauma to the chest may also cause an aortic rupture, injure the pericardium or coronary arteries, or cause valvular damage (Ketai, Brandt, & Schermer, 2000; Yates & Aldrete, 1991). Aortic injury is often fatal and must be given immediate attention if suspected. Ninety percent of people who suffer from aortic injury die before emergency care is instituted (Zink & Primack, 2000). Watch any athlete with a chest injury for breathing problems, fainting, decreases in heart rate and blood pressure, and complaints of severe chest pains.

For many years cardiopulmonary resuscitation (CPR) has been the standard method of attempting resuscitation of a person when the heart has stopped beating. Many CPR curricula now include training in both cardiac compression techniques and the use of an AED. The early use of an AED has been shown to increase the success rates of life-saving measures.

The prevention of injuries to the heart, lungs, and chest is primarily a function of protective equipment as part of the sport or activity (Figure 13.4). In baseball and softball the catcher is equipped with a chest protector. These days, chest protectors are made of materials that are much better at attenuating the shock from a ball traveling at high speeds. In football, hockey, lacrosse, and some other contact sports, part of the uniform is protective equipment designed to reduce possible impact to the heart and chest area. Some sports do not provide any preventative equipment protection from a blow to the chest area such as soccer and basketball. In these sports, the athlete must be trained to protect the chest when specific situations arise. Additionally, certified athletic trainers must be current in their CPR training and prepared with either an AED or an emergency action plan that would provide immediate care for a player with a significant chest contusion.

Lung Injuries

In addition to a cardiac contusion, an athlete may experience a pulmonary contusion. This injury can be a complication of a rib fracture, contusion, or some other type of pulmonary injury and can go undetected (Wagner, Sidhu, & Radcliffe, 1992). Pulmonary contusion has been reported in up to 70% of people experiencing blunt chest trauma (Zink & Primack, 2000). Ribs can fracture and puncture the pleural sac that surrounds the lung(s). If air gets into the pleural cavity, there is a possiblity of a lung collapse. When a lung collapses, it is termed a pneumothorax (Weissberg & Refaely, 2000).

There is also the possibility of spontaneous pneumothorax among athletes. Spontaneous pneumothorax occurs without a preceding traumatic event (Weissberg & Refaely, 2000). This has been reported among both runners and weight lifters (Wagner, Sidhu, & Radcliffe, 1992). This injury is significant and must be attended to by a physician. If blood gets into the pleural cavity, this is commonly called hemothorax; again, this can occur without a preceding traumatic event (Reuter, 1996). The coach or athletic trainer must be aware of the signs and symptoms of both cardiac and pulmonary contusions as well as pneumothorax. The progress of the athlete should be monitored over a period of days because some injuries have a tendency to exhibit complications later (Perkins & Sterling, 1991).

Signs and symptoms of a cardiac or pulmonary contusion and/or a pneumothorax include the following:

1. The athlete will complain of severe pain in the chest area, sometimes radiating to the thoracic spine.

2. The athlete will typically experience breathing problems—either shortness of breath or painful breathing exhibited by short, shallow breaths. Additionally, inspect for a loss of chest wall movement during breathing.

3. The athlete may exhibit a nonproductive cough and may have a tachycardiac heart rate.

First aid care:

1. Treat the athlete for possible shock.
2. Monitor vital signs continuously.
3. Arrange for transport to a medical facility.

More commonly, respiratory problems can lead to chest pain in the athlete (Steine, 1992). However, whenever a coach or athletic trainer has an athlete who reports chest pain, that player should be seen immediately by the team physician. Chest pain and heart conditions in athletes must be reviewed by the proper medical personnel as soon as possible.

Liver

The liver aids in the production of plasma proteins and the detoxification of alcohol and other substances; it also has various digestive functions (Farish, 1993). It is located in the upper right quadrant of the abdomen and can be susceptible to trauma, especially if the athlete has hepatitis and the organ is enlarged (Kulund, 1988). The liver may be implicated if a rib fracture occurs in the upper right abdominal quadrant. Otherwise, the liver is fairly safe from injury associated with sports participation. The liver is, however, susceptible to injury from the overuse of alcohol and drugs (especially massive amounts of steroids) as well as other internal insults.

Kidneys

The kidneys serve to maintain the proper levels of waste, gas, salt, water, and other chemicals in the bloodstream (Farish, 1993). The kidneys are located posteriorly and somewhat inferiorly on each side of the abdomen; they can be susceptible to injury from blunt trauma or heat (via extreme exercise in the heat of the day, for example). The body can experience acute renal failure, and the kidneys will cease to function. An athlete who has hematuria (blood in the urine) after being hit by an opponent in the lower back or after having exercised strenuously in the heat should be seen by a physician. Both of these scenarios can lead to kidney problems or damage. Many times an athlete's exercise regimen must be modified until the urine is once again clear of any blood.

Spleen

The chief function of the spleen is to maintain a reserve of ready-to-use blood cells for the body (Farish, 1993). It is located in the upper left quadrant of the abdomen and is somewhat protected by the ribs on the lower left side. Like most of the other internal organs, the spleen is susceptible to injury from both blunt trauma and internal disorders. An athlete who gets hit quite hard in the abdomen over the spleen can suffer a lacerated spleen. Nevertheless, the spleen has the capacity to splint or patch itself at the site of the injury because of its reservoir of red blood cells. If the spleen does patch itself and the athlete is allowed to continue participating, there remains the possibility that the patch may be disrupted by even a small amount of trauma. This can allow internal bleeding to resume, and death can occur even as long as days afterward (Kulund, 1988). If an athlete is hit hard in the upper left quadrant and later complains of pain in the abdomen and/or left shoulder and upper third of the left arm (sometimes the right shoulder), this is known as **Kehr's sign.** The athlete should be referred to a physician as soon as possible.

Additionally, if an athlete is suffering from mononucleosis, the spleen will probably be enlarged and susceptible to injury not only from blunt trauma but from excessive movement during sports participation. The athlete with mononucleosis needs to be restricted in activity until the physician can discern if the spleen has returned to normal size. Please refer to Chapter 19 for more information on mononucleosis.

Bladder

The bladder acts as a reservoir for the urine produced by the kidneys. It is located under the midline of the abdominal quadrants; this is a well-protected area, and the bladder is rarely injured by participation in sports and athletics. If the athlete receives a direct blow to the

Kehr's sign Pain radiating into the left shoulder that is normally associated with an injury to the spleen.

area of the bladder and injury does occur, the signs will be pain in the localized area and possibly blood in the urine. Avoiding injury to the bladder is best accomplished by emptying it before practice or competition.

Abdominal Pain

Various types of abdominal pain occur in athletes before, during, and after competition. Some of the more common abdominal pain complaints can be linked to multiple sites in the abdomen. If an athlete is experiencing chronic pain in the same location, the athlete should see a physician as soon as possible. Another reason for abdominal pain is referred pain, as noted with the spleen. The diaphragm can be irritated and result in shoulder tip pain (Morton & Callister, 2000). Calliet (1993) points out that esophageal problems are typically noted by the athlete as epigastric pain. Stomach problems such as duodenal ulcer are typically localized to the stomach area but have been known to produce low back pain complaints (Weiss, Conliffe, & Tata, 1998). Similarly, low back pain can be referred to other regions of the pelvic area from problems in the low back or iliac crest regions (Curtis, Gibbons, & Price, 2000).

Exercise-related transient abdominal pain (ETAP) is a problem commonly called "side ache" or "stitch in the side" by athletes. This problem typically occurs during running early in an exercise regimen of an unconditioned athlete. The actual cause of this problem has not been exactly determined, but different hypotheses have been put forth to try to explain why this problem might occur in athletes. Some possible explanations are ischemia in the diaphragm, stress on the visceral connective tissues, or a cramping of the local musculature (Morton & Callister, 2000). Other theoretical explanations address the time of onset (early in the exercise program) and hypothesize that the acute increase in venous return from the lower extremities to the liver results in the extra blood flow stretching the vein near the liver. This acute stretching of the vein initiates a pain response to the brain, and the brain recognizes a pain in the right side. In response to the pain the person typically slows his or her running pace or even stops. Following this decrease in exercise, blood flow equalizes and less stretch is placed on the vein, resulting in a decrease in the pain signal to the brain. When an athlete warms up appropriately, the incidence of this phenomenon reduces. Another theory for pain on the left side in the exercising athlete is that gas or fecal matter is being moved through the intestinal tract and that during exercise the timing is such that this movement is inhibited and could be stopped in one of the angles of the winding intestinal tract. Side aches do not appear to be a problem that eliminates athletes from participation in most sports, and most athletes learn how to deal with them on the rare occurrences they take place.

It is also possible to have right side pain that is not a result of any of the previous causes but which can be an early sign of acute appendicitis. Initially, the athlete will have a loss of appetite, followed by generalized abdominal pain. When the problem progresses, the chief complaint of the athlete with acute appendicitis will be severe pain in the lower right quadrant. At times this pain will be excruciating and the athlete can be rendered immobile. Additionally, the athlete will experience nausea and possibly vomiting and have a fever that increases over time. The athlete will be point tender to palpation in the lower right quadrant and should be taken to the hospital immediately. Without medical attention, the athlete can die from the complications associated with a ruptured appendix.

It may seem like there is a need for methods to circumvent problems associated with injury or preexisting conditions of the heart, lungs, and abdominal contents. Although some athletes may have preexisting cardiac abnormalities, as pointed out in Chapter 20, the uses of echocardiogram or echocardiography are not deemed necessary by the American Heart Association at the present time. It is important to review each athlete's history very closely to determine if a cardiac or respiratory problem may be exacerbated by an increased level of athletic participation. If an athlete has a family or personal history of cardiac or respiratory problems, the physician providing the preparticipation examination must make an informed decision as to the appropriateness of participation in a specific sport or activity for that athlete.

Preexisting conditions of the chest that may disqualify an athlete from participation can include but are not limited to problems such as hypertrophic cardiomyopathy (abnormal left ventricle growth), heart murmurs and arrhythmias, significantly decreased lung function from disease or a disorder such as cystic fibrosis, or chronic obstructive pulmonary disease. Disqualification from sports participation based on these conditions is dependent on the type of sport being considered, the amount of stress the activity will place on the dependent structures or systems, and the ability to control potential problems during the activity. Athletes with what might be considered a severe cardiac or respiratory disorder may be able to participate in specific activities depending on the control of their disorder, the type of activity, and the willingness of the physician to help the athlete make the necessary adjustments for participation at some level.

REVIEW QUESTIONS

1. *True or false:* Men and women have the same number of ribs.

2. Explain the difference between true ribs and floating ribs.

3. List the five main joints of the thorax.

4. With what necessary function do the intercostal muscles assist in the thorax?

5. *True or false:* Both lungs are the same size and configuration.

6. What is the name of the enclosed space where each lung is located?

7. *True or false:* The diaphragm separates the heart and lungs from the abdominal viscera.

8. Explain the difference between a pneumothorax and a hemothorax.

9. List the signs and symptoms of a costochondral separation.

10. What is the best indicator of kidney damage or disorder?

11. *True or false:* The spleen is able to splint itself if injured by blunt trauma.

12. Name the infection, prevalent among college-aged students, that causes the spleen to enlarge, requiring the athlete to reduce physical activity until the spleen is once again normal.

13. List four functions of the kidneys.

14. When pain occurs in the abdomen, what are some of the locations that the abdominal pain can be referred to?

15. Explain the best way to prevent bladder injury among athletes.

REFERENCES

Aubrey MJ, Cantu RC. (1989). Sudden death of a hockey player. *Phys Sportsmed.* 17(2):53–64.

Booher JM, Thibodeau GA. (2000). *Athletic Injury Assessment* (4th ed.). Boston: McGraw-Hill.

Calliet R. (1993). *Pain: Mechanisms and Management.* Philadelphia: F. A. Davis.

Curtis P, Gibbons G, Price J. (2000). Fibro-fatty nodules and low back pain: The back mouse masquerade. *J Fam Practice.* 49(4):345–348.

Farish DJ. (1993). *Human Biology.* Boston: Jones and Bartlett.

Gray H. (1974). *Anatomy, Descriptive and Surgical.* Philadelphia: Running Press.

Karofsky PS. (1990). Death of a high-school hockey player. *Phys Sportsmed.* 18:99–103.

Ketai L, Brandt MM, Schermer C. (2000). Nonaortic mediastinal injuries from blunt chest trauma. *J Thoracic Imaging.* 15(2):120–127.

Kulund DN. (1988). *The Injured Athlete* (2d ed.). Philadelphia: J. B. Lippincott.

Link MS, et al. (2002). Reduced risk of sudden death from chest wall blows (commotio cordis) with safety baseballs. *Pediatrics.* 109(5):873–877.

Maron BJ, et al. (2002). Clinical profile and spectrum of commotio cordis. *JAMA.* 287(9):1142–1146.

Moore K, Dalley AF. (1999). *Clinically Oriented Anatomy* (4th ed.). Baltimore: Williams and Wilkins.

Morton DP, Callister R. (2000). Characteristics and etiology of exercise-related transient abdominal pain. *Med Sci Sports Exerc.* 32(2):432–438.

Perkins RM, Sterling JC. (1991). Left lower chest pain in a collision athlete. *Phys Sportsmed.* 19(3):78–84.

Reuter M. (1996). Trauma of the chest. *Radiology.* 6:707–716.

Simoneauz SF, Murphy BJ, Tehranzadeh J. (1990). Spontaneous pneumothorax in a weight lifter. *Am J Sports Med.* 18(6):647–648.

Steine HA. (1992). Chest pain and shortness of breath in a collegiate basketball player: Case report and literature review. *Med Sci Sports Exerc.* 24:504–509.

Vincent GM, McPeak H. (2000). Commotio cordis, a deadly consequence of chest trauma. *Phys Sportsmed.* 28(11):31–32, 35–36, 39.

Wagner RB, Sidhu GS, Radcliffe WB. (1992). Pulmonary contusion in contact sports. *Phys Sportsmed.* 20(2):126–136.

Weiss DJ, Conliffe T, Tata N. (1998). Low back pain caused by a duodenal ulcer. *Arch Phys Med Rehabil.* 79(9):1139.

Weissberg D, Refaely Y. (2000). Pneumothorax. *Chest.* 117:1279–1285.

Widner PE. (1988). Thoracic injuries: Mechanisms, characteristics, management. *Athletic Training.* 23:148–151.

Yates MT, Aldrete V. (1991). Blunt trauma causing aortic rupture. *Phys Sportsmed.* 19(11):96–107.

Zink SE, Primack SL. (2000). Radiographic and CT findings in blunt chest trauma. *J Thoracic Imaging.* 15(2):87–96.

14

Injuries to the Hip and Pelvis

MAJOR CONCEPTS

This chapter includes a basic overview of the anatomy in the region of the hip and pelvis as well as a brief description of movements by the joints and actions of the musculature in the area. It discusses some of the more common hip and pelvis injuries incurred in sports and outlines emergency procedures. The chapter also includes a section about injuries to the area that are not common in sports. Coaches need to be aware of these types of injuries because of the possible negative long-term consequences that can result from improper care. The chapter reviews injuries to the male genitalia, including both testicular contusion and torsion. It also covers hernia and nerve problems and discusses proper referral.

http://health.jbpub.com/book/concepts/5e

The web site for this book offers many useful tools and is a great source for supplementary information for both students and instructors.

Visit the site at
http://health.jbpub.com/ book/concepts/5e
to link to the following organizations and sites:

- The Southern California Orthopedic Institute
- British Hernia Centre

ANATOMY REVIEW

The hip and pelvis form a "square" in the way they are constructed. This area comprises the two large, irregularly shaped pelvic bones on the lateral sides, the sacrum and coccyx posteriorly, and the articulation of the pubic bones anteriorly. The pelvic bones are also known as the innominate bones and are made up of three distinct parts: the ilium, the ischium, and the pubis. In the adult the three parts are fused and come together at a lateral point called the acetabulum, which is where the head of the femur articulates with the hip to form the hip joint (Figure 14.1).

The bony pelvis has several functions in the body: The lower extremities attach here, muscle attachments are prevalent, and it provides substantial protection for the entire pelvic region. In the female the pelvis becomes important in the birth process (Moore & Dalley, 1992).

The major articulations of the bony pelvis include the hip joint, the sacroiliac joints, and the symphysis pubis. The hip joint is the articulation of the head of the femur and the acetabulum in the hip bone; it is a true ball-and-socket joint that is well supported by strong ligaments. The sacroiliac joints are formed by the sacral bones and the iliac portion of the hip bones. The symphysis pubis is formed by the two pubic bones meeting in the anterior portion of the bony pelvis. All of these joints have strong ligamentous support that assists in joint stability.

Several nerves and blood vessels course through the bony pelvis (Figures 14.2 and 14.3). Some of the more important nerves are made up from the cauda equina. The spinal cord ends at the L-2 level, and the cauda equina exits the spinal cord beginning at L-2 and proceeding inferiorly (Gray, 1974). Nerves exiting the spinal cord below the L-1 level typically pass through the bony pelvis. These nerves include the formation of the lumbar plexus, the sacral plexus, the coccygeal plexus, and other individual nerves. Probably the most well known of these is the sciatic nerve, which is the largest in the body and is made up of nerve roots L-4 through S-3. The sciatic nerve passes through the posterior portion of the bony pelvis and down the posterior aspect of the leg. The blood vessels of the area include both arteries and veins that supply the pelvis and lower extremities. The more well known of these vessels include the iliac artery and vein.

Many of the muscles that attach to the bony pelvis are ones that move the lower extremities. The smaller muscles consist of the medial and lateral rotators of the femur. Some of the medial rotators include the tensor fasciae latae and gluteus minimus. These muscles are quite active in many movements of the lower extremity. The lateral rotators of the hip are small muscles located deep within the hip area that are also quite active in many movements of the lower extremity. Some of those more commonly injured include the piriformis, which attaches to the anterior surface of the sacrum and to the greater trochanter of the femur. The piriformis is a lateral rotator of the thigh; the sciatic nerve runs directly beneath the piriformis and can be irritated by the overuse of this muscle. Other external rotators of the thigh

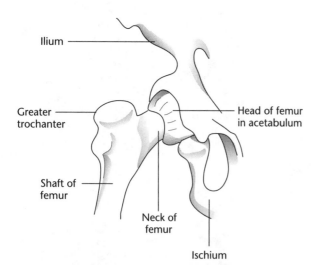

FIGURE 14.1 The ball-and-socket structure of the hip joint (anterior view).

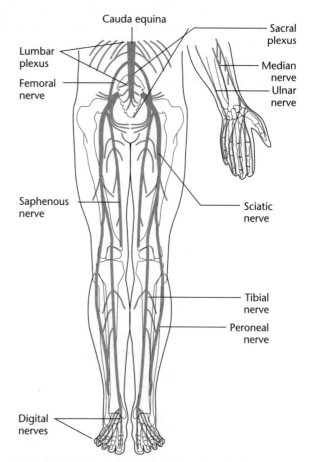

FIGURE 14.2 The nerves of the lower extremities.

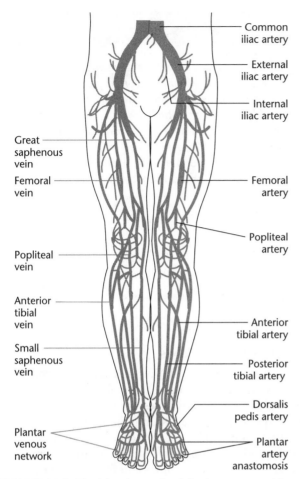

FIGURE 14.3 The blood vessels of the lower extremities.

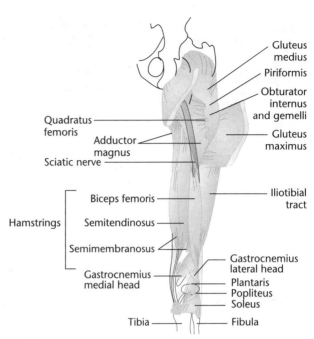

FIGURE 14.4 Hamstring and gluteal muscles (posterior view).

include the gemelli (superior and inferior), which attach on the ischium and run to the greater trochanter of the femur. All of these muscles (Figure 14.4) are small in comparison with the surrounding muscles, but they play an important part in the proper functioning of the hip and leg.

Many muscles attach on the pelvis and provide musculature for the leg, back, and abdomen. The muscles responsible for many of the large movements at the hip joint include flexors, extensors, adductors, and abductors. The main hip flexors include the rectus femoris, the iliopsoas group, the tensor fasciae latae, and the sartorious (Figure 14.5). The rectus femoris attaches at the anterior inferior iliac spine and runs down the front of the leg to the common attachment of the quadriceps group at the patellar tendon. The iliopsoas group is a combination of the iliacus and the psoas muscles, which attach on the anterior lumbar spine and iliac crest and come together as they run down to the lesser trochanter of the femur. The tensor fasciae latae and sartorius attach on the anterior iliac spine. The tensor fasciae latae runs to the lateral condyle of the tibia, whereas the sartorius runs across the anterior thigh and attaches to the anterior medial aspect of the tibia. The sartorius becomes one of the muscles of the pes anserinus group.

The main muscles of hip extension are the gluteals and the hamstrings (Figure 14.4). The gluteus maximus is the main hip extensor of the gluteals. The gluteus maximus attaches on the posterior surface of the ilium and runs inferiorly to the femur. The hamstrings attach mainly on the ischial tuberosity; then two of the muscles, the semitendinosus and semimembranosus, run more medially on the posterior leg and attach near the sartorius and on the posterior/medial condyle of the tibia, respectively. The biceps femoris runs more laterally on the posterior leg and attaches to the lateral aspect of the tibia and the head of the fibula.

The muscles that adduct the hip are located on the medial portion of the leg commonly called the groin area. The main muscles included in this group are the three adductors (brevis, longus, and magnus) as well as the pectineus and gracilis (Figure 14.5). The adductors attach on the pubis and run to the femur. The pectineus also attaches at the pubis and runs to the femur. The gracilis attaches on the inferior portion of the pubis and runs medially down the leg to the anterior medial portion of the tibia. The gracilis, sartorius, and the semitendinosus compose the pes anserinus group, to be discussed later.

Common Sports Injuries

The hip and pelvic regions are well designed anatomically: Sports-related injuries to the skeletal structures of the hip and pelvis are not common. Injuries to the soft tissues in the region are more common and can be quite debilitating to the athlete. Sports-related injuries to this

Athletic Trainers SPEAK Out

Acute avulsion fractures in the skeletally immature athlete are frequent injuries commonly associated with hip strains and hip pain. Most avulsion fractures are associated with the iliac crest, anterior superior iliac spine, and the ischial tuberocity. The skeletally immature high school athlete will not usually need surgical repair unless the avulsion fragment and related tissue damage are of appreciable size.

Most avulsion fractures can be treated with the same injury management as most muscle strains. Ice, rest, NSAIDs, and limited range of motion initially. A regimented strength and conditioning program should then be implemented as healing time and pain management are tolerated.

—*Jorge Garcia, BS, Sec Ed, LAT*

Jorge Garcia is a Licensed Athletic Trainer with Dr. Kip Owen Orthopedics, McAllen, Texas.

area commonly involve collision sports or forceful movements pursuant to an activity that requires power and speed of the lower extremities. However, one must remember that overuse injuries can also be associated with the hip and pelvis.

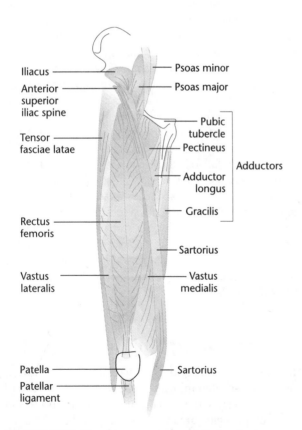

FIGURE 14.5 Quadriceps muscles (anterior view).

Skeletal Injuries

Fractures of the Pelvis

One of the most devastating injuries to the pelvic region is the fracture of one of the pelvic bones. Typically, a great deal of force is necessary to cause a fracture of this type. This is not a common injury related to sports participation. Still, it can occur in sports such as hockey, pole-vaulting, or football, in which there is the possibility of direct compression from another athlete, a fall from a height, or being twisted and hit by another player. Skeletal injuries to the pelvis in the adolescent population can be extremely serious, especially if the injury involves an open epiphysis. Any suspected skeletal injury to this area should be referred to a physician as quickly as possible.

Signs and symptoms of a fractured pelvis include the following:

1. Abnormal pain in the pelvic region after the injury.
2. There might be swelling at the site, with the rare occurrence of a visual or palpable deformity at the injury.
3. Pain is elicited when the iliac crests are pressed together by the examiner.
4. Associated injuries to internal organs such as the bladder are possible and should be ruled out only by the proper medical personnel. Blood in the urine (hematuria) must be immediately reported.

First aid care:

1. Treat for possible shock and internal bleeding.
2. Monitor the athlete's vital signs regularly.

3. Transport the athlete to the hospital on a long spine board with the foot of the board elevated to eliminate pooling of blood in the lower extremities.

A fracture of the pelvis is a serious injury and should be evaluated by a physician as soon as possible. Treatment will depend on the severity of the injury and should be complete before the athlete returns to practice or competition. Under no circumstances should an athlete with a suspected fracture of the pelvis return to competition before seeing a physician.

Other Adolescent Fractures

Femoral Neck Stress Fracture

This injury occurs more commonly in the thin amenorrheic athlete involved in running or endurance sport. The femoral neck stress fracture is a result of a loss in shock-absorbing capacity of the fatigued muscles in the hip area. This problem can also be a partial result of poor footwear, hard running surface, or hip deformities (Lacroix, 2000). Typically, athletes complain of severe anterior thigh or groin pain when they have a possible femoral neck stress fracture. The athlete will be able to walk but will experience pain during ambulation. Seeing a physician is necessary to get radiographs, which will help to discover the problem.

Slipped Capital Femoral Epiphysis

This problem occurs most commonly in 10- to 15-year-old boys. Typically, it occurs in a boy who is tall and has recently experienced a rapid growth period, or in boys who are overweight and in whom the secondary sex characteristics are late in appearing (Lacroix, 2000). The boy will exhibit a flexed hip, lack of hip motion, and pain in the anterior groin, hip, thigh, or knee. Lacroix (2000) points out that any child under the age of 12 who complains of knee pain should have a thorough hip evaluation by the physician to rule out any one of a number of hip pathologies that may exist in this population.

Hip Pointer

Probably the most common injury to the region is a contusion to the superior/anterior portion of the iliac crest, which is commonly referred to as a **hip pointer.** Typically, with this injury the athlete receives a direct blow to the area from an opponent's helmet or falls to the ground with great force. This can be an extremely painful and debilitating injury for the athlete, but it is not one that will require emergency attention or cause major complications if further activity is necessary.

Signs and symptoms of a hip pointer include the following:

1. Swelling at the site of injury.
2. Discoloration at the site of injury.
3. Pain and discomfort at the site of injury.
4. The athlete may walk with a slight limp on the affected side. Coughing, sneezing, and laughing may also produce pain at the site of injury.

First aid care:

1. Immediately apply ice to the injured area.
2. Have the athlete rest and avoid activity that involves the lower extremities.
3. If the injury is severe, walking with crutches may be necessary for a few days.

Long-term care for this type of injury is rather simple. The contusion has in most cases caused minimal damage to an area where several muscles attach directly to bone tissue. The muscular attachments in the abdominal region are the cause of pain when the athlete coughs, sneezes, or laughs. The player will usually be able to participate on a limited basis within 1 to 2 weeks, depending on the severity of the injury. It is important to note that if an athlete wishes to continue participating in sports while recovering from a hip pointer, the area should be padded well so that further damage will not occur if a similar incident happens before recovery is complete. This can be easily accomplished by securing a doughnut-shaped piece of foam padding over the area (Figure 14.6). Additionally, it is helpful to place hard plastic over the doughnut pad to provide even more protection to the area.

Other Hip Problems

Athletes who participate in excessive running as a part of their sport can experience what is known as "snapping hip syndrome." Snapping hip is a sensation that occurs when the athlete moves the hip in a specific direction. Usually, there is little if any pain associated with snapping hip. This problem is attributed to one of the muscles in the lateral hip riding over the top of the greater trochanter of the femur. The structures that could be involved include the iliotibial band, tensor fascia lata, and the gluteus medius. There could be subluxation of the hip or labral tears that induce extra movement of the femur during locomotion. Typically treatment consists of stretching tightened muscles that may contribute to the snapping sensation and correction of any biomechanical deviations of the area. The physician may also recommend anti-inflammatory

> **hip pointer** Contusion and associated hematoma to the superior/anterior portion of the iliac crest.

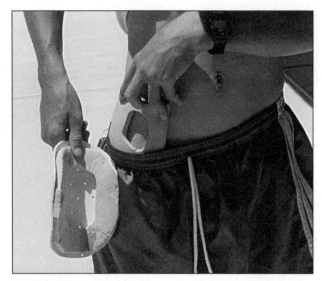

FIGURE 14.6 An athlete inserts a hip-pointer pad.

medications to the athlete. Rarely is any surgical intervention suggested for snapping hip syndrome.

Trochanteric bursitis is another rare problem experienced by some athletes. It is a problem seen most often in middle-aged people, but athletes, especially runners, are becoming more prone to trochanteric bursitis. This bursitis is usually a result of either acute trauma to the specific area or repeated microtrauma to the tendon attachments with secondary inflammation of the bursae in the area. The iliotibial band can be a source of the problem if it is tight and the athlete continues to run when he or she is experiencing signs and symptoms of trochanteric bursitis. When an athlete is experiencing the onset of trochanteric bursitis, he or she will initially complain of pain over the greater trochanter followed by pain radiating down the anterior or lateral thigh and to the buttock region. Most athletes will benefit from stretching the iliotibial band, taking nonsteroidal anti-inflammatory drugs, and using modality treatments that include cold and heat. In some athletes it may be necessary to pad the area if there is a chance of external trauma such as falling or being hit by another athlete in the hip. On rare occurences, athletes will not respond to conservative treatment and will benefit from surgical management (Slawski & Howard, 1997). Few athletes will need surgery if proper treatment is initiated early in the injury cycle.

Osteitis Pubis

Another type of skeletal injury to the pelvic area is **osteitis pubis,** a condition resulting from continued stress and possibly some degeneration in the symphysis pubis joint. This injury is commonly a result of overuse and chronic strain on the joint. Long-distance runners,

basketball and soccer players, and other athletes who experience repetitive pelvic movements in sports may complain of this condition. Athletes who produce repetitive shearing forces of the pelvis and have increased stresses on the lower abdominal structures during their sport participation are more susceptible to this problem. Osteitis pubis is a difficult injury to diagnose because of the many muscles and structures in the pelvic area, resulting in a delayed diagnosis or a nondiagnosed problem (Vitanzo & McShane, 2001).

The athlete will complain of an insidious onset of pain that worsens progressively. The athlete may indicate that the pain is in the groin area (unilateral or bilateral) and complain of testicular or scrotal pain along with anterior pubic, suprapubic, or even hip pain when experiencing osteitis pubis (Vitanzo & McShane, 2001; Morelli & Smith, 2001). An athlete complaining of symptoms should be referred to the appropriate doctor for complete evaluation. Because this is a chronic problem, first aid is typically not necessary, but the athlete will benefit from rest, ice, and anti-inflammatory medications such as aspirin or ibuprofen. This disorder typically responds well to therapy, with very few if any long-term side effects. An athlete may take anywhere from 3 months to a year to return to preinjury functioning levels. If osteitis pubis is diagnosed by the physician at early onset, the time frame for full return to activity may be reduced because treatment will be initiated early. Athletes who do not respond to conservative therapy may be candidates for surgery.

Injury of the Sacroiliac Joint

The sacroiliac (SI) joint, which is the articulation between the sacrum and the pelvis (Figure 14.7), is a common site of pain in the posterior aspect of the pelvis.

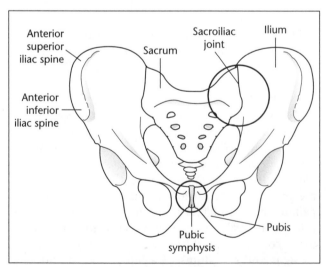

FIGURE 14.7 Common sites of hip injuries.

Movement at this joint is limited because of the configuration of the bones and numerous ligaments. This joint can present problems for the athlete if it becomes completely immobile or if it becomes inflamed from an injury or other problem. Injuries resulting in an immobile SI joint require specific movement techniques by a trained professional to restore the normal motion in this joint. Problems with inflammation in the SI joint can be treated by a certified athletic trainer or physical therapist under the direction of a physician.

Hip Dislocation

Infinitely more serious is a hip dislocation. This injury is actually quite rare in athletic events; however, it may occur to an athlete participating in contact sports. If a violent collision occurs between two players or between a player and another object (for example, the boards surrounding a hockey rink), this type of injury can happen. Typically, when this injury occurs the hip joint is in flexion, and the force is applied through the femur. Most often the hip will dislocate posteriorly, and the athlete will experience extreme pain and loss of movement in the affected extremity.

Signs and symptoms of a dislocated hip include the following:

1. Abnormal pain at the site of injury.
2. Swelling at the site of injury, with a palpable defect.

3. Knee of the involved extremity is angled toward the opposite leg.
4. This injury is typically quite visible to the observer.

First aid care:

1. Treat for possible shock.
2. Immobilize the athlete and transport to the nearest medical center.
3. Care should be given to monitor blood flow to the leg at all times.

Soft-Tissue Injuries

Because of the size and functions of the musculature in the hip and pelvic region, soft-tissue injuries are not very common in sports. The ligamentous support of the hip, sacrum, and other structures in the area is very strong; as a result, sprains rarely occur here. However, several muscles attach in the area of the pelvis, including the musculature on both the anterior and posterior aspects of the thigh, and these are subject to avulsion.

Avulsion Fractures

The possibility of muscle avulsions during forceful activity always exists. Skeletally immature athletes are more prone to avulsion fractures around the hip because their tendons are stronger than their cartilaginous growth centers. The mechanism of this type of injury is a sudden near-maximal muscle contraction. This results in the tendon pulling off a piece of bone at the attachment site. In a skeletally mature adult, this action usually results in a torn muscle or tendon because the bone is stronger than the tendon. In the adolescent, the tendon is stronger than the bone, so the result is an avulsion fracture. Avulsion fractures occur more commonly in adolescents who participate in sports requiring short bursts of maximal muscle contraction, such as soccer, tennis, sprinting, or jumping. The injured athlete will complain of severe localized pain and ecchymosis at the site of the injury. Common sites of injury in the adolescent are the anterior inferior iliac spine where the rectus femoris attaches, and the ischial tuberosities where the hamstrings attach.

Signs and symptoms of avulsion fractures in the pelvic region include the following:

1. Pain and swelling at the site of injury.
2. Inability to produce a specific movement that is usually accomplished easily.
3. Point tenderness over the affected area.

WHAT IF?

You are coaching a high school sophomore in the high hurdles on a cool, rainy afternoon in early spring. As the young man completes a start and five consecutive high hurdles, he grabs the back of his right leg, just below the buttock, and falls to the ground in obvious pain. You go to his aid immediately, and on examination you note that he is extremely tender in the region of the ischial tuberosity (origin of the hamstring muscles). He reports that he felt something tear and heard a pop while crossing the last hurdle, with immediate sharp pain. He has no history of a previous injury to this region. However, he has been complaining of tight hamstrings for the past several weeks. What type of injury may be present? What should be done for first aid? Should this athlete be referred to a physician?

osteitis pubis Inflammation of the bones in the region of the symphysis pubis.

4. Movement of the muscle closer to its opposite attachment when contracted. This is not easily detected in many avulsion injuries.

5. The athlete may report having felt or heard a snap or pop at the time of injury.

First aid care:

1. Immediately apply ice and require the athlete to rest.

2. Limit motion as much as possible. Walking with crutches may be necessary.

3. Have the athlete evaluated by a physician as soon as possible to determine the extent of the injury if an avulsion fracture is suspected. Radiographs done by the physician will document the avulsion fracture.

Avulsion fractures are debilitating and should be treated conservatively to reduce the amount of scar tissue that can result from these injuries. It is very wise to allow an athletic trainer or physical therapist to rehabilitate the athlete according to the recommendations of a physician. Without proper treatment and rehabilitation, this type of injury can be a problem in an athlete's future career.

Injuries to the Male Genitalia

An injury that is experienced by male athletes and is typically transient in nature is testicular contusion. Most male athletes competing in contact sports considered high-risk activities for testicular trauma wear a cup protector. However, this device does not always provide complete protection, nor do athletes always wear one. When the athlete receives a contusion to the testicular region there is extreme pain and usually a complete loss of mobility for a short period of time. Typically this pain and the resulting partial loss of movement are transitory; however, severe damage such as a ruptured testicle can be caused by extreme trauma to the testicles.

Signs and symptoms of testicular or scrotal contusions include the following:

1. Extreme pain and point tenderness.

2. Athlete may get into the fetal position and grasp his testicles.

3. The athlete will report a direct blow to the testicles.

First aid care:

1. Allow the athlete to rest on the sideline until he is ready to return to activity.

2. In severe cases, apply ice and allow the athlete to remain lying down in the locker room or athletic training facility when possible.

3. If there is swelling or lasting pain, refer the athlete to a physician as soon as possible.

The pain and debilitation associated with injuries to the testicles are transitory and should resolve without much intervention in a relatively short period of time (typically a few minutes). If the pain and debilitating effects last much longer than a few minutes, the athlete must see a physician to determine if severe damage has been sustained by the testicles at the time of injury.

Testicular torsion, or twisting of the testicles, can occur and should be recognized quickly; if this happens the athlete should be referred to a physician immediately. One of the testicles may, for any number of reasons, get twisted within the scrotum; as a result, the blood supply is compromised to or from the area, causing swelling to occur in the scrotum. The swelling may become quite uncomfortable, and the athlete needs to be transported to a medical facility as quickly as possible for treatment. Swelling in the scrotum can have serious side effects if not cared for immediately.

Hernias

A **hernia** is the protrusion of abdominal viscera through the abdominal wall; this typically occurs in the groin area. In males, inguinal hernias are more common; femoral hernias are more prevalent among female athletes (Lacroix, 2000; McCarthy, 1990). Most hernias will be detected during a preparticipation physical evaluation. However, an athlete who is suffering from a hernia will most likely have an abnormal protrusion in the groin area and experience pain in the groin and/or testicles. The athlete should seek proper medical advice promptly to discern how soon the hernia will have to be repaired. Athletes can experience "sports hernias" in which the posterior inguinal wall is weakened without any protrusion of abdominal contents through the abdominal wall. In this situation no palpable hernia is discovered during a routine physical examination, yet the athlete complains of continuing pain in the groin and lower abdominal regions. The sports hernia is difficult to diagnose for the physician and usually exhibits diffuse, deep groin pain that does not have a specific onset and gradually gets worse as the days pass. The athlete may complain of pain along the inguinal ligament and into the rectus muscles. It has been suggested that sports hernias may be the most common cause of chronic groin pain in athletes (Morelli & Smith, 2001).

Nerve Problems

A common complaint among many athletes is a burning or tingling sensation radiating from the hip and buttocks area and going down the back of the leg. These symptoms are often the result of irritation of the sciatic nerve. There are many reasons why this nerve becomes inflamed or painful. Typically, if an athlete continues to pursue the activity that has caused the irritation, then the pain will radiate farther down the leg to the foot and become more debilitating over time. The athlete must seek the advice of a physician and will need to rest and perform stretching and strengthening exercises depending on the cause of the problem.

Prevention

Many of the injuries to the hip and pelvis discussed in this chapter can be prevented by the use of proper conditioning and strengthening of the associated musculature. Adequate and appropriate conditioning of athletes will decrease the amount of stress placed on specific muscle groups and result in fewer soft-tissue types of injury. Groin strains, osteitis pubis, and some of the stress types of fractures can be avoided by conditioning and strengthening techniques that follow a planned protocol that includes proper rest periods. Rest is important for the body to repair micro damages incurred by the stresses of training.

Prevention of the hip pointer injury is typically a function of protective equipment as part of the uniform. Specifically, football pants include a hip pad, but other uniforms do not typically provide protection for injury to the anterior hip region. Athletes may ask the certified athletic trainer to custom-make a protective device if they have a tendency to experience the hip pointer injury.

The use of proper shoes for each activity can be helpful in preventing slipping or sliding by the athlete that might result in overstretch or tearing of muscles. Soccer players or similar types of athletes slipping on a wet field can sustain severe groin injury. Baseball players typically elect to wear a protective cup in an attempt to reduce trauma to the testicles from a hit by a baseball and catcher's masks now include a throat protector to deflect the shock of a foul tipped ball away from the throat. Other sports also have equipment specific to that sport that has been developed for protection from potential injury.

Even though injuries to the hip and pelvis are relatively uncommon as a result of sports participation, it is important to realize that injuries to this area do occur and that they can be debilitating to the athlete. Always take into consideration the possibility of severe injury when counseling an athlete about an injury to the hip and pelvis. First aid emergency care is important when treating these injuries. With most athletes, rehabilitation is also important if participants are to continue the enjoyment of specific sports.

> **hernia** Protrusion of a part of an organ or tissue through an abnormal opening.

REVIEW QUESTIONS

1. What type of joint is the hip joint?
2. Name the bones that make up the hip joint.
3. Explain the actions of the gluteal muscles.
4. Outline the location of the muscles that cause flexion, extension, adduction, and abduction of the hip.
5. List the bones in the hip area that are susceptible to fracture.
6. What structures are injured when an athlete suffers a hip pointer?
7. List the symptoms of osteitis pubis.
8. Explain the difference between testicular contusion and testicular torsion.
9. Define *hernia* and outline what a coach should do if one is suspected.
10. What should be done if an athlete is experiencing pain radiating down the back of the leg?

REFERENCES

Gray H. (1974). *Anatomy, Descriptive and Surgical.* Philadelphia: Running Press.

Lacroix VJ. (2000). A complete approach to groin pain. *Phys Sportsmed.* 28(1):66–78.

McCarthy P. (1990). Hernias in athletes: What you need to know. *Phys Sportsmed.* 18(5):115–122.

Moore K, Dalley AF. (1992). *Clinically Oriented Anatomy* (4th ed.). Baltimore: Williams and Wilkins.

Morrelli V, Smith V. (2001). Groin injuries in athletes. *Am Fam Phys.* 64(8):1405–1414.

Slawski DP, Howard RF. (1997). Surgical management of refractory trochanteric bursitis. *Am J Sports Med.* 25(1): 86–89.

Vitanzo PC, McShane JM..(2001). Osteitis pubis: Solving a perplexing problem. *Phys Sportsmed.* 29(7):33–34, 37–38, 48.

15

Injuries to the Thigh, Leg, and Knee

MAJOR CONCEPTS

Numerous injuries to the thigh and knee occur in a variety of sports to both male and female participants. Because this area is difficult to protect and is a major component of body contact with opponents, it can experience repeated trauma in contact and collision sports, thereby compounding earlier injuries. Knowledge about injuries to the thigh and knee is important for coaches dealing with young athletes.

This chapter begins with a brief anatomy overview that covers bones, ligaments, tendons, muscles, nerves, and blood vessels of the region; it goes on to describe the kinesiology of movements created by the muscles through the major joints.

The chapter continues with a description of soft-tissue injuries to the thigh that can become debilitating if not cared for properly, including contusions, strains, and various joint-related injuries. The knee joint, much like the foot and ankle, is required to provide both maximum stability and maximum mobility, thereby increasing the possibility of injury to this joint. The chapter covers problems such as osteochondritis dissecans, inflamed bursae, and patellar dislocation, along with injuries caused by chronic exercise. The knee joint is a complex configuration of bones, ligaments, and muscle tendons, any of which may be injured during sports participation. The chapter describes the four major ligaments of the knee and injuries to those ligaments; it also discusses the menisci (cartilage) within the knee joint that can be injured during sports participation. The chapter concludes with a discussion of prophylactic and functional knee bracing.

http://health.jbpub.com/book/concepts/5e

The web site for this book offers many useful tools and is a great source for supplementary information for both students and instructors.

Visit the site at
http://health.jbpub.com/book/concepts/5e
to link to the following organizations and sites:

- The Southern California Orthopedic Institute

ANATOMY REVIEW

The lower extremity is an area where many athletes experience some type of injury during their sports career. Injuries can occur to the thigh, knee, lower leg, ankle, or foot. The bones of this extremity include the femur, tibia, fibula, patella, and those of the foot (Gray, 1974). The femur or thigh bone is the longest, strongest, and heaviest bone in the body. It has a rounded, ball-like head that attaches to the hip bone with the help of a very strong network of ligaments. The head of the femur is attached to the shaft of the femur by a region known as the neck, which is highly susceptible to fractures. The femur becomes flatter and wider as it proceeds toward the knee, where it articulates with the tibia.

The thigh has a great deal of blood and nerve tissue going through it, both anteriorly and posteriorly. The anterior portion of the thigh contains the long saphenous vein and several branches of the femoral nerve. In the posterior section of the thigh are the deep femoral artery and the major nerve to the leg, the sciatic nerve. Most of the blood vessels and nerves are quite well protected by the musculature of the thigh.

The muscles of the thigh can be broken down into three basic regions. First, the anterior muscles of the thigh, commonly called the **quadriceps** (Figure 15.1), have two functions. The vastus lateralis, vastus intermedius, vastus medialis, and rectus femoris work together to extend the leg at the knee joint. Three of these muscles (vastus medialis, intermedius, and lateralis) attach on the femur and run down the thigh to the quadriceps tendon. The rectus femoris is the main working muscle of this group; it helps the hip flexors to flex the thigh and assists in steadying the hip joint in this position. The rectus femoris attaches on the hip bone at the anterior inferior iliac spine and runs down the leg to the quadriceps tendon. The other muscle in the anterior portion of the thigh is the sartorius; it also attaches on the hip bone and runs somewhat diagonally down the thigh to the anterior medial portion of the tibial condyle. This muscle is responsible for flexing, abducting, and laterally rotating the thigh at the hip.

Next, the main muscles of the medial aspect of the thigh include the adductor longus, adductor brevis, adductor magnus, and the gracilis (Moore & Dalley, 1999). These muscles attach on the pelvis and run to the femur; they are discussed in Chapter 14. The main function of these muscles is to adduct and help with flexion of the thigh. The third group of muscles in the thigh are in the posterior aspect of the thigh and are commonly known as the **hamstrings.** These include the semitendinosus, semimembranosus, and biceps femoris (Moore & Dalley, 1999). All these muscles attach on the pelvis and run down the leg to the tibia; they are discussed in Chapter 14. The main function of this group of

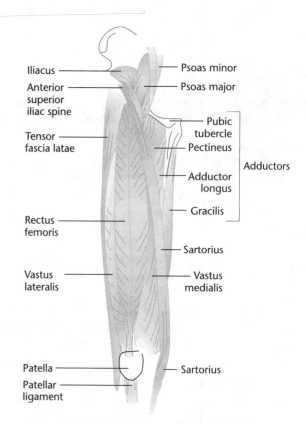

FIGURE 15.1 The quadriceps muscles of the anterior thigh serve two functions.

muscles is to flex the leg at the knee. Time Out 15.1 lists the thigh's muscle groups, actions, and innervations.

The knee is a very complex joint; it can be damaged through any number of accidents occurring during sports participation. The femur and the tibia articulate with each other (tibiofemoral joint) here, and the patella and the femur also have an articulation (patellofemoral joint). The patella is a sesamoid bone, which means that it is totally enclosed within a tendon, in this case the quadriceps tendon. The patella does not articulate with the tibia. There are many ligaments supporting the knee joint; however, four major ligaments serve as the primary stabilizers of this joint. They include the tibial or medial collateral ligament, the fibular or lateral collateral ligament, the anterior cruciate ligament, and the posterior cruciate ligament (Figure 15.2).

The tibial (medial) collateral ligament extends from the medial epicondyle of the femur down to the medial condyle of the tibia. The fibular (lateral) collateral ligament begins at the lateral epicondyle of the femur and extends to the head of the fibula. The fibular collateral ligament is the stronger of the two. Both ligaments help limit motion and/or disruption of the knee joint when movement at the joint is in a side-to-side direction, which is medically termed valgus (e.g., knock-knees) and varus (e.g., bow legs).

TIME OUT 15.1

Main Muscle Groups, Actions, and Innervations of the Thigh

Muscle Group	Action(s)	Innervation
Rectus femoris	Knee extension	Femoral
	Hip flexion	
Vastus medialis	Knee extension	Femoral
Vastus lateralis	Knee extension	Femoral
Vastus intermedius	Knee extension	Femoral
HAMSTRINGS	Knee flexion	
Semitendinosus	Knee flexion	Tibial
Semimembranosus	Knee flexion	Tibial
Biceps femoris	Knee flexion	Long head—Tibial
		Short head—Common peroneal
ADDUCTORS	Thigh adduction	
Adductor longus	Adduction	Obturator
Adductor magnus	Adduction	Obturator
Adductor brevis	Adduction	Obturator
ABDUCTORS		
Gluteus medius	Abduction	Superior gluteal
Gluteus minimus	Abduction	Superior gluteal
OTHER		
Sartorius	Knee flexion	Femoral
	Hip abduction, external rotation, flexion	Superior gluteal
Tensor fasciae latae	Hip flexion	
	Knee extension	Gracilis

The cruciate ligaments, unlike the collateral ligaments (which are located on the medial and lateral aspects of the knee joint proper), are situated on the inside of the joint. The anterior cruciate ligament attaches on the anterior portion of the intercondylar area of the tibia and runs superiorly and posteriorly to the internal aspect of the lateral femoral condyle. The posterior cruciate ligament attaches on the posterior aspect of the intercondylar area of the tibia and runs superiorly and anteriorly, passing the anterior cruciate ligament on the medial side and attaching to the internal aspect of the medial femoral condyle. The function of these two ligaments is primarily to reduce or prevent anterior and posterior displacement of the femur or the tibia.

Two semicircular fibrocartilaginous disks, commonly called cartilage and more specifically termed the **menisci,** are located within the space between the tibia and femur. The menisci assist with the lubrication and nourishment of the knee joint, aid in the distribution of weight and stress applied to the joint surfaces, and help with the biomechanics of the joint (Levangie & Norkin, 2005). Injuries to these disks, specifically the medial and lateral menisci, have caused the demise of many athletic careers.

Tendons of the muscles mentioned earlier in the description of the thigh run across the knee. Between the tendons and bone are several bursae, which reduce the friction of

quadriceps Four muscles of the anterior thigh: rectus femoris, vastus medialis, vastus intermedius, and vastus lateralis.

hamstrings The three muscles that make up the posterior thigh: biceps femoris, semimembranosus, and semitendinosus.

menisci Fibrocartilaginous structures that are between the hyaline cartilage surfaces in some synovial joints (e.g., the knee).

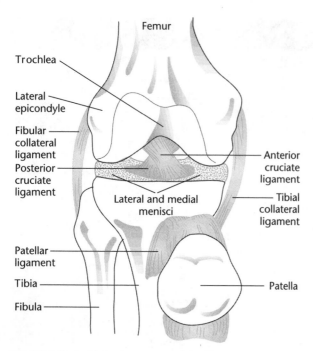

FIGURE 15.2 Major ligaments of the knee joint.

muscle tendons rubbing over a prominent area of bone, thereby adding some padding for the exposed bony areas of the knee.

Common Sports Injuries

Injuries to the thigh and knee can occur in almost any sport. In addition, this area can sustain injuries that are a result of overuse, trauma caused by an opponent, or trauma produced by the power and explosive movements required in some sports. The knee is an often-injured joint, and knee problems have caused a great many athletes to shorten their sports careers.

Because the knee is part of a complex mechanical system that includes the foot, ankle, lower leg, hip, and pelvis, there are times when another part of this system causes problems that can eventually be exhibited in the knee. For this reason, it is wise to obtain competent medical advice when athletes are experiencing knee pain or chronic problems with the joint.

Skeletal Injuries

Femoral Fractures

The femur is the longest bone in the body and is therefore subject to being fractured; however, this requires a great deal of force and is not a common occurrence in sports. If a fracture does occur to the shaft of the femur as a result of sports participation, the injury will be quite obvious; the athlete will be in a great deal of pain, and ambulation will be difficult with the affected leg (See Figure 15.3). The athlete should not attempt to walk on a femoral fracture. In such instances the athlete must be immediately transported to the nearest medical facility with the leg splinted and without bearing any weight on the affected limb. A femoral fracture requires urgent medical attention because the initial trauma can lead to multiple problems, including a lack of circulation, nervous innervation, or shock and other medical problems.

The neck of the femur can also be fractured. This occurs more often in sports than a fracture of the shaft, although neither happens frequently. Older children and teenagers are at risk for this injury because the fracture can occur through a growth plate. Among younger athletes these fractures can be the result of direct trauma or overuse. If direct trauma is the cause, the athlete will typically have a foot planted and then get hit in the hip or upper thigh with a great deal of force. When this injury does occur, it needs to be evaluated by a physician as soon as possible. One complication of a fracture in the neck of the femur is **avascular necrosis** of the femoral head; this is caused by a decrease in the blood supply to the femoral head, which can result in tissue death.

Signs and symptoms of a fracture of the femur include the following:

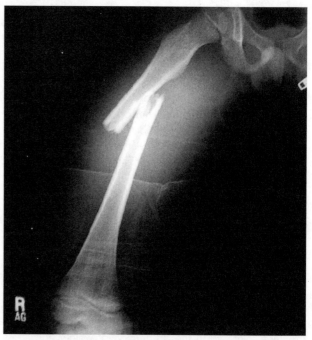

FIGURE 15.3 Femoral fracture of the right leg.

1. Pain at the site of injury.
2. Difficulty ambulating on the affected leg.
3. Swelling and/or deformity may occur.
4. Athlete may report a traumatic event as the cause.
5. The athlete may report having heard or felt a severe pop or snap at the time of injury.

First aid care:

1. Be prepared to treat the athlete for shock if necessary.
2. Splint the injured leg, preferably with a traction splint.
3. Apply sterile dressings to any related open wounds.
4. Monitor vital signs and circulation to the lower leg.
5. Arrange for transport to the nearest medical facility.

Patellar Fractures

Other skeletal problems that may arise include a fracture of the patella and dislocation of the knee or tibiofemoral joint. Although the patella can be fractured, this is not a common occurrence in sports participation. In most cases a patellar fracture is caused by violent trauma, and the athlete will be incapacitated for a short period of time following the trauma. There will be a great deal of pain associated with this injury, and the athlete will need to see a physician as soon as possible.

WHAT IF?

You are coaching a high school basketball game. It is late in the game; your team is on the defense, with their opponent's guard driving to the basket. Suddenly your post player, who was attempting to block the opponent's jump shot, falls to the floor, while simultaneously grabbing her left knee. On further examination she states that when she landed from jumping up to block the shot, her knee twisted and she felt something snap inside. You note that she also states that her knee feels very unstable. Given this information, what would you conclude? What would be the appropriate first aid for this injury?

Dislocation of Tibiofemoral Joint

Dislocation of the knee or **tibiofemoral joint** is possible and can compromise the blood flow to the lower leg in some instances. If there is a dislocation of the tibiofemoral joint, this will be outwardly apparent, and the athlete will experience marked pain. This injury must be splinted, and the athlete must be referred to the nearest medical facility without delay. Circulation and innervation to the knee and lower leg must not be compromised for even a brief period of time.

Soft-Tissue Injuries to the Thigh

Most of the soft-tissue injuries to the thigh are either the result of contact with an opponent or explosive movement by the athlete causing a self-inflicted muscle strain. Many sports, such as football and hockey, use some type of protective padding to prevent contact with an opponent to the thigh region. However, complete prevention is not always possible, and injuries do occur.

Myositis Ossificans

When an athlete receives a blow to the quadriceps muscle group from an opponent's knee, hip, or other anatomical part and there is a contusion to the musculature, bleeding and damage often occur. Depending on the force of impact and the muscles involved, the contusion may be of varying degrees of severity. In any case, the athlete must be counseled about the care of this injury and the long-term complications of improper care of a muscular contusion, which can include a condition called myositis ossificans. The initial muscular contusion causes bleeding; if not cared for properly, or if further insult occurs, there will be an increase in the amount of blood lost in the same area. Over a long period of time, continued bleeding and insult to the area can result in calcification within the muscle, abnormal bone growth, and further disability (Larson et al., 2002).

Signs and symptoms of a muscular contusion include the following:

1. The athlete will report a forceful impact to the area.
2. Muscular tightness and swelling may be present.

avascular necrosis Death of tissue caused by the lack of blood supply.

tibiofemoral joint Articulation (bicondylar) formed by the medial and lateral femoral condyles and the medial and lateral tibial condyles.

3. Decreased ability to forcefully contract the muscle.

4. Difficulties in ambulating with the affected leg.

First aid care:

1. Apply ice and compression immediately.

2. If the injury is severe, place the athlete on crutches.

3. Have the athlete rest and avoid any contact with the area.

With this type of injury, the athlete must be allowed plenty of rest and time to permit natural bodily processes to remove blood from the area so that healing will be complete. Early controlled, movement of the contused muscle will assist in regenerating the muscle when the athlete is ready to return to participation. The early mobilization in this case must be well controlled, and the athlete should not be allowed to participate in full-contact practice or competition until complete healing has occurred. Because further direct contact to the area may increase the risk of myositis ossificans, the area should be padded if the athlete continues to participate. Moreover, the player should be well aware of the long-term consequences of continued trauma to the area and should initiate treatment quickly if additional insult occurs.

Muscular Strains to the Thigh

Almost any of the muscles in the thigh region are susceptible to strains. Most of the strains to athletes, however, are to the hamstrings and adductor muscles. Strains to the adductor muscles are commonly known as groin pulls. Most strains occur to the muscle itself and not the tendon. Such strains are usually the result of muscles being stretched too far, which is the case with the adductor muscles. However, strains can be the result of miscommunication between **agonistic muscles** and **antagonistic muscles,** which is the case with many muscle strains involving the hamstrings.

If the muscle is stretched too far, the fibers of the muscle are damaged and bleeding occurs; the result is loss of contractibility, stiffness, and impaired movement. In the case of the previously mentioned miscommunication between agonistic and antagonistic muscles, the quadriceps musculature is contracting while the hamstrings are also contracting, causing the weaker muscle to be torn and damaged. Typically, the hamstrings are the weaker of the two groups; therefore, this is the musculature that is usually strained, with subsequent bleeding and hematoma formation.

Many athletes experience chronic tightness and repetitive strains to the muscles of the thigh adductor (groin) region. Specifically, the adductor brevis, longus,

and magnus muscles can exhibit problems, especially in athletes participating in activities requiring multiple changes in speed and/or direction. It is not uncommon for a track, soccer, football, or volleyball athlete to complain of tight, sore, or strained muscles in the groin region. The groin muscles are critical movers in speed and change of direction movements and are not easy to warm up and stretch. Special attention must be given to these muscles by the individual athletes as they are preparing for practice or competition.

These groin injuries can be debilitating if not cared for properly and quickly (see Time Out 15.2). Typically, when a strain to one or more of the groin muscles occurs, the athlete will feel a sharp pain in the medial side of the thigh, possibly associated with a "tearing" feeling. Not long after this incident, the athlete will complain of

TIME OUT 15.2

Case Study of a Ruptured Rectus Femoris Muscle

There is always a chance that a muscle injury can be more severe than first expected. The soccer player in this case study thought he had severely contused and strained his quadriceps muscle group during a soccer match when an opponent stepped on his thigh. There was abnormal swelling and a great deal of pain associated with the initial injury. Standard first aid procedures included ice, compression, and rest until the athlete attempted to play again on a wet field; at one point, when he planted his leg to start running, he felt something tear. At that point he decided to take some time off to let the injury heal. Months later, when the athlete was still having problems with pain and a lack of contractile ability, it was discovered that the injury to the quadriceps muscle was much more severe than thought during the initial evaluation. In this case study, the rectus femoris muscle had torn from its attachment at the patellar tendon and not been repaired in time to salvage the muscle attachment. As can be viewed in Figure 15.4, the muscle belly of the rectus femoris muscle draws up the leg when the athlete forcefully extends the lower leg. This athlete now must deal with a weak quadriceps mechanism and a strange feeling in his thigh each time he contracts his quadriceps muscles in that leg. This injury has eliminated his participation in collegiate soccer.

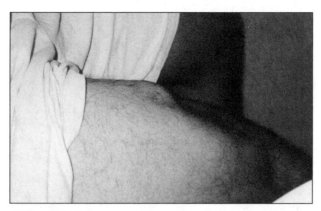

FIGURE 15.4 A soccer player with a ruptured rectus femoris muscle.

soreness, stiffness, and a lack of movement in the area. At times, even with continued use in even the most restricted situation, the muscle or muscles will take a long time to heal completely. This is because the muscles affected are being used unconsciously for many daily activities, movements of which cause small microtraumas that do not allow the damaged muscle to heal. To this end, constant attention must be paid to this injury until a complete recovery is made.

During and after recovery, athletes will need to implement a stretching program that specifically targets the adductor muscles. Stretching must be an integral part of the recovery from this and any other muscle strain injury because of the need to reduce scarring of the affected muscles.

Signs and symptoms of muscle strains to the thigh include the following:

1. A sharp pain in the affected muscle.
2. Swelling and inflammation in the immediate area.
3. Weakness and inability of the muscle to contract forcefully.
4. After a few days there may be discoloration of the area.
5. In severe cases, a visible defect is noted in the muscle.

First aid care:

1. Apply ice and compression immediately.
2. Have the athlete rest and use crutches if necessary.
3. Have the athlete evaluated by a member of the medical team.

Proper care for any injury to the thigh is important. Because a strain to the hamstrings or groin muscles is not considered serious, sometimes these injuries are not

cared for properly. The result can be a shortened career for the athlete.

Patellofemoral Joint Injuries

There are several injuries to the **patellofemoral joint**, both chronic and acute, that can become debilitating. Intervention is required if the athlete is to return to participation at peak level. Some of the problems causing injury are the result of faulty mechanics or growth in adolescents and are not due to anything that could be prevented initially. Many of the injuries to the patellofemoral joint, however, can be helped via intervention by the athletic trainer or physician, and the athlete can be participating at peak level in a very short time.

Osteochondritis Dissecans

Osteochondritis dissecans (OCD) has also been called "joint mice" because small pieces of bone that have been dislodged or chipped from the joint are floating within the joint capsule. In adolescents, OCD is the most common cause of a loose body in the joint space (Hixon & Gibbs, 2000). Damage to the joint surfaces caused by these osteochondral fragments can be a serious problem. When the joint surfaces are damaged and no longer make smooth contact with each other, further pain and joint damage are almost always inevitable. The piece of bone does not always have to be freely floating within the joint space: It may be dislodged yet still attached to the original bone and causing painful movement. If in fact the piece of bone is freely floating within the joint space, it can cause a blocking or locking action that limits the movement at the knee joint. The reason for this is not fully understood, although most experts believe it is a direct result of some type of trauma. When OCD occurs in juvenile athletes, the athlete should be referred to the proper physician for diagnosis and determination of the course of treatment. Many juvenile athletes will respond to conservative treatment, whereas others may require surgical intervention (Hixon & Gibbs, 2000).

Signs and symptoms of osteochondritis dissecans include the following:

1. Chronic knee pain with exertion that is generalized, not specific.
2. There may be chronic swelling present.

agonistic muscles Muscles in a state of contraction as related to opposing muscles.

antagonistic muscles Muscles that counteract the action of agonistic muscles.

patellofemoral joint Articulation (saddle) formed by the posterior surface of the patella and the anterior surface of the femoral condyles.

3. The knee may lock if there is a loose body within the joint. The athlete may be unable to fully extend the extremity.

4. The quadriceps group may atrophy.

5. One or both femoral condyles may be tender to palpation when the knee is flexed.

First aid care:

1. Apply ice and compression.

2. If the athlete has difficulty walking or the knee is locking, have the player use crutches.

3. Have the athlete see a physician for proper treatment.

Inflamed Bursae

A bursa is a small fluid-filled sac, located at strategic points throughout the body, that assists in the prevention of friction between bony surfaces, tendons, muscles, or skin that pass over it. There are several bursae in the knee joint; however, only a few are commonly irritated (Figure 15.5). A bursa can become inflamed as a result of trauma or infection. The inflammation can also be the result of chronic overuse and irritation of the bursa. In the case of trauma, a football player may hit a knee quite hard on another player's helmet or on the playing surface, thereby causing the prepatellar bursa to become swollen and enlarged (Figure 15.6). The prepatellar bursa is located just between the skin and the patella and is susceptible to direct trauma.

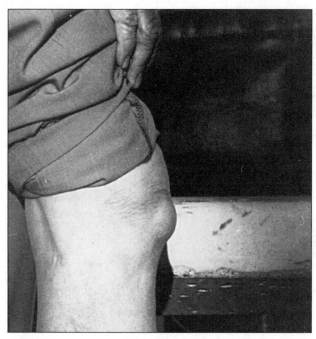

FIGURE 15.6 Prepatellar bursitis.

Most of the other bursae located in the knee are susceptible to chronic injury. The constant use of the legs and knees in some exercises creates too much friction in the area, and the bursae respond by becoming inflamed. It is also possible for these bursae to become inflamed from direct trauma, although this is not as common.

Signs and symptoms of an inflamed bursa include the following:

1. Swelling and tenderness at the site.

2. Increased pressure externally typically causes pain.

3. The athlete may report direct trauma or a chronic buildup of swelling.

First aid care:

1. Apply ice and compression.

2. Reduce activity for a short period of time.

3. In chronic cases, anti-inflammatory agents may be helpful.

Patellar Dislocation/Subluxation

When an athlete makes a quick, cutting motion to one side or another, a great deal of abnormal force is generated within the knee. As a result of this sudden abnormal force, the patella can move laterally instead of superiorly and inferiorly as it normally does. If the patella moves too far laterally, it can become dislocated. Whether the patella remains dislocated or returns to its normal position

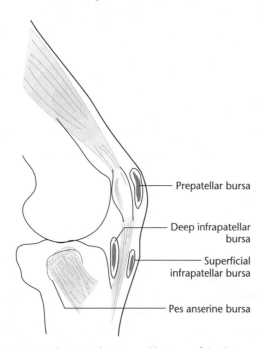

Prepatellar bursa

Deep infrapatellar bursa

Superficial infrapatellar bursa

Pes anserine bursa

FIGURE 15.5 Commonly irritated bursae of the knee.

spontaneously tends to be related to the number of times this type of incident has occurred in the past. In many cases, if the athlete is a chronic subluxor the patella will reduce (i.e., return to a normal position) without intervention. If it is the first time the patella has dislocated, it may or may not reduce itself. In most instances of patellar dislocation, the athlete will know that the patella has moved out of the normal position and will be somewhat disabled.

Signs and symptoms of a dislocation/subluxation of the patella include the following:

1. Athlete will report a great deal of pain and an abnormal movement of the patella when the injury occurred.
2. There will be associated swelling.
3. The knee and patella will be extremely tender, especially the medial aspect.

First aid care:

1. Apply ice immediately.
2. Compression and elevation will also be helpful.
3. Splint the entire leg.
4. Arrange for transport to the nearest medical facility.

When a patellar dislocation occurs, the patella will most often move laterally. In addition, when an athlete experiences a patellar dislocation there most likely will be accompanying soft-tissue damage to the medial aspect of the knee. If not cared for properly, this injury can become a chronic problem.

Osgood-Schlatter Disease and Jumper's Knee

The attachment of the patellar tendon at the tibial tubercle can be the site of two similar problems associated with athletes who do a great deal of jumping, although

WHAT IF?

You are teaching a junior high school weight-training class. One of the young boys in your class comes to you complaining of a chronic aching he has had for several days in the anterior knee, inferior to the patella, at the insertion of the patellar tendon. The boy reports the pain is worse in the mornings, especially when walking up and down stairs. Based on this history, what is the likely cause of this pain? What do you recommend for this child?

jumping is not a prerequisite to experiencing either Osgood-Schlatter disease or jumper's knee. These two injuries can be confused with one another if the certified athletic trainer does not look carefully at the age of the athlete and the signs and symptoms the athlete is experiencing. The main difference in these two conditions is the exact location of the injury. Osgood-Schlatter disease is typically a problem at the junction of the patellar tendon and the tibial tuberosity in the adolescent athlete. On the other hand, jumper's knee can exhibit itself at multiple sites within the patellar tendon along the entire tendon down to the tibial tuberosity attachment.

Osgood-Schlatter disease is technically defined as an osteochondritis of the epiphysis of the tibial tuberosity (Venes & Thomas, 2001). For this to occur there must be a growth plate at the site of the tibial tubercle; consequently, this condition is unique to children and adolescents. Constant jumping creates a pull on the patellar tendon and its attachment at the tibial tuberosity. During the growth phase there is an epiphyseal plate that is being pulled on simultaneously by the attachment of the patellar tendon at the tibia. This irritation causes inflammation and swelling to occur just below the patella.

Sign and symptoms of Osgood-Schlatter disease include the following:

1. Pain and tenderness about the patellar tendon complex.
2. Swelling in the associated area. This swelling may be more localized to the tibial tuberosity.
3. Decreased ability to use the quadriceps for running or jumping.
4. If the inflammation continues, the area over the tibial tuberosity may become more solid when palpated.
5. Symptoms seem to be exacerbated by activity.

First aid care:

1. Apply ice and compression to the area.
2. Have the athlete see a physician as soon as possible.
3. Rest is important until the inflammation subsides.

Jumper's knee is also an irritation of the patellar tendon complex between its attachments on the tibia and the patella. This problem is common to the athlete who must jump a great deal as part of sports participation.

Osgood-Schlatter disease Epiphyseal inflammation of the tibial tubercle.

Typically, the athlete will experience pain at one of three sites within this complex. The pain may be localized over the superior or inferior pole of the patella or at the tibial tuberosity (David, 1989). Regardless of the exact location of this condition, the athlete complains greatly of pain associated with jumping.

Sign and symptoms of jumper's knee include the following:

1. Pain and tenderness about the patellar tendon complex.
2. Swelling in the associated area. This swelling may spread from the patella to the tibial tuberosity.
3. Decreased ability to use the quadriceps for running or jumping.
4. Symptoms seem to be exacerbated by activity.

First aid care:

1. Apply ice and compression to the area.
2. Have the athlete see a physician for possible anti-inflammatory medications.
3. Rest will be helpful to the ailing athlete.

Patellofemoral Conditions

At times athletes will complain of nonspecific pain behind the patella. Sometimes this pain is caused by an increased Q angle, or it can be caused by any one of a number of other problems.

As can be seen in Figure 15.7, the **Q angle** is the difference between a straight line drawn from the anterior superior iliac spine and the center of the patella compared with one drawn from the center of the patella through the center of the tibia. The larger this angle, the greater the chance of the patella being pulled too far laterally during extension of the knee; consequently, the patella rubs on the condyle of the femur, causing pain and irritation. It is generally accepted that this angle is larger in females because of the width of the pelvis (Gould, 1990; Magee, 2002). Most authorities report that a Q angle of 15 to 20 degrees is acceptable. However, this is highly individual, as there are often associated problems with patellar tracking, such as weak musculature or an abnormal patellofemoral skeletal configuration.

If there is abnormal patellofemoral configuration as a result of some skeletal, muscular, or mechanical dysfunction, this too can create retropatellar (behind the patella) pain of an **idiopathic** nature. This typically occurs in athletes such as runners or gymnasts who perform a great deal of repetitive movements in their sports activities. If this problem is allowed to continue, the possibility of chondromalacia exists. **Chondromalacia** is a softening

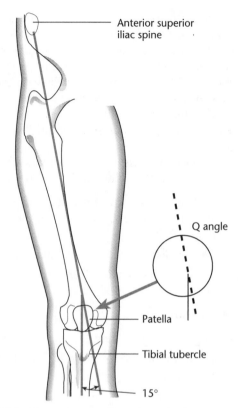

FIGURE 15.7 Measuring the Q angle at the knee.

and wearing out of the posterior cartilage surface of the patella. This is detrimental to the athlete's ability to perform in the future because there is associated pain and tenderness with this disorder that create difficulty in movement.

In the case of retropatellar pain and discomfort, the athlete will complain of chronic pain and disability. There is no immediate first aid care to be administered; however, the athlete may gain some comfort from rest, ice, compression, elevation, and the use of nonsteroidal anti-inflammatories. If the athlete has an abnormally large Q angle, muscular imbalances, or other predisposing conditions, he or she should seek the advice of a physician to assist in the care of retropatellar pain disorder.

Menisci Injuries

As mentioned earlier, the menisci have partial attachments to other structures about the knee joint such as the cruciate ligaments, the tibial tubercles, and other structures; this creates problems when either the menisci or various other structures are damaged. If a violent force injures the medial collateral ligament, there is also the possibility of damage to the medial meniscus because of a partial attachment between the two structures.

More commonly, a meniscus is damaged by being torn as a result of quick, sharp, cutting movements that occur when the foot is stabilized and does not turn with the body. This movement and others that cause excessive stress in abnormal planes will tear the meniscus at different points. A torn meniscus can affect the athlete in a variety of ways. Some athletes will be able to function normally; others will not be able to completely extend the leg at the knee joint because of a tear in the meniscus that causes a blocking or locking effect.

Signs and symptoms of a suspected torn meniscus include the following:

1. The athlete reports that a pop or snap was heard when the knee twisted.
2. The athlete may not have any swelling, depending on the structures involved in the injury.
3. The athlete may not complain of any pain.
4. Depending on the severity of the injury, there may be a loss of range of motion and/or movement with a blocking or locking effect.
5. The athlete may be able to continue participation with the injury.
6. The athlete may report a feeling of the knee "giving out" at times.

First aid care:

1. Apply ice and compression.
2. If the athlete has a blocked or locked knee, crutches should be used to aid in walking.
3. Encourage the athlete to see a physician as soon as possible.

Meniscus injuries do not necessarily have to end an athlete's playing season or career. New methods of surgery enable many athletes to return to participation relatively quickly. However, athletes should not be encouraged to finish the season with a suspected meniscus injury without first seeking the advice of a physician.

Knee Ligament Injuries

Several ligaments can be damaged through trauma; however, only four of the main ligaments will be discussed here. The four that are most commonly injured are the medial (tibial) collateral ligament, the lateral (fibular) collateral ligament, and the anterior and posterior cruciate ligaments. These ligaments are important stabilizers of the knee joint and are subject to many stresses, both internal and external. These ligaments, like any others in the body, can be traumatized and suffer first-, second-, or third-degree sprains. Refer to Chapter 1 for a review of ligament sprains.

The mechanisms by which ligaments can be injured include a broad range of maneuvers, from the athlete making a quick, sharp, cutting step and twisting the knee excessively to having an opposing lineman hit the knee from one side. Athletes also may be kicked in the tibia or attempt to stop an opponent and have the tibia driven forcefully anteriorly or posteriorly, all of which can damage one or more of the major supporting knee ligaments. It is important to remember that the knee can be injured by all types of forces, both internal and external, even when it does not seem that the athlete is in danger during the activity.

Collateral Ligament Injuries

One of the more common injuries to knee ligaments in athletics is a sprain to the medial collateral ligament (Figure 15.8). This occurs when an opponent is blocked or hits the athlete's leg and knee from the outside. The

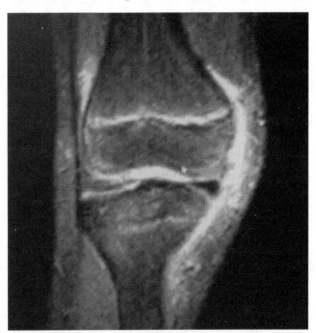

FIGURE 15.8 Coronal plane MRI image of a torn medial collateral ligament (MCL). Note the brightly colored region along the medial side of the knee indicating damage to the MCL.

Q angle Angle made by the rectus femoris and the patellar tendon as they attach to the tibial tuberosity.

idiopathic Cause of a condition is unknown.

chondromalacia Abnormal softening of cartilage, typically noted between the patella and femur.

FIGURE 15.9 Excessive stress on the medial collateral ligament.

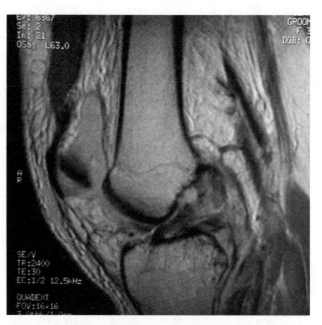

FIGURE 15.10 Sagittal plane MRI of a torn anterior cruciate ligament (ACL) in the right knee. Note the gap (lighter colored region) within the body of the ligament that is the area of the rupture.

opponent lands forcefully on the lateral side of the knee, resulting in the joint being pushed medially (valgus stress); this creates stress on the medial collateral ligament beyond what it can withstand (Figure 15.9).

If just the opposite mechanism occurs and an opponent lands on the inside of a player's knee and pushes the joint laterally (varus stress), then the lateral collateral ligament is stressed beyond the normal level and sprained.

Both of these ligament injuries render the knee unstable in side-to-side movements. Because the knee is a hinge joint and little sideways movement occurs there, this would seem to create very few problems for the athlete. However, the collateral ligaments are important in helping the knee with overall stability, and injury to either of these structures causes instability in the knee (Levangie & Norkin, 2005). The more severe the injury, the more unstable the knee.

Cruciate Ligament Injuries

The anterior cruciate ligament (ACL) can be injured by having the tibia moved forcefully in an anterior direction (Figure 15.10). This can occur when an athlete is making a very quick cutting motion on a hard surface, when an athlete gets hit from behind in the lower leg, or when the femur gets pushed backward while the tibia is held in place, as happens in contact sports. If the opposite occurs and the tibia is forced posteriorly, the posterior cruciate ligament can be disrupted and injured. The main function of these two ligaments is to stabilize the knee in anterior and/or posterior directions. In addition, quick rotational forces can injure the anterior cruciate ligament. A rotational injury can result from a noncontact mechanism. For example, a football player may make a very quick change in direction on a hard surface, and the upper body may go off balance, causing the knee to accept abnormal forces. If the circumstances are such

that the soft-tissue structures in the knee cannot withstand the extra forces, these structures will be damaged.

According to a review article written by a large group of individuals who have been researching the ACL for many years, the causes of noncontact ACL injury are still being debated (Griffin et al., 2000). Many ACL researchers are of the opinion that there is no evidence that prophylactic bracing reduces noncontact ACL injures. Most are of the opinion that there are some biomechanical considerations that must be made. There appears to be a relationship between the strength of the quadriceps activation during eccentric contraction and the risk of injury. The stronger the activation during eccentric contraction, the greater the chance of ACL damage, especially in female athletes. Additionally, there appears to be a shoe/surface interface reaction that needs to be researched further. The greater the shoe/surface friction, the more likely are ACL injuries. The cruciate ligaments work in conjunction with the collateral ligaments to create a stable knee; any time one or more of these ligaments is injured, the knee becomes unstable.

In 1999, as reported by Arendt, Agel, and Dick (1999) the number of ACL injuries in females participating specifically in soccer and basketball was significantly higher than for males in the same sports. Their study followed NCAA athletes during a 10-year period

(1989–1999) in all sports at the collegiate level. They did not report any reason why the injury rates were significantly higher in the females participating in these sports, and so other researchers began studying the phenomenon and creating hypotheses why this might be occurring. A similar study done over a 2-year period (1995–1997) on high school athletes also demonstrated that females encounter more knee and ACL injuries than their male counterparts (Powell & Barber-Foss, 2000). Many of these knee injuries to females are noncontact injuries. The increased risk and the incidence of noncontact ACL injuries in females are confusing to many researchers. Theories as to why female athletes are more at risk for this injury vary. One theory hypothesizes that intrinsic factors such as a narrowing of the femoral notch, which causes a pinching of the ACL when the athlete turns sharply with the foot planted, cause the ACL to tear. Another theory is that the Q angle of women is much larger because of the wider pelvis and that this again puts additional pressure on the ligament, enough to cause disruption when the athlete is making a cut or changing direction with the foot planted (Hayward, 2001). A number of researchers are looking at the correlation between hormonal changes during the menstrual cycle and ACL damage. Researchers report a correlation between the onset of the menstrual cycle and ACL damage (Slauterbeck et al., 2002). This theory is still being studied and cannot be considered the actual reason for ACL damage in the female athlete at this time. Other researchers are focusing on the development of the musculature of the quadriceps and hamstrings and how female athletes use these muscles when jumping and landing. Training techniques are being promoted that are suggested will help the female athlete learn how to use her thigh muscles more effectively in sports, thereby reducing the stress and damage to the ACL (Lephart, Abt, & Ferris, 2002; Myklebust et al., 2003). There appear to be many different reasons why female athletes are more prone to ACL injury, and some doctors and researchers believe that there are multiple factors contributing to this problem (Lephart, Ferris, & Fu, 2002).

Signs and symptoms of an injury to the knee ligaments include the following:

1. Athlete will report that the knee was forced beyond its normal range.
2. Athlete will complain of pain at the site of injury.
3. Swelling may occur in and around the knee.
4. Athlete may complain of an unstable feeling in the knee.
5. Athlete may report having felt a pop or tear or having heard a snapping sound.

First aid care:

1. Apply ice and compression immediately.
2. If the knee is unstable, have the athlete walk with crutches.
3. Have the athlete seek proper medical advice.

At times an athlete will receive a blow from the lateral side that will injure the medial collateral and anterior cruciate ligaments along with the medial meniscus. This has sometimes been called the terrible-triad injury. Obviously, injuring all of these structures creates a very unstable knee. Any time an athlete has a suspected injury to knee ligaments, caution must be exercised, and care by the proper medical personnel is critical.

Prevention

The quest to prevent injuries to the leg and knee continues for athletes, coaches, and certified athletic trainers. As discussed earlier, the increase in female ACL injuries has resulted in many different research teams looking for an answer or model for prevention of such injuries. In the future, research will continue in an attempt to outline techniques that will hopefully prevent the various injuries to the thigh, leg, and knee.

The prevention of strain injuries to the musculature of the thigh and leg is very similar to the techniques used in other areas of the body that contain a great deal of muscle tissue. To many athletes, proper warm-up and stretching of the muscles to be used is important in preparing for activity. Not all athletes require stretching before an activity, but some find it beneficial to their overall participation.

Preventing knee injuries has become much more of a focus. For many years, and in the present day, a variety of bracing options purport to provide peripheral mechanical stabilization for the ligaments of the knee when forces are applied externally. Today some football coaches require interior linemen and linebackers to wear bilateral prophylactic knee braces during practice and games. Much like stretching, knee bracing should be an individual choice for athletes. If athletes believe prophylactic knee bracing will benefit them, they should be provided the opportunity to use these devices.

The newest trend in prevention of ACL injuries is in using specific jump and landing training techniques. Some authors suggest that specialized proprioceptive training programs will decrease the number of ACL injuries in athletes (Griffin et al., 2000). Numerous jump and landing training programs are being promoted by certified athletic trainers, strength and conditioning specialists, physical therapists, and other health care

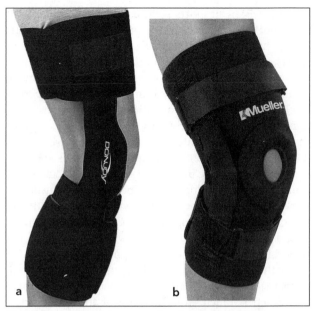

FIGURE 15.11 (a) An example of a prophylactic knee brace. (b) Neoprene knee sleeve with medial and lateral bracing. The neoprene is useful in keeping the joint warm during exercise.

professionals. These programs are designed to enhance the dynamic function of the leg musculature. The concept of this type of training is to train the appropriate muscles in the leg to contract or relax at appropriate moments with the idea that the muscles will assist the function of the ACL during activity. Many of the people promoting these programs claim that athletes (especially females) can benefit from this type of training and can reduce the chance of an ACL tear when they are participating in sports. It is worth looking into some of these proprioceptive training programs for athletes of any gender or sport, as this area of research appears to be quite promising for reducing ACL injuries.

Knee Bracing

One of the biggest controversies in sports medicine literature and in many athletic departments across the country is the use of prophylactic knee bracing with athletes. A prophylactic knee brace has two attachments: one above the knee and one below the knee, with either unilateral or bilateral braces running in between. The braces can be constructed of either metal or plastic and are typically lightweight. The bracing is meant to augment the stabilizing effect on each side of the knee joint (Figure 15.11 a & b).

One has only to look in almost any sports medicine journal to find a recent study analyzing the effects of prophylactic knee bracing. Reports of both epidemiological and biomechanical studies are being published

Athletic Trainers SPEAK Out

When evaluating injuries, it is important to be aware of biological variations. For example, discoloration caused by a direct blow to the thigh may not be as readily seen in athletes with dark skin pigmentation as compared to athletes with light skin pigmentation. I once had an athlete sustain a severe hamstring injury that turned deep purple in color. It was through very careful inspection that I was able to detect the discoloration, as the athlete had very dark skin. If I had not noticed the discoloration, I may not have realized the severity of the injury. In this case, careful inspection led to appropriate first aid care.

—*Rene Revis Shingles, PhD, ATC*

Rene Revis Shingles is an Assistant Professor in the Athletic Training Education Program at Central Michigan University.

regularly. Many of the epidemiological studies have been criticized for lacking proper methods of study design. The biomechanical studies are criticized for not incorporating proper mechanisms and forces to study the effects of prophylactic braces. One area of prophylactic knee brace research that is notable concerns the movement of the brace on the leg while the athlete is participating. It has been demonstrated that prophylactic braces will move up or down the leg, some more than others, and this movement can lead to sometimes negative changes in the muscle activity, biomechanics, speed, and overall agility of the athlete (Greene et al., 2000; Osternig & Robertson, 1993).

The general consensus regarding prophylactic knee braces indicates that these braces are not helpful in preventing knee ligament injury (Paluska & McKeag, 2000). Neither the American Academy of Orthopaedic Surgeons (AAOS) nor the American Academy of Pediatrics support the use of prophylactic knee braces in athletes (Martin, 2001; AAOS, 2004). Griffin and colleagues (2000) suggest that prophylactic bracing for noncontact ACL injuries is not helpful. More research in the area of ACL injuries resulting from contact and/or trauma needs to be completed before a definite recommendation can be made regarding the use of prophylactic knee braces.

Functional braces (i.e., braces specially constructed to assist an athlete after a knee injury who is returning to participation) appear to have a better record than prophylactic braces for assisting the athlete after surgical reconstruction. The functional brace (Figure 15.12) may change the biomechanics of the athlete's running, jumping, or landing, but the brace is constructed so that it provides some protection for the knee and minimizes future injury (Carlson, 2002). The athlete may be required by a physician to wear a functional knee brace after ACL reconstruction; therefore, the coach or athletic trainer will not be responsible for deciding whether the athlete should wear a knee brace. When the athlete is required to wear the brace during participation, the coach's or certified athletic trainer's role is to monitor compliance and make sure the athlete is wearing the brace until the physician releases the athlete to participate without the brace.

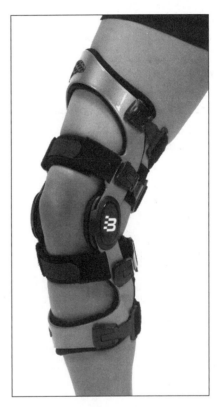

FIGURE 15.12 An example of a functional knee brace, used after ligament surgery or later in the healing/rehabilitation process.

REVIEW QUESTIONS

1. List the bones that comprise the knee joint.

2. Give the common name for the muscles located on the anterior portion of the thigh.

3. Give the common name for the muscles of the posterior thigh region.

4. Give the common name for the muscles located on the medial aspect of the thigh.

5. Where do the quadriceps attach on the lower leg?

6. Define a sesamoid bone using the patella as an example.

7. Explain the articulation of the knee joint, including the involvement of the patella.

8. List and explain the attachments of the four main ligaments of the knee.

9. *True or false:* There are two menisci located in the knee joint.

10. Explain the first aid care for a severe contusion of the thigh.

11. Explain which muscles of the thigh can experience strains through athletic participation.

12. *True or false:* If the patella dislocates, it will not return to its proper position without surgical intervention.

13. Define joint mice.

14. What age group is most susceptible to Osgood-Schlatter disease?

15. Describe how to care for an athlete with jumper's knee.

16. What population is more susceptible to Q-angle alignment problems?

17. *True or false:* An athlete with a torn meniscus will always have a great deal of swelling in the knee joint after the injury.

18. Explain the mechanism by which the medial and lateral collateral ligaments are damaged.

19. Define and list the structures damaged if an athlete experiences a terrible-triad injury.

20. Explain why an athlete should or should not choose to use a prophylactic knee brace.

REFERENCES

American Academy of Orthopaedic Surgeons (AAOS). (2004). The use of knee braces. Document #1124. Available: www.AAOS.org/wordhtml/papers/position/1124.htm.

Arendt EA, Agel J, Dick R. (1999). Anterior cruciate ligament injury patterns among collegiate men and women. *J Athl Training.* 34(2):86–92.

Carlson L. (2002). Use of functional knee braces after ACL reconstruction. *Ath Ther Today.* 7(3):48–49.

David JM. (1989). Jumper's knee. *J Orthop Sports Phys Ther.* 11(4):137–141.

Gould JA. (1990). *Orthopaedic and Sports Physical Therapy* (2d ed.). St. Louis: Mosby.

Gray H. (1974). *Anatomy, Descriptive and Surgical.* Philadelphia: Running Press.

Greene DL, et al. (2000). Effects of protective knee bracing on speed and agility. *Am J Sports Med.* 28(4):453–459.

Griffin LY, et al. (2000). Noncontact anterior cruciate ligament injuries: Risk factors and prevention strategies. *J Am Acad Orthop Surg.* 8:141–150.

Hayward RR. (2001). ACL injuries: Why more prevalent in women? *J Am Acad Phys Assist.* 14(8):38–40, 43–45.

Hixon AI, Gibbs LM. (2000). Osteochrondritis dissecans: A diagnosis not to miss. *Am Fam Phys.* 61(1):151–156.

Larson CM, et al. (2002). Evaluating and managing muscle contusions and myositis ossificans. *Phys Sportsmed.* 30(2):41–44, 49–50.

Lephart SM, Abt JP, Ferris CM. (2002). Neuromuscular contributions to anterior cruciate ligament injuries in females. *Curr Opin Rheumatol.* 14:168–173.

Lephart SM, Ferris CM, Fu FH. (2002). Risk factors associated with noncontact anterior cruciate ligament injuries in female athletes. *AAOS Instructional Course Lectures.* 51:307–310.

Levangie PK, Norkin CC. (2005). *Joint Structure and Function: A Comprehensive Analysis* (4th ed.). Philadelphia: F. A. Davis.

Magee DJ. (2002). *Orthopedic Physical Assessment* (4th ed.). Philadelphia: W. B. Saunders.

Martin, TJ. (2001). Technical report: Knee brace use in the young athlete. *Pediatrics.* 108(2):503–507.

Moore K, Dalley AF. (1999). *Clinically Oriented Anatomy* (4th ed.). Baltimore: Williams and Wilkins.

Myklebust G, et al. (2003). Prevention of anterior cruciate ligament injuries in female team handball players: A prospective intervention study over three seasons. *Clin J Sports Med.* 13(2):71–78.

Osternig LR, Robertson RN. (1993). Effects of prophylactic knee bracing on lower extremity joint position and muscle activation during running. *Am J Sports Med.* 21(5):733–738.

Paluska SA, McKeag DB. (2000). Knee braces: Current evidence and clinical recommendations for their use. *Am Fam Phys.* 61(2):411–418.

Powell JW, Barber-Foss KD. (2000). Sex-related injury patterns among selected high school sports. *Am J Sports Med.* 28(3):385–391.

Slauterbeck JR, et al. (2002). The menstrual cycle, sex hormones, and anterior cruciate ligament injury. *J Athl Training.* 37(3):275–280.

Venes D, Thomas CL (eds.). (2001). *Taber's Cyclopedic Medical Dictionary* (19th ed.). Philadelphia: F.A. Davis.

16

Injuries to the Lower Leg, Ankle, and Foot

MAJOR CONCEPTS

For an athlete to move well, there must be excellent functioning of the lower leg, ankle, and foot. The foot must provide a stable base of support and at the same time be flexible and extremely mobile. This chapter discusses the skeletal and muscular anatomy of the foot and lower leg, with emphasis on the ligaments of the ankle; it also covers the compartments of the lower leg, with an overview of the muscular actions of each compartment.

Sports participation can cause fractures of the bones of the lower leg and foot as a result of both acute trauma and chronic overuse. This chapter discusses such fractures as well as common sprains of ankle ligaments. Treatment of ankle sprains and control of possible future sprains are controversial issues and should be studied carefully.

Injuries to the tendons that cross the ankle joint are also quite common among athletes. This chapter reports on the recognition, care, and treatment of tendon injuries along with compartment problems and considers both the immediate and long-term effects of these disorders. It also focuses on the treatment and care of athletes with shin splints and considers ways to enhance the performance of these athletes.

Finally, the chapter discusses foot disorders such as plantar fasciitis, heel spurs, Morton's neuroma, arch problems, bunions, blisters, and calluses, providing guidelines for recognition, first aid treatment, and long-term care. It is critical to remember the importance of the lower leg, ankle, and foot when assisting the athlete to perform at peak levels; even small, seemingly insignificant injuries to this area can affect performance.

http://health.jbpub.com/book/concepts/5e

The web site for this book offers many useful tools and is a great source for supplementary information for both students and instructors.

Visit the site at
http://health.jbpub.com/book/concepts/5e
to link to the following organizations and sites:

- The Southern California Orthopedic Institute
- BioMechanics: The Magazine of Lower Extremity Movement

The lower leg, ankle, and foot work together to provide a stable base of support and a dynamic system for movement. The skeleton of the lower leg consists of the tibia and fibula bones. The tibia is the larger and stronger of the two and is commonly called the shin bone; it typically supports about 98% of body weight. The fibula is a smaller bone that supports about 2% of body weight; in addition, it acts as an attachment for various muscles and helps to provide a mechanical advantage for some of them.

The normal foot contains 26 bones (Figures 16.1 and 16.2) that are interconnected and supported by numerous ligaments. Many joints within the foot (Figures 16.1 and 16.2) also assist with support and movement. The ankle or **talocrural joint**, where the tibia, fibula, and talus join, provides mainly plantar flexion and **dorsiflexion** of the foot. The **subtalar joint**, which is the articulation of the talus and the calcaneus, is primarily responsible for **inversion** and **eversion of the foot**. Both of these joints are synovial joints, which means they are surrounded by a capsule and supported by ligaments.

The ankle (talocrural) joint is supported on the medial side by the large and strong deltoid ligament (Figure 16.3). On the lateral side of the ankle, the joint is supported by the anterior talofibular, the posterior talofibular, and the calcaneofibular

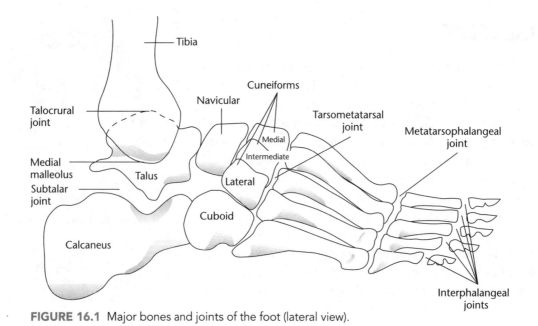

FIGURE 16.1 Major bones and joints of the foot (lateral view).

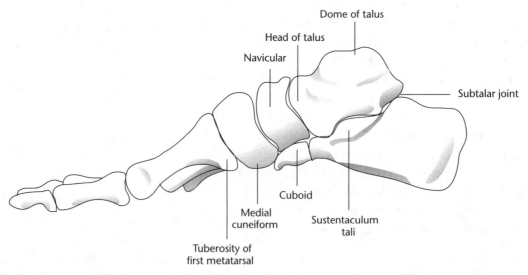

FIGURE 16.2 Major bones and joints of the foot (medial view).

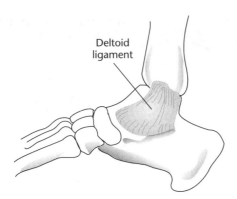

FIGURE 16.3 Major ligament of the ankle joint (medial view).

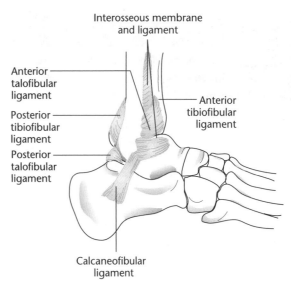

FIGURE 16.4 Major ligaments of the ankle joint (lateral view).

ligaments (Figure 16.4). These ligaments are not as large or as strong as the deltoid ligament. Additional lateral stability for the ankle joint is provided by the length of the fibula on the lateral side of the ankle. The ankle joint is strongest when it is placed in dorsiflexion because the talus fits much tighter between the tibia and fibula in this position. Conversely, the joint is weakest when placed in plantar flexion.

The joints, ligaments, and muscles help to create and maintain the two basic arches in the foot (Gray, 1974; Moore & Dalley, 1999). The longitudinal arch has medial and lateral divisions. There is one transverse arch running from side to side. These arches assist the foot as shock absorbers; they also provide propulsion off surfaces during movement.

As can be seen in Time Out 16.1, the muscles of the lower leg are divided into anterior, posterior, and lateral compartments. The muscles of the anterior compartment essentially produce dorsiflexion and extension of the toes. The muscles in this compartment include the tibialis anterior, extensor digitorum longus, extensor hallucis longus, and peroneus tertius. The anterior compartment is a very compact area with little room for any extra tissue or fluid.

The posterior compartment of the lower leg mainly functions to produce plantar flexion of the foot. This compartment is commonly referred to as the calf muscles. Many anatomy books subdivide this compartment into superficial and deep sections. In the superficial section are the gastrocnemius, soleus, and plantaris muscles. The gastrocnemius and soleus muscles have a common attachment on the calcaneus via the Achilles tendon. The plantaris muscle is small and insignificant in action and may be absent in some individuals. The deep section of this compartment houses the tibialis posterior, flexor digitorum longus, flexor hallucis longus, and popliteus muscles. With the exception of the popliteus, these muscles course behind the medial malleolus of the tibia and along the bottom of the foot: They help with plantar flexion as well as flexion of the toes. The popliteus

muscle is important in knee flexion: It actually initiates knee flexion by unlocking the knee.

The lateral compartment of the lower leg contains the peroneus longus and peroneus brevis muscles. These muscles are mainly evertors of the foot but do assist with some plantar flexion. Both of these muscles course behind the lateral malleolus of the fibula, which provides a mechanical advantage for these muscles. The peroneus longus courses under the lateral side of the foot and runs across the bottom to the first metatarsal and cuneiform bones. The peroneus brevis attaches at the base of the fifth metatarsal and is subject to **avulsion.** Also in this compartment is the peroneal nerve, a superficial nerve that is susceptible to injury. The posterior tibial artery supplies blood to the peroneal muscles because there is no major artery in the lateral compartment.

talocrural joint Articulation (ginglymus) formed by the distal tibia and fibula with the superior surface (dome) of the talus.

dorsiflexion Bending toward the dorsum or rear; the opposite of plantar flexion.

subtalar joint Articulation (arthrodial) formed by the inferior surface of the talus and the superior surface of the calcaneus.

inversion of the foot To turn the foot inward; inner border of the foot lifts.

eversion of the foot To turn the foot outward.

avulsion Forcible tearing away or separation.

TIME OUT 16.1

Main Muscle Groups, Actions, and Innervations of the Foot and Ankle

Muscle Group

Posterior Compartment	Action(s)	Innervation
Flexor digitorum longus	Flexion of 2–5 PIP and DIP Flexion of 2–5 MTP joints Assists in plantarflexion Assists in inversion	Tibial
Flexor hallicus longus	Flexion of 1st IP Assist in flexion of 1st MP Assist with inversion Assist with plantarflexion	Tibial
Gastrocnemius	Ankle plantarflexion Assist with knee flexion	Tibial
Soleus	Ankle plantarflexion	Tibial
Plantaris	Ankle plantarflexion Assist with knee flexion	Tibial
Popliteus	Tibial rotation Assist with knee flexion	Tibial

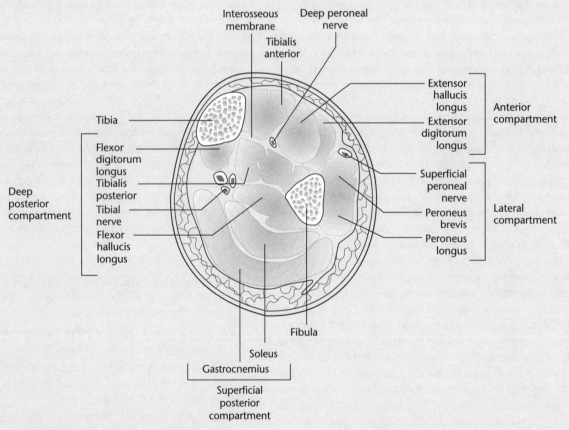

The muscle compartments of the lower leg.

(continued)

TIME OUT 16.1 (continued)

Main Muscles/Groups, Actions, and Innervations of the Foot and Ankle
Muscle Group

Anterior Compartment	Action(s)	Innervation
Extensior digitorum longus	Extension of 2–5 MTP Assist with extension of 2–5 DIP and PIP Assist with eversion Assist with dorsiflexion	Deep peroneal
Extensior hallucis longus	Extension of 1st MP Externsion of 1st IP	Deep peroneal
Peroneus tertius	Extension of foot Dorsiflexion of ankle	Deep peroneal
Tibialis anterior	Dorsiflexion of ankle Inversion	Deep peroneal
Lateral Compartment	**Action(s)**	**Innervation**
Peroneus brevis	Eversion Assists with plantarflexion	Superficial peroneal
Peroneus longus	Eversion Assists with plantarflexion	Superficial peroneal

WHAT IF?

One of your high school soccer players has just injured his ankle, apparently while moving the ball downfield. He has fallen to the ground and is in obvious pain, holding his right ankle. During your examination you note swelling and discoloration in the region of the lateral malleolus as well as point tenderness over the area of the lateral ankle ligaments. Based on this history and the signs and symptoms, what is the likely injury? What is the appropriate first aid for such injuries?

Common Sports Injuries

Many different sports-related injuries occur to the lower leg, ankle, and foot; some can be classified as traumatic, and others are chronic in nature. Traumatic injuries typically involve skeletal structures; chronic injuries usually involve damage to soft tissues in the area. However, there are definitely exceptions to this rule. There are times when overuse can be a factor in fractures, and there are occasions when trauma can be the cause of soft-tissue damage resulting in severe complications.

Skeletal Injuries

Fractures

Direct trauma through contact causes most fractures to the lower leg. The magnitude of contact necessary to fracture a bone such as the tibia or fibula can vary. (See Figure 16.5.) A fracture can be caused by being kicked by an opponent in a soccer match or by having a 300-pound lineman land on a leg in a professional football game. Fractures to the foot can also occur from trauma, for example, when an opponent lands forcefully on a player's foot. However, violent trauma is not always required in fractures of the bones of the leg and foot. Stress fractures can occur from overuse or **microtrauma**. In running, for example, each time the foot strikes the ground it produces a small amount of trauma to the bone. This trauma damages a few bone cells, which the body must repair as quickly as possible. When the body cannot maintain the repair process and keep up with repeated microtrauma to a specific bone, a stress fracture results (Malone, McPoil, & Nitz, 1996). Additionally, an avulsion fracture of the fifth metatarsal can occur in association with a lateral ankle sprain; therefore, the possibility of such a fracture should be examined when an athlete sprains his or her ankle (Simons, 1999).

microtrauma Microscopic lesion or injury.

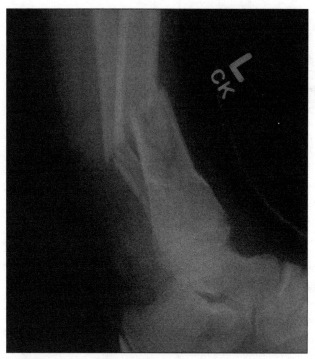

FIGURE 16.5 Fracture of the tibia and fibula in the left leg.

Signs and symptoms of a fracture in the lower leg or foot include the following:

1. Swelling and/or deformity at the location of the trauma.

2. Discoloration at the site of the fracture.

3. Possible broken bone end projecting through the skin.

4. Athlete reporting that a snap or a pop was heard or felt.

5. The athlete may not be able to bear weight on the affected extremity.

6. In the case of a stress fracture or a growth plate fracture that did not result from a traumatic event, the athlete will complain of extreme point tenderness and pain at the site of suspected injury.

First aid care:

1. Watch and treat for shock if necessary.

2. Apply sterile dressings to any related wounds (i.e., an open fracture).

3. Carefully immobilize the foot and leg using a splint.

4. Arrange for transport to a medical facility.

In the event that bones are fractured, the physician will apply a cast, and the athlete will be immobilized for a specified time. When the fracture has healed properly, the physician will release the athlete for rehabilitation, practice, and competition, in that order. There are extreme cases of athletes participating in sporting events with a broken bone in the lower leg or foot. This may

Athletic Trainers SPEAK Out

Most common injuries to the lower leg, often minimized by athletes and coaches, are traumatic contusions, which may progress to compartment syndrome. These injuries are commonly caused by kicks to the anterior lateral lower leg. Due to the anatomical compartments of the lower leg there is little room for expansion caused by hemorrhage.

An improperly recognized or treated contusion can result in increased pressure to nerves and blood vessels. This is especially true with injuries to the anterior compartment of the lower leg. These injuries can become life-long disabilities if not properly recognized and treated. As the effusion increases pressure, the area may need to be surgically decompressed. All trainers need to be aware of and concerned about the possibility of compartment syndrome when treating trauma to the lower leg. This is one area of the body where external pressure from elastic wraps should not be used as a method for control of swelling. The wrap may only increase the internal pressure and further hasten the symptoms of compartment syndrome.

—Dale Mildenberger, MS, ATC

Dale Mildenberger is Head Athletic Trainer for Utah State University.

happen in professional sports in which athletes get paid for participation in the activity. Participation while a fracture is healing is not recommended because it may slow the healing process. It is also important to note that there is a possibility of nonunion of a fracture, especially in the fifth metatarsal of the foot, as a result of a diminished blood supply (Simons, 1999; Omey & Micheli, 1999). Careful attention should be paid to the healing process of the broken bone.

Soft-Tissue Injuries

Ankle Injuries

One of the most common sports injuries to the lower leg and ankle is a sprained ankle (Figure 16.6 a & b). Sprains are abnormal stresses placed on ligamentous

a

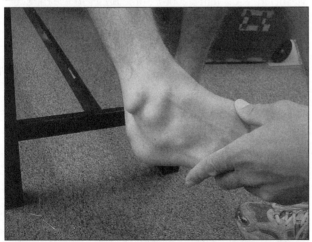

b

FIGURE 16.6 (a) Acute swelling after a second-degree ankle sprain. (b) The damage done to the lateral ligaments of the ankle from a sprain.

structures and cause various levels of damage. (Refer to Chapter 1 for a detailed description of degrees of sprains.) Sprains can occur to the lateral or medial ligaments of the ankle depending on which direction the foot moves when abnormal stress is placed on the ligaments and the foot rolls to one side.

By analyzing the anatomical relationships of the components of the ankle, it can be seen that the noncontractile structures on the lateral aspect of the ankle are most susceptible to injury. The formation of the bones of the ankle helps to stabilize the ankle; the fibula extends inferiorly, approximating the lateral talus completely. Also, the ligaments on the lateral side—the anterior talofibular, the posterior talofibular, and the calcaneofibular ligaments—are not as large or strong as the deltoid ligament on the medial side of the ankle joint. With the wide anterior superior aspect of the talus being securely wedged in the mortise formed by the inferior surfaces of the tibia and fibula, the joint is most stable in a dorsiflexed position, and weak in a position of plantar flexion. Therefore, when comparing the typical movements of the foot with the anatomical structure of the ankle joint, it becomes clear that the lateral ligaments are more prone to damage via excessive movement than the deltoid ligament on the medial aspect of the ankle. It has been estimated that 80% to 85% of ankle sprains experienced occur to the lateral ligaments (Ryan et al., 1986). An interesting note regarding ankle sprains is that authors are suggesting that serious ankle sprains in the adolescent athlete are unusual because the ligaments are typically stronger than the bones (Omey & Micheli, 1999).

Ankle sprains can occur in virtually any sport and can limit the abilities of the athlete in performance until resolution of the injury is complete. As the severity of the ankle sprain increases, so does the instability of the ankle. It is generally accepted that an eversion ankle sprain is more severe, with greater instability, and should be cared for more conservatively (Ryan et al., 1986). However, an inversion ankle sprain is more common, with the lateral ligaments being involved in 80% to 85% of all ankle sprains.

Signs and symptoms of a lateral ankle sprain include the following:

1. *First-degree sprain:* Pain, mild disability, point tenderness, little laxity, little or no swelling

2. *Second-degree sprain:* Pain, mild to moderate disability, point tenderness, loss of function, some laxity (abnormal movement), swelling (mild to moderate)

3. *Third-degree sprain:* Pain and severe disability, point tenderness, loss of function, laxity (abnormal movement), swelling (moderate to severe)

First aid care:

1. Immediately apply ice, compression, and elevation. A horseshoe- or doughnut-shaped pad kept in place by an elastic bandage aids at this stage in the compression and reduction of fluid (Figure 16.7).

2. Have the athlete rest and use crutches to ambulate with a three- or four-point gait if a second- or third-degree sprain has occurred.

3. If there is any question concerning the severity of the sprain, splint and transport the athlete to a medical facility for further evaluation by a physician.

It is important to recognize the possibility of a tibiofibular ("tib/fib") syndesmosis sprain in conjunction with or masquerading as a lateral ankle sprain. Too often a tib/fib syndesmosis sprain is treated as a lateral ankle sprain, which is inappropriate and will not allow the athlete to progress in the healing process as quickly as if the tib/fib syndesmosis sprain had been treated properly. To discern the difference in the two sprains, it is important to note that there is a significant difference in the etiology of the injury. With the lateral ankle sprain there is an inversion mechanism, which includes supination. In the tib/fib syndesmosis sprain, the mechanism is one of dorsiflexion followed by axial loading of the lower leg, with external rotation of the foot and internal rotation of the lower leg (Mangus, Hoffman, & Parry, 1999). Typically, athletes have their foot planted firmly with the foot in external rotation, and the lower leg twists medially, forcing the talus into the ankle mortise; the axial load forces the tibia and fibula to separate slightly and sprain the syndesmosis.

Signs and symptoms of a tib/fib syndesmosis sprain include the following:

1. The mechanism of injury is different from a lateral ankle sprain, with ankle dorsiflexion and foot external rotation combined with internal rotation of the lower leg.

2. The typical ankle sprain tests may be positive, but the athlete will complain of a great deal of pain and point tenderness in the area of the tib/fib syndesmosis.

3. Performing the "squeeze" test (squeezing the tibia and fibula together superior to the syndesmosis; Figure 16.8) will elicit pain in the syndesmosis area.

First aid care:

1. Immediately apply ice, compression, and elevation. A horseshoe- or doughnut-shaped pad kept in place by an elastic bandage aids at this stage in the compression and reduction of fluid (see Figure 16.7).

2. Have the athlete rest and use crutches to ambulate for the first 72 hours, followed by the use of a walking boot for a minimum of 3 days and preferably for 7 days following the initial injury (Mangus, Hoffman, & Parry, 1999).

3. If there is any question concerning the severity of the sprain, splint and transport the athlete to a medical facility for further evaluation by a physician.

The control of subsequent ankle sprains is a source of a great deal of research and debate in sports medicine literature, although it is recognized that either taping or bracing will reduce the number of ankle sprains (Verhagen, van Mechelen, & de Vente, 2000). Some prefer to use the standard ankle-taping procedure as a prophylactic treatment for ankles with no history of previous injury; others

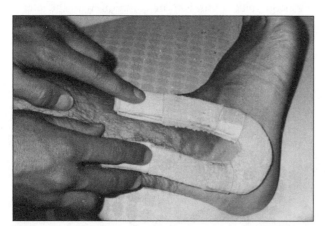

FIGURE 16.7 A horseshoe-shaped pad is used to ease inflammation after an ankle sprain.

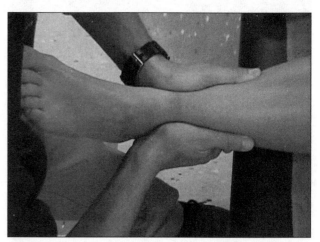

FIGURE 16.8 The "squeeze" test to determine if the tib/fib syndesmosis is involved in an injury.

choose to augment the taping procedure to prevent future ankle sprains if one has occurred before. In published research studies, ankle taping has been demonstrated to help with the neuromuscular response of the muscles (Lohrer, Alt, & Gollhofer, 1999) and to provide stability if done in a specific manner (Alt, Lohrer, & Gollhofer, 1999). Both of these factors will contribute to a reduction in ankle sprains. Most researchers agree that the best-known method of ankle support, the prophylactic adhesive-taping procedure, supports the ankle for only a short period of time after exercise begins (Frankeny et al., 1993; Paris, 1992). It is suggested that the reason ankle taping loses its prophylactic effect over time is that the soft tissues of the ankle region become more mobile as the athlete utilizes them and they become more flexible as the practice

or game progresses (Ricard, Schulthies, & Saret, 2000). Some researchers now maintain that bracing is better than taping for the prevention of ankle injuries, owing to the reduction in range of motion, either at excessive points or within normal ranges (Cordova, Ingersoll, & LeBlanc, 2000). There are now very good ankle braces on the market (Figures 16.9 through 16.11) that provide the necessary protection at a low overall cost. It has also been suggested that some high-top shoes may reduce the number of lateral ankle sprains (Ricard, Schulthies, & Saret, 2000). The combination of high-top shoes and taping or

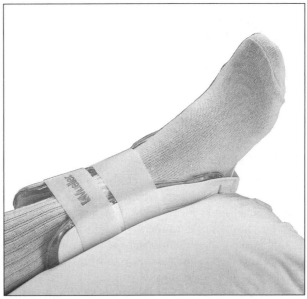

FIGURE 16.10 A rigid ankle brace is used for extra protection after an ankle has been sprained.

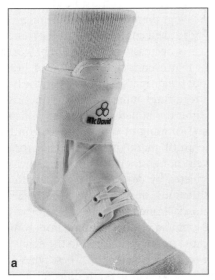

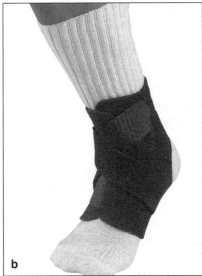

FIGURE 16.9 Companies have developed a wide variety of ankle braces. (a) Lace-up ankle braces are useful for prevention of ankle sprains. (b) This brace is neoprene (retains heat) and has supportive straps.

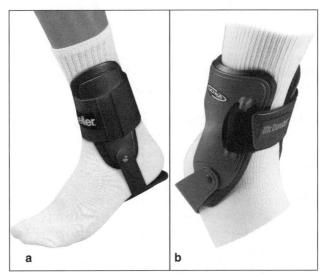

FIGURE 16.11 Rigid braces are also helpful in the prevention of ankle sprains.

bracing will be helpful to athletes in reducing the number of ankle sprains they experience. Proprioception and the ankle is a very intense area of study. Researchers report that proper ankle proprioception is a critical element in reducing chronic ankle instability (Hintermann, 1999). Proprioception training can also be an important part of both the preventive and rehabilitative aspects of ankle functioning (Hertel, 2000).

Whatever the choice of the coach or athlete, many factors must be considered in preventing ankle sprains. These include the type of activity, the compliance of the athlete in wearing braces or prophylactic taping, the cost to the school or athlete, and the effectiveness of the brace as reported in research studies. Even though most coaches believe that adhesive taping is effective in reducing ankle-related injuries, there are some serious consequences of poorly applied adhesive tape, including blisters, tape cuts, and loss of circulation. If ankle taping is to be part of an athlete's protective equipment, then it must be applied properly to perform correctly (see "Preventive Ankle Taping," later in this chapter).

Tendon-Related Injuries

The Achilles tendon is commonly injured by long-distance runners, basketball players, and tennis players (Leach, Schepsis, & Takai, 1991). The onset of tendinitis may be slow among runners, but much more rapid among basketball or tennis players, who make a great many short-burst movements requiring jumping or rapid motion from side to side.

Some controversy exists about the actual injury that constitutes Achilles tendinitis. The Achilles tendon itself, which attaches the gastrocnemius and soleus muscles to the calcaneus, can become inflamed. However, either the tendon sheath or the subcutaneous bursa dorsal to the tendon can become inflamed, both of which can be part of Achilles tendinitis (Leach, Schepsis, & Takai, 1991). Most agree that athletes who dramatically increase their running distance or workout times and who do so running on hard, uneven, or uphill surfaces are prone to Achilles tendinitis (Bazzoli & Pollina, 1989; Omey & Micheli, 1999).

Superficially, Achilles tendinitis can produce an increased temperature in the immediate area; moreover, the tendon is painful on touch and movement and appears thickened. The pain associated with this condition is localized to a small area of the tendon and typically intensifies when movement is initiated after rest (Bazzoli & Pollina, 1989). These signs and symptoms can be seen over an extended period of time (days to weeks) or over a shorter time period (days). Early detection of this problem usually enhances resolution of the symptoms and assists the athlete in returning earlier to practice and competition.

Treatment for chronic Achilles tendinitis is immediate rest until the swelling subsides. Usually the application of ice, nonsteroidal anti-inflammatories (e.g., aspirin or ibuprofen), and a small heel lift will assist in the reduction of swelling and the return to practice and competition. Stretching has also been shown to be beneficial to athletes with Achilles tendinitis (Taylor et al., 1990). Controlled stretching on a slant board or against a wall each day will aid in a return to participation. Additionally, if an athlete must exercise or run, it is advised that this be done in a controlled environment, perhaps in a swimming pool. Controlled gradual stressing exercises using the eccentric contraction of the Achilles, common to most activities, will assist the athlete in returning to activity (Humble & Nugent, 2001). An athlete's activity level and type of exercise must be closely monitored during the healing phase. Many times runners or other athletes will not accept complete rest as the route to healing. In such cases decreasing the amount of work may be the only way that even a small amount of healing will occur. Without the proper amount of rest, the body has a hard time repairing injury, thereby increasing the amount of time the athlete experiences difficulty with the condition. Running in water is an option for those athletes who must maintain conditioning or want to work out even though they are injured. Other exercises may be completed by doing them at slower rates or in controlled situations, in which the stress placed on the Achilles tendon is limited.

Explosive jumping or direct trauma from some type of impact can cause traumatic injuries to the Achilles tendon by tearing or rupturing the tendon. These types of injuries have been known to occur in many different sports.

Signs and symptoms of a ruptured Achilles tendon include the following:

1. Swelling and deformity at the site of injury.
2. The athlete will report a pop or snap associated with the injury.
3. Pain in the lower leg, which may range from mild to extreme.
4. Loss of function, mainly in plantar flexion.

First aid care:

1. Immediately apply ice and compression to the area.
2. Immobilize the foot by an air cast or splint.
3. Arrange for transportation to the nearest medical facility.

During the acute phase of the healing process, minimize dorsiflexion and eliminate forced dorsiflexion because this movement can produce more damage and inflammation to the area.

The long-term effects of a ruptured Achilles tendon depend on the severity or completeness of the rupture. If surgery is necessary, the athlete will most likely be out of commission for the rest of the season. In any case, the athlete will need to be careful and aware of the value of stretching and warming up in any future sports activity.

Other tendon problems typically occur with the tendons on the lateral side of the ankle, including those of the peroneus longus and peroneus brevis muscles. These muscles originate on the lateral aspect of the tibia and fibula; the tendons then run an inferior course behind the lateral malleolus in the peroneal groove and attach on the lateral and posterior aspects of the foot. There is a small retinaculum band attaching on the fibula and running posteriorly to the calcaneus, which assists in holding the tendons in place. As these tendons run their course behind the lateral malleolus, there is a possibility of their dislocating and/or subluxing due to trauma or extreme force and actually popping across the lateral malleolus. This can be very painful, but it is not usual for the athlete to experience.

The athlete with tendon problems should be seen by a member of the medical team, and a course of action outlined. Sometimes these problems can be controlled by taping or bracing and strengthening of the musculature in the area. Recurrent problems warrant further investigation by the physician; other modes of controlling recurrent subluxation are possible.

Compartment Syndrome

Another possible problem that can result from chronic or acute conditions is compartment syndrome. This syndrome is associated with the lower leg, which is divided into four very distinct compartments (see Time Out 16.1). The majority of compartment syndrome problems occur in the anterior compartment, which has very little room to expand if there is any extra swelling or effusion into it. This can be caused by chronic overuse that creates swelling of tissues in the compartment or by trauma that triggers bleeding and effusion (Black & Taylor, 1993). Some athletes chronically overuse the muscles in the anterior compartment. The resulting extra fluid creates a lack of space and places extreme pressure on the blood vessels and nerves in the compartment, thereby compromising their functions. In addition, trauma to the anterior portion of the leg (by being kicked or hit with a ball, for example) can create blood loss and swelling into the compartment. A similar scenario can cause the same results in the other compartments of the lower leg, which are so tightly packed with muscles, nerves, and blood vessels that there is little room for expansion when extra fluid is present.

Many soccer athletes tend to want to wear shin guards that are small (Figure 16.12). The athletes contend that large shin guards inhibit their play, and so they don't like to wear them. When athletes wear shin guards that are too small, however, they run the risk of being kicked in the lower leg (Figure 16.13). Fortunately for the athlete shown in Figure 16.13, the kick was to the medial side of the leg, which allowed the hematoma to be controlled and reduced in a short time. Being kicked on the lateral side could have resulted in anterior compartment pressure.

Signs and symptoms of compartment syndrome include the following:

1. Pain and swelling in the lower leg.
2. The athlete may complain of chronic or acute injury to the area.
3. There may be a loss of sensation or motor control to the lower leg and/or foot.
4. There can be a loss of pulse to the foot.
5. Inability to extend the great toe or dorsiflex the foot.

First aid care:

1. Apply ice and elevate. Do not apply compression, because the area is already compromised with too much pressure.
2. If the foot becomes numb, there is loss of movement, or there is loss of pulse to the foot, seek medical help immediately.
3. Seek proper medical advice early, because these problems can worsen very quickly.

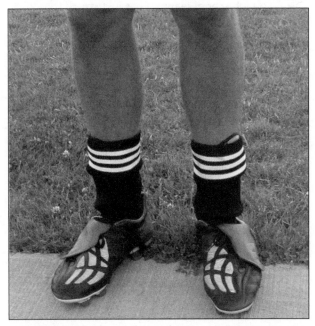

FIGURE 16.12 Some soccer players wear shin guards that are too small.

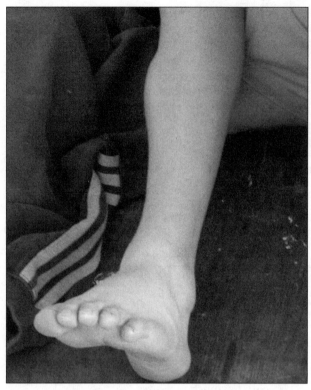

FIGURE 16.13 Severe contusion with hematoma formation on the medial aspect of the lower leg.

WHAT IF?

A high school gymnast has just struck the front of her lower left leg on the lower bar of the uneven bars. She immediately grabs her leg and complains loudly of extreme pain. On further examination you note that she has swelling and discoloration directly over the muscles of the anterior compartment. In addition, she states that she is unable to extend her big toe. What is the likely cause of these signs and symptoms? What would be the most appropriate first aid for this injury?

Shin Splints

Another very common disorder of the lower leg is **"shin splints,"** a term used to describe exercise-induced leg pain. Courture and Karlson (2002) define shin splints as "a wide variety of exercise induced lower-leg disorders." This is a dubious disorder that does not have definite parameters to follow for determining the exact problem that may exist in the lower leg. At one time medical professionals attempted to rename this problem using the descriptive term "medial tibial stress syndrome"—again, a name that really is more of a description than a diagnosis of the problem. The types of activities that produce this problem and the manifestations of the injury vary depending on the athlete. However, to date there has not been a positive link between any one specific cause and the resulting leg pain. Moreover, it is generally accepted that with rest the pain will subside and the athlete will be able once again to participate.

Signs and symptoms of shin splints include the following:

1. Lower leg pain either medially or posteromedially.
2. Typically, the athlete reports a chronic problem that gets progressively worse.
3. The pain and discomfort can be bilateral or unilateral.

First aid care:

1. Apply ice and have the athlete rest.
2. Nonsteroidal anti-inflammatory medications may help.

To help the athlete work through shin splints, suggest a change in workout routine. Recommend that the athlete run in water, reduce running, or eliminate the irritating stimulus altogether and use another type of exercise until there is an improvement. The athlete may also want to have his or her gait analyzed to look for biomechanical deficiencies such as overpronation. A myriad of related problems can exacerbate the pain and discomfort associated with shin splints. If the problem worsens, the athlete must seek professional medical advice so that long-term complications do not arise. An athletic trainer can assist the athlete with shin splints through preventive taping procedures and some therapies. However, long-term treatment with adhesive tape is not advised: The skin of the lower leg will become irritated, and many times this does not alleviate the initial problem causing the pain and discomfort (Holmes, Wilcox, & Fletcher, 2002). Each athlete responds differently to taping and therapy; therefore, a controlled progression of alternative taping procedures and therapy is important.

Foot Disorders

The foot contains many bones, joints, ligaments, muscles, and other tissues. It is important to remember that athletes participating in different sports will have different injuries associated with the foot. Some injuries are more common to specific sports.

Plantar Fasciitis

The plantar fascia is a dense collection of tissues, including muscles and tendons, that traverses from the plantar aspect of the metatarsal heads to the calcaneal tuberosity. If this collection of tissues becomes tight or inflamed by overuse or trauma, it can produce pain and disability in the bottom of the foot known as **plantar fasciitis.** A change in shoes, training technique, activity, or other factors may be precipitating factors in this injury. People who spend most of the week at a desk and then try to get in as much exercise as possible on the weekend are more susceptible to this problem than are full-time athletes (Simons, 1999). Plantar fasciitis in the young athlete typically is a combined problem with calcaneal apophysitis (Omey & Micheli, 1999). It is important to remember in the adolescent athlete that this condition may also include medial arch and/or heel pain (Omey & Micheli, 1999). To determine whether the condition is plantar fasciitis, you must take a thorough history. Ask the athlete if he or she experiences almost unbearable pain in the plantar aspect of the foot with the first steps taken on getting out of bed in the morning and whether the pain eases with each of the following steps. Also inquire if there is point tenderness on the plantar aspect of the calcaneal tuberosity. If both of these symptoms exist, there is a high probability that plantar fasciitis is the problem (Bazzoli & Pollina, 1989; Middleton & Kolodin, 1992).

Treatment of plantar fasciitis is typically conservative; it includes rest, anti-inflammatories, and the use of cold and heat alternatively to enhance healing (Taunton et al., 2002). A heel pad and stretching the Achilles tendon complex can assist in recovery and resolution. The use of semirigid orthoses has also been shown to be effective in recovering from plantar faciitis (Gross et al., 2002); however, many athletes find it difficult to participate in sports with such an orthotic in their shoes. Athletes will be tempted to continue exercising with this injury. However, the more the injury is aggravated by further insult to the same area, the longer it will take to heal, even when the healing process is being augmented with assorted therapeutic agents.

Heel Spurs

Heel spurs can also be related to plantar fasciitis: Sometimes with chronic cases of inflammation there is ossification at the site of the attachment on the plantar aspect of the calcaneus (Bazzoli & Pollina, 1989; Middleton & Kolodin, 1992). This results in long-term disability for many athletes because the heel spur can become problematic at any time during the exercise or activity program. Additionally, these small ossifications can occur on the posterior aspect of the calcaneus just below the attachment of the Achilles tendon. These too can become disabling to an athlete. The athlete needs to consult a physician to determine the proper treatment plan if these spurs become too incapacitating. Doughnut-shaped pads placed beneath the heel and some therapeutic interventions may assist the athlete to participate fully, but rarely do they ameliorate the problem.

Morton's Foot

Morton's foot typically involves either a shortened first metatarsal bone or an elongated second metatarsal bone. The result is that the majority of weight-bearing is done on the second metatarsal instead of along the first metatarsal and spreading out to the remainder of the foot. This problem can result in pain throughout the foot and difficulty in **ambulation.** The use of padding can help the athlete, but to have the problem correctly addressed the athlete should see a physician so that the proper treatment can be prescribed.

Also associated with this area is a condition called **Morton's neuroma.** This is a problem with the nerve, usually between the third and fourth metatarsal heads. As a result, pain radiates to the third and fourth toes. A **neuroma** is an abnormal growth on the nerve itself. Tight-fitting shoes have been blamed for irritation of the nerve in many cases of Morton's neuroma. Consequently, going barefoot is one of the best methods of pain relief for this problem. This condition is most often taken care of by a doctor, who should always be consulted regarding the early detection of foot problems.

Arch Problems

Athletes can experience several problems associated with the arches of the foot. Essentially, arch problems can be classified into two categories: **pes planus** (an abnormally flat foot) and **pes cavus** (an abnormally high

---

shin splints Medial or posteromedial leg pain brought about by walking, running, or related activities that decreases with rest.

plantar fasciitis Inflammation of the plantar fascia.

heel spur Ossification into the proximal attachment of the plantar fascia.

ambulation Move or walk about.

Morton's neuroma A nerve tumor (benign) related to the nerve between the third and fourth metatarsal heads with pain going to the third and fourth toes.

neuroma Tumor consisting mostly of nerve cells and nerve fibers.

pes planus An abnormally flat foot.

pes cavus Abnormally high arch of the foot.

arch in the foot). Both problems present difficulties to some athletes. Others with similar foot conditions may never complain of problems associated with arches.

Athletes with flat feet may have too much **foot pronation**, causing difficulties in the navicular bone and some of the joints around the ankle itself. This will lead to generalized discomfort around the foot and ankle. Several taping procedures have been developed to augment the arch in athletes. How long the effects of taping will enhance the arch has been evaluated by at least one research team, whose findings were consistent with those for ankle-taping procedures. There seems to be limited effectiveness in adhesive-strapping techniques for the person who walks for a minimum of 10 minutes continuously (Holmes, Wilcox, & Fletcher, 2002). However, it may be worth trying with an athlete to see if the acute application provides any benefit. It is definitely a low-cost alternative and could prove a good method of determining if the athlete could benefit from an **orthosis** (Figure 16.14) or some other type of augmentation for flat feet. A BOC-certified athletic

trainer can assist in providing direction in this taping procedure. Coaches should not attempt to apply adhesive tape to an athlete until they have received the proper training. Many athletes with flat feet can be helped in the long term by **orthotics** and proper shoe selection. It should be noted, however, that there is no evidence that the flat-footed athlete is a slower runner or has less motor ability than the athlete with a regular or high arch.

In many cases, the athlete with an excessively high arch also has foot problems. A foot with too much arch is often associated with plantar fasciitis and clawing of the toes. There have also been cases of athletes with too much arch having generalized discomfort about the foot and ankle because of the inability of the foot to absorb forces owing to the tightness of joints there. These athletes can also benefit from some orthotic help and proper shoe selection. The height of an athlete's arch need not hinder athletic performance if the proper attention and care are provided.

Bunions

Bunions are not very common in athletes at the high school and college level. Bunions can be simply a matter of inflamed bursae, or they can involve complicated bone and joint deformities. Many times bunions are caused by improperly fitting footwear. By getting the athlete into correctly fitting shoes the signs of a bunion should resolve. If an athlete has had a bunion for an extended period of time (weeks to months), then the athlete should seek the advice of a physician in the care of this condition.

Blisters and Calluses

Blisters and calluses are very common formations on athletes' feet. Excessive amounts of movement can produce a great deal of friction between the layers of skin in the foot and the shoe, resulting in the formation of either a blister or callus. If a blister forms, the layers of skin have been separated, and the friction has built up a fluid deposit. Always observe the color of the fluid within a blister. Most often the fluid will be clear, but on occasion it will be dark, which means there is blood in this small cavity. Many times the pain and discomfort from a blister will prevent the athlete from participating in sports. If the blister is large, the fluid should be drained and the area padded well to prevent further friction and blister formation. When a blister is drained, it is best to leave the top layer of skin in place until a new layer develops, thereby reducing the possibility of introducing infection into the area. In addition, place a doughnut-shaped pad made of felt or a large pad of thin adhesive felt directly over the blister to reduce friction. In case the blister

FIGURE 16.14 Soft orthotics can be placed in athletes' shoes to assist with some foot problems.

opens inadvertently (the top flap tears off for some reason), care needs to be taken to ensure that the area is clean and the possibility of infection is reduced. Any time the blister opens there is a possibility of infection entering the body. If the skin over the top of the blister tears, it is important to try to maintain the torn flap and keep it in contact with the blister if possible. This will maintain a little protection for the area. Apply an antibacterial ointment to the area and cover it as necessary.

When draining a blister, be sure to follow the recommended precautions regarding the human immunodeficiency virus (HIV) and hepatitis B:

1. Always use sterile instruments and keep the environment sterile.
2. Use latex gloves or some other barrier so that body fluids are not contacted.

According to the National Safety Council (1991), the following procedures should be followed when caring for a blister:

1. Initially wash the area with soap and warm water and sterilize the area with rubbing alcohol.
2. Using a sterile needle, puncture the base of the blister and gently drain by applying light pressure. This may need to be repeated several times in the first 24 hours. Do not remove the top of the blister; apply antibiotic ointment to the top of the blister and cover with a sterile dressing.
3. Check the area daily for redness or pus to determine if infection is occurring at the site.
4. After 3 to 7 days, gently remove the top of the blister, apply an antibiotic ointment, and cover with a sterile dressing.
5. Watch the area closely for signs of infection such as redness or pus and pad the area well with gauze pads or moleskin. This will allow for healing to occur without further irritation.

If the blister is small, padding the area to prevent further friction will usually suffice until the blister heals. Athletes should be encouraged to report the formation of any new blisters as soon as possible so that padding and protection can be provided. It is definitely best to help prevent blisters by having properly fitted footwear and giving new shoes a short break-in period before using them in practice or competition.

In addition to blisters, excessive tissue can build up on the bottom of the feet, which is commonly known as a callus. Calluses tend to build up over a bony area of the foot and should not be allowed to become large and extremely thick. If this happens, the callus can begin to move with the shoe and not with the foot. This creates an area of friction between the callus and layers of skin, causing a blister to form between the callus and the next lower layer of skin. This can cause problems because the blister is difficult to drain and can be very painful to the athlete. To prevent this from happening, a callus should be shaved regularly to allow for only a small amount of buildup, which then acts as a padding for the area. If a callus gets too large the athlete will begin to complain of pain and discomfort in the area.

Toe Injuries

The toes can also be injured during sports participation. In some sports the toes can be stepped on, resulting in torn-off nails or hematoma formation under the nail (Figure 16.15). This collection of blood under a nail will need to be released. Numerous techniques to remove this blood exist. Commercially available nail drills will bore a small hole in the nail and allow the trapped blood to be released. This will provide a great deal of relief to the athlete because this injury can produce a great deal of pain. If an athlete wears shoes that are too tight or small, this can also create a situation in which a toenail is smashed and blood collects under the nail. Shoes that are too small or too tight can also result in an ingrown toenail (Figure 16.16). Ingrown

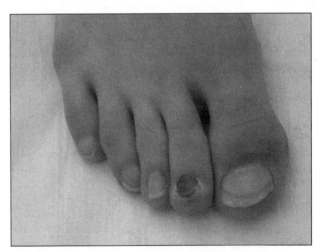

FIGURE 16.15 Players can get their toes stepped on, resulting in hematoma formation under the toenail; in some instances, as here, the nail can be torn off.

foot pronation Combined foot movements of eversion and abduction.

orthosis An appliance or apparatus used in sports to support, align, prevent, or correct deformities, or to improve function of a movable body part.

orthotics Field of knowledge relating to orthoses and their use.

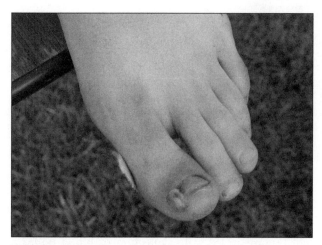

FIGURE 16.16 Shoes that are too tight can lead to ingrown toenails in the athlete.

toenails need to be treated early because delaying care can result in infection and serious problems. The ingrown nail can produce an open sore on the toe, and when the foot is placed in the sport shoe, bacteria can enter this open sore and result in further problems. Ingrown toenails should be treated by soaking them in a warm antibacterial solution. The nail needs to be elevated so that it will grow in a normal direction. This can be done by placing a small cotton roll under the affected part and leaving it there as the nail grows. It is important to address the situation that led up to the ingrown toenail. If the athlete is wearing shoes that are too small or too tight, he or she needs to get a shoe that has a more comfortable fit.

Preventive Ankle Taping

Applying preventive ankle taping to athletes is a popular practice among many high school, collegiate, and professional athletic trainers. Athletes commonly have their ankles taped as a routine procedure before practice or competition to prevent or reduce ankle injuries. The advantages and disadvantages of preventive ankle taping have been discussed widely, and a continuum of recommendations—from not using taping as a

preventive measure to always taping both ankles when participating in any sport—is advocated by various athletic trainers. Some athletic trainers promote the use of lace-up and other rigid braces rather than preventive taping. Paris, Vardaxis, and Kikkaliaris (1995) indicated through their research that ankle braces are just as effective, if not more so, as preventive taping in reducing inversion range of motion over a 30- to 60-minute time period (Paris, 1992). It has also been demonstrated that ankle braces do not detract from an athlete's ability to run, jump, or perform other skills as necessary during athletic competition.

Preventive ankle taping is an important skill that must be learned properly, practiced until a level of mastery is gained, and then applied in an athletic team setting. Taping is an art and a science, and each strip of tape has its own function. The following preventive taping outline is intended to provide the beginning student with the theoretical basis for the reasons the tape is applied. If students are interested in developing taping skills, it is recommended that they work under the direct supervision of a BOC-certified athletic trainer to learn and practice the art of taping.

As can be seen in Figure 16.17, the use of prewrap and anchoring strips is important in starting the taping procedure correctly. An adherent is used to help the prewrap to stay in place. If an adherent is not used, the tape will, in most situations, loosen and slide, diminishing the effectiveness of the taping procedure. The use of stirrups (Figures 16.18 to 16.20) is intended to maintain the foot in a normal or slightly everted position. Stirrups are combined with horseshoe strips, which help to hold the stirrups in place and reduce the gaps in the tape on the posterior portion of the foot. Figures 16.21 to 16.25 demonstrate the use of heel locks, which assist in stabilizing the subtalar joint. Heel locks are followed by the use of figure-eights (Figures 16.26 to 16.28), which are intended to help stabilize the talocrural joint and the transverse tarsal joint. From this point on, the procedure involves using finishing strips to make sure there are no gaps or holes between strips of tape, securing the tape at the bottom, and using a final covering to ensure that tape ends do not get rolled or wrinkled as the athlete puts on socks and shoes (Figures 16.29 and 16.30).

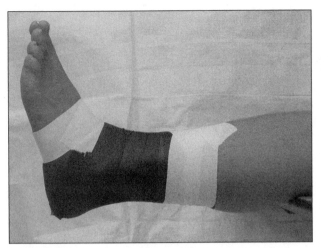

FIGURE 16.17 The application of prewrap and anchoring strips starts the ankle-taping procedure.

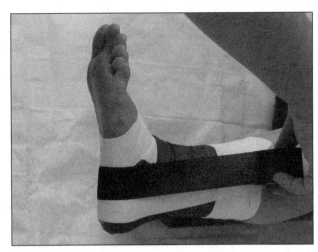

FIGURE 16.18 Stirrups are used to maintain a normal or slightly elevated foot position.

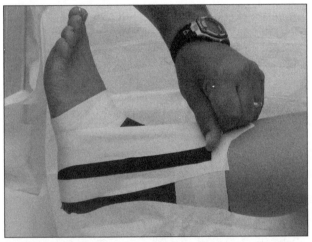

FIGURE 16.19 Overlapping stirrups, starting posteriorly and moving anteriorly.

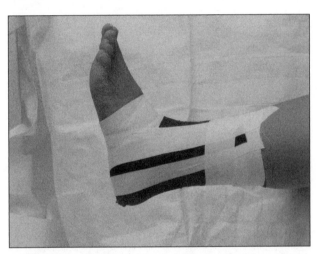

FIGURE 16.20 Stirrups are completed and anchored.

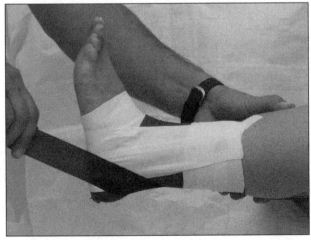

FIGURE 16.21 Applying the heel locks requires practice to perform correctly.

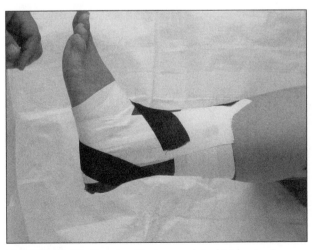

FIGURE 16.22 One heel lock completed (side view).

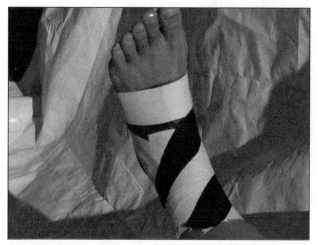

FIGURE 16.23 One heel lock completed (overhead view).

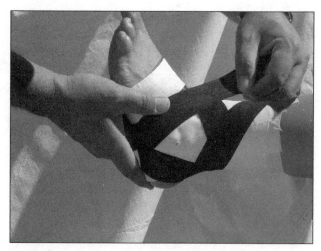

FIGURE 16.24 Second heel lock being applied.

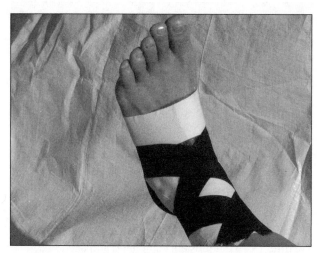

FIGURE 16.25 View of both heel locks after application.

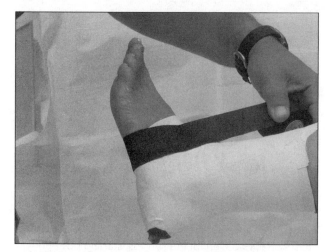

FIGURE 16.26 Starting the figure-eights also takes practice and proper direction of pull on the tape to be performed correctly.

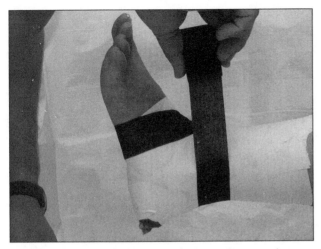

FIGURE 16.27 Completing the figure-eight procedure.

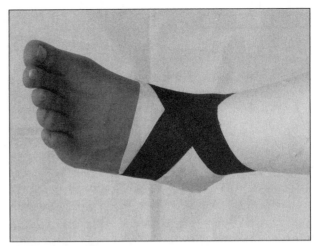

FIGURE 16.28 A completed figure-eight.

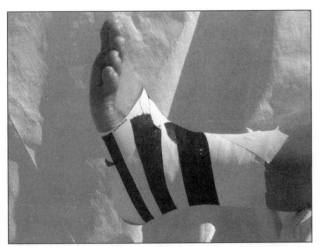

FIGURE 16.29 Finishing horseshoe stirrups are applied, alternating from distal to proximal.

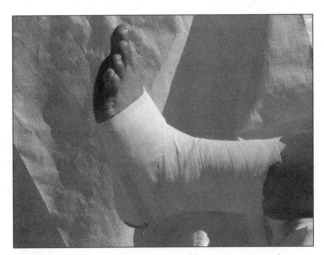

FIGURE 16.30 The completed ankle taping procedure.

REVIEW QUESTIONS

1. Name the two bones located in the lower leg.

2. Explain where the fibula is located and approximately how much body weight is supported by this bone.

3. What is the technical name for the ankle joint?

4. Name the strongest and largest of the ankle ligaments.

5. Draw or outline the compartments of the lower leg and describe the actions that the muscles in each compartment have on the foot.

6. Which compartment of the lower leg presents the most problems with fluid accumulation?

7. Outline the signs and symptoms of a fracture of the lower leg.

8. *True or false:* An inversion ankle sprain is more common than an eversion ankle sprain.

9. Explain which type of ankle sprain is more severe.

10. Describe where the Achilles tendon attaches and the signs, symptoms, and treatment of Achilles tendinitis.

11. Explain the possible long-term complications if problems with anterior compartment syndrome are left untreated.

12. Explain what types of changes (e.g., biomechanical, training) an athlete may need to make to alleviate and prevent further episodes of shin splints.

13. Outline the key signs and symptoms of plantar fasciitis and explain how heel spurs are associated with this condition.

14. What structures are involved in Morton's foot?

15. Explain the difference between pes cavus and pes planus.

16. Explain the difference between a blister and a callus.

17. Outline how a blister should be cared for when it is drained.

18. Explain how blisters can be prevented.

19. *True or false:* It is not possible for a callus to form over a blister.

20. *True or false:* Callus formation on the plantar aspect of the foot should be trimmed regularly to reduce friction.

REFERENCES

Alt W, Lohrer H, Gollhofer A. (1999). Functional properties of adhesive ankle taping: Neuromuscular and mechanical effects before and after exercise. *Foot Ankle Int.* 20:238–245.

Bazzoli AS, Pollina FS. (1989). Heel pain in recreational runners. *Phys Sportsmed.* 17(2):55–61.

Black KP, Taylor DE. (1993). Current concepts in the treatment of common compartment syndromes in athletes. *Sports Med.* 15(6):408–418.

Cordova ML, Ingersoll CD, LeBlanc MJ. (2000). Influence of support on joint range of motion before and after exercise: A meta-analysis. *J Orthop Sports Phys Ther.* 30:170–182.

Courture CJ, Karlson KA. (2002). Tibial stress injuries: Decisive diagnosis and treatment of "shin splints." *Phys Sportsmed.* 30(6):29–36, 51–52.

Frankeny JR, et al. (1993). A comparison of ankle-taping methods. *Clin J Sports Med.* 3(1):20–25.

Gray H. (1974). *Anatomy, Descriptive and Surgical.* Philadelphia: Running Press.

Gross MT, et al. (2002). The impact of custom semirigid foot orthotics on pain and disability for individuals with plantar fasciitis. *J Orthop Sports Phys Ther.* 32(4):149–157.

Hertel J. (2000). Functional instability following lateral ankle sprain. *Sports Med.* (29)5:361–371.

Hintermann B. (1999). Biomechanics of the unstable ankle joint and clinical implications. *Med Sci Sport Ex Suppl.* S459–469.

Holmes CF, Wilcox D, Fletcher JP. (2002). Effect of a modified, low-dye medial longitudinal arch taping procedure on the subtalar joint neutral position before and after light exercise. *J Orthop Sports Phys Ther.* 32(5):194–201.

Humble RN, Nugent LL. (2001). Achilles' tendonitis: An overview and reconditioning model. *Clin Podiatr Med Surg.* 18(2):233–254.

Leach RE, Schepsis AA, Takai H. (1991). Achilles tendinitis. *Phys Sportsmed.* 19(8):87–91.

Lohrer H, Alt W, Gollhofer A. (1999). Neuromuscular properties and functional aspects of taped ankles. *Am J Sports Med.* 27:69–75.

Malone T, McPoil T, Nitz AJ. (1996). *Orthopaedic and Sports Physical Therapy* (3rd ed.). St. Louis: Mosby.

Mangus BC, Hoffman MA, Parry SA. (1999). Management of tibiofibular syndesmosis injuries. *Ath Ther Today.* 4(5):47–50.

Middleton JA, Kolodin EL. (1992). Plantar fasciitis—heel pain in athletes. *J Athl Training.* 27(1):70–75.

Moore KL, Dalley AF. (1999). *Clinically Oriented Anatomy* (4th ed.). Baltimore: Williams and Wilkins.

National Safety Council. (1991). *First Aid and CPR.* Boston: Jones and Bartlett.

Omey ML, Micheli LJ. (1999). Foot and ankle problems in the young athlete. *Med Sci Sport Ex Suppl.* S470–486.

Paris DL. (1992). The effects of the Swede-O, New Cross, and McDavid ankle braces and adhesive ankle taping on speed, balance, agility, and vertical jump. *J Athl Training.* 27(3):253–256.

Paris DL, Vardaxis V, Kikkaliaris J. (1995). Ankle ranges of motion during extended activity periods while taped and braced. *J Athl Training.* 30(3):223–228.

Ricard MD, Schulthies SS, Saret JJ. (2000). Effects of high-top and low-top shoes on ankle inversion. *J Athletic Training.* 35(1):38–43.

Ricard MD, et al. (2000). Effects of tape and exercise on dynamic ankle inversion. *J Athl Training.* 35(1):31–37.

Ryan AJ, et al. (1986). Ankle sprains: A roundtable. *Phys Sportsmed.* 14(2):101–118.

Simons SM. (1999). Foot injuries of the recreational athlete. *Phys Sportsmed.* 27(1):57.

Taunton JE, et al. (2002). Plantar fasciitis: A retrospective analysis of 267 cases. *Phys Ther Sport.* 3(2):57–65.

Taylor DC, et al. (1990). Viscoelastic properties of muscle tendon units: The biomechanical effects of stretching. *Am J Sports Med.* 18(3):300–309.

Verhagen EAL, van Mechelen W, de Vente W. (2000). The effect of preventive measures on the incidence of ankle sprains. *Clin J Sport Med.* 10(4):291–296.

17

Skin Conditions in Sports

MAJOR CONCEPTS

The skin, the largest organ of the human body, is often involved in sports injuries, which range from simple wounds to a variety of bacterial, fungal, and viral infections. This chapter discusses the basic anatomy of the skin and describes the categories of wounds and their care. Obviously, the risk of HIV and HBV infection must be considered whenever a potential exposure to blood exists. The chapter presents the latest guidelines available for the prevention of accidental exposure to human blood.

Next, the chapter covers skin conditions related to excessive exposure to ultraviolet light, with an emphasis on prevention and safety precautions. Any number of microorganisms, ranging from minute viruses and bacteria to relatively large fungi, can produce skin infections. Information in this chapter introduces the reader to the common types of skin infections in sports, with helpful descriptions of signs and symptoms as well as recommended treatment and prevention protocols. The NCAA guidelines on wrestling and skin infections are included, along with a listing of conditions to be considered. This section also covers a related group of skin conditions resulting from allergic reactions to plant toxins and other materials.

http://health.jbpub.com/book/concepts/5e

The web site for this book offers many useful tools and is a great source for supplementary information for both students and instructors.

Visit the site at
http://health.jbpub.com/book/concepts/5e
to link to the following organizations and sites:

- The American Academy of Dermatology
- National Institute of General Medical Sciences
- Dermatology Online Atlas

The skin, or common integument, represents the largest organ of the human body. As can be seen in Figure 17.1, two major layers of tissues, the epidermis and dermis, combine to form this complex organ, which has a total surface area of 3,000 square inches on the average adult (AAOS, 1991). Located immediately beneath the skin is a layer of subcutaneous fat that helps to insulate the body from the external environment. Skin thickness varies regionally on the body: Thicker skin covers areas subject to pressure, such as the soles of the feet and palms of the hands; thinner skin covers areas where joint mobility is essential.

The skin serves a variety of purposes, not the least of which is protecting the body from the environment. It is also essential for controlling fluid balance within the body, protecting the body from disease organisms, and regulating body temperature. Furthermore, it houses nerves of sensation that register touch, temperature, and pressure. In addition, specialized cells within the skin produce vitamin D (AAOS, 1991).

The skin can be damaged in a variety of ways during participation in sports. External trauma can cause wounds, and damage can result from exposure to ultraviolet rays (sunlight) as well as burning or freezing temperatures. Skin infections can arise from a variety of organisms, including viruses, **bacteria,** and fungi. In addition, allergies can also affect the skin; these may be related to contact with plants or clothing and equipment that contain chemicals to which the athlete is sensitive.

Wounds

Sports injuries can cause many types of wounds, ranging from abrasions (scrapes, burns, and strawberry) to lacerations (cuts and gashes), all of which may result in infection as well as cosmetic complications (AMA, 1968). The primary goals of initial wound care are control of bleeding followed by prevention of infection through cleaning and bandaging. A primary concern when rendering first aid care for any wound is to avoid contact with whole blood that may transmit infectious organisms such as human immunodeficiency virus (**HIV**) or hepatitis B virus (**HBV**). The majority of wounds seen in sports are abrasions caused by rubbing, scraping, and burning; lacerations produced by a blunt object tearing the skin; and incisions caused by sharp objects. A special type of abrasion, known as turf burn, has been associated with playing surfaces in stadiums made of artificial turf. Turf burns are the result of falls sustained on artificial turf that produce friction and heat.

Treatment

Treatment of wounds in sports can be considered as a two-phase process. Initial first aid care is designed to control bleeding and guard the area from further injury. This is followed later with ongoing protection of the area so that return to participation is possible while

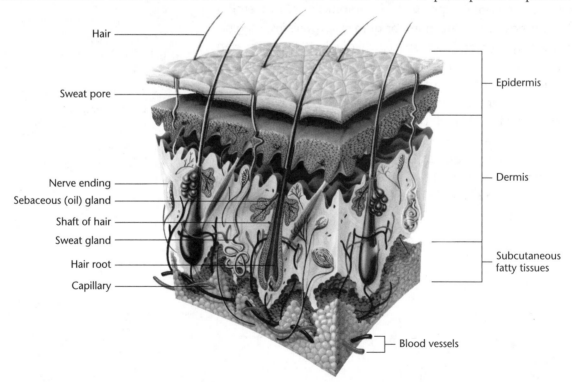

FIGURE 17.1 A cross section of human skin.

healing takes place. An important aspect of wound care is protection of fellow athletes, coaches, and other personnel from exposure to whole blood, which can result in the transmission of HIV and HBV organisms. Risk of exposure involves not only the wound itself, but also blood-soaked clothing as well as any blood that may be on playing surfaces.

Initial treatment of wounds follows first aid protocol described by the National Safety Council (1993). These are its guidelines:

1. Before rendering first aid, precautions should be taken against the possible transmission of HIV and HBV. Wear latex gloves and dispose of all waste in a storage container for biohazardous materials.
2. Remove clothing and/or equipment covering the wound.
3. Control bleeding with direct pressure over the wound site by applying some type of sterile dressing.
4. If dressing becomes soaked with blood, add more dressing on top. Do not remove blood-soaked dressings.
5. Although rare in sports, severe bleeding may not respond to direct pressure. In such cases, combine direct pressure with elevation.
6. Increased hemorrhage control can be achieved via the application of a pressure bandage to a point over either the brachial or femoral arteries, depending on location of the wound. Once pressure is applied to either of these points, it should not be released until the athlete is under the care of a physician.
7. Tourniquets should be applied only as a last resort; they are rarely needed in first aid for sports-related wounds.
8. All materials used to treat the wound—gauze pads, towels, and paper towels—should be stored for later disposal or cleaning in a container properly identified as containing biohazardous materials.

At the time of initial first aid, a decision must be made on whether the athlete will be allowed to return to participation. Obviously, the health and safety of the athlete must be the first priority; however, the majority of sports-related wounds are not life-threatening occurrences. Another consideration is protection of other participants, coaches, and personnel from exposure to whole blood from any wound. In sports such as wrestling, tackle football, and basketball, wounds must be dealt with in such a way to protect other athletes and the coaching staff from incidental exposure. Although research indicates the risk of transmission of HIV and HBV in such situations is remote, the possibility does exist (Calabrese, Haupt, & Hartman, 1993).

Once the initial bleeding is arrested, a commercially made dressing should be applied to the wound and held in place with an adhesive bandage. Small wounds are usually treatable by simply applying a bandage; larger wounds, such as a strawberry on the thigh or arm may require a large sterile gauze pad that is held in place with adhesive tape. Such bandages should be rechecked periodically during participation to ensure that they remain in proper position and bleeding has not resumed.

Lacerations and incisions, particularly those to the scalp or face, merit special attention because of their potential cosmetic impact. Such wounds should be referred to a physician for evaluation and possible stitches. As a general rule, any wound going below the dermal layer that is more than a centimeter in length—especially if it is on the face—should be seen by a physician for evaluation.

The National Safety Council (1993) provides the following guidelines for cleaning wounds:

1. Personnel rendering first aid should protect themselves from direct exposure to whole blood by wearing latex gloves.
2. Wash the wound with a sterile gauze pad saturated with soap and water. Hydrogen peroxide (3% solution) may be used to bubble away blood clots and related debris. This is especially helpful when treating abrasions containing significant amounts of dirt and other foreign material.
3. Flush the wound with large amounts of water; then dry the area with a sterile gauze pad.
4. Use isopropyl rubbing alcohol to clean the skin adjacent to the wound site; however, do not apply the alcohol directly to the wound.
5. Do not apply chemicals such as Mercurochrome, Merthiolate, or iodine to wounds; their effectiveness is minimal, and they may cause an allergic reaction.

bacteria Plural of bacterium. A Schizomycetes, unicellular microorganism that can either be parasitic or free-living and has a wide range of biochemical, often pathogenic, properties.

HIV Human immunodeficiency virus.

HBV Hepatitis B virus.

6. Apply a sterile, dry dressing and hold it in place with some type of bandage. For smaller wounds, Band-Aid bandages are effective; for larger wounds, sterile gauze pads held in place with elastic adhesive tape are recommended. By definition, a **dressing** is a sterile material, usually gauze, used to cover a wound to control bleeding and prevent contamination. A **bandage** is used to hold the dressing in place. Bandages need not be anything more than a folded cravat, strips of cloth, or commercially made elastic adhesive tape that can be directly applied to the skin and holds well even near a moving joint.

7. Severe wounds should be treated for control of bleeding and referred immediately for medical evaluation.

HIV/HBV and the Athlete

Although the majority of national focus regarding these two viral infections has focused primarily on HIV, HBV has been on the increase as well. It is estimated that 300,000 new HBV infections occur each year. In 1981, the first diagnosed case of acquired immune deficiency syndrome (AIDS) was reported. In 1986 there were approximately 2,000 people infected with HIV in the United States; recent data from the Centers for Disease Control and Prevention indicate an estimated 886,575 diagnosed cases of AIDS in the United States through 2002 (CDC, 2004).

Virtually anyone who is sexually active, including athletes, is at risk of contracting the AIDS virus. Athletes who inject anabolic steroids may also be at risk of infection, especially when sharing needles (Calabrese, 1989). The disease is spread primarily through intimate sexual contact or blood-to-blood exposure, which can easily occur when sharing needles during IV drug use. HBV is a bloodborne pathogen and is most easily spread via blood-to-blood contact with an infected person. Both HIV and HBV are carried within the blood of infected persons; therefore, any time such individuals sustain a bleeding wound, the possibility of transmission exists. This is especially true if another athlete who also has an open wound comes into contact with the blood of an infected person.

Although the chance of such an occurrence may be remote, some precautions are necessary, especially in sports in which external bleeding is likely. The Occupational Safety and Health Administration (**OSHA**) developed a comprehensive set of guidelines for health care workers regarding prevention of exposure to HIV and HBV (U.S. Department of Labor/U.S. Department of Health and Human Services, 1991). Although coaching personnel are not commonly thought of as health care providers, virtually all coaches find themselves dealing on a regular basis with open wounds on some of their athletes. Coaches and

athletes are routinely exposed to blood-contaminated towels, water bottles, playing surfaces, and blood-soaked bandaging materials. As a result, the prudent coach should make every effort to follow the basic preventive guidelines for HIV and HBV transmission that have been outlined by OSHA and are presented in Appendix 2.

Athletes participating in wrestling, tackle football, and boxing frequently sustain bleeding wounds. It is advised that coaches and officials remove players from participation when excessive bleeding is evident. Furthermore, those persons providing first aid care for such injuries should protect themselves by wearing latex gloves and perhaps even eye protection when treating a bleeding wound. In addition, athletes should be cautioned about sharing water bottles or blood-stained towels with fellow athletes (Calabrese, 1989). Athletes, coaches, and health care providers should wash hands and skin as soon as possible after being exposed to the blood of an injured athlete. Conversely, coaches and health care providers with open wounds should protect athletes from possible infection by wearing latex gloves or bandages and practicing good personal hygiene.

Education of athletes, coaches, and parents about the transmission and prevention of HIV and HBV is essential. Obviously, participation in organized sports presents a very low risk for the contraction of the viruses. Prudence dictates, however, that precautions be implemented, as sports participation does carry some risk to all parties involved—athletes, coaches, and sports medicine personnel (see Appendix 2).

Other Skin Conditions

Ultraviolet Light–Related Skin Problems

Outdoor sports played during the summer can result in exposure of large areas of the body to harmful rays of the sun. Typically, summer sportswear does not cover the arms and legs; in some sports, such as swimming and diving, major portions of the skin are unprotected. Medical evidence is substantial that even minor sunburn can be harmful to the skin; it may lead to serious, even lethal, complications such as skin-related carcinomas and melanomas (Reichel & Laub, 1992). Two different wavelengths of ultraviolet light are involved in the sunburn process: ultraviolet A (UVA) and ultraviolet B (UVB). UVB is a shorter wavelength than UVA and seems more related to the development of skin problems (Rustad, 1992).

It is well known that some individuals are at a higher risk for damage from sunlight exposure, including those with lighter skin, red hair, and freckles (Reichel & Laub,

1992). Exposure to sunlight at any time of day can result in sunburn; however, the most dangerous times are between 10:00 A.M. and 2:00 P.M.

Sunburn has two clinical phases. The first, known as the immediate erythema phase, involves reddening of the skin, which occurs during exposure to sunlight. The second phase, called the delayed erythema phase, normally develops within a few hours of exposure and peaks at 24 hours (Reichel & Laub, 1992). Although most cases of sunburn result in mild discomfort, with symptoms diminishing within a day or two, more severe cases can include the formation of blisters associated with chills and gastrointestinal distress.

The primary concern should be focused on protection of exposed skin when an athlete is participating in outdoor sports. Certain body areas may require special protection with a commercially prepared sunscreen—particularly the outer ear, nose, lips, back of the neck, forehead, and (if not covered by clothing) the forearms and hands. Though many sunscreen products are available, athletes should use only those rated with at least a sun protection factor (SPF) of 15. The SPF rating is derived by determining the sunscreen's ability to absorb harmful ultraviolet light over time. Thus, athletes using a product with an SPF rating of 15 will receive the same amount of ultraviolet light to the skin in 15 hours outdoors as they would have in 1 hour of unprotected exposure. Sunblocks are also available; they contain chemicals that block all light from reaching the skin. These products contain zinc oxide or titanium dioxide. Sunscreen products may contain a variety of chemicals that either absorb or reflect UVA and UVB light; these include *para*-aminobenzoic acid (**PABA**), cinnamates, salicylates, benzophenone-3, 3% avobenzone, and dibenzoylmethane (Rustad, 1992). For best results, sunscreens should be applied in advance of exposure to sunlight. Although many products are advertised as waterproof or water-resistant, athletes who perspire heavily or who are involved in water sports should periodically (every 60 minutes) reapply the product to maintain adequate protection.

Treatment of sunburn involves application of a commercially made topical anesthetic as well as a skin lotion to help relieve burning and dryness. In severe cases, medical attention may be warranted, and treatment may include the administration of anti-inflammatory medications.

Skin Infections

A variety of organisms can cause infections of the skin—including fungi, bacteria, and viruses. Although a detailed discussion of sports dermatology is beyond the scope of this book, some of the more common afflictions—along with their signs, symptoms, and

WHAT IF?

You are the wrestling coach at Johnson High School. Several of your athletes have reported similar skin lesions on their faces and arms. They appear as superficial, brownish-red, circular-shaped lesions. What might be causing these lesions and what, if any, action would you take?

treatment—are presented. It should also be remembered that many apparent skin infections can be symptoms of more serious infectious and/or allergic conditions, including Lyme disease, herpes, or contact dermatitis, and should be referred to a doctor for evaluation.

Tinea (Ringworm)

Tinea, commonly known as ringworm, is an infection of the skin caused by a group of fungi (Figure 17.2). In athletes, the common locations for tinea include the groin region (tinea cruris, commonly known as jock itch) and the feet and toes (tinea pedis). Tinea infections are common in these body areas because moisture and warmth make them ideal for fungal growth. Tinea can affect other parts of the body as well, including the scalp (tinea capitis) and the extremities. Although tinea infections are not serious, if left untreated they may persist and lead to secondary bacterial infections that can be cosmetically displeasing.

Signs and symptoms of tinea infections include the following:

1. Small, superficial, brownish-red, elevated lesions that tend to be circular in shape.
2. When infections involve the toes, lesions may include cracking between toes associated with oozing and crusting.
3. Itching and pain are associated with both tinea pedis and tinea cruris.

dressing Covering, either protective or supportive, that is applied to an injury or wound.

bandage Material used to cover a wound.

OSHA Occupational Safety and Health Administration.

PABA *Para*-aminobenzoic acid; the common active ingredient in sunscreen products.

tinea Group of fungi-related skin infections, commonly called ringworm, which can affect various parts of the body—groin (tinea cruris), feet and toes (tinea pedis), and scalp (tinea capitis).

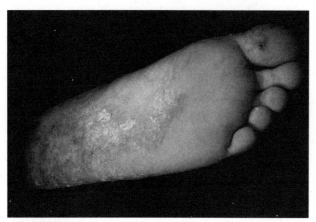

FIGURE 17.2 Tinea infection on the foot.

4. Scaling of the skin over the lesions may also be noted.

Treatment of tinea infections—according to Rustad (1992)—involves the following:

1. Vigilant cleaning of the involved areas, followed by drying.
2. Applying an over-the-counter topical treatment such as Tinactin.
3. Applying a moisture-absorbing powder to the area.
4. Wearing clothing made of natural fibers such as cotton.

Tinea Versicolor (TV)

This particular fungal infection is considered to be the most common warm-weather-related skin problem among teenagers and young adults (Rustad, 1992). **Tinea versicolor** gets its name from the symptoms it produces on the skin of the affected person. This infection is characterized by the appearance of lesions that are of a different color than the adjacent, normal skin. It is usually confined to the upper trunk, neck, and upper abdomen (AMA, 1968).

Signs and symptoms of tinea versicolor include the following:

1. Circular lesions that appear either lighter or darker than adjacent skin
2. Skin may appear white, in contrast to adjacent unaffected skin, after exposure to sunlight
3. Lesions normally found on the trunk

Treatment:

1. Prescription drugs, either oral or topical.
2. Treatment may require weeks or even months to be effective.

Bacterial Infections

Bacterial infections of the skin are relatively common in sports that involve close physical contact between participants. Known collectively as **pyoderma** (pus-producing infection of the skin), these infections are normally caused by two common bacteria, *Staphylococcus aureus* and *Streptococcus*. The former is related to conditions such as furuncles, carbuncles, and folliculitis; the latter causes impetigo (Figure 17.3) and cellulitis.

All of these conditions are characterized by infected, **purulent** (pus-producing) lesions on the skin. For example, in folliculitis the lesions are located at the base

Athletic Trainers SPEAK Out

Skin problems in wrestlers, such as fungal infections, seem to run a cyclic course through a season. No one is resistant and outbreaks tend to happen at the worst possible time, just before competition. Skin problems often go undiagnosed and unattended until the lesions start to spread or look bad enough to seek advice. This is a perplexing problem for coaches and athletes. Prevention is best spearheaded by universally instituted precautions and by early detection. Who should be charged with these duties? Everyone associated with the team should be sensitized to skin lesions as a fact of life in wrestling. Together, they should promote personal hygiene and develop a ready resource to assist with early recognition.

—Danny T. Foster, PhD, ATC, LAT

Dr. Foster is an Associate Director of Athletic Training at the University of Iowa.

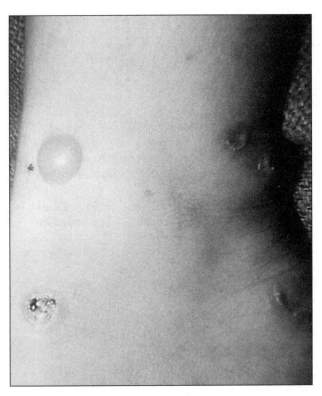

FIGURE 17.3 Impetigo on the ankle.

of a hair follicle. Furuncles are similar in appearance; however, they form large nodules around the hair follicles and may burst as the infection develops. Impetigo is similar in appearance, but may develop in areas with little or no hair.

Signs and symptoms of furuncles, carbuncles, and folliculitis:

1. The underlying symptom of all forms of pyoderma is a lesion, regardless of location, that is producing pus.

2. Folliculitis involves lesions located at the base of a hair follicle.

3. Furuncles, commonly called "boils," are lesions that form large nodules around the base of a hair follicle and may burst as the infection develops.

4. Boils can appear anywhere, but are more common on the arms, armpits, neck and chest, buttocks, and groin (Booher & Thibodeau, 2000).

5. Carbuncles are essentially a collection of boils that together form a weeping, pus-producing lesion typically found around the posterior neck and upper trunk regions.

Signs and symptoms of impetigo and cellulitis:

1. The underlying symptom of all forms of pyoderma is a lesion, regardless of location, that is producing pus.

2. Often seen on the face, impetigo presents groups of raised skin lesions that are honey-colored and crusty in appearance.

3. Cellulitis also is a skin infection; however, it affects the deeper layer of skin known as the dermis (Figure 17.1). The skin will appear red and warmer than adjacent skin and, in addition, will be painful to the touch.

Regardless of the specific condition, all pyodermal infections share a common characteristic: the presence of lesions that are obviously infected and associated with drainage and pus formation. Any athlete demonstrating such signs and/or symptoms as described should be removed from participation and referred for medical evaluation. If pyoderma is the diagnosis, the precautions outlined in Time Out 17.1 should be immediately instituted.

Viral Infections

Two of the more common viral-related skin problems in sports are plantar warts and herpes gladiatorum. As a skin problem, warts are quite common in the general population and occur as the result of infection by a specific group of viruses known collectively as the human papillomavirus (**HPV**), of which over 55 specific types have been identified. The majority of plantar warts are caused by two types: HPV-1 and HPV-4. The infection is contagious; however, some individuals seem more susceptible, with an **incubation period** ranging from 1 to 20 months (Ramsey, 1992). The most well-known characteristic of a wart is the abnormal

tinea versicolor Fungus infection resulting in the formation of circular skin lesions that appear either lighter or darker than adjacent skin.

pyoderma Pus-producing infection of the skin.

purulent Consisting of, or forming, pus.

HPV Human papillomavirus; approximately 55 specific types of these viruses have been identified, at least two of which are related to plantar warts.

incubation period The time between an exposure to an infectious agent and the appearance of symptoms of that infection.

TIME OUT 17.1

Official Statement from the National Athletic Trainers' Association on Community-Acquired MRSA Infections (CA-MRSA)

In an effort to educate the public about the potential risks of the emergence of community-acquired methicillin-resistant staphylococcus infection (CA-MRSA), the National Athletic Trainers' Association (NATA) recommends that health care personnel and physically active participants take appropriate precautions with suspicious lesions and talk with a physician.

According to the Centers for Disease Control and Prevention (CDC), approximately 25% to 30% of the population is colonized in the nose with *Staphylococcus aureus,* often referred to as "staph," and approximately 1% of the population is colonized with MRSA.[1]

Cases have developed from person-to-person contact, shared towels, soaps, improperly treated whirlpools, and equipment (mats, pads, surfaces, etc.). Staph or CA-MRSA infections usually manifest as skin infections, such as pimples, pustules, and boils, which present as red, swollen, painful, or have pus or other drainage. Without proper referral and care, more serious infections may cause pneumonia, bloodstream infections, or surgical wound infections.

Maintaining good hygiene and avoiding contact with drainage from skin lesions are the best methods for prevention.

Proper prevention and management recommendations may include, but are not limited to:
1. Keep hands clean by washing thoroughly with soap and warm water or using an alcohol-based hand sanitizer routinely.
2. Encourage immediate showering following activity.
3. Avoid whirlpools or common tubs with open wounds, scrapes, or scratches.
4. Avoid sharing towels, razors, and daily athletic gear.
5. Properly wash athletic gear and towels after each use.
6. Maintain clean facilities and equipment.
7. Inform or refer to appropriate health care personnel for all active skin lesions and lesions that do not respond to initial therapy.
8. Administer or seek proper first aid.
9. Encourage health care personnel to seek bacterial cultures to establish a diagnosis.
10. Care and cover skin lesions appropriately before participation.

[1]CA-MRSA Information for the Public. Centers for Disease Control and Prevention. Available online at: http://www.cdc.gov/ncidod/hip/aresist/ca_mrsa_public.htm.

Source: Official statement from the National Athletic Trainers' Association on community-acquired MSRA infections. Reprinted with permission.

---

buildup of epidermis around the region of actual infection; warts can vary in size from 1 millimeter in diameter to as large as 1 centimeter or more.

Plantar Warts

Plantar warts are simply warts that occur on the plantar surfaces of the feet. Although warts elsewhere generally rise up from the skin, the pressure of bearing weight drives the plantar wart inward on the bottom of the feet, often resulting in annoying if not painful symptoms.

Signs and symptoms of plantar warts include the following:

1. The warts are usually first noticed because they become painful when an athlete is walking or running because they are located on a weight-bearing surface.

2. Small thickened areas of skin may be noticeable, with tiny black or dark red dots appearing within the area (Ramsey, 1992).

3. Contrary to popular myth, these small dark spots are not seeds, but rather are small capillaries that have been destroyed within the wart.

4. Sometimes a group of warts will develop, causing a relatively large area to become involved. This is referred to as a mosaic wart.

Treatment of plantar warts ranges from the application of chemicals designed to dissolve the wart to actual surgical removal, although the latter is not recommended by the medical community. A variety of prescription products is available, most of which contain salicylic, pyruvic, and lactic acids. These compounds soften and erode the wart (the process is known technically as keratolysis); the ultimate goal is complete removal of the growth. Other treatment options exist, including the use of chemicals designed to stop the growth of the wart. Sometimes liquid nitrogen is applied to freeze the affected tissue; this is followed by surgical removal. Even a form of **laser** surgery has been developed for use on plantar warts (Ramsey, 1992).

Interestingly, in many athletes plantar warts terminate on their own with no long-term symptoms. Athletes who find plantar warts to be detrimental to participation in sports should consult a doctor to determine the best course of treatment. Coaches and athletes should not attempt treatment, as this may result in a worsening of the condition, infection, and even permanent scarring.

Herpes Gladiatorum

Herpes gladiatorum is the name given to herpes infections among athletes such as wrestlers. This virus, herpes simplex virus type 1 (**HSV-1**), is well known as the causative agent of the common cold sore or fever blister, which typically occurs on the outer lip area. Lesions are often associated with physical trauma, sunburn, emotional disturbances, fatigue, or infection (AMA, 1968). A unique aspect of herpes infection is its ability to remain dormant for long periods, sometimes months or even years, between active periods when lesions reappear. The infection is most contagious when open lesions are present. Once exposed to the virus, the incubation period may be as long as 2 weeks.

Signs and symptoms of herpes gladiatorum include the following:

1. Development of a lesion, often on the face, which is characterized by blistering associated with a red, infected area of skin.

2. Open, draining lesions may persist for a few days; afterward they become crusted and begin to heal.

3. General fatigue, body aches, and inflammation of lymph glands associated with tenderness (White, 1992).

Outbreaks of herpes must be controlled, or the infection can be devastating in a sport such as wrestling, in which acute outbreaks can involve many athletes. Coaches and athletes must be educated about the early signs and symptoms of HSV-1 infections. Moreover, any type of open lesion must be evaluated to rule out the possibility of infection. Athletes with active infections must be removed from participation until lesions have healed, a process that may take up to 5 days. It has been noted that once the crust of the lesion has come off, it is safe to resume activity (Olerud, 1989). Drugs are available for control of the infection; however, they must not be used without the supervision of a physician. In addition to drug therapy, athletes known to have an HSV-1 infection should wear sunscreen when exposed to sunlight, include foods high in lycine in their diets, and apply ice to lesions when they first appear (Olerud, 1989).

Wrestling and Skin Infections

Due to the nature of the sport of wrestling, participation with an active skin infection presents special hazards to the athletes involved. Common sense should prevail in such situations, and any open sore or skin lesion that cannot be covered adequately should be grounds for removal from participation until the infection subsides. The National Collegiate Athletic Association (NCAA) has published specific criteria for disqualification because of skin infections among wrestlers (Benson, 1995). The NCAA recommends that any infected area that cannot be protected adequately should be considered as cause for disqualification from practice and/or competition. The NCAA has included all of the following as infections worth considering under their recommendations (Benson, 1995):

1. Bacterial skin infections
   a. Impetigo
   b. Erysipelas
   c. Carbuncle
   d. Staphylococcal disease
   e. Folliculitis (generalized)
   f. Hidradentitis suppurative

2. Parasitic skin infections
   a. Pediculosis
   b. Scabies

3. Viral skin infections
   a. Herpes simplex
   b. Herpes zoster (chicken pox)
   c. Molluscum contagiosum

4. Fungal skin infections
   a. Tinea corporis (ringworm)

laser A device that concentrates high energies into a narrow beam of visible monochromatic light.

HSV-1 Herpes simplex virus type 1; related to infections in athletes commonly known as herpes gladiatorum.

WHAT IF?

A member of the cross-country team asks you to examine a strange rash he has developed on his legs. He reports that it developed about 12 to 24 hours after he used a topical analgesic with a wintergreen odor. What is a likely cause of this condition and what would you recommend to this athlete?

Allergic Reactions

Allergic skin reactions can be caused by exposure to any number of chemical agents from a variety of sources. For those susceptible, contact with the offending chemical results in a condition known as **contact dermatitis.** Plants such as poison ivy, poison oak, and poison sumac contain potent chemicals that cause reactions in susceptible people. Certain types of sports equipment and related clothing may also contain compounds causing allergic reactions.

According to the National Safety Council (1993), allergies to poison ivy, poison oak, and poison sumac result in skin reactions in 90% of adults. The sap of the plant contains the offending chemical; therefore, any direct contact with the plant can cause sap to be deposited onto the skin.

Contact with contaminated clothing or other materials can also result in reactions. The average time period between exposure and development of symptoms is 24 to 48 hours; the earliest symptoms include itching and redness in the affected area. These symptoms are followed by the development of blisters, which often break open and subsequently become crusted. Healing takes place within 1 to 2 weeks from the time of the initial reaction.

Athletes who know they are allergic to plants should learn to recognize poison ivy, poison oak, and poison sumac to avoid contact with them when participating in outdoor activities. Organizers of events that may place athletes in areas where these plants grow should alert participants to the potential problem. A good example is cross-country running, a traditional autumn sport in high schools across the nation. It is common for training runs, as well as races, to take the runners through areas where plants such as poison ivy flourish. Obviously, these athletes need to be able to recognize such vegetation. Coaches and organizers should also make every effort to keep courses well away from areas where such plants may grow.

Allergies related to chemicals contained in sports equipment or clothing have been receiving increased attention in sports medicine literature. It has been reported that products containing rubber, topical analgesics (pain relievers), resins found in athletic tape, and epoxy used in face gear are associated with allergic reactions in sensitive athletes. The chemicals initiating the allergic reaction are called sensitizers. They can produce classic symptoms of contact dermatitis—swelling and redness of the skin (erythema) followed by the development of pimple- or blisterlike lesions. Symptoms normally occur approximately 7 days after the initial exposure. In athletes with a history of previous allergic reactions, repeat exposures may yield symptoms within 24 hours (Fisher, 1993).

Major sensitizers include synthetic rubber additives commonly found in certain brands of tennis shoes, swim caps, swim goggles, nose clips, and earplugs as well as topical analgesics containing either salicylates or menthol. Adhesive athletic tapes made with formaldehyde resins, and face gear and helmets made with epoxy resins can also initiate allergic reactions (Fisher, 1993). For athletes with known allergies to any of these products, it is essential that alternative gear be identified if possible.

An athlete suspected of having allergic contact dermatitis should be referred to a dermatologist for specific diagnosis and treatment, which includes identification of the sensitizer and treatment of symptoms with anti-inflammatory drugs.

contact dermatitis Inflammation of the skin that is nonallergenic.

REVIEW QUESTIONS

1. Review the primary goals of initial wound care.

2. List the precautions that should be taken when treating an athlete with an open wound to avoid possible transmission of HIV and HBV.

3. Describe and differentiate between a wound dressing and a bandage.

4. *True or false:* With respect to the types of sunlight causing sunburn, evidence suggests that UVB is more connected with the development of skin-related problems.

5. Discuss the two clinical phases of sunburn as described in the chapter.

6. Explain the acronym *PABA.*

7. *True or false:* The term *pyoderma* implies a pus-producing infection of the skin.

8. Describe the recommended treatment(s) for plantar warts.

9. *True or false:* There is no evidence that synthetic materials such as tennis shoes, swim caps, and swim goggles can cause allergic skin reactions.

10. *True or false:* The first case of AIDS was reported in the United States in 1981.

REFERENCES

American Academy of Orthopaedic Surgeons (AAOS). (1991). *Athletic Training and Sports Medicine.* Park Ridge, Ill.: American Academy of Orthopaedic Surgeons.

American Medical Association (AMA). (1968). *Standard Nomenclature of Athletic Injuries.* Chicago: American Medical Association.

Benson M (ed.). (1995). *1995–96 Sports Medicine Handbook* (8th ed.). Overland Park, Kans.: The National Collegiate Athletic Association.

Booher JM, Thibodeau GA. (2000). *Athletic Injury Assessment* (2d ed.). Boston: McGraw-Hill.

Calabrese LH. (1989). AIDS and athletes. *Phys Sportsmed.* 17(1):127–132.

Calabrese LH, Haupt HA, Hartman L. (1993). HIV in sports: What is the risk? *Phys Sportsmed.* 21:172–180.

Centers for Disease Control and Prevention (CDC). (2004). Cumulative AIDS cases. Available: http://www.cdc.gov/hiv/stats.htm.

Cramer Products. (1994). OSHA regulations continue to raise questions. *The First Aider.* 64(2):1, 10.

Fisher AA. (1993). Allergic contact dermatitis: Practical solutions for sports-related rashes. *Phys Sportsmed.* 21(3):65–72.

National Safety Council. (1993). *First Aid and CPR* (2d ed.). Boston: Jones and Bartlett.

Olerud, J. (1989). Common skin problems. In Smith N (ed.). *Common Problems in Pediatric Sports Medicine.* Chicago: Year Book Medicine Publishers.

Ramsey ML. (1992). Plantar warts: Choosing treatment for active patients. *Phys Sportsmed.* 20(11):69–88.

Reichel M, Laub DA. (1992). From acne to black heel: Common skin injuries in sports. *Phys Sportsmed.* 20(2):111–118.

Rustad OJ. (1992). Outdoors and active: Relieving summer's siege on skin. *Phys Sportsmed.* 20(5):163–176.

U.S. Department of Labor/U.S. Department of Health and Human Services. (1991). *Joint Advisory Notice Protection Against Occupational Exposure to Hepatitis B (HBV) and Human Immunodeficiency Virus (HIV).* Washington, D.C.: Federal Register 56:235.

White J. (1992). Vigilance vanquishes herpes gladiatorum. *Phys Sportsmed.* 20(1):56.

18

Thermal Injuries

MAJOR CONCEPTS

Sports and athletic events are staged under a wide range of environmental conditions, indoors as well as a nearly infinite variety of outdoor settings. This chapter explores the body's response to extremes of both heat and cold, with particular attention given to life-threatening conditions. It is critical to note that a significant percentage of the deaths directly attributable to sports today result from heat-related problems.

In addition, the chapter discusses cold-related problems, including hypothermia, frostbite and frostnip, and a relatively unknown condition called cold urticaria.

http://health.jbpub.com/book/concepts/5e

The web site for this book offers many useful tools and is a great source for supplementary information for both students and instructors.

Visit the site at
http://health.jbpub.com/book/concepts/5e
to link to the following organizations and sites:

- Mark A. Jenkins, MD—Web site on Thermally Induced Medical Emergencies
- Dr. Pribut's Running Injuries Page

WHAT IF?

During practice in late August one of your football players, an offensive lineman, suddenly staggers away from the blocking sled, falls to the ground, and is unable to get to his feet. During your initial assessment you note that he is semiconscious and that his skin is dry, reddish in color, and hot to the touch. He is able to tell you that he is thirsty and that he has not had any water for over an hour. It is 95°F, approximately 78% humidity, and there is little wind. Given this scenario, most likely what is the problem? If you are correct, what is the appropriate first aid for this athlete?

Because of the great range of environmental conditions within which sports take place, a variety of temperature-related health emergencies occur each year; some result in death. The majority, if not all, of these deaths could be prevented if coaches, athletes, and administrators would take the time to consider the environmental conditions prior to allowing an event to begin.

Normal metabolism can be maintained within only a very narrow range of body **core temperatures,** ranging from between 98.0°F to 98.6°F when measured orally (Guyton, 1986). Heat is a natural product of metabolism; during exercise the metabolic rate can increase significantly, resulting in elevations of body temperature to 104°F. Excess heat must be eliminated from the body during exercise, or the body temperature can rise to dangerous levels in a short period of time. The body can rid itself of excess heat by taking advantage of basic physics through a complex process known as thermoregulation. Thermoregulation is controlled primarily by the temperature-regulating centers within the hypothalamus of the brain (Binkley et al., 2002; Wilmore & Costill, 1988). A variety of neurologic sensors throughout the body, both in the deep tissues and the skin, provide information regarding body temperature to the hypothalamus (Guyton, 1986).

Excess heat can be lost through **radiation** (via infrared light), **conduction** (absorbed into surrounding objects), **convection** (moving air currents), and evaporation (sweating). Each of these methods is effective, although during most exercise on dry land, evaporation is the most efficient. Its effectiveness as a form of thermoregulation can be severely compromised by extremes in relative humidity. Relative humidity represents the amount of water vapor suspended in the air, and it determines how much water can effectively evaporate from the skin during exercise. The higher the relative humidity, the less ability the surrounding air has to absorb fluid (sweat) from the skin surface. As a result, the higher the relative humidity the greater the potential for heat-related problems. In cases of outdoor activity during times of both extremely high temperatures and high humidity, coaches need to make modifications in the demands of the exercise session or consider delaying activity until conditions improve.

Athletes need to be given adequate time to adjust their systems to a major change in temperature. This process, known as **acclimatization** (Time Out 18.1), can take from 1 to 6 weeks, or longer, and occurs naturally when a person is exposed to continuous and significant climatic changes. As a general rule, those with a higher level of fitness tend to acclimatize more quickly; adolescents, obese individuals, and those with certain metabolic disorders take longer to readjust their systems.

As a result of proper acclimatization, the sweating mechanism can yield 1.5 to 2.5 liters (L) of sweat per hour, with a heat loss of at least 10 times the normal rate

TIME OUT 18.1

Physiologic Responses After Heat Acclimatization Relative to Nonacclimatized State

Physiologic Variable	After Acclimatization (10–14 Days) Exposure
• Heart rate	Decreases
• Stroke volume	Increases
• Body core temperature	Decreases
• Skin temperature	Decreases
• Sweat output/rate	Increases
• Onset of sweat	Earlier in training
• Evaporation of sweat	Increases
• Salt in sweat	Decreases
• Work output	Increases
• Subjective discomfort (rating of perceived exertion [RPE])	Decreases
• Fatigue	Decreases
• Capacity for work	Increases
• Mental disturbance	Decreases
• Syncopal response	Decreases
• Extracellular fluid volume	Increases
• Plasma volume	Increases

Source: Binkley HM, et al. (2002). National Athletic Trainers' Association position statement: Exertional heat illnesses. *J Athl Train.* 37(3):337. Reprinted with permission.

FIGURE 18.1 During hot-weather activity, adequate hydration is essential.

(Binkley et al., 2002; Guyton, 1986). During times of high ambient temperature, athletes need to consume from 4 to 10 L of fluids per day in order to avoid dehydration (Montain, Maughan, & Sawka, 1996). To put this amount into perspective, 4 L of fluid is roughly equivalent to consuming 17 eight-ounce glasses of water. Although this amount may seem large, it is important to remember that this figure represents consumption over a 24-hour period, and much of the food consumed during this time also contains some fluid.

Athletes, regardless of geographic region, can be susceptible to temperature-related disorders. For example, temperature extremes at both ends of the scale are common in the northern climates depending on time of year. Conversely, participants living in the so-called sun belt (southern climates) are routinely exposed to the combination of high temperature and high humidity. There, a typical scenario might involve a high school football player who has lost fitness over the summer and begins practices twice daily in August, when the temperature is 96°F and the relative humidity is 90%. Such athletes need to practice in the early morning or evening hours whenever possible to avoid the heat of the day. In addition, they need to be encouraged to drink water frequently (a minimum of 10 fluid ounces every 10 to 20 minutes) during practices (Casa et al., 2000; Figure 18.1). Evidence suggests that body fluid losses, representing as much as 2% of body weight, can occur before the athlete perceives the need to drink. Athletes may lose from 2% to 6% of body weight during exercise, which is significant in light of evidence that demonstrates that such losses can impair

performance by as much as 50%. It is critical to note that the process of heat acclimatization does *not* decrease the body's fluid needs; in fact, fluid needs are increased as the rate of sweating increases with improved fitness (Montain, Maughan, & Sawka, 1996).

Exertional Heat Illnesses

Exertional heat illnesses can involve any one of the following forms: dehydration, heat cramps, heat exhaustion, and heatstroke (Hubbard & Armstrong, 1989). They are presented here in the order of least severity, beginning with dehydration.

Dehydration

Given the very nature of physical activity and the metabolic processes associated with muscle contraction, a certain amount of dehydration is unavoidable. However, as long as the amount of dehydration is minimal (i.e., less than 2% body weight loss), the effects will not compromise performance or health. However, if dehydration is allowed to progress to a point of more than 2% body weight, both performance and thermoregulation can be negatively affected.

Signs and symptoms of dehydration include the following (NATA, 2003a):

1. Dry mouth
2. Thirst
3. Irritability or crankiness
4. Headache
5. Seeming bored or disinterested
6. Dizziness
7. Cramps
8. Excessive fatigue
9. Not able to run as fast or play as well as usual

core temperature Internal body temperature as opposed to shell or peripheral temperature.

radiation Emission and diffusion of rays of heat.

conduction Heating through direct contact with a hot medium.

convection Heating indirectly through another medium such as air or liquid.

acclimatization The adaptation of the body to a different environment.

Management:

1. Remove the athlete from the game or practice and move him or her to a cool location.

2. Rehydrate the athlete with either water or sports drink, preferably at a temperature of between 50° and 59°F (Casa et al., 2000).

3. If dehydration is minor (less than 2% body weight) and the athlete's symptoms are relieved, he or she may be returned to participation (NATA, 2003a).

4. If the athlete's symptoms persist after rehydration, seek medical attention.

Heat Cramps

Heat cramps generally develop within the muscles being exercised (e.g., the leg muscles in runners or the shoulder muscles in swimmers). The physiology of heat cramps is not clear; however, they are thought to occur as a result of water and mineral loss caused by sweating. As previously stated, air temperature and relative humidity work together to increase the likelihood of heat-related problems in athletes. The body rids itself of excess heat primarily through the evaporation of sweat from the skin surface. Under conditions of high relative humidity, however, the evaporation process becomes less effective, thereby contributing to elevations in body temperature. As can be seen in Table 18.1, apparent air temperature can vary significantly depending upon the relative humidity.

Signs and symptoms of heat cramps include the following:

1. Severe muscle cramps in the arms or legs, not related to muscle strain.

2. Muscle cramping may occur in the abdominal muscles.

3. Profuse sweating.

Management:

1. Immediate cessation of exercise.

2. Consumption of fluids, either water or sports drinks.

3. Static stretching of the involved muscles.

Heat Exhaustion

Heat exhaustion, as the term implies, involves generalized fatigue that occurs during exercise when excessive body fluids have been lost through sweating and are not adequately replaced. Though not in itself a life-threatening

TABLE 18.1

HEAT INDEX

Relative Humidity	Air Temperature (°F)										
	70	75	80	85	90	95	100	105	110	115	120
	Apparent Temperature (°F)										
0%	64	69	73	78	83	87	91	95	99	103	107
10%	65	70	75	80	85	90	95	100	105	111	116
20%	66	72	77	82	87	93	99	105	112	120	130
30%	67	73	78	84	90	96	104	113	123	135	148
40%	68	74	79	86	93	101	110	123	137	151	
50%	69	75	81	88	96	107	120	135	150		
60%	70	76	82	90	100	114	132	149			
70%	70	77	85	93	106	124	144				
80%	71	78	86	97	113	136					
90%	71	79	88	102	122						
100%	72	80	91	108							

Above 130°F = heatstroke imminent
105°–130°F = heat exhaustion and heat cramps likely, and heatstroke with long exposure and activity
90°–105°F = heat exhaustion and heat cramps with long exposure and activity
80°–90°F = fatigue during exposure and activity

condition, heat exhaustion can be a precursor to heatstroke, which is a true medical emergency. The prudent coach should constantly monitor athletes for the signs and symptoms of heat exhaustion when they must practice and compete in extreme climatic conditions of high heat and/or high humidity.

Signs and symptoms of heat exhaustion—according to Hubbard and Armstrong (1989) and the National Safety Council (1997)—include the following:

1. Moist, clammy skin
2. Profuse sweating
3. Muscle fatigue (general) and/or cramps
4. Nausea or related gastrointestinal distress
5. Dizziness and occasionally loss of consciousness
6. Severe thirst
7. Headache
8. Increased respiratory rate and rapid pulse
9. Body temperature ranging from 97°F to 104°F (Binkley et al., 2002)

Management:

1. Immediate cessation of exercise.
2. If the athlete is not nauseous, give fluids immediately—preferably cool water or commercial sports drink.
3. Move the athlete to a cool place.
4. Place the athlete in a supine position, with legs elevated 8 to 12 inches.
5. Loosen clothing and cool the athlete with wet towels or ice packs.
6. If the athlete is not fully recovered within 30 minutes, seek immediate medical attention.
7. Do not allow the athlete to return to participation for the remainder of that day.

Heatstroke

Heatstroke involves the body's inability to cool itself, with subsequent radical elevations in body temperature, sometimes exceeding 106°F. Two types of heatstroke have been identified, classic and exertional. Classic heatstroke occurs among nonathletes and is generally seen in obese people, the chronically ill or elderly, or diabetics. Such people often have circulatory problems and difficulty controlling body temperature. Exertional heatstroke is the form seen in athletes when they are exercising in a warm and/or humid environment. It is usually related to excessive fluid loss due to heavy sweating combined with a lack of adequate evaporation-related cooling. It is

critical to remember that heatstroke is a true medical emergency and must be treated accordingly.

Signs and symptoms of heatstroke include the following:

1. Sweating may or may not be present (Hubbard & Armstrong, 1989).
2. Hot, dry skin or clammy skin (if sweat is present on skin).
3. Mental confusion and possible loss of consciousness.
4. Gastrointestinal distress, including nausea and vomiting.
5. Severe motor disturbances and loss of coordination.
6. Rapid and strong pulse.
7. Rectal temperature higher than 104°F (athletic health care team should be trained to ascertain rectal core body temperature).

It must be emphasized that heatstroke can result in permanent damage to the central nervous system (CNS) as well as other systems within the body. Death can result if the body temperature is not controlled quickly; therefore, correct initial management of heatstroke is critical.

Management:

1. If emergency medical services (EMS) personnel, an athletic trainer, or a physician is present, immediate cooling of the athlete by using cold-water immersion is recommended to return body core temperature (measured rectally) to 101°F to 102°F. This can best be accomplished by removing the athlete's clothing and equipment and placing him or her into a tub of cold water (35°F to 58°F) (NATA, 2003b).
2. If they are not already on-site, summon EMS as per the emergency plan.
3. If cold-water immersion is not possible, move the athlete to a cool, humidity-controlled environment.

---

heat cramps Muscle spasms related to excessive heat buildup within the body.

heat exhaustion Generalized fatigue related to excessive heat buildup within the body; may be a precursor to heatstroke.

heatstroke Excessive heat buildup within the body resulting in the body's inability to cool itself, with core temperatures exceeding 106°F.

4. Wrap the athlete in wet sheets or towels or place cold packs in areas with abundant blood supply (e.g., neck, armpits, head, or groin).

5. Treat for shock and monitor temperature, not allowing it to drop below 102°F.

6. Keep the athlete in a semiseated position.

Prevention of Exertional Heat Illnesses

Ironically, heat-related illness causing death among athletes is a totally preventable problem. Application of a few simple guidelines and a dose of common sense are all that is needed to avoid possible tragedy. The National Athletic Trainers' Association (NATA) published a position statement entitled "Fluid Replacement for Athletes," with the objective "to present recommendations to optimize the fluid replacement practices of athletes" (Casa et al., 2000). All personnel involved with the supervision of young athletes should review the entire NATA document and make every effort to incorporate the recommendations.

To prevent heat disorders, athletes, coaches, and parents should comply with the following guidelines:

1. Utilize a weight chart. To determine if an athlete is consuming enough fluids during training, body weight should be recorded daily, before and after practice/competition, throughout the season. The preexercise weight is a good indicator of the athlete's rehydration over 24 hours, whereas postexercise weight provides an indication of the athlete's ability to drink adequate amounts of fluid during workouts, as well as how much fluid needs to be consumed after exercise to rehydrate adequately. A weight chart can be easily developed on a computer, with the weight being recorded by the coach or team manager. It is important that the same scale be used for all weighing. A program such as Microsoft Excel can be used to make the calculations as to percentage of body mass lost after exercise, as well as how much fluid needs to be consumed to get back to an adequate level of hydration.

To determine how much fluid the athlete needs to drink after practice/competition, calculate that for **every pound of weight loss, 24 oz. of fluid should be consumed** (GSSI, 1997). For example, a soccer player who weighs 165 lbs. at the beginning of practice and weighs 160 lbs. after practice has lost 5 lbs., or nearly 3% of body weight in fluid. This indicates a need to consume approximately 120 oz. of fluid to attain normal hydration. Postexercise rehydration should take place within 4 to 6 hours after the practice/competition (Casa et al., 2000). Such

---

Athletic Trainers SPEAK Out

A far too common type of injury is heat illness. This must be recognized in its early stages so that it can be easily managed. Refusing to recognize the signs and symptoms can quickly lead to heatstroke, which is a medical emergency and causes the most deaths among high school athletes. As a student athletic trainer, I experienced several situations in which aggressive treatment was prohibited by a well-meaning but ignorant coaching staff. We were often not allowed to administer assistance to the athletes until they dropped or lost consciousness. We were scolded for touching them to help break their falls as they fainted. These athletes fortunately did recover, but had to be hospitalized for three to seven days. The coaching staff was also replaced before the end of the academic year. [This problem] can be entirely avoided with proper preventive measures and aggressive management of those suspected of manifesting early signs and symptoms of heat stress.

— *Christine Stopka, PhD, ATC, LAT, CSCS, CAPE, MTAA*

Dr. Stopka is a Professor with the Department of Health Education & Behavior at the University of Florida.

a weight change also indicates that this athlete is not consuming enough fluid during exercise. Body weight should be monitored throughout the season, with significant changes being noted. The scale should be located in an easily accessible area, and coaches must require that athletes comply with the daily weight-monitoring protocols.

2. Consume fluids (17–20 oz.) 2 to 3 hours preceding activity and an additional 7 to 10 oz. 10 to 20 minutes prior to activity (Casa et al., 2000).

3. Consume fluids and avoid dehydration when participating in activities in warm and humid environments. Experts recommend the consumption of 7 to 10 oz. of fluids every 10 to 20 minutes during activity (Casa et al., 2000).

4. Avoid heavy exertion during times of extreme environmental conditions, especially when the temperature is above 95°F and there is high humidity.

5. Remember that restrictive garments can impair circulation of air, thus reducing the evaporation of sweat. Be aware that dark colors on uniforms and helmets may facilitate heat buildup.

6. Be reminded that fitness has a positive effect on the ability to function in extreme conditions. The process of developing a tolerance to extremes of climate, or acclimatization, normally requires a period of weeks.

Obviously, prevention of heatstroke must be a top priority for all those involved in organized sports. The

---

TABLE 18.2

FACTORS THAT INCREASE THE RISK OF HEATSTROKE

Drugs
Drugs such as cocaine or speed tend to increase physical activity and reduce the awareness of fatigue.

Alcohol
Decreases cardiac output and can cause hyperthermia.
Causes electrolyte disturbances in skeletal muscle.
Causes dehydration.

Illness
Particularly dangerous when fever is present.
Athletes are often reluctant to report illness for fear of losing their position on the team or being seen as a shirker.

Prescription Medications
Some cold medications act like amphetamines and increase heat production.
Antihistamines interfere with body cooling by reducing sweat production.
Many drugs for suppressing nausea or diarrhea also reduce sweating. So do many tranquilizers.
Diuretics are associated with loss of salt, potassium, and water.

Lack of Physical Conditioning
Poor physical condition predisposes an athlete to heatstroke.
Poor condition leads to inefficient performance that results in more heat production per unit of work performed.

Inappropriate Clothing
Being overdressed prevents the evaporation of sweat from the skin.

Environmental Factors
High temperature, high humidity, no breeze.
Physical exertion in the sun during the hottest part of the day.

Genetics
Obesity, or large, heavy physique.
Male gender.
Sickle cell trait.

Source: Knochel JP. (1996). Management of heat conditions. *Athletic Therapy Today.* 1(4):31. © 1996 by Human Kinetics Publishers, Inc. from Human Kinetics (Champaign, IL).

legal community has shown little tolerance for coaching personnel who are found to be negligent in the implementation of prudent heatstroke prevention procedures. All personnel should be well versed in the major risk factors for heatstroke; these are listed in Table 18.2. NATA's Position Statement on exertional heat illnesses is reproduced in Appendix 3.

Cold-Related Health Problems

Just as extremes in both heat and humidity can create problems for athletes, so can temperatures that are significantly lower than the body's core temperature. Exposure to cold can result in several conditions, including hypothermia, which can be a life-threatening situation.

Hypothermia

Hypothermia, another aspect of thermal-related injury, has to do with losing body heat too rapidly, resulting in total body cooling. Clinically, hypothermia involves a lowering of the body core temperature significantly below the norm of 98.6°F. Mild hypothermia begins to occur when core temperature drops to 95°F. Historically, the study of hypothermia has been limited to military personnel in the North Sea and those taking part in expeditions in extremely cold environments (Thornton, 1990). Recently, however, cases of clinical hypothermia have been documented in athletes involved in outdoor aerobic events like long-distance runs. Participants with the greatest risk are extremely lean athletes who have very little insulating body fat to help conserve heat. Surprisingly, hypothermia can occur at temperatures well above freezing. The combination of wind and moisture can cause rapid heat loss and the onset of hypothermia, during which the hypothalamus induces shivering in the skeletal muscles to generate heat. If this is unsuccessful, shivering will cease at around 87°F to 90°F; then, uncontrolled body cooling occurs.

Signs and symptoms of hypothermia—according to the National Safety Council (1997) and Thornton (1990)—include the following:

1. In *mild cases,* the athlete will display shivering, loss of motor control, slurring of speech, and mental problems such as confusion and loss of memory.

2. In *severe cases,* shivering will cease, and muscles will become stiff, giving the appearance of rigor mortis. Skin will become blue, and respiration and pulse rates will decrease. The athlete will be semiconscious or unconscious.

Management of mild hypothermia:

1. Move the athlete to a source of heat and out of the cold environment.

2. Remove any clothing that may be wet.

3. Wrap the athlete in warm, dry clothing or blankets.

4. Use an electric blanket or hot packs placed around the head and neck, armpits, groin, and chest.

Management of severe hypothermia (body temperature below 90°F):

1. Transport the athlete immediately to a health care facility.

2. Make no attempt to rewarm the athlete, but prevent further heat loss by moving the athlete to a warm environment and gently removing cold, wet clothing.

3. Treat the athlete gently, because cardiac-related problems are likely at low body temperatures.

4. Monitor vital signs and be prepared to administer artificial respiration or CPR.

As is the case with heat-related disorders, the best approach to the treatment of hypothermia is prevention. This can be accomplished in the majority of cases by following a few simple rules.

To prevent hypothermia, athletes should comply with the following guidelines:

1. Assess the risk by learning to use the windchill chart shown in Table 18.3. As can be seen, even on days when the temperature is moderate, the windchill factor can significantly increase the risk of hypothermia.

2. Do not embark on an outdoor activity of long duration, such as running or cycling, alone. Train with a friend or at least tell someone where you are going and when you plan to return.

3. Learn to recognize the early warning signs of hypothermia. If you have uncontrolled shivering in conjunction with loss of motor control, get to a warmer environment immediately.

4. Dress with appropriate cold-weather clothing. The synthetic materials now available allow body moisture to be wicked away from the skin surface while retaining body heat. It is also advised that you carry extra dry clothing whenever possible. When practical, keep your hands, feet, and head protected with extra insulation.

TABLE 18.3

WINDCHILL FACTOR

Estimated Wind Speed (in MPH)	Actual Thermometer Reading (°F)											
	50	40	30	20	10	0	−10	−20	−30	−40	−50	−60
	Equivalent Temperature (°F)											
Calm	50	40	30	20	10	0	−10	−20	−30	−40	−50	−60
5	48	37	27	16	6	−5	−15	−26	−36	−47	−57	−68
10	40	28	16	3	−9	−21	−33	−46	−58	−70	−83	−95
15	36	22	9	−5	−18	−32	−45	−58	−72	−85	−99	−112
20	32	18	4	−10	−25	−39	−53	−67	−82	−96	−110	−124
25	30	15	0	−15	−29	−44	−59	−74	−89	−104	−118	−133
30	25	13	−2	−18	−33	−48	−63	−79	−94	−109	−125	−140
35	27	11	−4	−20	−35	−51	−67	−82	−98	−113	−129	−145
40	26	10	−6	−21	−37	−53	−69	−85	−101	−117	−132	−148

(Wind speeds greater than 40 mph have little additional effect.)

Little danger (In less than 5 hours with dry skin. Greatest hazard is from false sense of security).

Increasing danger (Exposed flesh may freeze within 1 minute.)

Great danger (Flesh may freeze within 30 seconds.)

5. Make sure you remain properly hydrated and keep sufficient calories in your system to generate body heat. It is best to consume food and drink at regular intervals during long outdoor exposures. Also, avoid drugs such as alcohol, which creates the illusion of warmth but in fact contributes to heat loss.

Personnel rendering first aid to a victim of hypothermia should be versed in assessing body core temperature rectally. Oral thermometers are of little practical value when dealing with this form of medical emergency.

Frostbite and Frostnip

Exposure to extremely cold temperatures can result in skin-related problems, known commonly as frostbite and frostnip. The American Academy of Orthopaedic Surgeons (1991) defines frostbite as "freezing of tissues from excessive exposure to cold." Symptoms of frostbite include an initial feeling of burning and pain, followed by progressive loss of sensation. Damage in frostbite is caused by actual freezing of tissues as well as lack of blood (oxygen) supply to the tissues as a result of clotting. **Frostnip** is generally considered less severe than frostbite and involves freezing of only outer layers of skin, without damage to underlying tissue. Both these conditions can occur when the nose, ears, fingers, and feet are exposed to temperatures below 32°F for a long enough time period for freezing to occur. Skin temperatures must range between 28°F and 21°F for tissue freezing to occur. A temperature of −20°F is required for total freezing of exposed areas (Deivert, 1996). Medical evidence indicates that the most severe damage related to frostbite occurs when the frozen tissue thaws and then refreezes prior to medical treatment.

Fortunately, the risk of frostbite is minimal in most organized outdoor activities such as team sports. Typically such activities are held near school or community facilities so that participants can return to a warm environment before any significant freezing takes place. The probability of frostnip occurring is quite high, however, even under such circumstances because participants may not realize the severity of tissue cooling taking place. During activities in extreme conditions in which temperatures are below freezing and windchill is a factor, athletes should be instructed by coaching personnel to watch closely for the early warning signs of both frostbite and frostnip. Remember, the early signs of these problems are often noted by someone other than the victim.

hypothermia A body temperature below 33.3°C (95°F).

frostnip Less severe form of frostbite.

The National Safety Council (1997) has published criteria to aid in the treatment of both frostbite and frostnip; its guidelines are listed in Time Out 18.2. Tissue freezing can be categorized as either superficial or deep, depending on the duration and extent of exposure.

Signs and symptoms of superficial freezing include the following:

1. Skin color is white or grayish yellow.
2. Pain may occur early and later subside.
3. Affected part may feel very cold and numb. There may be a tingling, stinging, or aching sensation.
4. Skin surface will feel hard or crusty, and underlying tissue will be soft when depressed gently and firmly.

Signs and symptoms of deep freezing include the following:

1. Affected part feels hard, solid, and cannot be depressed.
2. Blisters appear in 12 to 36 hours.
3. Affected part is cold with pale, waxy skin.
4. A painfully cold part suddenly stops hurting.

Cold Urticaria

Another related problem of the skin associated with exposure to cold temperatures is **cold urticaria,** which involves a skin reaction of localized **edema** (fluid accumulation) associated with severe itching. The areas involved are usually those directly exposed to the cold or those not well protected by clothing. The exact mechanism of cold urticaria is unknown, but appears to be an allergic reaction to cold temperatures. Some individuals are more susceptible, including people with mononucleosis, syphilis, varicella (chickenpox), and hepatitis. In addition, those using certain drugs, such as penicillin and oral contraceptives, demonstrate a higher incidence of cold urticaria (Escher & Tucker, 1993).

Fortunately, symptoms of cold urticaria tend to be self-limiting, with the acute symptoms resolving within

---

TIME OUT 18.2

First Aid for Frostbite and Frostnip

1. For all hypothermic victims, stop further heat loss:

   - Get the victim out of the cold.
   - Handle the victim gently. Rough handling can cause a cardiac arrest.
   - Replace wet clothing with dry clothing.
   - Add insulation (blankets, towels, pillows, newspapers) beneath and around victim. Cover the victim's head (50% to 80% of the body's heat loss is through the head).
   - Keep the victim in a horizontal (flat) position. Do *not* raise the legs. (Elevating the legs would cause cold blood from the legs to flow into body core and adversely affect the heart.)
   - Do not let the victim walk or exercise. Do not massage the victim's body. Either activity could drive cold blood from the extremities to the torso and produce what is known as temperature afterdrop.

2. Call EMS for immediate medical transportation. Remember that hypothermia is more common in urban settings than in victims found in the wilderness.

3. For mild hypothermia in a remote or wilderness location, the goal is to prevent further heat loss. If protected from further heat loss, most mildly hypothermic victims are able to rewarm themselves by shivering, which generates heat.

4. For severe hypothermia in a remote or wilderness situation:

   - Check ABCs (airway, breathing, circulation).
   - Take 30–45 seconds to check the pulse before starting CPR.
   - Evacuate the victim by helicopter. Rewarming in a remote location is difficult and rarely effective.

a few hours after rewarming of the affected areas. For athletes who repeatedly suffer such symptoms, medical referral may be warranted. Treatment may include taking drugs such as antihistamines to control edema and itching. Athletes may also find certain types of outdoor clothing to be more effective in protecting the skin.

cold urticaria A condition in which the skin reacts to exposure to cold with localized edema associated with severe itching.

edema Swelling caused by the collection of fluid in connective tissue.

REVIEW QUESTIONS

1. Describe the normal range for body core temperature.

2. Explain how the body rids itself of excess heat.

3. What is the relationship between relative humidity and the process of evaporation?

4. *True or false:* Heat exhaustion is potentially more serious than simple heatstroke.

5. *True or false:* Heat cramps may be managed with rest, consumption of fluids, and static stretching of the involved muscles.

6. What is the recommended water intake during physical activity?

7. What is the fluid ounce equivalent of 4 L?

8. A fluid loss of from 2% to 6% can impair physical performance by how much?

9. At what core temperature does hypothermia begin?

10. At what body temperature does the shivering response cease?

11. What is the relationship between hypothermia and cardiac function?

12. Describe the signs and symptoms of cold urticaria.

13. Compute the fluid deficiency of an athlete who weights 5.5 pounds less after practice than he did prior to practice.

REFERENCES

American Academy of Orthopaedic Surgeons (AAOS). (1991). *Athletic Training and Sports Medicine.* Park Ridge, Ill.: American Academy of Orthopaedic Surgeons.

Binkley HM, et al. (2002). National Athletic Trainers' Association position statement: Exertional heat illnesses. *J Athl Train.* 37(3):329–343.

Casa DJ, et al. (2000). National Athletic Trainers' Association position statement: Fluid replacement for athletes. *J Athl Train.* 35(2):212–224.

Deivert RG. (1996). Adverse environmental conditions and athletes. *Athletic Therapy Today.* 1(4):5–10.

Escher S, Tucker A. (1993). Preventing, diagnosing, and treating cold urticaria. *Phys Sportsmed.* 21:125–133.

Gatorade Sports Science Institute (GSSI). (1997). Dehydration & heat injuries: Identification, treatment, and prevention.

Guyton AC. (1986). *Textbook of Medical Physiology.* Philadelphia: W. B. Saunders.

Hubbard RW, Armstrong LE. (1989). Hyperthermia: New thoughts on an old problem. *Phys Sportsmed.* 16(6): 97–113.

Montain SJ, Maughan RJ, Sawka MN. (1996). Fluid replacement strategies for exercise in hot weather. *Athletic Therapy Today.* 1(4):24–27.

National Athletic Trainers' Association (NATA). (2003a). How to recognize, prevent & treat exertional heat illnesses. NATA news release. Available: http://www.nata.org/newsrelease/archives/000056.html.

National Athletic Trainers' Association (NATA). (2003b, June). Inter-Association Task Force on Exertional Heat Illnesses consensus statement. *NATA News,* 24–29.

National Safety Council. (1997). *First Aid and CPR* (3d ed.). Boston: Jones and Bartlett.

Thornton JS. (1990). Hypothermia shouldn't freeze out cold-weather athletes. *Phys Sportsmed.* 18(1):109–113.

Wilmore JH, Costill DL. (1988). *Training for Sport and Activity: The Physiological Basis of the Conditioning Process.* Dubuque, Ia.: Wm. C. Brown.

Other Medical Concerns

MAJOR CONCEPTS

Athletes, like everyone else, occasionally become ill with infections that involve the respiratory and/or gastrointestinal systems. This chapter provides participation guidelines along with examples of typical signs and symptoms of the more common types of infections. The identification of several cases of Lyme disease within the athletic community has spurred growing concern over the last few years. This bacterial infection is transmitted primarily by ticks and can have serious, long-term implications for athletes. The chapter outlines early and late signs and symptoms, along with tips on how to avoid exposure to the disease-carrying ticks.

Next, the chapter examines several illnesses caused by viruses, including infectious mononucleosis and infectious strains of hepatitis A and B. All of these conditions pose a serious health risk to athletes; their signs and symptoms can assist the coach in identification.

The chapter concludes with a discussion of the current thinking regarding sports participation by athletes suffering from exercise-induced asthma (EIA), diabetes, or epilepsy. The emphasis is on identification of the major signs and symptoms of each of these conditions as well as on management and special precautions related to sports participation.

http://health.jbpub.com/book/concepts/5e

The web site for this book offers many useful tools and is a great source for supplementary information for both students and instructors.

Visit the site at
http://health.jbpub.com/book/concepts/5e
to link to the following organizations and sites:

- The CDC's Viral Hepatitis Web Page
- The Epilepsy Foundation of America

Exercise and Infectious Disease

Infectious disease is illness caused by some type of microorganism: viruses, bacteria, fungi, or protozoa. Although it is generally thought that physical activity helps to improve one's resistance to common infections, athletes remain vulnerable to the same illnesses as the general population. Research is ongoing in an effort to better identify the effects of long-term exercise on the immune system (Heath et al., 1991; Nieman & Nehlsen-Cannarella, 1991). The vast majority of infectious conditions affecting athletes involve either the respiratory or gastrointestinal systems.

Respiratory Infections

According to Afrasiabi and Spector (1991), respiratory infections can be categorized as upper respiratory infections (**URI**) involving the nose, throat, ears and sinuses, tonsils, and associated lymph glands, or lower respiratory infections (**LRI**) involving the lungs, bronchi, and larynx. The majority of upper and lower respiratory infections in athletes are caused by viruses.

Upper Respiratory Infections

Upper respiratory infections produce classic symptoms of the common cold or **rhinitis**—sore throat, stuffy nose, mild cough, mild fatigue, and fever. As a general rule, these infections are self-limited and last only a few days. Because the infection is related to a virus, antibiotic therapy will have no effect on the organism causing the illness. Athletes with colds should be cautioned not to borrow drugs such as antibiotics from a friend or parent, as this could result in drug-related poisoning or allergic reactions.

Athletes with URI can normally participate in competitive sports unless specific symptoms place them at obvious risk. For example, if an athlete has an ear infection affecting the vestibular system that results in **vertigo** (loss of balance), it may be unwise to allow participation in a

WHAT IF?

You are coaching track at a small college in the Midwest. Your best miler has been suffering from an upper respiratory infection for several days and, worse, the regional qualifying meet is in three days. What would you recommend to this young athlete and, further, what would you caution him regarding over-the-counter medication?

sport demanding a high degree of balance, for example, figure skating, gymnastics, or diving (Nelson, 1989). Scientific evidence regarding the effects of viral infections on both **endurance** and **muscular strength** are equivocal. Research by Eichner (1993) found that athletes with viral infections suffered decreases in both endurance and muscular strength. Weidner and associates found that URI did not negatively affect athletic performance (Weidner et al., 1997). Athletes involved in national or international events also must be warned not to treat themselves with over-the-counter medications such as decongestants or analgesics, as many of these drugs have been banned by sports regulatory organizations.

Infections of the upper respiratory system that persist for more than a few days may be related to bacterial infections such as streptococci. Symptoms of such infections are generally more pronounced, with visible lesions in the back of the throat (strep throat), severe sore throat, fever and chills, general discomfort, and swollen lymph glands in the neck and lower jaw. Athletes demonstrating such symptoms should not be allowed to participate, especially in team sports in which they are in close contact with other athletes, because such infections are routinely contagious. Medical evaluation is essential; it usually includes a physical assessment, throat culture (to identify the infectious agent), and in most cases a prescription for an antibiotic medication. The athlete should be advised to rest and drink plenty of nonalcoholic fluids until the major symptoms begin to subside. Return to activity can usually occur within a few days of treatment.

Lower Respiratory Infections

Infections of the lower respiratory system can impair performance for periods ranging up to several weeks. Normally related to a viral infection of the bronchi, the symptoms include cough, fever, and **malaise** (general discomfort). Obviously, athletes involved in aerobic sports—running, swimming, cycling, or cross-country skiing—will be directly and negatively affected by such an infection. As is the case with upper respiratory infections, athletes with lower respiratory infections should be isolated from their peers and referred to a physician for complete evaluation and treatment. Such cases are normally treated with rest and medication designed to control coughing and to relieve the associated aches and pains. More serious types of infections in the lower respiratory system include bronchitis and pneumonia (inflammation of the lungs), the latter can sometimes be life threatening. Symptoms of bronchitis include fever, coughing, and general feelings of illness. In addition the cough may yield sputum that appears greenish-yellow in color (Leaver-Dunn, Robinson, & Laubenthal, 2000).

The symptoms of pneumonia are more profound and also include coughing up of discolored sputum (AAOS, 1991). Diagnosis of either bronchitis or pneumonia must be made by a physician, and treatment includes rest, medication, and, in severe cases, hospitalization. Decisions regarding when to return to activity should be made on the advice of the attending physician as well as the athlete (or parents in the case of a minor).

Gastrointestinal Infections

Illnesses of the gastrointestinal (**GI**) system are typically related to viral, bacterial, or protozoan infections. Known collectively as **gastroenteritis** (inflammation of the stomach and intestines), these infections produce similar symptoms. Symptoms include abdominal cramping, nausea (often associated with vomiting), fever and chills, and diarrhea. When such symptoms occur, the best approach is to remove the athlete from participation, monitor the symptoms for 24 hours, and then make a decision regarding medical referral. Any athlete complaining of severe diarrhea or bloody stools should be referred immediately for a complete medical evaluation. Gastroenteritis, usually self-limiting within 1 to 3 days, is a generic problem that can be the result of a number of different causes, including pathogens such as viruses, bacteria, or protozoa. In addition, such symptoms can be the result of food allergies, food poisoning, and even psychological stress. The athlete should be encouraged to drink plenty of nonalcoholic fluid because dehydration can occur when vomiting and/or diarrhea persist. If symptoms continue for more than a few days, the athlete should consult a physician. Related conditions that may be more serious are caused by bacteria (in the case of typhoid fever) and protozoa (in the case of giardiasis). As a general rule, an athlete with GI symptoms—including severe (explosive or bloody) diarrhea, fever, extreme dehydration, and chills—should be referred to a physician for a complete physical evaluation and diagnosis.

A large and diverse number of problems of the gastrointestinal system can produce the symptoms of gastroenteritis. Evidence suggests that in some athletes the stress of physical activity may be the causative mechanism (Anderson, 1992). Other research has documented the reduction of GI symptoms in groups of athletes involved in aerobic activity (Halvorsen et al., 1990). Common GI-related problems include **gastritis** (inflammation of the stomach lining), **colitis** (inflammation of the colon), and **colic** (intra-abdominal pain). As with any recurrent and persistent clinical symptoms, referral to a physician is the prudent choice of action.

Other Infectious Diseases

Several other types of infections can affect athletes, and all present special problems with respect to identification, management, and prevention. The newest of this group is Lyme disease; although rarely a life-threatening illness, it can severely limit one's ability to participate in sports. Others include infectious mononucleosis, known in the 1960s as the kissing disease because of this common mode of transmission, and hepatitis A and B, both of which are extremely dangerous conditions.

Lyme Disease

Lyme disease is a bacterial (*Borrelia burgdorferi*) infection transmitted by the common deer tick (sometimes called bear tick in the western United States), which is widespread throughout the United States. Lyme disease gets its name from one of the towns where the first cases were identified in 1975: Lyme, Old Lyme, and East Haddam, Connecticut (Pinger, Hahn, & Sharp, 1991). Since that time Lyme disease has surpassed Rocky Mountain spotted fever as the most prevalent tick-borne infectious disease in the United States.

The disease is transmitted via a tick bite. Once a person is infected, initial symptoms may appear as early as 3 days later; however, symptoms may be absent for as long as 1 month after the bite. Regardless of the time period, the early symptom is the development of a circular area of reddened skin at the site of the bite. This is

URI Upper respiratory infection.

LRI Lower respiratory infection.

rhinitis The common cold.

vertigo Loss of balance.

endurance The ability of the body to engage in prolonged physical activity.

muscular strength The maximal force that can be applied by a muscle during a single maximal contraction.

malaise Discomfort and uneasiness caused by an illness.

GI Gastrointestinal.

gastroenteritis Inflammation of the stomach and intestines.

gastritis Inflammation of the stomach lining.

colitis Inflammation of the colon.

colic Intra-abdominal pain.

Lyme disease Bacterial infection transmitted by deer tick.

technically known as erythema chronicum migrans (ECM) and signifies the first stage of the infection. ECM will continue to develop for days; it can vary in size from a few inches to a foot or more. Additional symptoms include chills, fever, general aches and pains (malaise), and general fatigue. If left untreated the disease will become systemic and can affect the heart and central nervous system. In the majority of untreated cases arthritis will develop, with the knee being the most commonly affected joint (Pinger, Hahn, & Sharp, 1991). These symptoms may appear together or separately and can be accompanied by a repeated appearance of ECM. It is important to note that untreated Lyme disease can persist for years in the body and produce symptoms of a variety of disorders, thereby making recognition and diagnosis difficult.

Athletes who are involved in outdoor sports held in wooded areas are at risk of exposure to the deer tick; they should be taught how to perform a thorough inspection of their bodies for the presence of a tick. This may require assistance when inspecting hard-to-see areas, such as the hairline at the back of the neck, behind the ears, and the posterior torso. The deer tick is very small—about the size of a pinhead in the nymph stage, which is the time it is best able to transmit the disease. If a tick is found, it should be removed immediately because it has been found that length of attachment plays a role in likelihood of infection. Time Out 19.1 outlines recommended procedures for removal of a tick.

Treatment of Lyme disease involves the administration of antibiotic drugs. Cases have been reported in which even drug therapy was ineffective. Obviously, the best approach is prevention of the disease by avoiding an infectious tick bite. Sports organizations that promote outdoor activities during the summer months in wooded areas should check with local medical authorities regarding reports of deer tick activity. Every effort should be made to hold events in areas where the likelihood of tick exposure is minimal. Athletes should be encouraged to conduct tick checks regularly when they are participating in high-risk areas.

Several other viral-related illnesses can increase the chance of serious injury, even death, among athletes. Infectious mononucleosis is caused by the Epstein-Barr virus. Hepatitis A (HAV) and hepatitis B (serum hepatitis) (HBV) are both caused by viruses as well. The illnesses produce symptoms that can seriously impair performance; in the case of HBV infection, the disease can result in death.

Infectious Mononucleosis

Infectious mononucleosis is extremely common in the United States among young people and is caused by the Epstein-Barr virus, the same family of viruses responsi-

---

TIME OUT 19.1

Guidelines for Tick Removal

- Do not use the following popular methods of tick removal, which have proven useless.
  1. Petroleum jelly
  2. Fingernail polish
  3. Rubbing alcohol
  4. A hot match
- Pull the tick off, employing the following methods:
  1. Use tweezers or, if you have to use your fingers, protect your skin by using a paper towel or disposable tissue. Although few people ever encounter ticks infected with a disease, the person removing the tick may become infected by germs entering through breaks in the skin.
  2. Grasp the tick as close to the skin surface as possible and pull away from the skin with a steady pressure or lift the tick slightly upward and pull parallel to the skin until the tick detaches. Do not twist or jerk the tick because this may result in incomplete removal.
  3. Wash the bite site and your hands well with soap and water. Apply alcohol to further disinfect the area. Then, apply a cold pack to reduce pain. Calamine lotion might aid in relieving any itching. Keep the area clean.

---

ble for herpes infections. The reported incidence in the general population is very high by age 30, and 3% per year among college students (Eichner, 1996; McKeag & Kinderknecht, 1989). The initial symptoms of the infection are similar to the common cold—sore throat, fever, chills, and enlarged lymph nodes in the neck and jaw region. Infected persons often complain of extreme fatigue as well and may first notice the problem when they find it difficult to participate in sports. As the disease progresses other organs may become involved, including the liver and spleen.

Transmission of the disease usually occurs via contact with discharge from an infected person's mouth (airway). Once exposed, the incubation is variable; however, it usually ranges between 2 and 6 weeks (AAOS, 1991). Once the illness develops, its duration ranges from 5 to 15 days, with recovery beginning thereafter. Treatment is essentially symptomatic once the diagnosis is made by a physician; the emphasis is on rest and pain control with some type of analgesic drug.

Fortunately, infectious mononucleosis is a self-limited disease with no long-term effects.

A major concern with this illness, however, is its effect on the spleen. It has been well documented that acute cases result in enlargement of the spleen (splenomegaly) in 40% to 60% of all cases (McKeag & Kinderknecht, 1989). When the spleen experiences an episode of blunt trauma, as is common in many contact sports, splenomegaly predisposes this organ to rupture. Data regarding rupture are sparse; however, the available information indicates the incidence of rupture in the infected population to be approximately 1/1,000 cases (Eichner, 1996). (See Chapter 13.) Therefore, the attending physician is faced with the dilemma of determining when it is safe for an athlete to return to participation after recovering from infectious mononucleosis. It has been documented that most spleen ruptures occur between the 4th and 21st day of the illness; consequently, athletes never should be allowed to participate during this period (McKeag & Kinderknecht, 1989). Obviously, the coach, athlete, and parents must rely on the attending physician regarding the best time to resume participation.

Prevention of the spread of infectious mononucleosis is difficult when dealing with athletes involved in team sports in which they are in close contact with one another on a daily basis. Athletes should know that the major mode of transmission of this disease involves coming into contact with an infected person's saliva, such as during kissing. Preventive steps include advising athletes not to share water bottles or any other beverage containers. As a general precaution, towels and jerseys should not be shared by the athletes, as such items may be contaminated with respiratory discharge containing the virus. In addition, athletes should be taught the importance of reporting any symptoms of illness to the coach so he or she can decide a given athlete's participation status.

Hepatitis Infection

Hepatitis infection, either HAV or HBV, is serious, although HBV or serum hepatitis is considered to be the more serious and potentially life-threatening variety. HAV is transmitted via feces and is a serious problem

> **infectious mononucleosis** Viral infection characterized by general fatigue and enlargement of organs such as the spleen.

among food handlers who fail to wash their hands after going to the bathroom. Serum hepatitis is transmitted through the blood and sexual fluids of an infected person; it is routinely transmitted among IV drug users or accidentally by health care workers working with contaminated needles. It is also possible that transmission of HBV may occur during blood transfusions from an infected person. Guidelines for preventing the transmission of HBV were presented in Chapter 17.

Once a person is infected, the incubation period for HAV is 15 to 50 days; for HBV it is 45 to 160 days (Benenson, 1975). Symptoms of both HAV and HBV infection are varied, but symptoms of both strains include nausea, abdominal pain, vomiting, fever, and malaise. If untreated, both strains will begin to affect the liver, resulting in jaundice (yellowing of the skin). This indicates liver involvement; in severe cases this vital organ may be severely damaged, leading in some cases to death. Treatment for either form of hepatitis infection is limited; for HAV it appears that immediate innoculation with immune serum globulin (ISG) may confer passive immunity. There is some evidence that this also may be effective in treating cases of HBV exposure. Obviously, an athlete with HAV or HBV infection should be removed from participation and given prompt medical treatment. Because of the vulnerability of the liver during hepatitis infection, all decisions regarding return to participation for recovering athletes should be made by the attending physician.

Exercise-Induced Asthma

Exercise-induced asthma (EIA) has been defined as a constriction of the airway resulting in the typical symptoms associated with asthma (wheezing, chest tightness, dyspnea) resulting from participation in strenuous exercise. A less severe condition known as exercise-induced bronchospasm (EIB) is also associated with an exercise-induced restriction in the airways but does not result in asthmatic symptoms (Weiler, 1996). The highest incidence of EIA is found, not surprisingly, among chronic asthmatics: about 80% will develop an attack during exercise. However, EIA afflicts 12% to 15% of the general population as well (Afrasiabi & Spector, 1991).

The typical scenario for the onset and symptoms of EIA begins with exercise of sufficient magnitude to be considered intense. During exercise the airway will typically dilate; however, on cessation of exercise, airway restriction or bronchospasm will occur within minutes. EIA has been found to be more common among athletes engaging in continuous exercise lasting at least 6 to 8 minutes and less common among athletes involved in intermittent forms of exercise typical of team sports (Lemanske & Henke, 1989). Although the exact cause of EIA is unknown, the two most accepted theories are (1) the water-loss theory—rapid respiration results in a drying of the mucus of the airway, resulting in bronchoconstriction—and (2) the heat-exchange theory—immediately after exercise the bronchial vessels dilate in an effort to rewarm the airway tissues, resulting in a narrowing of the airway (Lacroix, 1999). Type of activity can also be a factor, as EIA is common among susceptible runners and less so among cyclists and walkers (Afrasiabi & Spector, 1991). Because indoor swimming pools usually provide a warm, humid environment, swimming in this setting is less likely to initiate an EIA attack.

Signs and symptoms of EIA include the following:

1. Coughing and tightness in the chest.
2. Shortness of breath.
3. Fatigue and stomachache (in children).
4. Some athletes may become alarmed.

Management of EIA generally involves the use of any one of a variety of drugs that prevent airway restriction or bronchospasm. Effective drugs are available and can be administered either orally or with an inhaler. The most common group of drugs used preemptively are the inhaled beta-2 agonists, which include the drugs albuterol, terbutaline sulfate, and salmeterol. The administration of choice is by way of a metered dose inhaler (MDI), a device that is held approximately 1.5 inches from the mouth that releases an aerosol form of the drug that is then inhaled slowly. Coaches should be aware of any athlete on their roster who suffers from EIA and who uses medication to control symptoms. It is important to note that certain drugs have been banned by some major sports-regulating agencies, including the National Collegiate Athletic Association and the International Olympic Committee. The NCAA continues to allow athletes with diagnosed EIA to self-treat with beta-2 agonists by way of an MDI. The IOC has prohibited the use of beta-2 agonists with the exception of albuterol, albuterol/ipratropium, salmeterol, and terbutaline, and these can only be administered via an inhaler. In addition, the athlete must have submitted written notification from his or her personal physician to the IOC (Lacroix, 1999).

Highly susceptible individuals may be required to avoid certain activities such as running or cycling, or at least be cognizant of environmental conditions and avoid such activity on cold, dry days. Sports involving short bursts of activity followed by periods of rest are excellent alternatives for high-risk athletes. For outdoor activities on cold, dry days, wearing a mask or scarf has been recommended (Afrasiabi & Spector, 1991). Warm-up

EIA Treatment

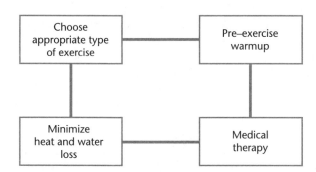

FIGURE 19.1 Overall treatment approaches for individuals with exercise-induced asthma.

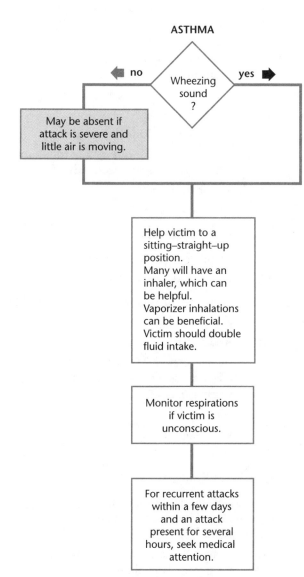

FIGURE 19.2 First aid procedures for asthma victims.

WHAT IF?

You are coaching high school softball. During practice one afternoon your right fielder comes to you complaining of extreme hunger and acting strangely. You notice during your conversation that she is perspiring heavily although it is a cool, cloudy afternoon. You know from her preseason physical evaluation that she has diabetes. What condition would these signs and symptoms indicate? What would be the appropriate first aid for this young athlete?

exercises have also been found to help reduce the likelihood of an attack (Lemanske & Henke, 1989). The National Athletic Trainers' Association has published a comprehensive position statement on the management of asthma in athletes, and it is available online at http://www.nata.org/statements/position/asthma.pdf. A schematic diagram of the major treatment approaches regarding EIA is shown in Figure 19.1.

The appropriate steps in the management of an athlete suffering an acute attack of EIA are shown in Figure 19.2.

The Athlete with Diabetes

Diabetes is defined by the National Safety Council (1993) as "the inability of the body to appropriately metabolize carbohydrates." The two most common forms of diabetes are (1) **type I—juvenile-onset** (insulin-dependent) **diabetes**, which requires an external source of insulin to control blood glucose levels, and (2) type II—adult-onset diabetes, which involves the body becoming resistant to the insulin produced by the pancreas. Blood glucose levels in an athlete with diabetes may fluctuate widely, ranging from excessive levels of blood glucose (**hyperglycemia**) to exceedingly low levels (hypoglycemia). Though a detailed explanation of the specific mechanisms for controlling levels of blood glucose is beyond the scope of this book, suffice it to say that the ability to either manufacture

juvenile-onset diabetes (type I) Insulin-dependent type of diabetes mellitus usually occurring in children and adolescents.

hyperglycemia Excessively high level of blood sugar.

insulin or utilize the insulin produced naturally is not possible for the athlete with diabetes. This can create significant problems for such an athlete, as both diet and exercise intensity can have profound effects on the blood glucose levels.

Exercise is now generally considered to be beneficial for children with insulin-dependent diabetes; however, certain problems can arise if exercise intensity, diet, and insulin dosage are not carefully monitored. This is best accomplished by working with a physician prior to the beginning of the playing season. Research by Robbins and Carleton (1989) has determined that any of three general reactions are possible in the athlete with diabetes who initiates an exercise session:

1. The athlete anticipates correctly the amount of insulin needed to keep levels of blood glucose between 100 and 200 milligrams per deciliter. In this situation, glucose utilization in muscles is equal to that produced by the liver.

2. If the athlete does not take into account the effects of exercise and starts working out with a low level of insulin and an elevated blood glucose, liver glucose production may actually increase. This may lead to a dangerously elevated level of blood glucose, a condition known as hyperglycemia.

3. In some cases, an athlete who begins exercising with a low level of insulin may react just the opposite to the preceding scenario. Liver glucose production may decrease whereas muscle glucose demand increases, causing dangerously low levels of blood glucose and leading to a condition known as hypoglycemia.

Research has shown that the type of exercise may determine what type of insulin response will occur (Horton, 1989). It has been found that sustained exercise of moderate intensity results in maintenance of, or even a decrease in, levels of blood glucose. It is recommended that diabetic athletes involved in triathlons or marathons decrease their insulin levels and increase caloric intake before a race or training session.

Interestingly, brief bouts of high-intensity exercise (80% or greater VO_2max) result in an increase in blood glucose levels. Sports such as tackle football, soccer, and basketball may contribute to this reaction; thus, athletes participating in these sports must be monitored to ensure they do not develop hyperglycemia and its complications.

The athlete with diabetes will benefit from learning how to monitor blood glucose levels; this is most easily accomplished through a test involving a finger-sticking technique. Periodic monitoring of blood glucose levels

allows the athlete to adjust caloric and insulin intake prior to, during, and even after exercise. Athletes should learn to estimate the caloric content of foods and the caloric demands of a given exercise session. With this information, the athlete can adjust diet prior to an event to compensate for the typical abnormal metabolic response seen in diabetics.

Coaches, parents, and fellow athletes need to be versed in the early recognition and first aid treatment of both hypoglycemia and hyperglycemia. Although both conditions present unique signs and symptoms, either condition can become life threatening. Hyperglycemia (high blood sugar) can lead to a condition known as diabetic coma or ketoacidosis. This occurs when fatty acids are metabolized to provide energy and yield ketones, which make the blood more acidic. Hypoglycemia occurs when too little sugar is available or too much insulin has been introduced into the body. In either case the body has too little glucose, and **hypoglycemic (insulin) shock** can occur.

Signs and symptoms of hyperglycemia include the following:

1. Symptoms develop slowly.
2. Fruity breath odor (indicates ketoacidosis).
3. The athlete will complain of extreme thirst and will have the urge to urinate frequently.
4. Nausea and/or vomiting.
5. Loss of consciousness.

Management of hyperglycemia:

1. Summon emergency medical services.
2. Treat for shock and monitor vital signs.

Signs and symptoms of hypoglycemia include the following:

1. Symptoms develop quickly.
2. The athlete may demonstrate unusual behavior—for example, aggression or confusion followed by loss of consciousness.
3. Profuse perspiration.
4. Loss of motor coordination.
5. Extreme hunger.

Management of hypoglycemia:

1. If the athlete is conscious, immediately administer a food or beverage containing sugar—for example, soda or fruit juice.
2. If the athlete does not improve within minutes, summon emergency medical services, treat for shock, and monitor vital signs.

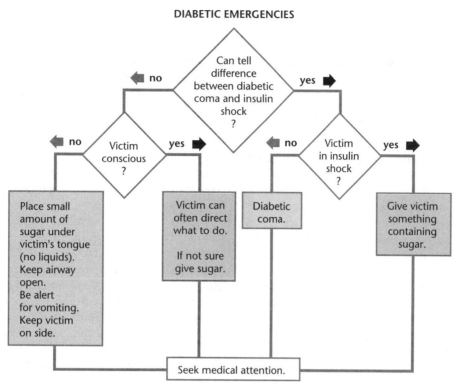

FIGURE 19.3 First aid procedures for diabetic emergencies.

A management flowchart covering the major treatment approaches for diabetic-related emergencies is shown in Figure 19.3.

Epilepsy and Sports Participation

Epilepsy is a disorder of the brain associated with a wide variety of symptoms. The most well-known symptom is a **seizure**—a sudden episodic change in behavior or internal psychic state associated with an abrupt paroxysmal discharge of electrical activity in the brain (Gates, 1991). Seizures take many forms and may involve motor systems, perceptions, and even the mood of the athlete. Epilepsy is not as common as popularly believed; it affects only 5 out of every 1,000 among the general population (Linschoten et al., 1990).

There are three forms of epileptic seizure the coach is likely to encounter among athletes (Gates, 1991). The first, a generalized tonic-clonic seizure known historically as the grand mal, involves perhaps the most dramatic type of epileptic disorder. This seizure is characterized by generalized convulsions involving a fall to the ground and uncontrolled shaking of the arms and legs as well as body twitching. During the seizure the person is unconscious,

although the eyes may be open, thereby creating the illusion that the person is awake. The typical generalized tonic-clonic (grand mal) seizure lasts from 2 to 5 minutes (National Safety Council, 1997).

The second type, called an absence attack, was previously known as a petit mal seizure. The classic symptoms are sudden loss of awareness of immediate surroundings associated with a blank stare that lasts for a few seconds. Immediately following the seizure the person will recover and may not know one has occurred.

The third form is known as a complex partial seizure. An athlete suffering this type of seizure will suddenly lose contact with surroundings and demonstrate any number of unusual behaviors, including mumbling,

hypoglycemic (insulin) shock Insulin shock resulting from an abnormally low sugar content in the blood.

epilepsy A chronic disorder characterized by sudden attacks of brain dysfunction, including altered consciousness, abnormal motor activity, sensory phenomena, and/or inappropriate behavior.

seizure Sudden onset of uncoordinated muscular activity and changes in consciousness lasting an unpredictable time.

picking at or removing clothing, or walking around in an apparently random fashion. This type of seizure may last for up to 5 minutes, after which time the athlete will recover but will remain confused and disoriented, possibly for a considerable time. The athlete will have no memory of activity during the seizure.

From the coach's standpoint, two major concerns must be addressed regarding an athlete with epilepsy—safety in the chosen activity and proper first aid care should a seizure occur. Many questions have been raised within both the lay and medical communities regarding what activities may pose a risk for the athlete with epilepsy. With the advent of anticonvulsant drugs, the vast majority of these athletes can control seizures. It has been reported that over half of epileptics taking antiseizure medication can remain free from seizures; another 30% will have infrequent attacks (Gates, 1991). The prevailing medical evidence suggests that high-risk activities for athletes afflicted with epilepsy include aquatic sports, sports in which falling is possible, and contact and collision sports (Gates, 1991; Linschoten et al., 1990).

Obviously, a seizure occurring while an athlete is in the water carries the risk of drowning; therefore, athletes who may suffer seizures should always swim with a buddy and alert pool personnel of their condition. However, it is generally advised that the benefits to a young athlete with epilepsy who is interested in water sports, such as competitive swimming, far outweigh any risks.

Athletes interested in sports capable of producing a dangerous fall, such as cycling, ice-skating or speed skating, skydiving, and horseback riding, should be discouraged from participating. In such activities the risks of injury related to a seizure exceed whatever benefits may be derived from participation.

A persistent myth has been that athletes with epilepsy should not be involved in contact and collision sports, as the potential jarring of the brain may increase the likelihood of seizure. Research, however, does not support this premise; in fact, it appears that athletes with epilepsy have no more risk of participation in such sports than does anyone else (Gates, 1991). Of course, athletes with epilepsy involved in such activities should take the same safety precautions as other athletes by wearing helmets, face masks, and mouth guards.

There is no reason why any youngster with epilepsy should be excluded from most school or community sports programs. In fact, such children can benefit a great deal from participation, particularly with regard to their self-esteem. It is important for coaching personnel to educate all participants about epilepsy in the event that an athlete suffers from a seizure. In this way, fear and anxiety on the part of teammates can be avoided.

First aid care for epileptic seizures is determined by the type of seizure and the immediate circumstances. Obviously, a generalized tonic-clonic seizure that takes place in the water will require quite different first aid than a complex partial seizure that occurs in the wrestling arena. For the most part, first aid for any type of seizure involves protection of the athlete from self-injury followed by psychological support. The appropriate first aid care for an athlete suffering an epileptic seizure is provided in Time Out 19.2.

TIME OUT 19.2

First Aid Care for Epileptic Seizure in an Athlete (Generalized Tonic-Clonic Seizure)

- Coaching staff should know who on their team has epilepsy, the specific type of the disorder, as well as any related medications the athlete is taking.
- Note the approximate time, to the minute, that the seizure began.
- If the seizure occurs in an aquatic setting, the priority must be to maintain the airway and remove the victim from the water immediately.
- Ask other athletes to move away from the victim and to resume their practice and/or game-related activities.
- Do not attempt to restrain the athlete during the seizure.
- Move potentially harmful objects away from the immediate area of the athlete.
- If the athlete is not wearing some type of helmet (football, lacrosse, hockey, etc.), place something soft under the head of the athlete.
- As the seizure passes, place the athlete onto his or her side, sometimes called the "recovery position."
- As the athlete regains consciousness be sure to provide psychological support.
- If the seizure last more than 5 minutes, or if another seizure occurs, initiate the emergency plan, including contacting EMS via 9-1-1 call.
- After the seizure, ask the athlete if he or she is taking the prescribed anticonvulsive medications as prescribed by his or her physician.

REVIEW QUESTIONS

1. Define the acronyms *URI* and *LRI*.
2. What types of organisms are related to the above infections?
3. Define the term *gastroenteritis*.
4. Describe briefly the history of Lyme disease in the United States.
5. What is the mode of transmission for Lyme disease?
6. Describe the major signs and symptoms of Lyme disease.
7. *True or false:* Lyme disease is caused by a virus.
8. What is the causative agent of infectious mononucleosis?
9. What is the risk related to collision sports and mononucleosis?
10. Describe the common signs and symptoms of EIA.
11. What are the recommended levels of blood glucose for the athlete with diabetes?
12. List the signs and symptoms of hyperglycemia.
13. List the signs and symptoms of hypoglycemia.
14. What is the difference between in-field management for the preceding two conditions?
15. Define *epilepsy*.
16. What are the management guidelines for an athlete suffering an epileptic seizure?

REFERENCES

Afrasiabi R, Spector SL. (1991). Exercise-induced asthma. *Phys Sportsmed.* 19(5):49–60.

American Academy of Orthopaedic Surgeons (AAOS). (1991). *Athletic Training and Sports Medicine.* Park Ridge, Ill.: American Academy of Orthopaedic Surgeons.

Anderson CR. (1992). A runner's recurrent abdominal pain. *Phys Sportsmed.* 20:81–83.

Benenson AS (ed.). (1975). *Control of Communicable Diseases in Man.* Washington, D.C.: American Public Health Association.

Eichner ER. (1993). Infection, immunity, and exercise: What to tell patients? *Phys Sportsmed.* 21:125–133.

Eichner ER. (1996). Infectious mononucleosis—recognizing the condition, reactivating the patient. *Phys Sportsmed.* 24:49–54.

Gates JR. (1991). Epilepsy and sports participation. *Phys Sportsmed.* 19:98–104.

Halvorsen FA, et al. (1990). Gastrointestinal disturbances in marathon runners. *Br J Sports Med.* 24:266–268.

Heath GW, et al. (1991). Exercise and the incidence of upper respiratory tract infections. *Med Sci Sports Exerc.* 23:152–157.

Horton ES. (1989). Exercise and diabetes in youth. In Gisolfi CV, Lamb DR (eds.). *Perspectives in Exercise Science and Sports Medicine,* Vol. 2: *Youth Exercise and Sport* (pp. 97–113). Indianapolis: Benchmark Press.

Lacroix VJ. (1999). Exercise-induced asthma. *Phys Sportsmed.* 27(12):75.

Leaver-Dunn D, Robinson JB, Laubenthal J. (2000). Assessment of respiratory conditions in athletes. *Athletic Therapy Today.* 5(6).

Lemanske RF, Henke KG. (1989). Exercise-induced asthma. In Gisolfi CV, Lamb DR (eds.). *Perspectives in Exercise Science and Sports Medicine,* Vol. 2: *Youth Exercise and Sport* (pp. 465–596). Indianapolis: Benchmark Press.

Linschoten R, et al. (1990). Epilepsy in sports. *Sports Med.* 10:10–19.

McKeag DB, Kinderknecht J. (1989). A basketball player with infectious mononucleosis. In Smith NJ (ed.). *Common Problems in Pediatric Sports Medicine* (pp. 191–203). Chicago: Year Book Medical Publishers.

National Safety Council. (1993). *First Aid and CPR* (2d ed.). Boston: Jones and Bartlett.

National Safety Council. (1997). *First Aid and CPR* (3d ed.). Boston: Jones and Bartlett.

Nelson MA. (1989). A young gymnast with an acute upper respiratory infection. In Smith NJ (ed.). *Common Problems in Pediatric Sports Medicine* (pp. 204–209). Chicago: Year Book Medical Publishers.

Nieman DC, Nehlsen-Cannarella SL. (1991). The effects of acute and chronic exercise on immunoglobulins. *Sports Med.* 11(3):183–201.

Pinger RR, Hahn DB, Sharp RL. (1991). The role of the athletic trainer in the detection and prevention of Lyme disease in athletes. *Athletic Training.* 26:324–331.

Robbins DC, Carleton S. (1989). Managing the diabetic athlete. *Phys Sportsmed.* 17(12):45–54.

Weidner TG, et al. (1997). Effect of rhinovirus caused upper respiratory illness on pulmonary function test and exercise response. *Med Sci Sports Exerc.* 29(5):604–609.

Weiler JM. (1996). Exercise-induced asthma: A practical guide to definitions, diagnosis, prevalence and treatment. *Allergy Asthma Proc.* 17(6): 315–325.

The Adolescent Athlete: Special Medical Concerns

Michael C. Koester, MD, ATC, CSCS, FAAP
Chris L. Amundson, MS, ATC, CSCS

INJURY TRENDS

Over 20 million youths between the ages of 6 and 16 years participate in a wide array of community-based organized sports nationwide. An additional 6 to 7 million children are involved in school-sponsored activities. With that large number of participants has come rather startling injury data. It is estimated that approximately 3 million injuries occur annually during sports participation among children and adolescents. Young girls playing organized sports have an estimated rate of 20 to 22 injuries per 100 participants per season, whereas boys are almost twice as likely to be injured, with a calculated risk of 39 injuries per 100 participants per season. Recent injury data show that sports and recreational activities account for 32.3% of all serious injuries in children aged 5 to 17 years.

Though young athletes suffer the greatest number of injuries of all sports participants, they often receive limited medical care. The availability and expertise of sports medicine providers, including physicians, NATABOC-certified athletic trainers (ATCs), and physical therapists, increases as athletes reach more elite levels of competition. Therefore, the relatively small number of athletes competing at the Olympic and professional levels have unlimited access to specialty medical care. Collegiate athletes usually have the services of a full-time ATC and one or more active team physicians. The situation changes drastically at the high school level, as a minority of schools employ ATCs to care for the millions of sports participants (see Chapter 1). Accordingly, at the youth sports level, there is rarely any involvement by trained medical personnel. As a result, coaches and parents are often left to provide initial care for injured athletes.

The web site for this book offers many useful tools and is a great source for supplementary information for both students and instructors.

Visit the site at
http://health.jbpub.com/book/concepts/5e
to link to the following organizations and sites:

- Cleveland Clinic Foundation—Musculoskeletal Concerns of the Pediatric Athlete: An Update
- American Academy of Pediatrics—Strength Training, Weight and Power Lifting and Body Building by Children and Adolescents

Youth Sports in America

Organized youth sports have been a part of American culture for over a century. As 19th-century America became increasingly industrialized and urbanized, local schools and churches formed youth sports organizations to help "build character" through physical activity. In the 1890s, the YMCA first began offering young men the opportunity to compete against each other. The founding of New York City's Public School Athletic League in 1903 ushered in the explosion of organized sports participation in the first half of the 20th century, which culminated with the birth of Little League Baseball in 1939.

In the 21st century, concerns continue to be raised about the potential for young athletes suffering physical and emotional harm from sports competition. For instance, many youth baseball and soccer leagues have stopped keeping score or recording wins and losses. Such concerns are nothing new. The 1930s saw a backlash against youth sports; educational leaders opposed competition, citing its potentially harmful psychological effects. Educators also observed a corresponding decrease in free play activities as children immersed themselves in organized sports. They feared "premature specialization" in certain sports would lead to injuries and interfere with the normal physical and mental development of childhood.

Many elementary school athletic programs were disbanded in the 1930s, beginning a shift in philosophy that has had repercussions in youth sports for the past 70 years. As physical educators and other teachers played a diminishing role in coaching school-sponsored sports, thousands of parents and others took their places. The majority of these well-meaning volunteers have no formal training in coaching or in child development. Despite continued opposition and calls for banning competitive leagues, youth sports have never been more popular. The 1970s saw an influx of girls and young women entering the traditionally male-dominated youth sports culture as barriers were overcome both legally and socially.

Factors in Youth Sports Participation

Why do children and adolescents play organized sports? Researchers have found a variety of answers. Not surprisingly, the primary motivating factor for many young athletes is "having fun." Other often-cited rationales have been making friends through team involvement, developing skills, and improving physical fitness. In what may be a reflection of the changing social structure in our country, researchers found that preadolescent boys in an urban club basketball league gave "having a coach to look up to" as a primary reason for participation.

Eventually, almost half of young athletes who go out for sports will discontinue participation prior to the end of their season. Unfortunately, the reasons for doing so are relatively few. Injury was found to be the most common factor in withdrawing from sports among high school students. Lack of playing time, overemphasis on competition, and dislike of the coach were also cited by high school students. Sadly, attrition among elementary school participants results from little success, lack of playing time, and "absence of fun."

The Growing Athlete
Puberty

Before proceeding with a discussion of common injury patterns, an understanding of the uniqueness of the growing athlete is required. It has often been said that children are not just "little adults." Nowhere does this saying apply more than in athletics. Emotionally and physically, children and adolescents respond far differently to the rigors of sports activity than do their adult counterparts.

Prior to reaching physical maturity, the young athlete's body is in a dynamic state. Change is constant as growth and development take place. Puberty is defined as the time when children develop secondary sexual characteristics, experience an increase in the rate of linear growth, and add muscle mass. Puberty usually begins at an average age of 10 years in girls and is signaled by the onset of breast development. At around the age of 12 years, boys will begin puberty, with an increase in testicular volume being the first physical sign. Growth during puberty may account for up to 20% of final adult height. The average boy will see a doubling of his total muscle mass between the ages of 10 and 17 years. Puberty may last from between 3 to 6 years.

Longitudinal growth accelerates during early puberty, with peak height velocity being attained at an average of age 12 years in girls and 14 years in boys. In young women, this time frame typically corresponds to just prior to the onset of menses. On average, menarche occurs 2 years after breast development begins. Most girls will see no more than 5 centimeters of height added after menarche. Boys attain peak height velocity later in puberty than do girls, corresponding to Tanner stage 3 or 4 of sexual maturity (near-adult pubic hair distribution and genital development). Peak height velocity may result in linear growth rates of almost 10 centimeters per year!

Growth

The longitudinal growth of bones arises from the physis (growth plate) located near the ends of long bones. Though a rather complex structure, the physis is basically an anatomic framework where rows of a cartilaginous matrix are progressively laid down to allow for longitudinal growth. Each layer undergoes a series of physiologic transformations, culminating in complete ossification (new bone formation). All bones continually lengthen beginning with embryonic development, but puberty signals a particularly rapid phase of bone growth. Bone growth ends once the physis closes, signaling the attainment of skeletal maturity. The average age of full skeletal development is approximately 14 years for girls and 16 years for boys, but there may be much variation.

The physes, apophyses, and the articular surfaces of long bones are three key anatomic structures susceptible to injury in the young athlete (Figure 20.1). All three share the presence of growth cartilage. The apophysis represents the site at which large muscle–tendon units attach to bones. Similar in structure to the physis, these tendon sites typically mature and completely ossify prior to the closure of the physes. The articular cartilage may be more susceptible to stress injury in young athletes, as the surface and underlying matrix have not yet achieved maturity. Therefore, it is likely unable to attenuate stress as well as the adult tissue.

Skeletal muscle has no corresponding "growth center" to that found in long bones. In fact, muscles grow in length in a similar manner as they grow in size—they respond to increasing forces. The progressive lengthening of the bone stimulates the muscles to correspondingly become longer. Therefore, muscles lag behind bones in length, setting up the potential for injury, particularly at times of rapid growth.

Injury Mechanisms

Two basic injury categories are seen in sports. Macrotrauma results from a single, high-force traumatic event. Examples include compound and comminuted fractures, joint dislocations, and tendon ruptures. Though young athletes may suffer these injuries, they are more likely to suffer trauma to the growth plate (physis) than to tear a ligament or fracture the shaft of a long bone. As with any structure, the weakest point is the most susceptible to damage when subjected to a force. The growth cartilage within the physis offers less resistance than the correspondingly stronger bones and joints. There is no evidence that organized sports contribute more to macrotraumatic injuries than does free play.

Microtrauma results from chronic, repetitive stress to local tissues. These injuries are increasingly common in children and adolescents and represent the majority of injuries seen in young athletes. Such injuries are often classified as overuse injuries, typically resulting from repetitive activities such as throwing, swimming, and distance running. There are multiple factors that lead to these injuries, which will be discussed in more detail throughout the chapter.

Ligament Injuries

Severe ligamentous injuries are less common in adolescent athletes than in adults, but they still do occur. An increased laxity of the ligaments prior to skeletal maturity contributes to this, as does the relative plasticity of the long bones, which may act to absorb some forces, thus attenuating many blows. As previously discussed, the physis offers less resistance to force than the ligaments and in many instances is the site of injury. For example, if a young athlete suffers a lateral blow to the knee, the valgus force will more likely result in a distal femoral or proximal physis fracture than in the medial collateral ligament sprain often seen in skeletally mature athletes (Figure 20.2).

Interestingly, an increasing body of evidence supports the fact that prior to puberty, ligamentous injuries may occur more commonly than previously thought. Prior to the pubertal growth spurt, the physis and its attachment site to the underlying bone may actually be stronger than the ligaments. When evaluating potential ligament injuries in adolescents, the basic principle of

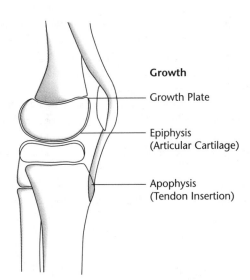

FIGURE 20.1 Long bone, showing physis, articular cartilage, and apophysis.

Growth

Growth Plate

Epiphysis
(Articular Cartilage)

Apophysis
(Tendon Insertion)

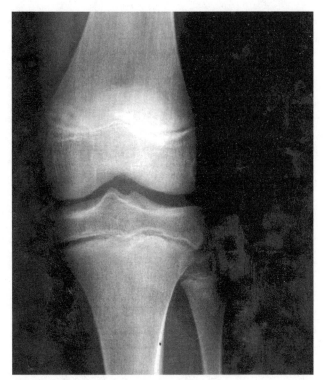

FIGURE 20.2 Stress X-ray of a fracture at the growth plate of a tibia in a skeletally immature athlete. Without the stress applied to the fracture by the radiology technologist to the medial aspect of the tibia, it would be difficult to visualize the fracture.

comparing the injured joint with the contralateral joint must always be remembered. The examiner may initially suspect ligamentous disruption owing to the increased laxity of immature joints. Similar laxity in the contralateral joint confirms a normal finding.

Tendon Injuries

Chronic, microtraumatic injuries to the immature apophysis and the resultant inflammation have long been recognized. Osgood (1903) and Schlatter each described traction injury at the tibial tubercle in 1903. Other commonly involved sites include the calcaneus and medial humerus (Table 20.1). Apophyseal injuries provide excellent examples of the multiple factors that lead to injury in the growing athlete. As discussed, muscles lengthen in response to bone growth. Therefore, a susceptible period exists when the muscle is shorter than necessary for optimal function in relation to the bone. The result is constant tension on the apophysis, which is exacerbated by repetitive activity. With repeated traction placed on the apophysis, there may be some weakening within the growth cartilage matrix, culminating in inflammation, pain, and loss of function.

Young athletes are more susceptible to **apophysitis** during times of rapid bone growth, but overtraining,

Athletic Trainers SPEAK Out

Providing athletic training services to the adolescent athletic population is both a rewarding experience for the certified athletic trainer and a critical component for the athlete as he/she matures mentally and physically. During the athlete's high school career, his/her body and mind move through an incredible transformation process in order to reach adult maturity. The first experience an athlete may have with an athletic trainer is likely to be at the high school level. The high school certified athletic trainer has to be knowledgeable of specific athletic injuries an adolescent may encounter during the athlete's developmental process.

A primary concern for high school athletic trainers, that can make a real difference in an athlete's career, is emphasizing the importance of injury prevention. Educating the athlete with regards to the proper development of flexibility, muscular strength, core stabilization, endurance, and sound nutrition can go a long way in minimizing injury severity. The role a high school certified athletic trainer serves is imperative in minimizing the severity of athletic injuries due to inappropriate prevention and care; therefore, decreasing the chance of an athlete's premature exit from high school athletics.

—*Eric Taylor, MS, LAT, ATC*

Eric Taylor is Head Athletic Trainer for Centennial High School, Boise, Idaho.

TABLE 20.1

COMMON SITES OF APOPHYSITIS

Anatomic Site	*Condition*
Tibial tubercle	Osgood-Schlatter disease
Calcaneus	Sever's disease
Medial distal humerus	Little League elbow
Fifth metatarsal base	Iselin's disease
Iliac crest	
Ischial tuberosity	

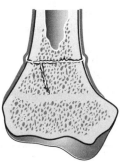

FIGURE 20.3 Rang-Ogden type IV injury.

FIGURE 20.4 Peterson type I injury.

poor technique, and chronic misuse all may inflict damaging forces across joints and contribute to injury. Infrequently, macrotraumatic injuries can also occur at the apophysis. High-force injuries may result in the complete disunion of the apophyseal growth cartilage, the adolescent equivalent of a complete tendon avulsion. Initial treatment of apophyseal injuries is similar to the treatment of other musculoskeletal injuries. Stretching of the involved muscle groups, changes in activity level, and anti-inflammatory medications may also help. Calcaneal apophysitis (Sever's disease) is often particularly amenable to the placement of a heel lift in the shoe of the involved foot. The heel lift acts to functionally shorten the pull of the gastrocnemius and soleus muscles, lessening the tension at the calcaneal apophysis.

Growth Plate Injuries

Injuries to the physis may result from microtrauma as well as macrotrauma. In the 1960s, Salter and Harris (1963) classified five injury patterns seen after trauma to the physis (see Figure 1.10). The Salter-Harris type I fracture is by far the most common physis injury and represents a "separation" of the cartilaginous zone. The diagnosis is most often made based on physical exam findings, because radiographs are typically normal (see Figure 20.2). Such an injury should always be suspected when the athlete presents with a joint injury, but with tenderness predominantly over the distal or proximal portion of the bone and a normal joint examination. Injuries to the distal fibula and distal radius are most often seen. Treatment consists of casting for 4 to 6 weeks, and complications are rare.

Injuries in the Salter-Harris classification system become progressively more serious as the corresponding type number increases. Types III and IV involve fractures of the bone's articular surface and usually require surgical repair. Type V injuries represent a compression of the growth plate and carry the highest incidence of premature closure and growth arrest. Over the years another type of growth plate injury has been recognized. Chronic, repetitive axial loading of a physis may lead to microvascular injury and resultant growth arrest. This injury is most commonly seen in gymnasts, who present with radial deviation of their hands secondary to overgrowth of the ulna as compared with the shortened radius.

Over the past several decades, a number of physeal injury classification systems have arisen. While the Salter-Harris system has stood the test of time and remains the most commonly used system, it does not adequately describe all possible fracture variants. Therefore, two additional physeal injuries deserve special mention. Rang and Ogden (1981) described an injury that may occur at the perichondral of the physis (Figure 20.3). In the early 1990s, Peterson (1994) proposed a classification system with many similarities to the Salter-Harris scheme. His main addition was that of the Peterson type I fracture—a transverse fracture of the metaphysis with a longitudinal extension into the physis, often seen in the distal radius (Figure 20.4).

apophysitis Inflammation of an apophysis.

WHAT IF?

A 15-year-old tackle football player, a linebacker, limps severely toward the sideline after having been involved in a tackle during a scrimmage. You remove his shoe, sock, and the athletic tape from his ankle. You note that he reports having felt his ankle twist severely, and that he experienced a popping, or "letting go" feeling, when the injury occurred. He has a full range of motion when compared with his other foot; however, he is extremely point tender over the area of the anterior talofibular ligament, as well as over the lateral malleolus. This pain was made worse by asking him to simply stand on the injured ankle. Based on the information presented in this chapter, what would you conclude are possible injuries given this athlete's injury history, signs, and symptoms?

Growth Cartilage

The articular surfaces of all bones are covered with cartilage. Immature growth cartilage differs biomechanically and biologically from that found in adults. As well as providing a low-friction articulating surface, cartilage acts to absorb and disperse forces in weight-bearing joints. Growth cartilage may be somewhat softer than its adult equivalent and subjects the underlying tissues to damage. Though less common than the two injury patterns mentioned earlier, injuries do occur. The primary example is osteochondritis of the radial head capitellum, found in Little League elbow (see Chapter 12). Such injuries may impart long-term damage to the articular cartilage.

Contributors to Injury

Sports medicine specialists nationwide are in agreement that sports-related injuries among adolescents and children have risen dramatically over the past two decades. Multiple factors are responsible for the rise and are most easily categorized as intrinsic and extrinsic contributors to injury. Though multiple factors exist, we will concentrate our discussion on those believed to be most important and amenable to change. It must also be remembered that many injuries are the result of a combination of factors rather than a single entity.

Intrinsic Factors

The most important intrinsic factor involved in youth sports injuries is the growing body itself. The susceptibility to injury of growth cartilage and the decreased flexibility of the muscle–tendon unit represent factors that are under only limited control.

Extrinsic Factors
Cultural Deconditioning

Despite record numbers of youngsters involved in organized sports, obesity among youths continues to rise. The degree of obesity in children and adolescents has been directly correlated to the amount of television watched by kids in the past; video games and computers have only worsened this trend. Concomitantly, *free play*, the spontaneous physical activity of childhood, has continued to decline. Along with the decrease in free play, simple activities such as walking to school or bicycling from one destination to another have also declined. At the time of its origin, organized youth activity was intended to be an adjunct to free play. Unfortunately, organized sports have become the basis of physical activity for most children. Therefore, we now see young athletes enter into sports with no underlying base of physical fitness, leaving them prone to acute and chronic injury.

WHAT IF?

A 14-year-old female cross-country runner has been complaining to you for the past week about hip pain. She reports that these symptoms began shortly after the team began running high-intensity sprint practice that included extremely explosive sprints with emphasis placed on driving the knees as high as possible. When asked to point to where the pain is most severe, she points to the area of the anterior superior iliac spine on her right hip. In addition, she reports that simply raising up her right leg, as if to bring her knee toward her face, causes considerable pain at that same site. Based on the information presented in this chapter, what would you conclude are possible injuries given this athlete's injury history, signs, and symptoms?

Training Error

There is no more important figure in the life of any young athlete than his or her coach. Unfortunately, there is a nationwide shortage of qualified individuals to fulfill these vital roles, as the need for coaches has quadrupled over the past 20 years. Over three quarters of all youth sports coaches have no formal training. As a result, many young athletes are never taught proper preseason conditioning methods, nor do they learn the basic fundamentals vital to their sport. In addition, athletes and coaches alike fall prey to the "more is better" philosophy of training, attempting to accomplish too much, too soon in an attempt to improve, but setting the stage for injury instead.

Formally trained or not, many coaches simply do not have the requisite knowledge base for instructing young athletes on the principles of sport techniques or conditioning. Volunteers without formal training often base their coaching style and teaching of fundamentals on personal experiences. Even trained coaches will likely have learned many of the technical aspects of their job by observing and listening to other coaches. Both of these styles of acquiring knowledge are prone to misinformation, with improper theory being perpetuated for years. Weight training (discussed in further detail later in the chapter) is a particularly important area where improper training can lead to serious injury.

Equipment

Although less important than the factors previously discussed, athletic equipment can play a role in injury. Football helmets must be up to current standards and fit properly. Shoulder pads also must be of the correct size and fit. Proper footwear can play a significant role in lower-extremity injuries among young distance runners. Footwear should be inspected for the quality of the impact absorption material, good fit, and ability to compensate for alignment changes, particularly during heel strike.

Playing Surfaces

The condition of athletic fields at the high school and youth sports levels may range from near professional quality to abysmal. All playing surfaces should be inspected prior to events to search for potential hazards such as sprinkler heads, holes, and other hazardous objects.

Injury Imitators

Any discussion of adolescent musculoskeletal injuries must include a review of pathologic conditions that may initially present with similar physical findings to common injuries. An old medical axiom is that "common illnesses happen commonly." However, we must always consider common presentations of uncommon conditions. This section briefly reviews some serious medical conditions that may be initially confused with musculoskeletal trauma. When evaluating injured adolescents, one must bear in mind three principles regarding such conditions:

1. *Physical findings inconsistent with injury history:* In general, the extent of the physical findings should be comparable to the severity of the injury described by the athlete or witnessed by others. Finding a complete rupture of the anterior talofibular ligament following an ankle inversion is consistent. Severe tenderness, edema, and erythema of the entire foot 2 to 3 days after a similar injury does not make sense. Additionally, absence of any trauma history coupled with physical exam findings consistent with injury (swelling, erythema, tenderness) should especially raise concerns for a more serious underlying pathologic process.

2. *Unusual local symptoms:* Exquisite tenderness, erythema, or pain out of proportion to the injury mechanism should all raise suspicion for other pathology. Severe night pain and pain on awakening in the morning are also unusual aspects of typical musculoskeletal injuries that should be further investigated.

3. *Systemic symptoms:* A young athlete with musculoskeletal complaints coupled with any combination of fevers, weight loss, night sweats, nausea, or vomiting requires urgent medical attention and a thorough evaluation.

Oncologic

Adolescence is the peak age for occurrence of long bone tumors. Such tumors are rare, yet their onset is typically insidious and the symptoms may be mistaken for a traumatic etiology early on in the course of illness. Unfortunately, delay in treatment can decrease chances for survival. Bone tumors often result in local pain, tenderness, edema, and night pain. Other complaints may include fever and weight loss. Osteosarcomas most commonly arise in the metaphyses of the femur, tibia, and humerus. Ewing's sarcoma is typically found in the midshaft of long bones, but also may arise in the pelvis. Diagnosis is made by plain radiographs and confirmed by biopsy. Treatment for each consists of tumor excision and intensive chemotherapy. Five-year survival rates are near 80%.

Rheumatologic

When an athlete presents with complaints of pain or swelling in more than one joint, particularly in the absence of trauma, a diagnosis of juvenile rheumatoid arthritis (JRA) must be considered. Pauciarticular JRA presents with involvement of only a few joints, typically of the lower limbs. Affected individuals initially complain of pain and stiffness on awakening in the morning, with symptoms improving with increased activity. Symptoms are progressive. There may also be inflammation of the sacroiliac joint. Though a thorough review of JRA is beyond the scope of our discussion, it may result in severe low back and lower extremity pain, disability, and additional systemic symptoms (fever, rash). Diagnosis is made by clinical history and blood testing.

Infectious

Variations in the blood supply to the joints and physes make young athletes more susceptible to bone and joint infections than their adult counterparts. Bone infections (osteomyelitis) may present similarly to bone tumors, with fevers being more common in infection. Plain radiographs are normal early in the course, with diagnosis typically made by bone scan or magnetic resonance imaging (MRI). Infections are treated with 4 to 6 weeks of antibiotics, usually intravenously. Adolescents are also at risk for localized muscle infections. Pyomyositis results from bacterial invasion of the muscle tissue. Symptoms include fever, pain, and local tenderness. Diagnosis may be made by MRI. Treatment typically requires surgical drainage and 4 to 6 weeks of intravenous antibiotics. Lyme disease may also present with joint involvement and other systemic symptoms; it is discussed in more detail in Chapter 19.

Neurovascular

Reflex neuropathic dystrophy (RND) merits discussion, because early intervention and treatment greatly aid in the resolution of symptoms. Though the exact pathogenesis is unknown, there is usually some degree of psychogenic overlay. Most common in girls between the ages of 9 and 16 years, RND is preceded by minor injury about half of the time and usually involves the lower extremities. Severe pain and dysfunction are the predominant presenting complaints. Physical findings include marked tenderness (hyperesthesia) and signs of local autonomic dysfunction, which may include cyanosis, coolness, diffuse edema, or increased perspiration. Laboratory tests are usually inconclusive. Once the diagnosis is made, patients are placed in an aggressive physical therapy program to regain function of the affected extremity. Treatment may also include individual or family counseling.

Psychologic

All members of the sports medicine team are familiar with athletes who malinger or seek secondary gain from their injuries. However, coaches and athletic trainers must also watch for the subtle signs of depression. Athletes presenting with a continuum of seemingly minor, yet troublesome, injuries should be further questioned about sleep habits, activities, and mood. An athlete's endorsement of symptoms such as poor sleep, early awakening, abandonment of pleasurable activities (anhedonia), and feelings of worthlessness indicate potential depression, and referral to a physician, psychologist, or school counselor is mandatory.

Strength Training

Adolescent strength training has become increasingly popular in recent years. Long thought of as being unnecessary, or even harmful, weight training for adolescents and preadolescents has come under a new focus with concentration on benefits, safety, and the appropriate age at which to begin participation. Studies examining the incidence and type of injuries incurred while weight training have shown varying results. Though a single study of young power lifters found a high injury rate, other studies have found rather low rates of injuries among young weight trainers. The former study's high injury rate may have resulted from improper supervision in combination with the nature of the sport—single lifts with maximum weight.

A concern in adolescent weight training is that skeletal immaturity may allow for growth plate injuries to occur. Although there have been reports of growth plate injury caused by weight training, many of these injuries were felt to be caused primarily by unsupervised training programs and the need to lift maximal weights. Because of this potential risk, the American Academy of Pediatrics (AAP) issued rather restrictive guidelines for adolescent weight training. The guidelines called for close supervision by knowledgeable coaches and medical professionals for children and adolescents who strength train; however, they also advised that adolescents reach Tanner stage 5 of sexual maturity before participating in vigorous weight training.

Besides being overly cautious, the AAP guidelines present a potential obstacle. For many coaches and strength specialists, attempting to determine whether or not an athlete has reached Tanner stage 5 can be confusing and possibly present legal concerns. There is a large body of literature supporting the initiation of resistance training at much younger stages of development with little or no risk of injury. Therefore, a simpler approach should be employed. Children should begin a strength training program if they have the desire to do so, are receptive to coaching, and can follow instructions. If a child is not coachable or loses interest in strength training, the program should be discontinued.

As with any sport, potential risks do exist, but strength training can be beneficial for children and adolescents. Before puberty, many of the gains achieved through strength training are attributable to neuromuscular adaptations. These adaptations may allow the young athlete to achieve greater and faster hypertrophy in the postpubertal stages because of the learning that occurred in the prepubertal stages.

Can strength training prevent injury? As mentioned, strength training increases neuromuscular coordination as well as muscle mass and strength. Assuming all other variables are equal, these neuromuscular adaptations may allow young athletes to perform better at their chosen sports. Also, these adaptations may make the young athlete less susceptible to the microtrauma of overuse injuries. Strength training should not be expected to prevent all serious acute injuries that are inherent in sports, but it may lessen the athlete's risk for injury.

Safety

Safety should be the focus of all adolescent weight-training programs. The main way to avoid injury is to provide the young athletes with proper supervision and guidelines. Other possible strategies may include, but are not limited to, eliminating use of single-repetition maximum lifts, limiting the use of Olympic and power-lifting techniques, and offering safer alternative techniques for lifting.

One area of concern with the adolescent population and strength training is the obsession with the measurement of strength. The predominant way to measure strength is through the use of the one-repetition maximum lift (1 RM). This technique is commonly used in squatting, the bench press, and other Olympic or power-lifting lifts. The 1 RM consists of a one-time maximal exertion of force used to move the weight. This one-time effort requires near-perfect execution of form and puts an inordinate amount of stress on the body. In adult populations this may be a valid and accurate way to assess strength, but not for adolescents. Their limited amount of training with regard to maintaining appropriate technique, combined with skeletal immaturity, may predispose them to injury while performing the 1 RM.

There are better and safer ways to assess an adolescent's strength. One such technique is to use a 1-RM equivalent. This would allow the athlete to estimate/assess maximum strength without the increased chance of injury. Example: (weight lifted × number of repetitions × 0.03) + weight lifted = 1 RM. Although this technique is not precise with regard to Olympic or power-lifting standards, it does provide a safer alternative for assessing strength in adolescent populations.

Another way to limit injury is to avoid placing the body in positions that may put the joints and limbs at a mechanical disadvantage, which increases the risk for injury. Following are four examples of safe lifting techniques.

Lat Pull Down
Problem

When the weight is pulled behind the neck, the neck is placed in excessive flexion, and the shoulder joints are loaded at the extreme of external rotation. Also, the line of pull with relation to the bar and the latissimus muscle is such that this position does not oppose the latissimus dorsi, thus not providing quality resistance.

Solution

A safer way to perform this exercise is to sit down with the bar directly overhead. Grabbing the bar with the hands approximately shoulder width apart, the athlete should lean back slightly so the bar just passes in front of the head, pulling the bar straight down in front of the head to chin level. This will allow for a more optimal line of pull on the latissimus dorsi and decrease stress on the shoulder joint. The torso should not rock back and forth while performing this exercise to avoid low back injury.

Bench Press
Problem

Hyperextension of the shoulders (dropping the bar to the chest or the elbows behind the plane of the body) puts the pectoralis major at a mechanical disadvantage, contributes to shoulder instability, and puts excessive stress on the acromioclavicular joint.

Solution

A safer way to perform this exercise is to keep the elbows even with the plane of the body (do not drop elbows beyond the level of the chest walls). This will decrease stress on the shoulder joint and allow for a better mechanical advantage, thus providing better resistance for the muscle. To ensure proper depth of the elbows, the use of a partner to watch elbow depth is beneficial. Once proper depth has been achieved, a towel placed on the chest may be used as a reminder. As the bar touches the towel, the push phase of the movement begins. When performing the chest press (or any exercise), control of the weight must be maintained. The bar should never be bounced off the chest.

Military Press

Problem

Extreme shoulder external rotation and abduction during a behind-the-neck military press puts stress on the shoulder capsule, contributing to shoulder instability.

Solution

A safer way to perform this exercise and eliminate these stresses is to do the military press in the front of the head. Also, by not allowing the shoulder to drop below 60° abduction, the deltoid muscle moves the weight through the range of motion without putting undue stress on the rotator cuff.

Squats

Problem

When performing a squat in which the thighs are parallel or lower to the floor, there is an excessive amount of shear force on the knee in a position where the articular cartilage is thinnest.

Solution

When weight training, the individual should avoid deep squats and maintain lumbar spine stability. Alternative lifts to the squat may include the leg press and the box squat. When employing the box squat, the box must only be used as a guide for appropriate depth of movement. The box itself should never be used to drop down to and rest on or bounce off of to gain momentum. When performing the leg press, the depth of the movement should entail not allowing the knees to be bent at greater than a 90° angle.

Adolescent weight training, like any activity, has the potential to result in musculoskeletal injury. However, the rate of injury does not seem to be any higher than that of other activities adolescents participate in on a daily basis. Through proper teaching, close supervision, adherence to suggested guidelines, and avoidance of one-repetition maximums, the low rate of injuries can be further lessened. Strength training is a safe and beneficial means of exercise for adolescent populations.

Prevention of Injury

Though all sports activities carry an inherent risk of injury, certain principles can be applied that will help lessen the number of injuries sustained. Strength and conditioning techniques have already been covered, and multiple studies show the benefits of such training for athletes of all ages. Other important areas of intervention include the following.

Preparticipation Physical Examination

All athletes should have a complete evaluation prior to their entry into organized sports. The preparticipation physical examination (PPE) is not intended to be a comprehensive medical examination but should be focused on sports participation. Particular attention should be paid to previous musculoskeletal injuries, as there is a high rate of recurrence if they have not been properly rehabilitated. Ideally, the exam should be conducted by a physician with training and specific knowledge in the adolescent athlete population (see Chapter 4). Though much attention has been placed on the detection of cardiovascular conditions that may result in sudden cardiac death, the American Heart Association does not endorse the routine use of echocardiograms or echocardiography as screening tools unless indicated by history or physical examination (Maron et al., 1996).

Rehabilitation of Previous Injuries

The relative lack of medical care for young athletes has resulted in injuries going undiagnosed and in diagnosed injuries not being properly rehabilitated. When an athlete is injured, he or she is highly susceptible to reinjury of that limb or joint over the next several years. New evidence suggests that improperly rehabilitated injuries may increase the risk for osteoarthritis years after the initial insult. Many of these "old injuries" can be assessed during the PPE, but coaches and athletic trainers must ensure that all injuries receive proper initial and follow-up care.

Stretching Programs

As we have discussed, muscles lengthen in response to longitudinal bone growth. Therefore, to lessen injury and improve overall flexibility, stretching and flexibility exercises should be a routine part of all conditioning programs prior to and during the sports season. Major muscle groups, including the quadriceps, hamstrings, and low back, should be targeted.

Coaching Techniques

Coaches can play a valuable role in the prevention of acute and chronic injuries among their young athletes. However, they must be knowledgeable in the fundamental techniques of their sport as well as know the proper principles of strength and conditioning. A basic understanding of the anatomical variations of young athletes is also helpful.

The overall training load and the progression toward more intense training early in the course of a sports season are major determinants in the development of overuse injuries, along with other factors previously discussed. In addition to placing increased stress on the muscles and joints, the body is more likely to fatigue, thus compromising form and technique. This increases the risk of injury even more. An increase in total training volume or intensity of no more than 10% per week has been suggested to provide coaches with a model of how to limit injury risk. For example, a young distance runner who begins the week running 3 miles per day would increase that to no more than 3.3 miles the next week. The same principle can be applied to young pitchers, swimmers, or gymnasts in regard to the overall length of their training sessions.

Female Athletes

At the time of the PPE, or if appropriate for a specific injury or complaint, a detailed menstrual history should be obtained from all female athletes. Any history of primary amenorrhea (absence of menses by age 16) or secondary amenorrhea (absence of menses for more than three consecutive cycles after regular monthly cycles have become established) should be further explored. Many female athletes believe that menstrual irregularities (absent menses or scant flow) during their competitive season are normal and will not perceive them as a problem unless specifically questioned. Such irregularity is typically indicative of poor nutritional intake, often the result of burning more calories than are being consumed. This energy (calorie) deficit may be unintentional (poor eating habits) or intentional (disordered eating).

Female athletes with a history of primary or secondary amenorrhea should be evaluated by a physician. Nutrition education or referral to a nutritionist may also be appropriate. Any history of previous stress fractures should also prompt a thorough training history (overload, poor technique, "too much, too soon") and a review of menstrual history and nutritional intake because such injuries should raise suspicion for the presence of the female athlete triad (anorexia, amenorrhea, and osteoporosis).

Prescription Stimulant Medications

The increasing use of stimulant medications for the treatment of attention deficit hyperactivity disorder (ADHD) is an emerging area of uncertainty in the sports medicine field. The majority of ADHD medications (Ritalin, Dexedrine, Adderall) are amphetamine derivatives and, therefore, are banned by the NCAA and IOC. In addition to the benefits seen in the classroom, when given appropriate medication young athletes with ADHD also show increased ability to concentrate on tasks during athletic practices, along with improvements in balance and coordination (perhaps secondary to improved concentration) (Hickey & Fricker, 1999). The ergogenic effects of these medications on this population are not known. Currently, athletes with ADHD should continue to take their medications as prescribed, regardless of athletic activity. Unfortunately, it seems likely that over time the potential for performance enhancement may lead to abuse of these medications. Future research should further define the ergogenic potency of these medications within the ADHD population.

REVIEW QUESTIONS

1. Females in organized sports have an estimated rate of 20 to 22 injuries per 100 participants. What is the figure for males?

2. What does research indicate is the primary motivating factor for children to engage in organized sports?

3. What is the most common cause reported for withdrawing from sports among high school students?

4. On average, boys will see how much of an increase in muscle mass between the ages of 10 and 17 years?

5. What is the anatomic term for the point on a long bone where large muscle–tendon units attach?

6. *True or false:* Changes in bone length occur more slowly than length changes in muscle–tendon structures.

7. What is the technical term for a growth plate?

8. *True or false:* Severe ligament injuries are more common in children than in adults.

9. The term *Salter-Harris fracture* refers to a type of fracture classification of what specific anatomic structure?

10. According to the text, what is the most important intrinsic factor related to youth sports injuries?

11. Define the term *cultural deconditioning* and describe how it contributed to sports injury.

12. What is the proportion of youth sport coaches that have no formal training?

13. Define the terms *osteomyelitis* and *pyomyositis*.

14. Explain briefly the guidelines on adolescent strength training in children that were presented by the American Academy of Pediatrics.

15. Using the 1-RM equivalent equation presented in the text, calculate the 1-RM equivalent for 120 pounds lifted for 10 repetitions on the bench press.

SUGGESTED READINGS

Abbassi V. (1998). Growth and normal puberty. *Pediatrics.* 102:507–511.

Faigenbaum AD, Micheli LJ. (2000). Preseason conditioning for the preadolescent athlete. *Pediatr Annals.* 29:156–161.

Koester MC. (2000). Youth sports: A pediatrician's perspective on coaching and injury prevention. *J Ath Training.* 35:466–470.

Micheli LJ. (1994). The child and adolescent. In Harries M, Williams C, Stanish WD, Micheli LJ (eds.). *Oxford Text-book of Sports Medicine* (pp. 646–652). New York: Oxford University Press.

Risser WL, Risser JM, Preston D. (1990). Weight-training injuries in adolescents. *Am J Dis Child.* 144:1015–1017.

Szer IS. (1996). Musculoskeletal pain syndromes that affect adolescents. *Arch Pediatr Adolesc Med.* 150:740–747.

Webb D. (1990). Strength training in children and adolescents. *Pediatr Clin North Am.* 37:1187–1207.

REFERENCES

Hickey G, Fricker P. (1999). Attention deficit hyperactivity disorder, CNS stimulants and sport. *Sports Med.* 27(1):11–21.

Maron BJ, et al. (1996). Cardiovascular preparticipation screening of competitive athletes. *Circulation.* 94(4):850–856.

Osgood RB. (1903). Tibial tubercle occurring during adolescence. *Boston Med Sci Journal.* 148:114.

Peterson HA. (1994). Physeal fractures. Part 3. Classification. *J Pediatr Orthop.* 14:439.

Rang M, Ogden JA. (1981). Injury to the growth mechanism of the immature skeleton. *Skeletal Radiol.* 6:237.

Salter RB, Harris WR. (1963). Injuries involving the epiphyseal plate. *J Bone Joint Surg.* 45A:587–622.

Appendix 1

CPR

Background Information

What Is CPR?

Cardiopulmonary resuscitation (CPR) combines rescue breathing (also known as mouth-to-mouth) and external chest compressions. *Cardio* refers to the heart and *pulmonary* refers to the lungs. *Resuscitation* means to revive. Proper and prompt CPR serves as a holding action by providing oxygen to the brain and heart until advanced cardiac life support can be provided.

When to Start CPR

Trained people need to be able to

- recognize the signs of cardiac arrest,
- provide CPR, and
- call for emergency medical services.

About two thirds of deaths that are the result of a heart attack in a nonhospital setting occur within 2 hours of the first signs and symptoms.
  Victims have a good chance of surviving if

- CPR is started with the first 4 minutes of heart stoppage, and
- they receive advanced cardiac life support within the next 4 minutes.

Brain damage usually begins within 4–6 minutes after the heart stops and is certain after 10 minutes when no CPR is given.

Start CPR as soon as possible!

EMS System

The emergency medical services (EMS) system consists of several components:

- First responders (law enforcement agency or fire service members or others designated in industry, government, and the private sector)

For more information go to
http://www.ECSInstitute.org.

- EMS dispatcher located at the local emergency communications center
- Emergency medical technicians (EMTs) with various levels of training working with well-equipped emergency vehicles
- Hospital emergency department staff (e.g., physicians, nurses)

EMS Telephone Numbers

Activate the EMS system by using

- 9-1-1 (covers majority of people in the United States), or
- seven-digit local number found on the inside front cover of the telephone directory because not all communities have 9-1-1, or
- 0 (zero or operator) as a last resort if unable to use the other numbers.

What Information to Give

Give the following to the EMS dispatcher:

- **The victim's location.** Give address, names of intersecting streets or roads, and other landmarks if possible.
- **Telephone number you are calling from.** This prevents false calls and also allows the center to call back for additional information if needed.
- **What happened.** Tell the nature of the emergency (e.g., heart attack, drowning, etc.).
- **Number of persons needing help and any special conditions.**
- **The victim's condition** (e.g., conscious, breathing, etc.) **and what is being done for the victim** (tell about CPR, rescue breathing).

Hang up the phone only after the dispatcher tells you to do so.

Disease Precautions
Disease Precautions During CPR Training

- There is concern about contracting diseases, such as HIV, which results in AIDS; hepatitis B virus (HBV); and respiratory tract infections (e.g., influenza, mononucleosis, and tuberculosis) from a CPR manikin during CPR training.
- CPR classes should follow the manikin manufacturers' recommendations for using and maintaining their manikins.
- The viral agent causing AIDS, known as HIV, is delicate and is inactivated in less than 10 minutes at room temperature by several kinds of disinfectants used for cleaning manikins.

Disease Precautions During Actual CPR

- Laypersons are most likely to perform CPR in the home and will usually know the health status of the victim.
- It should be assumed that certain body fluids may have the potential to spread disease either to the victim or the rescuer.
- HBV-positive saliva has not been shown to be infectious. A theoretical risk of HIV and HBV spread exists during rescue breathing if either the victim or rescuer has breaks in the skin, on or around the lips, or inside the mouth.
- Transmission of HBV and HIV infection during rescue breathing has not been documented.
- The Centers for Disease Control (CDC) and the Occupational Safety and Health Administration (OSHA) constructed guidelines that include the use of medical exam gloves and resuscitation masks with valves capable of diverting exhaled air from contacting the rescuer.
- Rescuers should not fear the transmission of a disease, but many may be unwilling to help a person in need because of that fear. Rescuers should learn how to use a mouth-to-barrier device (face mask or face shield).
- Two types of mouth-to-barrier devices exist:

1. **Mask devices.** These have a one-way valve so that exhaled air does not enter the rescuer's mouth. Those without one-way valves offer little protection.
2. **Face shields.** These have no exhalation valve, and air can leak around the shield.

- If a rescuer cannot start rescue breathing, he or she should at least

1. activate the EMS system,
2. open airway, and
3. give chest compressions until another rescuer arrives who will give rescue breathing.

When to Stop CPR

- Victim revives (regains pulse and breathing). Though revival is hoped for, most victims also require advanced cardiac procedures before ever regaining their heart and lung functions.
- Another trained rescuer or EMS professional takes over.
- Too exhausted to continue.
- Scene becomes unsafe for the rescuer.
- A physician tells you to stop.
- Cardiac arrest lasting longer than 30 minutes (with or without CPR except in cases of severe or profound hypothermia). This is a National Association of EMS Physicians' recommendation.

How Can an Untrained Rescuer Help?

Untrained rescuers can help by

- going for help,
- checking breathing and pulse following directions from a trained rescuer, and
- performing CPR following directions from a trained rescuer.

If exhausted, an untrained rescuer can give chest compressions while the trained rescuer gives rescue breaths. Tell the untrained rescuer to watch how to

- find hand position;
- keep fingers off victim's chest;
- keep arms straight and shoulders over victim's chest; and
- perform chest compressions, stop while trained rescuer gives breaths, then start another cycle of chest compressions and breaths.

If the untrained rescuer adequately performs chest compressions, allow him or her to continue helping you.

Precautions During Training

- Do not practice mouth-to-mouth resuscitation on people—practice on a manikin.
- Do not practice chest compressions on people—practice on a manikin.

- Do not practice abdominal or chest thrusts on people.
- Wash your hands before class.
- Clean the manikin before using it according to your instructor's directions (use either a solution of liquid bleach and water or rubbing alcohol).
- Do not put anything (chewing gum, food, drink, tobacco) in your mouth when manikins are being used.

Disease Precautions During CPR Training

Do *not* use a training manikin *if* you have any of the following:

- Sores on the hands, lips, or face (such as a cold sore)
- An upper respiratory infection (such as a cold or sore throat)
- Known positive hepatitis B virus
- Been infected by HIV or have AIDS
- An infection or recent exposure to an infectious source

Clean manikin between each student use:

1. Scrub the manikin's entire face and inside of mouth vigorously with a 4" × 4" gauze pad wet with 70% alcohol (isopropanol or ethanol).
2. Place the wet gauze pad over the manikin's mouth and nose for at least 30 seconds.
3. Allow manikin's face to dry.

During training, students should practice and become familiar with mouth-to-barrier devices.

CPR Performance Mistakes

Rescue breathing mistakes:

- Inadequate head tilt, airway not open
- Failing to pinch nose shut
- Not giving full breaths
- Too fast or too forceful
- Failing to watch chest and listen for exhalation
- Failing to maintain tight seal around victim's mouth (and/or nose)

Chest compression mistakes:

- Pivoting at knees instead of hips (rocking motion)
- Wrong compression site
- Bending elbows
- Shoulders not above sternum (arms not vertical)
- Fingers touching chest
- Heel of bottom hand not in line with sternum
- Quick, stabbing compressions
- Hand not staying in contact with chest between each compression

Dangerous Complications

- Vomiting may occur during CPR. If it happens, it is usually before CPR has begun or within the first minute after beginning CPR. Inhaling vomit (aspiration) into the lungs can produce a type of pneumonia that can kill even after successful rescue efforts. Vomiting happens at death or near death.

In case of vomiting:

1. Turn victim onto his or her side and keep him or her there until vomiting ends.
2. Wipe vomit out of victim's mouth with your fingers wrapped in a cloth to quickly clear the airway.
3. Reposition victim onto his or her back and resume rescue breathing/CPR if needed.

- Stomach (gastric) distention describes stomach bulging from air, especially common in children.

1. Caused by
   a. Rescue breaths given too fast
   b. Rescue breaths given too forcefully
   c. Partially or completely blocked airway
2. Dangerous because
   a. air in stomach pushes against lungs, making it difficult or impossible to give full breaths; and
   b. possibility of inhaling vomit into the lungs.
3. Prevent or minimize by doing the following:
   a. Try to blow just hard enough to make the chest rise.
   b. Retilt head to open airway.
   c. Use mouth-to-nose method.
   d. Do **not** try to push air out of stomach. Retilt the head and continue slow rescue breathing. If victim vomits, turn victim on his or her side, clean out mouth with your fingers covered by a cloth, roll victim onto back, and continue rescue efforts.

- Inhalation of foreign substances (known as aspiration).

1. Particulate matter aspiration—can stop up airway.

2. Nongastric liquid aspiration—mainly a result of fresh- and saltwater drowning.

3. Gastric acid aspiration—effects of gastric acid on lung tissue can be equated with a chemical burn.

- Help prevent vomiting by placing a nonbreathing victim on his or her left side. This position keeps the stomach from spilling contents into the esophagus by keeping the bottom end of the esophagus above the stomach.

- Chest compression–related injuries can happen even with proper compressions.

Injuries may include

1. Rib fractures

2. Rib separation

3. Bruised lung

4. Lung, liver, and spleen lacerations

To prevent or minimize:

1. Use proper hand location on chest—if too low, the sternum's tip can cut into the liver.

2. Keep fingers off victim's ribs by interlocking fingers.

3. Press straight down instead of sideways.

4. Give smooth, regular, and uninterrupted (except when breathing) compressions. Avoid sudden, jerking, jabbing, or stabbing compressions.

5. Avoid pressing chest too deeply.

- Dentures, loose or broken teeth, or dental appliances. Leave tight-fitting dentures in place to support victim's mouth during rescue breathing. Remove loose or broken teeth, dentures, and/or dental appliances.

One-Rescuer Adult CPR

If you are the only trained person at the scene, you must perform one-rescuer CPR.

When performing one-rescuer CPR—whether the patient is an adult, child, or infant—you must deliver chest compressions and rescue breathing at a ratio of 30 compressions to two breaths. Immediately give two rescue breaths after each set of 30 chest compressions. Because

ONE-RESCUER ADULT CPR

1

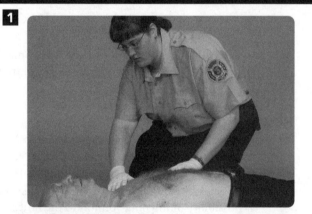

Establish the patient's level of consciousness. Ask the patient, "Are you okay?" Gently shake the patient's shoulder. If there is no response, call for additional help by activating the EMS system. (Even if you are alone, phone 9-1-1 before you begin CPR.) Turn the patient on his or her back, supporting the head and neck as you do.

2

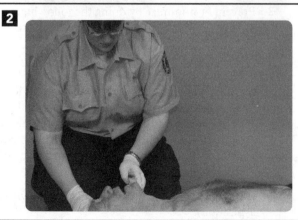

Open the airway. Use the head tilt–chin lift maneuver or, if the patient is injured, use the jaw-thrust maneuver. If the jaw-thrust maneuver does not adequately open the airway, carefully perform the head tilt–chin lift maneuver. Maintain the open airway.

3

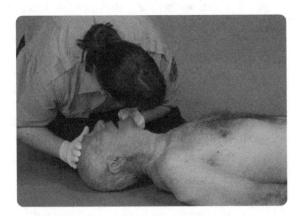

Check for breathing. Place the side of your face and your ear close to the nose and mouth of the patient. Look, listen, and feel for the movement of air: Look for movement of the chest, listen for sounds of air exchange, and feel for air movement on the side of your face. Your breathing check should last at least 5 seconds but no longer than 10 seconds. If there are no signs of breathing, begin rescue breathing. Use a mouth-to-mask ventilation device, if one is available, or place your mouth over the patient's mouth, seal the patient's nose with your thumb and index finger, and begin mouth-to-mouth rescue breathing.

4

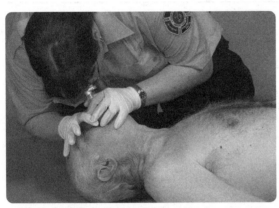

Give two breaths. Blow slowly for 1 second using just enough force to make the chest visibly rise. Allow the lungs to deflate between breaths.

5

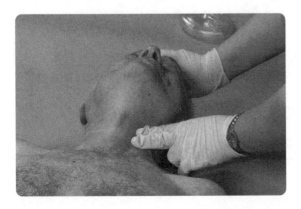

Check for signs of circulation by checking the carotid pulse and looking for signs of coughing or movement. Find the carotid pulse by locating the patient's larynx with your index and middle fingers, then sliding your fingers into the groove between the larynx and the muscles at the side of the neck. Check for at least 5 seconds but no more than 10 seconds. If the pulse is absent, proceed to the next step. If the pulse is present, continue rescue breathing every 5 to 6 seconds (10 to 12 breaths per minute).

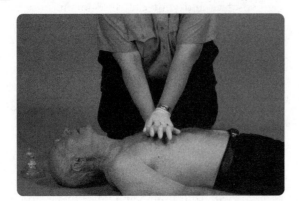

6

Begin chest compressions. Place the heel of one hand in the center of the patient's chest, in between the nipples. Place the other hand on top of the first, so the hands are parallel. Now press down to compress the chest about 1½ to 2 inches. Apply 30 compressions at the rate of 100 compressions per minute. Count the compressions out loud: "One and two and three and." After 30 chest compressions, give two rescue breaths. Continue alternating compressions and ventilations. Deliver a sequence of 30 compressions followed by two ventilations. After five cycles of CPR (about 2 minutes), check the carotid pulse. If there is no pulse, continue CPR and recheck the patient in 2 minutes.

One-Rescuer Adult CPR

Steps	Adequately Performed
1. Establish unresponsiveness. Activate the EMS system.	
2. Open airway using head tilt-chin lift maneuver. (If trauma is present, use jaw-thrust maneuver.) Check for breathing (look, listen, and feel).*	
3. Give two slow breaths at 1 second per breath. If chest does not rise, reposition head and try to ventilate again. Watch for chest rise; allow for exhalation between breaths.	
4. Check for signs of circulation. Check carotid pulse and look for signs of coughing and movement. If breathing is absent but pulse is present, provide rescue breathing (one breath every 5 to 6 seconds [10 to 12 breaths per minute]).	
5. If no pulse, give cycles of 30 chest compressions (100 compressions per minute) followed by two slow breaths.	
6. After five cycles of 30 to 2 (about 2 minutes), check pulse.* If no pulse, continue CPR and recheck the patient in 2 minutes.	

*If victim is unresponsive but breathing, place in the recovery position.

Source: Based on the 2005 CPR and ECC guidelines.

FIGURE A1.1 Skill performance sheet.

you must interrupt chest compressions to ventilate, you should perform each series of 30 chest compressions in about 20 seconds (a rate of 100 compressions per minute).

Although one-rescuer CPR can keep the patient alive, two-rescuer CPR is preferable because it is less exhausting for the rescuers. Whenever possible, CPR for an adult should be performed by two rescuers.

Two-Rescuer Adult CPR

In many cases, a second trained person will be on the scene to help you perform CPR. Two-rescuer CPR is more effective than one-rescuer CPR is. One rescuer can deliver chest compressions while the other performs rescue breathing. Chest compressions and ventilations can be given more regularly and without interruption. Two-rescuer CPR is also less tiring for the rescuers. However, to avoid rescuer fatigue—which may result in less effective chest compressions—two rescuers should switch roles after every five cycles of CPR (about every 2 minutes). Two rescuers should be able to switch roles quickly, interrupting CPR for 5 seconds or less. In any circumstance, CPR should not be interrupted for longer than 10 seconds.

In two-rescuer CPR, one rescuer delivers ventilations (mouth-to-mouth or mouth-to-mask breathing) and the other gives chest compressions. If possible, position yourselves on opposite sides of the patient—one near the head and the other near the chest. The sequence of steps is the same as for one-rescuer CPR, but the tasks are divided:

TWO-RESCUER ADULT CPR

1

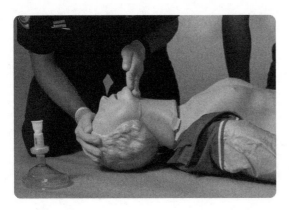

Rescuer One (at the patient's head) determines the patient's level of consciousness by asking, "Are you okay?" If there is no response, the rescuer gently shakes the person's shoulder. Call 9-1-1 to activate the EMS system if the patient is unconscious. If other people are present, ask them to call for EMS. If two rescuers are present, but no bystanders are present, one rescuer should call 9-1-1 as the other continues to assess the patient. Turn the patient on his or her back. Turn the patient as a unit, supporting the head and neck to protect the spine.

2

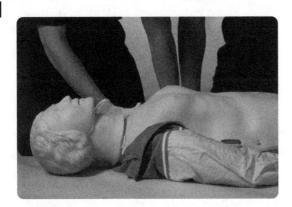

Rescuer One opens the airway using the head tilt–chin lift or jaw-thrust maneuver. If the jaw-thrust maneuver does not adequately open the airway, carefully perform a head tilt–chin lift.

3

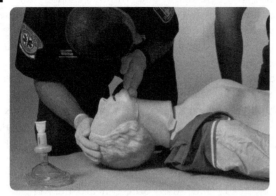

Rescuer One checks for breathing by placing the side of his or her face close to the mouth and nose of the patient to look for chest movements, listen for breathing sounds, and feel for air movement for at least 5 seconds but no more than 10 seconds. If there are no signs of breathing, proceed to the next step.

4

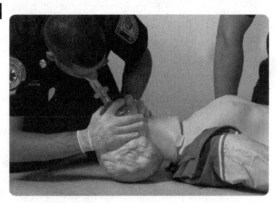

Rescuer One gives two breaths (1 second per breath). Allow time for complete deflation of the lungs between breaths. Rescuer One checks for signs of circulation by checking for the presence of a carotid pulse and looking for signs of coughing and movement. Check the pulse for at least 5 seconds but no more than 10 seconds. If there is no carotid pulse, proceed to the following step.

5

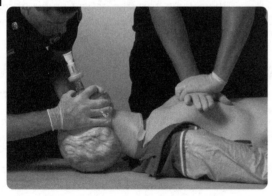

Rescuer Two performs 30 chest compressions at a rate of 100 compressions per minute. Count "one and two and three" to maintain the proper rate of compressions and to let Rescuer One know when to ventilate.

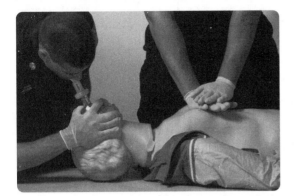

6

After Rescuer Two completes 30 chest compressions, Rescuer One gives two ventilations. Rescuer Two should pause just long enough for Rescuer One to ventilate twice. Periodically, Rescuer One should place his or her fingers on the carotid pulse of the patient as Rescuer Two continues the compressions. If the compressions are being done correctly, Rescuer One should feel a pulse with each compression. This confirms that the CPR is adequate. After five cycles of CPR (about 2 minutes), Rescuer One should ask Rescuer Two to stop compressions as he or she rechecks the patient's pulse. If the patient's heart starts beating on its own, Rescuer One will continue to feel a pulse. In this case, Rescuer Two can stop doing compressions. Rescue breathing should be continued at a rate of 10 to 12 breaths per minute (one breath every 5 to 6 seconds) until spontaneous breathing resumes. If there is no pulse, CPR should be resumed.

Compressions and ventilations should remain rhythmic and uninterrupted. By counting out loud, Rescuer Two can continue to deliver compressions at the rate of 100 per minute, briefly pausing as Rescuer One delivers two rescue breaths. Once you and your partner establish a smooth pattern of CPR, you should limit interruptions in CPR to 10 seconds or less, such as when checking for a pulse or moving the patient.

Early Defibrillation by First Responders

Each year in the United States about 250,000 people die of coronary heart disease in a prehospital setting. More than 70% of all prehospital cardiac arrest patients have an irregular heart electrical rhythm called ventricular fibrillation. This condition, often referred to as V-fib, is the rapid, disorganized, and ineffective vibration of the heart. An electric shock applied to the heart will defibrillate it and reorganize the vibrations into effective heartbeats. A patient in cardiac arrest stands the greatest chance for survival when early defibrillation is available.

A first responder is often the first emergency care provider to reach a patient who has collapsed in cardiac arrest. A first responder who performs effective CPR helps to keep the patient's brain and heart supplied with oxygen until a defibrillator and advanced life support can arrive on the scene.

To get defibrillators to cardiac arrest patients more quickly, increasing numbers of EMS systems are equipping first responders with automated external defibrillators (AEDs) (Figure 13.3). These machines accurately identify ventricular fibrillation and advise you to deliver a shock if needed. Such equipment allows the first responder to combine effective CPR with early defibrillation to restore an organized heartbeat.

AEDs may be appropriate for your community if you work to strengthen all links of the cardiac Chain of Survival. The links of the Chain of Survival include:

- Early recognition of cardiac arrest and activation of the 9-1-1 system
- Early CPR: Early bystander CPR
- Early defibrillation by first responders or other EMS personnel
- Early advanced care by paramedics and hospital personnel

AEDs vary in their operation, and so learn how to use your specific AED. You must have the training required by your medical director in order to practice this procedure. Practice until you can perform the

Two-Rescuer Adult CPR

Steps	Adequately Performed
RESCUER ONE	
1. Establish unresponsiveness. If unresponsive, have someone activate the EMS system if not already done.	
2. Open airway using head tilt-chin lift maneuver. (If trauma is present, use jaw-thrust maneuver.) Check breathing (look, listen, and feel); try to ventilate; if the chest does not rise, reposition head and try to ventilate again.	
3. Give two slow breaths (1 second per breath), watch for chest rise, and allow for deflation between breaths.	
4. Check for circulation. Check carotid pulse and look for signs of coughing and movement.	
RESCUER TWO	
5. If no pulse, give cycles of 30 chest compressions (100 compressions per minute) followed by two slow breaths by Rescuer One.	
RESCUER ONE	
6. After five cycles of CPR (about 2 minutes), check pulse.* If no pulse, continue CPR and recheck the patient in 2 minutes.	

*If victim is unresponsive but breathing, place in the recovery position.
Source: Based on the 2005 CPR and ECC guidelines.

FIGURE A1.2 Skill performance sheet.

procedure quickly and safely. Because the recommended guidelines for performing AED change, always follow the most current Emergency Cardiac Care (ECC) guidelines.

CPR Training

As a first responder, you should successfully complete a CPR course through a recognized agency such as the Emergency Care and Safety Institute (ECSI). You should also regularly update your skills by successfully completing a recognized recertification course. You cannot achieve proficiency in CPR unless you have adequate practice on adult, child, and infant manikins. Your department should schedule periodic reviews of

CPR theory and practice for all people who are trained as first responders.

Legal Implications of CPR

Living wills, advance directives, and Do Not Resuscitate (DNR) orders are legal documents that specify the patient's wishes regarding specified medical procedures. First responders sometimes wonder if they should start CPR on a person who has a living will or an advance directive. Because you are not in a position to determine if the living will or advance directive is valid, CPR should be started on all patients unless signs of obvious death are present (such as rigor

One-Rescuer Child CPR

Steps	Adequately Performed
1. Establish unresponsiveness. If a second rescuer is available, have him or her activate the EMS system.	
2. Open airway using head tilt-chin lift maneuver. (If trauma is present, use jaw-thrust maneuver.) Check breathing (look, listen, and feel).*	
3. Give two effective breaths (1 second per breath); if chest does not rise, reposition head and try to ventilate again. Watch for chest rise; allow for exhalation between breaths.	
4. Check for signs of circulation. Check carotid pulse and look for signs of coughing or movement. If breathing is absent but pulse is present, provide rescue breathing (one breath every 3 to 5 seconds, [12 to 20 breaths per minute]).	
5. If no pulse, perform 30 chest compressions (rate 100 compressions per minute) followed by two slow breaths.	
6. After five cycles of CPR (about 2 minutes), check pulse.* If rescuer is alone, activate the EMS system and return to the patient. If no pulse, continue CPR.	

*If victim is unresponsive but breathing, place in the recovery position.

Source: Based on the 2005 CPR and ECC guidelines.

FIGURE A1.3 Skill performance sheet.

mortis or decapitation). If a patient has a living will or advance directive, the physician at the hospital will determine whether you should stop CPR. Follow your department's protocols regarding advance directives, living wills, and DNR orders.

Do not hesitate to begin CPR on a pulseless, non-breathing patient. Without your help, the patient will certainly die. You may have legal problems if you begin CPR on a patient who does not need it and this action harms the patient. However, the chances of this happening are minimal if you assess the patient carefully before beginning CPR.

Another potential legal pitfall is abandonment—the discontinuation of CPR without the order of a licensed physician or without turning the patient over to someone who is at least as qualified as you are. If you avoid these pitfalls, you need not be overly concerned about the legal implications of performing CPR. Your most important protection against a possible legal suit is to become thoroughly proficient in the theory and practice of CPR.

Management of Foreign Body Airway Obstructions

Airway Obstruction in an Adult

The steps to treat severe airway obstruction vary, depending on whether the patient is conscious or unconscious. If the patient is conscious, stand behind the patient and

EARLY DEFIBRILLATION BY FIRST RESPONDERS

1

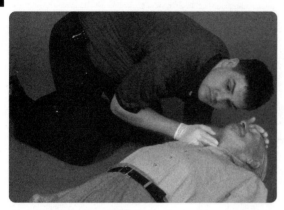

If you arrive on the scene before an AED is available, check the patient for responsiveness, airway, breathing, and circulation. If the patient is unresponsive, is not breathing, and has no pulse, you should begin CPR.

2

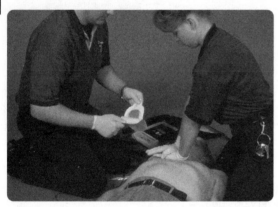

If you arrive with an AED and have been trained in its use, first check the patient for responsiveness, airway, breathing, and circulation. If the patient's cardiac arrest was not witnessed, perform five cycles of CPR (about 2 minutes) before beginning the AED procedure. If the cardiac arrest was witnessed, apply the AED as soon as possible.

3

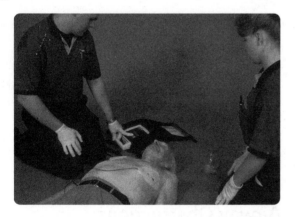

Once the AED is brought to the scene, quickly attach the adhesive electrode pads to the patient. Minimize interruptions in performing CPR.

4

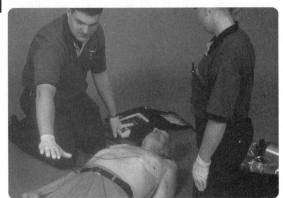

Stop CPR and remove your hands from the patient before you turn on the defibrillator. No one should touch the patient once the machine has been turned on and is analyzing the heart rhythm. Allow the defibrillator to analyze for a shockable rhythm. If a shockable rhythm is found, the machine quickly recommends defibrillation. You should first say, "Clear the patient" and ensure that no one is touching the patient before you press the "shock" button on the defibrillator.

5

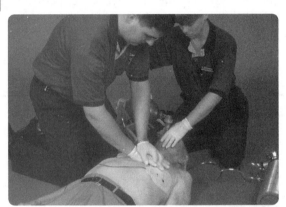

After one shock is delivered, immediately resume CPR. Perform five cycles of CPR (about 2 minutes) starting with chest compressions. Stop CPR and remove your hands from the patient. Press the defibrillator to analyze the heart rhythm. If another shock is recommended, "clear" the patient, and administer another shock. Continue the sequence of five cycles of CPR, analyze, and shock until the defibrillator recommends no further shocks.

6

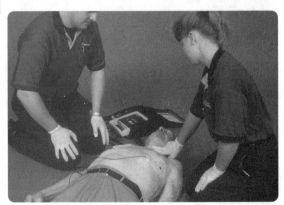

Check the patient's pulse. If a pulse is present, check breathing and support ventilations if necessary. If no pulse, resume five cycles of CPR (about 2 minutes) starting with chest compressions. Check rhythm every five cycles. Continue until adranced life support (ALS) providers take over or the patient starts to move.

If, after five cycles (about 2 minutes) of CPR, the defibrillator advises no shock, check the patient's pulse for at least 5 seconds but no more than 10 seconds. If the pulse is absent, resume CPR. If the pulse is present, check the breathing. Support ventilations if necessary. When advanced life support personnel arrive at the scene, they will assume control and responsibility for the patient's care.

perform the abdominal thrusts while the patient is standing or seated in a chair.

Locate the xiphoid process (the bottom of the sternum) and the navel. Place one fist above the navel and well below the xiphoid process, thumb side against the patient's abdomen. Grasp your fist with your other hand. Then, apply abdominal thrusts sharply and firmly, bringing your fist in and slightly upward. Do not give the patient a bear hug; rather, apply pressure at the point where your fist contacts the patient's abdomen. Each thrust should be distinct and forceful. Repeat these abdominal thrusts until the foreign object is expelled or until the patient becomes unresponsive.

If the patient is obese or in the late stages of pregnancy, use chest thrusts instead of abdominal thrusts. Chest thrusts are done by standing behind the patient and placing your arms under the patient's armpits to encircle the patient's chest. Press with quick backward thrusts.

If the patient becomes unresponsive, ensure that the EMS system has been activated and begin CPR:

- Open the airway by using the head tilt–chin lift maneuver.
- Look into the mouth for any foreign object. Use finger sweeps only if you can see a foreign object.
- Give two rescue breaths.
- Begin chest compressions.

Continue these steps of CPR until more advanced EMS personnel arrive.

Recent studies have shown that performing chest compressions on an unresponsive patient increases the pressure in the chest similar to performing abdominal thrusts and may relieve an airway obstruction. Therefore, performing CPR on a patient who has become unresponsive has the same effect as performing the Heimlich maneuver on a conscious patient.

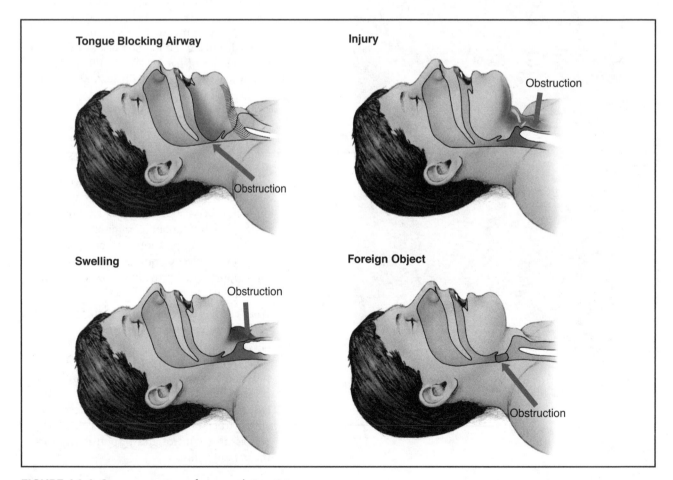

FIGURE A1.4 Common causes of airway obstruction.

MANAGEMENT OF FOREIGN BODY AIRWAY OBSTRUCTION

1

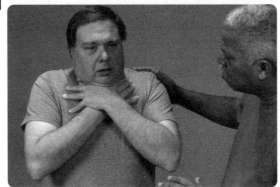

Ask, "Are you choking? Can you speak?" If there is no response, assume that the airway obstruction is complete.

2

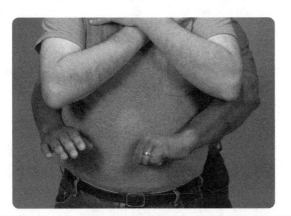

Stand behind the patient and position the thumb side of your fist just above the patient's navel.

3

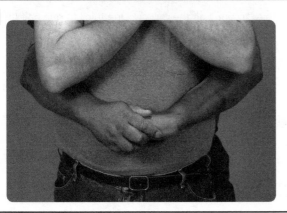

Press into the patient's abdomen with a quick upward thrust. Repeat the abdominal thrusts until either the foreign body is expelled or the patient becomes unresponsive.

TABLE A1-1

CPR AND AIRWAY OBSTRUCTION REVIEW

These eight steps are the same for all motionless victims regardless of age:

1. *Check responsiveness:* Tap a shoulder and ask if the victim is okay. If the victim is unresponsive, have someone call 9-1-1.
2. *Open airway:* Head tilt–chin lift maneuver.
3. *Check breathing:* Look at the chest to see it rise and fall, and listen and feel for breathing for 5–10 seconds.
4. *Place victim in recovery position:* If victim is breathing but unresponsive, place him or her in recovery position.
5. *Give breaths:* If victim is not breathing, give two breaths (1 second per breath).
6. *Perform CPR:* If breaths cause the chest to rise, begin CPR——cycles of 30 chest compressions and two breaths for five cycles (2 minutes). Rate should be 100 compressions per minute. Recheck breathing after every five cycles.
7. *Retilt and retry:* If first breath does not cause the chest to rise, retilt victim's head and try a second breath.
8. *Perform CPR:* Whether the second breath is successful or not, perform CPR——30 compressions and 2 breaths for five cycles (2 minutes). In the case of an unresponsive victim with an airway obstruction, look for an object in the victim's mouth before giving the two breaths, and remove it if you see it.

Action	Adult (≥ 8 years)	Child (1–8 years)	Infant (< 1 year)
1. Breathing methods	Mouth-to-barrier device Mouth-to-mouth Mouth-to-nose Mouth-to-stoma	Mouth-to-barrier device Mouth-to-mouth Mouth-to-nose Mouth-to-stoma	Mouth-to-mouth and nose Mouth-to-barrier device Mouth-to-nose
2. Chest compressions			
Locations	On the breastbone, between nipples	On the breastbone, between nipples	On the breastbone, just below nipple line
Method	Two hands: Heel of one hand on breastbone between nipples; other hand on top	One or two hands	Two fingers
Depth	1.5 to 2 inches	One third to one half the depth of the chest	One third to one half the depth of the chest
Rate	100 per minute	100 per minute	100 per minute
Ratio of chest compressions to breaths	30:2	30:2	30:2
3. When to activate EMS when alone	Immediately after determining unresponsiveness	After 5 cycles of CPR	After 5 cycles of CPR
4. Use of AED	Yes; deliver one shock as soon as possible, followed by 5 cycles of CPR	Yes; use special electrode pads if available	No
5. Responsive victim and airway obstruction	Heimlich maneuver	Heimlich maneuver	Back blows and chest thrusts

Adult: Foreign Body Airway Obstruction

Steps	Adequately Performed
1. Ask "Are you choking?"	
2. Give abdominal thrusts (chest thrusts for pregnant or obese victim).	
3. Repeat thrusts until foreign body is dislodged or until patient becomes unresponsive.	
If the patient becomes unresponsive:	
4. Ensure that the EMS system has been activated.	
5. Begin CPR: ■ Open the airway by using the head tilt-chin lift maneuver. ■ Look into the mouth for any foreign object. Use finger sweeps only if you can see a foreign object. ■ Give two rescue breaths. ■ Begin chest compressions.	
6. Continue these CPR steps until more advanced EMS personnel arrive.	

Source: Based on the 2005 CPR and ECC guidelines.

FIGURE A1.5 Skill performance sheet.

Appendix 2

Bloodborne Pathogens

What Is the OSHA Bloodborne Pathogens Standard?

The OSHA Bloodborne Pathogens Standard (also referred to as 29 CFR 1910.1030) was issued in 1991 to protect employees from occupational exposure to bloodborne pathogens (Figure A2.1). These regulations require employers to use a combination of engineering and work practice controls, personal protective clothing and equipment, medical surveillance, and additional safety precautions in the workplace. Any employees who are required to handle human blood or other potentially infectious materials (OPIMs) must receive training in bloodborne pathogens as well as onsite training to implement the requirements of specific work environments properly.

The standard has greatly improved employee safety through training and prevention measures. It has also influenced manufacturers to introduce new engineering controls (such as needleless systems) and produce a wide variety of products that create a safer work environment and provide greater personal protection. Despite these advances, however, bloodborne pathogens pose a significant occupational health risk for employees handling blood or OPIMs, and the requirements of the OSHA Bloodborne Pathogens Standard remain an essential component to maintaining a safe working environment.

OSHA Bloodborne Pathogens Standard

OSHA Bloodborne Pathogens Regulations Section 1910.1030

Part 1910-[Amended]

Subpart Z-[Amended]

1. The general authority citation for subpart Z of 29 CFR part 1910 continues to read as follows and a new citation for 1910.1030 is added:

Authority: Secs. 6 and 8, Occupational Safety and Health Act, 29 U.S.C. 655, 657, Secretary of Labor's Orders Nos. 12-71 (36 CFR 8754), 8-76 (41 CFR 25059), or 9-83 (48 CFR 35736), as applicable; and 29 CFR part 1911.

* * *

Section 1910.1030 also issued under 29 U.S.C. 853.

* * *

2. Section 1910.1030 is added to read as follows:

1910.1030 Bloodborne Pathogens.

(a) Scope and Application

This section applies to all occupational exposure to blood or other potentially infectious materials as defined by paragraph (b) of this section.

(b) Definitions

For purposes of this section, the following shall apply:

Assistant Secretary means the Assistant Secretary of Labor for Occupational Safety and Health, or designated representative.

Blood means human blood, human blood components, and products made from human blood.

Bloodborne Pathogens means pathogenic microorganisms that are present in human blood and can cause disease in humans. These pathogens include, but are not limited to, Hepatitis B Virus [HBV] and Human Immunodeficiency Virus [HIV].

Clinical Laboratory means a workplace where diagnostic or other screening procedures are performed on blood or other potentially infectious materials.

Contaminated means the presence or the reasonably anticipated presence of blood or other potentially infectious materials on an item or surface.

Contaminated Laundry means laundry which has been soiled with blood or other potentially infectious materials or may contain sharps.

Contaminated Sharps means any contaminated object that can penetrate the skin including, but not limited to, needles, scalpels, broken glass, broken capillary tubes, and exposed ends of dental wires.

Decontamination means the use of physical or chemical means to remove, inactivate, or destroy bloodborne pathogens on a surface or item to the point where they are no longer capable of transmitting infectious particles and the surface or item is rendered safe for handling, use, or disposal.

Director means the Director of the National Institute for Occupational Safety and Health, U.S. Department of Health and Human Services, or designated representative.

Engineering Controls means controls (e.g., sharps disposal containers, self-sheathing needles) that isolate or remove the bloodborne pathogens hazard from the workplace.

Exposure Incident means a specific eye, mouth, other mucous membrane, non-intact skin, or parenteral contact with blood or other potentially infectious materials that results from the performance of an employee's duties.

Handwashing Facilities means a facility providing an adequate supply of running potable water, soap, and single use towels or hot air drying machines.

Licensed Health Care Professional is a person whose legally permitted scope of practice allows him or her to independently perform the activities required by paragraph (f) Hepatitis B vaccination and Post-Exposure Evaluation and Follow-Up.

HBV means Hepatitis B Virus.

HIV means Human Immunodeficiency Virus.

Occupational Exposure means reasonably anticipated skin, eye, mucous membrane, or parenteral contact with blood or other potentially infectious materials that may result from the performance of an employee's duties.

Other Potentially Infectious Materials means

(1) The following human body fluids: semen, vaginal secretions, cerebrospinal fluid, synovial fluid, pleural fluid, pericardial fluid, peritoneal fluid, amniotic fluid, saliva in dental procedures, any body fluid that is visibly contaminated with blood, and all body fluids in situations where it is difficult or impossible to differentiate between body fluids;

(2) Any unfixed tissue or organ (other than intact skin) from a human (living or dead); and

(3) HIV-containing cell or tissue cultures, organ cultures, and HIV- or HBV-containing culture medium or other solutions; and blood, organs, or other tissues from experimental animals infected with HIV or HBV.

Parenteral means piercing mucous membranes or the skin barrier through such events as needlesticks, human bites, cuts, and abrasions.

FIGURE A2.1 OSHA Bloodborne Pathogen Standard.

Who Needs OSHA Bloodborne Pathogens Training?

The scope of the standard is not limited to employees with job classifications that may have occupational exposure to blood and OPIMs. For example, employees trained in first aid and identified by their employer as responsible for administering medical assistance on the job need to receive training in bloodborne pathogens.

The standard includes the potential for exposure, not just actual exposure. For example, emergency department intake personnel may not have an actual exposure to a bleeding patient, but the potential for exposure may exist.

Employees

Any employee who has occupational exposure to blood or OPIMs is included within the scope of the standard. This includes part-time, temporary health care workers known as "per diem" employees and volunteers.

OSHA jurisdiction extends only to private business employees in the workplace. It does *not* extend to the following:

- Students if they are not considered an employee (students participating in internships are covered)

For more information go to http://www.ECSInstitute.org.

- State, county, or municipal employees
- Health care professionals who are sole practitioners or partners
- Those who are self-employed

Any employee who has potential for occupational exposure to blood or OPIMs is required to receive training (Figure A2.2). The following job classifications may be associated with tasks that have occupational exposure to blood or OPIMs, but the standard is not limited to employees in these positions:

- Physicians, physician's assistants, nurses, nurse practitioners, and other health care employees in clinics and physicians' offices
- Employees of clinical and diagnostic laboratories
- Housekeepers in health care and other facilities
- Personnel in hospital laundries or commercial laundries that service health care or public-safety institutions
- Tissue bank personnel
- Employees in blood banks and plasma centers who collect, transport, and test blood
- Freestanding clinic employees (eg, hemodialysis clinics, urgent care clinics, health maintenance organization clinics, and family planning clinics)
- Employees in clinics in industrial, educational, and correctional facilities (e.g., those who collect blood and clean and dress wounds)
- Employees designated to provide emergency first aid

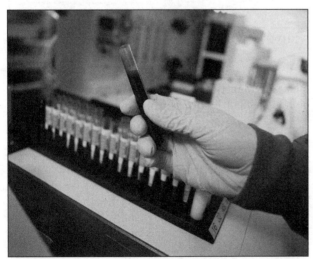

FIGURE A2.2 Any employee who has potential for occupational exposure to blood or OPIMs is required to receive training.

- Dentists, dental hygienists, dental assistants, and dental laboratory technicians
- Staff of institutions for the developmentally disabled
- Hospice employees
- Home health care workers
- Staff of nursing homes and long-term care facilities
- Employees of funeral homes and mortuaries
- Human immunodeficiency virus (HIV) and hepatitis B virus (HBV) research laboratory and production facility workers
- Employees handling regulated waste; custodial workers required to clean up contaminated sharps or spills of blood or OPIMs
- Medical equipment service and repair personnel
- Emergency medical technicians, paramedics, and other emergency medical service providers
- Fire fighters, law enforcement personnel, and correctional officers
- Maintenance workers (e.g., plumbers) in health care facilities and employees of substance abuse clinics

Employers and Employment Agencies

Employment agencies are not required to provide training because the agency is not considered the employer. The company or institution that uses the workers (such as a hospital) therefore is responsible for providing training according to the standard.

Personnel Services and Multiemployer Worksite Guidelines

Personnel service firms employ medical care staff who are assigned to work at hospitals and other health care facilities that contract with the firm. Often the employees are paid by the personnel services firm, but day-to-day supervision of the work is provided by the medical facility. When the medical facility (host employer) exercises day-to-day supervision over the personnel services worker, the worker is the employee of the host employer *and* the personnel service. The shared responsibilities of both employers are referred to as multiemployer worksite guidelines.

Under these circumstances, the personnel service firm can be held accountable for meeting the following provisions of the standard:

- Providing hepatitis B vaccinations
- Managing postexposure evaluation and follow-up

- Keeping records
- Providing generic training
- Exercising reasonable diligence to ensure that the host workplace facility is in compliance with the standard
- When violations of the standard at the host workplace are known, taking reasonable steps to have the host employer correct the violation

The host employer must comply with all provisions of the standard, such as providing appropriate engineering controls, an exposure control plan that is clearly explained and available to the worker, and personal protective equipment in the appropriate size and type. The host employer is obligated to take reasonable measures to ensure that the personnel service firm has complied with the provisions listed above.

Home Health Services

The employees of home health service companies may provide health services in private homes. Because the employer does not control the home work environment, the application of the bloodborne pathogens standard is restricted in the home health services industry.

The private home work environment is not free from bloodborne pathogen hazards, however. Employees should follow work practice guidelines and use personal protective equipment to prevent exposure.

OSHA has determined that the employer will not be held responsible for the following site-specific violations (such as violations occurring in a private home):

- Housekeeping requirements, such as the maintenance of a clean and sanitary worksite
- Handling and disposal of regulated waste
- Ensuring the use of personal protective equipment
- Ensuring that specific work practices are followed (such as handwashing with running water)
- Ensuring the use of engineering controls

The employer will be held responsible for all non–site-specific requirements of the standard, such as the following:

- The non–site-specific requirements of the exposure control plan
- Providing hepatitis B vaccinations
- Postexposure evaluation and follow-up
- Record keeping
- Providing generic training that is not workplace specific in detail and content

- Providing appropriate personal protective equipment to employees

Physicians and Health Care Professionals in an Independent Practice

Physicians may be employers or employees. In applying the provisions of the standard in situations involving physicians, the status of the physician is important. The responsibilities under the standard are similar to those of personnel services firms.

In general, professional corporations are the employers of their physician-members when they work at host employer sites and must comply with the hepatitis B vaccination, postexposure evaluation and follow-up, record keeping, and site-specific training provisions. The host employer is not responsible for these provisions for physicians with staff privileges, but the host employer must comply with all other provisions of the standard in accordance with the multiemployer worksite guidelines.

Independent Contractors

Independent contractors provide a service, such as a radiology service, to host employers. These contractors provide supervisory personnel and other personnel to carry out a service. Both the company and the host employer are responsible for complying with all provisions of the standard in accordance with multiemployer worksite guidelines.

Other Industries

The bloodborne pathogens standard does not apply to the construction, agricultural, marine terminal, and longshoring industries, although these industries are not free from the hazards of bloodborne pathogens.

Good Samaritan Assistance

Employees who do not fall within the scope of the standard may still experience a specific exposure incident at work that is unrelated to the performance of their job duties. An employee may choose to aid another person who is injured or ill, which is considered Good Samaritan assistance.

Why Do I Need This Information?

The OSHA-specific bloodborne pathogens guidelines should be used with your worksite-specific training. You are encouraged to gather worksite-specific details on various work pages throughout this appendix.

This appendix will not make you an expert in bloodborne pathogens or the treatment of diseases caused by bloodborne pathogens. It does give you important and necessary information as required by the OSHA Bloodborne Pathogens Standard. Your instructor may expand on the information according to worksite-specific practices. The OSHA-required categories of information must be included in all training.

Meeting OSHA Standards

The goal of training is to educate employees regarding bloodborne pathogen issues and how to minimize or eliminate the exposure to bloodborne pathogens by using a combination of universal precautions, work practice controls, engineering controls, and personal protective equipment.

Employees being trained must have direct access to a qualified trainer. Educating employees solely by means of a film, video, or computer CD-ROM without the opportunity for a discussion period is not acceptable and constitutes a violation of the standard. The trainer must be familiar with the manner in which the elements in the training program relate to the workplace practices. This may also be accomplished by having two trainers: one to discuss generic bloodborne pathogen issues and one to discuss site-specific information (Figure A2.3).

All employees at the time of initial assignment to tasks with occupational exposure to blood or OPIMs, before actually performing any of the tasks, must receive training on the hazards associated with blood and OPIMs and the protective measures to be taken to minimize the risk of occupational exposure.

Thereafter, training is provided at least annually and must be provided within 1 year of the original training. Whenever a change in an employee's responsibilities, procedures, or work situation is such that an employee's occupational exposure is affected, additional training or, as stated in the standard, "retraining" must take place. Retraining is not the same as annual training. Retraining must occur when new equipment is brought to the worksite that might affect the employee's possible exposure.

Annual training must cover the topics listed in the standard to the extent needed and must emphasize new information or procedures. In other words, if individuals are sitting through their fifth renewal class, the instructor may not need to cover the material to the depth that would be required in an initial training. Additionally, the course should be tailored to the group that the instructor is teaching.

The provisions for employee training are based on the employee's job responsibilities, with flexibility in training

FIGURE A2.3 Annual training is necessary to ensure employee safety.

permitted to allow the program to be tailored to the employee's background and responsibilities or other site-specific needs. The categories of information presented in this manual must be included in any and all training.

OSHA requires that any training (including written material, oral presentations, films, videotapes, computer programs, or audiotapes) be presented in the employee's language and at the employee's education level. The trainer or an interpreter may convey the information.

It is necessary to record information about the dates of training sessions, a summary of the training content, and the names and job titles of the employees who attend the training.

OSHA-Required Categories of Information

A. An accessible copy of the Standard and an explanation of its contents

B. A general explanation of the epidemiology and symptoms of bloodborne disease

C. An explanation of the modes of transmission of bloodborne pathogens

D. An explanation of the employer's exposure control plan and the means by which the employee can obtain a copy of the written plan (supplied by your company directly or through the instructor)

E. An explanation of the appropriate methods for recognizing tasks and other activities that may involve exposure to blood and OPIMs

F. An explanation of the use and limitations of methods that will prevent or reduce exposure, including appropriate engineering controls, work practices, and personal protective equipment

G. An explanation of the requirements to evaluate, select, and use needleless systems and sharps with engineered sharps injury protections, which requires employee input, appropriate to circumstances of the workplace

H. Information on the types, proper use, location, removal, handling, decontamination, and disposal of personal protective equipment

I. An explanation of the basis for selection of personal protective equipment

J. Information on the hepatitis B vaccine, including information on its efficacy, safety, method of administration, the benefits of being vaccinated, and that the vaccine and vaccination will be offered free of charge to employees covered by the standard

K. Information on the appropriate actions to take and persons to contact in an emergency (exposure outside the normal scope of work) involving blood or OPIMs

L. An explanation of the procedure to follow if an exposure incident occurs, including the method of reporting the incident and the medical follow-up that will be made available

M. Information on the postexposure evaluation and follow-up that the employer is required to provide for the employee following an exposure incident

N. An explanation of the signs, labels, and/or color coding required

O. An opportunity for interactive questions and answers with the person conducting the training session (during and after training session)

The Ryan White Act

The Centers for Disease Control and Prevention is in the process of preparing the final list of diseases required by the passage of the Public Law 101-381, the Ryan White Comprehensive AIDS Resources Emergency Act. The act creates a notification system for emergency response employees listed as police, fire, and EMS who are exposed to diseases such as *M tuberculosis*, hepatitis B or hepatitis C, and HIV.

OSHA-Required Record Keeping

Record keeping needs to comply with 29 CFR 1904 using *Log of Work-Related Injuries and Illness* (Form 300) and *Injury and Illness Incident Report* (Form 301) and must record the following:

1. Any needlestick injury or cut from a sharp object that is contaminated with another person's blood or OPIMs

2. Any case requiring an employee to be medically removed under the requirements of an OSHA health standard

3. Tuberculosis infection as evidenced by a positive skin test or diagnosis by a physician or other licensed health care professional after exposure to a known case of active TB

This is in accordance with CPL2-0.131, effective January 1, 2002.

Additionally, there must be a sharps injury log maintained independently from the OSHA 300. This log must be confidential, and person-specific data should not be contained on the sharps injury log. At a minimum, the log must record the type and brand of the device involved, department or area of incident, and description of incident. The log should be reviewed on a regular basis, and action should be taken to correct any problems that are leading to needlestick or sharps injury.

What Are Bloodborne Pathogens?

Bloodborne pathogens are disease-causing microorganisms (viruses, bacteria, and parasites) that may be present in human blood. They may be transmitted during exposure to blood or OPIMs.

Mode of Transmission of Bloodborne Pathogens

Bloodborne pathogens are transmitted when blood or OPIMs come in contact with mucous membranes or nonintact skin. Nonintact skin includes, but is not limited to, cuts, abrasions, burns, rashes, acne, paper cuts, and hangnails. Bloodborne pathogens may also be transmitted by blood splashes or sprays, handling or touching contaminated items or surfaces, and injection under the skin by puncture wounds or cuts from contaminated sharps (Figure A2.4).

Most occupational transmission of HIV has occurred through puncture injuries from contaminated sharps; however, there have been documented transmissions through nonintact skin and mucous membranes. One worker became HIV positive after a splash of HIV-contaminated blood to the eyes. Contact with blood or OPIM should be avoided.

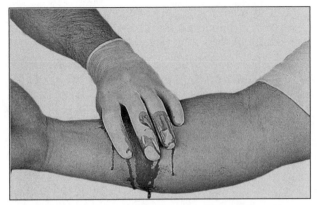

FIGURE A2.4 Always wear gloves to prevent contamination.

OSHA Expectations Regarding Exposure

The objective of the standard is to minimize or eliminate the hazard posed by exposure to blood or OPIMs; however, occupational exposure to a bloodborne pathogen may occur.

If there is a risk of exposure or injury, it is important to know the following:

1. If there is a way to prevent infection as a result of exposure to the pathogen (such as immunization)

2. The symptoms caused by infection with the pathogen, as well as the natural course of the infection

3. Counseling specific to the exposure incident is available

4. The postexposure treatments and follow-up that may be provided

If you are exposed to bloodborne pathogens, a confidential medical evaluation is to be made *immediately* available to you, the injured employee. The word *immediately* is used in the standard to emphasize the importance of prompt medical evaluation and prophylaxis. An exact timeframe cannot be stated because the effectiveness of postexposure prophylactic measures varies depending on the infecting organism.

Medical evaluation must be confidential and protect your identity and test results.

If you go for a medical evaluation, the following information will be made available to the health professional:

1. A copy of the OSHA guidelines section 1910.1030. This is the OSHA standard that dictates the requirement for all aspects of bloodborne pathogens and infectious diseases. The OSHA standard provides the necessary procedures for the medical evaluation.

2. A description of how the incident occurred as it relates to your employment

3. The results of the source individual's testing (if available)

4. All medical records that are relevant for your proper treatment (if treatment is necessary), including a copy of your hepatitis B vaccination status with the dates of all the hepatitis B vaccinations and any medical records relative to your ability to receive the vaccination

You and your employer should expect that current Centers for Disease Control and Prevention (CDC) guidelines will be used to guide postexposure prophylaxis and treatment.

It is the employer's responsibility to ensure that your medical records are kept confidential. Your records cannot be disclosed without your express written consent to any person within or outside the workplace, except as required by law. Your employer will have a copy of the health care provider's written opinion regarding the incident.

During consultation with the health care professional, decisions will be made about the need for hepatitis B vaccination, and laboratory tests and information will be provided about available postexposure prophylaxis and treatments.

The health care professional will discuss the laboratory test results with you. A plan will be created that identifies any necessary follow-up or treatments, including initiation of hepatitis B immunization, if indicated. Postexposure treatments and follow-up plans should be in accordance with the current CDC guidelines.

Reporting Requirements
What Is an Occupational Exposure Incident?

An occupational exposure incident occurs if you are in a work situation and come in contact with blood or OPIM.

For OSHA 2000 record keeping purposes, an occupational bloodborne pathogens exposure incident (such as a needlestick, laceration, or splash) is classified as an *injury* because it is usually the result of an instantaneous event or exposure (Figure A2.5).

After an occupational exposure to blood or OPIM has occurred, the employee's name and job classification are listed on the OSHA 2000 log. The job classification should be reviewed, and a determination should be made as to which employees, if any, in that classification should be covered under the standard.

Exposure Determination

The employer must identify and document the job classifications in which exposure occurs. The exposure determination must have been made without taking into consideration the use of personal protective clothing or equipment. The exposure control plan should identify the person responsible for the determination and assessment of an exposure incident.

Reporting an Incident

The goal of reporting an incident is to ensure that an employee receives timely access to medical services and to identify and adopt other methods or devices to prevent exposure incidents from recurring.

At sites where an exposure incident has occurred, it should be determined whether OSHA Standards were properly followed through interviews and reviews of incident reports or medical records.

The employee needs to report the incident to his or her supervisor. OSHA requires that the following information be reported:

- Date and time of the exposure incident
- Job classification of the exposed employee
- Worksite location where the exposure incident occurred
- Work practices being followed
- Engineering controls in use at the time including a description of the device in use (such as type

FIGURE A2.5 An uncapped needle can cause an injury.

and brand of sharp involved in the exposure incident)
- Protective equipment or clothing that was used at the time of the exposure incident
- Procedure being performed when the incident occurred
- Your training for the activity

The California OSHA also requires the following:

- Identifying the body part involved in the exposure incident
- The engineering controls in use at the time if the sharp had engineered sharps injury protection
- Whether the protective mechanism was activated and whether the injury occurred before the protective mechanism was activated, during activation of the mechanism, or after activation of the mechanism, if applicable
- If the sharp had no engineered sharps injury protection, the injured employee's opinion as to whether and how such a mechanism could have prevented the injury
- The employee's opinion about whether any other engineering, administrative, or work practice control could have prevented the injury

After an incident has been reported, your employer will need to identify and document the source individual and obtain consent and make arrangements to have the source individual tested as soon as possible to determine HIV, HCV, and HBV infection. It should be documented when legally required consent to test the blood is not obtained.

It may not always be feasible to identify the source individual. Examples of when you may be unable to identify the source individual include needlesticks caused by unmarked syringes left in laundry or those involving blood samples that are not properly labeled, as well as incidents occurring where state or local laws prohibit such identification.

Your blood may be tested for HBV, HCV, and/or HIV only with your consent. OSHA encourages employees to consent to blood collection at the time of exposure. The results of HIV testing must be made in person and cannot be given over the telephone or by mail. Even if you choose not to undergo testing, counseling and evaluation of reported illnesses are available to you.

You may choose to have your blood drawn but not tested and stored for 90 days. The 90-day time frame allows the employee to have the opportunity to obtain knowledge about baseline serologic testing after exposure incidents and to participate in further discussion, education, or counseling. If you elect not to have the blood tested, the sample will be disposed of after 90 days.

HBV

Hepatitis B can affect anyone. Each year in the United States, 140,000 to 320,000 people will become infected with the virus. Studies conducted by the CDC have shown a steady decline in the incidence of HBV infection. This decline is attributed to the widespread use of HBV vaccine and the implementation of other prevention methods, such as engineering and work practice controls, personal protective equipment, and universal precautions.

It is estimated that 1 to 1.25 million Americans are chronically infected with HBV.

Prevention and Control

The HBV vaccine has been available since 1982. The vaccine does not contain any live components. The vaccine is given in a series of three shots (Figure A2.6).

Immunization

All people who have routine occupational exposure to blood or OPIM have the right to receive the immunization series against HBV at no personal expense. The standard includes temporary and part-time workers and volunteers.

There are several reasons why you may choose not to receive the HBV vaccine. Among the most common reasons are as follows:

1. Documentation exists that you have previously received the series.
2. Antibody testing reveals that you are immune.
3. Medical evaluation shows that vaccination is contraindicated.
4. You are allergic to any component of the vaccine.

Exception for HBV Vaccination

Designated first aid providers who have occupational exposure are not required to be offered HBV vaccine if the following conditions exist:

1. The primary job assignment of the designated first aid provider is not the rendering of first aid.
2. Any first aid rendered by the first aid provider is rendered only as a collateral duty responding solely to injuries resulting from workplace incidents and generally at the location where the incident occurred.
3. This provision does not apply to designated first aid providers who render assistance on a regular

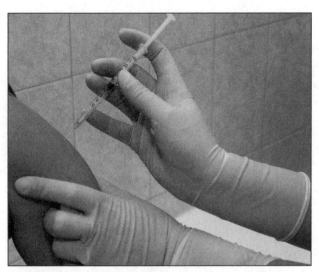

FIGURE A2.6 Immunization against HBV is possible.

basis, for example, at a first aid station, clinic, dispensary, or other location where injured employees routinely go for such assistance, and emergency or public safety personnel who are expected to render first aid in the course of their work.

Prescreening antibody testing is not required, and your employer may not make prescreening a requirement for receiving the vaccine. If an employer wishes prescreening, it must be made available to you at no cost. If you choose to have prescreening, the testing must be done at an accredited laboratory.

The standard requires that your employer offer the vaccine at a convenient time and place to you, during normal work hours. If travel is required away from the worksite, your employer is responsible for that cost. The standard includes temporary and part-time workers.

Your employer cannot require you to pay for testing and then reimburse you if you remain employed for a specific time. Nor are you required to reimburse your employer for the cost of the vaccine if you leave your job.

HIV

Human immunodeficiency virus (HIV) is the virus that causes AIDS. Two types of HIV have been identified (HIV-1 and HIV-2). HIV infection causes suppression of the immune system and can lead to opportunistic infections and unusual types of cancer.

The differences between HIV-1 and HIV-2 should be noted. HIV-2 AIDS develops more slowly and may be milder. There are few reported cases of HIV-2 in the United States. HIV-2 is predominately found in Africa. Hereafter, all references to HIV mean HIV-1.

The CDC reports that in 2003 there were an estimated 1,039,000 people in the United States with HIV/AIDS. Approximately 25% of infected persons are undiagnosed and unaware of their infection.

The annual rate of infection with HIV is 16.5 cases per 100,000 population (Figure A2.7).

Prevention and Control

There is no vaccination for HIV.

Prevention recommendations are directed toward the use of engineering and work practice controls, personal protective equipment, and universal precautions.

Clinical Features and History of HIV

The only way to determine for sure whether you are infected is to be tested. The incubation period with HIV from the time of HIV infection to the development of AIDS may take 8 to 10 years. This time varies greatly from person to person.

You cannot rely on symptoms to know whether you are infected with HIV. Many people who are infected with HIV experience no symptoms for many years. The symptoms of AIDS are similar to the symptoms of many other infections and might include night sweats, weight loss, fever, fatigue, gland pain or swelling, and muscle or joint pain.

Postexposure Prophylaxis and Follow-up for HIV

There is no cure for infection with HIV.

All decisions about postexposure laboratory testing and prophylaxis are made in consultation with your health care professional. Testing for the HIV antibody should be done as soon as possible after exposure and, thereafter, periodically for at least 6 months. Antibodies usually become detectable within 3 months of infection.

Decisions regarding treatment need to be made after discussion with an infectious diseases specialist. Postexposure treatment is not recommended for all occupational exposures; 99.7% of the exposures do not lead to HIV infection. If treatment with antiviral medications plus a protease inhibitor is recommended, treatment should begin within hours of the exposure.

The CDC reports that t!he risk of infection after a needlestick or cut exposure to HIV-infected blood is about 0.3%.

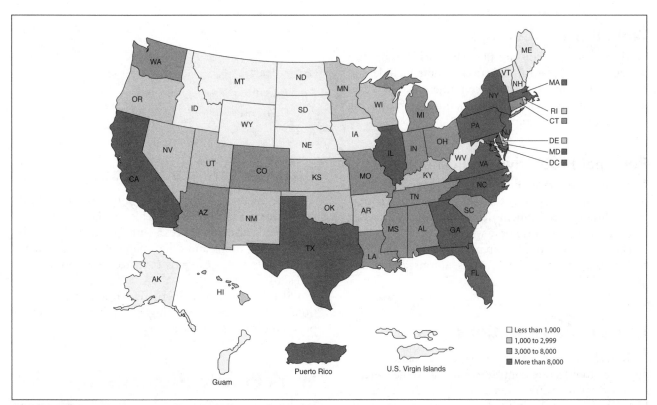

FIGURE A2.7 Estimated number of persons living with AIDS.

Source: The Kaiser Family Foundation, statehealthfacts.org. Data Source: HIV/AIDS Surveillance Report: Cases of HIV Infection and AIDS in the United States, 2005, Volume 16, National Center for HIV, STD and TB Prevention, Centers for Disease Control and Prevention, Department of Health and Human Services, 2006.

Prevention

The Occupational Safety and Health Administration (OSHA) defined four principal strategies to prevent or reduce exposure to bloodborne pathogens. These strategies are used in combination to offer you maximum protection. It is OSHA's view that preventing exposures requires a comprehensive program, including engineering controls (such as needleless devices, shielded needle devices, and plastic capillary tubes) and proper work practices (such as no-hands procedures in handling contaminated sharps). If engineering and work practice controls do not eliminate exposure, the use of personal protective equipment (PPE) (such as eye protection) and universal precautions is required.

All these strategies combined promote worker safety and provide a safer working enviroment.

Engineering Controls

Engineering controls are structural or mechanical devices the company provides. Examples include hand-washing facilities, eye stations, sharps containers, and biohazard labels.

Work Practice Controls

Work practice controls are the behaviors necessary to use engineering controls effectively. These include, but are not limited to, using sharps containers, using an eye-wash station, and washing your hands after removing personal protective equipment.

Personal Protective Equipment

Personal protective equipment is equipment provided by your employer at no cost to you. It is to your advantage to use this equipment. Report to your supervisor when any equipment is not in working order.

Personal protective equipment includes materials such as medical exam gloves, masks, aprons, gowns, and face shields.

Universal Precautions

Universal precautions is an aggressive, standardized approach to infection control. According to the concept of universal precautions, you should treat all human blood and certain body fluids as if they are known to contain HIV, HBV, HCV, or other bloodborne pathogens, regardless of the perceived risk of the source. Examples of incidents that do and do not required universal precautions are included in the table.

Materials That Require Universal Precautions

Universal precautions apply to the following potentially infectious materials:

- Blood
- Semen
- Vaginal secretions
- Cerebrospinal fluid
- Synovial fluid
- Pleural fluid
- Any body fluid with visible blood
- Any unidentifiable body fluid
- Saliva from dental procedures

Materials That Do Not Require Universal Precautions

Universal precautions do not apply to the following body fluids unless they contain visible blood:

- Feces
- Nasal secretions
- Sputum
- Sweat
- Tears
- Urine
- Vomitus

Body Substance Isolation

Another method of infection control is called body substance isolation (BSI). This method defines *all* body fluids and substances as infectious. BSI includes not only the fluids and other materials covered by this standard, but also expands coverage to all body fluids and substances.

BSI is an acceptable alternative to universal precautions provided facilities using BSI adhere to all other provisions of this standard.

Work Practice Controls

Work practice controls are the behaviors necessary to use engineering controls effectively. These include, but are not limited to, using sharps containers, using an eye-wash station, and washing your hands after removing PPE. An example of a work practice control would be to immediately place contaminated sharps into a sharps container.

All procedures involving blood or OPIMs must be performed in a manner that minimizes or eliminates splashing, spraying, splattering, and generation of droplets of these substances. Not only does this decrease the chances of direct exposure through spraying or splashing of infectious materials onto you, but it also reduces contamination of surfaces in the general work area.

Work practice controls must be evaluated and updated on a regular schedule to ensure their effectiveness.

Mouth pipetting or suctioning of blood or OPIMs is prohibited. This procedure should never occur unless it is part of a specialized procedure such as DeLee suctioning; however, even then there must be a one-way valve between the patient and the practitioner.

Eating, drinking, smoking, applying cosmetics or lip balm, and handling contact lenses are prohibited in work areas where there is a reasonable likelihood of occupational exposure to blood or OPIMs.

Employees are permitted to eat and drink in an ambulance cab, for example, as long as the employer has implemented procedures to permit employees to wash up and change contaminated clothing before entering the ambulance cab and to ensure that patients and contaminated material remain behind the separating partition.

Hand cream is not considered a cosmetic and is permitted under the standard; however, some petroleum-based hand creams can adversely affect glove integrity.

Food or drink must not be kept in refrigerators, freezers, shelves, cabinets, countertops, or benches where blood or OPIMs are present.

You must remove all PPE and wash your hands before leaving the work area. To prevent contamination of employee eating areas, you should not enter eating or break areas while wearing PPE (Figure A2.8).

Handwashing and Handwashing Facilities

Handwashing is one of the most effective methods of preventing transmission of bloodborne pathogens. It is required that you wash your hands after removal of gloves and other PPE (Figure A2.9).

Employers are required to provide handwashing facilities that are readily accessible to all employees. The standard specifies that the handwashing facility must be situated so that you do not have to use stairs, doorways, and corridors, which might result in environmental surface contamination.

When the provision of handwashing facilities is not feasible (such as in an ambulance or police car), the

Determining the Need for Universal Precautions

Incident	Universal Precautions Needed?	Suggested Action
Nurse is going to change dressing on a recent wound.	Yes	Nurse should wear latex or vinyl gloves and/or PPE whenever at risk of exposure to blood or potentially infectious materials.
Teacher is approached by young, hysterical student with a bloody nose.	Yes	If required to attend to the student, the teacher should reassure child, put on latex or vinyl gloves, and follow routine procedures.
A neighbor is called to a home where an older man appears to have had a heart attack. The man is conscious and able to speak.	No	There is no immediate blood or infectious materials, although the neighbor may need to perform CPR in the event of cardiac or respiratory arrest. Note: In the event of cardiac or respiratory arrest, work practice controls and PPE may be required.
A police officer pulls over a car that has a burned-out headlight.	No	It is unlikely that the police officer will come in contact with blood or potentially infectious materials.
A laboratory worker is testing urine for evidence of infection. The specimen appears to have a trace of blood.	Yes	The laboratory worker should be using PPE whenever dealing with any specimens with visible blood.

FIGURE A2.8 Properly dispose of protective equipment in biohazard containers.

FIGURE A2.10 Antiseptic wipes can be used when hand-washing is not an option.

FIGURE A2.9 Handwashing is a primary means of preventing transmission of bloodborne pathogens.

employer must provide either an appropriate antiseptic hand cleanser with clean cloth or paper towels or antiseptic towelettes. If you use antiseptic hand cleansers or towelettes, you must wash your hands (or other affected area) with soap and warm water as soon as possible after contact with blood or OPIMs (Figure A2.10).

Employers must ensure you wash your hands, and any other contaminated skin, with soap and at least tepid running warm water (or flush mucous membranes with water) as soon as possible after contact with blood or OPIMs. Groups that may need to use alternative washing methods such as antiseptic hand cleansers and towelettes are ambulance-based EMTs, fire fighters, police, and mobile blood collection personnel.

Handwashing is required after the removal of gloves because although gloves (vinyl or latex) form a barrier they are not completely impermeable.

Cleaning Work Surfaces

The term *work area* means the area where work involving exposure or potential exposure to blood or OPIMs exists, along with the potential contamination of surfaces.

The term *worksite* not only refers to permanent fixed facilities such as hospitals, dental/medical offices, or clinics, but also covers temporary nonfixed workplaces. Examples of such facilities include, but are not limited to, ambulances, bloodmobiles, temporary blood collection centers, and any other nonfixed worksites that have a reasonable possibility of becoming contaminated with blood or OPIMs.

Your employer will identify which work surfaces require inspection for contamination with blood or OPIMs and have regularly scheduled decontamination. This could include, but is not limited to, wastebaskets, exam tables, counters, floors, ambulance interiors, and police cars.

After a regular inspection and cleaning schedule is established, it will need to be followed. The schedule must consider location (exam room versus patient waiting area), type of surface (carpet versus hard floor), type of soil present (gross contamination versus minor splattering), and procedure and tasks performed (laboratory analysis versus patient care). The cleaning schedule must occur at least weekly or after completion of tasks or procedures, after contamination of surfaces, or at the end of a shift if there is a possibility of contamination.

Receptacles

All bins, pails, cans, and similar receptacles intended for reuse that have a reasonable likelihood for becoming contaminated with blood or OPIMs should be inspected and decontaminated on a regularly scheduled basis. These receptacles should be cleaned and decontaminated immediately or as soon as feasible upon visible contamination.

Protective Coverings

Protective coverings, such as plastic wrap, aluminum foil, or imperviously backed absorbent paper used to cover equipment and environmental surfaces, should be removed and replaced as soon as feasible when they become overtly contaminated or at the end of the work shift if they may have become contaminated during the shift.

Work Practices

Work surface decontamination should be performed at the end of the work shift if the work surface may have become contaminated since the last cleaning by, for example, setting down contaminated instruments or specimens on the work surface. This requirement is based on the existence of a contaminated work surface rather than a particular worksite location. It does not, for example, encompass desks or countertops that remain uncontaminated.

Where procedures are performed on a continual basis throughout a shift or a day, as may be the case with a clinical laboratory technician performing blood analyses, it is not necessary for the work surface to be decontaminated before the technician can proceed to the next analysis. Rather, the contaminated work surfaces must be decontaminated after the procedures are completed (in this example, a set of analyses). The completion of procedures might also occur when the employee is going to leave the work area for a period of time.

While cleaning up potentially infectious materials, you must wear disposable medical exam gloves and use an Environmental Protection Agency–approved solution. Follow the label instructions regarding the amount of disinfectant and the length of time it must remain wet on the surface. The effectiveness of a disinfectant is governed by strict adherence to the instructions on the label.

Cleansing Solutions

An example of an inexpensive approved solution is 10% bleach and water. Fresh solutions of diluted household bleach made up daily (every 24 hours) are also considered appropriate for disinfecting environmental surfaces and for decontamination of sites following initial cleanup of spills of blood or OPIMs. You should use disposable towels to clean up the spill, and then dispose of the towels in a biohazard-labeled bag.

Do not clean up with your hands any broken glass that may be contaminated. Instead, use a dust pan and brush, cardboard, or tongs. The tools used in cleanup (such as forceps) must be properly decontaminated or discarded after use. Contaminated broken glass must be placed in a biohazard sharps container. Placing broken glass in a plastic bag may put others at risk for an occupational exposure incident. You must be given specific information and training with respect to this task.

1. When cleaning up broken glass, wear gloves and/or other PPE (Step 1).

2. Do not clean up broken glass with your hands. Instead use a dust pan and brush, cardboard, or tongs (Step 2).

3. Broken glass must be placed in an appropriate sharps container. Placing broken glass in plastic bag may put others at risk for exposure (Steps 3 and 4).

Contaminated Sharps

OSHA defines contaminated sharps as any contaminated object that can penetrate the skin, including, but not limited to, needles, scalpels, broken capillary tubes, and exposed ends of dental wires.

Contaminated needles or other contaminated sharps must not be bent, recapped, or removed unless it can be demonstrated that no alternative is feasible or that such action is required by a specific medical procedure.

If a procedure requires shearing or breaking of needles, this procedure must be specified in the company's exposure control plan. An acceptable means of demonstrating that no alternative to bending, recapping, or removing contaminated needles is feasible or that such action is required by a specific medical procedure would be a written justification (supported by reliable evidence). This also needs to be included as part of the exposure control plan. The justification must state the basis for the determination that no alternative is feasible or must specify that a particular medical procedure requires, for example, the bending of the needle and the use of forceps to accomplish this.

Needle removal or recapping needles must be accomplished through a one-handed technique or the use of a mechanical device.

Nurses (RNs and LPNs) were injured more often than any other type of health care worker. An overwhelming majority (93%) of the injuries were caused by needles that did not have a safe design. The needles were not shielded, recessed, or retractable.

Laundry

Contaminated laundry should be sent to a facility following the OSHA standard. Your employer must determine whether the facility to which laundry is shipped uses universal precautions when handling all laundry. If not, all bags or containers of contaminated laundry must be labeled or color coded. Because red bags can indicate materials for disposal, many agencies use yellow bags with the biohazard symbol affixed to them to avoid confusion. The biohazard symbol must be affixed to any biohazard waste or contaminated materials such as laundry.

Do not handle laundry any more than necessary. Reducing the amount of manual handling of contaminated laundry reduces the risk of exposure to blood or OPIMs and will also reduce contamination of work surfaces in the laundry area.

CLEANING A CONTAMINATED SPILL

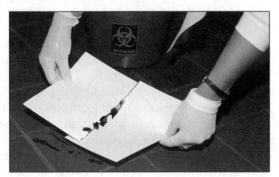

1 When cleaning up broken glass, wear gloves and/or other PPE.

2 Do not clean up broken glass with your hands. Instead use a dust pan and brush, cardboard (as shown), or tongs.

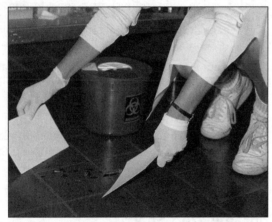

3 Slide pieces of cardboard under broken glass.

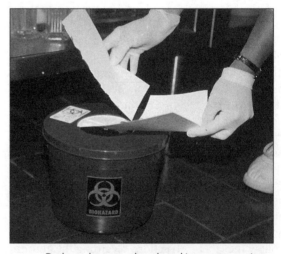

4 Broken glass must be placed in an appropriate sharps container. Placing broken glass in a plastic bag may put others at risk for exposure.

Contaminated laundry should be bagged or placed in an approved container at the location where it was used and should not be sorted or rinsed in the location of use.

Contaminated laundry should be placed and transported in bags or containers labeled or color coded in accordance with the standard. When a facility uses universal precautions in the handling of all soiled laundry, alternative labeling or color coding is sufficient if it permits all employees to recognize that universal precautions are required in handling the containers (Figure A2.11).

Whenever contaminated laundry is wet and presents a reasonable likelihood of soaking through or leaking from the bag or container, the laundry should be placed and transported in bags or containers that prevent soak-through and/or leakage of fluids to the exterior.

ONE-HANDED TECHNIQUE

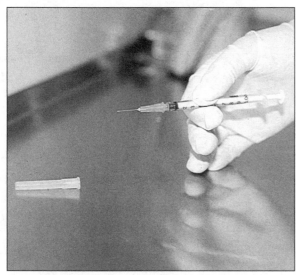

1 Needle removal or recapping must be accomplished through the use of a mechanical device or one-handed technique to prevent puncture wounds.

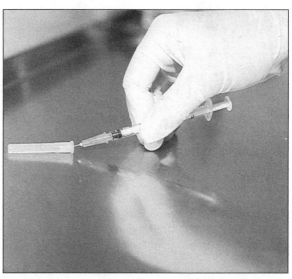

2 The one-handed technique uses a nearby wall or heavy object to stabilize the needle cover.

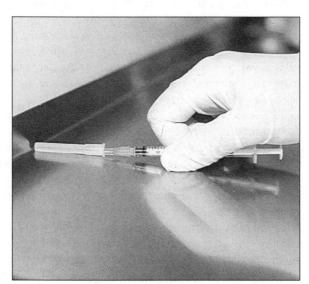

3 Using one hand, gently slide the needle into the needle cover.

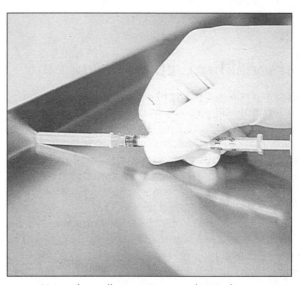

4 Using the wall as support, apply gentle pressure to secure the needle cover. Dispose of the needle and syringe in nearest sharps container.

FIGURE A2.11 Contaminated laundry should be clearly labeled and placed in leakproof containers.

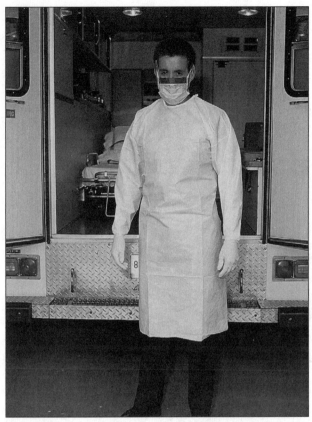

FIGURE A2.12 Full PPE includes gloves, gown, mask, and eye shield.

You must wear protective gloves (e.g., utility gloves) and any other appropriate PPE to prevent or reduce contact exposure to blood or OPIMs when handling laundry or waste materials.

Personal Protective Equipment

PPE is specialized clothing or equipment worn or used by you for protection against hazard. This includes equipment such as latex or vinyl gloves, gowns, aprons, face shields, masks, eye protection, laboratory coats, CPR microshields, and resuscitation bags. PPE prevents blood or OPIMs from passing through to or contacting your work or street clothes, undergarments, skin, eyes, mouth, or other mucous membranes (Figure A2.12).

Resuscitator devices must be readily available and accessible to employees who can reasonably be expected to perform resuscitation procedures. Emergency ventilation devices also fall under the scope of PPE and therefore must be provided by the employer for use in resuscitation. This includes masks, mouthpieces, resuscitation bags, and shields/overlay barriers (Figure A2.13).

Reasonably anticipated spattering or generation of droplets would necessitate use of eye protection and mask or a face shield to prevent contamination of the mucous membranes of the eyes, nose, and mouth. Whenever you need to wear a face mask, you must also wear eye protection. If you are wearing your personal glasses, you must use side shields and plan to decontaminate your glasses and side shields according to the schedule determined by your employer.

PPE is acceptable if it prevents blood or OPIMs from contaminating work clothes, street clothes, undergarments, skin, eyes, mouth, or other mucous membranes. You must use PPE such as gloves or a mask whenever you might be exposed to blood or OPIMs.

Your employer is responsible for providing PPE at no expense to you. PPE must be provided in appropriate sizes and placed within easy reach for all employees. Your employer must evaluate the task and the type of exposure expected and, based on the determination, select the "appropriate" personal protective clothing. For example, laboratory coats or gowns with long sleeves must be used for procedures in which exposure of the forearm to blood or OPIMs is reasonably anticipated to occur.

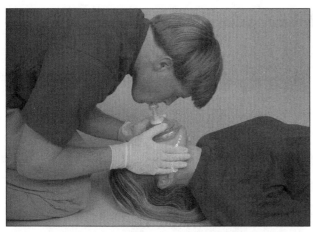

FIGURE A2.13 Using a pocket mask during CPR prevents exposure to potentially infectious body fluids.

Laboratory coats and uniforms that are used as PPE must be laundered by the employer and not sent home with the employee for cleaning. Although many employees have traditionally provided and laundered their own uniforms or laboratory coats if the item's intended function is to act as PPE, it is your employer's responsibility to provide, clean, repair, replace, and/or dispose of it.

It is necessary for you to be trained in the proper use of PPE. Report to your supervisor when any equipment is not available (such as a missing protective shield) or not in working order (such as a hole in an apron).

If blood or OPIMs contaminate your clothing, you must remove them as soon as feasible and place them in an appropriately designated area or container.

If a pullover scrub or shirt becomes contaminated, you must remove it in such a way as to avoid contact with the outer surface—for example, rolling up the garment as it is pulled toward the head for removal; however, if the blood penetrates the scrub or shirt and contaminates the inner surface, the penetration of the garment itself would constitute an exposure. If the scrub or shirt cannot be removed without contamination of the face, it is recommended that the shirt be cut and removed.

1. If a pullover shirt becomes contaminated, you must remove it in such a way as to avoid contact with the outer surface (Step 1).

2. Rolling the garment as it is pulled toward the head will decrease the chance of contact with the contaminated area (Step 2).

3. After rolling up the shirt, carefully pull it over the head to avoid contact with the face or mucous membranes (Step 3).

4. If the shirt cannot be removed without contamination, it is recommended that the shirt be cut off (Step 4).

If blood or OPIMs have penetrated your PPE, it is recommended that you check your body for cuts or scrapes or other nonintact skin when removing your equipment. The penetration itself would constitute an exposure of the skin.

You must remove all PPE before leaving the work area to prevent transmission of bloodborne pathogens to coworkers in other departments and family and to prevent contamination of environmental surfaces.

Gloves

Gloves must be used where there is reasonable anticipation of employee hand contact with blood, OPIMs, mucous membranes, or nonintact skin; when performing vascular access procedures; or when handling or touching contaminated surfaces or items.

Gloves are not necessary when administering intramuscular or subcutaneous injections as long as bleeding that could result in hand contact with blood or OPIMs is not anticipated. Gloves are not necessary when blood or OPIMs are not present or do not have the possibility of occurring.

It is important to consider that the use of gloves is required for any situation that might reasonably be anticipated to result in an exposure to blood or OPIMs. For example, the use of pneumatic tube systems for the transport of laboratory specimens requires that all employees should regard the contents as hazardous and must wear gloves when removing specimens from the tube system carrier.

Hypoallergenic gloves, glove liners, powderless gloves, or other similar alternatives must be readily available and accessible at no cost to those employees who are allergic to the gloves normally provided.

What Is an Acceptable Container?

A sharps container must meet four criteria to be considered acceptable.

It must be closable, puncture resistant, leakproof on sides and bottom, and labeled or color coded.

A sharps container may be made of a variety of products, including cardboard or plastic, as long as the four criteria are met. Duct tape may be used to secure a sharps container lid, but it is not acceptable if it serves as the lid itself.

Using Sharps Containers

Contaminated sharps must be discarded immediately in an acceptable sharps container. Sharps containers must be easily accessible to personnel and located as close as

REMOVING CONTAMINATED EQUIPMENT

1 If a pullover shirt becomes contaminated, remove it in such a way as to avoid contact with the outer surface.

2 Roll the garment as you pull it toward your head.

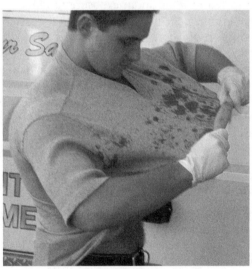

3 After rolling up the shirt, carefully pull it over your head to avoid contact with the face or mucous membranes.

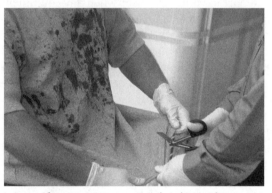

4 If you cannot remove the shirt without contaminating yourself, cut the shirt off.

feasible to the immediate area where sharps are used or can be reasonably anticipated to be found.

Sharps containers must be maintained upright throughout use and replaced routinely. The replacement schedule must be clearly outlined in the Exposure Control Plan.

If leakage is possible or if the outside of the container has become contaminated, the sharps container must be placed in a secondary container.

Areas such as correctional facilities, psychiatric units, or pediatric units may have difficulty placing sharps containers in the immediate use area. If a mobile cart is used by health care workers in these units, an alternative would be to lock a sharps container in the cart.

Laundries that handle contaminated laundry must have sharps containers easily accessible due to the incidence of needles mixed with laundry.

Facilities that handle shipments of waste that may contain contaminated sharps must also have sharps containers easily accessible in the event a package accidentally opens and releases sharps.

Labeling Regulated Waste
What Is Regulated Waste?

The term *regulated waste* refers to the following categories of waste that require special handling, at a minimum:

- Liquid or semiliquid blood or other potentially infectious materials (OPIMs)
- Items contaminated with blood or OPIMs and that would release these substances in a liquid or semiliquid state if compressed
- Items that are caked with dried blood or OPIMs and are capable of releasing these materials during handling
- Contaminated sharps
- Pathological and microbiological wastes containing blood or OPIMs

When Is Labeling Regulated Waste Necessary?

Labels must be provided on containers of regulated waste, on refrigerators and freezers that are used to store blood or OPIMs, and on containers used to store, dispose of, transport, or ship blood or OPIMs.

Equipment that is being sent to another facility for servicing or decontamination must have a label attached stating which portions of the equipment remain contaminated to warn other employees of the hazard and encourage them to use proper precautions.

Labeling Regulated Waste

Regulated waste containers must be labeled with the biohazard label or color coded to warn individuals who may have contact with the containers of the potential hazard posed by their contents.

Even if your facility considers *all* of its waste to be regulated waste, the waste containers must still bear the required label or color coding to protect new employees and individuals and employees from outside facilities.

Regulated waste that has been decontaminated need not be labeled or color coded; however, your employer must have controls in place to determine whether the decontamination process is successful.

Blood and blood products that bear an identifying label as specified by the Food and Drug Admin-istration and that have been screened for hepatitis B virus (HBV), hepatitis C virus (HCV), and HIV antibodies and released for transfusion or other clinical uses are exempted from the labeling requirements.

When blood is being drawn or laboratory procedures are being performed on blood samples, the individual containers housing the blood or OPIMs do not have to be labeled, provided the larger container into which they are placed for storage, transport, shipment, or disposal (such as a test tube rack) is labeled.

Biohazard Labels

Biohazard labels may be attached to bags containing potentially infectious materials. These labels must be fluorescent orange or orange-red with letters or symbols in a contrasting color. These are attached to any container that is used to store or transport potentially infectious materials.

What Is an Exposure Control Plan?

The exposure control plan exists as a guideline for employees to know what to do when an exposure occurs. You do not have time to determine what to do *during* an exposure event. A well-documented exposure control plan resolves most of the questions that might arise about an exposure. In addition, the exposure control plan is a key provision of the Occupational Safety and Health Administration (OSHA) Bloodborne Pathogens Standard. A requirement of the plan is for the employer to identify the individuals who should receive training, protective equipment, vaccination, and other protections of the standard.

A hard copy of the exposure control plan must be made available to an employee within 15 working days of his or her request (Figure A2.14).

FIGURE A2.14 All employees must be made aware of an employer's exposure control plan.

Exposure Control Plan Requirements

According to OSHA, the exposure control plan should contain an exposure determination, including the following:

- *The exposure determination*: Each employer must determine which employees potentially have an occupational exposure to blood or OPIMs. This determination is made by reviewing job descriptions to see which employees could be exposed to blood or OPIMs on the job. The employer has to create the list of all tasks and procedures where occupational exposure could occur. This exposure determination has to be made without regard to the use of personal protective equipment.

- The schedule and method of implementation for each of the applicable subsections:
  - Methods of compliance
  - HIV, hepatitis B virus, and hepatitis C virus research laboratories and production facilities
  - Hepatitis B vaccination and postexposure evaluation and follow-up
  - Communication of hazards to employees
  - Record keeping of this standard

- Each employer needs to ensure that a copy of the exposure control plan is accessible to employees in accordance with 29 CFR 1910.1020(e).

- The exposure control plan is required to be reviewed and updated at least annually and whenever necessary to reflect new or modified tasks and procedures that affect occupational exposure and to reflect new or revised employee positions with occupational exposure. The review and update of such plans also need to do the following:

  - Reflect changes in technology that eliminate or reduce exposure to bloodborne pathogens
  - Document annually consideration and implementation of appropriate commercially available and effective safer medical devices designed to eliminate or minimize occupational exposure

The exposure control plan must include the procedure for evaluating the circumstances surrounding exposure incidents.

Any employer who is required to establish an exposure control plan also needs to solicit input from nonmanagerial employees responsible for direct patient care who are potentially exposed to injuries from contaminated sharps in the identification, evaluation, and selection of effective engineering and work practice controls and shall document the solicitation in the exposure control plan.

The exposure control plan needs to be made available to the assistant secretary and the director upon request for examination and copying.

Tuberculosis

This section contains information about tuberculosis (TB), an airborne disease. Since 1985, the incidence of TB in the general U.S. population has increased approximately 14%, reversing a 30-year downward trend. Recently, drug-resistant strains of *Mycobacterium tuberculosis (M tuberculosis)* have become a serious concern, and cases of multidrug-resistant (MDR) TB have occurred in 40 states. This overview of the risks of tuberculosis exposure (although it is not a bloodborne pathogen) has been added because many employees with occupational exposure to bloodborne pathogens may potentially have occupational exposure to persons with TB.

Nationwide, at least several hundred health care workers (HCWs) have become infected with TB and have required medical treatment after workplace exposure to TB. Twelve of these HCWs have died of TB. In general, persons who become infected with TB have approximately a 10% risk for developing TB in their lifetimes.

2005 Centers for Disease Control and Prevention TB Guidelines

OSHA has not released a standard specific to tuberculosis (as of this printing); however, the Centers for Disease Control and Prevention (CDC) has released the 2005 TB Guidelines for the protection of HCWs. OSHA believes the CDC's 2005 TB Guidelines reflect an industry recognition of the hazard as well as appropriate, widely recognized, and accepted standards of practice to be followed by employers in carrying out their responsibilities under the act.

The CDC is not a regulatory agency. The focus of the 2005 CDC TB Guidelines is to minimize the number of HCWs exposed to *M tuberculosis* while maintaining optimum care of patients with active infection with *M tuberculosis*. The guidelines can be found in the *Morbidity and Mortality Weekly Report*, vol. 54, December 30, 2005, No. RR-17, "Recommendations and Reports: Guidelines for Preventing the Transmission of *Mycobacterium tuberculosis* in Health-Care Facilities."

Occupational Safety and Health Act of 1970

OSHA is a regulatory agency. OSHA regulations are written to protect the employee from recognized hazards in the workplace. OSHA can and does enforce the worker protection by invoking the Occupational Safety and Health Act of 1970, or the General Duty Clause. The General Duty Clause (Public Law 91-596) states that "each employer shall furnish to each of his employees employment and a place of employment which are free from recognized hazards that are causing or are likely to cause death or serious physical harm to his employees: shall comply with occupational safety and health standards promulgated under this Act. Each employee shall comply with occupational safety and health standards and all rules, regulations, and orders issued pursuant to this Act which are applicable to his own actions and conduct."

Methods are available to minimize the hazards posed by employee exposure to TB. It is the employer's responsibility to see that these protections are in place and are readily available. It is your (the employee's) responsibility to use these protections.

Who Needs This Section?

Any employee who has potential for occupational exposure to *M tuberculosis* needs this section. The 2005 CDC TB Guidelines specify several potentially hazardous work settings:

- Health care facilities
- Long-term care facilities for older persons
- Homeless shelters
- Drug and treatment centers
- Correctional facilities

Health care facilities include inpatient settings (emergency departments, patient rooms), outpatient settings (medical offices, dialysis units), and nontraditional facility-based settings (EMS, home-based health care). The CDC also notes that TB patients might be encountered in other settings as well, such as laundry facilities, pharmacies, and law enforcement settings.

The following is a list of HCWs whose tasks may lead them to occupational exposure to *M tuberculosis*. The potential for occupational exposure is not limited to employees in these positions.

- Physicians
- Nurses
- Aides
- Home health care workers
- Dental workers
- Technicians
- Workers in laboratories and morgues
- Emergency medical service personnel
- Students
- Part-time personnel
- Temporary staff not employed by the health care facility
- Persons not directly involved with patient care, but who are potentially at risk for occupational exposure to *M tuberculosis* (e.g., air ventilation system workers)

Meeting the General Duty Clause

The 2005 CDC TB Guidelines specify steps to be taken to minimize exposure to *M tuberculosis*. To ensure a safe working environment and meet the OSHA General Duty Clause requirements, employers should provide the following:

1. An assessment of the risk for transmission of *M tuberculosis* in the particular work setting

2. A protocol for the early identification of individuals with active TB

3. Training and information to ensure employee knowledge of the method of TB transmission, its signs and symptoms, medical surveillance and therapy, and site-specific protocols, including the purpose and proper use of controls (failure to provide respirator training is citable under OSHA's general industry standard on respirators)

4. Medical screening, including preplacement evaluation; administration and interpretation of Mantoux skin tests

5. Evaluation and management of workers with positive skin tests or a history of positive skin tests who are exhibiting symptoms of TB, including work restrictions for infectious employees

6. AFB (acid-fast bacilli) isolation rooms for suspected or confirmed infectious TB patients. These AFB isolation rooms and areas in which high-hazard procedures are performed should be single-patient rooms with special ventilation characteristics that are properly installed, maintained, and evaluated to reduce the potential for airborne exposure to *M tuberculosis*.

7. Institution of exposure controls specific to the workplace which include the following:

   - Administrative controls are policies and procedures to reduce the risk of employee exposure to infectious sources of *M tuberculosis*. An example is a protocol to ensure rapid detection of people who are likely to have an active case of TB.

   - Engineering controls attempt to design safety into the tools and workspace organization. An example is High Efficiency Particulate Air (HEPA) filtration systems.

   - Personal respiratory protective equipment is used by the employee to prevent exposure to potentially infectious air droplet nuclei, for example, a personal respirator.

What Is Tuberculosis?

- *M tuberculosis* is the bacteria responsible for causing TB in humans.

- TB is a disease that primarily spreads from person to person through droplet nuclei suspended in the air.

- TB may cause disease in any organ of the body. The most commonly affected organ is the lung, which accounts for about 85% of all infection sites. Other sites may include lymph nodes, the central nervous system, kidneys, and the skeletal system.

- TB is a serious and often fatal disease if left untreated.

- Symptoms of TB include weight loss, weakness, fever, night sweats, coughing, chest pain, and coughing up blood.

- The prevalence of infection is much higher in the close contacts of TB patients than in the general population.

- There is a difference between TB infection (positive TB skin test) and TB disease.

Transmission

TB is spread from person to person in the form of droplet nuclei in the air. When a person with TB coughs, sings, or laughs, the droplet nuclei are released into the air. When uninfected people breathe in the droplet nuclei, they may become infected with TB.

For an employee to develop TB infection, he or she must have close contact to a sufficient number of air droplet nuclei. The employee's health is also considered as contributing to the susceptibility for TB infection and the possible development of TB disease. Among the medical risk factors for developing TB are diabetes, gastrectomy (removal of the stomach), long-term corticosteroid use, immunosuppressive therapy, cancers and other malignancies, and HIV infection.

Symptoms

Symptoms of TB also occur in people with more common diseases such as a cold or flu. The difference is that the symptoms of TB disease last longer than those of a cold or flu and must be treated with prescription antibiotics. The usual symptoms of TB disease include cough, production of sputum, weight loss, loss of appetite, weakness, fever, night sweats, malaise, fatigue, and, occasionally, chest pain. Hemoptysis, the coughing up of blood, may also occur, but usually not until after a person has had TB disease for some time.

Diagnosis

TB disease is diagnosed when there is a positive AFB sputum smear or when three successive early morning sputum specimens are cultured and there is growth of *M tuberculosis* from at least one culture. When extrapulmonary (not in the lungs) TB is being considered, it may also be diagnosed by culture techniques. The difference is that the specimen is cultured from the site where TB is considered as the cause of the infection.

Prevention

The 2005 CDC TB Guidelines recommend a hierarchy of controls to minimize TB transmission. These strategies are used in combination to promote workplace safety and to provide the employee with maximum protection against occupational exposure to *M tuberculosis*. Under these guidelines, the control of TB is to be accomplished through the early identification, isolation, and treatment of persons with TB; the use of engineering and administrative procedures to reduce the risk of exposure; and through the use of respiratory protection. The CDC 2005

TB Guidelines also stress the importance of the following measures: (1) use of risk assessments for developing a written TB control plan (e.g., incidence of TB in your community, number of patients with TB admitted to your facility), (2) TB screening programs for HCWs, (3) HCW training and education, and (4) evaluation of TB infection-control programs.

TB Screening

Who Should Receive TB Screening?

According to the 2005 CDC TB Guidelines, HCWs are at increased risk for TB infection and should be provided with TB skin testing. This testing must be provided at no cost to employees at risk of exposure. The general population of the United States is thought to be at low risk for TB and should not be routinely tested.

Frequency of Testing

The frequency of testing is determined by the number of active cases of TB within a worksite of the facility. HCWs should receive TB skin testing before work in an area at increased risk for active cases of TB. A two-step TB skin testing process should be used (see What Is the Booster Effect?). Testing should be repeated each year or more frequently for an employee assigned to a high-risk worksite or after a known exposure to a person with active TB.

What Is the TB Skin Test?

The tuberculin skin test of choice is the Mantoux test, which uses an intradermal injection of purified protein derivative (PPD). There are three strengths of PPD available; intermediate-strength (five tuberculin units) PPD is the standard test material.

A skin test is done by injecting a very small amount of PPD just under the skin (usually the forearm is used). A small bleb (bump) will be raised. The bleb will disappear. The injection site is then checked for reaction by your clinician about 48 to 72 hours later. If you fail to have the injection site evaluated in 72 hours and no induration (swelling) is present, the tuberculin skin test will need to be repeated.

What Types of Reactions Occur?

Induration, the hard and bumpy swelling at the injection site, is used for determining a reaction to the PPD. Interpretation of results are best understood when the general health and risk of exposure to active TB cases are considered in the assessment. The injection site may also be red, but that does not determine a reaction to the PPD nor indicate a positive result. We recommend that the interpretation guidelines of the American Thoracic Society–CDC Advisory panel be used to assess the measured induration at the injection site.

What Does a Positive Result Mean?

A positive skin test means an infection with *M tuberculosis* has occurred, but does not prove TB disease. Referral for further medical evaluation is required to determine a diagnosis of TB disease. People found to have TB disease must be provided effective treatments. These treatments would be provided to the employee by the employer if the illness was found to be work related.

Possible False-Positive Results

Close contacts of a person with TB disease who have had a negative reaction to the first skin test should be retested about 10 weeks after the last exposure to the person with TB disease. The delay between tests should allow enough time for the body's immune system to respond to an infection with *M tuberculosis*. A second test will result in a positive reaction at the injection site if an infection with *M tuberculosis* has occurred.

Contraindications to TB Screening

If you have tested positive to the TB skin test in the past, it is not recommended that you receive the test again. If you have had a vaccine called BCG (sometimes used in foreign countries), you should not have a TB skin test because it will be positive.

Pregnancy does not exclude an HCW from being tested. Many pregnant workers have been tested for TB without documented harm to the fetus. You should consult with your doctor if you are pregnant and have any questions about receiving a TB skin test.

Postexposure Reporting

What Determines an Occupational Exposure?

Occupational exposure to *M tuberculosis* is defined as employees working in one of the types of facilities whose workers have been identified by the CDC as having a higher incidence of TB than the general population, and whose employees have exposure defined as follows:

1. Potential exposure to the exhaled air of an individual with suspected or confirmed TB disease

2. Exposure to a high-hazard procedure performed on an individual with suspected or confirmed TB disease, which could generate potentially infectious airborne droplet nuclei

What Is the Booster Effect?

Sensitivity to the TB skin test may decrease over time, causing an initial skin test to be negative but at the same time stimulating or boosting the immune system's sensitivity to tuberculin, thereby producing a positive reaction the next time the test is given. When repeated skin testing is necessary, concern about the booster effect and the misinterpretation of skin test results can be avoided by using a two-step testing process. This is why your employer should require the two-step test as soon as you start employment. The two-step test helps to eliminate any confusion over whether an employee was infected at the worksite or was previously infected (see Record Keeping).

Postexposure Evaluation and Testing

Record Keeping

Records of employee exposure to TB, skin tests, and medical evaluations and treatment must be maintained by your employer.

Active tuberculosis disease is an illness that must be reported to public health officials. Every state has reporting requirements.

For OSHA Form 200 record-keeping purposes, both tuberculosis infections (positive TB skin test) and tuberculosis disease are recordable. A positive skin test for tuberculosis, even on initial testing (except preassignment screening), is recordable on the OSHA 200 log because of the presumption of work relatedness in these settings, unless there is clear documentation that an outside exposure occurred.

Requirements

TB Exposure Control Plan

Employers having employees with exposure to TB shall establish a written exposure control plan designed to eliminate or minimize employee exposure. This plan involves the following:

- Schedule and method of implementation of the control plan
- PPD testing
- Respiratory protection
- Communication of hazards to employees
- Postexposure evaluation and follow-up
- Record keeping

Relationship to HIV

1. People infected with HIV and *M tuberculosis* are at a very high risk of developing active TB. Seven percent to 10% of persons infected with both TB and HIV will develop active disease each year.

2. Extrapulmonary TB (i.e., outside the lungs) is more common in people with HIV infections.

3. Miliary TB (infection that has spread to other organs by the blood or lymph system) and lymphatic TB (infection of the lymphatic glands) are more common in HIV-infected persons.

4. The HIV epidemic is a major contributing factor to the recent increase in cases of active TB.

Appendix 3

NATA Position Statement: Exertional Heat Illnesses

A Message from the National Athletic Trainers' Association Board of Directors Disclaimer for Exertional Heat Illnesses Consensus Statement

Background Information

Heat illness is one of the most pressing issues in athletics today, particularly considering the untimely deaths of several high-profile athletes. In response to the need for information on this topic, the National Athletic Trainers' Association (NATA) Pronouncements Committee developed a position statement titled "National Athletic Trainers' Association Position Statement: Exertional Heat Illnesses" (referred to as the "position statement"), which was published in the September 2002 *Journal of Athletic Training*.

The position statement also served as the basis for the document released by the Inter-Association Task Force on Exertional Heat Illnesses, a group convened at the request of NATA to develop universal guidelines for reducing the risk of heat illness. The Inter-Association Task Force on Exertional Heat Illnesses Consensus Statement (referred to as the "consensus statement") was published on pages 24–29 of the June *NATA News* and is supported by representatives of several distinguished organizations, including the American Academy of Pediatrics, American Orthopaedic Society for Sports Medicine and American College of Sports Medicine.

This Issue

Since publication of the Inter-Association Task Force consensus statement, several NATA members have questioned the wet bulb globe temperature chart (WBGT) information shown on Table 1, which is also referenced in NATA's official position statement as Table 3. However, according to Douglas Casa, PhD, ATC, chair of both the NATA Pronouncements Committee and the Inter-Association Task Force on Exertional Heat Illnesses, the intent of both documents is to *serve as flexible statements* that can and should be modified to meet the needs of ATCs working in different climates and within different financial and staffing situations.

"Certified athletic trainers work in a variety of professional and geographic settings, and as an organization we understand and appreciate the diversity within this group," Casa said. "Our goal with these statements is to provide our colleagues with cutting-edge information that will serve as a starting point for the development of policies and procedures that meet the needs of our members' individual settings and circumstances. Obviously the ATC in Florida will adapt the recommendations to his or her environment, while the ATC in Maine will make different adjustments."

The Solution

As a result of this discussion, the NATA Board of Directors opted to add the following disclaimer to the Inter-Association Task Force consensus statement. The disclaimer was developed by NATA College University Athletic Trainers' Committee Chair Ron Courson, ATC, PT, and approved by NATA legal counsel.

Athletic trainers should recognize that temperature ranges might vary widely based upon geographic regions. Athletic trainers may practice in regions, such as the southeastern United States, where the WBGT is routinely in the high or extreme or hazardous level of risk throughout a significant part of the year. In these regions, while it may not be practical to reschedule or delay events, the athletic trainer must recognize that the level of risk is high and take appropriate steps to reduce risk.

Future Statements

Other organizations involved in the development of the consensus statement will be asked to include this disclaimer when releasing the document. In addition, all future NATA position statements will include a disclaimer, written by NATA legal counsel and approved by the NATA Board, noting the flexibility of the documents.

According to NATA District Three Director Rod Walters, DA, ATC, who initiated discussions regarding the heat illness issue after hearing from members in the southern areas of the United States, this approach is a logical one. By adding the disclaimer, NATA is providing certified athletic trainers with important information and guidelines while acknowledging that circumstances vary from member to member.

"It is very important that NATA continue to research and publish position statements, and I am proud of the Pronouncements Committee's work in this area," Walters said. "But as an athletic trainer working in the trenches, I understand that some of the challenges we face in the field may make it impossible to implement our guidelines in all circumstances. By adding a three-sentence statement, we are recognizing that situations vary—depending on location, staffing and financial issues and a host of other variables."

Introduction

Heat illness is inherent to physical activity and its incidence increases with rising ambient temperature and relative humidity. Athletes who begin training in the late summer (eg, football, soccer, and cross-country athletes) experience exertional heat-related illness more often than athletes who begin training during the winter and spring.[1–5] Although the hot conditions associated with late summer provide a simple explanation for this difference, we need to understand what makes certain athletes more susceptible and how these illnesses can be prevented.

Purpose

This position statement provides recommendations that will enable certified athletic trainers (ATCs) and other allied health providers to (1) identify and implement preventive strategies that can reduce heat-related illnesses in sports, (2) characterize factors associated with the early detection of heat illness, (3) provide on-site

Source: Binkley HM, Beckett J, Casa DJ, Kleiner DM, Plummer PE. (2002). National Athletic Trainers' Association position statement: Exertional heat illnesses. *J Athl Train.* 37(3):329–343. © by the National Athletic Trainers' Association, Inc. Reprinted with permission.

first aid and emergency management of athletes with heat illnesses, (4) determine appropriate return-to-play procedures, (5) understand thermoregulation and physiologic responses to heat, and (6) recognize groups with special concerns related to heat exposure.

Organization

This position statement is organized as follows:

1. Definitions of exertional heat illnesses, including exercise-associated muscle (heat) cramps, heat syncope, exercise (heat) exhaustion, exertional heat stroke, and exertional hyponatremia;

2. Recommendations for the prevention, recognition, and treatment of exertional heat illnesses;

3. Background and literature review of the diagnosis of exertional heat illnesses; risk factors; predisposing medical conditions; environmental risk factors; thermoregulation, heat acclimatization, cumulative dehydration, and cooling therapies;

4. Special concerns regarding exertional heat illnesses in prepubescent athletes, older athletes, and athletes with spinal-cord injuries;

5. Hospitalization and recovery from exertional heat stroke and resumption of activity after heat-related collapse; and

6. Conclusions.

Definitions of Exertional Heat Illnesses

The traditional classification of heat illness defines 3 categories: heat cramps, heat exhaustion, and heat stroke.[6–8] However, this classification scheme omits several other heat- and activity-related illnesses, including heat syncope and exertional hyponatremia. The signs and symptoms of the exertional heat illnesses are listed in Table 1.

Heat illness is more likely in hot, humid weather but can occur in the absence of hot and humid conditions.

Exercise-Associated Muscle (Heat) Cramps

Exercise-associated muscle (heat) cramps represent a condition that presents during or after intense exercise sessions as an acute, painful, involuntary muscle

TABLE 1

SIGNS AND SYMPTOMS OF EXERTIONAL HEAT ILLNESSES

Condition Sign or Symptom*

Exercise-associated muscle (heat) cramps[6,9–11]
  Dehydration
  Thirst
  Sweating
  Transient muscle cramps
  Fatigue
Heat syncope[10,12]
  Dehydration
  Fatigue
  Tunnel vision
  Pale or sweaty skin
  Decreased pulse rate
  Dizziness
  Lightheadedness
  Fainting
Exercise (heat) exhaustion[6,9,10,13]
  Normal or elevated body-core temperature
  Dehydration
  Dizziness
  Lightheadedness
  Syncope
  Headache
  Nausea
  Anorexia
  Diarrhea
  Decreased urine output
  Persistent muscle cramps
  Pallor
  Profuse sweating
  Chills
  Cool, clammy skin
  Intestinal cramps
  Urge to defecate
  Weakness
  Hyperventilation
Exertional heat stroke[6,9,10,14]
  High body-core temperature (>40°C [104°F])
  Central nervous system changes
    Dizziness
    Drowsiness
    Irrational behavior

  Confusion
 Central nervous system changes (continued)
    Irritability
    Emotional instability
    Hysteria
    Apathy
    Aggressiveness
    Delirium
    Disorientation
    Staggering
    Seizures
    Loss of consciousness
    Coma
  Dehydration
  Weakness
  Hot and wet or dry skin
  Tachycardia (100 to 120 beats per minute)
  Hypotension
  Hyperventilation
  Vomiting
  Diarrhea
Exertional hyponatremia[15–18]
  Body-core temperature <40°C (104°F)
  Nausea
  Vomiting
  Extremity (hands and feet) swelling
  Low blood-sodium level
  Progressive headache
  Confusion
  Significant mental compromise
  Lethargy
  Altered consciousness
  Apathy
  Pulmonary edema
  Cerebral edema
  Seizures
  Coma

---

*Not every patient will present with all the signs and symptoms for the suspected condition.

---

contraction. Proposed causes include fluid deficiencies (dehydration), electrolyte imbalances, neuromuscular fatigue, or any combination of these factors.[6,9–11,19]

Heat Syncope

Heat syncope, or orthostatic dizziness, can occur when a person is exposed to high environmental temperatures.[19] This condition is attributed to peripheral vasodilation,

postural pooling of blood, diminished venous return, dehydration, reduction in cardiac output, and cerebral ischemia.[10,19] Heat syncope usually occurs during the first 5 days of acclimatization, before the blood volume expands,[12] or in persons with heart disease or those taking diuretics.[10] It often occurs after standing for long periods of time, immediately after cessation of activity, or after rapid assumption of upright posture after resting or being seated.

Exercise (Heat) Exhaustion

Exercise (heat) exhaustion is the inability to continue exercise associated with any combination of heavy sweating, dehydration, sodium loss, and energy depletion. It occurs most frequently in hot, humid conditions. At its worst, it is difficult to distinguish from exertional heat stroke without measuring rectal temperature. Other signs and symptoms include pallor, persistent muscular cramps, urge to defecate, weakness, fainting, dizziness, headache, hyperventilation, nausea, anorexia, diarrhea, decreased urine output, and a body-core temperature that generally ranges between 36°C (97°F) and 40°C (104°F).[6,9,10,13,19]

Exertional Heatstroke

Exertional heatstroke is an elevated core temperature (usually >40°C [104°F]) associated with signs of organ system failure caused by hyperthermia. The central nervous system neurologic changes are often the first marker of exertional heatstroke. Exertional heatstroke occurs when the temperature regulation system is overwhelmed because of excessive endogenous heat production or inhibited heat loss in challenging environmental conditions[20] and can progress to complete thermoregulatory system failure.[19,21] This condition is life threatening and can be fatal unless promptly recognized and treated. Signs and symptoms include tachycardia, hypotension, sweating (although skin may be wet or dry at the time of collapse), hyperventilation, altered mental status, vomiting, diarrhea, seizures, and coma.[6,10,14] The risk of morbidity and mortality is greater the longer an athlete's body temperature remains above 41°C (106°F) and is significantly reduced if body temperature is lowered rapidly.[22–24]

Unlike classic heatstroke, which typically involves prolonged heat exposure in infants, elderly persons, or unhealthy, sedentary adults in whom body heat-regulation mechanisms are inefficient,[25–27] exertional heatstroke occurs during physical activity.[28] The pathophysiology of exertional heatstroke is caused by the overheating of organ tissues that may induce malfunction of the temperature-control center in the brain, circulatory failure, or endotoxemia (or a combination of these).[29,30] Severe lactic acidosis (accumulation of lactic acid in the blood), hyperkalemia (excessive potassium in the blood), acute renal failure, rhabdomyolysis (destruction of skeletal muscle that may be associated with strenuous exercise), and disseminated intravascular coagulation (a bleeding disorder characterized by diffuse blood coagulation), among other medical conditions, may result from exertional heatstroke and often cause death.[25]

Exertional Hyponatremia

Exertional hyponatremia is a relatively rare condition defined as a serum-sodium level less than 130 mmol/L. Low serum-sodium levels usually occur when activity exceeds 4 hours.[19] Two, often-additive mechanisms are proposed: an athlete ingests water or low-solute beverages well beyond sweat losses (also known as water intoxication), or an athlete's sweat sodium losses are not adequately replaced.[15–18] The low blood-sodium levels are the result of a combination of excessive fluid intake and inappropriate body water retention in the water-intoxication model and insufficient fluid intake and inadequate sodium replacement in the latter. Ultimately, the intravascular and extracellular fluid has a lower solute load than the intracellular fluids, and water flows into the cells, producing intracellular swelling that causes potentially fatal neurologic and physiologic dysfunction. Affected athletes present with a combination of disorientation, altered mental status, headache, vomiting, lethargy, and swelling of the extremities (hands and feet), pulmonary edema, cerebral edema, and seizures. Exertional hyponatremia can result in death if not treated properly. This condition can be prevented by matching fluid intake with sweat and urine losses and by rehydrating with fluids that contain sufficient sodium.[31,32]

Recommendations

The National Athletic Trainers' Association (NATA) advocates the following prevention, recognition, and treatment strategies for exertional heat illnesses. These recommendations are presented to help ATCs and other allied health providers maximize health, safety, and sport performance as they relate to these illnesses. Athletes' individual responses to physiologic stimuli and environmental conditions vary widely. These recommendations do not guarantee full protection from heat-related illness but should decrease the risk during athletic participation. These recommendations should be considered by ATCs and allied health providers who work with athletes at risk for exertional heat illnesses to improve prevention strategies and ensure proper treatment.

Prevention

1. Ensure that appropriate medical care is available and that rescue personnel are familiar with exertional heat illness prevention, recognition, and treatment. Table 2 provides general guidelines that should be considered.[7] Ensure that ATCs and other health care providers attending practices or

TABLE 2

PREVENTION CHECKLIST FOR THE CERTIFIED ATHLETIC TRAINER*

1. Pre-event preparation
   _____ Am I challenging unsafe rules (e.g., ability to receive fluids, modify game and practice times)?
   _____ Am I encouraging athletes to drink before the onset of thirst and to be well hydrated at the start of activity?
   _____ Am I familiar with which athletes have a history of a heat illness?
   _____ Am I discouraging alcohol, caffeine, and drug use?
   _____ Am I encouraging proper conditioning and acclimatization procedures?
2. Checking hydration status
   _____ Do I know the preexercise weight of the athletes (especially those at high risk) with whom I work, particularly during hot and humid conditions?
   _____ Are the athletes familiar with how to assess urine color?
   _____ Is a urine color chart accessible?
   _____ Do the athletes know their sweat rates and, therefore, know how much to drink during exercise?
   _____ Is a refractometer or urine color chart present to provide additional information regarding hydration status in high-risk athletes when baseline body weights are checked?
3. Environmental assessment
   _____ Am I regularly checking the wet-bulb globe temperature or temperature and humidity during the day?
   _____ Am I knowledgeable about the risk categories of a heat illness based on the environmental conditions?
   _____ Are alternate plans made in case risky conditions force rescheduling of events or practices?
4. Coaches' and athletes' responsibilities
   _____ Are coaches and athletes educated about the signs and symptoms of heat illnesses?
   _____ Am I double checking to make sure coaches are allowing ample rest and rehydration breaks?
   _____ Are modifications being made to reduce risk in the heat (e.g., decrease intensity, change practice times, allow more frequent breaks, eliminate double sessions, reduce or change equipment or clothing requirements, etc.)?
   _____ Are rapid weight-loss practices in weight-class sports adamantly disallowed?
5. Event management
   _____ Have I checked to make sure proper amounts of fluids will be available and accessible?
   _____ Are carbohydrate-electrolyte drinks available at events and practices (especially during twice-a-day practices and those that last longer than 50 to 60 minutes or are extremely intense in nature)?
   _____ Am I aware of the factors that may increase the likelihood of a heat illness?
   _____ Am I promptly rehydrating athletes to preexercise weight after an exercise session?
   _____ Are shaded or indoor areas used for practices or breaks when possible to minimize thermal strain?
6. Treatment considerations
   _____ Am I familiar with the most common early signs and symptoms of heat illnesses?
   _____ Do I have the proper field equipment and skills to assess a heat illness?
   _____ Is an emergency plan in place in case an immediate evacuation is needed?
   _____ Is a kiddy pool available in situations of high risk to initiate immediate cold-water immersion of heatstroke patients?
   _____ Are ice bags available for immediate cooling when cold-water immersion is not possible?
   _____ Have shaded, air-conditioned, and cool areas been identified to use when athletes need to cool down, recover, or receive treatment?
   _____ Are fans available to assist evaporation when cooling?
   _____ Am I properly equipped to assess high core temperature (i.e., rectal thermometer)?
7. Other situation-specific considerations

_____
*Adapted with permission from Casa.[7]

events are allowed to evaluate and examine any athlete who displays signs or symptoms of heat illness[33,34] and have the authority to restrict the athlete from participating if heat illness is present.

2. Conduct a thorough, physician-supervised, preparticipation medical screening before the season starts to identify athletes predisposed to heat illness on the basis of risk factors[34–36] and those who have a history of exertional heat illness.

3. Adapt athletes to exercise in the heat (acclimatization) gradually over 10 to 14 days. Progressively increase the intensity and duration of work in the

heat with a combination of strenuous interval training and continuous exercise.[6,9,14,33,37–44] Well-acclimatized athletes should train for 1 to 2 hours under the same heat conditions that will be present for their event.[6,45,46] In a cooler environment, an athlete can wear additional clothing during training to induce or maintain heat acclimatization. Athletes should maintain proper hydration during the heat-acclimatization process.[47]

4. Educate athletes and coaches regarding the prevention, recognition, and treatment of heat illnesses[9,33,38,39,42,48–51] and the risks associated with exercising in hot, humid environmental conditions.

5. Educate athletes to match fluid intake with sweat and urine losses to maintain adequate hydration.* (See the "National Athletic Trainers' Association Position Statement: Fluid Replacement in Athletes."[52]) Instruct athletes to drink sodium-containing fluids to keep their urine clear to light yellow to improve hydration[33,34,52–55] and to replace fluids between practices on the same day and on successive days to maintain less than 2% body-weight change. These strategies will lessen the risk of acute and chronic dehydration and decrease the risk of heat-related events.

6. Encourage athletes to sleep at least 6 to 8 hours at night in a cool environment,[41,35,50] eat a well-balanced diet that follows the Food Guide Pyramid and United States Dietary Guidelines,[56–58] and maintain proper hydration status. Athletes exercising in hot conditions (especially during twice-a-day practices) require extra sodium from the diet or rehydration beverages or both.

7. Develop event and practice guidelines for hot, humid weather that anticipate potential problems encountered based on the wet-bulb globe temperature (WBGT) (Table 3) or heat and humidity as measured by a sling psychrometer (Figure 1), the number of participants, the nature of the activity, and other predisposing risk factors.[14,51] If the WBGT is greater than 28°C (82°F, or "very high" as indicated in Table 3, Figure 1), an athletic event should be delayed, rescheduled, or moved into an air-conditioned space, if possible.[69–74] It is important to note that these measures are based on the risk of environmental stress for athletes wearing shorts and a T-shirt; if an athlete is wearing additional clothing (i.e., football uniform, wetsuit, helmet), a

*References 9, 29, 37, 38, 40, 41, 43, 52–66.

lower WBGT value could result in comparable risk of environmental heat stress (Figure 2).[75,76] If the event or practice is conducted in hot, humid conditions, then use extreme caution in monitoring the athletes and be proactive in taking preventive steps. In addition, be sure that emergency supplies and equipment are easily accessible and in good working order. The most important factors are to limit intensity and duration of activity, limit the amount of clothing and equipment worn, increase the number and length of rest breaks, and encourage proper hydration.

Modify activity under high-risk conditions to prevent exertional heat illnesses.[19,21] Identify individuals who are susceptible to heat illnesses. In some athletes, the prodromal signs and symptoms of heat illnesses are not evident before collapse, but in many cases, adept medical supervision will allow early intervention.

8. Check the environmental conditions before and during the activity, and adjust the practice schedule accordingly.[29,38,41,42,60] Schedule training sessions to avoid the hottest part of the day (10 A.M. to 5 P.M.) and to avoid radiant heating from direct sunlight, especially in the acclimatization during the first few days of practice sessions.[9,29,33,34,38,40,50,60]

9. Plan rest breaks to match the environmental conditions and the intensity of the activity.[33,34] Exercise intensity and environmental conditions should be the major determinants in deciding the length and frequency of rest breaks. If possible, cancel or postpone the activity or move it indoors (if air conditioned) if the conditions are "extreme or hazardous" (see Table 3) or "very high" (see Figure 1) or to the right of the circled line (see Figure 2). General guidelines during intense exercise would include a work:rest ratio of 1:1, 2:1, 3:1, and 4:1 for "extreme or hazardous" (see Table 3) or "very high" (see Figure 1), "high," "moderate," or "low" environmental risk, respectively.[41,77] For activities such as football in which equipment must be considered, please refer to Figure 2 for equipment modifications and appropriate work:rest ratios for various environmental conditions. Rest breaks should occur in the shade if possible, and hydration during rest breaks should be encouraged.

10. Implement rest periods at mealtime by allowing 2 to 3 hours for food, fluids, nutrients, and electrolytes (sodium and potassium) to move into

TABLE 3

WET-BULB GLOBE TEMPERATURE RISK CHART[62–67]*

WBGT	Flag Color	Level of Risk	Comments
<18°C (<65°F)	Green	Low	Risk low but still exists on the basis of risk factors
18–23°C (65–73°F)	Yellow	Moderate	Risk level increases as event progresses through the day
23–28°C (73–82°F)	Red	High	Everyone should be aware of injury potential; individuals at risk should not compete
>28°C (82°F)	Black	Extreme or hazardous	Consider rescheduling or delaying the event until safer conditions prevail; if the event must take place, be on high alert

*Adapted with permission from Roberts.[67]

the small intestine and bloodstream before the next practice.[34,50,77]

11. Provide an adequate supply of proper fluids (water or sports drinks) to maintain hydration[9,34,38,40,50,60] and institute a hydration protocol that allows the maintenance of hydration status.[34,49] Fluids should be readily available and served in containers that allow adequate volumes to be ingested with ease and with minimal interruption of exercise.[49,52] The goal should be to lose no more than 2% to 3% of body weight during the practice session (due to sweat and urine losses).[78–82] (See the "National Athletic Trainers' Association Position Statement: Fluid Replacement in Athletes."[52])

12. Weigh high-risk athletes (in high-risk conditions, weigh all athletes) before and after practice to estimate the amount of body water lost during practice and to ensure a return to prepractice weight before the next practice. Following exercise athletes should consume approximately 1–1.25 L (16 oz) of fluid for each kilogram of body water lost during exercise.[†]

13. Minimize the amount of equipment and clothing worn by the athlete in hot or humid (or both) conditions. For example, a full football uniform prevents sweat evaporation from more than 60% of the body.[29,33,40,51,77] Consult Figure 2 for possible equipment and clothing recommendations. When athletes exercise in the heat, they should wear loose-fitting, absorbent, and light-colored clothing; mesh clothing and new-generation cloth blends have been specially designed to allow more effective cooling.[‡]

14. Minimize warm-up time when feasible, and conduct warm-up sessions in the shade when possible to minimize the radiant heat load in "high" or "very high" or "extreme or hazardous" (see Table 3, Figure 1) conditions.[77]

15. Allow athletes to practice in shaded areas and use electric or cooling fans to circulate air whenever feasible.[66]

16. Include the following supplies on the field, in the locker room, and at various other stations:

- A supply of cool water or sports drinks or both to meet the participants' needs (see the "National Athletic Trainers' Association Position Statement: Fluid Replacement in Athletes"[52] for recommendations regarding the appropriate composition of rehydration beverages based on the length and intensity of the activity)[29,34,38]

- Ice for active cooling (ice bags, tub cooling) and to keep beverages cool during exercise[29,38]

- Rectal thermometer to assess body-core temperature[39,74,75,87,88]

- Telephone or 2-way radio to communicate with medical personnel and to summon emergency medical transportation[38,39,48]

- Tub, wading pool, kiddy pool, or whirlpool to cool the trunk and extremities for immersion cooling therapy[35,65]

†References 6, 9, 29, 33, 38, 40, 49, 60, 77, 83.

‡References 8, 9, 29, 33, 38, 40, 53, 59, 84–86.

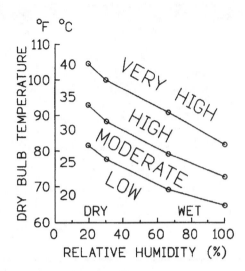

FIGURE 1 Risk of heat exhaustion or heatstroke while racing in hot environments. However, Figure 2 may be better suited for estimating heatstroke risk when equipment is worn. Reprinted with permission from Convertino VA, Armstrong LE, Coyle EF, et al. American College of Sports Medicine position stand: exercise and fluid replacement. *Med Sci Sports Exerc.* 1996;28:i–vii.[31]

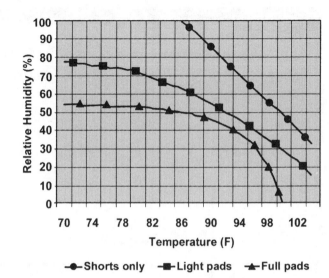

FIGURE 2 Heat stress risk temperature and humidity graph. Heatstroke risk rises with increasing heat and relative humidity. Fluid breaks should be scheduled for all practices and scheduled more frequently as the heat stress rises. Add 5° to temperature between 10 AM and 4 PM from mid May to mid-September on bright, sunny days. Practices should be modified for the safety of the athletes to reflect the heat-stress conditions. Regular practices with full practice gear can be conducted for conditions that plot to the left of the triangles. Cancel all practices when the temperature and relative humidity plot is to the right of the circles; practices may be moved into air-conditioned spaces or held as walk-through sessions with no conditioning activities.

Conditions that plot between squares and circles: increase rest-to-work ratio with 5-to 10-minute rest and fluid breaks every 15 to 20 minutes; practice should be in shorts only with all protective equipment removed.

Conditions that plot between triangles and squares: increase rest-to-work ratio with 5-to 10-minute rest and fluid breaks every 20 to 30 minutes; practice should be in shorts with helmets and shoulder pads (not full equipment).

Source: Adapted with permission from Kulka J, Kenney WL. Heat balance limits in football uniforms: how different uniform ensembles alter the equation. *Physician Sportsmed.* 2002;30(7):29–39.[68]

17. Notify local hospital and emergency personnel before mass participation events to inform them of the event and the increased possibility of heat-related illnesses.[41,89]

18. Mandate a check of hydration status at weigh-in to ensure athletes in sports requiring weight classes (e.g., wrestling, judo, rowing) are not dehydrated. Any procedures used to induce dramatic dehydration (e.g., diuretics, rubber suits, exercising in a sauna) are strictly prohibited.[52] Dehydrated athletes exercising at the same intensity as euhydrated athletes are at increased risk for thermoregulatory strain (see the "National Athletic Trainers' Association Position Statement: Fluid Replacement in Athletes"[52]).

Recognition and Treatment

19. Exercise-associated muscle (heat) cramps:

   • An athlete showing signs or symptoms including dehydration, thirst, sweating, transient muscle cramps, and fatigue is likely experiencing exercise-associated muscle (heat) cramps.

   • To relieve muscle spasms, the athlete should stop activity, replace lost fluids with sodium-containing fluids, and begin mild stretching with massage of the muscle spasm.

   • Fluid absorption is enhanced with sports drinks that contain sodium.[52,60,87] A high-sodium sports product may be added to the rehydration beverage to prevent or relieve cramping in athletes who lose large amounts of sodium in their sweat.[19] A simple salted fluid consists of two 10-grain salt tablets dissolved in 1 L (34 oz) of water. Intravenous fluids may be required if nausea or vomiting limits oral fluid intake; these must be ordered by a physician.[6,7,52,90,91]

- A recumbent position may allow more rapid redistribution of blood flow to cramping leg muscles.

20. Heat syncope:

- If an athlete experiences a brief episode of fainting associated with dizziness, tunnel vision, pale or sweaty skin, and a decreased pulse rate but has a normal rectal temperature (for exercise, 36°C to 40°C [97°F to 104°F]), then heat syncope is most likely the cause.[19]

- Move the athlete to a shaded area, monitor vital signs, elevate the legs above the level of the head, and rehydrate.

21. Exercise (heat) exhaustion:

- Cognitive changes are usually minimal, but assess central nervous system function for bizarre behavior, hallucinations, altered mental status, confusion, disorientation, or coma (see Table 1) to rule out more serious conditions.

- If feasible, measure body-core temperature (rectal temperature) and assess cognitive function (see Table 1) and vital signs.[19] Rectal temperature is the most accurate method possible in the field to monitor body-core temperature.[34,74,75,87,88] The ATC should not rely on the oral, tympanic, or axillary temperature for athletes because these are inaccurate and ineffective measures of body-core temperature during and after exercise.[75,89,92]

- If the athlete's temperature is elevated, remove his or her excess clothing to increase the evaporative surface and to facilitate cooling.[6,93]

- Cool the athlete with fans,[94] ice towels,[29,38] or ice bags because these may help the athlete with a temperature of more than 38.8°C (102°F) to feel better faster.

- Remove the athlete to a cool or shaded environment if possible.

- Start fluid replacement.[6,52,93,95]

- Transfer care to a physician if intravenous fluids are needed[6,52,90,91,96] or if recovery is not rapid and uneventful.

22. Exertional heatstroke:

- Measure the rectal temperature if feasible to differentiate between heat exhaustion and heatstroke. With heatstroke, rectal temperature is elevated (generally higher than 40°C [104°F]).[19]

- Assess cognitive function, which is markedly altered in exertional heatstroke (see Table 1).

- Lower the body-core temperature as quickly as possible.[34,70,77] The fastest way to decrease body temperature is to remove clothes and equipment and immerse the body (trunk and extremities) into a pool or tub of cold water (approximately 1°C to 15°C [35°F to 59°F]).[32,91,92,97–99] Aggressive cooling is the most critical factor in the treatment of exertional heat stroke. Circulation of the tub water may enhance cooling.

- Monitor the temperature during the cooling therapy and recovery (every 5 to 10 minutes).[39,87] Once the athlete's rectal temperature reaches approximately 38.3°C to 38.9°C (101°F to 102°F), he or she should be removed from the pool or tub to avoid overcooling.[40,100]

- If a physician is present to manage the athlete's medical care on site, then initial transportation to a medical facility may not be necessary so immersion can continue uninterrupted. If a physician is not present, aggressive first-aid cooling should be initiated on site and continued during emergency medical system transport and at the hospital until the athlete is normothermic.

- Activate the emergency medical system.

- Monitor the athlete's vital signs and other signs and symptoms of heatstroke (see Table 1).[34,95]

- During transport and when immersion is not feasible, other methods can be used to reduce body temperature: removing the clothing; sponging down the athlete with cool water and applying cold towels; applying ice bags to as much of the body as possible, especially the major vessels in the armpit, groin, and neck; providing shade; and fanning the body with air.[39,95]

- In addition to cooling therapies, first-aid emergency procedures for heat stroke may include airway management. Also a physician may decide to begin intravenous fluid replacement.[87]

- Monitor for organ-system complications for at least 24 hours.

23. Exertional hyponatremia:

- Attempt to differentiate between hyponatremia and heat exhaustion. Hyponatremia is characterized by increasing headache, significant mental compromise, altered consciousness, seizures, lethargy, and swelling in the extremities. The athlete may be dehydrated, normally hydrated, or overhydrated.[19]

- Attempt to differentiate between hyponatremia and heat stroke. In hyponatremia, hyperthermia is likely to be less (rectal temperature less than 40°C [104°F]).[19] The plasma-sodium level is less than 130 mEq/L and can be measured with a sodium analyzer on site if the device is available.

- If hyponatremia is suspected, immediate transfer to an emergency medical center via the emergency medical system is indicated. An intravenous line should be placed to administer medication as needed to increase sodium levels, induce diuresis, and control seizures.

- An athlete with suspected hyponatremia should not be administered fluids until a physician is consulted.

24. Return to activity

- In cases of exercise-associated muscle (heat) cramps or heat syncope, the ATC should discuss the athlete's case with the supervising physician. The cases of athletes with heat exhaustion who were not transferred to the physician's care should also be discussed with the physician. After exertional heatstroke or exertional hyponatremia, the athlete must be cleared by a physician before returning to athletic participation.[92] The return to full activity should be gradual and monitored.[8,87]

Background and Literature Review

Diagnosis

To differentiate heat illnesses in athletes, ATCs and other on-site health care providers must be familiar with the signs and symptoms of each condition (see Table 1). Other medical conditions (e.g., asthma, status epilepticus, drug toxicities) may also present with similar signs and symptoms. It is important to realize, however, that an athlete with a heat illness will not exhibit all the signs and symptoms of a specific condition, increasing the need for diligent observation during athletic activity.

Nonenvironmental Risk Factors

Athletic trainers and other health care providers should be sensitive to the following nonenvironmental risk factors, which could place athletes at risk for heat illness.

Dehydration. Sweating, inadequate fluid intake, vomiting, diarrhea, certain medications,[89,101–103] and alcohol[104,105] or caffeine[106] use can lead to fluid deficit. Body-weight change is the preferred method to monitor for dehydration in the field, but a clinical refractometer is another accurate method (specific gravity should be no more than 1.020).[34,49,107–110] Dehydration can also be identified by monitoring urine color or body-weight changes before, during, and after a practice or an event and across successive days.[53,54]

The signs and symptoms of dehydration are thirst, general discomfort, flushed skin, weariness, cramps, apathy, dizziness, headache, vomiting, nausea, heat sensations on the head or neck, chills, decreased performance, and dyspnea.[52] Water loss that is not regained by the next practice increases the risk for heat illness.[110]

Barriers to Evaporation. Athletic equipment and rubber or plastic suits used for "weight loss" do not allow water vapor to pass through and inhibit evaporative, convective, and radiant heat loss.[111,112] Participants who wear equipment that does not allow for heat dissipation are at an increased risk for heat illness.[113] Helmets are also limiting because a significant amount of heat is dissipated through the head.

Illness. Athletes who are currently or were recently ill may be at an increased risk for heat illness because of fever or dehydration.[114–116]

History of Heat Illness. Some individuals with a history of heat illness are at greater risk for recurrent heat illness.[8,117]

Increased Body Mass Index (Thick Fat Layer or Small Surface Area). Obese individuals are at an increased risk for heat illness because the fat layer decreases heat loss.[118] Obese persons are less efficient and have a greater metabolic heat production during exercise. Conversely, muscle-bound individuals have increased metabolic heat production and a lower ratio of surface area to mass, contributing to a decreased ability to dissipate heat.[119–121]

Wet-Bulb Globe Temperature on Previous Day and Night. When the WBGT is high to extreme (see Table 3), the risk of heat-related problems is greater the next day; this appears to be one of the best predictors of heat illness.[121] Athletes who sleep in cool or air-conditioned quarters are at less risk.

Poor Physical Condition. Individuals who are untrained are more susceptible to heat illness than are trained athletes. As the VO_2 max of an individual improves, the ability to withstand heat stress improves independent of acclimatization and heat adaptation.[122] High-intensity work can easily produce 1,000 kcal/h and elevate the core temperature of at-risk individuals (those who are unfit, overweight, or unacclimatized) to dangerous levels within 20 to 30 minutes.[123]

Excessive or Dark-Colored Clothing or Equipment. Excessive clothing or equipment decreases the ability to thermoregulate, and dark-colored clothing or equipment may cause a greater absorption of heat from the environment. Both should be avoided.[113]

Overzealousness. Overzealous athletes are at a higher risk for heat illness because they override the normal behavioral adaptations to heat and decrease the likelihood of subtle cues being recognized.

Lack of Acclimatization to Heat. An athlete with no or minimal physiologic acclimatization to hot conditions is at an increased risk of heat-related illness.[8,37,83,124]

Medications and Drugs. Athletes who take certain medications or drugs, particularly medications with a dehydrating effect, are at an increased risk for a heat illness.[101–106,125–136] Alcohol, caffeine, and theophylline at certain doses are mild diuretics.[106,137,138] Caffeine is found in coffee, tea, soft drinks, chocolate, and several over-the-counter and prescription medications.[139] Theophylline is found mostly in tea and anti-asthma medications.[140]

Electrolyte Imbalance. Electrolyte imbalances do not usually occur in trained, acclimatized individuals who engage in physical activity and eat a normal diet.[141] Most sodium and chloride losses in athletes occur through the urine, but athletes who sweat heavily, are salty sweaters, or are not heat acclimatized can lose significant amounts of sodium during activity.[142] Electrolyte imbalances often contribute to heat illness in older athletes who use diuretics.[143,144]

Predisposing Medical Conditions

The following predisposing medical conditions add to the risk of heat illness.

Malignant Hyperthermia. Malignant hyperthermia is caused by an autosomal dominant trait that causes muscle rigidity, resulting in elevation of body temperature due to the accelerated metabolic rate in the skeletal muscle.[145–147]

Neuroleptic Malignant Syndrome. Neuroleptic malignant syndrome is associated with the use of neuroleptic agents and antipsychotic drugs and an unexpected idiopathic increase in core temperature during exercise.[148–151]

Arteriosclerotic Vascular Disease. Arteriosclerotic vascular disease compromises cardiac output and blood flow through the vascular system by thickening the arterial walls.[115,152]

Scleroderma. Scleroderma is a skin disorder that decreases sweat production, thereby decreasing heat transfer.[149,153]

Cystic Fibrosis. Cystic fibrosis causes increased salt loss in sweat and can increase the risk for hyponatremia.[154,155]

Sickle Cell Trait. Sickle cell trait limits blood-flow distribution and decreases oxygen-carrying capacity. The condition is exacerbated by exercise at higher altitudes.[156,157]

Environmental Risk Factors

When the environmental temperature is above skin temperature, athletes begin to absorb heat from the environment and depend entirely on evaporation for heat loss.[113,158,159] High relative humidity inhibits heat loss from the body through evaporation.[61]

The environmental factors that influence the risk of heat illness include the ambient air temperature, relative humidity (amount of water vapor in the air), air motion, and the amount of radiant heat from the sun or other sources.[2,9,41] The relative risk of heat illness can be calculated using the WBGT equation.[2,43,50,69,77,160,161] Using the WBGT index to modify activity in high-risk settings has virtually eliminated heat-stroke deaths in United States Marine Corps recruits.[159] Wet-bulb globe temperature is calculated using the wet-bulb (wb), dry-bulb (db), and black-globe (bg) temperature with the following equation[49,62,85,162,163]:

$$WBGT = 0.7T_{wb} + 0.2T_{bg} + 0.1T_{db}$$

When there is no radiant heat load, $T_{db} = T_{bg}$, and the equation is reduced[62] to

$$WBGT = 0.7T_{wb} + 0.3T_{db}$$

This equation is used to estimate risk as outlined in Table 3.[13,40,50,61,85] This index was determined for athletes wearing a T-shirt and light pants.[158] The WBGT calculation can be performed using information obtained from electronic devices[42] or the local meteorologic service, but conversion tables for relative humidity and Tdb are needed to calculate the wet-bulb temperature.[50,162] The predictive value from the meteorologic service is not as accurate as site-specific data for representing local heat load but will suffice in most situations. When WBGT measures are not possible, environmental heat stress can be estimated using a sling psychrometer (see Figures 1, 2).

Several recommendations have been published for distance running, but these can also be applied to other continuous activity sports. The Canadian Track and

Field Association recommended that a distance race should be cancelled if the WBGT is greater than 26.7°C (80°F).[39] The American College of Sports Medicine guidelines from 1996 recommended that a race should be delayed or rescheduled when the WBGT is greater than 27.8°C (82°F).[31,72,73] In some instances, the event will go on regardless of the WBGT; ATCs should then have an increased level of suspicion for heat stroke and focus on hydration, emergency supplies, and detection of exertional heat illnesses.

Thermoregulation

Thermoregulation is a complex interaction among the central nervous system (CNS), the cardiovascular system, and the skin to maintain a body-core temperature of 37°C.[9,43,51,164] The CNS temperature-regulation center is located in the hypothalamus and is the site where the core temperature setpoint is determined.[9,43,82,158,164–166] The hypothalamus receives information regarding body-core and shell temperatures from peripheral skin receptors and the circulating blood; body-core temperature is regulated through an open-ended feedback loop similar to that in a home thermostat system.[158,165,167,168] Body responses for heat regulation include cutaneous vasodilation, increased sweating, increased heart rate, and increased respiratory rate.[38,43,51,164,165]

Body-core temperature is determined by metabolic heat production and the transfer of body heat to and from the surrounding environment using the following heat-production and heat-storage equation[166,167]:

$$S = M \pm R \pm K \pm Cv - E$$

where S is the amount of stored heat, M is the metabolic heat production, R is the heat gained or lost by radiation, K is the conductive heat lost or gained, Cv is the convective heat lost or gained, and E is the evaporative heat lost.

Basal metabolic heat production fasting and at absolute rest is approximately 60 to 70 kcal/h for an average adult, with 50% of the heat produced by the internal organs. Metabolic heat produced by intense exercise may approach 1000 kcal/h,[51,164] with greater than 90% of the heat resulting from muscle metabolism.[9,40,42,166]

Heat is gained or lost from the body by one or more of the following mechanisms[9,85]:

Radiation. The energy is transferred to or from an object or body via electromagnetic radiation from higher to lower energy surfaces.[9,43,51,85,166]

Conduction. Heat transfers from warmer to cooler objects through direct physical contact.[9,43,51,85,166] Ice packs and cold-water baths are examples of conductive heat exchange.

Convection. Heat transfers to or from the body to surrounding moving fluid (including air).[9,43,51,85,166] Moving air from a fan, cycling, or windy day produces convective heat exchange.

Evaporation. Heat transfers via the vaporization of sweat[§] and is the most efficient means of heat loss.[51,158,169] The evaporation of sweat from the skin depends on the water saturation of the air and the velocity of the moving air.[170–172] The effectiveness of this evaporation for heat loss from the body diminishes rapidly when the relative humidity is greater than 60%.[9,20,164]

Cognitive performance and associated CNS functions deteriorate when brain temperature rises. Signs and symptoms include dizziness, confusion, behavior changes, coordination difficulties, decreased physical performance, and collapse due to hyperthermia.[168,173] The residual effects of elevated brain temperature depend on the duration of the hyperthermia. Heat stroke rarely leads to permanent neurologic deficits[51]; however, some sporadic symptoms of frontal headache and sleep disturbances have been noted for up to 4 months.[168,174,175] When permanent CNS damage occurs, it is associated with cerebellar changes, including ataxia, marked dysarthria, and dysmetria.[174]

Heat Acclimatization

Heat acclimatization is the physiologic response produced by repeated exposures to hot environments in which the capacity to withstand heat stress is improved.[14,43,75,176,177] Physiologic responses to heat stress are summarized in Table 4. Exercise heat exposure produces progressive changes in thermoregulation that involve sweating, skin circulation, thermoregulatory setpoint, cardiovascular alterations, and endocrine adjustments.[29,43,178] Individual differences affect the onset and decay of acclimatization.[29,45,179] The rate of acclimatization is related to aerobic conditioning and fitness; more conditioned athletes acclimatize more quickly.[43,45,180] The acclimatization process begins with heat exposure and is reasonably protective after 7 to 14 days, but maximum acclimatization may take 2 to 3 months.[45,181,182] Heat acclimatization diminishes by day 6 when heat stress is no longer present.[180,183] Fluid replacement improves the induction and effect of heat acclimatization.[184–187] Extra salt in the diet during the first few days of heat exposure also improves acclimatization; this can be accomplished by encouraging the athlete to eat salty foods and to use the salt shaker liberally during meals.

§References 9, 40, 43, 50, 51, 85, 159, 165, 166.

TABLE 4

PHYSIOLOGIC RESPONSES AFTER HEAT ACCLIMATIZATION RELATIVE TO NONACCLIMATIZED STATE

Physiologic Variable	After Acclimatization (10–14 Days' Exposure)
Heart rate	Decreases[46,145]
Stroke volume	Increases[145,147]
Body-core temperature	Decreases[145]
Skin temperature	Decreases[152]
Sweat output/rate	Increases[46,47,149]
Onset of sweat	Earlier in training[46,145]
Evaporation of sweat	Increases[47,152]
Salt in sweat	Decreases[9,50]
Work output	Increases[46,50]
Subjective discomfort (rating of perceived exertion [RPE])	Decreases[50,145]
Fatigue	Decreases[50]
Capacity for work	Increases[46,50]
Mental disturbance	Decreases[50]
Syncopal response	Decreases[9,50]
Extracellular fluid volume	Increases[50]
Plasma volume	Increases[50,150]

Cumulative Dehydration

Cumulative dehydration develops insidiously over several days and is typically observed during the first few days of a season during practice sessions or in tournament competition. Cumulative dehydration can be detected by monitoring daily prepractice and postpractice weights. Even though a small decrease in body weight (less than 1%) may not have a detrimental effect on the individual, the cumulative effect of a 1% fluid loss per day occurring over several days will create an increased risk for heat illness and a decrease in performance.[110]

During intense exercise in the heat, sweat rates can be 1 to 2.5 L/h (about 1 to 2.25 kilograms [2 to 5 pounds] of body weight per hour) or more, resulting in dehydration. Unfortunately, the volume of fluid that most athletes drink voluntarily during exercise replaces only about 50% of body-fluid losses.[188] Ideally, rehydration involves drinking at a rate sufficient to replace all of the water lost through sweating and urination.[60,77] If the athlete is not able to drink at this rate, he or she should drink the maximum tolerated. Use caution to ensure that athletes do not overhydrate and put themselves at risk for the development of hyponatremia. However, hydration before an event is essential to help decrease the incidence of heat illnesses. For more information on this topic, see the "National Athletic Trainers' Association Position Statement: Fluid Replacement in Athletes."[52]

Cooling Therapies

The fastest way to decrease body-core temperature is immersion of the trunk and extremities into a pool or tub filled with cold water (between 1°C [35°F] and 15°C [59°F]).[39,88,91,97] Conditions that have been associated with immersion therapy include shivering and peripheral vasoconstriction; however, the potential for these should not deter the medical staff from using immersion therapy for rapid cooling. Shivering can be prevented if the athlete is removed from the water once rectal temperature reaches 38.3°C to 38.9°C (101°F to 102°F). Peripheral vasoconstriction may occur, but the powerful cooling potential of immersion outweighs any potential concerns. Cardiogenic shock has also been a proposed consequence of immersion therapy, but this connection has not been proven in cooling heatstroke patients.[39] Cold-water immersion therapy was associated with a zero percent fatality rate in 252 cases of exertional heat stroke in the military.[89] Other forms of cooling (water spray; ice packs covering the body; ice packs on axillae, groin, and neck; or blowing air) decrease body-core temperature at a slower rate compared with cold-water immersion.[97] If immersion cooling is not being used, cooling with ice bags should be directed to as much of the body as possible, especially the major vessels in the armpit, groin, and neck regions (and likely the hands and feet), and cold towels may be applied to the head and trunk because these areas have been demonstrated on thermography[173,189] to have the most rapid heat loss.

Special Concerns

Most research related to heat illness has been performed on normal, healthy adults. Child athletes, older athletes, and athletes with spinal-cord injuries have been studied less frequently. The following are suggestions for special populations or those with special conditions.

Children (Prepubescents)

Exercise in hot environments and heat tolerance are affected by many physiologic factors in children. These include decreased sweat gland activity,[190] higher skin temperatures,[191–193] decreased cardiac output (increased heart rate and lower stroke volume) as a result of increased peripheral circulation,[194] decreased exercise economy,[195] decreased ability to acclimatize to heat (slower and takes longer),[192] smaller body size (issues related to body surface-to-mass ratio), maturational differences,[190] and predisposing conditions (obesity, hypohydration, childhood illnesses, and other disease states).[190,192,196]

- Decrease the intensity of activities that last longer than 30 minutes,[197] and have the athlete take brief rests[50] if the WBGT is between 22.8°C and 27.8°C (73°F and 82°F); cancel or modify the activity if the WBGT is greater than 27.8°C (82°F).[31,69–73] Modification could involve longer and more frequent rest breaks than are usually permitted within the rules of the sport (e.g., insert a rest break before halftime).

- Encourage children to ingest some fluids at least every 15 to 30 minutes during activity to maintain hydration, even if they are not thirsty.[197]

- Use similar precautions as listed earlier for adults.

Older Athletes (>50 Years Old)

The ability of the older athlete to adapt is partly a function of age and also depends on functional capacity and physiologic health status.[198–206]

- The athlete should be evaluated by a physician before exercise, with the potential consequences of predisposing medical conditions and illnesses addressed.[9,34–36] An increase has been shown in the exercise heart rate of 1 beat per minute for each 1°C (1.8°F) increase in ambient temperature above neutral (23.9°C [75°F]).[207] Athletes with known or suspected heart disease should curtail activities at lower temperatures than healthy athletes and should have cardiovascular stress testing before participating in hot environments.

- Older athletes have a decreased ability to maintain an adequate plasma volume and osmolality during exercise,[198,208] which may predispose them to dehydration. Regular fluid intake is critical to avoid hyperthermia.

Athletes with Spinal-Cord Injuries

As sport participation for athletes with spinal-cord injuries increases from beginner to elite levels, understanding the disability,[209,210] training methods, and causes of heat injury will help make competition safer.[211] For example, the abilities to regulate heart rate, circulate the blood volume, produce sweat, and transfer heat to the surface vary with the level and severity of the spinal-cord lesion.[208,212–218]

- Monitor these athletes closely for heat-related problems. One technique for determining hyperthermia is to feel the skin under the arms of the distressed athlete.[211] Rectal temperature may not be as accurate for measuring core temperature as in other athletes because of decreased ability to regulate blood flow beneath the spinal-cord lesion.[218–220]

- If the athlete is hyperthermic, provide more water, lighter clothing, or cooling of the trunk,[211,213] legs,[211] and head.[213]

Hospitalization and Recovery

After an episode of heatstroke, the athlete may experience impaired thermoregulation, persistent CNS dysfunction,[221,222] hepatic insufficiency, and renal insufficiency.[39,223] For persons with exertional heatstroke and associated multisystem tissue damage, the rate of recovery is highly individualized, ranging up to more than 1 year.[8,86,221] In one study, 9 of 10 patients exhibited normal heat-acclimatization responses, thermoregulation, whole-body sodium and potassium balance, sweat-gland function, and blood values about 2 months after the heatstroke.[8] Transient or persistent heat intolerance was found in a small percentage of patients.[83] For some athletes, a history of exertional heatstroke increases the chance of experiencing subsequent episodes.[39]

An athlete who experiences heatstroke may have compromised heat tolerance and heat acclimatization after physician clearance.[35,224,225] Decreased heat tolerance may affect 15% to 20% of persons after a heatstroke-related collapse,[226,227] and in a few individuals, decreased heat tolerance has persisted up to 5 years.[35,224,228] Additional heat stress may reduce the athlete's ability to train and compete as a result of impaired cardiovascular and thermoregulatory responses.[115,228–230]

After recovery from an episode of heatstroke or hyponatremia, an athlete's physical activity should be restricted[8,86] and the gradual return to sport individualized by his or her physician. The athlete should be monitored on a daily basis by the ATC during exercise.[86] During the return-to-exercise phase, an athlete may experience some detraining and deconditioning not directly related to the heat exposure.[8,86] Evaluate the athlete over time to determine whether there has been a complete recovery of exercise and heat tolerance.[8,86]

Conclusions

Athletic trainers and other allied health providers must be able to differentiate exercise-associated muscle (heat) cramps, heat syncope, exercise (heat) exhaustion, exertional heatstroke, and exertional hyponatremia in athletes.

This position statement outlines the NATA's current recommendations to reduce the incidence, improve the recognition, and optimize treatment of heat illness in athletes. Education and increased awareness will help to reduce both the frequency and the severity of heat illness in athletes.

Acknowledgments

This pronouncement was reviewed for the NATA by the Pronouncements Committee, Edward R. Eichner, MD, FACSM, and William O. Roberts, MD, MS, FACSM. T. Kyle Eubanks, MA, ATC, and Paul C. Miller, PhD, provided assistance in the preparation of the manuscript.

REFERENCES

1. Hawley DA, Slentz K, Clark MA, Pless JE, Waller BF. Athletic fatalities. *Am J Forensic Med Pathol.* 1990;11:124–129.

2. Mueller FO, Schindler RD. Annual survey of football injury research 1931–1984. *Athl Train J Natl Athl Train Assoc.* 1985;20:213–218.

3. Bijur PE, Trumble A, Harel Y, Overpeck MD, Jones D, Scheidt PC. Sports and recreation injuries in US children and adolescents. *Arch Pediatr Adolesc Med.* 1995;149: 1009–1016.

4. Tucker AM. Common soccer injuries: diagnosis, treatment and rehabilitation. *Sports Med.* 1997; 23:21–32.

5. Martin DE. Influence of elevated climatic heat stress on athletic competition in Atlanta, 1996. *New Stud Athl.* 1997;12:65–78.

6. Rich B. Environmental concerns: heat. In: Sallis RE, Massimino F, eds. *Essentials of Sports Medicine.* St Louis, Mo: Mosby Year Book; 1997: 129–133.

7. Casa DJ. Exercise in the heat, II: critical concepts in rehydration, exertional heat illnesses, and maximizing athletic performance. *J Athl Train.* 1999; 34:253–262.

8. Armstrong LE, De Luca JP, Hubbard RW. Time course of recovery and heat acclimation ability of prior exertional heatstroke patients. *Med Sci Sports Exerc.* 1990;22:36–48.

9. Brewster SJ, O'Connor FG, Lillegard WA. Exercise-induced heat injury: diagnosis and management. *Sports Med Arthrosc Rev.* 1995;3:206–266.

10. Knochel JP. Environmental heat illness: an eclectic review. *Arch Intern Med.* 1974;133:841–864.

11. Bergeron MF. Heat cramps during tennis: a case report. *Int J Sport Nutr.* 1996;6:62–68.

12. Hubbard R, Gaffin S, Squire D. Heat-related illness. In: Auerbach PS, ed. *Wilderness Medicine.* 3rd ed. St Louis, Mo: Mosby Year Book; 1995: 167–212.

13. Armstrong LE, Hubbard RW, Kraemer WJ, DeLuca JP, Christensen EL. Signs and symptoms of heat exhaustion during strenuous exercise. *Ann Sports Med.* 1987;3:182–189.

14. Epstein Y. Exertional heatstroke: lessons we tend to forget. *Am J Med Sports.* 2000;2:143–152.

15. Epstein Y, Armstrong LE. Fluid-electrolyte balance during labor and exercise: concepts and misconceptions. *Int J Sport Nutr.* 1999;9:1–12.

16. Maughan RJ. Optimizing hydration for competitive sport. In: Lamb DR, Murray R, eds. *Optimizing Sport Performance.* Carmel, Ind: Cooper Publishing; 1997:139–183.

17. Armstrong LE, Curtis WC, Hubbard RW, Francesconi RP, Moore R, Askew W. Symptomatic hyponatremia during prolonged exercise in the heat. *Med Sci Sports Exerc.* 1993;25: 543–549.

18. Garigan T, Ristedt DE. Death from hyponatremia as a result of acute water intoxication in an Army basic trainee. *Mil Med.* 1999;164:234– 238.

19. Casa DJ, Roberts WO. Considerations for the medical staff in preventing, identifying and treating exertional heat illnesses. In: Armstrong LE, ed. *Exertional Heat Illnesses.* Champaign, Ill: Human Kinetics; 2003.

20. Cabanac M, White MD. Core temperature thresholds of hyperpnea during passive hyperthermia in humans. *Eur J Appl Physiol Occup Physiol.* 1995;71:71–76.

21. Casa DJ, Armstrong LE. Heatstroke: a medical emergency. In: Armstrong LE, ed. *Exertional Heat Illnesses.* Champaign, Ill: Human Kinetics: 2003.

22. Vicario SJ, Okabajue R, Haltom T. Rapid cooling in classic heatstroke: effect on mortality rates. *Am J Emerg Med.* 1986;4:394–398.

23. Assia E, Epstein Y, Shapiro Y. Fatal heatstroke after a short march at night: a case report. *Aviat Space Environ Med.* 1985;56:441–442.

24. Graham BS, Lichtenstein MJ, Hinson JM, Theil GB. Nonexertional heatstroke: physiologic management and cooling in 14 patients. *Arch Intern Med.* 1986;146:87–90.

25. Hart GR, Anderson RJ, Crumpler CP, Shulkin A, Reed G, Knochel JP. Epidemic classical heat stroke: clinical characteristics and course of 28 patients. *Medicine (Baltimore).*1982;61:189–197.

26. Thomas C, ed. *Taber's Cyclopedic Medical Dictionary.* Philadelphia, Pa: FA Davis; 1993.

27. Akhtar MJ, Al-Nozha M, al-Harthi S, Nouh MS. Electrocardiographic abnormalities in patients with heat stroke. *Chest.* 1993;104:411–414.

28. Partin N. Internal medicine: exertional heatstroke. *Athl Train J Natl Athl Train Assoc.* 1990;25:192–194.

29. Knochel J. Management of heat conditions. *Athl Ther Today.* 1996;1: 30–34.

30. Hubbard RW, Armstrong LE. Hyperthermia: new thoughts on an old problem. *Physician Sportsmed.*1989;17(6):97–98,101,104,107–108, 111–113.

31. Convertino VA, Armstrong LE, Coyle EF, et al. American College of Sports Medicine position stand: exercise and fluid replacement. *Med Sci Sports Exerc.* 1996;28:i–vii.

32. Armstrong LE, Casa DJ, Watson G. Exertional hyponatremia: unanswered questions and etiological perspectives. *Int J Sport Nutr Exerc Metab.* In press.

33. Francis K, Feinstein R, Brasher J. Optimal practice times for the reduction of the risk of heat illness during fall football practice in the Southeastern United States. *Athl Train J Natl Athl Train Assoc.* 1991;26:76– 78,80.

34. Shapiro Y, Seidman DS. Field and clinical observations of exertional heat stroke patients. *Med Sci Sports Exerc.* 1990;22:6–14.

35. Epstein Y, Shapiro Y, Brill S. Role of surface area-to-mass ratio and work efficiency in heat intolerance. *J Appl Physiol.* 1983;54:831–836.

36. Kenney WL. Physiological correlates of heat intolerance. *Sports Med.* 1985;2:279–286.

37. Mitchell D, Senay LC, Wyndham CH, van Rensburg AJ, Rogers GG, Strydom NB. Acclimatization in a hot, humid environment: energy exchange, body temperature, and sweating. *J Appl Physiol.* 1976;40:768– 778.

38. Davidson M. Heat illness in athletics. *Athl Train J Natl Athl Train Assoc.* 1985;20:96–101.

39. Brodeur VB, Dennett SR, Griffin LS. Exertional hyperthermia, ice baths, and emergency care at the Falmouth Road Race. *J Emerg Nurs.* 1989; 15:304–312.

40. Allman FL Jr. The effects of heat on the athlete. *J Med Assoc Ga.* 1992; 81:307–310.

41. Bernard TE. Risk management for preventing heat illness in athletes. *Athl Ther Today.* 1996;1:19–21.

42. Delaney KA. Heatstroke: underlying processes and lifesaving management. *Postgrad Med.* 1992;91:379–388.

43. Haymes EM, Wells CL. *Environment and Human Performance.* Champaign, Ill: Human Kinetics; 1986:1–41.

44. Gisolfi C, Robinson S. Relations between physical training, acclimatization, and heat tolerance. *J Appl Physiol.* 1969;26:530–534.

45. Armstrong LE, Maresh CM. The induction and decay of heat acclimatisation in trained athletes. *Sports Med.* 1991;12:302–312.

46. Fortney SM, Vroman NB. Exercise, performance and temperature control: temperature regulation during exercise and implications for sports performance and training. *Sports Med.* 1985;2:8–20.

47. Dawson B. Exercise training in sweat clothing in cool conditions to improve heat tolerance. *Sports Med.* 1994;17:233–244.

48. Kleiner DM, Glickman SE. Medical considerations and planning for short distance road races. *J Athl Train.* 1994;29:145–146,149–151.

49. Murray B. Fluid replacement: the American College of Sports Medicine position stand. *Sport Sci Exch.* 1996;9(4S):63.

50. Elias SR, Roberts WO, Thorson DC. Team sports in hot weather: guidelines for modifying youth soccer. *Physician Sportsmed.* 1991;19(5):67–68, 72–74,77,80.

51. Knochel JP. Heat stroke and related heat stress disorders. *Dis Month.* 1989;35:301–377.

52. Casa DJ, Armstrong LE, Hillman SK, et al. National Athletic Trainers' Association position statement: fluid replacement for athletes. *J Athl Train.* 2000;35:212–224.

53. Armstrong LE, Maresh CM, Castellani JW, et al. Urinary indices of hydration status. *Int J Sport Nutr.* 1994;4:265–279.

54. Armstrong LE, Soto JA, Hacker FT Jr, Casa DJ, Kavouras SA, Maresh CM. Urinary indices during dehydration exercise and rehydration. *Int J Sport Nutr.* 1997;8:345–355.

55. Heat and humidity. In: Armstrong LE. *Performing in Extreme Environments*. Champaign, Ill: Human Kinetics; 2000:15–70.

56. Nadel ER, Fortney SM, Wenger CB. Effect of hydration state on circulatory and thermal regulations. *J Appl Physiol*. 1980;49:715–721.

57. Keithley JK, Keller A, Vazquez MG. Promoting good nutrition: using the Food Guide Pyramid in clinical practice. *Medsurg Nurs*. 1996;5:397– 403.

58. Achterberg C, McDonnell E, Bagby R. How to put the Food Guide Pyramid into practice. *J Am Diet Assoc*. 1994;94:1030–1035.

59. Laywell P. Guidelines for pre-event eating. *Texas Coach*. 1981;25:40– 41,59.

60. Terrados N, Maughan RJ. Exercise in the heat: strategies to minimize the adverse effects on performance. *J Sports Sci*. 1995;13(suppl):55–62.

61. Armstrong LE, Hubbard RW, Szlyk PC, Matthew WT, Sils IV. Voluntary dehydration and electrolyte losses during prolonged exercise in the heat. *Aviat Space Environ Med*. 1985;56:765–770.

62. Sandor RP. Heat illness: on-site diagnosis and cooling. *Physician Sports med*.1997;25(6):35–40.

63. Squire DL. Heat illness: fluid and electrolyte issues for pediatric and adolescent athletes. *Pediatr Clin North Am*. 1990;37:1085–1109.

64. Murray R. Fluid needs in hot and cold environments. *Int J Sports Nutr*. 1995;5(suppl):62–73.

65. Gisolfi CV. Fluid balance for optimal performance. *Nutr Rev*. 1996;54(4 Pt 2, suppl):159–168.

66. Sawka MN, Coyle EF. Influence of body water and blood volume on thermoregulation and exercise performance in the heat. *Exerc Sport Sci Rev*. 1999;27:167–218.

67. Roberts WO. Medical management and administration manual for long distance road racing. In: Brown CH, Gudjonsson B, eds. *IAAF Medical Manual for Athletics and Road Racing Competitions: A Practical Guide*. Monaco: International Amateur Athletic Federation Publications; 1998: 39–75.

68. Kulka TJ, Kenney WL. Heat balance limits in football uniforms: how different uniform ensembles alter the equation. *Physician Sportsmed*. 2002;30(7):29–39.

69. Department of the Army. Prevention Treatment and Control of Heat Injury. Washington, DC: Department of the Army; 1980. Technical bulletin TBMED 507:1–21.

70. Hughson RL, Staudt LA, Mackie JM. Monitoring road racing in the heat. *Physician Sportsmed*. 1983;11(5):94–102.

71. American College of Sports Medicine. ACSM position statement: prevention of thermal injuries during distance running. *Med Sci Sports Exerc*. 1987;19:529–533.

72. Armstrong LE, Epstein Y, Greenleaf JE, et al. American College of Sports Medicine position stand: heat and cold illnesses during distance running. *Med Sci Sports Exerc*. 1996;28:i–x.

73. Rozycki TJ. Oral and rectal temperatures in runners. *Physician Sportsmed*. 1984;12(6):105–110.

74. Knight JC, Casa DJ, McClung JM, Caldwell KA, Gilmer AM, Meenan PM, Goss PJ. Assessing if two tympanic temperature instruments are valid predictors of core temperature in hyperthermic runners and does drying the ear canal help [abstract]. *J Athl Train*. 2000;35(suppl):S21.

75. Shapiro Y, Pandolf KB, Goldman RF. Predicting sweat loss response to exercise, environment and clothing. *Eur J Appl Physiol Occup Physiol*. 1982; 48:83–96.

76. Shvartz E, Saar E, Benor D. Physique and heat tolerance in hot dry and hot humid environments. *J Appl Physiol*. 1973;34:799–803.

77. Murray R. Dehydration, hyperthermia, and athletes: science and practice. *J Athl Train*. 1996; 31:248–252.

78. Pichan G, Gauttam RK, Tomar OS, Bajaj AC. Effects of primary hypohydration on physical work capacity. *Int J Biometerorol*. 1988;32: 176–180.

79. Walsh RM, Noakes TD, Hawley JA, Dennis SC. Impaired high-intensity cycling performance time at low levels of dehydration. *Int J Sports Med*. 1994;15:392–398.

80. Cheung SS, McLellan TM. Heat acclimation, aerobic fitness, and hydration effects on tolerance during uncompensable heat stress. *J Appl Physiol*. 1998;84:1731–1739.

81. Bijlani R, Sharma KN. Effect of dehydration and a few regimes of rehydration on human performance. *Indian J Physiol Pharmacol*. 1980; 24: 255–266.

82. Nielsen B. Solar heat load: heat balance during exercise in clothed subjects. *Eur J Appl Physiol Occup Physiol*. 1990;60:452–456.

83. Maughan RJ, Shirreffs SM. Preparing athletes for competition in the heat: developing an effective acclimatization strategy. *Sports Sci Exchange*. 1997;10:1–4.

84. Lloyd EL. ABC of sports medicine: temperature and performance—II: heat. *BMJ.* 1994;309: 587–589.

85. Pascoe DD, Shanley LA, Smith EW. Clothing and exercise, I: biophysics of heat transfer between the individual clothing and environment. *Sports Med.* 1994;18:38–54.

86. Anderson MK, Hall SJ. *Sports Injury Management.* Philadelphia, Pa: Williams & Wilkins; 1995:66–75.

87. Roberts WO. Assessing core temperature in collapsed athletes: what's the best method? *Physician Sportsmed.* 1994;22(8):49–55.

88. Armstrong LE, Maresh CM, Crago AE, Adams R, Roberts RO. Interpretation of aural temperatures during exercise, hyperthermia, and cooling therapy. *Med Exerc Nutr Health.* 1994;3:9–16.

89. Adner MM, Scarlet JJ, Casey J, Robinson W, Jones BH. The Boston Marathon medical care team: ten years of experience. *Physician Sportsmed.* 1988; 16(7):99–108.

90. Casa DJ, Maresh CM, Armstrong LE, et al. Intravenous versus oral rehydration during a brief period: responses to subsequent exercise in the heat. *Med Sci Sports Exerc.* 2000;32:124–133.

91. Noakes T. Failure to thermoregulate. In: Sutton J, Thompson M, Torode M, eds. *Exercise and Thermoregulation.* Sydney, Australia: The University of Sydney; 1995:37.

92. Deschamps A, Levy RD, Coslo MG, Marliss EB, Magder S. Tympanic temperature should not be used to assess exercise-induced hyperthermia. *Clin J Sport Med.* 1992;2:27–32.

93. Gonzalez-Alonso J, Mora-Rodriguez R, Coyle EF. Supine exercise restores arterial blood pressure and skin blood flow despite dehydration and hyperthermia. *Am J Physiol.* 1999;277(2 Pt 2):H576–H583.

94. Germain M, Jobin M, Cabanac M. The effect of face fanning during the recovery from exercise hyperthermia. *Can J Physiol Pharmacol.* 1987;65: 87–91.

95. Roberts WO. Exercise-associated collapse in endurance events: a classification system. *Physician Sportsmed.* 1989;17(5):49–55.

96. Matthew CB. Treatment of hyperthermia and dehydration with hypertonic saline in dextran. *Shock.* 1994;2:216–221.

97. Armstrong LE, Crago AE, Adams R, Roberts WO, Maresh CM. Whole-body cooling of hyperthermic runners: comparison to two field therapies. *Am J Emerg Med.* 1996;14:355–358.

98. Marino F, Booth J. Whole body cooling by immersion in water at moderate temperature. *J Sci Med Sport.* 1998;1:73–82.

99. Clements JM, Casa DJ, Knight JC, et al. Ice-water immersion and cold-water immersion provide similar cooling rates in runners with exercise-induced hyperthermia. *J Athl Train.* 2002;37: 146–150.

100. Ash CJ, Cook JR, McMurry TA, Auner CR. The use of rectal temperature to monitor heat stroke. *Mo Med.* 1992;89:283–288.

101. Brechue WF, Stager JM. Acetazolamide alters temperature regulation during submaximal exercise. *J Appl Physiol.* 1990;69:1402–1407.

102. Kubica R, Nielsen B, Bonnesen A, Rasmussen IB, Stoklosa J, Wilk B. Relationship between plasma volume reduction and plasma electrolyte changes after prolonged bicycle exercise, passive heating and diuretic dehydration. *Acta Physiol Pol.* 1983; 34:569–579.

103. Claremont AD, Costill DL, Fink W, Van Handel P. Heat tolerance following diuretic induced dehydration. *Med Sci Sports.* 1976;8:239–243.

104. Desruelle AV, Boisvert P, Candas V. Alcohol and its variable effect on human thermoregulatory response to exercise in a warm environment. *Eur J Appl Physiol Occup Physiol.* 1996;74:572–574.

105. Kalant H, Le AD. Effect of ethanol on thermoregulation. *Pharmacol Ther.* 1983;23:313–364.

106. Vanakoski J, Seppala T. Heat exposure and drugs: a review of the effects of hyperthermia on pharmacokinetics. *Clin Pharmacokinet.* 1998;34: 311–322.

107. Shirreffs SM, Maughan RJ. Urine osmolality and conductivity as indices of hydration status in athletes in the heat. *Med Sci Sports Exerc.* 1998; 30:1598–1602.

108. Kaplan A, Szabo LL, Opheim KE. *Clinical Chemistry: Interpretations and Techniques.* 2nd ed. Philadelphia, Pa: Lea & Febiger; 1983.

109. Ross D, Neely AE. *Textbook of Urinalysis and Body Fluids.* Norwalk, Conn: Appleton-Century-Crofts; 1983.

110. Armstrong L. The impact of hyperthermia and hypohydration on circulation strength endurance and health. *J Appl Sport Sci Res.* 1998;2: 60–65.

111. Montain SJ, Sawka MN, Cadarette BS, Quigley MD, McKay JM. Physiological tolerance to uncompensable heat stress: effects of exercise intensity, protective clothing, and climate. *J Appl Physiol.* 1994;77:216–222.

112. Kenney WL, Hyde DE, Bernard TE. Physiological evaluation of liquid-barrier, vapor-permeable protective clothing ensembles for work in hot environments. *Am Ind Hyg Assoc J.* 1993;54:397–402.

113. Mathews DK, Fox EL, Tanzi D. Physiological responses during exercise and recovery in a football uniform. *J Appl Physiol.* 1969;26:611–615.

114. Armstrong LE. The nature of heatstroke during exercise. *Natl Strength Condition J.* 1992;14:80.

115. Wetterhall SF, Coulombier DM, Herndon JM, Zaza S, Cantwell JD. Medical care delivery at the 1996 Olympic Games: Centers for Disease Control and Prevention Olympics Surveillance Unit. *JAMA.* 1998;279: 1463–1468.

116. Cooper KE. Some responses of the cardiovascular system to heat and fever. *Can J Cardiol.* 1994; 10:444–448.

117. Epstein Y. Heat intolerance: predisposing factor or residual injury? *Med Sci Sports Exerc.* 1990;22: 29–35.

118. Chung NK, Pin CH. Obesity and the occurrence of heat disorders. *Mil Med.* 1996;161:739–742.

119. Gardner JW, Kark JA, Karnei K, et al. Risk factors predicting exertional heat illness in male Marine Corps recruits. *Med Sci Sports Exerc.* 1996; 28:939–944.

120. Hayward JS, Eckerson JD, Dawson BT. Effect of mesomorphy on hyperthermia during exercise in a warm, humid environment. *Am J Phys Anthropol.* 1986;70:11–17.

121. Kark JA, Burr PQ, Wenger CB, Gastaldo E, Gardner JW. Exertional heat illness in Marine Corps recruit training. *Aviat Space Environ Med.* 1996; 67:354–360.

122. Piwonka RW, Robinson S, Gay VL, Manalis RS. Preacclimatization of men to heat by training. *J Appl Physiol.* 1965;20:379–384.

123. Noakes TD, Myburgh KH, du Plessis J, et al. Metabolic rate, not percent dehydration, predicts rectal temperature in marathon runners. *Med Sci Sports Exerc.* 1991;23:443–449.

124. Nadel ER, Pandolf KB, Roberts MF, Stolwijk JA. Mechanisms of thermal acclimation to exercise and heat. *J Appl Physiol.* 1974;37:515–520.

125. Walter FF, Bey TA, Ruschke DS, Benowitz NL. Marijuana and hyperthermia. *J Toxicol Clin Toxicol.* 1996;34:217–221.

126. Watson JD, Ferguson C, Hinds CJ, Skinner R, Coakley JH. Exertional heat stroke induced by amphetamine analogues: does dantrolene have a place? *Anaesthesia.* 1993;48:1057–1060.

127. Epstein Y, Albukrek D, Kalmovitc B, Moran "DS, Shapiro Y. Heat intolerance induced by antidepressants. *Ann N Y Acad Sci.* 1997;813: 553– 558.

128. Stadnyk AN, Glezos JD. Drug-induced heat stroke. *Can Med Assoc J.* 1983;128:957–959.

129. Forester D. Fatal drug-induced heat stroke. *JACEP.* 1978;7:243–244.

130. Sarnquist F, Larson CP Jr. Drug-induced heat stroke. *Anesthesiology.* 1973;39:348–350.

131. Zelman S, Guillan R. Heat stroke in phenothiazine-treated patients: a report of three fatalities. *Am J Psychiatry.* 1970;126:1787–1790.

132. Gordon NF, Duncan JJ. Effect of beta-blockers on exercise physiology: implications for exercise training. *Med Sci Sports Exerc.* 1991;23:668– 676.

133. Freund BJ, Joyner MJ, Jilka SM, et al. Thermoregulation during prolonged exercise in heat: alterations with beta-adrenergic blockade. *J Appl Physiol.* 1987;63:930–936.

134. Kew MC, Hopp M, Rothberg A. Fatal heat-stroke in a child taking appetite-suppressant drugs. *S Afr Med J.* 1982;62:905–906.

135. Lomax P, Daniel KA. Cocaine and body temperature: effect of exercise at high ambient temperature. *Pharmacology.* 1993;46:164–172.

136. Chen WL, Huang WS, Lin YF, Shieh SD. Changes in thyroid hormone metabolism in exertional heat stroke with or without acute renal failure. *J Clin Endocrinol Metab.* 1996;81:625–629.

137. Wemple RD, Lamb DR, McKeever KH. Caffeine vs caffeine-free sports drinks: effect on urine production at rest and during prolonged exercise. *Int J Sports Med.* 1997;18:40–46.

138. Odlind B. Site and mechanism of the action of diuretics. *Acta Pharmacol Toxicol (Copenh).* 1984; 54(suppl 1):5–15.

139. Stookey JD. The diuretic effects of alcohol and caffeine and total water intake misclassification. *Eur J Epidemiol.* 1999;15:181–188.

140. Schlaeffer F, Engelberg I, Kaplanski J, Danon A. Effect of exercise and environmental heat on theophylline kinetics. *Respiration.* 1984;45:438–442.

141. Armstrong LE, Hubbard RW, Askew EW, et al. Responses to moderate and low sodium diets during exercise-heat acclimation. *Int J Sport Nutr.* 1993;3:207–221.

142. Armstrong LE, Szlyk PC, DeLuca JP, Sils IV, Hubbard RW. Fluid-electrolyte losses in uniforms during prolonged exercise at 30 degrees C. *Aviat Space Environ Med.* 1992;63:351–355.

143. Mendyka BE. Fluid and electrolyte disorders caused by diuretic therapy. *AACN Clin Issues Crit Care Nurs.* 1992;3:672–680.

144. Melby JC. Selected mechanisms of diuretic-induced electrolyte changes. *Am J Cardiol.* 1986; 58:1A–4A.

145. Bourdon L, Canini F. On the nature of the link between malignant hyperthermia and exertional heatstroke. *Med Hypotheses.* 1995;45:268–270.

146. Dixit SN, Bushara KO, Brooks BR. Epidemic heat stroke in midwest community: risk factors, neurological complications, and sequelae. *Wis Med J.* 1997;96:39–41.

147. Hunter SL, Rosenberg H, Tuttle GH, DeWalt JL, Smodie R, Martin J. Malignant hyperthermia in a college football player. *Physician Sportsmed.* 1987;15(12):77–81.

148. Lazarus A. Differentiating neuroleptic-related heatstroke from neuroleptic malignant syndrome. *Psychosomatics.* 1989;30:454–456.

149. Rampertaap MP. Neuroleptic malignant syndrome. *South Med J.* 1986; 79:331–336.

150. Addonizio G, Susman V. Neuroleptic malignant syndrome and heat stroke. *Br J Psychiatry.* 1984;145:556–557.

151. Martin ML, Lucid EJ, Walker RW. Neuroleptic malignant syndrome. *Ann Emerg Med.* 1985;14: 354–358.

152. Virmani R, Robinowitz M. Cardiac pathology and sports medicine. *Hum Pathol.* 1987;18:493–501.

153. Buchwald I, Davis PJ. Scleroderma with fatal heat stroke. *JAMA.* 1967; 201:270–271.

154. Smith HR, Dhatt GS, Melia WM, Dickinson JG. Cystic fibrosis presenting as hyponatraemic heat exhaustion. *BMJ.* 1995;310:579–580.

155. Andrews C, Mango M, Venuto RC. Cystic fibrosis in adults. *Ann Intern Med.* 1978;88:128–129.

156. Kerle KK, Nishimura KD. Exertional collapse and sudden death associated with sickle cell trait. *Am Fam Physician.* 1996;54:237–240.

157. Gardner JW, Kark JA. Fatal rhabdomyolysis presenting as mild heat illness in military training. *Mil Med.* 1994;159:160–163.

158. Kenney WL. Thermoregulation during exercise in the heat. *Athl Ther Today.* 1996;1:13–16.

159. Tilley RI, Standerwick JM, Long GJ. Ability of the Wet Bulb Globe Temperature Index to predict heat stress in men wearing NBC protective clothing. *Mil Med.* 1987;152:554–556.

160. Rasch W, Cabanac M. Selective brain cooling is affected by wearing headgear during exercise. *J Appl Physiol.* 1993;74:1229–1233.

161. Sheffield-Moore M, Short KR, Kerr CG, Parcell AC, Bolster DR, Costill DL. Thermoregulatory responses to cycling with and without a helmet. *Med Sci Sports Exerc.* 1997;29:755–761.

162. Shapiro Y, Pandolf KB, Avellini BA, Pimental NA, Goldman RF. Physiological responses of men and women to humid and dry heat. *J Appl Physiol.* 1980;49:1–8.

163. Yaglou CP, Minard D. Control of heat casualties at military training centers. *Arch Ind Health.* 1957;16:302–305.

164. Bracker MO. Hyperthermia: man's adaptation to a warm climate. *Sports Med Dig.* 1991;13:1–2.

165. Johnson SC, Ruhling RO. Aspirin in exercise-induced hyperthermia: evidence for and against its role. *Sports Med.* 1985;2:1–7.

166. Werner J. Central regulation of body temperature. In: Gisolfi C, ed. *Exercise, Heat, and Thermoregulation.* Carmel, Ind: Cooper Publishing; 1993:7–35.

167. Galaski MJ. Hyperthermia. *J Can Athl Ther.* 1985;12:23–26.

168. Yaqub BA. Neurologic manifestations of heatstroke at the Mecca pilgrimage. *Neurology.* 1987; 37:1004–1006.

169. Armstrong LE. *Keeping Your Cool in Barcelona: The Effects of Heat Humidity and Dehydration on Athletic Performance Strength and Endurance.* Colorado Springs, Colo: United States Olympic Committee Sports Sciences Division; 1992:1–29.

170. Anderson GS, Meneilly GS, Mekjavic IB. Passive temperature lability in the elderly. *Eur J Appl Physiol Occup Physiol.* 1996;73:278–286.

171. Candas V, Libert JP, Vogt JJ. Influence of air velocity and heat acclimation on human skin wettedness and sweating efficiency. *J Appl Physiol.* 1979;47:1194–2000.

172. Berglund LG, Gonzalez RR. Evaporation of sweat from sedentary man in humid environments. *J Appl Physiol.* 1977;42:767–772.

173. Gabrys J, Pieniazek W, Olejnik I, Pogorzelska T, Karpe J. Effects of local cooling of neck circulatory responses in men subjected to physical exercise in hyperthermia. *Biol Sport.* 1993;10:167–171.

174. Royburt M, Epstein Y, Solomon Z, Shemer J. Long-term psychological and physiological effects of heat stroke. *Physiol Behav.* 1993;54:265–267.

175. Mehta AC, Baker RN. Persistent neurological deficits in heat stroke. *Neurology.* 1970;20: 336–340.

176. McArdle WD, Katch FI, Katch VL. *Exercise Physiology.* 3rd ed. Philadelphia, Pa: Lea & Febiger; 1991:556–570.

177. Avellini BA, Kamon E, Krajewski JT. Physiological responses of physically fit men and women to acclimation to humid heat. *J Appl Physiol.* 1980; 49:254–261.

178. Geor RJ, McCutcheon LJ. Thermoregulatory adaptations associated with training and heat acclimation. *Vet Clin North Am Equine Pract.* 1988; 14:97–120.

179. Nielsen B. Heat stress and acclimation. *Ergonomics.* 1994;37:49–58.

180. Gisolfi CV, Wenger CB. Temperature regulation during exercise: old concepts, new ideas. *Exerc Sport Sci Rev.* 1984;12:339–372.

181. Morimoto T, Miki K, Nose H, Yamada S, Hirakawa K, Matsubara D. Changes in body fluid and its composition during heavy sweating and effect of fluid and electrolyte replacement. *Jpn J Biometeorol.* 1981;18: 31–39.

182. Pandolf KB, Cadarette BS, Sawka MN, Young AJ, Francesconi RP, Gonzalez RR. Thermoregulatory responses of middle-aged and young men during dry-heat acclimation. *J Appl Physiol.* 1998;65:65–71.

183. Pandolf KB, Burse RL, Goldman RF. Role of physical fitness in heat acclimatisation, decay and reinduction. *Ergonomics.* 1977;20:399–408.

184. Cadarette BS, Sawka MN, Toner MM, Pandolf KB. Aerobic fitness and the hypohydration response to exercise-heat stress. *Aviat Space Environ Med.* 1984;55:507–512.

185. Buskirk ER, Iampietro PF, Bass DE. Work performance after dehydration: effects of physical conditioning and heat acclimatization. *J Appl Physiol.* 1958;12:789–794.

186. Adams J, Fox R, Grimby G, Kidd D, Wolff H. Acclimatization to heat and its rate of decay in man. *J Physiol.* 1960;152:26P–27P.

187. Czerkawski JT, Meintod A, Kleiner DM. Exertional heat illness: teaching patients when to cool it. *Your Patient Fitness.* 1996;10:13–20.

188. Wyndham C, Strydom N, Cooks H, et al. Methods of cooling subjects with hyperpyrexia. *J Appl Physiol.* 1959;14:771–776.

189. Hayward JS, Collis M, Eckerson JD. Thermographic evaluation of relative heat loss areas of man during cold water immersion. *Aerosp Med.* 1973;44:708–711.

190. Tsuzuki-Hayakawa K, Tochihara Y, Ohnaka T. Thermoregulation during heat exposure of young children compared to their mothers. *Eur J Appl Physiol Occup Physiol.* 1995;72:12–17.

191. Bar-Or O. Children's responses to exercise in hot climates: implications for performance and health. *Sports Sci Exerc.* 1994;7:1–5.

192. Davies CT. Thermal responses to exercise in children. *Ergonomics.* 1981;24:55–61.

193. Docherty D, Eckerson JD, Hayward JS. Physique and thermoregulation in prepubertal males during exercise in a warm, humid environment. *Am J Phys Anthropol.* 1986;70:19–23.

194. Armstrong LE, Maresh CM. Exercise-heat tolerance of children and adolescents. *Pediatr Exerc Sci.* 1995;7:239–252.

195. Gutierrez GG. Solar injury and heat illness: treatment and prevention in children. *Physician Sportsmed.* 1995;23(7):43–48.

196. Nash HL. Hyperthermia: risks greater in children. *Physician Sportsmed.* 1987;15(2):29.

197. American Academy of Pediatrics Committee on Sports Medicine. Climatic heat stress and the exercising child. *Pediatrics.* 1982;69:808–809.

198. Kenney WL, Hodgson JL. Heat tolerance, thermoregulation, and ageing. *Sports Med.* 1987;4: 446–456.

199. Wagner JA, Robinson S, Tzankoff SP, Marino RP. Heat tolerance and acclimatization to work in the heat in relation to age. *J Appl Physiol.* 1972;33: 616–622.

200. Pandolf KB. Heat tolerance and aging. *Exp Aging Res.* 1994;20:275–284.

201. Pandolf KB. Aging and human heat tolerance. *Exp Aging Res.* 1997;23: 69–105.

202. Kenney W. The older athlete: exercise in hot environments. *Sports Sci Exerc.* 1993;6:1–4.

203. Inoue Y, Shibasaki M, Hirata K, Araki T. Relationship between skin blood flow and sweating rate and age related regional differences. *Eur J Appl Physiol Occup Physiol.* 1998;79:17–23.

204. Sagawa S, Shiraki K, Yousef MK, Miki K. Sweating and cardiovascular responses of aged men to heat exposure. *J Gerontol.* 1988;43:M1–M8.

205. Inoue Y, Shibasaki M. Regional differences in age-related decrements of the cutaneous vascular and sweating responses to passive heating. *Eur J Appl Physiol Occup Physiol.* 1996;74:78–84.

206. Inoue Y, Shibasaki M, Ueda H, Ishizashi H. Mechanisms underlying the age-related decrement in the human sweating response. *Eur J Appl Physiol Occup Physiol.* 1999;79:121–126.

207. Pandolf KB, Cafarelli E, Noble BJ, Metz KF. Hyperthermia: effect on exercise prescription. *Arch Phys Med Rehabil.* 1975;56:524–526.

208. Zappe DH, Bell GW, Swartzentruber H, Wideman RF, Kenney WL. Age and regulation of fluid and electrolyte balance during repeated exercise sessions. *Am J Physiol.* 1996;207(1 Pt 2):R71–R79.

209. Binkhorst RA, Hopman MT. Heat balance in paraplegic individuals during arm exercise at 10 and 35°C. *Med Sci Sports Exerc.* 1995;27.

210. Clark MW. The physically challenged athlete. *Adolesc Med.* 1998;9: 491–499.

211. Bloomquist LE. Injuries to athletes with physical disabilities: prevention implications. *Physician Sportsmed.* 1986;14(9):96–100,102,105.

212. Hopman MT, Binkhourst RA. Spinal cord injury and exercise in the heat. *Sports Sci Exerc.* 1997;10:1–4.

213. Armstrong LE, Maresh CM, Riebe D, et al. Local cooling in wheelchair athletes during exercise-heat stress. *Med Sci Sports Exerc.* 1995;27:211–216.

214. Sawka MN, Latzka WA, Pandolf KB. Temperature regulation during upper body exercise: able-bodied and spinal cord injured. *Med Sci Sports Exerc.* 1989;21(5 suppl):132–140.

215. Hopman MT, Oeseburg B, Binkhorst RA. Cardiovascular responses in persons with paraplegia to prolonged arm exercise and thermal stress. *Med Sci Sports Exerc.* 1993;25:577–583.

216. Petrofsky JS. Thermoregulatory stress during rest and exercise in heat in patients with a spinal cord injury. *Eur J Appl Physiol Occup Physiol.* 1992;64:503–507.

217. Bracker MD. Environmental and thermal injury. *Clin Sports Med.* 1992; 11:419–436.

218. Hopman MT. Circulatory responses during arm exercise in individuals with paraplegia. *Int J Sports Med.* 1994;15:126–131.

219. Yamaski M, Kim KT, Choi SW, Muraki S, Shiokawa M, Kurokawa T. Characteristics of body heat balance of paraplegics during exercise in a hot environment. *J Physiol Anthropol Appl Human Sci.* 2001;20:227–232.

220. Gass GC, Camp EM, Nadel ER, Gwinn TH, Engel P. Rectal and rectal vs. esophageal temperatures in paraplegic men during prolonged exercise. *J Appl Physiol.* 1998;64:2265–2271.

221. Yaqub BA, Al-Harthi SS, Al-Orainey IO, Laajam MA, Obeid MT. Heat stroke at the Mekkah pilgrimage: clinical characteristics and course of 30 patients. *Q J Med.* 1986;59:523–530.

222. Hubbard RW. The role of exercise in the etiology of exertional heatstroke. *Med Sci Sports Exerc.* 1990;22:2–5.

223. Holman ND, Schneider AJ. Multi-organ damage in exertional heat stroke. *Neth J Med.* 1989;35: 38–43.

224. Shibolet S, Coll R, Gilat T, Sohar E. Heatstroke: its clinical picture and mechanism in 36 cases. *Q J Med.* 1965;36:525–548.

225. Gummaa K, El-Mahrouky S, Mahmoud H, Mustafa K, Khogall M. The metabolic status of heat stroke patients: the Makkah experience. In: Khogali M, Hale JR, eds. *Heat Stroke and Temperature Regulation.* New York, NY: Academic Press; 1983:157–169.

226. Garcia-Rubira JC, Aguilar J, Romero D. Acute myocardial infarction in a young man after heat exhaustion. *Int J Cardiol.* 1995;47:297–300.

227. Senay LC, Kok R. Body fluid responses of heat-tolerant and intolerant men to work in a hot wet environment. *J Appl Physiol.* 1976;40:55–59.

228. Shvartz E, Shibolet S, Merez A, Magazanik A, Shapiro Y. Prediction of heat tolerance from heart rate and rectal temperature in a temperate environment. *J Appl Physiol.* 1977;43:684–688.

229. Strydom NB. Heat intolerance: its detection and elimination in the mining industry. *S Afr J Sci.* 1980;76: 154–156.

230. Robergs RA, Roberts SO. *Exercise Physiology: Exercise, Performance, and Clinical Applications.* St Louis, MO: Mosby; 1997:653–662.

Appendix 4

Weight Loss in Wrestlers

Summary

Despite a growing body of evidence admonishing the behavior, weight cutting (rapid weight reduction) remains prevalent among wrestlers. Weight cutting has significant adverse consequences that may affect competitive performance, physical health, and normal growth and development. To enhance the education experience and reduce the health risks for the participants, the ACSM recommends measures to educate coaches and wrestlers toward sound nutrition and weight-control behaviors, to curtail weight cutting, and to enact rules that limit weight loss.

Introduction

For more than half a century, rapid weight loss, weight cutting as practiced by wrestlers, has remained a concern among educators, health professionals, exercise scientists, and parents (14,28,55,63). Since the American College of Sports Medicine first published the position statement Weight Loss in Wrestlers (3) in 1976, a plethora of research articles has been published on this topic. On a weekly basis, rapid weight loss in high school and collegiate wrestlers has been shown to average 2 kg and may exceed 2.7 kg among 20% of the wrestlers (41,55,61). One-third of high school wrestlers have reported repeating this process more than 10 times in a season (41,61). These practices have been documented over the past 25 years (61,62), and during that

Source: American College of Sports Medicine. (1996). Position stand on weight loss in wrestlers. *Med. Sci. Sports. Exerc.* 28(2)ix–xii. This pronouncement was written for the American College of Sports Medicine by Robert A. Oppliger, PhD, FACSM, (Chair), H. Samuel Case, PhD, FACSM, Craig A. Horswill, PhD, Gregory L. Landry, MD, and Ann C. Shelter, MA, RD. Reprinted with permission.

time their prevalence appears to have changed little (41,55,61).

Weight Loss in Wrestlers

Although wrestlers may believe they have excess fat, studies show that in the off-season high school wrestlers have 8% to 11% body fat, well below their high school peers, who average 15% (6,21,24,60). Estimates made during the season have found body fat to be as low as 3% and to average 6% to 7% (17,23,27,38,42,43,58). Consequently, loss of fat contributes minimally to weight reduction whereas the primary methods for weight loss (e.g., exercise, food restriction, fasting, and various dehydration methods) affect body water, glycogen content, and lean body mass (23,51,56,67,69). These weight-loss techniques are used by 25% to 67% of wrestlers (32,41,61,69). Use of pharmacological agents, including diuretics, stimulants, and laxatives to reduce weight has been reported among a few of these athletes (32,41,55). The weight-loss techniques have been passed down from wrestler to wrestler, or coach to wrestler, and have changed little over the past 25 years. Seldom do parents and health professionals provide input on how to lose weight appropriately (32,41,61). Recently, a small but growing number of females have begun to participate in wrestling. No data exist on the weight-control behaviors of this select group of wrestlers. If these females also practice weight cutting, the same health and performance concerns apply to them as to their male counterparts.

Wrestlers practice these weight-loss techniques believing their chances of competitive success will increase. Ironically, weight cutting may impair performance and endanger the wrestler's health. Weight loss in wrestlers can be attributed to reductions in body water, glycogen, lean tissue, and only a small amount of fat. The combination of food restriction and fluid deprivation creates a synergistic, adverse physiologic effect on the body, leaving the wrestler ill prepared to compete. In addition, most forms of dehydration (e.g., sweating and catharsis) contribute to the loss of electrolytes as well as water (5,9). Wrestlers hope to replenish body fluids, electrolytes, and glycogen in the brief period (30 min– 20 h) between the weigh-in and competition. However, reestablishing fluid homeostasis may take 24 to 48 h (10), replenishing muscle glycogen may take as long as 72 h (11,25), and replacing lean tissue might take even longer. In short, weight cutting appears to adversely influence the wrestler's energy reserves and fluid and electrolyte balances.

The singular or combined effects of weight cutting on physiological function and performance are presented in Table 1. These functions are indicators of performance on the mat; however, no research to date has investigated the relationship between wrestling performance and weight loss. Although the scientific data are not conclusive, these weight cutting practices may also alter hormonal status (59), diminish protein nutritional status (20), impede normal growth and development (18), affect psychological state (19,32,37,41,55), impair academic performance (8,13,64), and have severe consequences such as pulmonary emboli (12), pancreatitis (34), and reduced immune function (30). Use of diuretics may result in more profound effects on the cardiovascular systems and electrolyte balance than other forms of weight loss (5,7).

For these reasons, the National Federation of State High School Associations supports the opinion that each state implement rules that include an effective weight-control program (39). Several states have successfully instituted programs that require body composition assessment and nutrition education (personal communications, 40), and more states appear poised to follow. Scientists, physicians, dieticians, coaches, athletic administrators, trainers, and other health professionals should work toward implementation of these recommended changes nationwide.

TABLE 1	
EFFECTS OF "WEIGHT CUTTING" ON PHYSIOLOGICAL PERFORMANCE	
[a,c]	Little or no increase (1,17,50,53,63,68) and possible reduction in muscle strength (23,46,66)
[a,c]	Little or no increase (26,44,46) and possible decrease in anaerobic power capacity (35,66)
[b,c]	Lower plasma and blood volume (2,31,49,65), increased resting and submaximal heart rate (2,49), decreased cardiac stroke volume (2), resulting in decreased ability to sustain work at a constant rate, i.e., reduced endurance capacity (45,47)
[a]	Lower oxygen consumption (36,57)
[c,d]	Impaired thermoregulatory processes, which could decrease endurance capacity and increase the risk of heat illness during practice (7,48,49)
[c]	Decreased renal blood flow and kidney filtration of blood (70–72)
[a,b]	Depletion of muscle (23) and possibly liver glycogen (25), which will reduce muscle endurance capacity (19,29), the body's ability to maintain blood glucose levels, and accelerate the breakdown of the bodys protein (4,15)
[a,c,d]	Depletion of electrolytes resulting in impaired muscle function (5), coordination (29), and possibly cardiac arrhythmias

Superscript identifies methods that contribute to this physiological effect: [a] = food restriction or fasting; [b] = exercise; [c] = dehydration; [d] = catharsis (diuretic or laxatives).

Conclusions and Recommendations

Because of the equivocal benefits and the potential health risks created by the procedures used for "weight cutting" by wrestlers (particularly adolescents), the ACSM makes the following recommendations:

1. Educate coaches and wrestlers about the adverse consequences of prolonged fasting and dehydration on physical performance and physical health.

2. Discourage the use of rubber suits, steam rooms, hot boxes, saunas, laxatives, and diuretics for "making weight."

3. Adopt new state or national governing body legislation that schedules weigh-ins immediately prior to competition.

4. Schedule daily weigh-ins before and after practice to monitor weight loss and dehydration. Weight lost during practice should be regained through adequate food and fluid intake.

5. Assess the body composition of each wrestler prior to the season using valid methods for this population (42,60). Males 16 years old and younger with a body fat below 7% or those over 16 with a body fat below 5% need medical clearance before being

allowed to compete. Female wrestlers need a minimal body fat of 12% to 14% (33).

6. Emphasize the need for daily caloric intake obtained from a balance diet high in carbohydrates ($> 55\%$ of calories), low in fat ($< 30\%$ of calories) with adequate protein (15% to 20% of calories, 1.0 to 1.5g·kg^{-1} body weight) determined on the basis of RDA guidelines and physical activity levels (16,22,54). The minimal caloric intake for wrestlers of high school and college age should range from 1,700 to 2,500 kcal·d^{-1}, and rigorous training may increase the requirement up to an additional 1,000 calories per day (16). Wrestlers should be discouraged by coaches, parents, school officials, and physicians from consuming less than their minimal daily needs. Combined with exercise, this minimal caloric intake will allow for gradual weight loss. After the minimal weight has been attained, caloric intake should be increased sufficiently to support the normal developmental needs of the young wrestler (16).

The ACSM encourages:

Permitting more participants per team to compete by adding weight classes between 119 lb. and 151 lb. or by allowing more than one representative at a given weight class just as swimming and track teams do in competition.

Standardization of regulations concerning the eligibility rules at championship tournaments so that severe and rapid weight loss is discouraged at the end of the season (e.g., a wrestler dropping one or more weight classes).

Cooperative efforts between coaches, exercise scientists, physicians, dietitians, and wrestlers to systematically collect data on the body composition, hydration state, energy and nutritional demands, growth, maturation, and psychological development of wrestlers.

Through this position statement, the ACSM hopes to further the sport of wrestling by providing a positive educational environment for the primary, secondary, or collegiate wrestler. The ACSM believes these recommendations will enable the athlete to better focus on skill acquisition, fitness enhancement, psychological preparation, and the social interactions offered by the sport.

Acknowledgments

This position stand replaces the 1976 ACSM position paper, "Weight Loss in Wrestlers."

This pronouncement was reviewed for the American College of Sports Medicine by members-at-large, the Pronouncements Committee, and by: Jack Harvey, MD, FACSM, Michael Sharratt, PhD, FACSM, Suzanne Steen, PhD, and Charles Tipton, PhD, FACSM.

REFERENCES

1. Ahlman K, Karvonen MJ. (1961). Weight reduction by sweating in wrestlers and its effect on physical fitness. *J Sports Med.* 1:58–62.

2. Allen TE, Smith DP, Miller DK. (1977). Hemodynamic response to submaximal exercise after dehydration and rehydration in high school wrestlers. *Med Sci Sports Exerc.* 9:159–163.

3. American College of Sports Medicine. (1976). Position statement: Weight loss in wrestlers. *Med Sci Sports.* 8:xi–xiii.

4. Cahill GF. (1970). Starvation in man. *N Engl J Med.* 282:668–675.

5. Caldwell JE, Ahonen E, Nousiainen U. (1984). Differential effects on sauna-, diuretic-, and exercise-induced hypohydration. *J Appl Physiol.* 57:1018–1023.

6. Cisar CJ, Johnson, GO, Fry AC, et al. (1987). Preseason body composition, build, and strength as predictors of high school wrestling success. *J Appl Sports Sci Res.* 1:66–70.

7. Claremont AD, Costill DL, Fink WJ, Vanhandel P. (1976). Heat tolerance following diuretic induced dehydration. *Med Sci Sports Exerc.* 8:239–243.

8. Conners CK, Bouin AG. (1982). Nutritional effects on behavior of children. *Psychiatry Res.* 17:193–201.

9. Costill DL, Cote P, Fink WJ. (1976). Muscle water and electrolytes following varied levels of dehydration in man. *J Appl Physiol.* 40:6–11.

10. Costill DL, Sparks KE. (1973). Rapid fluid replacement following thermal dehydration. *J Appl Physiol.* 34:299–303.

11. Coyle EF, Coyle E. (1993). Carbohydrates that speed recovery from training. *Physician Sportsmed.* 21:111–123.

12. Croyle PH, Place RA, Hilgenberg AD. (1979). Massive pulmonary embolism in a high school wrestler. *JAMA.* 241:827–828.

13. DeFeo P, Gallia V, Mazzotta G. (1988). Modest decrements in plasma glucose concentration cause early impairment in cognitive function and later activation in glucose counterregulation in absence of hypoglycemic symptoms in normal man. *J Clin Invest.* 82:436–444.

14. Doshner N. (1944). The effect of rapid weight loss upon the performance of wrestlers and boxers and upon the physical proficiency of college students. *Res Q* 15:317–324.

15. Felig P, Owen OE, Wahren J, Cahill GF. (1969). Amino acid metabolism during prolonged starvation. *J Clin Invest.* 48:584–594.

16. Food and Nutrition Board. (1989). *Recommended Dietary Allowances,* 10th ed. Washington, DC: National Academy of Sciences, pp. 24–37, 65, 66.

17. Freischlag J. (1984). Weight loss, body composition, and health of high school wrestlers. *Physician Sportsmed.* 12:121–126.

18. Hansen NC. (1978). Wrestling with "making weight." *Physician Sportsmed.* 6:106–111.

19. Horswill CA, Hickner RC, Scott JR, Costill DL, Gould D. (1990). Weight loss, dietary carbohydrate modifications and high intensity physical performance. *Med Sci Sports Exerc.* 22:470–476.

20. Horswill CA, Park SH, Roemmich JN. (1990). Changes in the protein nutrition status of adolescent wrestlers. *Med Sci Sports Exerc.* 22:599–604.

21. Horswill CA, Scott J, Galea P, Park SH. (1988). Physiological profile of elite junior wrestlers. *Res Q Exerc Sports.* 59:257–261.

22. Houck J, Slavin J. (1991). Protein nutrition in the athlete. In: Berning JR, Steen SN (eds.). *Sports Nutrition for the 90s: The Health Profession's Handbook.* Gaithersburg, Md: Aspen Publishers, pp. 1–12.

23. Houston ME, Marrin DA, Green HJ, Thomson JA. (1981). The effect of rapid weight reduction on physiological functions in wrestlers. *Physician Sportsmed.* 9:73–78.

24. Hughes RA, Housh TJ, Johnson GO. (1992). Anthropometric estimations of body composition across a season. *J Appl Sports Sci Res.* 5:71–76.

25. Hultman E, Nilsson L. (1973). Liver glycogen as glucose-supplying source during exercise. *Limiting Factors of Physical Performance,* pp. 179–189.

26. Jacobs I. (1980). The effects of thermal dehydration on performance of the Wingate anaerobic test. *Int J Sports Med* 1:21–24.

27. Kelly JM, Gorney BA, Kalm KK. (1978). The effect of a collegiate wrestling season on body composition, cardiovascular fitness, muscular strength, and endurance. *Med Sci Sports Exerc.* 10:119–124.

28. Kenny HE. (1930). The problem of making weight for wrestling meets. *J Health Phys Ed.* 1:24.

29. Klinzing JE, Karpowicz W. (1986). The effect of rapid weight loss and rehydration on a wrestling performance test. *J Sports Med.* 26:139–145.

30. Kono I, Kitao H, Matsuda M, Haga S, Fukushmia H. (1988). Weight reduction in athletes may adversely affect phagocytic function of monocytes. *Physician Sportsmed.* 16:56–65.

31. Kozlowski S, Saltin B. (1964). Effects of sweat loss on body fluids. *J Appl Physiol.* 19:1119–1124.

32. Lakin JA, Steen SN, Oppliger RA. (1990). Eating behaviors, weight loss methods, and nutritional practices of high school wrestlers. *J Community Health Nurs.* 7:223–234.

33. McArdle WD, Katch FI, Katch VL. (1991). *Exercise Physiology: Energy, Nutrition, and Human Performance.* 3d ed. Malvern, Pa: Lea & Febiger, p. 488.

34. McDermott WV, Bartlett MK, Culver PJ. (1956). Acute pancreatitis after prolonged fast and subsequent surfeit. *N Engl J Med.* 254:379–380.

35. McMurray RG, Proctor CR, Wilson WL. (1991). Effects of caloric deficit and dietary manipulation on aerobic and anaerobic exercise. *Int J Sports Med.* 12:167–172.

36. Melby CL, Schmidt WD, Corrigan D. (1990). Resting metabolic rate in weight-cycling collegiate wrestlers compared with physically active, noncycling control subjects. *Am J Clin Nutr.* 52:409–414.

37. Morgan WP. (1970). Psychological effects of weight reduction in the college wrestler. *Med Sci Sports Exerc.* 2:24–27.

38. Nagle FJ, Morgan WP, Hellickson RO, Serfass RC, Alexander JF. (1975). Spotting success traits in Olympic contenders. *Physician Sportsmed.* 3:31–34.

39. National Federation of High School Associations. (1992). *Wrestling Rules 1992–93.* Kansas City, Mo: National Federation of High School Associations.

40. Oppliger RA, Harms RD, Herrmann DL, Streich CM, Clark RR. (1995). The Wisconsin wrestling minimal weight project: A model for wrestling weight control. *Med Sci Sports Exerc.* 27:1220–1224.

41. Oppliger RA, Landry GL, Foster SA, Lambrecht AC. (1993). Bulimic behaviors among high school wrestlers: A statewide survey. *Pediatr Res.* 94:826–831.

42. Oppliger RA, Neilsen DH, Thompson CG. (1991). Minimal weight predicted by bioelectrical impedance and anthropometric equations. *Med Sci Sports Exerc.* 23:247–253.

43. Oppliger RA, Tipton CM. (1985). Weight prediction equation tested and available. *Iowa Med.* 75:449–452.

44. Park SH, Roemmich JN, Horswill CA. (1990). A season of wrestling and weight loss by adolescent wrestlers: Effect on anaerobic arm power. *J Appl Sports Sci. Res.* 4:1–4.

45. Ribisl PM, Herbert WG. (1970). Effect of rapid weight reduction and subsequent rehydration upon the physical working capacity of wrestlers. *Res Q.* 41:536–541.

46. Roemmich JN, Sinning WE. (1996). Sport seasonal changes in body composition, growth, power, and strength of adolescent wrestlers. *Int J Sports Med.* 17:92–99.

47. Saltin B. (1964). Aerobic and anaerobic work capacity after dehydration. *J Appl Physiol.* 19:1114–1118.

48. Saltin B. (1964). Circulatory response to submaximal and maximal exercise after thermal dehydration. *J Appl Physiol.* 19:1125–1132.

49. Sawka MN, Francesconi RP, Pandolf KB, Young AJ. (1984). Influence of hydration level and body fluids on exercise performance in the heat. *JAMA.* 252:1165–1169.

50. Serfass RC, Stull GA, Alexander JF, Ewing JL. (1984). The effects of rapid weight loss and attempted rehydration on strength and endurance of the hand muscle in college wrestlers. *Res Q Exerc Sports.* 55:46–52.

51. Sherman WM, Costill DL, Fink WJ, Hagerman FC, Armstrong LE, Murray TS. (1983). Effect of 42.2 m footrace and subsequent rest or exercise on muscle glycogen and enzymes. *J Appl Physiol.* 55:1219–1224.

52. Short SH, Short WR. (1983). Four year study of university athletes' dietary intake. *J Am Diet Assoc.* 82:632–645.

53. Singer RN, Weiss SA. (1968). Effects of weight reduction on selected anthropometric, physical, and performance measures of wrestlers. *Res Q.* 39:361–369.

54. Steen SN. (1991). Nutritional considerations for the low body-weight athlete. In: Berning JR, Steen SN (eds.). *Sports Nutrition for the 90s: The Health Profession's Handbook.* Gaithersburg, Md: Aspen Publishers, pp. 160–164.

55. Steen SN, Brownell KD. (1990). Patterns of weight loss and regain in wrestlers: Has the tradition changed? *Med Sci Sports Exerc.* 22:762–768.

56. Steen SN, McKinney S. (1986). Nutritional assessment of college wrestlers. *Physician Sportsmed.* 14:100–116.

57. Steen SN, Oppliger RA, Brownell KD. (1988). Metabolic effects of repeated weight loss and regain in adolescent wrestlers. *JAMA.* 260:47–50.

58. Stine G, Ratliff R, Shierman G, Grana WA. (1979). Physical profile of the wrestlers at the 1977 NCAA Championships. *Physician Sportsmed.* 7:98–105.

59. Strauss RH, Lanese RR, Malarkey WB. (1985). Weight loss in amateur wrestlers and its effect on serum testosterone. *JAMA.* 254:3337–3338.

60. Thorland WG, Tipton CM, Bowers RW, et al. (1991). Midwest wrestling study: Prediction of minimal weight for high school wrestlers. *Med Sci Sports Exerc.* 23:1102–1110.

61. Tipton CM, Tcheng TK. (1970). Iowa wrestling study: Weight loss in high school students. *JAMA.* 214:1269–1274.

62. Tipton CM, Tcheng TK, Paul WD. (1969). Evaluation of the Hall method for determining minimum wrestling weights. *J Iowa Med Soc.* 59:571–574.

63. Tuttle WW. (1943). The effects of weight loss by dehydration and withholding of food on the physiologic response of wrestlers. *Res Q.* 14:158–166.

64. Tuttle WW, Daum K, Myers L, Martin C. (1950). Effect of omitting breakfast on the physiologic response of men. *J Am Diet Assoc.* 26:332–335.

65. Vaccaro P, Zauner CW, Cade JR. (1976). Changes in body weight, hematocrit, and plasma protein

concentration due to dehydration and rehydration in wrestlers. *J Sports Med Phys Fitness* 16:45–53.

66. Webster S, Rutt R, Weltman A. (1990). Physiological effects of a weight loss regimen practiced by college wrestlers. *Med Sci Sports Exerc.* 22:229–234.

67. Weissinger E, Housh TJ, Johnson GO, Evans SA. (1991). Weight loss behavior in high school wrestling: Wrestler and parent perception. *Pediatr Exerc Sci.* 3:64–73.

68. Widerman PM, Hagen RD. (1982). Body weight loss in a wrestler preparing for competition: A case report. *Med Sci Sports Exerc.* 14:413–418.

69. Woods ER, Wilson CD, Masland RP. (1988). Weight control methods in high school wrestlers. *J Adolesc Health Care.* 9:394–397.

70. Zambraski EJ, Foster DT, Gross PM, Tipton CM. (1976). Iowa wrestling study: Weight loss and urinary profiles of collegiate wrestlers. *Med Sci Sports.* 8:105–108.

71. Zambraski EJ, Tipson CM, Jordan HR, Palmer WK, Tcheng TK. (1974). Iowa wrestling study: Urinary profiles of state finalists prior to competition. *Med Sci Sports.* 6:129–132.

72. Zambraski EJ, Tipton CM, Tcheng TK, Jordan HR, Vailas AC, Callahan AK. (1975). Iowa wrestling study: Changes in urinary profiles of wrestlers prior to and after competition. *Med Sci Sports.* 7:217–220.

Appendix 5

Generic First Aid Kit for Sports Injuries (Checklist)

The following is a comprehensive listing of supplies that should enable coaching personnel to handle the majority of common sports injuries, regardless of sport. However, it is critical to note that some sports may present unique problems, such as in the case of tackle football, with respect to airway management and face mask removal. In such cases, coaching personnel should include specialty items such as a set of Trainers Angels for face mask removal, in addition to the items listed below.

Check Item

_____ alcohol preps

_____ antibiotic ointment

_____ antifungal cream

_____ approved biohazard container (for storage of all materials exposed to blood or other body fluids)

_____ athletic tape (1.5″ width, nonelastic)

_____ Band-Aids—variety of shapes and sizes including those for fingers, knuckles, and large joints

_____ Betadine skin disinfectant

_____ Chapstick (with sunscreen)

_____ cloth ties for splints (can be made from old sheets)

_____ Conform (elastic athletic tape)

_____ contact-lens cleaning kit

_____ cotton tip applicators (Q-tips)

_____ elastic wraps (Ace bandages in sizes ranging from 4″ to 6″)

_____ emergency information cards for all athletes—should include all pertinent information regarding each athlete, such as drug allergies, preexisting medical conditions, home phone number, insurance policy information, name and phone number of family physician

_____ face mask, one-way valve (artificial respiration)

_____ fingernail clippers

_____ foam padding material (open- and closed-cell foams)

_____ hydrogen peroxide solution

_____ inhalers (for exercise-induced asthma attack)

_____ medical soap (used for wound cleaning)

_____ medically approved eye protection (goggles)

_____ nonsterile latex examination gloves (sizes small, medium, large)

_____ nonstick sterile gauze pads (variety of sizes)

_____ note pad and pencil or pen

_____ padding material for splints (wool or cotton blankets)

_____ paper bag (for treatment of hyperventilation)

_____ pen light (with extra batteries)

_____ petroleum jelly or other lubricant for skin

_____ plastic (sandwich) bags (for use with crushed ice)

_____ prewrap (used in conjunction with athletic tape)

_____ quarters and dimes (for public phone)

_____ rolled sterile gauze (self-adhering)

_____ skin tape

_____ Spenco Second Skin

_____ splints (Sam Splint)

_____ sterile gauze pads (variety of sizes from 2″ × 2″ to 4″ × 4″)

_____ Steri-Strips (for management of wounds on the face)

_____ sunscreen product (waterproof)

_____ tape scissors

_____ thermometers (oral and rectal)

_____ tongue depressors

_____ triangular bandages (cravat bandages)

_____ tweezers

_____ wooden splints (variety of sizes suitable for arm and leg fractures)

Appendix 6
Rehabilitation: An Overview

Throughout their competitive careers, many athletes incur injuries, the majority of which are minor enough not to need rehabilitation. However, there are several sports-related injuries that are severe enough to require a formal rehabilitation program. Unfortunately, sometimes this program is not completed because of an athlete's, coach's, or parent's impatience for a return to play. Such a situation may arise when there is no one available who is experienced in and understands the rehabilitation process. It may be that the coach, athlete, or parent does not understand the importance of restoration before returning to activity and how a rehabilitation process can enhance an athlete's level of functioning after return. However, a knowledgeable professional, willing to spend a little time working with an athlete recovering from an injury, can only enhance the restoration process.

The rehabilitation or reconditioning of sports-related injuries is both an art and a science when properly completed. Rehabilitation can be defined as the restoration of an injured part to normal or near normal function. To return an athlete to activity functioning as close to 100% as possible is a valuable asset both for the athlete and the team. An untrained person may propose a strength training regimen but, without the basic understanding of the healing process and the basis for a gradual progression through a rehabilitation program, the outcome may not be positive. For example, weight training too early after injury can actually create more of a problem for an athlete by increasing damage to already injured tissues.

Rehabilitation programs can be created by working with a certified athletic trainer or a physical therapist. Sometimes, though, these are just "written recipes" for the athlete to follow that include a series of exercises. This type of program, "by the numbers," does not account for the recognition of daily gains or setbacks, swelling or pain, or other variables that might accompany the rehabilitation process. A well-structured and supervised rehabilitation program will include a set of detailed

Source: Idaho Sports Medicine Institute, Boise, Idaho. Reprinted with permission.

guidelines to follow and will include a qualified therapist, who can discern variables that could be counterproductive to healing the injury. The next sections present the science of the rehabilitation process as well as the art of the entire process. Finally, there are some generic sample programs for rehabilitating the ankle, shoulder, and knee.

The Science of Rehabilitation

For a detailed outline of the inflammatory process, see the section "Physiology of Sports Injury" in Chapter 8. The final phase of the inflammatory process is regeneration and repair. Here, the circulatory system brings fibroblasts to the damaged area; these fibroblasts mature and provide the necessary collagen for the repair of damaged tissues. The collagen fibers are randomly placed in the damaged area and take time to initiate collagen cross-linking to native tissue. It is during this time that it is important both to protect the damaged area and to promote movement there. The injury must be protected from further damage by undue stresses. However, the collagen is being deposited randomly, and before the collagen cross-linking is completed, controlled movement in a proper direction will assist the newly deposited collagen to assimilate a corresponding direction to the native fibers. With controlled movement as the healing process continues, the collagen fibers will align themselves in the direction of pull and, as time progresses, they will lay down a cross-linking system with native tissues. This process will provide the injured tissue both a structural base and an elastic component, allowing it to function as close to normal as possible. However, if the new collagen is allowed to migrate to the injured area and set up cross-links in a random fashion, a less pliable and less structurally sound tissue will result. This uncontrolled scarring will not allow the injured soft tissue to function in as close to normal capacity as possible, and therefore the athlete will be unable to perform at his or her highest level.

All of the phases in the inflammatory process, including the regeneration and repair phase, have generalized time lines depending on the severity of the injury. In this case, the regeneration and repair phase can last anywhere from one week to one year, again, depending on the severity of the injury and the intervention provided by the athletic trainer or physician.

Once the time line for the regeneration and repair phase is understood, the rehabilitation program becomes a series of steps that build on one another. The first step is designed to decrease swelling and pain to make it easier to move and exercise the injured part. When the swelling and pain are essentially absent from the injured area, the rehabilitation can proceed to the second step, reestablishing the range of motion (ROM). It is critical to restore normal, preinjury levels of ROM, as any loss of joint mobility may contribute to reinjury. Range-of-motion exercises incorporate either passive movements (the coach or therapist moves the joint) or active movements (the athlete moves the joint). There are times when other, more-intensive ROM measures need to be incorporated, but this decision should be made by the attending physician. When an athlete has regained approximately 90% of ROM, he or she can move into the third step of the rehabilitation program. The goal of this portion of the program is to return muscle strength to the level of what it was prior to the injury. That can be accomplished best by incorporating a progressive resistive exercise (PRE) program that takes advantage of the overload principle. A variation of the PRE program is the daily adjusted progressive resistive exercise (DAPRE) program, developed by Dr. Ken Knight. The DAPRE protocol provides the athletic trainer with an objective method for adjusting the amount of weight being lifted in a given rehabilitation workout. An outline of the DAPRE protocol designed specifically for the

---

TABLE 2

GUIDELINES FOR ADJUSTMENT OF WORKING WEIGHT

Number of Repetitions	Fourth Set Adjustment	Next Session
0–2	Decrease 2–5 kg	Redo set
3–4	Decrease 0–2 kg	Same weight
6–7	Same weight	Increase 2–5 kg
8–12	Increase 2–5 kg	Increase 2–7 kg
13+	Increase 5–7 kg	Increase 5–10 kg

Source: Knight KL. (1985). Quadriceps strengthening with the DAPRE technique: Case studies with neurological implications. *Med Sci Sports Exer.* 17(6): 646–650.

---

quadriceps is shown in Table 1. Guidelines for adjusting the weight used during rehabilitation are shown in Table 2.

When strength is restored to 85% to 90% of the uninjured limb, the athlete is ready to proceed to the fourth step of the rehabilitation program: to train the nervous system to regain normal proprioception and to reestablish muscle power, speed, and skill. This is accomplished using many different types of equipment and exercises. Proprioception in the lower extremities is commonly reestablished by performing simple balance exercises such as standing on one foot or on the toes of both feet. As proprioception improves, more challenging exercises can be introduced, such as the slide board or the biomechanical ankle platform system (BAPS) board. Power can be improved by way of high-velocity, high-intensity resistive exercises such as Olympic lifts (power clean, high pull, hang cleans) or with plyometric (bounding) exercises. Skill is best reestablished by practicing sport-specific drills. What type of exercise is appropriate at this stage of the rehabilitation is based on the athletic trainer's experience and an understanding of the athlete's needs on returning to activity.

When athletes can efficiently accomplish the tasks outlined in the fourth category, they are ready for a functional test to determine readiness to return to competition. These functional tests put the athlete through complete movements and drills similar to those needed in participation at a competitive level.

The five steps of the rehabilitation process are summarized as

1. Control pain and swelling
2. Increase ROM
3. Increase strength

TABLE 1

KNIGHT'S DAPRE PROGRAM

Set	Weight	Repetitions
1	50% of maximum	10
2	75% of maximum	6
3	100% of maximum	Max*
4	Adjust weight	Max**

*Repetitions in the third set determine the adjusted working weight for the fourth set, according to the guidelines in Table 2.

**Repetitions in the fourth set determine the adjusted working weight for the next day according to the guidelines in Table 2.

4. Restore proprioception and reestablish muscle power, speed, and skill

5. Functional testing

The Art of Rehabilitation

The actual implementation of the rehabilitation program takes great skill. One must understand the injury, the time lines the injury requires for complete healing, the psychological makeup of the athlete and how that athlete will respond to the injury. In addition, it is essential to be familiar with both the equipment needed and the equipment available to assist in the rehabilitation process. It is important that the athlete have some short-term and long-term goals for rehabilitation. The coach or athletic trainer can assist the athlete in setting reasonable and attainable goals. Too many times after an injury, athletes are determined to be back in play for the next game. In many cases, such an attitude results in a delay of healing and, frequently, a reinjury or secondary injury of another stucture.

If there is specific equipment needed to complete the rehabilitation process and it is not available on-site, the coach or athletic trainer needs to develop a viable alternative. The alternative piece of equipment may not look as fancy, but will do the job that is necessary in the process. If an alternative piece of equipment cannot be devised, the coach or athletic trainer may need to locate and acquire the equipment to complete the rehabilitation.

The coach or athletic trainer must have the time and patience to participate fully in the rehabilitation process. There will be times when an athlete needs to slow down after a rehabilitation sessions because of an increase in swelling or pain. Time and patience are necessary for the healing process to continue. Goals must be set and maintained, and the athlete needs positive feedback about his or her role in the rehabilitation process.

The final portion of this appendix includes some sample generic rehabilitation protocols. These protocols are not meant to be used generally, but rather in specific rehabilitation situations. Please do not feel that by following one of these protocols step-by-step the athlete will be totally rehabilitated from an injury. These sample protocols are intended to give the reader an idea of how programs are structured and the exercises are progressed through. These programs should not be used, as presented, by an athlete until he or she is fully evaluated by an athletic trainer or physical therapist. Any rehabilitation program should be individualized and supervised by a qualified practitioner such as an athletic trainer or physical therapist.

Shoulder Rehabilitation Exercises Weight/Tubing Strengthening Program

Perform the following exercises _____ times per week. This program has been designed for *your* specific needs. *Do not* change it without your doctor's or therapist's consent and instruction. Weight strengthening exercises should be done *after* activity.

Rotator Cuff Exercises

1. *Internal Rotation*
   Stand with involved side toward the door. Grasp tubing with hand and position elbow so it is bent to 90°. Place a towel roll under your arm for correct starting position. Pull from the starting position toward your stomach, rotating the shoulder inward. Start exercises pulling from *high* to *low*. Keep exercise pain free.

   Repeat _____ sets of _____ repetitions.

2. *External Rotation*
   Stand with uninvolved side toward the door. Grasp tubing with hand and position elbow so it is bent to 90°. Place a towel roll under your arm for correct starting position. Pull from your stomach out away from your body. Rotate

outward until pain or shoulder starts to move. Start exercise by pulling from *low* to *high*.

Repeat _____ sets of _____ repetitions.

3. *Marshall Exercise*

This exercise is performed by lying on your back as in the position shown. With dumbbell weights in your hands, rotate your arms from palm of hand to back of hand lightly touching the floor. If full range of motion is painful, try to accomplish as much of the range as possible. Perform continuously for 2 to 3 minutes, checking to maintain elbows at shoulder height. Use 3- to 5-lb weights.

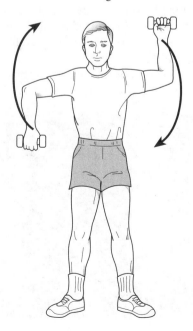

Shoulder Rehabilitation Exercises

Perform the following exercises _____ times per week. This program has been designed for *your* specific needs. *Do not* change it without your doctor's or therapist's consent and instruction. Shoulder strengthening exercises should *not* be done *before* sports activities. Keep all exercises pain free.

1. *Upright Rowing*

Shoulder rhythm is very important when doing this exercise. Watch the shoulders carefully to be sure you do not let one shoulder "hike up" higher than the other. *Do not* increase weight at the expense of sacrificing proper rhythm.

Lift the bar up to your chin keeping the elbows *higher* than your wrists. The weights should be held close to your body.

Repeat _____ sets of _____ repetitions.

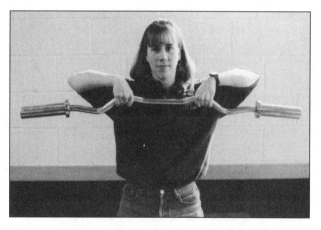

2. *Bent Over Lateral Raises*

This exercise is also a rhythm exercise and should be done smoothly. Raise weights out to your side until your arms are level with the top of shoulder. Pause and slowly lower arms to starting position.

Repeat _____ sets of _____ repetitions.

3. *Marshall Exercise*
   This exercise is performed by lying on your back, as in the position shown below.

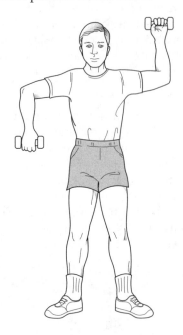

With dumbbells in your hand, rotate your arms doing 3 sets of 10 repetitions.
   Repeat _____ sets of _____ repetitions.

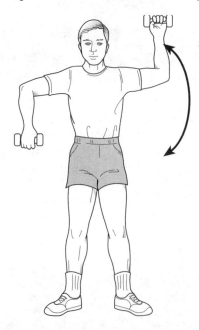

4. *Ice*
   a. Fill a plastic bag with ice. Place the bag around the shoulder and wrap it with a towel.
   b. Ice for 10 to 15 minutes.
   c. Icing should be done immediately following the exercise, if possible.

Ankle Rehabilitation Exercises

Perform the following exercises _____ times per week. This program has been designed for *your* specific needs. *Do not* change it without your doctor's or therapist's consent and instruction. Ankle strengthening exercises should *not* be done *before* sports activities. Keep all exercises pain free.

1. *Ankle Inversion*
   Sit on a chair next to the rubber bands with knee bent to 45°. Pull your foot out and away from the rubber bands. Keeping the thigh still, pivot just on the heel to the *inside* and then back to the starting position.
      As above, perform with straight knee.
      Repeat _____ sets of _____ repetitions.

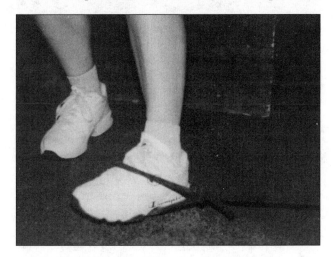

2. *Ankle Eversion*
   Bend the knee to 45° and attach rubber band to mid-foot area. Keeping the thigh still, pivot just on the heel to the *outside* and then back to starting position.
      As above, perform with straight knee.
      Repeat _____ sets of _____ repetitions.

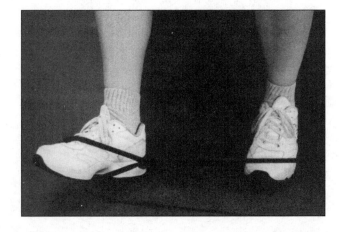

3. *Toe Raises*

Stand at the edge of a 2″-high board. Point your toes in slightly so that your feet are in a bit of a "pigeon-toed" position. Raise up and down on your tiptoes, making sure to go both directions as far as possible. Keep your weight equally distributed on both legs.

Repeat _____ sets of _____ repetitions. single leg

Repeat _____ sets of _____ repetitions. double leg

4. *Dorsiflexion*

Attach the rubber bands to the mid-foot area. Pull your toes toward your shins and back to the original position.

Repeat _____ sets of _____ repetitions.

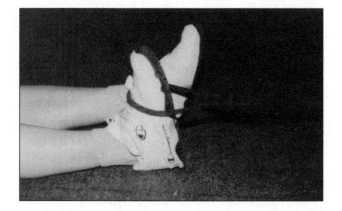

5. *Ice*
   a. Fill a plastic bag with ice. Place the bag around the ankle and wrap it with a towel.
   b. Ice 10 to 15 minutes.
   c. Icing should be done no later than 15 minutes after exercises or immediately following exercises, if possible.

Knee Rehabilitation Exercises

Perform the following exercises _____ times per week. This program has been designed for *your* specific needs. *Do not* change it without your doctor's or therapist's consent and instruction. Weight strengthening exercises should *not* be done *before* sports activities. Keep all exercises pain free.

1. *Toe Raises*

Stand at the edge of a 2″-high board. Point your toes in slightly so that your feet are a bit "pigeontoed." Raise up and down on your tiptoes, making sure to go both directions as far as possible. Keep your weight equally distributed on both legs.

Repeat _____ sets of _____ repetitions.

2. *Short-Arc Leg Extensions*
   Use a knee bench through an angle of _____ degrees. Sit with your foot under the resistance pad and straighten (extend) leg. Pause, and lower weight under control.

   Repeat _____ sets of _____ repetitions, single leg

   Repeat _____ sets of _____ repetitions, double leg

4. *Ice*
   a. Fill a plastic bag with ice. Place the bag around the knee and wrap it with a towel.
   b. *Ice 10 to 15 minutes.*
   c. Icing should be done no later than 15 minutes after exercises or immediately following exercise, if possible.

3. *Hamstring Curls*
   Use a knee bench. Lie on your stomach with your kneecaps slightly off the edge of the bench. Place your heels under the resistive pad.

   Bend your knee so your heel approaches your buttocks. Pause, and lower the weight in control.

   Repeat _____ sets of _____ repetitions, single leg

   Repeat _____ sets of _____ repetitions, double leg

Appendix 7
Equipment Fitting

Many times at the high school and sometimes at the college level the coach or athletic trainer becomes the equipment personnel for the team. For this and other reasons, it is important for the coach and/or athletic trainer to have a working knowledge of equipment fitting. The purpose of this appendix is to provide an overview of some of the more common equipment fitting procedures. In this appendix we will discuss the fitting of football and ice hockey helmets, football shoulder pads, mouth guards, shin guards for soccer, baseball helmets, baseball/softball catcher's equipment, and general eye protection concepts.

It is important to remember there are numerous liability issues related to the equipment used in many sports. We suggest that the person responsible for the issuing or fitting of equipment for a specific sport or group of athletes become familiar with the rules, regulations, and liability of the equipment they are issuing and/or fitting. For example, if a coach or athletic trainer issues and/or fits a football helmet to an athlete and that helmet is not approved by the National Operating Committee on Safety for Athletic Equipment (NOCSAE), there can be legal repercussions for the coach or athletic trainer.

Football Helmets

It is important to follow a few basic steps when issuing or fitting a football helmet. The following is a generic outline of football helmet fitting steps to ensure proper fit.

1. Carefully read and follow all manufacturer's guidelines when fitting football helmets. Manufacturers will produce different models of helmets, and fitting them can differ from model to model.

2. Ensure that the football helmet has been approved by NOCSAE. Visually inspect the helmet for the following: *Cracks* (look closely around all drilled or formed holes in the shell); all *interior padding* for "spring back" capability or, if air equipped, do all areas hold air; and *face mask*—is it cracked, broken or have metal showing through?

3. Have the athlete wet his hair, as this will simulate a practice or game condition, which is the necessary conditions for proper fitting.

4. Measure the head to get an approximate size for the helmet.

5. Have the athlete put the helmet on by pulling out on the ear holes and sliding the helmet on from back to front. It is easier to fit the helmet without a face mask attached to the helmet.

6. Check the height of the helmet. Does the front of the helmet rest just above the eyebrows (about one to a maximum of two finger breaths)?

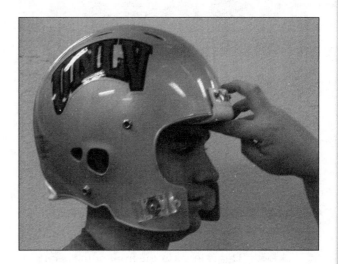

7. Check the rear of the helmet. Does the back of the helmet cover the base of the skull?

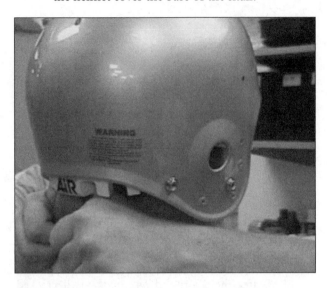

8. Check the ear holes to see that they line up with the ears properly.

9. Check the inside of the helmet to see that the jaw pads are touching the skin of the jaw. The application of the chin strap and face mask will tighten this area, so don't get the jaw pads too snug.

10. Attach the face mask and chin strap and check all of the preceding once again.

Test for Proper Fit of the Helmet

1. Try to forcefully push the top of the helmet down. This is to check the front of the helmet to see if it depresses enough to travel past the eyebrows and onto the bridge of the nose. If the front of the helmet travels down past the eyebrows, you will want to adjust the height via the size of the padding or the amount of air in the air pockets.

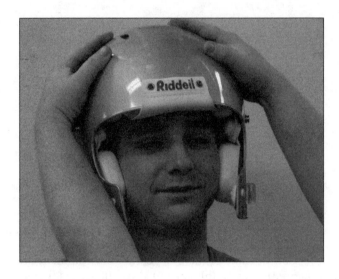

2. Try to rotate the helmet from side to side. Watch the skin on the forehead, as it should move and wrinkle slightly. The helmet should stay in contact with the skin at all times during this test. The jaw pads should be carefully observed, as any excess movement here should be adjusted for with a wider pad.

3. Check the chin strap for fit and comfort. The chin strap should help with control of all the preceding movements, but needs to be comfortable.

Ice Hockey Helmets

The ice hockey helmet is fit much like the football helmet. The following are some general guidelines for fitting ice hockey helmets. Remember to review the manufacturer's instructions for each different type of helmet.

1. Use a soft tape measure to determine the size of the helmet needed. Many manufacturers use a sizing chart, so make sure you check the appropriate sizing chart when selecting a helmet.

2. Have the athlete put the helmet on with the chin strap attached to both sides of the helmet. Check to see that the chin strap fits properly and is snug without pinching or binding.

3. Check the ear holes to see that the holes line up properly with the ears. This will ensure that the athlete can hear properly.

4. Check to make sure the posterior aspect of the skull is properly covered. Additionally, the front of the helmet should rest just above the eyebrows (about 1″ is adequate).

5. Twist the helmet to see that there is limited side-to-side movement. Push down on the top of the helmet to see that there is adequate but limited movement in this direction as well. Ask the athlete if he or she feels any abnormal pain, discomfort, or pressure during these movements.

6. The athlete should have normal vision; check for limited peripheral vision. Also check the movement of the head and neck for full range of motion.

Football Shoulder Pads

As with football helmet fitting, it is wise to always review the manufacturer's recommendations for fitting shoulder pads as manufacturers may have special fitting procedures that will maximize protection. The following is a generic fitting procedure that can be followed for assistance in fitting shoulder pads.

1. Ask the athlete about any previous injuries that may require special fitting or special padding procedures.

2. Ask the athlete what position he is going to be playing. Quarterbacks, receivers, running backs, linebackers, linemen, and other positions will use different size and styles of shoulder pads.

3. Begin with a measurement of the athlete. This measurement will usually be directed by the manufacturers' instructions. Typically this measurement is from shoulder tip to shoulder tip and will give you a starting point for sizing.

4. The shoulder pads should fit snugly about the chest and through the axillary straps.

5. If a cantilever pad is used, the cantilever strap should rest approximately 1″ above the clavicle.

6. Around the neck the athlete should have approximately ½- to ¾-inch clearance from neck to pad. At this stage it is important to check that the pads cover the sternoclavicular (SC) joint on each side. If the SC joints are not covered, the pads are too large for this athlete.

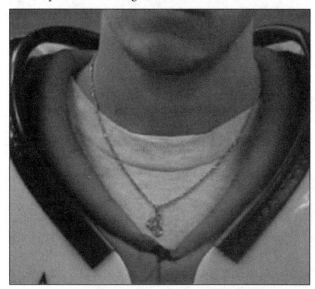

7. Check the fit of the pad at the shoulders. The end of the pad under the deltoid camp should be centered over the midpoint of the deltoid muscle. Place your hand under the pad at the shoulder and feel for a gap. There needs to be a gap under this space for shock absorption purposes.

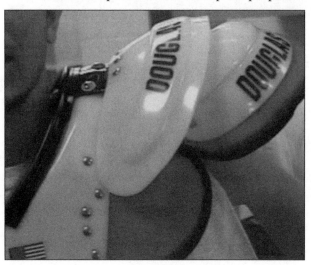

8. The epaulet (plastic flap over the deltoid pad) should extend past the middle of the deltoid muscle. This is the main contact area and must cover the AC joint and the deltoid muscle.

9. The rear of the pads should extend down the back to cover each scapula and be centered over the spine.

10. Recheck the shoulder pads for comfort and proper coverage.

See specific manufacturers' Web pages for fitting of individual equipment.

Mouth Guards

Mouth guards come in basically two different types. You can purchase a mouthpiece from the local sporting goods store that can be boiled in water and fitted to the athlete's mouth while it is hot. This type of mouth guard is commonly called a "dip and bite" mouth guard. This type of mouth guard has been demonstrated to provide adequate protection. The second type of mouth guard is the form-fitted mouth guard that is custom made from a dental impression. The custom-made mouth guard has been shown to provide maximal protection for the teeth in different sports.

To fit a dip-and-bite mouth guard, boil a small amount of water in a pan and turn the heat off. Dip the mouth guard in the water as per the manufacturer's instructions, allow the mouthpiece to cool a little, place

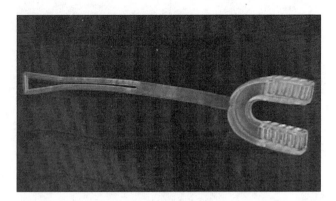

the mouth guard in the athlete's mouth, and have him or her bite down. Hold the biting position until the mouth guard starts to regain firmness. The dip-and-bite mouth guard can be redipped if necessary, but do not redip the mouth guard more than twice for fitting. One of the biggest problems with this type of mouth guard is its generic length. For the athlete with a small mouth, the mouth guard can extend too far into the back of the mouth. In this situation, the coach or athletic trainer should look to see how far back the mouth guard needs to extend to cover all the teeth and can then trim off the excess. Take care to not trim off too much of the material, as this results in loss of the protective function of the mouth guard. If the athlete receives a blow to the jaw, the mouth guard acts to absorb some of that shock, and if the mouthpiece is too short, the teeth will be touching and transmit the shock from the jaw to the head. If the shock to the jaw that is transmitted to the head is great enough, there is a possibility this will contribute to a concussion. Remind athletes not to cut off the ends of their dip-and-bite mouth guards without checking the proper length for full dental coverage.

Custom-fit mouth guards are just that—they are custom made from a dental impression. Making a custom-fit mouth guard is typically, by state law, a dental procedure. You may want to check your local state dentistry laws

before attempting to custom make mouth guards. If your team dentist will not make the mouth guards for the athletes, the athlete may want to go to his or her own dentist for a custom-made mouth guard. The disadvantage of this type of mouth guard is the expense of making the custom mold. The custom-made mouth guard does have a greater protective capacity and is far more comfortable for the athlete.

Soccer Shin Guards

Soccer is played with a minimum of protective equipment. The incidence of lower-extremity injuries is also very high in this sport. Therefore, the minimal amount of equipment used needs to be used properly. When players choose the shin guards they are going to wear, it is important to choose some that fit properly. Soccer shin guards come in a variety of sizes for the adult and junior player. In the photo you can see that the shin guard on the right leg fits properly. It covers the majority of the tibia from the ankle to just below the patella. If the shin guard is too long, it will extend into the area of the patella and cause the patella to bump into the guard, causing pain and discomfort to the athlete. If the shin guard is too short, as on the left leg in the photo, the tibia is not covered adequately, and there is an increased opportunity for injury. Sometimes athletes will select shin guards that are very small and place them either very high or very low on the tibia, just covering a small portion of the tibia. Choosing very small shin guards

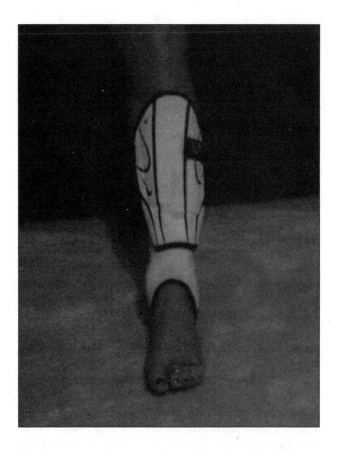

meets the minimum rule interpretation; however, it does not provide adequate coverage and places the athlete in greater danger for injury.

Athletes may also choose shin guards with built-in ankle guards, as seen in the photo here. The younger athlete (under 12 years old) is better off with the shin guard and ankle protection, as there is a greater tendency for the young athlete to be kicked in the ankle by a competitor. The extra ankle protection is sometimes too bulky for the skilled athlete, and he or she chooses to use only shin guard protection. Again, it is important to ensure the shin guard covers the tibia adequately no matter what the age of the athlete.

Baseball/Softball
Helmets

Baseball/softball helmets are manufactured in a common look and come in regular sizing. They have a hard shell on the outside, have padding on the inside, and are typically shared by many athletes on the same team. Athletes should be encouraged to select a helmet that fits them properly and does not have excessive movement up and down or side to side when they will be

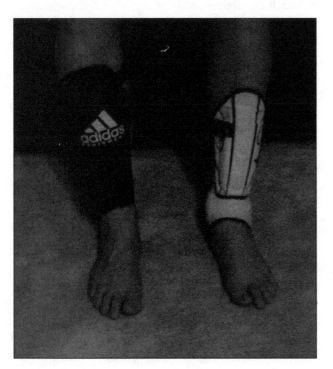

batting or running. Minimally, batting helmets should have ear protection on the side of the helmet facing the pitcher. As with other helmets, the ear hole of the ear protector must line up with the ear so the athlete will be able to hear clearly.

Catcher's Equipment

The catcher in baseball and softball will be required to wear face, chest, and shin protection. The catcher's mask is commercially produced and needs to cover the front of the head to protect the face from pitched balls or balls foul tipped from a batter. Some catchers choose to wear a throat protector that hangs from the chin of the face mask and provides some protection to the throat much like the face mask for the face. Catchers will also sometimes choose a hard-shell head protector to increase protection to their head.

Chest protection is important for the catcher and is also commercially manufactured in multiple sizes from youth to adult. It is important that the chest protector cover the chest and stomach and not have large gaps below the neck or above the belt line. If a chest protector is too small or too large and there are gaps in specific areas, this will allow a hard thrown or foul tipped ball to damage soft tissues not covered properly. If the chest protector is too large, there is also the possibility of the protector getting in the way of normal movements by the catcher and not allowing the catcher to throw the ball properly. Improper throwing motion can lead to secondary injury. The youth chest protector for the young male catcher should also have an extension to cover the external genital area, which should also be covered with a hard protective cup. The female chest protector may also be made specifically for the female athlete with breast molds and increased padding in the breast area. Most catchers will select the chest protection that is most comfortable and functional for them. The coach or athletic trainer should make sure the chest protector covers appropriately and provides adequate protection in all areas.

Eye Protection

Protective eyewear used by athletes in practice and competition should be approved by one of the two major eyewear approval institutes. The largest protective eyewear approval institution is the American Society for Testing and Materials (ASTM). This institute is a nonprofit organization that utilizes both object impact and realistic competition conditions to test eyewear for protective capacity. The ASTM mandates reviews of standards regularly to ensure that new technology is keeping up with proper protection. The other approval institute is the American National Standards Institute (ANSI) and is generally oriented toward the safety and protection of industrial eyewear. Even though the ANSI is oriented toward industrial protection, many of their standards are adequate for the athlete wearing eyewear.

Generally, eyewear should be impact resistant when used in athletic competition. The eyewear should be able to dissipate impact forces coming into it without shattering. The protective eyewear must be fit correctly and be secured to the head to reduce movement. If there is movement of the eyewear during activity, it will reduce the protective effectiveness and cause the athlete to lose concentration.

An athlete that needs visual correction in his or her protective eyewear must use a qualified medical provider to obtain protective eyewear for use during sport. Do not try to modify or make protective eyewear from an old pair of eyeglasses. Regular street or dress types of eyewear do not provide adequate protection during high levels of activity. Additionally, many times dress or street-type eyewear has sharp edges and can cut the wearer or a competitor.

Many athletes are using sunglasses to assist with comfort as they participate or to protect their eyes if they use contact lenses. Sunglasses need to fit properly and be impact resistant, due to the probability of impact during activity. If the sunglasses are also used to help protect the eye that contains a contact lens, it is important that the lenses cover enough of the eye to keep dirt and dust particles out of the eyes.

Glossary

A

abduction Movement of a body part away from the midline of the body.

abrasion Rubbing or scraping off of skin.

accident Occurring by chance or without intention.

acclimatization The adaptation of the body to a different environment.

acromioclavicular (AC) joint Articulation (arthrodial) formed by the distal end of the clavicle and the acromion process.

acute injury Characterized by rapid onset, resulting from a traumatic event.

adduction Movement of a body part toward the midline of the body.

ad libitum Amount desired.

adult-onset diabetes (type II) Mild form of diabetes mellitus typically occurring in adults; controlled mainly through diet and exercise.

AFB Acid fast bacilli.

afferent nerves Nerves that transport messages toward the brain.

agonistic muscles Muscles in a state of contraction as related to opposing muscles.

airborne Capable of being transmitted by air particles.

ambient Environing or surrounding (e.g., temperature that surrounds the immediate environment).

ambulation Move or walk about.

amenorrhea Absence or suppression of menstruation.

analgesia Pain inhibition.

analgesic Agent that relieves pain without causing a complete loss of sensation.

anaphylactic shock Shock caused by an allergic reaction.

anaphylaxis Increased susceptibility or sensitivity to a foreign protein or toxin as the result of previous exposure to it.

androgen A generic term for a substance that aids in the development of and controls the appearance of male characteristics.

anesthesia Partial or complete loss of sensation.

angiogenesis Formation of capillaries, which interconnect, resulting in the formation of new vessels.

anisocoria Rare, but naturally occurring condition where the pupils are of unequal size, not related to any acute condition such as head injury.

anomaly Deviation from the normal.

anorexia Diminished or loss of appetite; aversion to food.

anorexia nervosa Characterized by a pattern of self-starvation with a concomitant obsession with being thin and an overwhelming fear of being fat.

anoxia Lack of oxygen.

antagonistic muscles Muscles that counteract the action of agonistic muscles.

anterior Before or in front of.

anti-inflammatories Drugs designed to prevent swelling. Two basic categories are currently in use: steroidal and nonsteroidal.

antipyretic Agent that relieves or reduces fever.

anxiety A feeling of uncertainty or apprehension.

apophysis Bony outgrowth to which muscles attach.

apophysitis Inflammation of an apophysis.

arachidonic acid Chemical released when cells are damaged that serves as a precursor to the formation of other inflammatory chemicals including leukotrienes and prostaglandins.

arrhythmic movement Irregular movement.

arthrography Radiopaque material injected into a joint to facilitate the taking of X-rays.

arthrokinematics Physiological and accessory movements of the joint.

arthroscopic examination Viewing the inside of a joint through an arthroscope using a small video-camera lens.

aspiration Taking a foreign matter into the respiratory tract during inhalation.

asymmetry (body) Lack of symmetry of sides of the body.

atrophy Decrease in size of a tissue or an organ.

aura Preepileptic seizure phenomenon involving a sensory stimulatory effect.

automatism Automatic behavior before consciousness or full awareness has been achieved after a brain concussion.

avascular Devoid of blood circulation.

avascular necrosis Death of tissue caused by the lack of blood supply.

avulsion Forcible tearing away or separation.

axilla Armpit.

B

bacteria Plural of bacterium. A Schizomycetes, unicellular microorganism that can either be parasitic or free-living and has a wide range of biochemical, often pathogenic, properties.

bacteriostatic Inhibiting or retarding the growth of bacteria.

ballistic stretching Stretching technique that uses repetitive bouncing motions.

bandage Material used to cover a wound.

Bennett's fracture Fracture and/or dislocation of the first metacarpal bone away from the greater multangular bone of the wrist.

biomechanics Branch of study that applies the laws of mechanics, internal or external, to the living body.

BLS Basic life support; its primary objective is to maintain life until medical assistance arrives at the scene of the injury.

BMR Basal metabolic rate.

boutonnière deformity Buttonhole deformity whereby the proximal interphalangeal joint of the finger is forced through the central band of the tendon of the extensor digitorum muscle.

boxer's fracture Fracture of the proximal fourth and/or fifth metacarpal bones.

bradycardia Slow heartbeat; adults below 60 BPM, children below 70 BPM.

bradykinin Inflammatory chemical released when tissues are damaged; it results in increased pain in the area and may play a role in the production of other inflammatory chemicals such as prostaglandins.

bulimia Binge-purge eating disorder.

bulimia nervosa Characterized by repeated bouts of binge eating followed by some form of purging, e.g., vomiting, use of laxatives, fasting, or vigorous and excessive exercise.

bursa Small synovial sac typically located over bony prominences that assists in cushioning and reducing friction.

bursitis Inflammation of a bursa.

C

calcific tendinitis Deposition of calcium in a chronically inflamed tendon.

calisthenic Exercise involving free movement without the aid of equipment.

carpal tunnel Anatomic region of the wrist where the median nerve and the majority of the tendons of the forearm pass into the hand.

carpal tunnel syndrome A complex of symptoms resulting from pressure on the median nerve as it passes through the carpal tunnel of the wrist, causing soreness and numbness.

catastrophic injury One involving damage to the brain and/or spinal cord that presents a potentially life-threatening situation or the possibility of permanent disability.

catecholamine Active amines, such as epinephrine and norepinephrine, that affect the nervous and cardiovascular systems.

cerebral concussion A clinical syndrome characterized by immediate and transient impairment of neurologic function secondary to mechanical forces.

cerebral contusion Bruising of brain tissue.

cerebrovascular accident Stroke.

chafing Irritation of the skin caused by friction.

charitable immunity Legal doctrine holding that a person sponsoring a charitable function should not be held accountable for negligent acts.

chiropractor One who practices a method for restoring normal health by adjusting segments of the spinal column.

Chlamydia trachomatis A genus of microorganism that can cause a wide variety of diseases in humans, one of which is venereal and causes nonspecific urethritis.

chondromalacia Abnormal softening of cartilage, typically noted between the patella and femur.

chronic injury One characterized by a slow, insidious onset, implying a gradual development of structural damage.

circadian rhythm Biological time clock of body functions.

circuit training Exercise stations that incorporate combinations of weight training, stretching exercises, calisthenics, and aerobic exercises.

circumduct Act of moving a limb such as the arm or hip in a circular manner.

CNS Central nervous system.

cold urticaria A condition in which the skin reacts to exposure to cold with localized edema associated with severe itching.

colic Intra-abdominal pain.

colitis Inflammation of the colon.

collagen The major protein of connective tissue.

Colles' fracture Transverse fracture of the distal radius.

collision sport One in which collisions between athletes are expected.

commission A legal liability arising when a person commits an act that is not legally his to perform.

communicable disease One that may be transmitted directly or indirectly from one individual to another.

comprehensive evaluation Assessment of an injured athlete that commences once the initial assessment is completed. The objective is to collect as much information about the injury as possible under the circumstances.

computerized axial tomography (CAT) Computer-assisted X-ray scan that provides detailed images of tissues based on their relative density. Also called CAT scan.

concentric contraction Occurs when a muscle shortens and there is movement at the joint accompanied by contraction against resistance.

conduction Heating through direct contact with a hot medium.

conjunctiva Mucous membrane that lines the eyes.

connective tissue The most common tissue in the body; includes ligaments, bones, retinaculum, joint capsules, cartilage, fascia, and tendons.

contact allergen External agent that causes inflammation of the skin.

contact dermatitis Inflammation of the skin that is nonallergenic.

contact sport Sport in which athletes are expected to make physical contact but not with the intent to produce bodily injury.

contrecoup brain injury Trauma occurring when the brain continues to move within the skull following a blow to the head, resulting in injury to the brain on the side opposite the initial force.

contributory negligence Negligence arising when an injured party is at least partly responsible for an act that causes his own injury.

contusion Bruise or injury to soft tissue that does not break the skin.

convection Heating indirectly through another medium such as air or liquid.

conversion Heating by other forms of energy, e.g., electricity.

convulsions Involuntary muscular spasms or jerking.

core temperature Internal body temperature as opposed to shell or peripheral temperature.

corticosteroid Steroid produced by the adrenal cortex.

coryza Profuse nasal discharge.

counterirritant Agent that produces mild inflammation and acts in turn as an analgesic when applied locally to the skin, e.g., liniment.

crepitation Crackling sound heard during the movement of a broken bone.

critical force Magnitude of a single force by which an anatomical structure is damaged.

cryokinetics Cold application combined with exercise.

cryotherapy Therapeutic use of cold.

CSF Cerebrospinal fluid.

cubital fossa Triangular area on the anterior aspect of the forearm directly over the elbow joint.

cyanosis Bluish, grayish, or dark purple discoloration of the skin caused by a reduced amount of hemoglobin in the blood.

D

DAPRE Daily adjustable progressive resistive exercise.

débride Removal of dirt and dead tissue from a wound.

deconditioning The loss of a competitive fitness level.

degeneration Deterioration of tissue.

dehydration Decrease of fluid contained within the body.

de Quervain's disease Inflammation of sheaths surrounding the extensor tendons of the thumb.

dermatome Segmental skin area innervated by various segments of the spinal cord.

diabetes mellitus Disorder characterized by the inability of the body to appropriately metabolize carbohydrates.

diastolic blood pressure The residual pressure when the heart is between beats.

DIP Distal interphalangeal joint.

diplopia Double vision.

dislocation The displacement of contiguous surfaces of bones comprising a joint.

distal Farthest from the center, midline, or trunk.

distal interphalangeal (DIP) joint The joint formed by the articulation between the intermediate and distal phalanges of the digits (hinge type of joint).

doping The use of a drug designed to improve a competitor's performance.

dorsiflexion Bending toward the dorsum or rear; the opposite of plantar flexion.

dorsum The back of a body part.

dressing Covering, either protective or supportive, that is applied to an injury or wound.

drug Any substance that when taken into a living organism may modify one or more of its functions.

dysesthesia Impairment of the sense of touch.

dysmenorrhea Painful menstruation.

dyspnea Difficult or painful breathing.

dysrhythmia Irregular heartbeats.

E

eccentric contraction The simultaneous processes of muscle contraction and stretching of the muscle–tendon unit by an extrinsic force.

ecchymosis Black-and-blue discoloration of the skin caused by hemorrhage.

ectopic calcification Calcification occurring in an abnormal place.

edema Swelling caused by the collection of fluid in connective tissue.

effleurage Stroking massage technique.

electrolyte Solution that is a conductor of electricity.

embolus A mass of undissolved matter occluding a blood vessel.

emetic Agent that induces vomiting.

endurance The ability of the body to engage in prolonged physical activity.

enzyme An organic catalyst that can cause chemical changes in other substances without being changed itself.

epicondylitis Inflammatory response at the epicondyle.

epidemiology The study of the distribution of disease or injury within a population and its environment.

epidural hematoma Bleeding between the dura and the cranial bones.

epilepsy A chronic disorder characterized by sudden attacks of brain dysfunction, including altered consciousness, abnormal motor activity, sensory phenomena, and/or inappropriate behavior.

epiphysis Cartilaginous growth region of a bone.

epistaxis Nosebleed.

ergogenic aid Food or beverages that have the potential to increase the work output of the person using them.

erythema Swelling and red discoloration of the skin.

ethics Principles of morality and professional conduct.

etiology Science dealing with causes of disease.

eversion of the foot To turn the foot outward.

exercise-induced asthma (EIA) Acute, reversible, self-limiting bronchospasm occurring during or after exercise.

exostosis Bony outgrowths that protrude from the surface of a bone where there is not a typical bony formation.

extraoral mouth guard Protective device that fits outside the mouth.

extrapulmonary Outside of the lungs.

extravasation Escape of a fluid from its vessels into the surrounding tissues.

exudate Exuded matter such as fluid that accumulates in an area.

F

facilitation To assist the progress of or help with the healing process.

fascia Fibrous membrane that covers, supports, and separates muscles.

fasciitis Inflammation of fascia.

fibrinogen Blood plasma protein that is converted into a fibrin clot.

fibroblast Immature, fiber-producing cells of connective tissue that can mature into one of several different cell types.

fibrocartilage Type of cartilage that contains visible collagenous fibers.

fibrosis Development of excessive fibrous connective tissue; fibroid degeneration.

flexibility The range of motion (ROM) in a given joint or combination of joints.

foot pronation Combined foot movements of eversion and abduction.

foot supination Combined foot movements of inversion and abduction.

fracture A break or crack in a bone.

fracture-dislocation An injury resulting in both the fracture of a bone and dislocation at the joint.

friction Heat producing.

frostbite Freezing of tissues from excessive exposure to cold.

frostnip Less severe form of frostbite.

G

gamekeeper's thumb Sprain of the ulnar collateral ligament of the metacarpophalangeal joint of the thumb.

ganglion Herniation of the synovium surrounding a tendon and subsequent filling of the area with synovial fluid, resulting in a visible bump seen through the skin.

gastritis Inflammation of the stomach lining.

gastroenteritis Inflammation of the stomach and intestines.

genitourinary Pertaining to the reproductive and urinary organs.

genu recurvatum Hyperextension at the knee joint.

genu valgum Knock knee.

genu varum Bowleg.

GI Gastrointestinal.

glenohumeral (GH) joint Articulation (spheroid) formed by the head of the humerus and the glenoid fossa of the scapula.

glycogen Storage form of glucose found in both the liver and skeletal muscles.

glycosuria Abnormally high proportion of sugar in the urine.

golfer's elbow Medial humeral epicondylitis related to incorrect golf technique.

H

hamstrings The three muscles that make up the posterior thigh: biceps femoris, semimembranosus, and semitendinosus.

HBV Hepatitis B virus.

heat cramps Muscle spasms related to excessive heat buildup within the body.

heat exhaustion Generalized fatigue related to excessive heat buildup within the body; may be a precursor to heatstroke.

heatstroke Excessive heat buildup within the body resulting in the body's inability to cool itself, with core temperatures exceeding 106°F.

heel spur Ossification into the proximal attachment of the plantar fascia.

hemarthrosis Blood in a joint.

hematolytic Pertaining to the degeneration and disintegration of the blood.

hematoma A localized collection of extravasated blood, usually clotted, that is confined within an organ, tissue, or space.

hematuria Blood in the urine.

hemoglobin The red respiratory protein of erythrocytes that transports oxygen from the lungs to the tissues.

hemoglobinuria Hemoglobin in the urine.

hemolysis Destruction of red blood cells.

hemophilia Hereditary blood disease in which coagulation is prolonged or nonexistent.

hemopoietic Forming blood cells.

hemorrhage Discharge of blood.

hemothorax Bloody fluid in the pleural cavity.

HEPA High-efficiency particulate air filter.

hernia Protrusion of a part of an organ or tissue through an abnormal opening.

herniated disk Rupture or protrusion of the nucleus pulposus through the annulus fibrosus of an intervertebral disk.

hip pointer Contusion and associated hematoma to the superior/anterior portion of the iliac crest.

hirsutism Excessive hair growth and/or presence of hair in unusual places, especially in women.

histamine Powerful inflammatory chemical that causes an increase in vascular permeability as well as vasodilation.

HIV Human immunodeficiency virus.

homeostasis Maintenance of a steady state in the body's internal environment.

HPV Human papillomavirus; approximately 55 specific types of these viruses have been identified, at least two of which are related to plantar warts.

HSV-1 Herpes simplex virus type 1; related to infections in athletes commonly known as herpes gladiatorum.

humeroradial joint Articulation (arthrodial) formed by the proximal end of the radius and the distal end of the humerus, specifically the capitulum.

humeroulnar joint Articulation (ginglymus) formed by the proximal end of the ulna, specifically the trochlear notch, with the distal end of the humerus, specifically the trochlea.

hyperallergenic Material(s) that result in allergic reactions.

hyperemia Unusual amount of blood in a body part.

hyperextension Extreme stretching of a body part.

hyperflexibility Flexibility beyond a joint's normal range.

hyperglycemia Excessively high level of blood sugar.

hyperhidrosis Excessive sweating; excessive foot perspiration.

hyperkeratosis Increased callus development.

hypermobility Extreme mobility of a joint.

hyperpnea Hyperventilation; exaggerated deep breathing that is also more rapid than normal.

hypertension High blood pressure; abnormally high tension.

hyperthermia Abnormally high body temperature.

hypertonic Having a higher osmotic pressure than a comparable solution.

hypertrophy Enlargement of a part caused by an increase in the size of its cells.

hyperventilation Abnormally deep breathing that is prolonged, causing a depletion of carbon dioxide, a fall in blood pressure, and fainting.

hyphema Bleeding into the anterior portion of the eye.

hypoglycemic (insulin) shock Insulin shock resulting from an abnormally low sugar content in the blood.

hypothermia A body temperature below 33.3°C (95°F).

hypovolemic shock Inability of the cardiovascular system to maintain adequate circulation to all parts of the body.

hypoxia Lack of an adequate amount of oxygen.

I

ICE Ice, compression, and elevation.

idiopathic Cause of a condition is unknown.

incubation period The time between an exposure to an infectious agent and the appearance of symptoms of that infection.

infectious mononucleosis Viral infection characterized by general fatigue and enlargement of organs such as the spleen.

initial check Evaluation of an injured athlete to determine if the player's life is in immediate jeopardy.

injury Act that damages or hurts.

innervation Nerve stimulation of a muscle.

interosseous membrane Connective tissue membrane between bones.

intertrigo Chafing of the skin.

interval training Alternating periods of work with active recovery.

intracerebral hematoma Bleeding within the brain tissues.

intracranial injury Head injury characterized by disruption of blood vessels, either veins or arteries, resulting in the development of a hematoma or swelling within the confines of the cranium.

inunctions Oily or medicated substances (e.g., liniments) that are rubbed into the skin to produce a local or systemic effect.

inversion of the foot To turn the foot inward; inner border of the foot lifts.

ions Electrically charged atoms.

iontophoresis Using an electrical current to drive a chemical directly through the skin.

ipsilateral Situated on the same side.

ischemia Local anemia.

isokinetic muscle resistance Accommodating and variable resistance.

isometric exercise Exercise that contracts a muscle statically without a concurrent range of motion.

isotonic exercise Exercise that shortens and lengthens a contracted muscle through a range of motion.

J

joint capsule Sac-like structure that encloses the ends of bones in a diarthrodial joint.

juvenile-onset diabetes (type I) Insulin-dependent type of diabetes mellitus usually occurring in children and adolescents.

K

Kehr's sign Pain radiating into the left shoulder that is normally associated with an injury to the spleen.

keratolytic Loosening of a horny layer of skin.

keratosis Excessive growth of a horny layer of skin tissue.

kilocalorie Amount of heat required to raise one kilogram of water one degree Celsius.

kinesthesia Sensation or feeling of movement; the awareness one has of the spatial relationships of the body and its parts.

kyphosis Exaggeration of the normal curve of the thoracic spine.

L

laser A device that concentrates high energies into a narrow beam of visible monochromatic light.

LBW Lean body weight.

leukocytes White blood cells.

liability Legal responsibility to perform an act in a reasonable and prudent manner.

Little League elbow Condition related to excessive throwing that results in swelling of the medial epicondyle of the elbow, i.e., medial humeral epicondylitis.

locus of control People's belief, or lack thereof, of being in control of events occurring in their lives.

lordosis Abnormal curvature of the lumbar vertebrae.

LRI Lower respiratory infection.

luxation Complete dislocation of a joint.

Lyme disease Bacterial infection transmitted by deer tick.

lysis To break down.

M

macerated skin Skin that has been softened through wetting.

malaise Discomfort and uneasiness caused by an illness.

mallet finger Deformity of the distal interphalangeal joint of the finger caused by an avulsion of the tendon of the extensor digitorum muscle from the distal phalanx.

margination Accumulation of leukocytes on the walls of blood vessels at the site of injury during early stages of inflammation.

massage Using the hands to systematically manipulate soft tissues of the body.

mast cells Connective tissue cells that contain heparin and histamine.

menarche Onset of menstrual function.

menisci Fibrocartilaginous structures that are between the hyaline cartilage surfaces in some synovial joints (e.g., the knee).

metatarsalgia A general term to describe pain in the ball of the foot.

microtrauma Microscopic lesion or injury.

modalities Physical agents that help create an optimal healing environment.

mode of transmission The manner in which an infection is spread.

Morton's neuroma A nerve tumor (benign) related to the nerve between the third and fourth metatarsal heads with pain going to the third and fourth toes.

MP Metacarpophalangeal joint.

muscle contracture Permanent contraction of a muscle as a result of spasm or paralysis.

muscular endurance The ability to perform repetitive muscular contractions against some resistance.

muscular strength The maximal force that can be applied by a muscle during a single maximal contraction.

myocarditis Inflammation of the heart muscle.

myoglobin Respiratory protein in muscle tissue that is an oxygen carrier.

myositis Inflammation of muscle.

myositis ossificans Myositis marked by ossification within a muscle.

N

negative resistance Slow, eccentric muscle contraction against a resistance.

negligence The failure to do what a reasonably careful and prudent person would have done under the same or like circumstances, or doing something that a reasonably careful and prudent person would not have done under the same or like circumstances.

nerve entrapment Compression of a nerve between bone or soft tissue.

neuritis Inflammation of a nerve.

neuroma Tumor consisting mostly of nerve cells and nerve fibers.

nociceptor Receptor of pain.

noncontact sport Sport in which athletes are not expected to be involved in any physical contact.

NSAID Nonsteroidal anti-inflammatory drugs.

nuclei A particle that makes up a nucleus of an atom.

nystagmus Constant involuntary movement of the eyeball, which may be back and forth, up and down, or rotary.

O

omission Liability arising when a person fails to perform a legal duty.

orthopedic surgeon Physician who corrects deformities of the musculoskeletal system.

orthosis An appliance or apparatus used in sports to support, align, prevent, or correct deformities, or to improve function of a movable body part.

orthotics Field of knowledge relating to orthoses and their use.

Osgood-Schlatter disease Epiphyseal inflammation of the tibial tubercle.

OSHA Occupational Safety and Health Administration.

osteitis pubis Inflammation of the bones in the region of the symphysis pubis.

osteoarthritis Chronic disease involving joints, especially weight-bearing joints, in which the articular cartilage is damaged and there is a degeneration of the joint.

osteochondral Refers to relationship of bone and cartilage.

osteochondritis Inflammation of bone and cartilage.

osteochondritis dissecans Condition in which a fragment of cartilage and underlying bone is detached from the articular surface.

osteochondrosis Diseased state of a bone and its articular cartilage.

P

PABA *Para*-aminobenzoic acid; the common active ingredient in sunscreen products.

palpation The act of feeling with the hands for the purpose of determining the consistency of the part beneath.

paraplegia Paralysis of lower portion of the body and both legs.

paresis Slight or incomplete paralysis.

paresthesia Abnormal or morbid sensation such as itching or prickling.

patellofemoral joint Articulation (saddle) formed by the posterior surface of the patella and the anterior surface of the femoral condyles.

pathogenic Causing disease.

pathology Area of specialization concerned with the manifestations of disease.

pathomechanics Act of applying mechanical forces to an organism that can adversely affect the structure and function of that organism.

pediatrician Physician specializing in the treatment of children's diseases.

periodization The organization of training into a cyclical structure in order to attain the optimal development of an athlete's performance capacities.

permeable Permitting the passage of a substance through a vessel wall.

pes anserinus tendinitis Irritation of the tibial attachment of the pes anserine, associated most often with runners and cyclists.

pes cavus Abnormally high arch of the foot.

pes planus An abnormally flat foot.

pétrissage Kneading type of massage.

phagocytosis Destruction of injurious cells or particles by phagocytes (white blood cells).

phalanges Anatomical name for the bones of both the fingers and/or toes.

phalanx Any one of the bones of the fingers and toes.

pharmacology The science of drugs—their preparation, uses, and effects.

phonophoresis Introduction of ions of soluble salt into the body through ultrasound.

photophobia Unusual intolerance to light.

physical exam Checking a victim of an emergency for signs and symptoms associated with injury and/or illness.

piezoelectric Production of an electric current as a result of pressure on certain crystals.

PIP Proximal interphalangeal joint.

plantar fasciitis Inflammation of the plantar fascia.

plyometric exercise Exercise that utilizes the stretch reflex to increase athletic power.

pneumonia Inflammation of the lungs.

pneumothorax Collapse of a lung as a result of air in the pleural cavity.

podiatrist Medical practitioner who specializes in the study and care of the foot.

point tenderness Pain produced when an injury site is palpated.

polymers Natural or synthetic substances formed by the combination of two or more molecules of the same substance.

posterior Toward the rear or back.

post-traumatic amnesia Inability to recall events that have occurred from the moment of injury.

prognosis Prediction as to probable outcome of a disease or injury.

prophylaxis Guarding against injury or disease.

proprioceptive neuromuscular facilitation (PNF) Stretching techniques that involve combinations of alternating contractions and stretches.

proprioceptor One of several sensory receptors located in muscles, tendons, and joint capsules.

prostaglandins Perhaps some of the most powerful chemicals produced within the body. Related to the inflammatory process, they cause a variety of effects including vasodilation, increased vascular permeability, pain, fever, and clotting.

prosthesis An artificial replacement of an absent body part.

proximal Nearest to the point of reference.

proximal interphalangeal (PIP) joint The joint formed by the articulation between the proximal and intermediate phalanges of the digits (hinge type of joint).

psychogenic Of psychic origin; that which originates in the mind.

purulent Consisting of, or forming, pus.

pyoderma Pus-producing infection of the skin.

Q

Q angle Angle made by the rectus femoris and the patellar tendon as they attach to the tibial tuberosity.

quadriceps Four muscles of the anterior thigh: rectus femoris, vastus medialis, vastus intermedius, and vastus lateralis.

quadriplegia Paralysis affecting all four limbs.

R

radiation Emission and diffusion of rays of heat.

radiocarpal joint Articulation (ellipsoidal) formed by the distal end of the radius and three bones of the wrist: navicular, lunate, and triquetral.

radioulnar joints Two articulations (pivot) formed by the proximal and distal radius and ulna, known commonly as the proximal and distal radioulnar joints.

Raynaud's phenomenon Condition in which exposure to cold causes vasospasm of digital arteries.

regeneration Repair, regrowth, or restoration of a part, such as tissue.

residual The remaining amount.

resorption Removal by absorption.

respirator A mechanical device used to assist breathing. In this case it refers to a device used to filter particles from the air.

retrograde amnesia Inability to recall events that occurred just prior to an injury.

retroversion Tilting or tuning backward of a part.

revascularize Restoration of blood circulation to an injured area.

rhinitis The common cold.

risk factor Causative agent in a sports injury.

ROM Range of motion.

rotation Turning around an axis in an angular motion.

rotator cuff Group of four muscles of the glenohumeral joint: subscapularis, supraspinatus, infraspinatus, and teres minor.

S

SAID principle Specific adaptation to imposed demands.

scoliosis Lateral and/or rotary curvature of the spine.

seizure Sudden onset of uncoordinated muscular

activity and changes in consciousness lasting an unpredictable time.

septic shock Shock caused by bacteria, especially gram-negative bacteria commonly seen in systemic infections.

sequela Pathological condition that occurs as a consequence of another condition or event.

serotonin Hormone and neurotransmitter.

shin splints Medial or posteromedial leg pain brought about by walking, running, or related activities that decreases with rest.

shoulder pointer Contusion and subsequent hematoma in the region of the acromioclavicular joint.

sign Objective evidence of an abnormal situation within the body.

soft tissue Includes muscles, fascia, tendons, joint capsules, ligaments, blood vessels, and nerves.

spearing A practice in tackle football whereby a player performs either a tackle or a block using the head as the initial point of contact.

spheroid joint A ball-and-socket articulation.

spondylolisthesis Forward slippage of vertebra, usually between the fifth lumbar and the sacrum.

spondylolysis A defect in the neural arch (pars interarticularis) of the vertebrae.

sports medicine Branch of medicine concerned with the medical aspects of sports participation.

sprain Injury to a joint and the surrounding structures, primarily ligaments and/or joint capsules.

Staphylococcus Genus of gram-positive bacteria normally present on the skin and in the upper respiratory tract and prevalent in localized infections.

stasis Blockage or stoppage of circulation.

static stretching Passively stretching an antagonistic muscle by placing it in a maximal stretch and holding it there.

sternoclavicular (SC) joint Articulation (arthrodial) formed by the union of the proximal clavicle and the manubrium of the sternum.

strain Injury involving muscles and tendons or the junction between the two, commonly known as the musculotendinous junction.

Streptococcus Genus of gram-positive bacteria found in the throat, respiratory tract, and intestinal tract.

stress fracture Small crack or break in a bone related to excessive, repeated overloads; also known as overuse fracture or march fracture.

stressor Anything that affects the body's physiological or psychological condition and upsets the homeostatic balance.

subdural hematoma Bleeding below the dura mater.

subluxation Partial or incomplete dislocation of an articulation.

subtalar joint Articulation (arthrodial) formed by the inferior surface of the talus and the superior surface of the calcaneus.

symptom Subjective evidence of an abnormal situation within the body.

syndrome Group of typical symptoms or conditions that characterize a deficiency or disease.

synergy To work in cooperation with.

synovitis Inflammation of the synovium.

synthesis To build up.

systolic blood pressure The pressure caused by the pumping of the heart.

T

tachycardia Rapid or abnormally high pulse rate.

tackler's exostosis Formation of a benign growth projecting from the humerus that is caused by repeated blows to the upper arm region; common in tackle football.

talocrural joint Articulation (ginglymus) formed by the distal tibia and fibula with the superior surface (dome) of the talus.

tapotement Percussion.

TB disease Having the organism that causes tuberculosis (TB) in the body, in its active state. A person with TB disease usually has symptoms and can transmit the disease to others.

TB infection Having the organism that causes tuberculosis (TB) in the body, but not having the active disease. A person having TB infection is asymptomatic and cannot transmit TB unless the organism converts to an active state.

team physician A medical doctor who agrees to provide at least limited medical coverage to a particular sports program or institution.

tendinitis Inflammation of a tendon.

tenosynovitis Inflammation of the sheath of a tendon.

tetanus An acute, often fatal, condition characterized by tonic muscular spasm, hyperreflexia, and sometimes lockjaw.

tetanus toxoid Tetanus toxin modified to produce active immunity against *Clostridium tetani.*

thermotherapy Therapeutic use of heat.

thoracic cage Thoracic vertebrae, their corresponding ribs, and the sternum.

thrombi Plural of thrombus, a blood clot that blocks small blood vessels or a cavity of the heart.

tibiofemoral joint Articulation (bicondylar) formed by the medial and lateral femoral condyles and the medial and lateral tibial condyles.

tinea Group of fungi-related skin infections, commonly called ringworm, which can affect various parts of the body—groin (tinea cruris), feet and toes (tinea pedis), and scalp (tinea capitis).

tinea versicolor Fungus infection resulting in the formation of circular skin lesions that appear either lighter or darker than adjacent skin.

tinnitus Ringing in the ears.

TMJ Temporomandibular joint.

tonic muscle spasm Rigid muscle contraction that lasts over a period of time.

torsion Act or state of being twisted.

tort Harm, other than a breach of contract, done to another for which the law holds the wrongdoer responsible.

training effect Result achieved when stroke volume increases while heart rate is reduced at a given exercise load.

trait anxiety A general disposition or tendency to perceive certain situations as threatening and to react with an anxiety response.

transcutaneous electrical nerve stimulation (TENS) Modality of electrical stimulation typically applied to the body for the purpose of pain reduction.

transitory paralysis Temporary paralysis.

trauma Wound or injury.

traumatic Pertaining to an injury or wound.

trigger points Small areas within a muscle that can become highly irritated.

tunnel of Guyon Anatomic region formed by the hook of the hamate bone and the pisiform bone, whereby the ulnar nerve passes into the hand.

turf toe Sprain of the metatarsophalangeal joint of the great toe.

U

URI Upper respiratory infection.

V

valgus Position of a body part that is bent outward.

varus Position of a body part that is bent inward.

vasoconstriction Decrease in the diameter of a blood vessel resulting in a decreased blood flow.

vasodilation Increase in the diameter of a blood vessel resulting in an increased blood flow.

vasospasm Spasm of a blood vessel.

vehicle The substance in which a drug is transported.

verruca Wart caused by a virus.

vertigo Loss of balance.

vibration Rapid shaking.

viscoelastic Any substance having both viscous and elastic properties.

viscosity Resistance to flow.

volar Pertaining to the palm or the sole.

Volkmann's contracture Contracture of muscles of the forearm related to a loss of blood supply caused by a fracture and/or dislocation of either of the bones in the forearm or the humerus.

Index

Photo Credits

Unless otherwise indicated, photographs are under copyright of Jones and Bartlett Publishers, courtesy of Dan Evans Photography or courtesy of the Maryland Institute of Emergency Medical Service Systems, or have been supplied by the American Academy of Orthopaedic Surgeons.

p. xiv, © Larry St. Pierre/ShutterStock, Inc.; p. 2, (T) © Larry St. Pierre/ShutterStock, Inc., (B) © Shawn Pecor/ShutterStock, Inc.; p. 4, (TL) © Christoph & Friends/Das Fotoarchiv/Alamy Images, (BL) © Rubberball Productions; p. 5, (TL) © Bruce Yeung/ShutterStock, Inc., (TR) © Photodisc, (BL) © Photodisc; p. 6, Courtesy of Malissa Martin, College of Mount St. Joseph; p. 10, Courtesy of Kevin G. Shea, MD, Intermountain Orthopaedics, Boise, Idaho; p. 14, © PhotoLink/Photodisc/Getty Images; p. 15, © Photodisc; p. 16, (L) © Peter Weber/ShutterStock, Inc., (R) © Digital Vision/Getty Images; p. 17, © Photodisc; p. 22, Courtesy of Central Michigan University; p. 28, © David Young-Wolff/PhotoEdit; p. 29, Courtesy of Ariko Iso, Pittsburgh Steelers; p. 32, © Photodisc; p. 34, © Photodisc; p. 37, Courtesy of Barrie Steele, University of Idaho; p. 42, Courtesy of Central Michigan University; p. 44, © Larry St. Pierre/ShutterStock, Inc.; p. 46, Courtesy of Daniel H. Ruiz, Mark Morris High School; p. 54, Courtesy of Central Michigan University; p. 56, © Pétur Ásgeirsson/ShutterStock, Inc.; p. 58, Courtesy of Gary Craner, Boise State University; p. 59, © Lario Tus/ShutterStock, Inc.; p. 60, © John Lumb/ShutterStock, Inc.; p. 66, © LiquidLibrary; p. 70, Courtesy of Karen Lew, Southeastern Louisiana University; p. 73, © Photodisc; p. 87, © DigitalVues/Alamy Images; p. 88, © Photodisc; p. 95, (T) Courtesy of Yasuo Fukuda, (B) Courtesy of Kenji Sasaki, Iwate Amatuer Sports Association; p. 98, Courtesy of Central Michigan University; p. 102, Courtesy of Richard Leander, Moscow School District; pp. 105–107, Courtesy of Ron Pfeiffer; p. 109, © Photodisc; p. 112, © Digital Vision/PictureQuest; p. 121, Courtesy of Rick Griffin, Seattle Mariners; p. 123, Courtesy of Ron Pfeiffer; p. 131, (TL) Courtesy of Ron Pfeiffer, (ML) Courtesy of Ron Pfeiffer, (BR) Courtesy of Ron Pfeiffer; p. 140, © Patrick Gardin/AP Photos; p. 144, Courtesy of Doris Flores, California State University, Sacramento; p. 148, Courtesy of Ron Pfeiffer; p. 150, © Gregory Kendall/ShutterStock, Inc.; p. 156, (TR) Courtesy of Kevin G. Shea, MD, Intermountain Orthopaedics, Boise, Idaho, (BR) Courtesy of Ron Pfeiffer; p. 159, Courtesy of Kevin G. Shea, MD, Intermountain Orthopaedics, Boise, Idaho; p. 162, Courtesy of Katie Walsh, East Carolina University; p. 166, Courtesy of Central Michigan University; p. 171, Courtesy of Kevin G. Shea, MD, Intermountain Orthopaedics, Boise, Idaho; p. 173, Courtesy of Sue Lerner, University of Southern California; p. 179, Courtesy of Kevin G. Shea, MD, Intermountain Orthopaedics, Boise, Idaho; pp. 190, 191, Courtesy of Brent Mangus; p. 194, Courtesy of Central Michigan University; p. 199, Courtesy of Larry J. Leverenz, Purdue University; p. 200, (L) Courtesy of Physio-Control, a division of Medtronic, (R) Courtesy of Schutt Sports; p. 204, © Jeff Hinds/ShutterStock, Inc.; p. 208, Courtesy of Jorge Garcia, Dr. Kip Owen Orthopedics, McAllen, TX; p. 210, Courtesy of Brent Mangus; p. 214, © Adam Tinney/ShutterStock, Inc.; p. 218, Courtesy of Kevin G. Shea, MD, Intermountain Orthopaedics, Boise, Idaho; pp. 221, 222, Courtesy of Brent Mangus; p. 225, Courtesy of Kevin G. Shea, MD, Intermountain Orthopaedics, Boise, Idaho; p. 226, (L) © Alessandro Bianchi/Reuters/Landov, (R) Courtesy of Kevin G. Shea, MD, Intermountain Orthopaedics, Boise, Idaho; p. 228, (L) Courtesy of DJO Incorporated, (R) Courtesy of Mueller Sports Medicine, (B) Courtesy of Rene Revis Shingles, Central Michigan University; p. 229, Courtesy of Bledsoe Brace Systems; p. 232, © Marko Risovic/Alamy